Microsoft® SQL Server™ 2008

DELIVERING BUSINESS INTELLIGENCE

Brian Larson

McGraw Hill

New York Chicago San Francisco Lisbon
London Madrid Mexico City Milan
New Delhi San Juan Seoul Singapore
Sydney Toronto

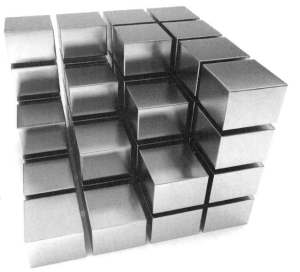

The **McGraw·Hill** Companies

Library of Congress Cataloging-in-Publication Data

Larson, Brian.
   Delivering business intelligence with Microsoft SQL server TM 2008/
Brian Larson.
      p.   cm.
   Includes bibliographical references and index.
   ISBN 978-0-07-154944-8 (alk. paper)
   1. Business intelligence. I. Title.
HD38.7.L36   2009
658.4'038—dc22   2008044462

McGraw-Hill books are available at special quantity discounts to use as premiums and sales promotions, or for use in corporate training programs. To contact a special sales representative, please visit the Contact Us page at www.mhprofessional.com.

Delivering Business Intelligence with Microsoft® SQL Server™ 2008

23456789 DOC DOC   1543210

ISBN   978-0-07-154944-8
MHID   0-07-154944-7

Sponsoring Editor
   Wendy Rinaldi

Editorial Supervisor
   Patty Mon

Project Manager
   Madhu Bhardwaj,
   International Typesetting and Composition

Acquisitions Coordinators
   Mandy Canales
   Jennifer Housh

Technical Editor
   Robert Bruckner

Copy Editor
   Lisa McCoy

Proofreader
   Bev Weiler

Indexer
   Kevin Broccoli

Production Supervisor
   Jean Bodeaux

Composition
   International Typesetting and Composition

Illustration
   International Typesetting and Composition

Art Director, Cover
   Jeff Weeks

Cover Designer
   Jeff Weeks

Microsoft® SQL Server™ 2008

DELIVERING BUSINESS INTELLIGENCE

About the Author

Brian Larson is a Phi Beta Kappa graduate of Luther College in Decorah, Iowa, with degrees in physics and computer science. Brian has 23 years of experience in the computer industry and 19 years experience as a consultant creating custom database applications. He is currently the Chief of Technology for Superior Consulting Services in Minneapolis, Minnesota, a Microsoft Consulting Partner for Reporting Services. Brian is a Microsoft Certified Solution Developer (MCSD) and a Microsoft Certified Database Administrator (MCDBA).

Brian served as a member of the original Reporting Services development team as a consultant to Microsoft. In that role, he contributed to the original code base of Reporting Services.

Brian has presented at national conferences and events, including the SQL Server Magazine Connections Conference, the PASS Community Summit, and the Microsoft Business Intelligence Conference, and has provided training and mentoring on Reporting Services across the country. He has been a contributor and columnist for *SQL Server Magazine*. In addition to this book, Brian is the author of *Microsoft SQL Server 2008 Reporting Services,* also from McGraw-Hill.

Brian and his wife Pam have been married for 23 years. Pam will tell you that their first date took place at the campus computer center. If that doesn't qualify someone to write a computer book, then I don't know what does. Brian and Pam have two children, Jessica and Corey.

About the Technical Editor

Robert M. Bruckner is a senior developer with the SQL Server Reporting Services (SSRS) product group at Microsoft. Prior to this role at Microsoft, he researched, designed, and implemented database and business intelligence systems as a scientific researcher at Vienna University of Technology, and as a system architect at T-Mobile Austria. Robert joined the Reporting Services development team in early 2003 and has been specializing on the data and report processing engine that is running inside server and client components of Reporting Services. Ever since the initial beta release of SSRS 2000, Robert has been sharing insights, tips, tricks, and expert advice about RDL, data and report processing, and SSRS in general, helping people learn about, understand, and succeed with SSRS (e.g., by posting on newsgroups and MSDN forums, publishing whitepapers, and speaking at conferences). Robert holds Master and PhD degrees with highest distinctions in Computer Science from Vienna University of Technology, Austria.

This book is dedicated to my parents. To my father, Robert, who even after 40-plus years as a junior high mathematics teacher and computer instructor, has a love of teaching. He has shown me a real commitment to sharing knowledge with others. To my mother, Beverly, who was my first editor, coaching me through elementary school papers on this state or that president. She taught me the value of sticking with a job and seeing it through to the end. I owe them both a debt of love, caring, and support that can never be adequately repaid.

Contents at a Glance

Contents

Part V   Delivering

Acknowledgments

No project of this size is the work of a single person. I need to thank a number of people for their assistance, professionalism, dedication, and support. So, a *gianormous* thank you …

To Wendy Rinaldi, who allowed me to lean on her as part editor, part coach, part literary agent, and part psychoanalyst. Her professionalism, humor, understanding, and faith truly made this project possible.

To Madhu Bhardwaj, who put up with my temperamental author moments and kept me on track and organized through two simultaneous book projects.

To Robert Bruckner, who provided vital insight and product knowledge.

To the rest of the McGraw-Hill Professional staff, who saw it through to the end and made sure there really was a book when all was said and done.

To John Miller, who founded Superior Consulting Services as a place where people can grow and learn, produce solid technology solutions, serve customers, and have a good time to boot.

To Jessica and Corey, my children, who allowed me time to pursue this passion.

To my wife, Pam, who continues to be gracious in her understanding of my affliction with the writing bug. She has given generously of her time to proof and review this book and its Learn By Doing exercises. Her incredible attention to detail has made this a better product.

Last, but certainly not least, to you, the reader, who plunked down your hard-earned cash for this purchase. I hope you view this as a helpful and informative guide to all of the truly exciting business intelligence features in SQL Server 2008.

All the best,
Brian Larson
blarson@teamscs.com

The Maximum Miniatures Databases and Other Supporting Materials

All of the samples in this book are based on business scenarios for a fictional company called Maximum Miniatures, Inc. You can download the data, image files, and other supporting materials from the book's web page on the McGraw-Hill Professional website. This download also includes the complete source code for all of the Learn By Doing activities and the applications demonstrated in the book.

The download is found on this book's web page at www.mhprofessional.com. Search for the book's web page using the ISBN, which is 0071549447. Use the "Code" link to download the zip file containing the book's material. Follow the instructions in the individual zip files to install or prepare each item as needed.

Part I

Business Intelligence

Chapter 1

Equipping the Organization for Effective Decision Making

In This Chapter

- ▶ **Effective Decision Making**
- ▶ **Keys to Effective Decision Making**
- ▶ **Business Intelligence**

"Would you tell me please, which way I ought to go from here?" asked Alice.
"That depends a good deal on where you want to get to," said the Cat.
"I don't much care where," said Alice.
"Then, it doesn't matter which way you go," said the Cat.

Alice's Adventures in Wonderland
—Lewis Carroll

Life is filled with decisions. Should I have the burger and fries or the salad for lunch? Should I get my significant other that new watch they've had their eye on, or should I buy them a new vacuum cleaner? Do I invest my holiday bonus or head for the casino? Should I buy this book or go browse the comics section? (Here is your first bit of business intelligence: Buy this book!)

The choices we make can have life-changing consequences. Even seemingly trivial decisions can have big consequences down the road. It's like your parents always told you: The key to success in life is to make good choices!

Effective Decision Making

Good decision making is as important in the working world as it is in the rest of our lives. Every day a number of decisions must be made that determine the direction and efficiency of the organizations we work for. Decisions are made concerning production, marketing, and personnel. Decisions are made affecting costs, sales, and margins. Just as in our personal lives, the key to organizational success is to make good choices. The organization must have effective decision making.

Who Is a Decision Maker?

Just who is it that must make good choices within an organization? At first blush, it may seem that only the person at the top, the chief executive officer (CEO), the president, or the chairperson needs to be an effective decision maker. If that person makes appropriate strategic decisions, the organization will succeed!

Unfortunately, it is not that easy. There are countless examples throughout history where absolutely brilliant strategic plans went awry because of poor decisions made by those responsible for their implementation. As emperor and leader of "La Grande Armée," Napoleon Bonaparte had a fairly decent strategic plan for his campaign in Belgium. However, due to some poor decision making by his marshals, Napoleon suffered a major defeat at a little place called Waterloo.

Given this, perhaps it is important for the next level of management to be effective decision makers as well. The chief financial officers (CFOs), CIOs, vice presidents, assistant chairpersons, and department heads (and marshals of the army) must make good choices when creating the policies and setting the priorities to implement the strategic plan. With all of upper management making effective decisions, the organization is guaranteed to go places!

In fact, success is not even assured when this is true. Effective plans and policies created at the top of the organization can be undone by poor decisions made further down as those plans and policies are put into action. The opposite is also true. Good decisions made by those working where the rubber meets the road can be quickly overwhelmed by poor decisions made further up the line.

The answer, then, is to have effective decision makers throughout an organization. Those lower down the organizational chart will have much better morale and will invest more energy in an activity if they have some assurance that their efforts will not be undone by someone higher up. In addition, the success of the person in the corner office is, in large part, simply a reflection of the effective decisions and successes of the people who report to them. Effective decision making at every level leads to success.

What Is an Effective Decision?

The organization that has the desired products or services, provided in the proper place, at the correct time, produced at the appropriate cost, and backed by the necessary customer support will be successful. This, of course, is fairly obvious. Any business plan or mission statement worth its salt professes to do just this.

What is not so obvious is how an organization goes about making sure it provides what is desired, proper, correct, appropriate, and necessary. The answer, as we learned in the last section, is to have people making effective decisions at all levels of the organization. But what exactly is an effective decision?

DEFINITION

Effective decisions *are choices that move an organization closer to an agreed-on set of goals in a timely manner.*

An effective decision moves an organization toward its goals in a timely manner. This definition is extremely broad. In fact, this makes a good slogan, but is too broad to be of much use in day-to-day operations. Using this definition, however, we can define three key ingredients necessary for making effective decisions:

▶ First, there must be a set of goals to work toward.

▶ Second, there must be a way to measure whether a chosen course is moving toward or away from those goals.

▶ Third, information based on those measures must be provided to the decision maker in a timely manner.

This information serves as both the foundation for the initial decision making and as feedback showing the results of the decision. Defining effective decision making is the easy part. Taking this rather nebulous definition and turning it into concrete business practices requires a bit more work.

DEFINITION

Foundation information *serves as the basis for making a particular decision as that decision is being made.*

DEFINITION

Feedback information *is used to evaluate the effectiveness of a particular decision after that decision is made.*

Keys to Effective Decision Making

In the previous section, we learned that three keys are necessary for effective decision making: specific goals, concrete measures, and timely foundation and feedback information, as shown in Figure 1-1. In this section, we take a detailed look at each of these three keys to learn how to encourage effective decision making.

Are We Going Hither or Yon?

In Mel Brooks's film, *The Producers,* Max and Leopold set out to stage an absolutely horrible Broadway musical, certain to fail, so they can abscond with the investor's money. Aside from this entertaining exception, organizations do not set out to fail. On the contrary, they come together, raise capital, create organizational charts,

Figure 1-1   *Three keys to effective decision making*

draw up business plans, prepare massive presentations, and have endless meetings, all to succeed. The first, largest, and ultimately fatal problem for many of these organizations is they do not define exactly what that success looks like. They don't know what the destination is.

An organization may have some nebulous goals in its mission statement. Phrases such as "superior customer satisfaction," "increased profit margin," or "better meeting our community's needs" grace the reception area, the annual report, and the entryway to the shareholders' meeting. These are great slogans for building a marketing campaign or generating esprit de corps among the employees. They do not, however, make good milestones for measuring business performance.

"Superior customer satisfaction" is a wonderful goal. (The world would be a much happier place if even half the companies that profess to strive toward superior customer satisfaction would actually make some progress in that direction.) The issue is how to measure "customer satisfaction." How do we know when we have reached this goal or if we are even making progress in that direction? What is required is something a bit more concrete and a lot more measurable.

Rather than the ill-defined "superior customer satisfaction," a better goal might be "to maintain superior customer satisfaction as measured by repeat customer orders with a goal of 80% repeat orders." This goal may need a few more details filled in, but it is the beginning of a goal that is specific and measurable. We can measure whether our decisions are taking us in the right direction based on the increase or decrease in repeat orders.

"Increased profit margin" makes the shareholders happy. Still, the organization must decide what operating costs impact profit margin and how they are divvied up among a number of concurrent projects. We may also want to state how large the increase to profit margin must be in order to satisfy the investors. Does a 1% increase put a smile on the shareholders' faces, or does our target need to be more in the 5% range? Once these details are added, we have a specific target to work toward.

"Better meeting our community's needs" is a noble goal, but what are those needs and how can we tell when they are met? Instead, we need to select a specific community need, such as increasing the number of quality, affordable housing units. We can then define what is meant by quality, affordable housing and just what size increase we are looking to achieve.

To function as part of effective decision making, a goal must:

▶ Contain a specific target.

▶ Provide a means to measure whether we are progressing toward that target.

As with the dartboard in Figure 1-2, we need both a bullseye to aim for and a method for scoring how close we came to that target.

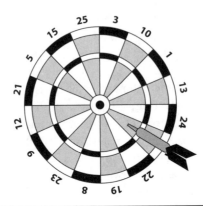

Figure 1-2 *Required elements of a goal to be used in effective decision making*

Is Your Map Upside-Down?

Goals are important. In fact, they are essential to effective decision making, as discussed in the previous section. However, goals are useless without some sort of movement toward reaching them. The finish line can only be reached if the ladies and gentlemen start their engines and begin the race.

This is where decision making comes into play. Each decision moves the company in a particular direction. Some decisions produce a giant leap. These are the policy and priority decisions usually made in the upper levels of management. These decisions determine the general course the organization is going to take over a lengthy period of time, a fiscal year, a school calendar period, or perhaps even the entire lifetime of the organization. It is essential that these decisions point the organization toward its goals if those goals are ever going to be reached.

Some decisions cause the organization to make smaller movements one way or another. These decisions range from workgroup policies to daily operating decisions. It could even come down to the way a particular employee decides to handle a specific customer complaint or which phone number a sales representative decides to dial next. These small variations in the organization's direction, these small steps forward or backward, when added together become a large determinant of whether the organization ultimately reaches its goals. For this reason, effective decision making is needed at all levels of the organization.

But how do we know when a decision moves the organization, either by a leap or a baby step, toward the goal? We need a method of navigation. As shown in Figure 1-3, we need a map or, these days, perhaps a global positioning system (GPS), to tell us where we are relative to our goal and to show us if we are moving in the right direction.

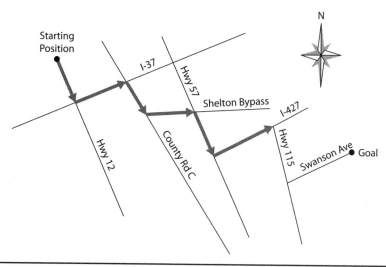

Figure 1-3   *Measuring progress toward the goal*

This is the reason why goals must include a means of measuring progress. By repeatedly checking these measures, we can determine whether the organization is making effective decisions. When the measures show we are heading away from the goals, the decision making can be adjusted accordingly. As long as our measures are correctly defined to match our goals, we have a good chance of moving ever closer to those goals.

Panicked Gossip, the Crow's Nest, or the Wireless

The sinking of the *Titanic* provides a catastrophic illustration of poor decision making. The ship was traveling at high speed in ice-laden waters—an unfortunate decision. This tragedy also provides us with an illustration of how important it is to receive feedback information in a timely manner.

News that there were "icebergs about" reached different people aboard the ship at different times. Most passengers found out about the fatal iceberg through panicked gossip as they were boarding the lifeboats. Of course, the passengers were not in a position to take direct action to correct the situation and, by the time they found out, it was far too late.

The ship's captain got news of the iceberg from the lookout in the crow's nest of the *Titanic*. This warning was received before the collision, and the captain attempted to correct the situation. However, the *Titanic* could neither stop nor turn on a dime so, ultimately, this warning turned out to be too late.

Another warning had been received earlier on board the *Titanic*. The wireless operator received an ice warning from another ship, the *America*, and even passed that warning on to a land-based wireless station. This message was received hours ahead of the collision—plenty of time to take precautions and avoid the tragedy. Because of the large workload on the wireless operator, however, this warning was never relayed to anyone on the *Titanic* with the authority to take those precautions. The feedback information aboard the *Titanic* is shown in Figure 1-4.

In the previous section, we learned about the need to use defined measures to get information to our decision makers. As the story of the *Titanic* illustrates, the timing of this feedback information is as important as its content. Feedback information that does not reach the proper decision makers in a timely manner is useful only to those investigating the tragedy after it has occurred. The goal of effective decision making is to avoid the tragedy in the first place!

As with the passengers on the *Titanic*, information in our organizations may come in the form of panicked gossip among lower-level personnel. Unlike those passengers, these people might even pick up some important information in advance of a calamity. Even if this is the case, these people are not in a position to correct the problem. Furthermore, we need to base our decision making on solid information from well-designed measures, not gossip and rumors.

Like the captain of the *Titanic*, the decision makers in our organizations often get feedback information when it is too late to act. The information may be extremely

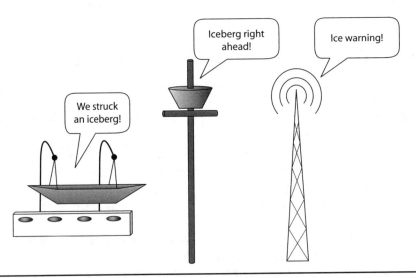

Figure 1-4   *Aboard the Titanic, feedback information was not given to the decision makers in a timely manner.*

accurate, but if it does not get to the decision makers in time to make corrections, it is not helpful. The numbers in the year-end report are not helpful for making decisions during the current year.

Similar to the wireless operator, our organizations often have a person who has the appropriate information at the appropriate time. The situation breaks down when this person does not pass the information along to the appropriate decision maker. This may occur, as in the case of the *Titanic's* wireless operator, because that person is overworked and has too much information to get out to too many people. It may also occur because organizational policies or structures prevent the flow of information. Finally, this may occur because the infrastructure is not in place to facilitate this communication.

Business Intelligence

The first step in effective decision making is to set specific, measurable goals. As these goals are being set, the objective is to get accurate, useful information to the appropriate decision makers to serve as a foundation for the decision and as feedback on the effectiveness of that decision. Having the foundation and feedback information available at the appropriate time is extremely important. The question becomes: How does an organization go about obtaining and distributing this information? As the title of this book suggests, the answer is through the use of business intelligence. In fact, this objective serves as our definition of business intelligence.

DEFINITION

Business intelligence *is the delivery of accurate, useful information to the appropriate decision makers within the necessary timeframe to support effective decision making.*

Business intelligence is not simply facts and figures on a printed report or a computer screen. Rows upon rows of numbers showing detailed sales figures or production numbers may be extremely accurate, but they are not business intelligence until they are put in a format that can be easily understood by a decision maker who needs to use them. Concise summaries of customer satisfaction or assembly-line efficiency may be easily understood, but they are not business intelligence until they can be delivered in time to meaningfully affect daily decision making.

We also discovered earlier in this chapter that effective decision making is important at all organizational levels. Timely foundation and feedback information is needed as part of that effective decision making. Therefore, we need to make business intelligence available throughout our organizations.

Business Intelligence and Microsoft SQL Server 2008

Fortunately, Microsoft SQL Server 2008 provides tools to support all aspects of business intelligence. Integration Services enables us to create automated processes to cleanse data and move it into a business intelligence warehouse, when necessary, to ensure we have accurate information available in a timely manner. Numerous online analytical processing (OLAP) features, such as Key Performance Indicators (KPIs), multidimensional expression (MDX) queries and scripts, and the Unified Dimensional Model (UDM) enable us to slice, dice, and summarize information so it can be presented in a meaningful manner. *Data mining* permits us to find and present patterns and behavior predictors that might not otherwise be found in the data. Finally, Reporting Services and Microsoft Office Business Intelligence Accelerators facilitate the delivery of this information to decision makers throughout the entire organization.

In Chapter 2 of this book, we learn more about the concepts used when creating and delivering business intelligence. We see the types of questions business intelligence can help us answer. We also examine the kinds of information and the timeliness of that information required at various levels within an organization.

Finally, we become acquainted with Maximum Miniatures, Incorporated, the sample company we use throughout the remainder of the book. To make the business intelligence features of SQL Server 2008 easier to understand, we perform several hands-on exercises to create business intelligence solutions. Rather than looking at code snippets without any business context, we use the business needs of Maximum Miniatures. The goal of this book is not to enable you to use this or that feature of SQL Server 2008, but to help you understand how to use those features to meet business needs.

Chapter 2

Making the Most of What You've Got—Using Business Intelligence

In This Chapter

- ▶ **What Business Intelligence Can Do for You**
- ▶ **Business Intelligence at Many Levels**
- ▶ **Maximum Miniatures, Inc.**
- ▶ **Building the Foundation**

Out of clutter find simplicity.
From discord find harmony.

—Albert Einstein's First Two Rules of Work

In the previous chapter, we discussed the importance of effective decision making to the success of any organization. We also learned that effective decision making depends on specific goals, concrete measures to evaluate our progress toward those goals, and foundation and feedback information based on those measures. The latter two items, concrete measures and foundation/feedback information, we referred to as business intelligence.

In this chapter, we take a look at the types of questions this business intelligence can help us answer. We also discuss the types of business intelligence that are needed at various levels of an organization. The chapter ends by talking about Maximum Miniatures, Incorporated, the company we are going to use for our examples throughout the book.

What Business Intelligence Can Do for You

In Chapter 1, we saw how business intelligence is used to support effective decision making. It provides foundational information on which to base a decision. Business intelligence also provides us with feedback information that can be used to evaluate a decision. It can provide that foundational and feedback information in a number of different ways.

When We Know What We Are Looking For

In some cases, we know what information we are looking for. We have a set of particular questions we want answered. What is the dollar amount of the sales or services our organization is providing in each region? Who are our top salespeople? In some of these situations, we not only know what we are looking for, but we also have a good idea where to find the information when we design the business intelligence solution.

Layout-led Discovery

When we know the question we want answered and have a good idea where that answer is going to be found, we can use printed reports to deliver our business intelligence. This is the most common form of business intelligence and one we are all familiar with. For many situations, this format works well.

For example, if we want to know the dollar amount of the sales or services provided in each region, we know where to find this information. We can design a report to retrieve the information, and the report will consistently deliver what we need. The report serves as an effective business intelligence tool.

This is an example of layout-led discovery. With *layout-led discovery,* we can only learn information that the report designer thought to put in the report layout when it was first designed. If the information wasn't included at design time, we have no way to access it at the time the report is read.

Suppose our report shows the dollar amount for a given region to be unusually low. If the report designer did not include the supporting detail for that region, we have no way to drill into the region and determine the cause of the anomaly. Perhaps a top salesperson moved to another region. Maybe we have lost a key client. The report won't give us that information. We quickly come to a dead end.

Data-led Discovery

In some cases, we know the question, but we don't know exactly where to look for our answer. This often occurs when the information we initially receive changes the question slightly. As in the example from the previous section, an anomaly in the information may cause us to want to look at the data in a slightly different way. The unusually low dollar amount for sales or services provided in a specific region led us to want detailed numbers within that region.

In other cases, we know where to look, but it is not practical to search through all of the detailed information. Instead, we want to start at an upper level, find a number that looks interesting, and then drill to more detail. We want to follow the data that catches our attention to see where it leads.

This is *data-led discovery:* The information we find determines where we want to go next. The developer of this type of solution cannot know everywhere the report user may want to go. Instead, the developer must provide an interactive environment that enables the user to navigate at will.

To implement data-led discovery, we need some type of drilldown mechanism. When we see something that looks interesting, we need to be able to click that item and access the next level of detail. This is, of course, not going to happen on a sheet of paper. Data-led discovery must be done online.

Discovering New Questions and Their Answers

In some cases, our data may hold answers to questions we have not even thought to ask. The data may contain trends, correlations, and dependencies at a level of detail that would be impossible for a human being to notice using either layout-led or data-led discovery. These relationships can be discovered by the computer using data mining techniques.

DEFINITION

Data mining *uses a complex mathematical algorithm to sift through detail data to identify patterns, correlations, and clustering within the data.*

Where layout-led discovery and data-led discovery usually start with summarized data, data mining works at the lowest level of detail. Highly sophisticated mathematical algorithms are applied to the data to find correlations between characteristics and events. Data mining can uncover such nuggets as the fact that a customer who purchased a certain product is more likely to buy a different product from your organization (we hope a product with a high profit margin). Or, a client receiving a particular service is also likely to need another service from your organization in the next three months.

This type of information can be extremely helpful when planning marketing campaigns, setting up cross-product promotions, or doing capacity planning for the future. It can also aid in determining where additional resources and effort would produce the most effective result.

Business Intelligence at Many Levels

In Chapter 1, we discussed the fact that business intelligence should be utilized at all levels of an organization to promote effective decision making. While it is true that business intelligence is useful throughout the organization, the same type of information is not needed at each level. Different levels within the organization require different types of business intelligence for effective decision making.

As we look at what is required at each level, keep in mind the Effective Decisions Triangle from Figure 1-1. We will transform that triangle into a pyramid as we examine the specific goals, concrete measures, and the timing of the foundation and feedback information required at each level. (See Figure 2-1, Figure 2-2, and Figure 2-3.)

The Top of the Pyramid

Decision makers at the upper levels of our organizations must look at the big picture. They are charged with setting long-term goals for the organization. Decision makers need to have a broad overview of their area of responsibility and not get caught up in the minutiae.

Figure 2-1   *Specific goals at each level of the organization*

Highly Summarized Measures

The business intelligence utilized at this level needs to match these characteristics. The measures delivered to these decision makers must be highly summarized. In many cases, each measure is represented, not by a number, but by a status indicator showing whether the measure is in an acceptable range, is starting to lag, or is in an unacceptable range. These highly summarized measures are known as Key Performance Indicators.

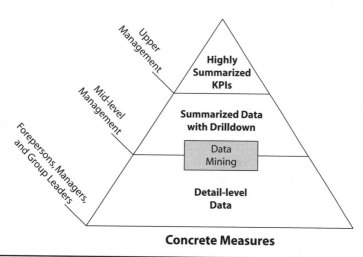

Figure 2-2   *Concrete measures at each level of the organization*

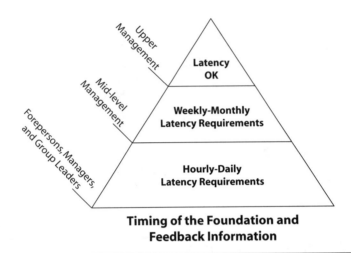

Figure 2-3 *Timing of the foundation and feedback information at each level of the organization*

DEFINITION

Key Performance Indicators (KPIs) are highly summarized measures designed to quickly relay the status of that measure. They usually reflect the most vital aspects of the organization.

KPIs are used to provide these high-level decision makers with a quick way to determine the health of the essential aspects of the organization. KPIs are often presented as a graphical icon, such as a traffic light or a gauge, designed to convey the indicator's status at a glance. We discuss KPIs in greater detail in Chapter 10 of this book.

Higher Latency

Because these upper-level decision makers are dealing in long-term policies and direction, they do not need up-to-the-minute business intelligence. Another way to state this is to say they can have more *latency* in their business intelligence. These decision makers need to see downward trends in time to make corrections. They do not need to see the daily blips in the organization's operation.

DEFINITION

The latency *of business intelligence is the amount of time between the occurrence of a transaction and the loading of that transaction's information into the business intelligence system.*

Mid-Level

Mid-level decision makers are managing the operation of departments and other working units within the organization. They are setting short-term goals and doing the planning for the functioning of these areas. Mid-level decision makers are still at a level where they should not be in the details of day-to-day processes.

Summarized Measures with Drilldown

These mid-level decision makers need business intelligence that is still summarized, but they often need to drill down into this information to get at more detail. Therefore, these decision makers can utilize printed reports, along with interactive systems, allowing data-led discovery. These decision makers can also make use of information from data mining.

Some Latency Acceptable

Because these decision makers are closer to the everyday functions, they may require business intelligence with less latency. In some cases, they may need to see measures that are updated daily. In other cases, these decision makers are looking for trends discernable from weekly or monthly loads.

The Broad Base

At the broad base of our business intelligence pyramid are the forepersons, managers, and group leaders taking care of daily operations. These people are setting daily operational goals and making decisions on resource allocation for the next week, the next day, or perhaps the next shift. They are planning the next sales campaign or maybe just the next sales call. These decision makers usually need business intelligence systems with high availability and high responsiveness.

Measures at the Detail Level

These decision makers are dealing with the details of the organization's operations. They need to be able to access information at the detail level. In some cases, the work groups these decision makers are responsible for are small enough that they can see the detail for the work group directly without being overwhelmed. In other cases, measures need to be summarized, but drilldown to the detail level will probably be required. These decision makers may utilize some forms of data mining to help discern trends and correlations in daily information.

Low Latency

Because these low-level decision makers are managing day-to-day operations, they need to react quickly to changes in feedback information. For this reason, they can tolerate little latency. In some cases, these decision makers require data that is no more than one day old, one hour old, or even less.

Maximum Miniatures, Inc.

Throughout the remainder of this book, Maximum Miniatures, Incorporated serves as the basis for all of our examples. Maximum Miniatures, or Max Min, Inc., as it is referred to by most employees, manufactures and sells small, hand-painted figurines. It has several product lines, including the Woodland Creatures collection of North American animals; the Mythic World collection, which includes dragons, trolls, and elves; the Warriors of Yore collection, containing various soldiers from Roman times up through World War II; and the Guiding Lights collection, featuring replica lighthouses from the United States. The miniatures are made from clay, pewter, or aluminum.

Max Min markets these miniatures through three different channels. It operates five of its own "Maximum Miniature World" stores dedicated to selling the Max Min product line. Max Min also operates MaxMin.com to sell its products online. In addition, Max Min sells wholesale to other retailers.

Business Needs

Max Min, Inc. has experienced rapid growth in the past three years, with orders increasing by over 300 %. This growth has put a strain on Max Min's only current source of business intelligence, the printed report. Reports that worked well to support decision making just a few years ago now take an hour or more to print and even longer to digest. These reports work at the detail level with little summarization. Max Min's current systems provide few, if any, alternatives to the printed reports for viewing business intelligence.

In addition, Max Min, Inc. is facing tough competition in a number of its product areas. This competition requires Max Min to practice effective decision making to keep its competitive edge. Unfortunately, Max Min's current business intelligence infrastructure, or lack thereof, is making this extremely difficult.

Because of these issues, Max Min has launched a new project to create a true business intelligence environment to support its decision making. This project includes the design of a data warehouse structure, the population of that data warehouse from its current systems, and the creation of analysis applications to serve decision makers at all levels of the organization.

The new business intelligence platform is based on SQL Server 2008. After an extensive evaluation, it was decided that the SQL Server 2008 platform would provide the highest level of business intelligence capability for the money spent. SQL Server 2008 was also chosen because it features the tools necessary to implement the data warehouse in a relatively short amount of time.

We will examine each step of Max Min's implementation project as we learn about the various business intelligence tools available in SQL Server 2008. Before we begin, let's take a quick look at Max Min's current systems.

Current Systems

Max Min has five data processing systems that are expected to serve as sources of business intelligence (see Figure 2-4).

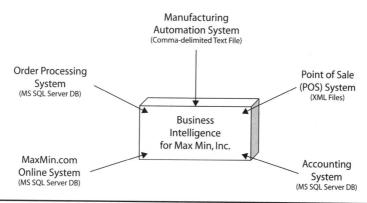

Figure 2-4   *Sources of business intelligence at Max Min, Inc.*

Manufacturing Automation

The manufacturing automation system tracks the materials used to make each product. It also stores which products are manufactured on which production lines. Finally, this system tracks the number of items manufactured during each shift.

The manufacturing automation system uses a proprietary data-storage format. Data can be exported from the manufacturing automation system to a comma-delimited text file. This text file serves as the source for loading the manufacturing data into the business intelligence systems.

Order Processing

The order processing system manages the inventory amounts for all products. It tracks wholesale orders placed by non–Max Min retailers. The system also records product amounts sold through the Max Min retail stores and the Max Min online store to maintain inventory amounts.

The order processing system tracks order fulfillment, including product shipping. It also generates invoices and handles the payment of those invoices. In addition, this system records any products returned from the retailer.

The order processing system uses a Microsoft SQL Server database as its backend.

Point of Sale

The point of sale (POS) system manages the cash registers at each of the five Max Min–owned retail stores. This system also tracks the inventory at each retail store using Universal Product Code (UPC) barcode stickers placed on each item. The POS system handles both cash and credit card transactions. It also tracks information on any products returned by the customer.

Information from each of the five POS systems is exported to an XML file. This XML file is transferred nightly, using File Transfer Protocol (FTP), to a central location. These XML files serve as the source for loading the POS data into the business intelligence systems.

MaxMin.com

The MaxMin.com online store is an ASP.NET application. It uses SQL Server as its backend database. All sales through the online store are paid with a credit card. All customers of the online store must provide name, address, phone number, and e-mail address with each purchase.

The online store tracks the shipping of orders. It also handles any products returned by customers. Finally, the online store saves information on product promotions and discounts that are run on the store site.

Accounting

The accounting system tracks all the financial transactions for Max Min, Inc. This includes the purchase of raw materials for manufacturing. The accounting system uses a SQL Server database for its backend.

Building the Foundation

In Chapter 3, you will learn more about the foundations of our business intelligence systems. We explore possible sources for our business intelligence data. We also look at what the structure of those data sources might look like.

Chapter 3

Seeking the Source— The Source of Business Intelligence

In This Chapter

▶ **Seeking the Source**
▶ **The Data Mart**
▶ **Snowflakes, Stars, and Analysis Services**

Planning ahead is a good idea. It wasn't raining when Noah built the ark.

—Anonymous

In the previous chapter, we discussed the various ways business intelligence can aid in making effective business decisions. We also looked at the characteristics of the business intelligence used at different levels within our organizations. Finally, we were introduced to Maximum Miniatures, Incorporated, the source for all sample data in this book.

In this chapter, we begin planning the database structures to serve as the source of our business intelligence. In some cases, we can extract our business intelligence information directly from the same database used to store the data from our daily business operations. In many cases, however, we need to move that data into another location before we can use it as business intelligence. This "other location" is known as a data mart.

Seeking the Source

We have seen that business intelligence is important for effective decision making in our organizations. This, however, leads to a big question. Just where is this business intelligence going to come from? Is business intelligence a form of corporate espionage? Do we need to send up spy satellites to watch our competitors and tap the phone lines of our clients? Should we be hiring secret agents to infiltrate our rivals' facilities? Of course not!

Does business intelligence require us to take the pulse of the people? Do we need to commission large studies of our potential customers? Do we need to conduct a survey to determine what people are thinking about our products or services? While some business intelligence may come from customer satisfaction surveys or market research, the customer's buying behavior is a better gauge of their tendencies and satisfaction. At any rate, this is not what we are going to focus on in this book.

The bulk of business intelligence for most organizations comes from something they already have: their transactional data.

Transactional Data

Most organizations need to keep track of the things they do to conduct their business. Orders taken, products produced, services rendered, payments received from clients, and payments made to vendors are all interactions that usually result in one or more entries in some type of data store. Each of these interactions is a business transaction, so we refer to this as transactional data.

DEFINITION

Transactional data *is the information stored to track the interactions, or business transactions, carried out by an organization.*

The business transactions of an organization need to be tracked for that organization to operate. Payments must be collected for products and services. Payments must be made for goods and services received. Orders and service requests need to be fulfilled. In general, the organization needs to keep track of what it has done and what it needs to do. When these transactions are stored on and managed by computers, we refer to this as online transaction processing, or OLTP.

DEFINITION

Online transaction processing (OLTP) systems record business interactions as they happen. They support the day-to-day operation of an organization.

The sum of these transactions stored in OLTP systems is the history of an organization. This transactional data contains the raw numbers necessary to calculate the measures we discussed in the previous chapter. Here, then, is the data we need to create our business intelligence.

Difficulties Using Transactional Data for Business Intelligence

OLTP systems are the treasure chests holding the raw data we need to calculate measures and create business intelligence. Problems arise, however, when we try to extract these nuggets of raw data from our OLTP systems. Let's take a look at some of the difficulties.

The Nature of the Beast   Well-designed OLTP systems are optimized for efficiently processing and storing transactions. This means breaking data up into small chunks using the rules of database normalization. This allows OLTP systems to process a number of transactions at the same time without one transaction getting in another's way. Information of this type is best stored in a relational database.

The measures we are using for business intelligence, on the other hand, are not designed to reflect the events of one transaction, but to reflect the net result of a number of transactions over a selected period of time. Business intelligence measures are often aggregates of hundreds, thousands, or even millions of individual transactions. Designing a system to provide these aggregates efficiently requires an entirely different set of optimizations.

DEFINITION

An aggregate *is a number that is calculated from amounts in many detail records. An aggregate is often the sum of many numbers, although it can also be derived using other arithmetic operations or even from a count of the number of items in a group. For example, the total amount invoiced to a client in a given year is the aggregate sum of all the invoice amounts for that client in the given year.*

OLTP systems, because of the way they are designed, are usually not good at delivering large aggregates. This is not what they were intended to do. We need to look to a different type of data storage optimization to make these aggregates work efficiently.

Interfering with Business Operations   OLTP systems are used by our organizations to support their daily operations. In many cases, the organizations' operation depends on the performance of these systems. If the order processing system or the client management system becomes too bogged down, our organizations can grind to a halt.

We've already discussed the fact that OLTP systems are not good at delivering the aggregates needed for business intelligence. When OLTP systems are called on to produce such aggregates, they typically use a large amount of processing power and take a long time to produce a result. It is also possible that a large number of records will be locked while the aggregate is being produced, rendering those records unavailable to participate in transactional processing. Either of these two events can have a serious impact on transactional processing efficiency.

In other words, requiring an OLTP system to create business intelligence aggregates can tax the system. This can have a detrimental effect on our organizations' daily operations.

Archiving   Because OLTP systems are concerned with the day-to-day operations, they aren't too worried about data from the distant past. These systems may only save data for a relatively short period of time (and/or the data may only represent the current state, such as current quantity in stock). The data may be saved for a year, and then a year-end process may remove it from the database. It may be archived in another format, a text file or a database backup file, or it might simply be deleted. Whether deleted or archived, the data is no longer easily accessible.

OLTP systems use this archive process to ensure that the system continues to operate efficiently. If a transaction table contains too many records, the OLTP system can become bogged down and begin to operate slowly. Archiving allows an OLTP system to stay lean and mean.

This archiving causes problems for business intelligence. When we are looking for trends in our measures, we want to compare last year's numbers to this year's numbers. We may even want to compare numbers over several years of operation. This is hard to do when the data from past years has been archived or deleted.

Divided They Stand   Our organizations probably use a number of different OLTP systems to manage different aspects of their operations. One system is used for order processing, a different system for accounting, another for manufacturing, and still another for personnel. As we saw in the previous chapter, Maximum Miniatures, Incorporated has five different systems that can provide data for business intelligence. Even with the move toward integrated Enterprise Resource Planning (ERP) systems, it is unlikely that all of an organization's transactional data will be in one location.

The measures used to provide business intelligence, on the other hand, do not respect these lines of separation. Instead, they treat the organization as a whole. For example, a reasonable measure to require is the profit margin for a particular product. To calculate this measure, we need the list of raw materials from the manufacturing system, the cost of those materials from the accounting system, the cost of labor required to produce the product from the time entry system, and the amount paid for the product from the order processing system. To calculate this type of a measure, then, we need to combine data across systems to get what we need.

Aside from the necessity for communication between systems, this need to cross systems leads to another problem. Each of these systems maintains its own set of product numbering schemes, codes, and calendars. The same product may be known as "12593" in the manufacturing system and "SD125RDS" in the order processing system. The payroll system may work on two-week pay periods, while the accounting system works on fiscal months. When data from these disparate systems is brought together, we need to find some common ground.

The Data Mart

A number of problems can result when we try to use our organizations' OLTP systems as the source for our business intelligence. What we need to do is take the information stored in these OLTP systems and move it into a different data store. This intermediate data store can then serve as the source for our measure calculations. We need to store the data so it is available for our business intelligence needs somewhere outside of our OLTP systems. When data is stored in this manner, it is referred to as a data mart.

DEFINITION

A data mart is a body of historical data in an electronic repository that does not participate in the daily operations of the organization. Instead, this data is used to create business intelligence. The data in the data mart usually applies to a specific area of the organization.

NOTE

In this book, we discuss the creation of data marts, rather than the perhaps more familiar term, data warehouse. Data warehouses tend to be large, one-stop-shopping repositories where all the historical data for the organization would be stored. Nothing is wrong with this as a concept; however, attempting to create a data warehouse often led to huge, multiyear technology projects that were never quite finished or were outdated when they finally did get done. In this book, we concern ourselves with creating data marts—smaller undertakings that focus on a particular aspect of an organization.

Features of a Data Mart

Because the data mart is meant to serve as a source for business intelligence rather than managing the organization's day-to-day transactions, it is not designed the same as an OLTP database. Instead of being built around the rules of normalization, data marts are built for speed of access. A data mart is still a relational database, but it is designed to require fewer table joins when data is output for analysis and reporting. In a data mart, it is acceptable to have data repeated (denormalized) for the sake of speed.

When designing a data mart, the rules of normalization are replaced by a different method of design organized around "facts." These new design approaches are called stars and snowflakes. We discuss stars and snowflakes in the sections "The Star Schema" and "The Snowflake Schema." Stars and snowflakes may seem like the stuff of children's fantasies, but, in reality, they provide quite grownup and down-to-earth approaches to creating information that is quick and easy to access.

Not Real-Time Data

OLTP systems store data from business transactions as they occur throughout the day. Data marts, on the other hand, are updated at set intervals. Data is copied from the OLTP systems periodically and written to the data mart. This is known as a *data load*.

Because the data mart exists separately from the OLTP systems, accessing the data mart for business intelligence information does not put any stress on the transactional systems vital to the business' operation. The only exception to this is during the data load. During the data load, the OLTP systems may have to work hard to prepare the data for copying to the data mart. The good news here is the data load is an automated process that can be scheduled to run during off-peak hours.

As we discussed in Chapter 2, information in a data mart has some latency. In most cases, some time elapses between the moment a transaction is completed and the moment when the transaction is copied to the data mart. If a data mart load is scheduled to run each month right after the month-end processing, then the data mart has a latency of one month. If the data load runs nightly, the data mart can have a latency of up to one day.

The latency of the data mart must be set properly to fulfill the business intelligence requirements of that data mart. The information provided by the data mart must be up-to-date enough to facilitate effective decision making. However, the data loads should not occur so often that they cause unneeded stress on the OLTP systems.

Consolidation and Cleansing

Data from a number of different OLTP systems may be combined into a single data mart. This enables us to calculate some complex measures for our business intelligence. As we discussed earlier, this may also cause problems. Multiple OLTP systems can have different ways of representing data. Inconsistent data types used for the same data, dissimilar unique identifiers used for the same entity, and different time periods and calendar systems can all cause a great deal of difficulty when trying to combine data from heterogeneous systems.

In fact, problems can even arise when using data from a single system. The business rules necessary for a meaningful measure calculation may be stricter than those enforced within the OLTP system itself. If this is the case, some of the data coming from the OLTP system may not meet the stricter rules. Inconsistencies with data types and unique identifiers could also exist within the same system if the database has been poorly designed or poorly maintained.

These problems must be resolved before the data can be stored in the data mart. We must scrub out all the problem data. To do this, the data is put through a data cleansing process.

DEFINITION

Data cleansing removes inconsistencies and errors from transactional data so it has the consistency necessary for use in a data mart.

Data cleansing transforms data into a format that does not cause problems in the data mart environment. It converts inconsistent data types into a single type. Data cleansing translates dissimilar identifiers to a standard set of codes for the data mart. In addition, it repairs or removes any data that does not meet the business rules required by the measures calculated from this data mart.

Data cleansing is usually done as part of a larger process. This process extracts the data from the OLTP systems and loads it into the data mart. Thus, the entire procedure is known as extract, transform, and load—or ETL.

DEFINITION

The Extract, Transform, and Load (ETL) process extracts data to copy from one or more OLTP systems, performs any required data cleansing to transform the data into a consistent format, and loads the cleansed data by inserting it into the data mart.

Data Mart Structure

The data we use for business intelligence can be divided into four categories: measures, dimensions, attributes, and hierarchies. These four types of data help us to define the structure of the data mart. Let's look at each of these types of data and see how they are stored in the data mart.

Measures

The measure forms the basis of everything we do with business intelligence. In fact, without measures, there would be no business intelligence. As we learned in Chapter 1, the measures are the whole reason for pursuing business intelligence. They are the basic building blocks for effective decision making.

DEFINITION

A measure is a numeric quantity expressing some aspect of the organization's performance. The information represented by this quantity is used to support or evaluate the decision making and performance of the organization. A measure can also be called a fact.

Measures are the facts we use for our foundational and feedback information. Therefore, the tables that hold measure information are known as *fact tables*. Don't let the name fool you, though, Sergeant Friday—fact tables hold more than just the facts.

Dimensions

Total sales is an example of a measure that is often required for effective decision making. However, it is not often that decision makers want to see one single aggregate representing the total sales for all products for all salespersons for the entire lifetime of the organization. Instead, they are more likely to want to slice and dice this total into smaller parts. Dimensions are used to facilitate this slicing and dicing.

DEFINITION

A dimension is a categorization used to spread out an aggregate measure to reveal its constituent parts.

A dimension enables us to apply a categorization to an aggregate measure. The categorization lets us see the constituent numbers that create the aggregate measure. For example, we can think of the measure of total sales as a single point of information. In geometry, a point has no dimensions.

Total Sales

$145,346,834

We can apply a categorization or a dimension to that single point of data to spread it out. In this case, let's spread the total sales out into the total sales for each year.

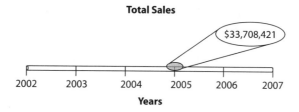

Total Sales

$33,708,421

2002   2003   2004   2005   2006   2007

Years

We now have a line made up of measures of total sales at various points along that line, one point for each year in the dimension. In geometry, a line is a one-dimensional object. Thus, we have added a dimension to our measure: 2002, 2003, 2004, 2005, 2006, and 2007 are each said to be *members* of the year dimension.

We can again spread out the total sales, this time for each product type.

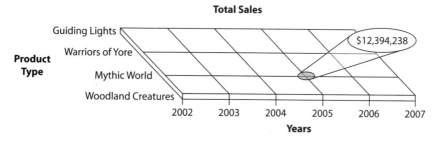

Total Sales

Guiding Lights
Warriors of Yore
Product Type
Mythic World
Woodland Creatures

$12,394,238

2002   2003   2004   2005   2006   2007

Years

The measures of total sales are now arranged in a square. Because a square is a two-dimensional object, we have added another dimension to our measure. Woodland Creatures, Mythic World, Warriors of Yore, and Guiding Lights are each members of the product type dimension.

Let's spread out the total sales once more—this time by sales region. The measure of total sales has become a cube, which is a three-dimensional object. You can see that each time we add a new criteria to spread out the measure, we increase the dimensionality of our measure, thus, the name dimension.

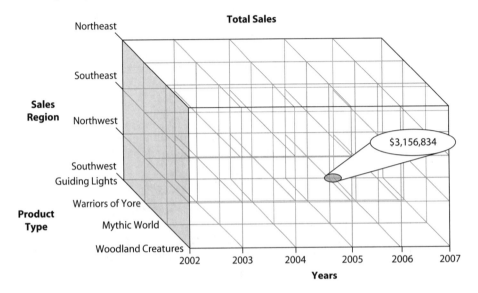

We can continue to spread out the measure using additional dimensions, such as a marketing campaign dimension and a buyer's age bracket dimension, to get a four-dimensional object, and then a five-dimensional object. Even though this becomes difficult to represent in an illustration, it is a perfectly valid thing to do. Also, because we are more familiar with three-dimensional objects than four- or five-dimensional ones, if there is such a thing, we continue to refer to these structures with four, five, or even more dimensions as cubes. We talk more about cubes in Chapter 4.

The Star Schema

Measures and dimensions are stored in the data mart in one of two layouts, or schemas. First, we look at the star schema. The name of this schema comes from the shape formed by the relational database diagram for the data mart, as we will see in a moment. The star schema uses two types of tables: fact tables and dimension tables.

DEFINITION

A star schema is a relational database schema used to hold measures and dimensions in a data mart. The measures are stored in a fact table, and dimensions are stored in dimension tables.

SalesFact
⧫ YearID
⧫ ProductTypeID
⧫ SalesRegionID
⧫ MarketingCampaignID
⧫ BuyersAgeGroupID
Total Sales

Figure 3-1   *The SalesFact table*

The center of the star is formed by the fact table. The fact table has a column for the measure and a column for each dimension containing the foreign key for a member of that dimension. The primary key for this table is created by concatenating all of the foreign key fields. This is known as a *composite key*. Fact tables are named for the set of measures they contain, with the word "Fact" added to the end. The fact table for the example in the previous section is shown in Figure 3-1.

The dimensions are stored in dimension tables. The dimension table has a column for the unique identifier of a member of the dimension, usually an integer or a short character value. The dimension table has another column for a description of the member. One dimension is stored in each dimension table, with one row for each member of the dimension. Dimension tables are named for the dimension they contain, with the letters "Dim" added to the beginning. The rows of the DimProductType dimension table would be:

ProductTypeID	ProductTypeDescription
1	Woodland Creatures
2	Mythic World
3	Warriors of Yore
4	Guiding Lights

When we add the dimension tables to the schema, we get the characteristic star design, as shown in Figure 3-2.

Potentially, one row will be in the fact table for every unique combination of dimension members. The word "potentially" is used here because there may be some combinations of dimension members that do not have a value. In some cases, a particular combination of dimension members may not even make sense.

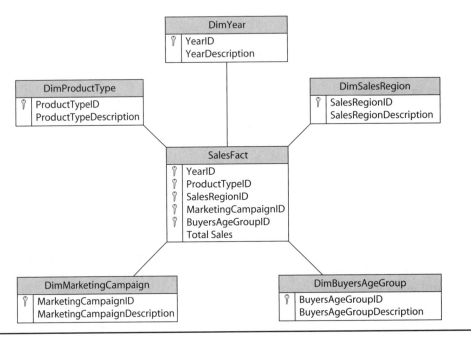

Figure 3-2   *The star schema*

In our example, if History Magazine Spring Ad is a member of the marketing campaign dimension, some of the rows in the SalesFact table would be:

Year	Product Type	Sales Region	Marketing Campaign	Buyer's Age	Total Sales
2003	Mythic World	Northeast	History Mag Spring Ad	0–25	56,342
2003	Mythic World	Northeast	History Mag Spring Ad	25–35	104,547
2003	Mythic World	Northeast	History Mag Spring Ad	35–45	234,385
2003	Mythic World	Northeast	History Mag Spring Ad	45–55	534,532
2003	Mythic World	Northeast	History Mag Spring Ad	55–65	829,282
2003	Mythic World	Northeast	History Mag Spring Ad	65+	284,540

If, in our example, we assume there are eight members of the marketing campaign dimension to go along with six members of the year dimension, four members of the product type dimension, four members of the sales region dimension, and six members of the buyer's age dimension, we have a potential for

$8 \times 6 \times 4 \times 4 \times 6$

or 4608 rows in the SalesFact table. This is not a huge number, but you can see when you have dimensions with tens or hundreds of members, the size of the fact table can grow rather large.

In reality, the fact table should contain the identifiers for the dimension members, rather than their descriptions. This cuts down on the size required to store each fact row. This becomes important in fact tables with a potential for millions or even hundreds of millions of rows.

In addition, a single fact table may contain multiple measures. This can occur when two or more measures use exactly the same dimensions. Putting a number of measures with the same dimensions in the same fact table is also a way to save on storage space required for the data mart.

Attributes

In some cases, we may want to store additional information about dimension members in our data mart. This helps us further define the members of the dimension. These bits of additional information are known as attributes of the dimension.

DEFINITION

An attribute *is an additional piece of information pertaining to a dimension member that is not the unique identifier or the description of the member.*

Attributes can be used to more fully describe dimension members. They may contain information about a dimension member that the users are likely to want as part of their business intelligence output. Attributes are also used to store information that may be used to limit or filter the records selected from the data mart during data analysis. They are stored as additional columns in the dimension tables, as shown in Figure 3-3.

Hierarchies

In many cases, a dimension is part of a larger structure with many levels. This structure is known as a hierarchy. In our sample, the year, product type, and sales region dimensions are each part of their own hierarchy.

DEFINITION

A hierarchy *is a structure made up of two or more levels of related dimensions. A dimension at an upper level of the hierarchy completely contains one or more dimensions from the next lower level of the hierarchy.*

The year dimension contains quarters. Further, the quarters contain months. The product type dimension contains product subtypes, which, in turn, contain products. The sales region dimension contains sales territories.

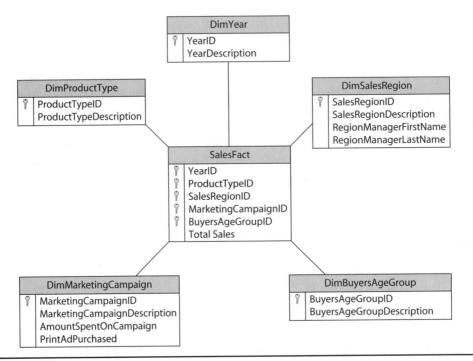

Figure 3-3 *Attribute columns in the dimension tables*

Hierarchies enable the users to navigate to different levels of granularity within the measures of the data mart. Users can look at the measures at one level of the hierarchy, then drill into a selected member to see the next lower level. For example, a user can look at the product subtypes within the Mythic World product type. He or she can look at the sales territories within the Northeast sales region. A user can also look at the months within Q1, 2007. In fact, all of these can be combined at once so the user can view the sales totals by the product subtypes of the Mythic World product type, by sales territories of the Northeast sales region, and by months in Q1, 2007. By moving up and down the hierarchy, users can find exactly the right measure to aid in making the decision at hand.

In a star schema, the information about the hierarchies is stored right in the dimension tables, as shown in Figure 3-4. The primary key in each of the dimension tables is at the lowest level of the hierarchy. Because of this, the fact table must be changed so its foreign keys point to the lowest levels in the hierarchies as well. This means, then, the fact table will have one row (and one set of measures) for each unique combination of members at the lowest level of all the hierarchies.

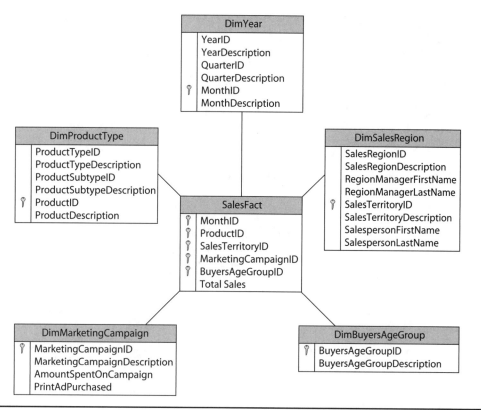

Figure 3-4   *A star schema with hierarchies*

Measures for hierarchy levels above the lowest level are not stored in the data mart. Instead, these measures have to be calculated by taking an aggregate of the measures stored at the lowest level. For example, if the user wants to see the total sales for the Northeast sales region, that measure has to be calculated by aggregating the total sales for all of the territories within the Northeast sales region. In this case, the aggregation is the sum of the total sales of the territories.

The Snowflake Schema

An alternative to the star schema is the snowflake schema. The *snowflake schema* represents hierarchies in a manner that is more familiar to those of us who have been working with relational databases. In a snowflake schema, each level of a hierarchy is stored in a separate dimension table. This is shown in Figure 3-5. These chains of dimension tables are supposed to resemble the intricate patterns of a snowflake. Although the resemblance may not be too strong in Figure 3-5, this is how the snowflake schema got its name.

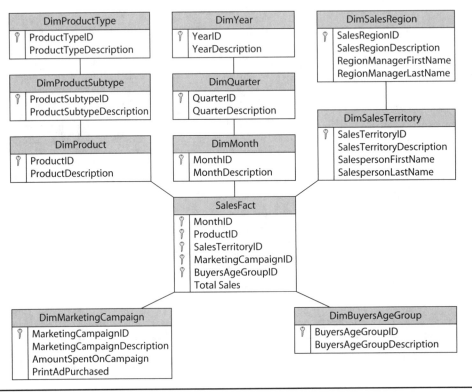

Figure 3-5   *The snowflake schema*

As with the star schema, the foreign keys in the fact table at the center of the snowflake schema point to the lowest level of each hierarchy. Therefore, the fact table in the snowflake schema also contains one row for each unique combination of members at the lowest level of each hierarchy. Measures for hierarchy levels above the lowest level have to be calculated by taking an aggregate, just as they were with the star schema.

Snowflakes, Stars, and Analysis Services

The snowflake schema has all the advantages of good relational design. It does not result in duplicate data and is, therefore, easier to maintain. It also looks more proper to those of us who have been working with relational databases.

The disadvantage of the snowflake design is that it requires a number of table joins when aggregating measures at the upper levels of the hierarchy. In larger data marts or in data marts that experience heavy utilization, this can lead to performance problems.

In both the snowflake and the star schemas, we have to calculate aggregates on the fly when the user wants to see data at any level above the lowest level in each dimension. In a schema with a number of dimensions or with dimensions that have a large number of members, this can take a significant amount of time. The whole idea of business intelligence is to make information readily available to our decision makers.

We could calculate all the measures at every level of our hierarchy and store them in the data mart. However, this would make the data mart much too complex and, therefore, much harder to maintain. How do we get good performance from our data mart at every level of the hierarchy without driving the data mart administrator crazy? The answer is Microsoft SQL Server 2008 Analysis Services, as we see in Chapter 4.

Chapter 4

One-Stop Shopping— The Unified Dimensional Model

In This Chapter

▶ **Online Analytical Processing**

▶ **The Unified Dimensional Model**

▶ **Tools of the Trade**

Snowflakes are one of nature's most fragile things, but just look at what they can do when they stick together.

—Vesta M. Kelly

I n Chapters 1 and 3, we learned how business intelligence can be used to support effective decision making. In Chapter 3, we began the search for the data that serves as the source for this business intelligence. In most cases, the data we need can be found in our online transaction processing (OLTP) systems.

On close examination, we discovered that an OLTP system is not a good candidate for the direct source of business intelligence. OLTP systems are designed for processing business transactions and storing the detail from each of these transactions. They are not optimized for delivering the aggregated information typically required for business intelligence.

The shortcomings of OLTP systems as a source for business intelligence led us to the data mart. The *data mart* is a relational database structure specifically designed for storing large amounts of historical data. Data must be copied from the OLTP systems into the data mart.

At the end of Chapter 3, we were left with a concern about the data mart. Namely, how do we improve performance when the user wants to view aggregate information derived from a large number of detail records? For the answer to this, we look to online analytical processing.

Online Analytical Processing

In 1993, E. F. Codd, one of the fathers of relational database and OLTP theory, proposed a different type of system that would be tuned to the needs of data analysts. He called this an online analytical processing, or OLAP, system. The criteria Codd originally laid out for an OLAP system were not widely accepted. However, the OLAP name continues to be used for systems designed to quickly provide users with business intelligence.

DEFINITION

Online analytical processing (OLAP) systems enable users to quickly and easily retrieve information from data, usually in a data mart, for analysis. OLAP systems present data using measures, dimensions, hierarchies, and cubes.

As the first word—online—in the name implies, OLAP is designed to let the user interact with the data during analysis. It is geared toward having the user online with the data, slicing and dicing the data to view it in different ways, drilling down into the data to see more detail. This is a different approach from the static reports produced by most OLTP systems.

Building OLAP—Out of Cubes

An OLAP system is designed to provide its users with quick and easy access to business data. That data is usually stored in a data mart. The OLAP system simply provides a mechanism for viewing and analyzing the data mart information quickly. Within the OLAP system, the business data takes the form of measures, dimensions, hierarchies, and cubes.

In fact, OLAP systems focus on cubes. We briefly discussed cubes in Chapter 3. Before we get into the specifics of OLAP systems, let's take a more detailed look at cubes. We again create a cube using the total sales measure. This time, we use month, product, and salesperson as our dimensions. The resulting cube is shown in Figure 4-1.

DEFINITION

A cube is a structure that contains a value for one or more measures for each unique combination of the members of all its dimensions. These are detail, or leaf-level, values. The cube also contains aggregated values formed by the dimension hierarchies or when one or more of the dimensions is left out of the hierarchy.

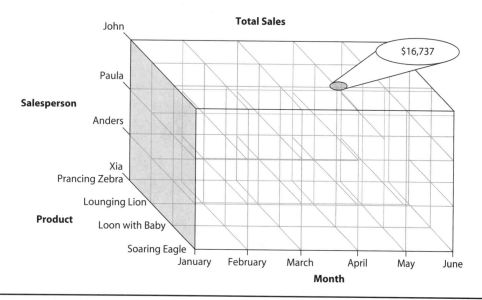

Figure 4-1   *Total Sales cube*

Within the cube is a measure value for each intersection of members of the three dimensions. Figure 4-1 illustrates the total sales for the Loon with Baby figurine by John in April. Loon with Baby is a member of the product dimension. John is a member of the salesperson dimension. April is a member of the month dimension. The total sales at this intersection are $16,737.

A measure value that exists at an intersection of all of the dimensions is called a *detail*, or *leaf-level*, *value*. In Figure 4-1, total sales for the Loon with Baby figurine by John in April is an example of a leaf-level value. This is a leaf-level value because members (John, April, and Loon with Baby) are specified for each dimension (salesperson, month, and product).

To determine the total sales by John in April, we need to add together John's total sales of each individual product in April. In other words, John's total sales for April are equal to John's total sales of Soaring Eagle in April, plus his total sales of Loon with Baby in April, plus his total sales of Lounging Lion in April, plus John's total sales of Prancing Zebra in April. In OLAP terminology, we aggregate all the leaf-level values from the product dimension using the sum aggregation. This is shown in Figure 4-2.

DEFINITION

An **aggregate** *is a value formed by combining values from a given dimension or set of dimensions to create a single value. This is often done by adding the values together using the sum aggregate, but other aggregation calculations can also be used.*

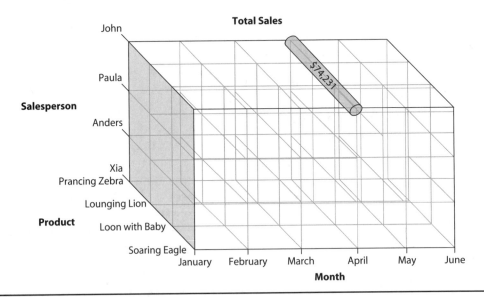

Figure 4-2   *Total Sales cube with an aggregation for John's total sales for April*

To determine the total sales for April for all salespersons, we need to do another aggregation. This time, we need to aggregate all the total sales for all the salespersons across all the products they sold in April (see Figure 4-3).

We also use aggregate values within the cube when we traverse the hierarchy of one or more dimensions. Recall that salespersons can be grouped, or rolled up, into sales regions, products can be rolled up into product subtypes and product types, and months can be rolled up into quarters and years. Each time one level of a hierarchy is rolled up into a higher level, aggregations are used to combine values from the lower level into the groupings at the upper level. For example, the total sales for the Loon with Baby figurine by John in Quarter 1 would be the total sales for the Loon with Baby figurine by John in January, plus the total sales for the Loon with Baby figurine by John in February, plus the total sales for the Loon with Baby figurine by John in March.

You can see that cubes with a number of dimensions and a number of hierarchies require quite a few aggregate calculations as the user navigates through the cube. This can slow down analysis to a large extent. To combat this, some or all of the possible data aggregates in the cubes are calculated ahead of time and stored within the cube itself. These stored values are known as *preprocessed aggregates*.

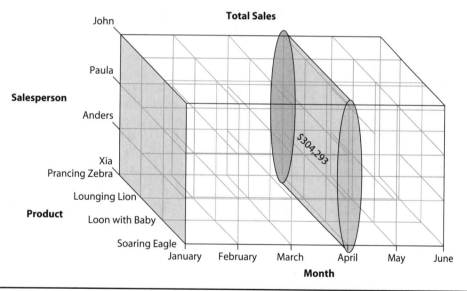

Figure 4-3   *Total Sales cube with an aggregation for total sales for all salespersons for April*

Features of an OLAP System

An OLAP system offers many advantages for us as we seek to produce business intelligence. It provides an architecture that is focused on the presentation of information for analysis. This focus makes the OLAP system a natural environment for users looking to use information for effective decision making.

Multidimensional Database

An OLAP system is built around data that is structured as measures, dimensions, hierarchies, and cubes. This multidimensional approach makes it easy for users to slice and dice information as needed. Users can use dimensions to view the data in different ways. They can use hierarchies to drill into the data and find more detail when needed.

DEFINITION

A multidimensional database is structured around measures, dimensions, hierarchies, and cubes rather than tables, rows, columns, and relations.

A multidimensional database is the most natural way to store information used for business intelligence, when measures are analyzed by dimensions. Aside from this innate fit, the multidimensional database offers another big advantage. It provides the structure for storing preprocessed aggregates.

Preprocessed Aggregates

In a data mart, when a decision maker wants to see the value of a measure for a certain set of dimension members, that value must be calculated on the fly. The decision maker must wait while the aggregate value is calculated from all the detail information that rolls up into that aggregate. This can cause a significant delay that distracts from productive research and leads to frustration.

If the goal of an OLAP system is to get the decision maker to interact with the data, then aggregates must be returned quickly. For this reason, OLAP systems preprocess a portion of the aggregates that are found throughout the cube. This preprocessing is done as part of the background task that loads or updates the data in the OLAP database. Because this is done as part of a background task, the time taken to do the preprocessing does not impact any users. As the aggregates are preprocessed, they are stored within the cube in the multidimensional database.

Now, when a decision maker wants to see the value of a measure for a certain set of dimensional members, that value can be read from the database rather than being calculated on the fly. This greatly improves the responsiveness of the system, which, in turn, encourages online interaction and provides the decision maker with a higher probability of finding the correct piece or pieces of information necessary to make an effective decision.

Easily Understood

In OLTP systems, the data is normalized and dependencies are represented by complex foreign key relationships; the goal is to reduce redundant data. Any decision maker querying this data must reconstruct the dependencies with the appropriate INNER JOINs and OUTER JOINs. Business rules that define the way a measure is to be calculated are kept in programmatic structures that are used for transaction processing, not reporting. When including a measure, the decision maker must re-create these calculations each time they are used in a report.

Fields and tables in an OLTP system are given names that make sense to the developer, but not necessarily the end user. The database system may impose a limit on the length of a name, or the database administrator may not like typing long names in his or her maintenance scripts. In either case, the result is cryptic abbreviations in field and table names. The decision maker must decipher the code to be sure the correct data is being queried from the tables.

In an OLAP system, just the opposite is true. The structure of the data is represented by dimensions and hierarchies. If the OLAP system is designed properly, these dimensions and hierarchies should match the structure of the organization. Thus, the data structure is familiar to the decision maker using the system.

The business rules that pertain to each measure in the OLAP system are contained within the calculation defined for that measure. The user does not need to re-create this calculation each time that particular measure is used. For example, suppose your organization defines net profit as:

```
Selling Price - (Cost of Materials + Cost of Labor + Sales Commmissions)
```

In a relational environment, net profit might be incorrectly reported as

```
Selling Price - (Cost of Materials + Cost of Labor)
```

in one place and as

```
Selling Price - (Cost of Materials + Sales Commissions)
```

in another. This inconsistency can lead to confusion and, worse yet, poor decisions. In the OLAP system, the measure for net profit is defined in one place, so it is always calculated properly whether the decision maker is looking at net profit by product, net profit by month, or net profit by sales region.

Finally, because the OLAP system exists solely for producing business intelligence, all of the measures, dimensions, and hierarchies are given names that can be easily understood by the decision maker. In many cases, an OLAP system allows additional metadata, such as a long description, to be stored along with the name of the object.

This provides the decision maker with enough information to ensure they know exactly what business information they are looking at.

Architecture

The key part of the OLAP system is the cube and the preprocessed aggregates it contains. OLAP systems typically use one of three different architectures for storing cube data. Each architecture has certain advantages and disadvantages. The basics of each are shown in Figure 4-4.

Relational OLAP

Relational OLAP (ROLAP) stores the cube structure in a multidimensional database. The leaf-level measures are left in the relational data mart that serves as the source of the cube. The preprocessed aggregates are also stored in a relational database table.

When a decision maker requests the value of a measure for a certain set of dimension members, the ROLAP system first checks to determine whether the dimension members specify an aggregate or a leaf-level value. If an aggregate is specified, the value is selected from the relational table. If a leaf-level value is specified, the value is selected from the data mart.

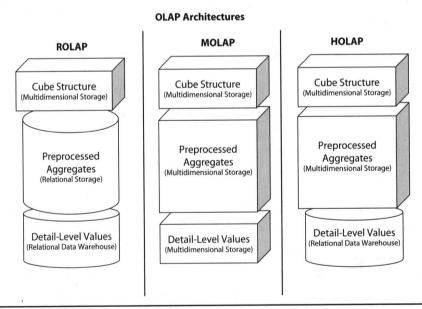

Figure 4-4 *OLAP architectures*

A ROLAP architecture, because of its reliance on relational tables, can store larger amounts of data than other OLAP architectures. Also, because the ROLAP architecture retrieves leaf-level values directly from the data mart, the leaf-level values returned by the ROLAP system are always as up-to-date as the data mart itself. In other words, the ROLAP system does not add latency to leaf-level data. The disadvantage of a ROLAP system is that the retrieval of the aggregate and leaf-level values is slower than the other OLAP architectures.

Multidimensional OLAP

Multidimensional OLAP (MOLAP) also stores the cube structure in a multidimensional database. However, *both* the preprocessed aggregate values and a copy of the leaf-level values are placed in the multidimensional database as well. Because of this, all data requests are answered from the multidimensional database, making MOLAP systems extremely responsive.

Additional time is required when loading a MOLAP system because all the leaf-level data is copied into the multidimensional database. Because of this, times occur when the leaf-level data returned by the MOLAP system is not in sync with the leaf-level data in the data mart itself. A MOLAP system, therefore, does add latency to the leaf-level data. The MOLAP architecture also requires more disk space to store the copy of the leaf-level values in the multidimensional database. However, because MOLAP is extremely efficient at storing values, the additional space required is usually not significant.

Hybrid OLAP

Hybrid OLAP (HOLAP) combines ROLAP and MOLAP storage. This is why we end up with the word "hybrid" in the name. HOLAP tries to take advantage of the strengths of each of the other two architectures while minimizing their weaknesses.

HOLAP stores the cube structure and the preprocessed aggregates in a multidimensional database. This provides the fast retrieval of aggregates present in MOLAP structures. HOLAP leaves the leaf-level data in the relational data mart that serves as the source of the cube.

This leads to longer retrieval times when accessing the leaf-level values. However, HOLAP does not need to take time to copy the leaf-level data from the data mart. As soon as the data is updated in the data mart, it is available to the decision maker. Therefore, HOLAP does not add latency to the leaf-level data. In essence, HOLAP sacrifices retrieval speed on leaf-level data to prevent adding latency to leaf-level data and to speed the data load.

Disadvantages

OLAP systems have a number of advantages that make them desirable tools for producing business intelligence. However, drawbacks exist in OLAP systems that must be dealt with.

Complexity to Administer

OLAP systems provide a comfortable environment for the end user. To attain that ease of use, a certain amount of complexity is shifted to the developer and administrator. This complexity increases the level of knowledge required to create business intelligence systems.

All of the dimensions, hierarchies, and measures need to be identified and created. These items must then be organized into cubes. This requires an intimate knowledge of the organization, its goals, and its operation. In addition, the development and maintenance team must be competent with the data mart and OLAP tools selected for the project.

Of course, as the knowledge and experience requirements for the development and maintenance team increase, so does the cost. Business intelligence projects can be extremely expensive because of the high-priced expertise that must be assembled to get the project done right. This factor alone has prevented a number of organizations from pursuing business intelligence undertakings.

Data Mart Required

In most cases, an OLAP system requires a data mart with a star or snowflake layout. Data must be copied from the OLTP systems into the data mart. Scheduled routines need to be created to perform this data copy, along with any data cleansing necessary to get it ready for use. If any of the OLTP systems change, the corresponding copy and cleansing routines need to be changed as well.

Latency

Because a data mart is required by OLAP, there is automatically some latency in the business intelligence. Time is required to run the routines that copy the data from the OLTP systems to the data mart. Furthermore, we probably do not want these copy routines running constantly. Instead, they are run at scheduled intervals. Between the times that the copy routines run, the data in the data mart can get old or "stale."

Read-Only

In some cases, it is desirable to update a piece of information while doing OLAP analysis. Perhaps the decision maker wants to look at the effects of certain "what if" scenarios: "What would the impact on profits be if commissions were raised by 1 percent?"

In another situation, the decision maker may want to adjust projections or modify quotas based on OLAP information. Rather than having to open a second application to make these adjustments, and then wait for them to propagate through to the data mart, it would be easier to make the changes, or "write back," to the OLAP data.

In most cases, however, OLAP data is read-only. Even if our OLAP system does support cube writeback, we are writing to the data mart. Our changes will not be reflected in the OLTP data.

The Unified Dimensional Model

With SQL Server 2005, Microsoft introduced a new technology called a Unified Dimensional Model (UDM). A UDM is designed to provide all the benefits of an OLAP system with multidimensional storage and preprocessed aggregates. A UDM, however, avoids a number of the drawbacks of more traditional OLAP systems.

Structure

A *UDM* is a structure that sits over the top of a data mart and looks exactly like an OLAP system to the end user. One of the major advantages of a UDM, however, is that it does not require a data mart. You can also build a UDM over one or more OLTP systems. You can even mix data mart and OLTP system data in the same UDM. The UDM can even include data from databases from other vendors and Extensible Markup Language (XML)-formatted data.

A UDM can define measures, dimensions, hierarchies, and cubes, either from star and snowflake schemas, or directly from relational database tables. This latter capability enables us to provide business intelligence without first having to build a data mart. However, there are still some reasons for choosing to build a data mart, which we discuss in Chapter 6.

Data Sources

A UDM begins with one or more data sources. A data source stores the information necessary to connect to a database that provides data to the UDM. The data source includes the server name, database name, and the database logon credentials, among other things. A number of OLE DB providers are available for accessing different databases, including Oracle and Microsoft Directory Services.

Data Views

Once the data sources have been defined, data views are used to determine which tables and fields are utilized. The data view can combine tables and fields from a number of different data sources. For instance, tables from the order processing system can be combined with tables from the sales management system so a measure of actual sales versus sales quota can be created. This multiple data source capability of data views is what puts the "Unified" in Unified Dimensional Model.

Once the tables and fields have been added to the data view, the data view can then be used to filter out unnecessary items in the database. Only those tables and fields being used to create business intelligence are included in the view. The underlying table structures in the data sources are not changed. The data view merely controls what is available as building blocks for the next step in the definition process.

This is especially helpful when a data source is a large, highly normalized OLTP system. The data view makes available only those tables that contain the data for the measures, dimensions, and hierarchies we need to define. The same is true within a table. Only those fields that contain required data are visible. All the extraneous tables and fields are filtered out by the data view.

To make the data view even easier to understand, user-friendly names and descriptions can be assigned to tables and fields. This metadata is used throughout the UDM. Any measures, dimensions, and hierarchies created from these fields will utilize the user-friendly names.

In addition, we can use the data view to make virtual additions to the table and field structures. These additions are not made in the database itself, but in the virtual view that exists only in the UDM. Therefore, we can make these virtual additions without any fear of breaking the OLTP systems that use the relational tables.

One example of these virtual additions is the creation of a relationship between two tables that is not defined in the database itself. Another example is the addition of a calculated field in a database table. For instance, a calculation involving a number of different fields from different tables can be created for use as a measure. Or, a number of strings can be concatenated together for use as a dimension. These calculated fields are given names and descriptions, so they appear just like any other field included in the UDM.

Once the data view is completed, its content is used to create measures, dimensions, hierarchies, and cubes.

Proactive Caching

To obtain the same performance benefits of traditional OLAP systems, a UDM uses preprocessed aggregates. To facilitate high availability, these preprocessed aggregates are stored in the *proactive cache*.

This structure is referred to as cache because it is created when needed and is changed when the underlying data or the underlying structure changes. It works much the same way Internet Information Services (IIS) caches web pages, as shown in Figure 4-5. The results of a processed web page are stored in the IIS page cache, so subsequent

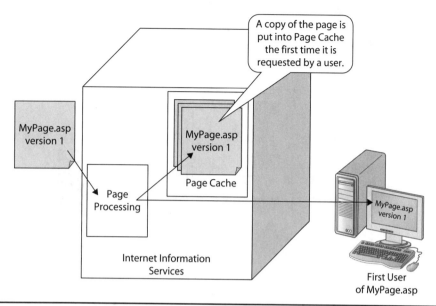

Figure 4-5   *Creating a cached web page in Internet Information Services*

accesses to that page are faster, as shown in Figure 4-6. When changes are made to the underlying page, that page is deleted and eventually re-created in the page cache, as in Figure 4-7.

The major difference between UDM caching and other caching mechanisms, such as the IIS example, is summed up in the word "proactive." With IIS, a page is put into cache only after it has been accessed the first time. The first user to request a particular page must wait until the page is read from the disk and processed before the user receives the contents of the page, as you see in Figure 4-5.

The UDM, on the other hand, uses proactive caching. Items are created in the cache before they have been requested by a user. With UDM, the preprocessed aggregates are created automatically, as shown in Figure 4-8. Even the first users receive their requested aggregates from the proactive cache, as in Figure 4-9.

The UDM monitors the data in the data source. As this data is modified, the UDM checks the options selected for the associated proactive cache. We look at just what these caching options are in Chapter 10. At the appropriate time, as defined by the caching options, the UDM deletes the current cache and rebuilds it with up-to-date values, as shown in Figure 4-10.

The proactive cache can be built using MOLAP, ROLAP, or HOLAP. The UDM provides an easy mechanism to assist you with the decision among these three architectures. It points out the tradeoffs these three architectures make between latency

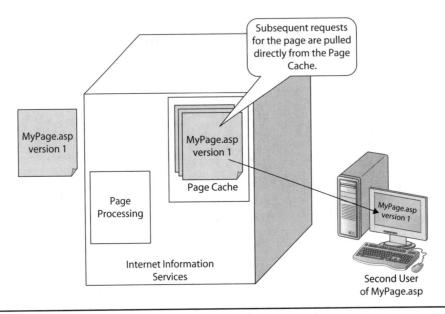

Figure 4-6 *Retrieving a web page from the Internet Information Services page cache*

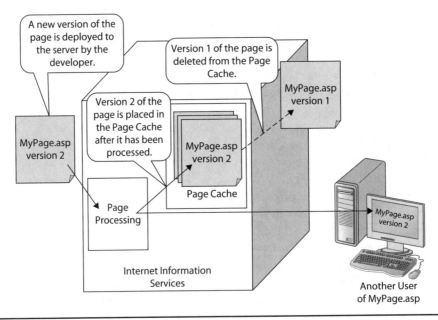

Figure 4-7 *Updating the Internet Information Services page cache when a web wage is modified*

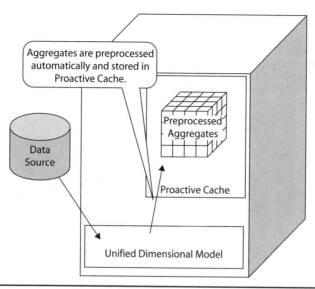

Figure 4-8   *Proactive caching with a Unified Dimensional Model*

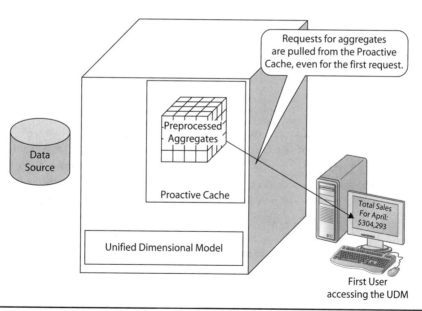

Figure 4-9   *Even the first user receives the requested aggregate from the proactive cache.*

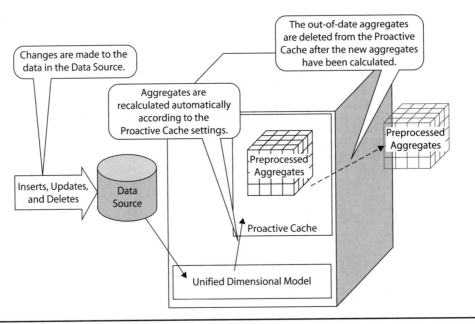

Figure 4-10   *The proactive cache is deleted and re-created in response to changes in the data source.*

and responsiveness. This enables you to determine which architecture to use based on the business needs without getting lost in the technical details.

XML Definitions

The definitions of all the objects in the UDM are stored as XML text files. Each of the data source, data view, dimension, and cube definitions is stored in its own text file. These XML text files do not contain any of the data for the object—the dimension text file does not contain any of the members of the dimension; the cube text file does not contain any of the preprocessed aggregates. The XML text files simply contain the definitions—the dimension text file tells which table and field hold the members of the dimension; the cube text file contains the information on how the preprocessed aggregates will be managed.

In short, these XML text files act as the source code for the UDM.

Advantages

The UDM features a novel architecture boasting a unique set of capabilities. These capabilities provide us with a number of advantages over more traditional OLAP implementations. They go a long way toward solving the problems and frustrations that often accompany business intelligence implementation.

OLAP Built on Transactional Data

The UDM allows OLAP cubes to be built directly on top of transactional data. The UDM does not need a strict star or snowflake schema data mart as its data source. Instead, any well-structured, relational database works just fine.

This eliminates the effort necessary to copy data from the OLTP system into a data mart. With UDM, the data can be utilized directly from the OLTP system without a large extract, transform, and load process. This greatly simplifies an OLAP implementation project, providing savings of both time and money.

Extremely Low Latency

By building our OLAP system directly on top of the OLTP system, we can eliminate much of the latency required in data warehousing systems. In fact, we can have real-time or near real-time performance. However, we must take care to balance the need for real-time business intelligence with the load that is placed on the OLTP system. Still, if the computing power is available, real-time performance is attainable in a straightforward environment.

Ease of Creation and Maintenance

The UDM architecture removes much of the complexity that accompanies most OLAP projects. The UDM eliminates the need to create and maintain a data mart, and it does away with the extract, transform, and load routines that must accompany it. This alone makes creating business intelligence with the UDM orders of magnitude simpler than other OLAP architectures.

On top of this, the *Business Intelligence Development Studio* provides a user-friendly environment for creating, reviewing, and maintaining all of the items in a UDM. Dimension and Cube Wizards guide you step-by-step through the creation of these objects, making suggestions along the way. In short, it has never been easier to provide the benefits of an OLAP system to your decision makers.

Design Versioning with Source Control

Because the definition for each of the objects in the UDM is stored in its own XML text file, the objects in the UDM can be managed by a source code utility. The source code utility can track these objects as you develop your UDM. It can also provide version control in case you need to undo a change to an object's definition and roll it back to an earlier version.

Tools of the Trade

In Chapter 5, we look at the business intelligence tools available in SQL Server 2008. We use two major development and management environments throughout this book. We are introduced to both, the Business Intelligence Development Studio and the SQL Server Management Studio, in the next chapter.

First Steps—Beginning the Development of Business Intelligence

In This Chapter

▶ **The Business Intelligence Development Studio**

▶ **The SQL Server Management Studio**

▶ **Don Your Hardhat**

There is a great satisfaction in building good tools for other people to use.

—Freeman Dyson

Now that we have discussed the basics of business intelligence and online analytical processing (OLAP), it is time to become acquainted with the tools that we are going to be using. Microsoft has created a special tool for creating and managing business intelligence (we use the acronym BI to refer to business intelligence throughout the book). This is the Business Intelligence Development Studio.

We begin this chapter with a tour of this tool. The Business Intelligence Development Studio looks familiar to those of you who have used Microsoft Visual Studio as part of front-end or middleware development projects. In fact, the Business Intelligence Development Studio is Visual Studio with some special functionality.

With home improvement, having the right tool for the job makes things faster and easier. The same is true with BI development. Let's see how the Business Intelligence Development Studio can make our job faster and easier.

The Business Intelligence Development Studio

The Business Intelligence Development Studio is our primary work environment for almost this entire book. All the work we do creating and querying OLAP structures, all the work we do building and training data mining models, and all the work we do developing reports will be done in the Business Intelligence Development Studio. Because of this, it is important to become comfortable with the interface and capabilities of this product.

Visual Studio

The Business Intelligence Development Studio is, in fact, Visual Studio, the same integrated development environment (IDE) used by Visual Basic and C# developers. Visual Studio is also used to author reports for use with SQL Server Reporting Services. Visual Studio provides the business intelligence developer with a robust environment that has been tested and proven by millions of developer hours of use.

Project Organization

Visual Studio organizes each development effort into projects. Each project produces its own type of output: a Windows application, a web service, or a set of Reporting Services reports. SQL Server 2008 provides two additional project types: an Integration Services package and an Analysis Services project.

Projects are grouped together in solutions. Each solution represents a solution to a particular business problem. A solution could be an e-commerce website with a Visual Basic web application project to produce the ASP.NET user interface pages and an Analysis Services project to define the data mining model used to do cross-selling. Another solution might contain a complete business intelligence application, with a C# Windows application project to produce the front-end application, an Analysis Services project to create the OLAP structures, and a Reporting Services project that produces reports for presenting the analysis to the user. This grouping of projects into solutions makes it easier to manage software systems built from several different parts.

Editing and Debugging Tools

Visual Studio also provides a rich set of editing and debugging tools. Some of you may say that color-coded editors and single-step debugging are only for wimps. After all, many of us grew up writing stored procedures in a text editor and debugging them with embedded PRINT statements, and we did just fine. Believe me, once you have these tools available, you will never want to go back!

Source Code Management Integration

Another benefit of using the Visual Studio environment for BI projects is source control. *Source control* copies the source code for your item definitions and report layouts to a central database. Source control then manages access to those definitions and layouts to provide version control and prevent two developers from trying to change the same item at the same time.

Each version of these items is saved. This makes it possible for us to roll back changes if we discover we have gone down the wrong path. It also makes it possible to determine what changed between two versions of an item. This can be helpful for troubleshooting or when copying changes from one server to another.

Source code also enables multiple developers or administrators to work on the same project at the same time without the danger of one person overwriting another's changes. You must check out an item from source control before you can edit it. Only one person can have a given item checked out at a given time. Once changes are made, the item is checked back in for the next person to use.

Visual Studio makes this check-out and check-in process straightforward. In fact, it is simply part of the editing process itself. No additional applications to open. No extra steps writing things out to temporary files.

Navigating the Business Intelligence Development Studio

The Business Intelligence Development Studio is found on the Start menu under Microsoft SQL Server 2008, as shown in Figure 5-1. After the splash screen, you see the empty Business Intelligence Development Studio. No solution has been opened.

In this section, we create a solution and an Analysis Services project within that solution. Then, we explore the menus, toolbar, and windows within the Business Intelligence Development Studio. In the next section, we look at some of the ways to customize this development environment.

Creating a Solution and an Analysis Services Project

The empty Business Intelligence Development Studio is not too exciting. Therefore, we begin by creating a solution and an Analysis Services project within that solution. We can then explore all of the windows, menu choices, and toolbar buttons available to us when working in this type of project.

In the Business Intelligence Development Studio, we do not choose to create a solution. Instead, we create a new project. At the same time that project is created, we can create the solution that will contain that project.

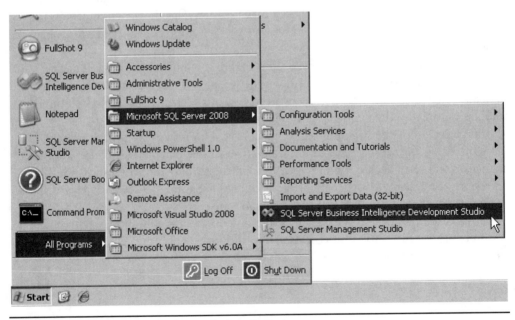

Figure 5-1   *Business Intelligence Development Studio on the Start menu*

Figure 5-2   *The New Project Toolbar button*

We can create a new project in the Business Intelligence Development Studio in four ways.

▶   Select File | New | Project from the menu.

▶   Press CTRL-SHIFT-N.

▶   Click the New Project button on the toolbar, as shown in Figure 5-2.

▶   Click the Create: Project link in the Recent Projects portion of the Start tab.

No matter how you get there, once you request a new project, you see the New Project dialog box, shown in Figure 5-3. The left side of the dialog box contains a list of

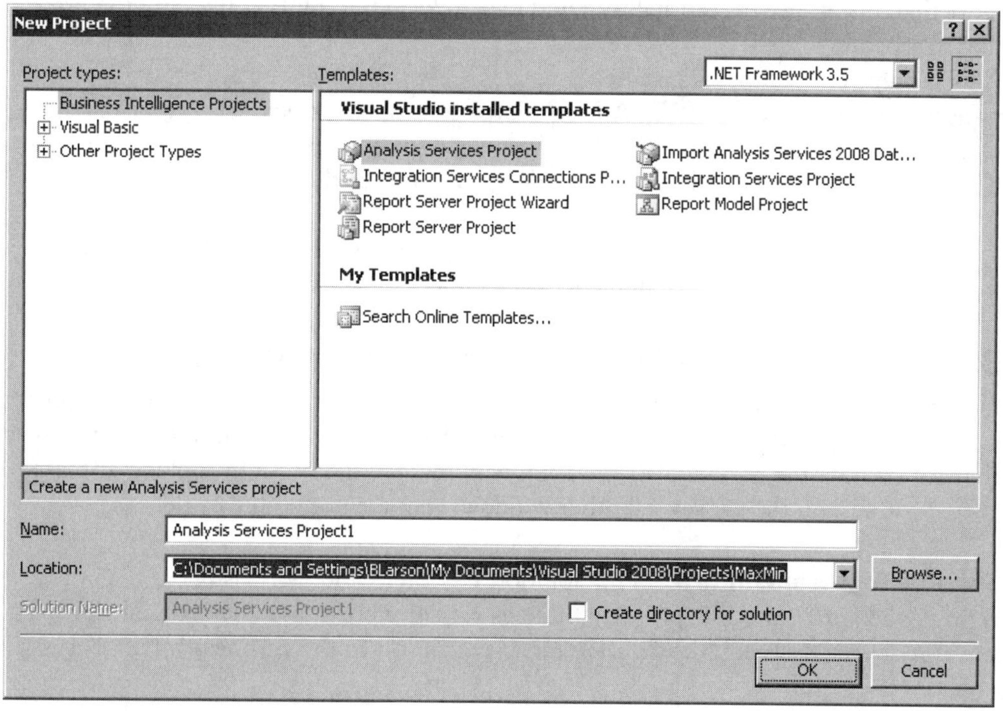

Figure 5-3   *The New Project dialog box*

the Visual Studio project types installed on your development machine. In this book, we are interested in Business Intelligence Projects. Click this project type to select it, if it is not already highlighted.

The right side of the dialog box displays the various BI projects available to us. These can be displayed as large icon, or as small icons as shown in Figure 5-3. You can toggle between the two sizes using the buttons in the upper-right corner of the dialog box.

The lower portion of the dialog box displays the path and filename for the project we are about to create. Name is the name of the new project. Location is the file path where the new solution and project are to be stored. Solution Name is the name of the new solution.

By default, solutions and projects are stored in the Visual Studio 2008 Projects folder under My Documents. You can use the Browse button to navigate to a different folder, if desired. When the Create directory for solution check box is not checked, only one folder is created. Both the new solution files and the new project files are placed in this folder.

When the Create directory for solution check box is checked, two folders are created. One folder is created to hold the solution files, and a second folder is created within this solution folder to contain the project files. By default, the solution folder and the project folder have the same name. You can override this default behavior by entering a unique name for both the Name and the Solution Name. If the solution is going to contain more than one project, it is usually a good idea to keep the solution files and the project files in separate folders.

If a source control tool is installed on your PC, we also have the option of placing the project under source control. An Add to source control check box will appear under the Create directory for solution check box. If you are going to use source control for your BI projects, it is a good idea to use this check box to place them under source control right from the start.

To create our empty Analysis Services project, select Business Intelligence Projects for the project types, select Analysis Services Project for the template, and click OK.

Business Intelligence Development Studio Windows

Now that we have a solution and a project open, the Business Intelligence Development Studio appears as shown in Figure 5-4. We now have some content in the two windows that are open on the right side of the main window. We can begin by looking at these two windows, and then at several other windows that are not visible by default.

Solution Explorer Window   The Solution Explorer window is visible in the upper-right portion of Figure 5-4. Just as Windows Explorer provides a hierarchical view of the Windows file system, the *Solution Explorer* window in the Business Intelligence

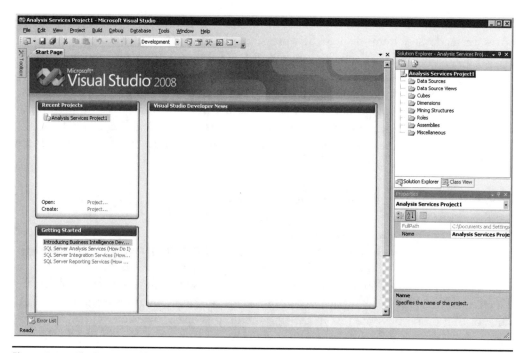

Figure 5-4 *The Business Intelligence Development Studio with an empty Analysis Services project*

Development Studio provides a hierarchical view of your solution and the projects it contains. Both Windows Explorer and the Solution Explorer window use a tree view to let us navigate the hierarchical structure. We can browse through our solution to find and open any item it contains.

Each project node displays the name of the project. Within the project nodes are folders for each type of item the project can create. The number of folders and their labels vary, depending on the project type. In Figure 5-4, you can see that an Analysis Services project contains eight folders, one for each of the eight different types of items it can create.

In addition to the toolbar at the top of the Business Intelligence Development Studio (where we found the New Project button), each window has its own toolbar. The content of this toolbar varies depending on which item or folder is selected. The leftmost toolbar button shown in the Solution Explorer window in Figure 5-4 is the Properties button. If this toolbar button is clicked when a project node is highlighted, the Project Property Pages dialog box is displayed.

Most other items in the solution do not have their own custom property pages dialog boxes. Instead, these items display their properties in the Properties window, which we discuss next. Clicking the Properties button in the Solution Explorer toolbar when any of these other items is highlighted causes the Properties window to gain focus.

The other button shown on the Solution Explorer toolbar in Figure 5-4 is the Show All Files toggle. This toggle causes all the supporting files to be displayed for a project, as shown in Figure 5-5. In most cases, this is not necessary and toggling it on clutters up the Solution Explorer. However, at times, it is helpful to know exactly which files are being used by a project.

Properties Window   Below the Solution Explorer window in Figure 5-4 is the Properties window. This window displays the property settings of the item highlighted in the Solution Explorer window or elsewhere in the Business Intelligence Development Studio. The drop-down list at the top of the Properties window shows the name of the item whose properties are currently displayed.

The main portion of the *Properties* window is composed of a list with two columns. The left column shows the name of each property. The right column shows the current value of that property. If the text in the right column is black, the value of that property can be changed in the Properties window. If the text in the right column is gray, the value is read-only.

The lower portion of the screen provides a little more information about the selected property. The name of the selected property is displayed in bold, along with a description of this property. This description can often help users understand a property without having to consult the online help.

Figure 5-5   *The Solution Explorer window with the Property and Show All Files Toolbar buttons*

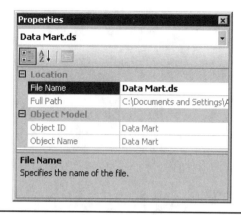

Figure 5-6   *The Properties window with categorized properties*

There are three buttons on the Properties window toolbar. The left button causes the properties to be displayed by category. The category headings are shown as light gray bands within the properties list. Figure 5-6 shows the properties of the Data Mart data source. These properties are divided into two categories: Location and Object Model.

The middle button on the Properties window toolbar causes the properties to be displayed in one continuous, alphabetical list without any grouping. Personally, I never remember which grouping contains the property I want to see, so I use the alphabetical list setting. However, you may find it more helpful to have properties grouped. Use whichever setting works best for you.

The right button on the Properties window toolbar displays the Property Pages dialog box for the selected item. However, only some items have a Property Pages dialog associated with them. Therefore, this toolbar button does not function for all items.

Toolbox Window   On the left side of Figure 5-4 is a tab labeled Toolbox. This tab provides access to the *Toolbox* window, which is set to auto hide. The *auto hide* setting causes the window to remain out of the way until it is needed. A window that is set to auto hide can be displayed by hovering the mouse pointer over the window's tab, as shown in Figure 5-7.

The auto hide feature is controlled by the pushpin icon at the top of the window. When auto hide is on, the pushpin is sideways, as shown in Figure 5-7. When auto hide is off, the pushpin is vertical. You can see this at the top of the Solution Explorer and Properties windows in Figure 5-4. To toggle the auto hide setting for a window, click its pushpin icon.

The Toolbox window contains components used to build items in our projects. The contents of the Toolbox window change to match the type of item being built.

Figure 5-7 *Displaying the Toolbox window when it is set to auto hide*

It contains data transformation tasks when we are creating Data Integration Services packages. The Toolbox window contains report items when we are building Reporting Services reports. The toolbox for report designing is shown in Figure 5-7.

Opening Windows Not Visible in the Business Intelligence Development Studio   Any window in the Business Intelligence Development Studio, including the three already discussed, can be closed using the close icon in the upper-right corner of the window. Because this is the case, we obviously need a way to open a window that is not visible on the screen. This is done using the View menu. The Solution Explorer, Properties, and Toolbox windows are available right from the View menu, as shown in Figure 5-8. Additional windows are found in the Other Windows submenu.

In addition to the View menu, windows can be opened directly using buttons on the toolbar. These toolbar buttons are illustrated in Figure 5-9.

Task List Window   The *Task List* window can be opened from the View menu. This window provides a convenient place for us to make note of to-do items for this solution. We can assign priorities that are signified by the exclamation point (high priority), blank (normal priority), and down arrow (low priority). When items are completed, they can be checked off. Completed items are displayed with a strike-through. The Task List window is shown in Figure 5-10.

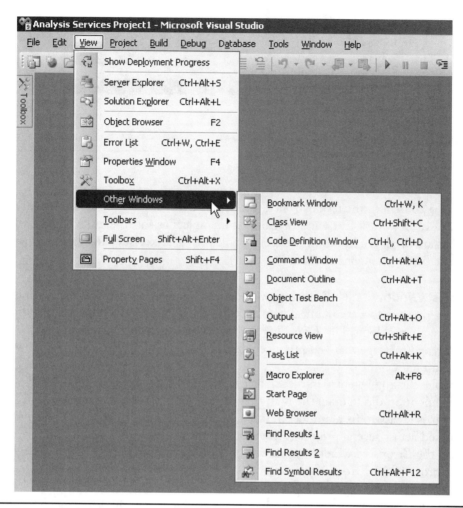

Figure 5-8   *The View menu*

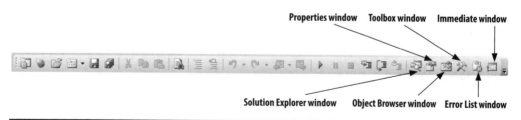

Figure 5-9   *Toolbar buttons for opening Business Intelligence Development Studio windows*

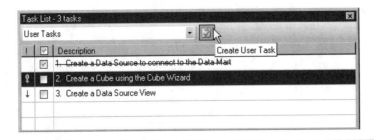

Figure 5-10   *The Task List window*

To add an item to the task list, click the Create User Task button, as shown in Figure 5-10. The Task List window Context menu lets us sort the tasks, control which columns are displayed in the window, copy an existing task, or delete a task. Right-click a task to display the Context menu.

Error List Window   The Error List window can be opened from the View menu. In addition, this window automatically opens when we try to build a project or solution and there are problems. The *Error List* window contains an entry for each error, warning, and message that was produced during the build. The Error List window is shown in Figure 5-11.

Double-clicking an entry in the Error List window causes the Business Intelligence Development Studio to open the item that caused the error, warning, or message. This makes it easy to fix a number of build errors that have occurred in various items distributed across several projects. As with the Task List window, right-clicking an entry in the Error List window displays a Context menu for controlling the sorting and display order of the Error List entries.

Output Window   The Output window can be opened from the View menu. In addition, this window automatically opens when we try to build a project or solution. The *Output* window contains a narrative of the events that occurred during the most recent build attempt. The Output window is shown in Figure 5-12.

	Description	File	Line	Column	Project
1	Dimension 'Store' : The source is not specified.		0	-1	
2	Dimension 'Promotion' : The source is not specified.		0	-1	
3	Dimension 'Product' : The source is not specified.		0	-1	
4	Dimension 'Time' : The source is not specified.		0	-1	

Figure 5-11   *The Error List window*

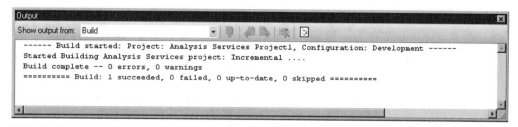

Figure 5-12   *The Output window*

Like the Error List window, the Output window notes errors, warnings, and messages from the last build attempt. Unlike the Error List window, the Output window also notes successful tasks completed. The Output window includes toolbar buttons for clearing its contents and for toggling word wrap within the window.

Find Results Windows   The Find Results windows can be opened from the View menu. In addition, one of these windows automatically opens whenever we perform a Find in Files or a Replace in Files operation. The Find Results 1 window is shown in Figure 5-13.

When we execute a find or replace operation, we can choose to display the results in either the Find Results 1 window or the Find Results 2 window. In this way, we can move between the results of two different find operations. The *Find Results* window contains a list of all of the places where the desired text was found. We can move to any of these locations by double-clicking that line in the Find Results window.

Designer Window   All of the windows we have discussed so far are usually found along the left, right, top, or bottom edge of the Business Intelligence Development Studio (although they don't have to be, as we discuss in the next section). That leaves us with the large area in the center. This area is occupied by the Designer window.

The Designer window appears any time we view the code or the design of an item. In fact, the *Designer* window is where most of the work of creating business intelligence

Figure 5-13   *The Find Results 1 window*

gets done. Figure 5-14 shows the Designer window with several designers and source code editors open (note the three tabs across the top). The Cube designer is open for the Min Max Sales cube. The Data Source View designer is open for the Min Max Sales DV data view. The Dimension source code editor is open for the store dimension. (We can tell this is a source code editor rather than a designer because of the "[XML]" in the tab. We talk more about code editors and designers throughout the rest of this book.)

A tab is created each time an item is opened in a code editor or a designer. The tabs enable us to move quickly from one item's designer or source code editor to another item's designer or source code editor with a single click. We can open an item's designer by doing one of the following:

▶ Selecting the item in the Solution Explorer window, and then selecting View | Designer from the Main menu

▶ Right-clicking the item in the Solution Explorer window and selecting View Designer from the Context menu

▶ Double-clicking the item in the Solution Explorer window

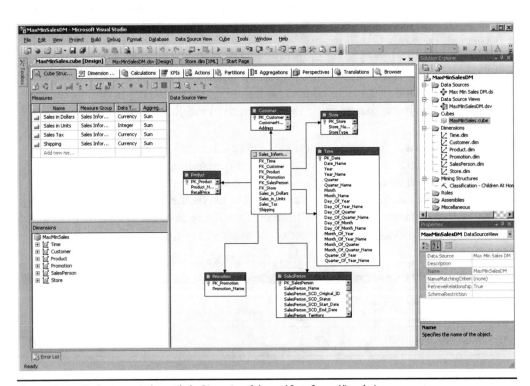

Figure 5-14 *The Designer window with the Dimension, Cube, and Data Source View designers open*

We can open an item's code editor by doing one of the following:

▶ Selecting the item in the Solution Explorer window, and then selecting View | Code from the Main menu

▶ Right-clicking the item in the Solution Explorer window and selecting View Code from the Context menu

We can close an item's designer or code editor by selecting the appropriate tab, and then clicking the Close button (the *X*) to the right of the tabs.

We discuss each designer and code editor as we use them to create and modify the various items in the Business Intelligence Development Studio.

Window Management

The windows of the Business Intelligence Development Studio can be rearranged any way that we like. This is done by setting various windows to be docked along the sides or bottom, to float, or to auto hide. In this way, each person can arrange the windows to suit their development style.

Each window can be set to one of five states:

▶ Floating

▶ Dockable

▶ Tabbed Document

▶ Auto Hide

▶ Hide

We can set a window's state by selecting that window, and then selecting Floating, Dockable, Tabbed Document, Auto Hide, or Hide from the Window menu. Alternately, we can right-click the title bar of a window and set its state using the Context menu. This is shown in Figure 5-15.

Floating Windows   When a window's state is set to floating, it exists as a separate *floating* window on top of the rest of the Business Intelligence Development Studio windows. A floating window can be moved anywhere around the screen on top of any other part of the user interface. This is shown in Figure 5-16.

Dockable Windows   When a window's state is set to *dockable,* it is able to dock with the left, right, top, or bottom edge of the Business Intelligence Development Studio.

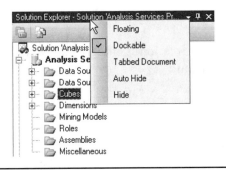

Figure 5-15 *Changing a window's state*

After a floating window's state is set to dockable, the window may be dragged to a docking position. To drag a dockable window, click the window's title bar and hold down the left mouse button while you move the window into the appropriate place.

As soon as you begin dragging the window, several blue docking guides appear on the screen. These docking guides make it easy to dock the window in the desired location. The docking guides are linked to each of the possible docking locations on the screen.

By moving the mouse pointer over one of the docking guides while dragging a dockable window, we can see exactly where that window is going to dock if the mouse button is released at that point. The possible docking location linked to the docking guide under your mouse pointer displays as a blue shadow on the screen. If this is not the desired docking location, we can drag the window to another docking guide.

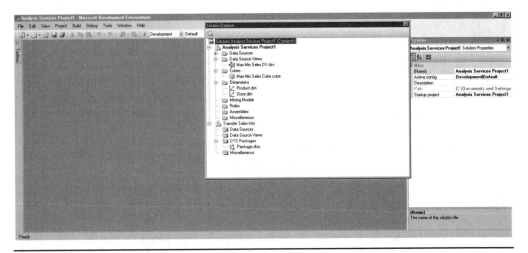

Figure 5-16 *The Solution Explorer as a floating window*

When we find the docking guide linked to the desired location, we simply release the mouse button and the window docks in the selected location.

There are docking guides for the top, bottom, left, and right sides of the Business Intelligence Development Studio. Using one of these docking guides, we can dock the window along the entire length of that side. Any other windows that might butt up against that side are moved out of the way. Also, a set of docking guides in the form of a diamond is in the center of the current window. Using one of the docking guides at the points of this diamond docks the window at the side of this current window. As we drag from one window to another, this diamond-shaped docking guide switches so that it is always in the center of the window we are dragging over.

In the center of the diamond is a tabbed-icon docking guide. Using this tabbed-icon docking guide causes the window being docked to fill the current window. The two windows now form a tabbed grouping. Figure 5-17 shows the Properties window and the Solution Explorer window combined to create a tabbed grouping. Note the tabs at the bottom of the window for switching between the Solution Explorer and the Properties window. To remove a window from a tabbed grouping, simply click that window's tab, hold down the left mouse button, and drag the window away.

Tabbed Document   You can even create a tabbed grouping with the Designer window. In Figure 5-18, the Solution Explorer is part of the tabbed grouping in the Designer window. When this is done, the window's state changes from dockable to tabbed document. Remember, this is only true when a window is in a tabbed group in the Designer window. A window in a tabbed group outside of the Designer window continues to have a dockable window state.

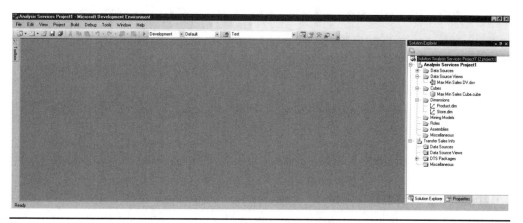

Figure 5-17   *The Properties window and the Solution Explorer window combined in a tabbed window*

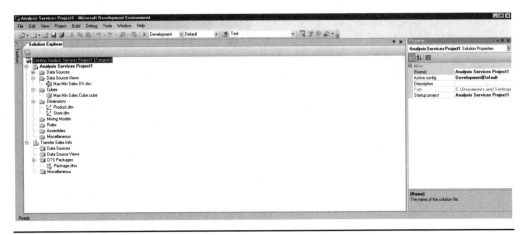

Figure 5-18   *The Solution Explorer window in a tabbed grouping on the Designer window*

Auto Hide   We have already seen the behavior of an auto hide window when we examined the Toolbox window. Note, a window's state cannot be changed to auto hide unless it is already docked. A window must have auto hide turned off, using the pushpin icon, before it can be changed to another state.

Hide   The final window state is the simplest one of all. This is the hide state. When a window is in the *hide state*, it is closed and no longer appears on the screen. If we want to view a hidden window, we need to use the Windows menu or the toolbar, as discussed previously.

Business Intelligence Development Studio Options

In addition to the capability to rearrange the windows to our liking, the Business Intelligence Development Studio can be customized using the Options dialog box. The Options dialog box is accessed by selecting Tools | Options from the Main menu. It is shown in Figure 5-19.

The Options dialog box provides the capability to modify a great number of settings for the Business Intelligence Development Studio. We only discuss a few of those settings here. Feel free to explore this dialog further on your own to learn about more of the customization options.

MDI Environment

The first option we look at is in the Environment | General options shown in Figure 5-19. At the top of the dialog box are two radio buttons: Tabbed documents and Multiple

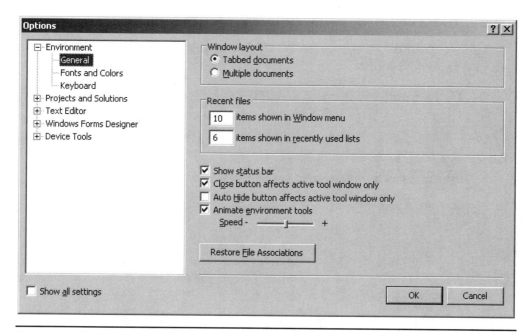

Figure 5-19   *The Options dialog box*

documents. These radio buttons control the behavior of the Designer window. As we discussed earlier, each designer and code editor opened in the Designer window becomes a tab. This is the default behavior of the Designer window, but it is not the only option.

If you are more comfortable with a multidocument interface (MDI) from previous versions of Visual Studio or from Microsoft Office products, you can switch the Designer window from using tabbed documents to using MDI. Simply click the Multiple documents radio button and click OK to exit the dialog box. Once this is done, the Designer window looks similar to Figure 5-20. For the remainder of this book, however, we use the Designer window with its default, tabbed document setting.

Fonts and Colors

Further down under the Environment options is the Fonts and Colors entry. This area lets us customize the font and color used for any category of text within the Business Intelligence Development Studio. This is shown in Figure 5-21. The fonts and colors options can be used to change font size or typeface to make certain items more readable. They can also be used to change the color of a particular set of text to make it stand out.

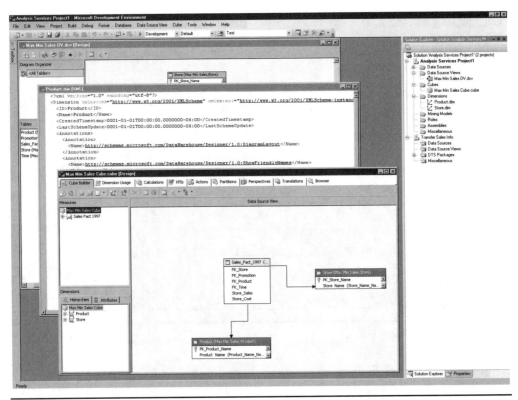

Figure 5-20   *The Designer window with an MDI interface*

To make a change, we first make a selection from the Show Settings For drop-down list. Next, we select the text we want to change from the Display items list. Finally, we make the desired font and color changes, and then click OK to apply the changes.

Default File Locations

Another area that often needs customizing is the default location for creating solution and project files. This can be changed in the General area under Projects and Solutions, as shown in Figure 5-22. The path in the Projects location text box is the default location for creating new solutions and projects. To change this, we simply browse to or type in a new path and click OK to apply the changes. Now, whenever the New Project dialog box is displayed, Location shows our updated path. (Refer to Figure 5-3 for another look at the New Project dialog box.)

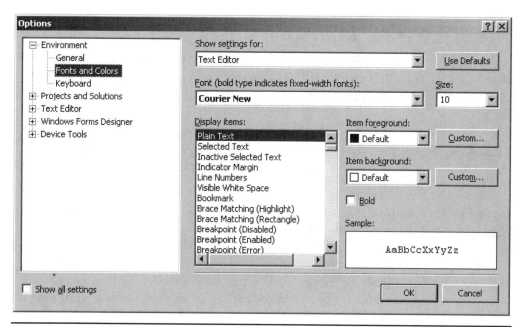

Figure 5-21   *Fonts and Colors options*

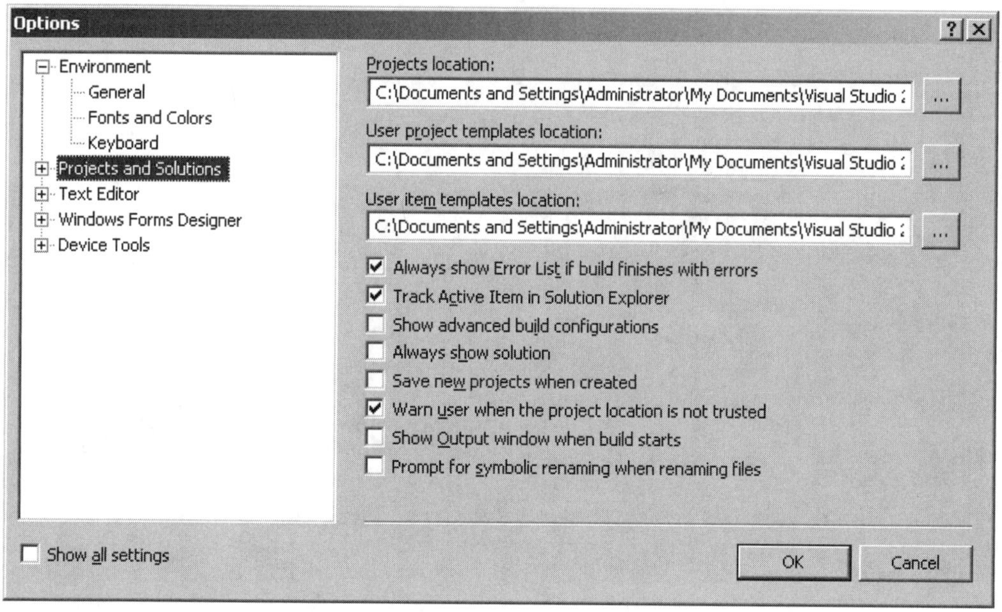

Figure 5-22   *Projects and Solutions - General options*

The SQL Server Management Studio

As we have seen in the previous section, we use the Business Intelligence Development Studio to develop OLAP structures. We use another tool to manage our relational and OLAP databases during day-to-day operations. This is the SQL Server Management Studio.

The SQL Server Management Studio User Interface

The SQL Server Management Studio has a user interface similar to the Business Intelligence Development Studio. It has the same type of window states (floating, dockable, and so forth), and it features a tabbed work area. Let's take a quick look at the SQL Server Management Studio so we have some familiarity with it when it is time to use this tool for managing databases.

The SQL Server Management Studio is found on the Start menu under Microsoft SQL Server 2008, as shown in Figure 5-23. When the SQL Server Management Studio starts up, it attempts to connect to the last server we were working with. The Connect to Server dialog box is displayed, as shown in Figure 5-24. To connect to the server, we need to provide logon credentials, if necessary, and then click Connect.

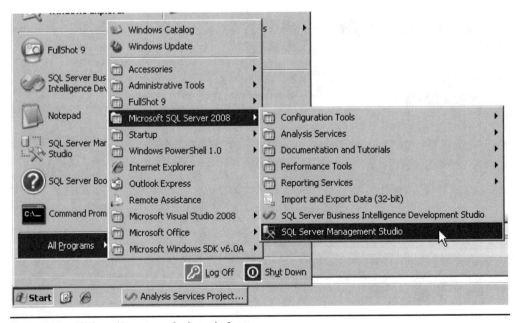

Figure 5-23   *SQL Server Management Studio on the Start menu*

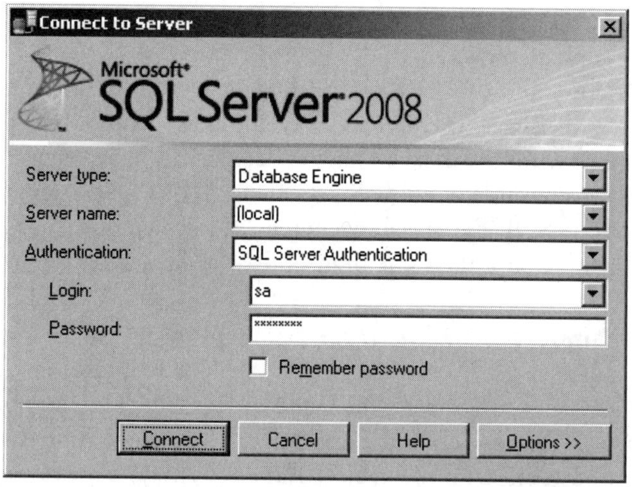

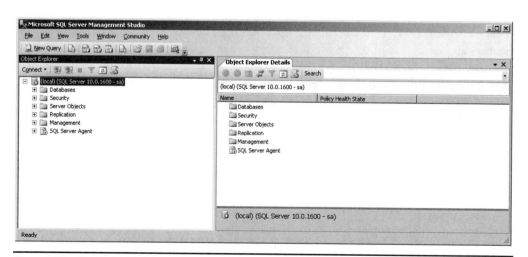

Figure 5-24   *Connecting to a server on startup*

We can also enter the SQL Server Management Studio without connecting to a server by clicking Cancel.

The SQL Server Management Studio Windows

By default, the SQL Server Management Studio has two windows open, as shown in Figure 5-25. The Object Explorer window is on the left side, and the Object Explorer Details window is a tabbed document inside the Designer window. As with the

Figure 5-25   *The SQL Server Management Studio default window layout*

Business Intelligence Development Studio, additional windows can be displayed when needed using the View menu.

The Object Explorer and Object Explorer Details windows function similarly to the dockable windows in Business Intelligence Development Studio. We can make them float over other windows or set them to auto hide. We can have them form tabbed groupings with other dockable windows or set them to be tabbed documents in the Designer window. The SQL Server Management Studio windows use the same menus, the same docking guides, and the same drag-and-drop functionality.

Object Explorer Window The *Object Explorer* window lets us view and manage the objects on a particular server. These objects are displayed in a tree view, as shown in Figure 5-26. In most cases, objects are managed by right-clicking an object to display its Context menu and then selecting the appropriate action from the Context menu. We discuss the various objects in the Object Explorer window as we work with them in future chapters.

When the SQL Server Management Studio first opens, the Object Explorer window displays objects for the server you connected to using the Connect to Server dialog box. We can add other servers to the Object Explorer window by clicking Connect in the Object Explorer window toolbar. The servers appear one below the next in the Object Explorer window's tree view.

Object Explorer Details Window The *Object Explorer Details* window provides a brief overview of the entry currently selected in the Object Explorer window. If the selected entry is a folder, the Details window shows the contents of that folder. If the selected entry is an object, the Details window shows the current status of that object.

Query Windows One of the functions of the SQL Server Management Studio is the creation and execution of queries. These queries may be Transact-SQL for relational databases, MDX or XMLA for Analysis Services databases, DMX for data mining, or SQL Compact Edition for hand-held devices. Each type of query has its own specific type of query window. We discuss how to use these query windows throughout the rest of this book.

DEFINITION

Multidimensional Expression (MDX) *language provides the programming language for OLAP Cube navigation.*

DEFINITION

Data Mining Expression (DMX) *language provides the commands to easily set up and analyze data mining structures.*

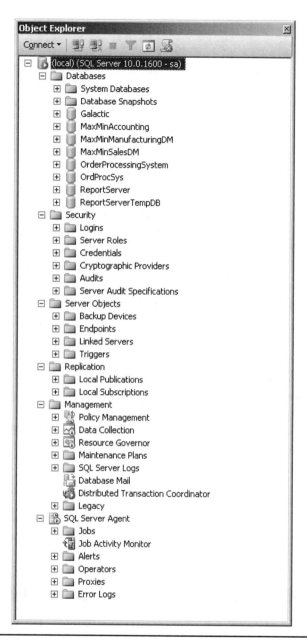

Figure 5-26   *The Object Explorer window*

DEFINITION

XML for Analysis Services (XMLA) *is an open, XML-based standard protocol for interacting with Microsoft SQL Server 2008 Analysis Services data over a Hypertext Transfer Protocol (HTTP) connection, such as an intranet or the Internet. XMLA uses the Simple Object Access Protocol (SOAP). (Being an open standard, XMLA is used by other vendors' OLAP tools as well.)*

To create and execute queries, we need to open a query window of the appropriate type. This is done using the query buttons on the toolbar. These buttons are shown in Figure 5-27. The New Query button opens the default type of query window for the database selected in the Object Explorer window. We can also select the specific type of query window we want to open by selecting the appropriate toolbar button. We can also open a query window by selecting the appropriate option under File on the Main menu or by using the Context menu for objects in the Object Explorer window. Figure 5-28 shows the SQL Server Management Studio with a SQL Server Query window open in the designer area.

The SQL Server Management Studio Projects

The *SQL Server Management Studio* enables us to create solutions and projects to manage and store our queries. Three types of projects are supported: SQL Server scripts, Analysis Services scripts, and SQL Compact Edition scripts. A *script* is simply one or more queries. The SQL Server Management Studio includes a Solution Explorer window and a Properties window to help us manage our solutions and projects. They function in much the same manner as the Solution Explorer window and Properties window in the Business Intelligence Development Studio.

Figure 5-29 shows the same query as Figure 5-28; however, this time, it is part of a solution and a project.

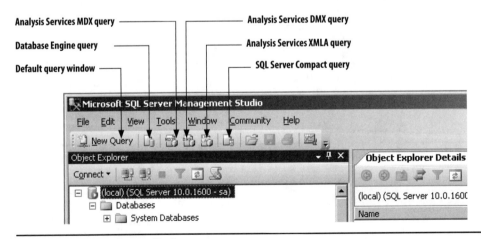

Figure 5-27   *The New Query toolbar buttons*

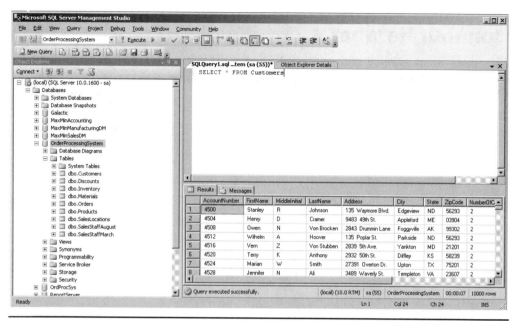

Figure 5-28   *The SQL Server Management Studio with a SQL Server Query window*

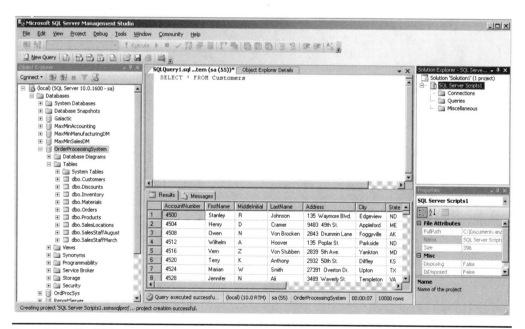

Figure 5-29   *The SQL Server Management Studio with a solution and a project*

Don Your Hardhat

Now that you are familiar with these SQL Server 2008 business intelligence tools, it is time to start building. In Chapter 6, we return to our sample company, Maximum Miniatures, Incorporated. We look at some of their specific business intelligence needs and begin to build the structures to help them meet those needs. Specifically, we build two data marts—one from scratch and one using the Business Intelligence Development Studio Cube Wizard. After these data marts are built, we will determine how to populate them using Integration Services.

Strap on your tool belt and let's go!

Part II

Defining Business
Intelligence Structures

Chapter 6

Building Foundations— Creating Data Marts

In This Chapter

- ▶ Data Mart
- ▶ Designing a Data Mart
- ▶ Table Compression
- ▶ The Benefits of Integration

*He who has not first laid his foundations may be able with great ability to lay them
afterwards, but they will be laid with trouble to the architect and danger to the building.*

The Prince
—Niccolò Machiavelli

N ow that you have been introduced to the business intelligence and database
management tools in SQL Server 2008, it is time to get to work. The first
thing we need to do is lay some foundations. We need to examine our data
sources and determine if we can use the Unified Dimensional Model (UDM) to pull the
information directly from each source or if we need to create one or more data marts.

We look at the criteria to use when determining whether a data mart is needed.
Next, we walk through the steps necessary for designing a data mart. Finally, we look
at two different methods for creating data marts: using the SQL Server Management
Studio and using the Business Intelligence Development Studio.

Data Mart

In Chapter 3, we were introduced to the concept of the data mart. We learned that
a data mart is a repository for data to be used as a source for business intelligence.
The data mart is not used as part of day-to-day operations. Instead, the data mart
periodically receives data from the online transactional processing (OLTP) systems.
The data in the data mart is then made available to Analysis Services for creating cubes
with preprocessed aggregates. This is shown in Figure 6-1.

Who Needs a Data Mart Anyway?

In Chapter 4, we learned about a feature introduced in SQL Server 2005 called the Unified
Dimensional Model (UDM). The UDM makes it possible for business intelligence to be
extracted right from the OLTP systems in a manner that does not put undue stress on
these systems, thus eliminating the need for data marts. This is shown in Figure 6-2.

So, why are we back to talking about data marts? Why don't we skip over all of this
and get right to the UDM? The answer is this: Even with the UDM, situations still
exist where a data mart may be the best choice as a source for business intelligence data.
These situations are shown in Figure 6-3.

Legacy Databases

The UDM's data sources utilize Windows OLE DB providers to make a connection to
OLTP systems. A number of different OLE DB providers are available for use when
creating data sources. However, some database systems do not have an appropriate

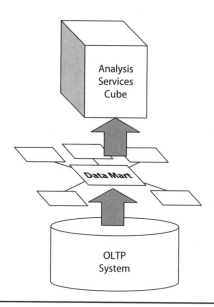

Figure 6-1   *An Analysis Services cube receiving data from a data mart*

OLE DB provider to make this connection. In fact, some systems, especially legacy systems, do not have any way to allow the type of external access required by an OLE DB provider.

In these situations, the data must be exported from the legacy system and copied into a database that can be utilized by the UDM. This database is the data mart. The data

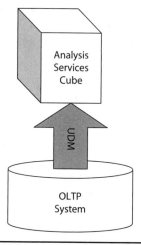

Figure 6-2   *The Unified Dimensional Model eliminates the need for a data mart.*

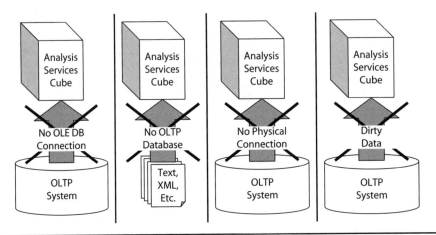

Figure 6-3   *Situations where UDM cannot be used*

must be exported from the legacy system into a format that can then be imported into the data mart. Usually, this is in the form of some type of text file: delimited columns, fixed-width columns, or, perhaps, Extensible Markup Language (XML).

Each time the export is run, a text file is created. This file is then imported into the data mart. The import is accomplished using Integration Services.

Data from Non-database Source

In some cases, the data needed for business intelligence is not even stored in a database. Production information from the automated manufacturing system could be written to a text file. Customer service call records might be logged to an XML file. Perhaps customer orders only exist on paper forms.

Again, in these situations, we need to import the data into a data mart before it can be utilized by a UDM. The text and XML files can be imported directly by Integration Services. The paper order forms must be scanned in or entered by hand into an electronic format that can be imported into the data mart.

No Physical Connection

In other cases, the data may exist in an OLTP database that has an OLE DB provider, but does not have a full-time connection to the location where the business intelligence must be utilized. The UDM requires some type of a connection that will support an OLE DB connection. If there is none, we again need to set up a data mart to serve as a repository for this data at the location where the business intelligence is utilized.

Of course, we also need some way to transport an export file from the OLTP database to the data mart so it can be imported. This might mean performing a File Transfer Protocol (FTP) transfer over a dial-up connection. It could mean putting the export file on a backup tape or burning it on a DVD-R and carrying it or shipping it between the two sites. However the data is transported, it is once again imported into the data mart using Integration Services.

Dirty Data

Dirty data can also trigger the need for a data mart. If the data in our OLTP systems contains a number of errors, inconsistencies, or duplicate information, we may need to clean the data before we can use it as a source of accurate business intelligence. Because of limitations in the OLTP systems, it may not be possible to properly cleanse the data in the OLTP database. Instead, the data must be exported from the OLTP system, and then cleaned up as it is imported into a data mart by Integration Services.

Designing a Data Mart

Once you establish the need for a data mart, it is time to create a design. As we learned in Chapter 3, a data mart is made up of measures, dimensions organized in hierarchies, and attributes. We begin our design by identifying the information that our decision makers need for effective decision making. We then need to reconcile this with the data we have available from our OLTP systems and organize this data into the data mart components: measures, dimensions, hierarchies, and attributes. When this is complete, we can build the database structure for the data mart using either a star or snowflake schema.

We discuss each step of the data mart design process in the following sections. This is followed by a section called "Learn By Doing." The Learn By Doing section lets you make the concepts more concrete by applying what you just learned to a business scenario from Maximum Miniatures, Incorporated. I encourage you to work through these Learn By Doing exercises to make what can be complex and overwhelming concepts more tangible and straightforward. As Aristotle said, "One must learn by doing the thing, for though you think you know it, you have no certainty until you try."

Decision Makers' Needs

Business intelligence design should never be done in a vacuum. As we discussed in Chapter 1, the goal of business intelligence is to provide the tools for effective decision making. Therefore, any business intelligence design must start with the decision makers themselves. What foundation and feedback information do they need? How do they need that information sliced and diced for proper analysis? To create truly effective business intelligence, these questions need to be answered by the decision makers themselves.

There are two important reasons to have the decision makers involved in this design process. First, the decision makers are the ones in the trenches. They know the choices that are made each day in the organization's operation. They also have a pretty good idea of what information can aid them in making those choices.

Second, the decision makers are the ones who ultimately determine the success or failure of a project. They do this through their willingness or unwillingness to use the resulting business intelligence tools. Your tool may produce dynamite information, but, ultimately, it is a failure if no one uses that information to produce more effective decisions.

Involving decision makers in the design of the data mart structures distributes the perceived ownership of the project. Most people who get their brainstorming ideas on the whiteboard during a design meeting or who are allowed to submit a design suggestion via e-mail, feel some sense of having contributed to the project. They feel a small piece of ownership in the project. Just as the owner of a single share in a billion-dollar corporation cares whether the company's stock goes up or down, the person who feels ownership in a project, no matter how small their actual contribution might be, cares about the success or failure of that project. A decision maker who has taken a small piece of ownership in our business intelligence project is far more likely to use the resulting tool and, if appropriate, to push for others to make use of it as well.

So, with the goal of both gaining important insight into the decision makers' needs and creating a sense of ownership among the future users of our business intelligence tool, we need to have our decision makers answer the following questions:

- ▶ What facts, figures, statistics, and so forth do you need for effective decision making? (foundation and feedback measures)
- ▶ How should this information be sliced and diced for analysis? (dimensions)
- ▶ What additional information can aid in finding exactly what is needed? (attributes)

The answers to these questions form half of the required design information. The other half comes from the OLTP data itself.

Available Data

The input and the ownership buy-in of the decision makers are important to our data mart design. Next comes the reality check. The fact is we cannot place any measures, dimensions, hierarchies, or attributes in the data mart if they are not represented in the OLTP data source.

We need to analyze the data to be received from the data source to make sure that all of the information requested by the decision makers can be obtained from there. Measures and attributes can come directly from fields in the OLTP data or from calculations based on those fields. Dimensions and hierarchies must be represented in the data and relationships contained in the OLTP data.

If a piece of requested information is not present in the OLTP data source, we need to determine if it is present in another data source. If so, data from these two data sources can be joined during the population of the data mart to provide the decision makers with the desired result. If the requested information is unavailable, we have to work with the decision makers to either determine a method to gather the missing information in the future, or identify an alternative bit of information already present in the OLTP data source.

Data Mart Structures

We are now ready to specify the structures that will be in our data mart. These are the measures, dimensions, hierarchies, and attributes. These structures lead us to the star or snowflake schema that is going to define our data mart.

Measures

We start our data mart design by specifying the measures. The *measures* are the foundation and feedback information our decision makers require. We reconcile these requirements with what is available in the OLTP data to come up with a list of measures, as shown in Figure 6-4.

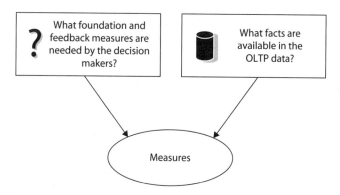

Figure 6-4   *Designing the measures in a data mart*

In Chapter 4, we learned measures are numeric quantities. The following are some examples of numeric data that can be used as measures:

Monetary Amounts

▶ The cost of raw materials

▶ The value of a sale

▶ Operational expenses

▶ Labor expenses

Counts

▶ The number of items produced

▶ The number of items ordered

▶ The number of items shipped

▶ The number of items returned

▶ The number of calls to customer service

Time Periods

▶ The number of minutes or hours required to produce a product

▶ The number of days required to fill an order

▶ Mean time between failure of a product

In the design, we need to note the following for each measure:

▶ Name of the measure

▶ What OLTP field or fields should be used to supply the data

▶ Data type (money, integer, decimal)

▶ Formula used to calculate the measure (if there is one)

As previously discussed, the data cannot appear out of thin air. It must be copied from or calculated from somewhere else. Therefore, identifying the OLTP fields that supply the data is important.

Refer to the "Learn By Doing—Designing the Maximum Miniatures Manufacturing Data Mart" section for an example of measure design.

Dimensions and Hierarchies

As we learned in Chapter 3, *dimensions* are used to spread a measure into its constituent parts. Hierarchies are used to organize dimensions into various levels. Dimensions and hierarchies are used to drill down into a measure to move from more general information to more specific information. While measures define *what* the decision makers want to see, the dimensions and hierarchies define *how* they want to see it.

When the decision makers tell us they want to see "total sales by salesperson by year," they are describing a measure, total sales, and two dimensions: salesperson and date. In discussions with decision makers, dimensions often are preceded with the words "by," "for each," or "for every." When the decision makers tell us they want to be able to "roll up salespersons into sales regions" or "drill down from year into quarter," they are describing hierarchies. The sales region dimension is above the salesperson dimension and the year dimension is above the quarter dimension in the hierarchy they are describing. These are all indications of how the decision makers want to view the measure.

We again reconcile the requested dimensions and hierarchies with what is available from the OLTP data to come up with the list of dimensions and their hierarchies for our design. This is shown in Figure 6-5. In the design, we need to have the following listed for each dimension:

▶ Name of the dimension

▶ What OLTP field or fields are to be used to supply the data

▶ Data type of the dimension's key (the code that uniquely identifies each member of the dimension)

▶ Name of the parent dimension (if there is one)

Refer to the "Learn By Doing—Designing the Maximum Miniatures Manufacturing Data Mart" section for an example of dimension and hierarchy design.

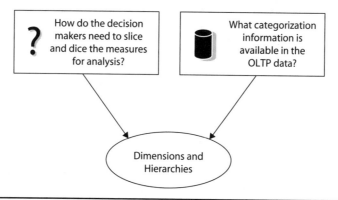

Figure 6-5   *Designing the dimensions and hierarchies in a data mart*

Attributes

Attributes provide additional information about a dimension. They may result from information decision makers want to have readily available during analysis. Attributes may also result from information decision makers want to filter on during the analysis process.

As before, we need to reconcile the requested attributes with the data available from the OLTP database to come up with the list of attributes in our design. This is shown in Figure 6-6. In the design, we need to include the following for each attribute:

▶ Name of the attribute

▶ What OLTP field or fields are to be used to supply the data

▶ Data type

▶ Name of the dimension to which it applies

Refer to the "Learn By Doing—Designing the Maximum Miniatures Manufacturing Data Mart" section for an example of attribute design.

Stars and Snowflakes

Data marts are architected using either a star schema or a snowflake schema. Refer to Chapter 3 if you need a refresher on these two layouts. Our last step is to turn our lists into either a star or a snowflake schema. Figure 6-7 shows a star schema, while Figure 6-8 shows a snowflake schema.

Recall that all the measures are placed in a single table called the fact table. The dimensions at the lowest level of the hierarchies are each placed in their own

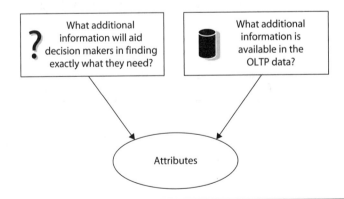

Figure 6-6 *Designing the attributes in a data mart*

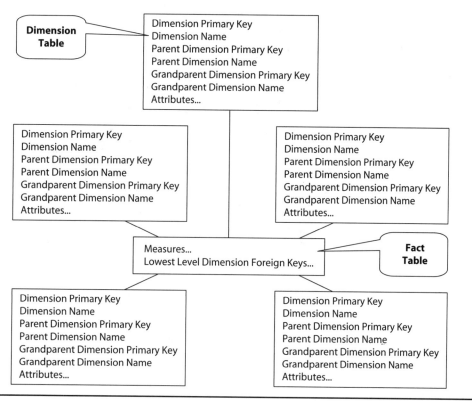

Figure 6-7   *A star schema*

dimension table. In the *star schema,* all the information for a hierarchy is stored in the same table. The information for the parent (or grandparent or great-grandparent, and so forth) dimension is added to the table containing the dimension at the lowest level of the hierarchy.

The snowflake schema works a bit differently. In the *snowflake schema,* each level in the dimensional hierarchy has its own table. The dimension tables are linked together with foreign key relationships to form the hierarchy. Refer to Chapter 3 for a discussion of the advantages and disadvantages of star and snowflake schemas.

Once we create our schema, we are ready to implement that schema in a database. Before we look at implementing the schema, however, let's walk through an example of data mart design.

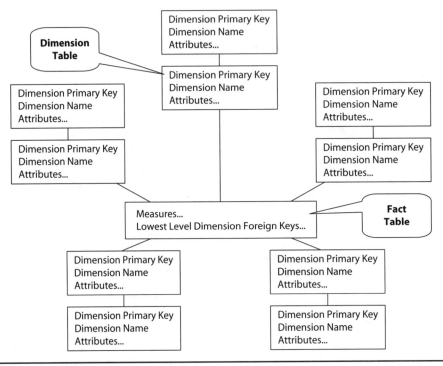

Figure 6-8 *A snowflake schema*

Learn By Doing—Designing the Maximum Miniatures Manufacturing Data Mart

Feature Highlighted

▶ Designing a data mart

In this section, we apply the knowledge gained in the previous sections to complete a sample task for Maximum Miniatures, Incorporated. In this case, we design the Manufacturing data mart to hold information that is initially logged by the manufacturing automation system in comma-delimited text files.

Business Need The vice president (VP) of production for Max Min, Inc. wants to analyze the statistics available from the manufacturing automation system. He would like an interactive analysis tool, rather than printed reports, for this analysis. In keeping with Max Min's new business intelligence strategy, Microsoft SQL Server 2008 Analysis

Services is the platform for this analysis tool. Because the manufacturing automation system does not use a database, logging everything to comma-delimited text files instead, a data mart must be designed and built as a repository for this information.

The manufacturing automation system controls all the machines used by Max Min to create its figurines. Each machine handles all the steps in the manufacturing process of a figurine. This includes the following:

▶ Filling a mold with the raw material (clay, pewter, or aluminum)

▶ Aiding the hardening of this material

▶ Removal from the mold when hardening is complete

▶ Computerized painting of the figurine, if necessary (pewter figurines are not painted)

▶ Curing the paint, if necessary

Multiple painting and curing cycles may be necessary, depending on the intricacy of the paint job required by a product. A quality assurance check is done by the machine operator as the figurine is completed.

Operators log onto a machine. As part of this logon process, the operator tells the manufacturing automation system what product is being produced, along with the batch number of the raw material being used by that machine. The operator also makes an entry in the system when a figurine is rejected.

An interview with the VP of production yielded the following data requirements for effective decision making:

▶ Number of accepted products by batch, by product, by machine, by day

▶ Number of rejected products by batch, by product, by machine, by day

▶ Elapsed time for molding and hardening by product, by machine, by day

▶ Elapsed time for painting and curing by paint type, by product, by machine, by day

▶ Product rolls up into product subtype, which rolls up into product type

▶ Machine rolls up into machine type, which rolls up into material (clay, pewter, or aluminum)

▶ Machine also rolls up into plant, which rolls up into country

▶ Day rolls up into month, which rolls up into quarter, which rolls up into year

▶ The information should be able to be filtered by machine manufacturer and purchase date of the machine

The export file from the manufacturing automation system contains one row for each product produced. Each row includes the following information:

- ▶ Product
- ▶ Batch number of the raw material
- ▶ Machine number
- ▶ Operator employee number
- ▶ Start of manufacture date and time (when the batch run begins)
- ▶ End of manufacture date and time (when the batch run is complete)
- ▶ Reject flag

Steps

> **NOTE**
>
> *In this particular Learn By Doing exercise, you don't have that much to do except follow along and make sure you understand each step. You can use these steps as a guideline when you have to create your own data mart design. Subsequent "Learn By Doing" sections require you to use the SQL Server 2008 tools to create part of a working business intelligence solution.*

1. Prepare a list of the measures requested by the VP of production. This is shown in the Measure column of Figure 6-9.

2. Determine which fields in the OLTP data source supply the data for these measures. This is shown in the OLTP Fields column of Figure 6-9. The Reject Flag field tells us whether a product has been accepted or rejected. This can be used to determine the number of accepted and number of rejected products. The manufacturing system does not track the time spent in each individual production step. It only tracks the date and time at the start of manufacture and the date and time at the end of manufacture. Therefore, we need to put NOT AVAILABLE for these two items.

Measure	OLTP Fields
Number of Accepted Products	Reject Flag
Number of Rejected Products	Reject Flag
Elapsed Minutes for Molding and Hardening	NOT AVAILABLE
Elapsed Minutes for Painting and Curing	NOT AVAILABLE

Figure 6-9   *Requested measures for the Manufacturing data mart*

Measure	OLTP Fields	Data Type	Formula
Number of Accepted Products	Reject flag	Int	Count when reject flag is false
Number of Rejected Products	Reject flag	Int	Count when reject flag is true
Elapsed Minutes for Manufacturing	Start of manufacture date and time, End of manufacture date and time	Decimal(6,2)	DATEDIFF(mi, [Start of manufacture date and time], [End of manufacture date and time])

Figure 6-10   *Finalized measures for the Manufacturing data mart*

3. Resolve any problems with information that is unavailable. In this case, a follow-up interview with the VP reveals he will be satisfied with knowing the elapsed minutes for the entire manufacturing process. When our list is updated with this information, it appears as shown in the Measure and OLTP Fields columns of Figure 6-10.

4. Add the data types and calculations to the list. This is shown in the Data Type and Formula columns of Figure 6-10.

5. Prepare a list of the dimensions requested by the VP of production. This is shown in the Dimension column of Figure 6-11.

6. Determine which fields in the OLTP data source are going to supply the data for these dimensions. This is shown in the OLTP Fields column of Figure 6-11.

7. Resolve any problems with information that is not available. The manufacturing automation system does not include information on the hierarchies within Max Min. To include these hierarchies in the data mart, we need to pull data from

Dimension	OLTP Fields
Product	Product
Product Subtype	NOT AVAILABLE
Product Type	NOT AVAILABLE
Batch	Batch
Machine	Machine
Machine Type	NOT AVAILABLE
Material	NOT AVAILABLE
Plant	NOT AVAILABLE
Country	NOT AVAILABLE
Day	Start of Manufacture Date and Time
Month	Start of Manufacture Date and Time
Quarter	Start of Manufacture Date and Time
Year	Start of Manufacture Date and Time
Paint Type	NOT AVAILABLE

Figure 6-11   *Requested dimensions for the Manufacturing data mart*

Dimension	OLTP Fields	Data Type	Parent Dimension
Product	Product	Int	Product Subtype
Product Subtype	Accounting System.ProductSubtype	Int	Product Type
Product Type	Accounting System.ProductType	Int	None
Batch	Batch	Int	None
Machine	Machine	Int	Machine Type, Plant
Machine Type	Accounting System.MachineType	Nvarchar(30)	Material
Material	Accounting System.Material	Nvarchar(30)	None
Plant	Accounting System.Plant	Int	Country
Country	Accounting System.Country	Nchar(3)	None
Day	Start of Manufacture Date and Time	Int	Month
Month	Start of Manufacture Date and Time	Int	Quarter
Quarter	Start of Manufacture Date and Time	Int	Year
Year	Start of Manufacture Date and Time	Int	None

Figure 6-12   *Finalized dimensions and hierarchies for the Manufacturing data mart*

another system. It turns out that the accounting system has the data we need. We remove the Paint Type dimension because this data is not available electronically. When our list is updated with this information, it appears as shown in the Dimension and OLTP Fields columns of Figure 6-12.

8. Add the data type of the dimension's key, along with the name of the parent dimension. This is shown in the Data Type and Parent Dimension columns of Figure 6-12.

9. Prepare a list of the attributes requested by the VP of production. This is shown in the Attribute column of Figure 6-13.

10. Determine which fields in the OLTP data source will supply the data for these attributes. Remember, some of this data needs to come from the accounting system. This is shown in the OLTP Fields column of Figure 6-13.

11. Resolve any problems with information that is unavailable. In this case, we do not have any problem attributes, so no changes need to be made to the list.

12. Add the data type of the attribute, along with the name of the dimension it is associated with. This is shown in the Data Type and Dimension columns of Figure 6-13.

Attribute	OLTP Fields	Data Type	Dimension
Machine Manufacturer	Accounting.Equipment	Nvarchar(50)	Machine
Date of Purchase	Accounting.Equipment	Datetime	Machine

Figure 6-13   *Finalized attributes for the Manufacturing data mart*

ManufacturingFact	
Field Name	**Data Type**
AcceptedProducts	Int
RejectedProducts	Int
ElapsedTimeForManufacture	Decimal(6,2)

Figure 6-14 *The Manufacturing data mart schema with measures in a fact table*

13. Turn the lists in Figure 6-10, Figure 6-12, and Figure 6-13 into your choice of a star schema or a snowflake schema. In this case, we use a snowflake schema. Place the measures and their data types in the ManufacturingFact table, as shown in Figure 6-14.

14. Place each dimension into its own dimension table, as shown in Figure 6-15. Include a table name beginning with "Dim" and a primary key designation in each table.

ManufacturingFact	
Field Name	**Data Type**
AcceptedProducts	Int
RejectedProducts	Int
ElapsedTimeForManufacture	Decimal(6,2)
DateOfManufacture	DateTime

DimProduct	
Field Name	**Data Type**
ProductCode (PK)	Int
ProductName	Nvarchar(50)

DimProductSubtype	
Field Name	**Data Type**
ProductSubtypeCode (PK)	Int
ProductSubtypeName	Nvarchar(50)

DimProductType	
Field Name	**Data Type**
ProductTypeCode (PK)	Int
ProductTypeName	Nvarchar(50)

DimBatch	
Field Name	**Data Type**
BatchNumber (PK)	Int
BatchName	Nvarchar(50)

DimMachine	
Field Name	**Data Type**
MachineNumber (PK)	Int
MachineName	Nvarchar(50)

DimMachineType	
Field Name	**Data Type**
MachineType (PK)	Nvarchar(30)

DimMaterial	
Field Name	**Data Type**
Material (PK)	Nvarchar(30)

DimPlant	
Field Name	**Data Type**
PlantNumber (PK)	Int
PlantName	Nvarchar(30)

DimCountry	
Field Name	**Data Type**
CountryCode (PK)	Char(3)
CountryName	Nvarchar(30)

Figure 6-15 *The Manufacturing data mart schema with dimension tables added*

> **NOTE**
>
> *The time-related dimensions of day, month, quarter, and year do not need dimension tables. Instead, a single datetime field is placed in the ManufacturingFact table (DateOfManufacture). The entire time-related hierarchy will be extrapolated from this field when we create a cube based on this data mart in a later chapter. This is done using a feature of SQL Server Analysis Services.*

15. Create the dimensional hierarchies by adding foreign keys to the dimension tables. This is shown in Figure 6-16.

16. Link the lowest-level dimensions to the fact table by adding foreign keys to the fact table. Also, add the attributes to the dimension tables. The final Manufacturing data mart schema is shown in Figure 6-17. This may be a pretty funny looking snowflake, but it is, indeed, a snowflake schema.

The design of the Manufacturing data mart is complete. Next, we learn how to turn that design into a reality.

ManufacturingFact

Field Name	Data Type
AcceptedProducts	Int
RejectedProducts	Int
ElapsedTimeForManufacture	Decimal(6,2)
DateOfManufacture	DateTime

DimBatch

Field Name	Data Type
BatchNumber (PK)	Int
BatchName	Nvarchar(50)

DimMachine

Field Name	Data Type
MachineNumber (PK)	Int
MachineName	Nvarchar(50)
MachineType (FK)	Nvarchar(30)
PlantNumber (FK)	Int

DimProduct

Field Name	Data Type
ProductCode (PK)	Int
ProductName	Varchar(50)
ProductSubtypeCode (FK)	Int

DimProductSubtype

Field Name	Data Type
ProductSubtypeCode (PK)	Int
ProductSubtypeName	Nvarchar(50)
ProductTypeCode (FK)	Int

DimMachineType

Field Name	Data Type
MachineType (PK)	Nvarchar(30)
Material (FK)	Nvarchar(30)

DimMaterial

Field Name	Data Type
Material (PK)	Nvarchar(30)

DimPlant

Field Name	Data Type
PlantNumber (PK)	Int
PlantName	Nvarchar(30)
CountryCode (FK)	Char(2)

DimProductType

Field Name	Data Type
ProductTypeCode (PK)	Int
ProductTypeName	Nvarchar(50)

DimCountry

Field Name	Data Type
CountryCode (PK)	Char(2)
CountryName	Nvarchar(30)

Figure 6-16 *The Manufacturing data mart schema with hierarchies added*

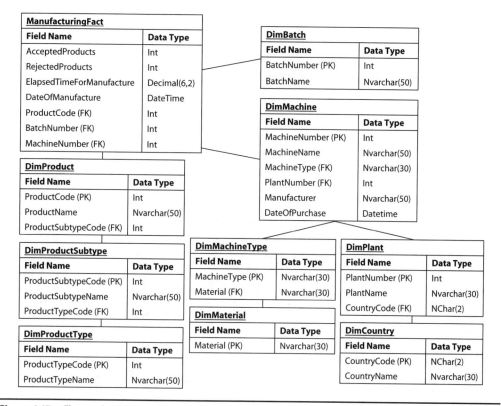

Figure 6-17   *The completed Manufacturing data mart schema*

Creating a Data Mart Using the SQL Server Management Studio

Now that we have a design for our data mart based on the decision maker's requests and the data available from the OLTP systems, it is time to turn that design into database tables. We are going to build the relational data mart as shown in Figure 6-18. We use the schema in Figure 6-17 to create a database with a fact table and several dimension tables.

Even though we identified several foreign key relationships amongst our tables, we are not going to create foreign key constraints in our data mart. Foreign key constraints put a strain on the database engine during a large data load. Large data loads are quite common in the data mart environment. Instead of using foreign key constraints, we will depend on our data extract, transform, and load (ETL) process in SQL Server Integration Services to enforce data integrity. We will see this in action in Chapter 8.

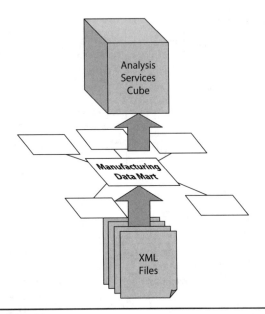

Figure 6-18   *Building the relational data mart*

Follow the steps in the "Learn By Doing—Creating the Maximum Miniatures Manufacturing Data Mart Using the SQL Server Management Studio" section to create the Manufacturing data mart.

Learn By Doing—Creating the Maximum Miniatures Manufacturing Data Mart Using the SQL Server Management Studio

Features Highlighted

- Creating a data mart database
- Creating dimension tables
- Creating a fact table

Business Need   The business need was stated in the previous Learn By Doing section, where we created the schema for the Manufacturing data mart. In this section, we implement the Maximum Miniatures Manufacturing data mart schema using the SQL Server Management Studio.

Steps

1. Open the SQL Server Management Studio, as we discussed in Chapter 5.

2. Connect to a development or test SQL server. (Do *not* perform this or any other Learn By Doing activity on a server used for production database operations!)

3. Right-click the Databases folder in the Object Explorer window. The context menu appears, as shown in Figure 6-19.

4. Select New Database from the context menu. The New Database dialog box appears, as shown in Figure 6-20.

5. Enter **MaxMinManufacturingDM** for Database Name. Select the Options page and select Simple from the Recovery model drop-down list. Click OK to create the database.

NOTE

Because this is not a transactional database, there is no need to recover the content of this database using the transaction log. The simple recovery model truncates the transaction log on checkpoint, keeping the size of the transaction log small. The Full and Bulk-logged recovery models require a backup of the transaction log before it is truncated.

6. Expand the Databases folder and expand the MaxMinManufacturingDM database entry. Right-click the Tables folder and select New Table from the context menu. A Table Designer tab appears, as shown in Figure 6-21.

7. We use both the Properties window and the Column Properties window as we create our tables. If the Properties window is not visible, as shown in Figure 6-21, select Properties Window from the View menu. Be sure to note whether the entries in the following steps are being made in the Properties window or in the Column Properties window.

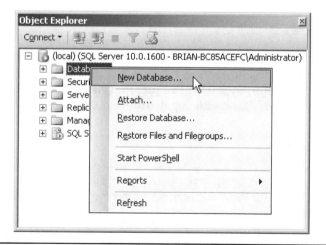

Figure 6-19   *The Database folder context menu*

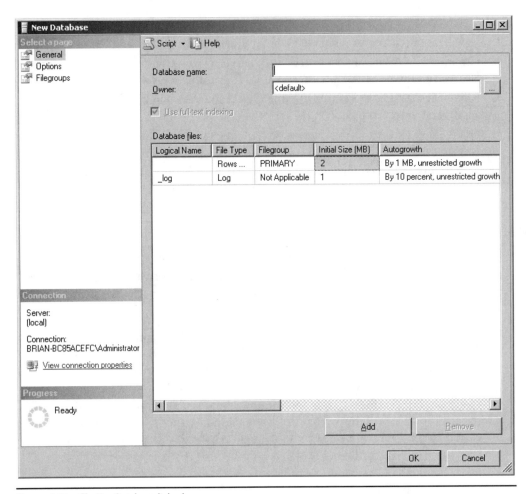

Figure 6-20 *The New Database dialog box*

8. Begin by creating the DimProduct table from the schema (see Figure 6-17). In the Properties window, enter **DimProduct** for (Name) and **Product Dimension populated from the Manufacturing Automation System export file.** for Description.

NOTE

To use a larger editing area when entering the description, click the ellipses button (...) at the end of the Description property entry area. This opens a dialog window with a multiline entry area for typing the description.

9. In the first row of the Table Designer tab, enter **ProductCode** under Column Name, select int under Data Type, and uncheck Allow Nulls. Click the Set Primary Key button in the toolbar to make this the primary key for this table.

Table Designer Tab   Properties Window

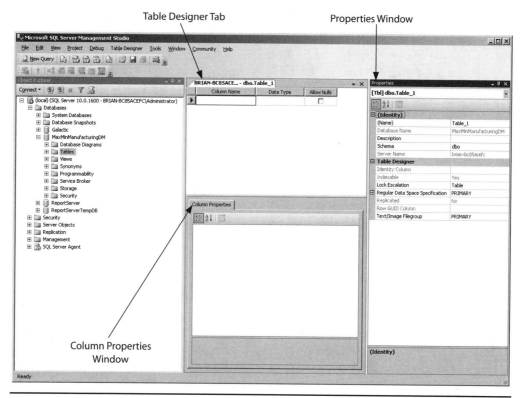

Figure 6-21   *The SQL Server Management Studio ready to create a table*

10. In the second row of the Table Designer tab, enter **ProductName** under Column Name, select nvarchar(50) under Data Type, and uncheck Allow Nulls. (Leave Length in the Column Properties window set to the default value of 50.)

11. In the third row of the Table Designer tab, enter **ProductSubtypeCode** under Column Name, select int under Data Type, and uncheck Allow Nulls.

12. Click the Save toolbar button to save this table design. This creates the table in the database. Next, click the Close button in the upper-right corner of the Table Designer tab.

13. Next, create the DimProductSubtype table from the schema. Right-click the Tables folder and select New Table from the context menu. In the Properties window, enter **DimProductSubtype** for (Name) and **ProductSubtype Dimension populated from the Accounting System.ProductSubtype table**. for Description.

14. In the first row of the Table Designer tab, enter **ProductSubtypeCode** under Column Name, select int under Data Type, and uncheck Allow Nulls. Click the Set Primary Key button in the toolbar to make this the primary key for this table.

15. In the second row of the Table Designer tab, enter **ProductSubtypeName** under Column Name, select nvarchar(50) under Data Type, and uncheck Allow Nulls. (Leave Length in the Column Properties window set to the default value of 50.)

16. In the third row of the Table Designer tab, enter **ProductTypeCode** under Column Name, select int under Data Type, and uncheck Allow Nulls.

17. Click the Save toolbar button to create the table, and then click the Close button in the upper-right corner of the Table Designer tab.

18. Use the same process to create the DimProductType, DimBatch, DimMachine, DimMachineType, DimMaterial, DimPlant, and DimCountry dimension tables based on the schema in Figure 6-17. Be sure to uncheck Allow Nulls for all fields and to enter the appropriate data type along with the appropriate length in the Column Properties window. Also, create a primary key for each field that is followed by a (PK) in Figure 6-17.

19. Right-click the MaxMinManufacturingDM database entry in the Object Explorer window and select Refresh from the context menu. When you expand the node for columns under each table, the entries should appear just as in Figure 6-22 and Figure 6-23.

NOTE

If you notice any mistakes as you compare Figure 6-22 and Figure 6-23 with your tables, right-click the table that is in error and select Design from the context menu. Make the necessary changes to the table structure to correct the error. Be sure to click the Save toolbar button when you are done. You need to refresh the contents of the Object Explorer window after your changes before again comparing to Figure 6-22 and Figure 6-23. You may need to enable table changes in the SQL Server Management Studio. If you receive an error, select Tools | Options from the main menu. In the Options dialog box, select the Designers | Table and Database Designers page. Uncheck the Prevent saving changes that require table re-creation check box and click OK.

20. Now, create the ManufacturingFact table. Right-click the Tables folder and select New Table from the context menu. In the Properties window, enter **ManufacturingFact** for (Name) and **Manufacturing Fact populated from the Manufacturing Automation System export file**. for Description.

21. Using the schema in Figure 6-17, create the entries for the seven columns in the ManufacturingFact table. When creating the ElapsedTimeForManufacture field definition, select decimal under Data Type, and then enter **6** for Precision and **2** for Scale. (Continue to uncheck Allow Nulls for all fields.)

NOTE

The decimal data type is used to store real numbers. The precision determines the total number of digits contained in the number. The scale tells how many of those digits are to the right of the decimal. The ElapsedTimeForManufacture field has a maximum of six digits, with two of those digits to the right of the decimal. Therefore, the largest number that can be stored in this field is 9999.99.

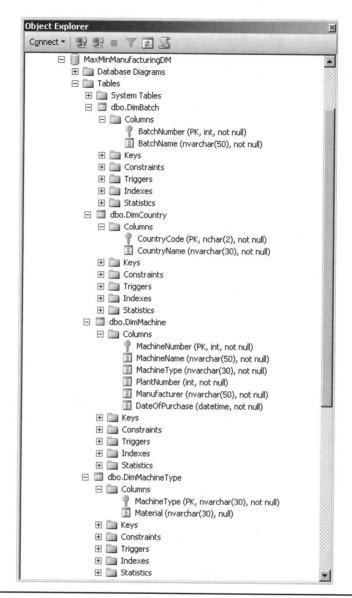

Figure 6-22   *The tables in the MaxMinManufacturingDM with columns (Part 1)*

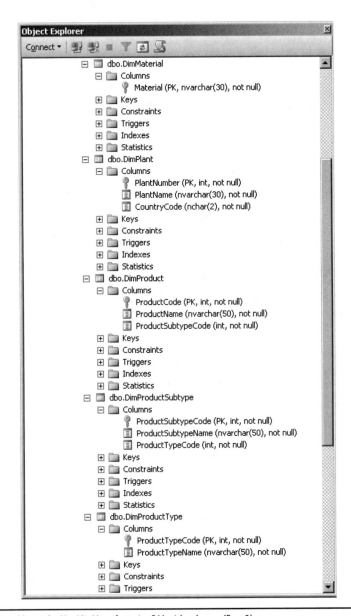

Figure 6-23 *The tables in the MaxMinManufacturingDM with columns (Part 2)*

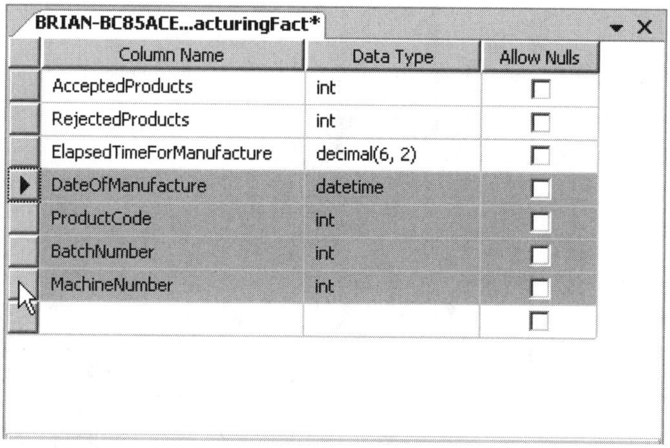

Figure 6-24   *Selecting multiple fields to create a compound primary key*

22. Click the square to the left of the DateOfManufacture field definition. Hold down SHIFT and click the square to the left of the MachineNumber field definition. This selects these two field definitions and all the field definitions in between, as shown in Figure 6-24. Click the Set Primary Key button in the toolbar to make these four fields a compound primary key for this table.

23. Click the Save toolbar button, and then click the Close button in the upper-right corner of the Table Designer tab.

We have now manually built the Manufacturing data mart structure using the SQL Server Management Studio. Even though this process took 23 steps, we are only halfway done. In Chapter 8, we complete the other half of the process by creating an Analysis Services cube that uses this data mart as its data source.

Creating a Data Mart Using the Business Intelligence Development Studio

In the previous section, we completed the first half of a two-step process for creating a relational data mart and an Analysis Services cube built on that data mart. This is a long and, as you will see, somewhat redundant process. The Business Intelligence Development Studio comes to our rescue here. We will now use this tool to create the Analysis Services cube and its underlying relational data mart for the Maximum Miniatures sales data at the same time. This is shown in Figure 6-25. The Cube Wizard creates an Analysis Services cube, and then creates the matching dimension and fact tables in the Sales data mart based on the cube definition.

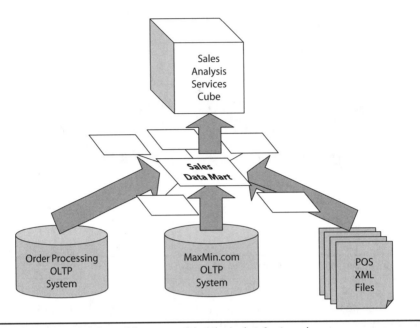

Figure 6-25 *Building the Sales relational data mart and the Sales Analysis Services cube*

Follow the steps in the "Learn By Doing—Creating the Maximum Miniatures Sales Data Mart Using the Business Intelligence Development Studio" section to create the Sales data mart through the Cube Wizard.

Learn By Doing—Creating the Maximum Miniatures Sales Data Mart Using the Business Intelligence Development Studio

Features Highlighted

▶ Creating an Analysis Services cube using the Cube Wizard in the Business Intelligence Development Studio

▶ Creating a relational data mart from a cube definition in the Business Intelligence Development Studio

Business Need   The VP of sales for Max Min, Inc. would like to analyze sales information. This information is collected by three OLTP systems: the Order Processing System, the Point of Sale (POS) System, and the MaxMin.com Online System (refer to Figure 2-4). The Order Processing System and the MaxMin.com Online System both use Microsoft SQL Server as their back-end databases. The POS System uses XML files to transfer data from each of the five Max Min–owned retail stores.

Microsoft SQL Server 2008 Analysis Services is the platform for this analysis tool. Because the data must come from three different systems and because one of these systems is file-based, a relational data mart is created to hold the information that is to serve as the data source for the cube.

The VP of sales would like to be able to analyze the following numbers:

▶ Dollar value of products sold

▶ Number of products sold

▶ Sales tax charged on products sold

▶ Shipping charged on products sold

These numbers should be viewable by:

▶ Store

▶ Sales Promotion

▶ Product

▶ Day, Month, Quarter, and Year

▶ Customer

▶ Salesperson

An analysis of the three data sources shows that all of this information is available from at least one data source.

In the previous Learn By Doing exercise, we first created our data mart structure on paper, and then implemented it in SQL Server. This time around, we will let the Cube Wizard guide us through the creation of the data mart structures.

NOTE

We need to use the SQL Server Management Studio to create a database for our Max Min Sales data mart. The Business Intelligence Development Studio creates the dimension and fact tables in this database later in the process.

Steps

1. Open the SQL Server Management Studio and connect to your development or test SQL server. Create a new database called MaxMinSalesDM, which uses the Simple recovery model. If you have any questions about creating this database, refer to Steps 3–5 in the "Learn By Doing—Creating the Maximum Miniatures Manufacturing Data Mart Using the SQL Server Management Studio" section of this chapter.

2. Close the SQL Server Management Studio.

3. Open the SQL Server Business Intelligence Development Studio, as we discussed in Chapter 5.

4. Click the New Project button in the toolbar.

5. Make sure Business Intelligence Projects is selected in the Project types pane, and then select Analysis Services Project from the Templates.

6. Enter **MaxMinSalesDM** for Name and set the Location to the appropriate folder. Leave Create Directory for Solution checked.

NOTE

You should create a folder to hold all of the Learn By Doing activities in this book. Make sure this folder is clearly named so it does not become confused with production source code.

7. Click OK to create the project.

8. Once the project is open, right-click the Cubes folder in the Solution Explorer and select New Cube from the context menu. The Cube Wizard dialog box appears.

9. On the Welcome page, click Next.

10. On the Select Creation Method page, select the Generate tables in the data source radio button. Leave (None) selected in the Template drop-down list. Click Next.

11. Click the highlighted cell in the Add new measures grid. Enter **Sales in Dollars** in the Measure Name column.

12. Enter **Sales Information** in the Measure Group column.

13. Select Currency in the Data Type column. Sum should be selected by default in the Aggregation column.

14. Click the cell containing "Add new measure" in the Add new measures grid.

15. Enter **Sales in Units** in the Measure Name column.

16. Enter **Sales Information** in the Measure Group column. This should be selected by default.

17. Select Integer in the Data Type column. Sum should be selected by default in the Aggregation column.

18. Click the cell containing "Add new measure" in the Add new measures grid.

19. Enter **Sales Tax** in the Measure Name column.

20. Enter **Sales Information** in the Measure Group column. This should be selected by default.

21. Select Currency in the Data Type column. Sum should be selected by default in the Aggregation column.

22. Click the cell containing "Add new measure" in the Add new measures grid.

23. Enter **Shipping** in the Measure Name column.

24. Enter **Sales Information** in the Measure Group column. This should be selected by default.

25. Select Currency in the Data Type column. Sum should be selected by default in the Aggregation column. The Define New Measures page should appear as shown in Figure 6-26.

26. Click Next.

27. The Select dimensions from template grid at the top of the Define New Dimensions page will create the Time dimension for us from a time dimension template. Make sure the Time dimension line remains checked.

28. Click the cell containing "Add new dimension" in the Add new dimensions grid.

29. Enter **Customer** in the Name column.

30. Click the cell containing "Add new dimension" and enter **Product** in the Name column.

31. Click the cell containing "Add new dimension" and enter **Promotion** in the Name column.

32. Click the cell containing "Add new dimension" and enter **Sales Person** in the Name column.

33. Check the box under SCD in the SalesPerson row.

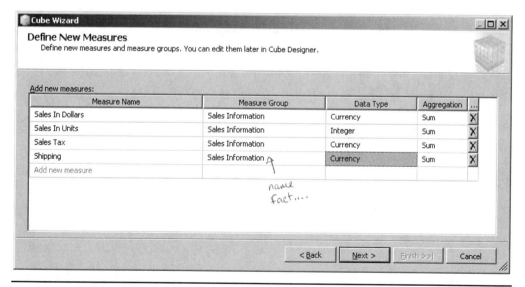

Figure 6-26   *After defining the measures in the Cube Wizard*

DEFINITION

A Slowly Changing Dimension (SCD) varies over time. Of course, the data in many dimensions can change over time. What differentiates an SCD is the fact that the history of that change is important and must be tracked in the business intelligence information. For example, the salesperson dimension changes as salespeople are transferred from one sales territory to another. We need to track which territory a salesperson was in last year versus which territory they are in this year so sales can be rolled up into the correct territory for year-to-year comparisons.

34. Click the cell containing "Add new dimension" and enter **Store** in the Name column. The Define New Dimensions page should appear as shown in Figure 6-27.

35. Click Next.

36. The Define Time Periods page enables us to specify range, format, and hierarchy for the time dimension. Select Sunday, January 01, 2006 from the First calendar day date picker. Check Month, Quarter, and Year in Time periods. (Leave Date checked as well.) The Define Time Periods page appears as shown in Figure 6-28.

NOTE

If we use week in a time hierarchy, we can specify the first day of the week to use with this dimension. We can also specify the language to use for the members of the time dimension.

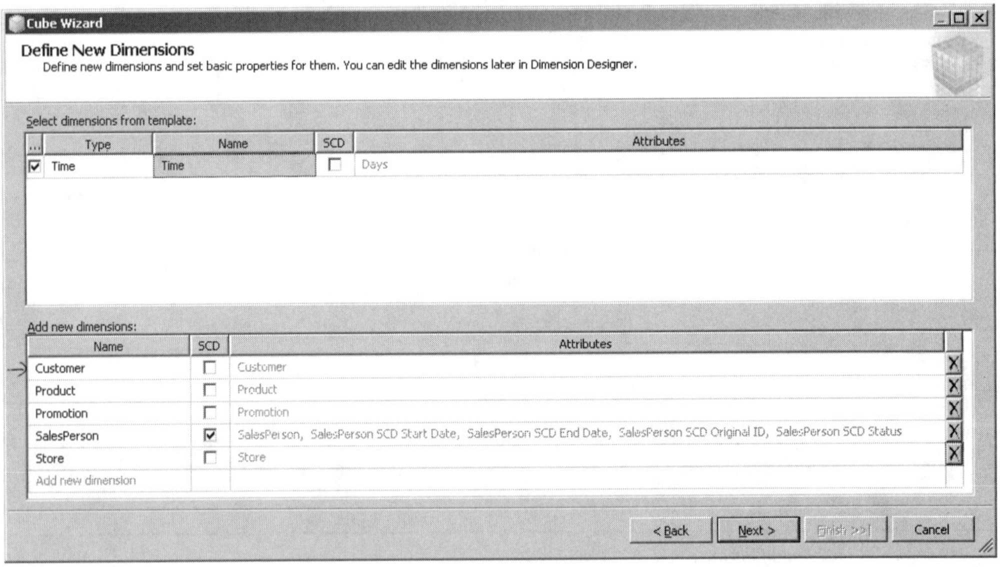

Figure 6-27   *After defining dimensions in the Cube Wizard*

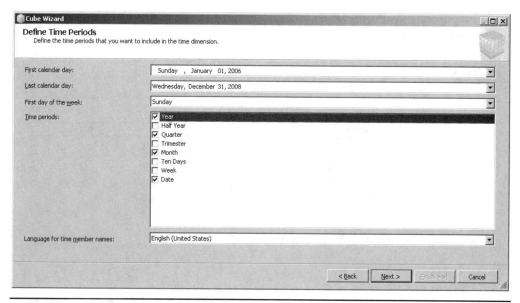

Figure 6-28 *After defining the time periods for the time dimension in the Cube Wizard*

37. Click Next.

38. The Specify Additional Calendars page lets us add additional calendars other than the standard 12-month calendar to the time dimension. The Specify Additional Calendars page is shown in Figure 6-29. This might include a calendar for a fiscal year that starts on a day other than January 1 or the ISO 8601 standard calendar. Max Min tracks sales based on the standard 12-month calendar, so simply click Next.

39. The Define Dimension Usage page enables us to specify which dimensions are related to each group of measures. The Max Min Sales data mart is only using one group of measures, called Sales Information, so we want all the dimensions to apply to this group. Check the box in the Sales Information column for all of the dimensions, as shown in Figure 6-30. Click Next.

40. The Completing the Wizard page lets us review the cube we defined. Enter **MaxMinSales** for the Cube Name. We can expand the nodes in Preview to view the measures and dimensions that are to be created in this cube. Note, only the Time dimension has a hierarchy. We add additional hierarchies manually. When all the nodes except the Attributes nodes are expanded, the Preview should appear as shown in Figure 6-31.

41. Check Generate Schema Now. This causes the Cube Wizard to create the relational database to hold the data mart that serves as the source for this cube.

42. Click Finish.

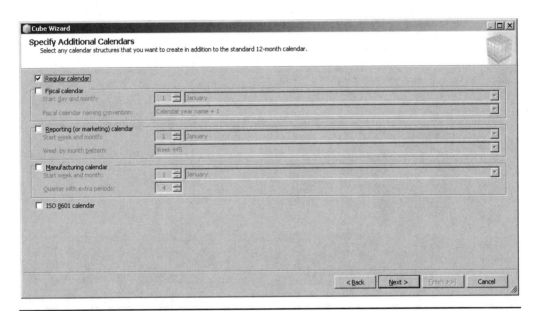

Figure 6-29   *Specifying additional calendars in the Cube Wizard*

43. Because we checked Generate Schema Now, the Schema Generation Wizard is automatically launched. On the Welcome to the Schema Generation Wizard page, click Next.

44. The Specify Target page enables us to select the database server where the data mart relational database is created. This is done by creating a data source and a data source view. Click New. The Data Source Wizard appears.

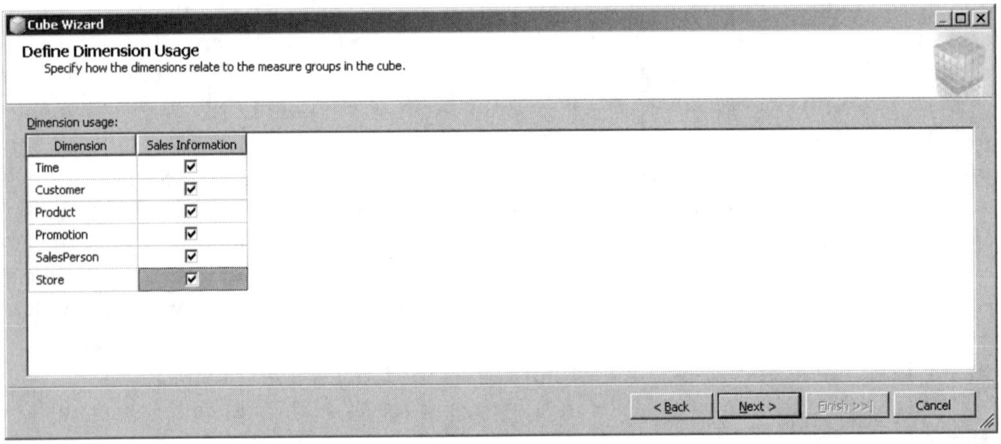

Figure 6-30   *Setting the dimension usage in the Cube Wizard*

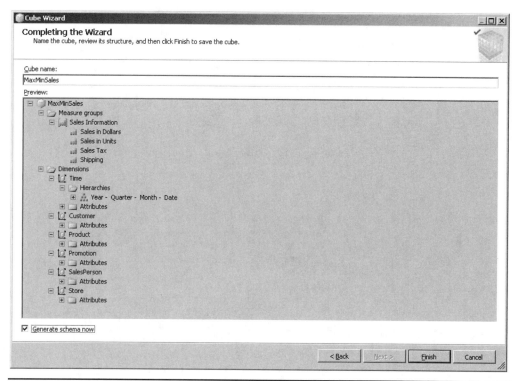

Figure 6-31   *Completing the cube in the Cube Wizard*

45. On the Welcome to the Data Source Wizard page, click Next. On the Select how to define the connection screen, click New.

46. The Connection Manager dialog box lets us define a connection string used to access a database. Provider enables you to select between Native OLE DB providers and the .NET providers for either SQL Server or Oracle. In this case, we leave Provider set to Native OLE DB\SQL Server Native Client. For Server Name, enter the name of the database server where you created the MaxMinSalesDM database in Step 2 of this section.

47. Select Use Windows Authentication under Log On to the Server. The Schema Generation process requires Windows Authentication. Make sure that your current Windows credentials have rights to create tables in the MaxMinSalesDM database.

48. Select MaxMinSalesDM from the Select or Enter the Database Name drop-down list. (A valid set of credentials must be specified before the drop-down list is populated.) The Connection Manager will appear, as shown in Figure 6-32.

49. Click OK to exit the Connection Manager dialog box.

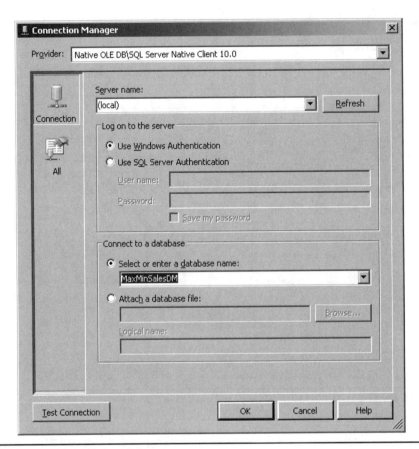

Figure 6-32 *The Connection Manager dialog box*

50. In the Select how to define the connection dialog box, click Next.

51. On the Impersonation Information page, if you are using Windows Authentication in your data connection, select "Use a specific Windows user name and password" and enter a valid Windows user name and password for database access. If you entered a specific SQL Server logon in the data connection, you do not need to worry about impersonation. Click Next. The Completing the Wizard page will appear.

NOTE

Analysis Services needs to access the data mart relational database in order to populate and update the information in the OLAP cube. This is done using the information in the data connection selected in Step 46. The Analysis Services updates may run as a background process. This can be an issue if the data connection specifies Windows Authentication or if the connection is to a file-based database such as Access. In these situations, Analysis Services needs to know what Windows credentials to use when accessing the data source. In other words, it needs to impersonate a Windows identity while accessing the data.

52. The Completing the Wizard page shows the finished connection string. Click Finish to exit the Data Source Wizard.

53. We are now back to the Specify Target page of the Schema Generation Wizard. Click Next.

54. The Subject Area Database Schema Options page lets us select the operations we want the Schema Generation Wizard to perform. Uncheck the Enforce referential integrity check box. As stated earlier, we will let our ETL process enforce referential integrity. Populate should be selected from the Populate Time Table(s) drop-down list. Click Next.

NOTE

There are three options for handling the population of the table for the time dimension. The Populate option creates records in the time dimension table for the timeframe specified on the Define Time Periods page in Step 36.

55. The Specify Naming Conventions page enables us to determine how the tables and fields in the data mart are named. We use all the default settings. Click Next.

56. The Completing the Wizard page provides a summary of the schema generation we defined. Click Finish.

57. The Schema Generation Progress dialog box appears. This dialog box shows each step as the data mart (called the subject area database) is created. When the process has completed, the dialog box should appear similar to Figure 6-33. Click Close.

58. Click the Save All toolbar button.

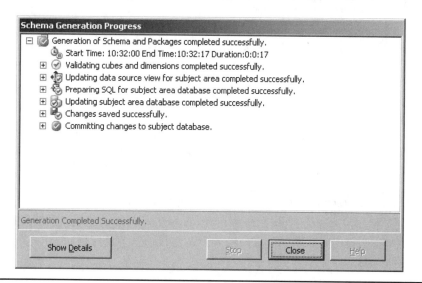

Figure 6-33   *The Schema Generation Progress dialog box with a successful process completion*

NOTE

If an error occurs during the process, a red asterisk appears next to the last step, as shown in Figure 6-34. The text next to the red asterisk describes the error. If an error occurs, use the description to determine the cause of the error, click Stop to terminate the process, click Close, and then repeat the process with the problem corrected. The cube and the dimensions may have been created in the Analysis Services project before the error occurred. To restart the entire process, the cube and dimensions need to be deleted from the project. The most common cause of an error is not using Windows Authentication in the data source or being logged onto Windows with credentials that do not have rights to create tables in the MaxMinSalesDM database.

59. Beyond the basic fields created for us in the Sales data mart, we need to add some fields to hold additional information coming from our data sources. We add these fields using the SQL Server Management Studio. Close the Business Intelligence Development Studio.

60. Open the SQL Server Management Studio and connect to the SQL server hosting the MaxMinSalesDM database.

61. Expand the Databases folder, and then expand the MaxMinSalesDM database. Finally, expand the Tables folder.

62. Right-click the dbo.Customer table entry and select Design from the context menu.

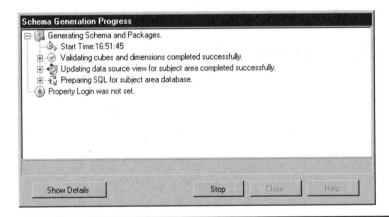

Figure 6-34 *The Schema Generation Progress dialog box after an error has occurred*

63. Add the following columns to the Customer table:

Column Name	Data Type	Allow Nulls
Address	nvarchar(50)	Checked
City	nvarchar(50)	Checked
State	nchar(2)	Checked
ZipCode	nvarchar(10)	Checked
Homeowner	nchar(1)	Checked
MaritalStatus	nchar(1)	Checked
NumCarsOwned	smallint	Checked
NumChildrenAtHome	smallint	Checked

64. Close the table design tab. Click Yes when asked if you want to save changes.
65. Right-click the dbo.Product table entry and select Design from the context menu.
66. Add the following columns to the Product table:

Column Name	Data Type	Allow Nulls
RetailPrice	money	Checked
Weight	real	Checked

67. Close the table design tab. Click Yes when asked if you want to save changes.
68. Right-click the dbo.Sales_Person table entry and select Design from the context menu.
69. Add the following columns to the SalesPerson table:

Column Name	Data Type	Allow Nulls
SalesPerson_Territory	int	Checked

70. Close the table design tab. Click Yes when asked if you want to save changes.
71. Right-click the dbo.Store table entry and select Design from the context menu.
72. Add the following columns to the Store table:

Column Name	Data Type	Allow Nulls
StoreType	nvarchar(50)	Checked

73. Close the table design tab. Click Yes when asked if you want to save changes.

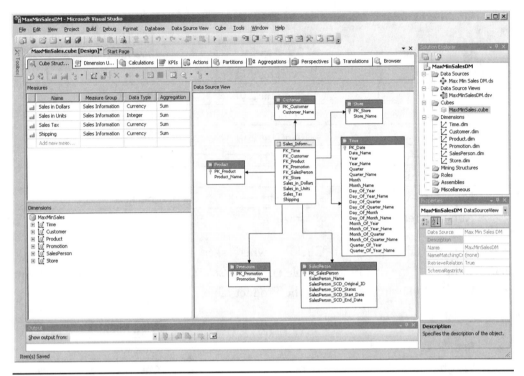

Figure 6-35   *The Max Min Sales star schema*

The Sales Data Mart

We now have a Sales data mart along with an Analysis Services cube built on that data mart. The star schema that defines both the data mart and the cube is shown in Figure 6-35. (Note, the data source view shown in Figure 6-35 does not include the fields we manually added to the tables.) We can tell this is a star schema rather than a snowflake schema because all the levels in the time hierarchy are contained in a single Time table, rather than multiple linked tables. We will add additional fields to these tables and additional hierarchies to this cube later.

Also, note the fields in the SalesPerson table. Several fields contain SCD in the field name. These fields are included to help maintain the history of a member of this dimension. We see this in action in future examples.

Table Compression

Our relational data warehouses may be called upon to store a copious amount of data. This can cause our fact tables and perhaps even some of our dimension tables to grow very large. Fortunately, SQL Server 2008 provides some relief in the form of table compression.

Table compression modifies the way data is physically stored on the disk drive in order to save space. It does not change the structure of a table nor does it change the syntax used to SELECT, INSERT, UPDATE, or DELETE data in a table. Table compression is completely transparent to applications making use of the data. It simply makes more efficient use of disk space.

Types of Table Compression

SQL Server offers two flavors of table compression for us to take advantage of. The first is *row compression*. Row compression works within each row of data.

The second type of table compression is *page compression*. Page compression works within the page structure that SQL Server uses to store data. Let's take a closer look at each of the compression types.

Row Compression

Row compression reduces the space required to store a row of data. It does this by only using the bytes required to store a given value. For example, without row compression, a column of type int normally occupies 4 bytes. This is true if we are storing the number 1 or the number 1 million. SQL Server allocates enough space to store the maximum value possible for the data type.

When row compression is turned on, SQL Server makes smarter space allocations. It looks at the actual value being stored for a given column in a given row, and then determines the storage required to represent that value. This is done to the nearest whole byte.

Of course, this added complexity adds some overhead as data is inserted or updated in the table. It also adds a smaller amount of overhead when data is retrieved from that table. In most cases, the time taken for this additional processing is negligible. In fact, in some cases, the saving in disk read and disk write time can even be greater than the calculation time required for data compression.

Page Compression

Page compression takes things a bit further than row compression. In fact, page compression starts by utilizing row compression. It then adds two other compression techniques: *prefix compression* and *dictionary compression*.

Prefix compression looks for values of a given column that have a common beginning within a page of data. If the rows are sorted by account number, then the account number fields that fall within a given page will probably start with the same digits. The same is true if the rows are sorted by last name. The last name fields that fall within a given page are all likely to start with the same characters.

Prefix compression is designed to take advantage of these situations. It determines these common prefixes, and then stores a representative of this common beginning, or prefix, in a reference row in the page header. Rather than storing this repeating prefix data in every row, a pointer to the reference row is used. The pointer to the reference row can even show where a given value diverges from the reference row.

Dictionary compression is applied after prefix compression. This compression scheme looks for repeating values within the page. A representative of the repeated value is placed in the page header. A pointer to the header entry is then used in place of each occurrence of the repeated value.

It is not necessary to understand the technical details of table compression. What is important is to know that we have ways to reduce the storage space required by large tables and in general, make these tables more manageable. Fortunately, using table compression is much easier than understanding what is happening under the hood.

Learn By Doing—Enabling Table Compression

Features Highlighted

▶ Turning on table compression

▶ Using the sp_estimate_data_compression_savings stored procedure

Business Need We want to decrease the disk space required by our fact tables. These tables will grow quite large as we gather a number of years' worth of manufacturing and inventory data for reporting.

Steps

1. Open the SQL Server Management Studio, if it is not already open, and connect to the SQL server hosting the MaxMinManufacturingDM database.
2. Click New Query to open a query window.
3. Select the MaxMinManufacturingDM database from the drop-down list in the Toolbar.
4. Execute the following set of statements:

```
ALTER TABLE ManufacturingFact

REBUILD WITH (DATA_COMPRESSION = PAGE)
```

This statement turns on page compression for the fact table in the MaxMinManufacturingDM database.

5. Locate the ManufacturingFact table in the Object Explorer window. Right-click the ManufacturingFact table entry and select Properties from the context menu. The Table Properties dialog box appears.

6. Select the Storage page of the Table Properties dialog box. Note the Compression type shown near the top of the page. This is shown in Figure 6-36.

7. Click OK to exit the Table Properties dialog box.

8. Click in the Query window and select the MaxMinSalesDM database from the drop-down list in the Toolbar.

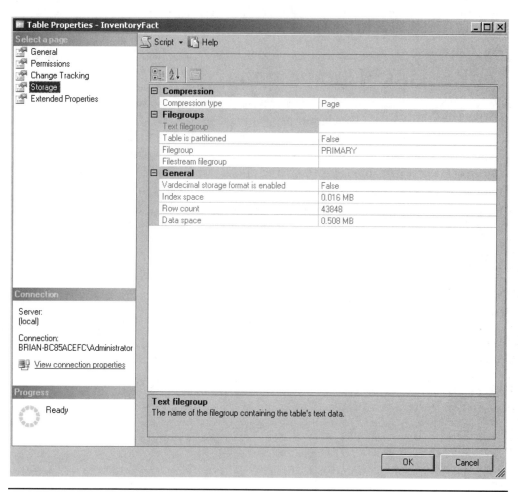

Figure 6-36   *The Table Properties dialog box showing page compression turned on*

9. Execute the following statement:

```
EXEC sp_estimate_data_compression_savings 'dbo',
                    'Sales_Information', NULL, NULL, 'PAGE'
```

This system stored procedure calculates the amount of space that would be saved if page compression was applied to the Sales_Information table. This stored procedure works by sampling the actual data in the table to estimate compression savings. Of course, because we don't yet have any data in the Sales_Information table, we don't get any meaningful results from the stored procedure. Try executing this stored procedure again after you fill the Sales_Information table with data.

The Benefits of Integration

We now have designed two data mart structures to serve as the source for Analysis Services cubes. You might have noticed, however, if you look into either of these data marts, that they are completely empty (expect for the MaxMinSalesDM.Time table). There is not much business intelligence to be gleaned from an empty data mart!

We need to get data into our data marts. This is done using Integration Services. In the next two chapters, we look at the many and varied capabilities of Integration Services. We also develop and utilize some working Integration Services packages to populate our all-too-empty data marts, making them much more useful.

Chapter 7

Transformers—Integration Services Structure and Components

In This Chapter

▶ **Integration Services**
▶ **Package Items**
▶ **Getting Under the Sink**

There are painters who transform the sun to a yellow spot, but there are others who with the help of their art and their intelligence, transform a yellow spot into the sun.

—Pablo Picasso

I n the previous chapter, we created two data marts on our relational database server. As we pointed out at the end of Chapter 6, these data marts are not much use to us or our decision makers until they contain useful data. Fortunately, SQL Server 2008 has a tool designed for just such a purpose. This tool is Integration Services.

Integration Services enables us to change the location of data by copying it from our online transaction processing (OLTP) databases and other locations into the data mart. As it is being copied, we can also transform the data from the format required by the OLTP systems to the format required by the OLAP systems we are creating. Finally, we can verify foreign key values as we load the data. This enables us to implement our data mart database without foreign key constraints.

Integration Services

Integration Services was introduced with SQL Server 2005. Prior to that, moving data from a data source to a data destination was done with a tool called Data Transformation Services (DTS). DTS offered a limited ability to change data as it was moved from source to destination. Integration Services provides all of the functionality of DTS in an environment that simultaneously offers more capabilities, with less programming and scripting required. In addition, Integration Services offers a large performance boost over DTS. In fact, performance is even better in the SQL Server 2008 incarnation of Integration Services!

Package Structure

Integration Services and its predecessor, DTS, both create structures called packages, which are used to move data between systems. Packages in both tools contain data sources and data destinations. After that, however, the similarities between these two utilities come to an end. Integration Services represents a complete rethinking of Microsoft's approach to data transfer. The result is an easy-to-use, extremely flexible, exceedingly capable, and highly scalable data Extract, Transform, and Load (ETL) tool.

One of the most obvious departures from DTS is in the design of the packages themselves. Where DTS combined control of the package's operation and the mapping of the data flow into one graphical layout, Integration Services splits the two apart. Separating these two related, but ultimately distinct, areas makes Integration Services packages easier to create and certainly much easier to maintain.

A package's overall operation is defined by the control flow. The *control flow* is the sequence of tasks that will be performed by the package. These may be tasks such as transferring a file using File Transfer Protocol (FTP), logging an event, truncating a table in preparation for a data load, or even e-mailing a status message to an administrator. Of course, one of the most-used control flow tasks is the *data flow task*, which moves data from one place to another.

The data flow task provides the plumbing for moving data from one or more sources to one or more destinations. Along the way, the data may be subjected to any number of transformation processes. Data can now be manipulated as it is flowing through "the pipeline" without having to be deposited in a temporary, working table, as in DTS. This capability to massage the data on-the-fly yields a cleaner and more streamlined ETL process and a much more efficient package.

Integration Services packages are created using an Integration Services project in the Business Intelligence Development Studio. When we are working on an Integration Services project, the Designer window contains four tabs, as shown in Figure 7-1.

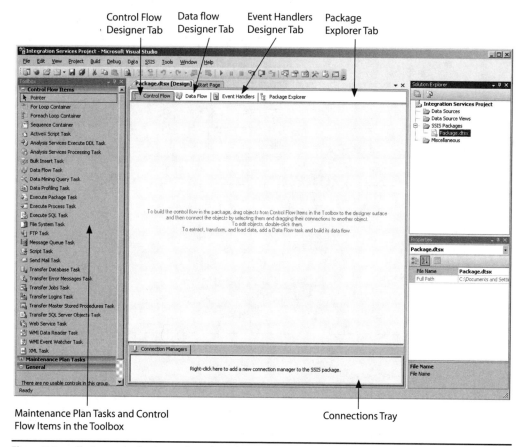

Figure 7-1   *The Integration Services package design layout in the Business Intelligence Development Studio*

The first three tabs—the Control Flow Designer tab, the Data Flow Designer tab, and the Event Handlers Designer tab—let us define various types of functionality for the package. The final tab—the Package Explorer—provides an alternative view of the contents of the package. In addition to the tabs, there is a special area at the bottom of the Designer window for defining Connection Managers, which is called the *Connections tray.*

As stated earlier, each Integration Services package contains a control flow to define the overall operation of the package. This is shown in Figure 7-2. The control flow is defined by dragging items from the Toolbox onto the Control Flow Designer tab. When the Control Flow Designer tab is selected, only those tasks that can be used on this tab are displayed in the Toolbox, as shown in Figure 7-1.

An Integration Services package may contain several data flows. Each data flow is represented by a data flow task placed on the Control Flow Designer tab, as shown in Figure 7-2. A data flow task is created by dragging a Data Flow item from the Toolbox and placing it in the control flow. We need to drill down into a data flow task to define the contents of that data flow, as shown in Figure 7-3. This is done by double-clicking a data flow task on the Control Flow Designer tab or clicking the Data Flow Designer

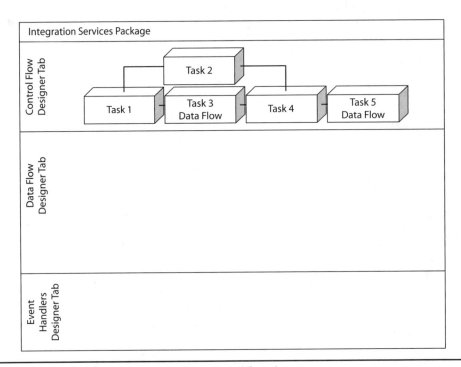

Figure 7-2   *The Integration Services package structure Control Flow tab*

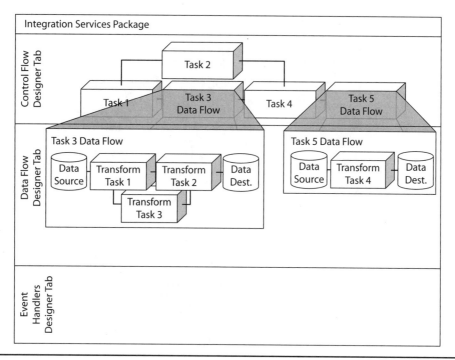

Figure 7-3 *The Integration Services package structure Data Flow Designer tab*

tab and selecting the correct data flow task from the drop-down list. We can now define the details of the data flow on the Data Flow Designer tab. As might be expected, only Data Flow control items are displayed in the Toolbox when the Data Flow Designer tab is selected.

Integration Services packages are event-driven. This means we can specify routines to execute when a particular event occurs. An *event* can be the completion of a task or an error that occurs during task execution. The routine for the event is known as an *event handler* and is defined as a *control flow*. However, event handler control flows are created on the Event Handlers Designer tab rather than on the Control Flow Designer tab, as shown in Figure 7-4.

The same control flow items that can be used on the Control Flow Designer tab can also be used to create event handler tasks on the Event Handlers Designer tab. These might include sending an e-mail to update the administrator on the status of a package or executing an alternative data flow when a task fails. When a data flow task is used in an event handler, the details of the data flow are defined on the Data Flow Designer tab, as shown in Figure 7-5.

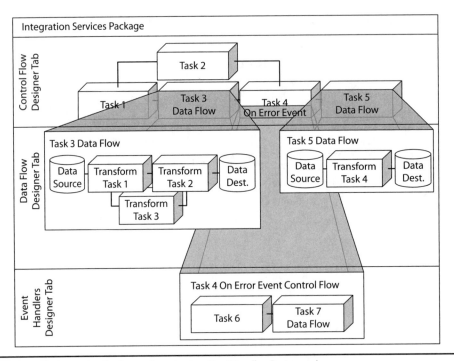

Figure 7-4   *The Integration Services package structure Event Handlers Designer tab*

The rightmost tab of the Designer window in Figure 7-1 provides access to the Package Explorer. The *Package Explorer* displays all the contents of the Integration Services package in a single tree-view structure. In addition to the control flow tasks, data flow tasks, and event handler tasks, the Package Explorer displays all the variables available for use in the package. We discuss the use of variables in Integration Services packages in Chapter 8.

The Connections tray is used to manage all the connections in the package. This includes paths to flat files and connection strings for databases. Rather than having this spread throughout the package, all this connection information is stored in the Connections tray. This makes it much easier to locate and manage the connection information as paths, server names, and login credentials change, or as the package is used in different server environments.

Drag-and-Drop Programming

Creating nontrivial data transfer packages with DTS usually required someone with a programming background. A certain amount of Visual Basic script or SQL queries were generally required to accomplish even the most straightforward data loading and

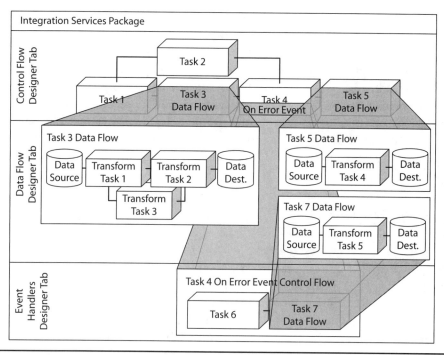

Figure 7-5   *Defining a data flow task in an event handler control flow*

data cleansing tasks. This blurred the line between database administration tasks and development tasks, while tending to complicate database management.

In a number of cases, the data could not be cleansed prior to loading it into the database. It was just too complicated to implement the aggregations, lookups, and validations as operations in the DTS pipeline. In these situations, the data had to be placed in a staging table in SQL Server. SQL queries would then be developed to do the cleansing tasks, again requiring someone with database development know-how. The SQL queries, not the DTS package, were ultimately responsible for copying the data to its final destination. This has been referred to as ELT (Extract, Load, and Transform) rather than the more traditional, and far more efficient, ETL.

Integration Services is designed to eliminate both the need for a developer and the need for any ELT-mode operations. Integration Services uses a drag-and-drop development style. Task items are dragged from the Toolbox and placed on the Designer workspace. The behavior of these tasks is controlled by setting properties in the dialog box associated with each task and by connecting the output from one task to the input of another. Some expressions may be required, but these tend to be straightforward, single-line comparison statements, rather than more complicated, multiline programming constructs.

Almost all the data manipulations that required staging tables in DTS can now be done through Integration Services tasks without writing the data to disk. These tasks work with the data in buffers kept in physical memory. Pointers to these memory buffers are passed from one task to another throughout the processing. The only time data is written to disk during a data pipeline process is when it exceeds the size of the physical memory available. All of this makes it easy to develop complex packages while ensuring fast, efficient operation.

Control Flow Tasks

As we create our Integration Services packages, we use a top-down approach. First, we use the Control Flow Designer tab to define the tasks that the package will perform. Next, we use precedence arrows to define the tasks' order of execution and any dependencies between them. Then, we drill down into each of the data flow tasks to define their operation. Finally, we add any event handlers or other programming needed to get the package functioning in the manner required.

We begin, then, on the Control Flow Designer tab, by specifying the tasks that must be accomplished by the package. We create tasks by dragging Control Flow items from the Toolbox and placing them on the Control Flow Designer tab. Each item taken from the Toolbox becomes a control flow task. This is shown in Figure 7-6.

The red octagon with the white X on the control flow task indicates that the task is in an error state because some of the required properties for the task have not been set or have been set improperly. Hovering the mouse over a task with this symbol displays a message explaining the error. In other situations, a yellow triangle with a black exclamation point appears on a task. This indicates a warning message is associated with this task. Again, hovering the mouse over the task displays the warning message. A task with a warning executes, but a task with an error does not.

We can set the properties of a task by double-clicking the task to display its Editor dialog box. This is shown in Figure 7-7. We can also select the task and modify its properties using the Properties window. We look at the properties of each task in detail in the next section of this chapter.

When creating an Integration Services package, it is important to change the default name for each task that is placed in the package. The names should be changed to a phrase that accurately describes the functionality performed by that task. It is also a good idea to enter a short explanation of each task in the Description property of the task. The description is displayed when we hover over the task on the Control Flow tab.

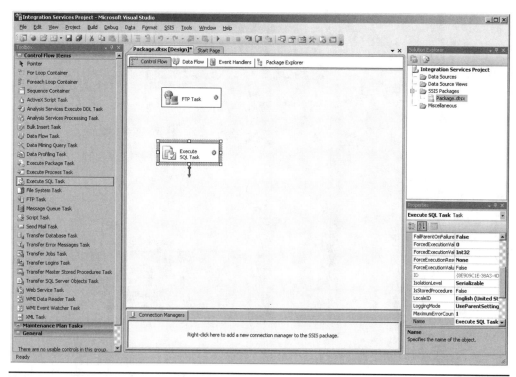

Figure 7-6 *Creating control flow tasks from the Toolbox*

Entering meaningful information for each task makes the package self-documenting and, consequently, much easier to test, debug, and maintain.

Connection Managers

Any time a control flow task must make a connection to a database or to the file system, this connection information is stored in a Connection Manager in the Connections tray. This makes it easier to move packages from one server to another or from a development environment to a production environment. When database connection information or file system paths need to be modified to work on a different server, we do not need to look for them throughout the package. Instead, they are conveniently located in one place: the Connections tray.

We take a look at creating some of the most commonly used connections in the "Learn By Doing" sections in Chapter 8.

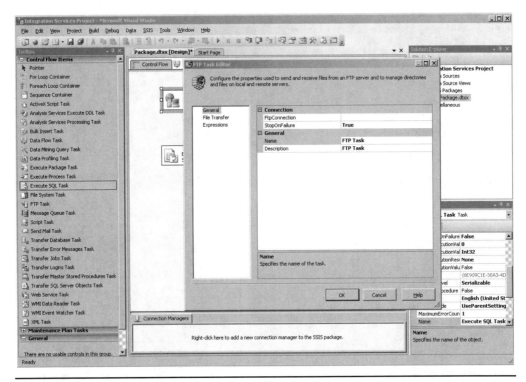

Figure 7-7 *Setting the properties of a task using the task's Editor dialog box*

Precedence Arrows

We control the order in which tasks are executed by connecting the precedence arrow from one task to the task that is to run after it. To do this, we select a task and then click the green arrow that appears below that task. We drag this arrow until the mouse pointer is over the task that should follow during execution. This is shown in Figure 7-8.

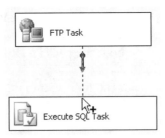

Figure 7-8 *Making a precedence connection between two tasks*

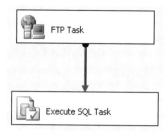

Figure 7-9   *The precedence arrow*

When we release the mouse button, the green arrow connects the two tasks, as shown in Figure 7-9. This is known as a *precedence constraint* because it constrains one task to run after another.

By default, the precedence arrow is green, meaning the second task will execute only after the successful completion of the first task. This is the "Success" precedence. When we right-click the arrow, a context menu appears, as shown in Figure 7-10. Three options on the context menu—Success, Failure, and Completion—allow us to select the type of precedence the arrow represents.

When we select Failure from the context menu, the precedence arrow changes from green to red. With "Failure" precedence, the second task executes only after the failure of the first task. When we select Completion from the context menu, the precedence arrow changes to blue. With "Completion" precedence, the second task executes after the first task has completed without regard to whether the first task succeeded or failed.

Figure 7-10   *The precedence arrow context menu*

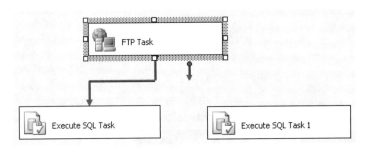

Figure 7-11 *A control flow task with a second precedence arrow*

A single task can have multiple precedence arrows connecting it to other tasks. When we select a task that already has its precedence arrow connected to another task, a second precedence arrow automatically appears. This is shown in Figure 7-11. This second arrow can be connected to another task. When a task has two precedence arrows connected to subsequent tasks, a third arrow appears. And so on. Each of these precedence arrows can be set to Success, Failure, or Completion as appropriate. The result can be a complex sequence of tasks, such as the one shown in Figure 7-12.

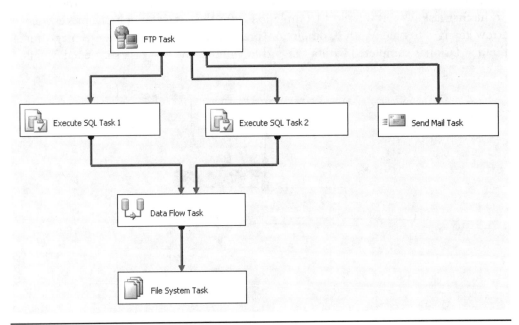

Figure 7-12 *Using precedence arrows to make a complex sequence of tasks*

We can double-click a precedence arrow or right-click the arrow and select Edit from the context menu to access the Precedence Constraint Editor dialog box, shown in Figure 7-13. The Value drop-down list on this dialog box provides another way to select among Success, Failure, and Completion. If these three options do not provide enough flexibility, we can also attach expressions to a precedence arrow.

If the Evaluation Operation drop-down list is set to Expression, then the contents of the expression must evaluate to true before this precedence path is taken. If the Evaluation Operation drop-down list is set to Expression and Constraint, the contents of the expression must be true and the constraint selected in the Value drop-down list must match the result of the task execution. If the Evaluation Operation drop-down list is set to Expression or Constraint, either the contents of the expression must be true or the constraint selected in the Value drop-down list must match the result of the task execution. We discuss Integration Services expressions in Chapter 8.

The Multiple Constraints section at the bottom of the Precedence Constraint Editor dialog box determines the behavior when more than one precedence arrow connects to a single task. The data flow task in Figure 7-12 is a good example. The Success precedence constraints from both Execute SQL Task 1 and Execute SQL Task 2 lead to the data flow task. When the Multiple Constraints setting is Logical AND, both

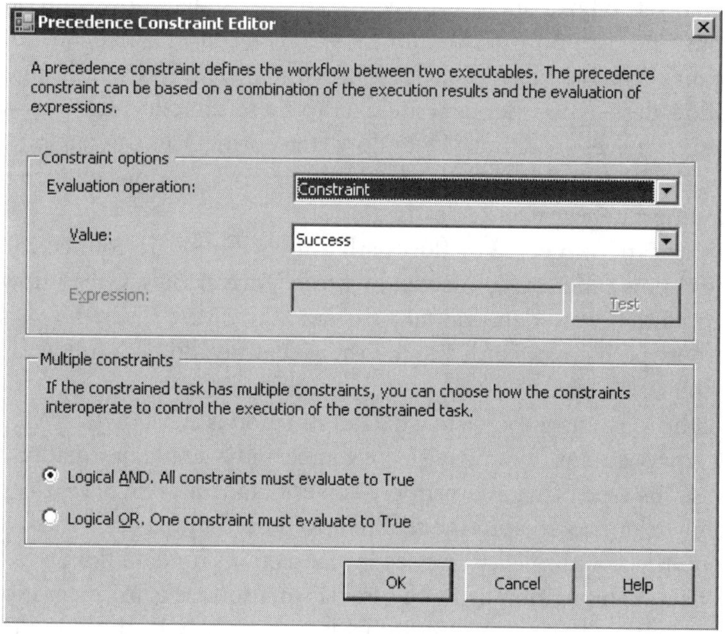

Figure 7-13 *The Precedence Constraint Editor dialog box*

Execute SQL Task 1 and Execute SQL Task 2 must finish successfully before the data flow task executes. If either one or both of the Execute SQL tasks fails, the data flow task cannot execute. When the Multiple Constraints setting is Logical OR, the data flow task executes if either one or the other of the Execute SQL tasks is successful. Changing the Multiple Constraints setting on any one of the precedence arrows leading into a task changes the Multiple Constraints setting for all of the precedence arrows leading into that task.

It is possible to have one or more control flow tasks in a package that are not connected by precedence arrows to any other task. These tasks are not constrained to execute in any particular order, and they are not constrained by the success or failure of any other task. These disconnected tasks execute every time the package is run, no matter what happens with the other tasks in the package.

Data Flow

Once we set the precedence constraints for the control flow tasks in the package, we can define each of the data flows. This is done on the Data Flow Designer tab. Each data flow task that was added to the control flow has its own layout on the Data Flow Designer tab. We can switch between different data flows using the Data Flow Task drop-down list located at the top of the Data Flow tab.

The Data Flow Toolbox contains three types of items: data flow sources, data flow transformations, and data flow destinations. Data flow sources enable us to read data from any vendor's relational database, flat file, or Extensible Markup Language (XML) source. Data flow destinations let us write data to these same locations, as well as to certain Analysis Services structures. Data flow transformations operate on the data as it moves through the data flow. In most cases, the transformations change the data to increase its appropriateness for the destination.

Data flow tasks are connected by flow path arrows. These are connected in the same way that control flow tasks are connected by precedence arrows. Green flow path arrows indicate the route that valid data will take through the task. This is the output flow of the task. Red flow path arrows indicate the route that invalid data follow. This is the error flow of the task.

The flow path from a data source to a data destination is called a *data flow segment*. The simplest data flow segment has only a single source and a single destination, connected by a flow path. This type of segment simply copies data from one place to another. Transformation tasks are added to the segment to modify the data as it moves from the source to the destination. In fact, as we see in the sections on data flow, we can do some sophisticated data manipulation using the transformation tasks in Integration Services.

Data flow segments may contain multiple data sources, with the data flow from each source being combined with a merge or union task. Likewise, a segment may have multiple data destinations, with the data flow being divided by an error path, a conditional split task, or a multicast task. We gain even more flexibility with the ability to have multiple, distinct data segments in the same data flow.

When a data flow has multiple segments, the order in which the segments are executed is determined by the execution plan created at run time. This means that we cannot depend on the order in which multiple segments are executed within a single data flow. If the multiple segments are performing independent tasks, such as loading data into different dimensions of a data mart, this is not a problem. However, if these multiple segments are performing dependent tasks, such that one segment must be completed before another segment can begin, the segments should be split up into different data flow tasks. The order of execution can then be enforced by a precedence arrow from one data flow task to the other on the Control Flow Designer tab.

Package Items

In this section, we take a look at the Control Flow and Data Flow items that can be used in an Integration Services package. We discuss how each item can be used in a package and we look at the task dialog box provided for configuring each task. Because of the tremendous amount of capability and flexibility available from Integration Services tasks, it would take the remainder of this book, and then some, to provide a complete description. Instead, this section is intended to give you some familiarity with the purpose and capabilities of each task.

Control Flow

The Control Flow Toolbox is divided into two areas: Control Flow items and Maintenance Plan tasks. (We will not be concerned with the General area of the Toolbox, which is empty.) Most components, Control Flow items, or Maintenance Plan tasks, have an editor dialog box that lets us configure that component in a straightforward manner. The editor dialog box is launched by double-clicking the component in the design area or right-clicking the item and selecting Edit from the Context menu.

Control Flow Items

We begin by looking at the Control Flow items. These items are presented in the order in which they appear in the Control Flow Toolbox. The Control Flow items are grouped into containers and tasks, with the containers at the top of the list. *Containers* are a special type of item that can hold other Control Flow items and Maintenance Plan tasks.

NOTE

Each section of the Toolbox starts with an entry called Pointer. These pointer entries enable us to switch back to the mouse pointer if we begin a drag-and-drop operation, and then change our mind. The pointer entries do not create tasks on the designers.

For Loop Container   The *For Loop container* enables us to repeat a segment of a control flow. In this way, it functions much the same as a FOR... NEXT loop in Visual Basic or a *for* loop in C#. The For Loop container in Figure 7-14 executes the Execute SQL task and the Data Flow task multiple times.

The number of times the content of the container is executed is controlled by three properties of the For Loop container: InitExpression, EvalExpression, and AssignExpression. These properties are shown in the For Loop Editor dialog box in Figure 7-15. The InitExpression is executed once at the beginning of the loop to initialize the variable (or other item) that is controlling the loop. The EvalExpression is then evaluated. If the EvalExpression evaluates to true, the loop's content is executed. If the EvalExpression is false, the loop is exited. After each execution of the loop's contents, the AssignExpression is evaluated, followed by another evaluation of the EvalExpression.

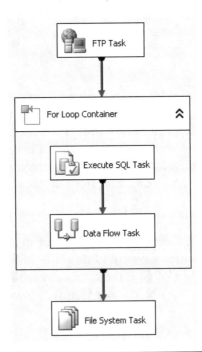

Figure 7-14   *A For Loop container in a control flow*

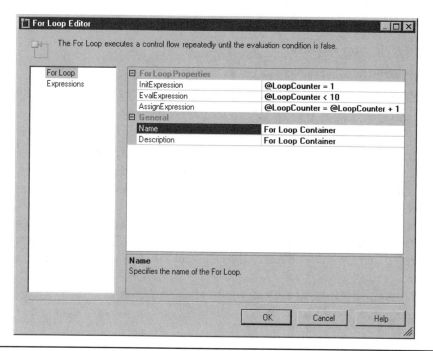

Figure 7-15   *The For Loop Editor dialog box*

The For Loop in Figure 7-15 is using a variable called @LoopCounter in the expressions to control the number of times the loop is executed. (We discuss variables and Integration Services expressions in Chapter 8.) We don't need to use an explicit loop counter variable to control the loop. In fact, any valid expression that results in a true value while the loop should continue and a false value when it is complete can be used in the EvalExpression property to control the number of iterations. The InitExpression and AssignExpression properties can be left empty if the mechanism controlling the number of iterations does not require a separate expression for initialization or modification of the counter.

Foreach Loop Container

Like the For Loop container, the Foreach Loop container also provides a way of repeating a segment of a control flow. However, rather than have an expression to control when the loop is exited, the *Foreach Loop container* iterates one time for each item in a collection. The following collections can be used:

▶   Each file in a given folder matching a given file specification

▶   Each row of the first table in an ADO recordset or an ADO.NET dataset

▶ Each row of all tables in an ADO.NET dataset

▶ Each table in an ADO.NET dataset

▶ Each item from a variable that holds a collection

▶ Each node in an XML nodelist

▶ Each object in an SMO collection

Each time the Foreach Loop iterates, it selects a different object from the collection. The name of this object can then be mapped to one or more properties of the control flow tasks inside the container. In this way, the tasks inside the container can operate on each object in the collection.

For example, Figure 7-16 shows the Nightly Transfer package. This package uses FTP to transfer data files from a mainframe to the C:\FTP_RCV directory on the server. Several .dat files may be received by a given transfer. After the FTP transfer is

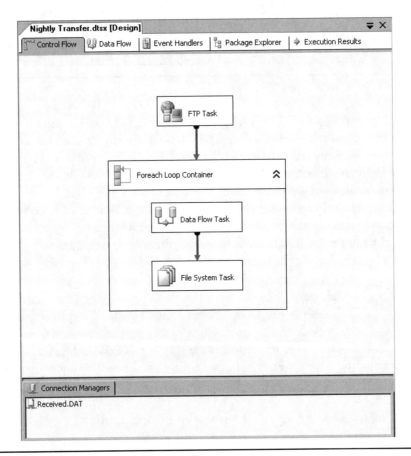

Figure 7-16 *The Nightly Transfer package using a Foreach Loop container*

complete, the Foreach Loop processes each of the files that are received. The Collection page of the Foreach Loop Editor dialog box in Figure 7-17 shows the configuration of the Foreach Loop necessary to accomplish this task.

The Data Flow task and the File System task within the Foreach Loop use the Received.DAT Files connection, shown at the bottom of Figure 7-16, to operate on a given data file received from the mainframe. For the Data Flow task and the File System task to operate on each file received, we need a way to change the connection string of the Received.DAT connection for each iteration of the loop. To do this, we first assign the fully qualified filename to a variable. This is done on the Variable Mappings page of the Foreach Loop container as follows:

Variable	Index
User::FileName	0

User::FileName is a user variable in the package. The entry in the Index column is an index to the Foreach Loop collection. When used with a collection of files, index 0 contains the file specification and is the only valid index. Next we create an expression in the Received.DAT Connection Manager to assign the value of the User::FileName to its ConnectionString.

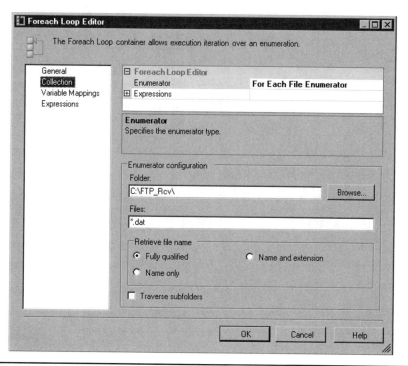

Figure 7-17 *The Collection page of the Foreach Loop container in the Nightly Transfer package*

Sequence Container   Unlike the For Loop and Foreach Loop containers, the Sequence container does not change the control flow. Instead, the purpose of the *Sequence container* is to help organize tasks in a package. The Sequence container can be used to do the following:

▶ Organize a large package into logical sections for easier development and debugging

▶ Manage properties for a group of tasks by setting the properties on the container, rather than on the individual tasks

▶ Allow a group of tasks to be easily enabled or disabled to aid package development and debugging

▶ Provide a variable scope that includes multiple tasks, but does not include the entire package

All of the container objects—For Loop, Foreach Loop, and Sequence—have the capability to hide their content. Figure 7-18 shows two Sequence containers. Sequence Container 2 is hiding its content. The content of a container is hidden or shown by clicking the chevron, indicated by the mouse pointer in Figure 7-18.

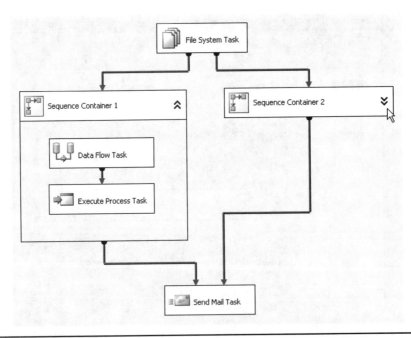

Figure 7-18   *Sequence Container 1 is showing its content. Sequence Container 2 is hiding its content.*

ActiveX Script Task   The *ActiveX Script task* enables us to define scripts using

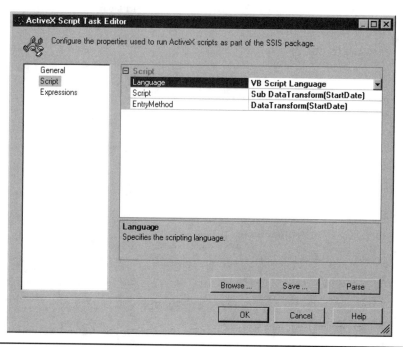

either VBScript or JScript. These scripts can be used to implement transformations or business logic that cannot be created using the other Integration Services tasks. The scripts can perform complex calculations and even use ActiveX COM objects to access database values or interact with the operating system.

Figure 7-19 shows the Script page of the ActiveX Script Task Editor dialog box. This page lets us select the language of the script using the drop-down list for the Language property. Select the Script property, and then click the ellipsis (...) button to enter the contents of the script. The script can also be loaded from a file by clicking Browse or saved to a file by clicking Save. The method that serves as the entry point to the script is specified in the EntryMethod property.

Using the ActiveX Script task in our Integration Services packages has three disadvantages. First, the ActiveX scripts are interpreted at run time. This can negatively impact performance and scalability. Second, the ActiveX scripts can be a security issue. A malicious script can use its direct access to server resources to do all kinds of bad things. Third, the ActiveX script editor does not provide any programmer aids, such as autocomplete, context-sensitive help, or debugging.

Figure 7-19   *The Script page of the ActiveX Script Task Editor dialog box*

As an alternative, use the Script task in place of the ActiveX Script task. The Script task supports modules written in any .NET language. The Script task modules can be precompiled for better performance and scalability. All of the security features of the .NET Framework are in place when a Script task executes. Finally, the Script task provides a rich environment for script development.

Analysis Services Execute DDL Task   The *Analysis Services Execute DDL task* enables us to run a statement on an Analysis Services server. The statement must be a valid Data Definition Language (DDL) query, which lets us create, modify, delete, and process Analysis Services objects, such as cubes and dimensions. The Analysis Services Execute DDL Task Editor dialog box is shown in Figure 7-20.

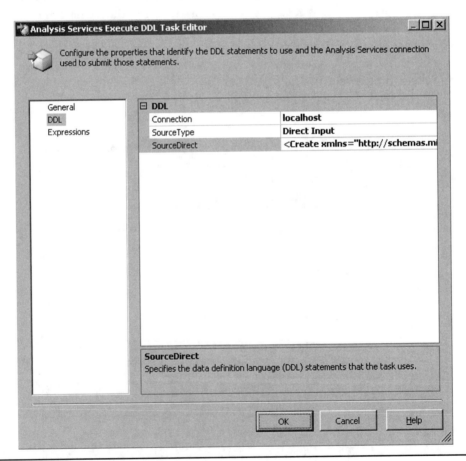

Figure 7-20   *The Analysis Services Execute DDL Task Editor dialog box*

Analysis Services Processing Task   The *Analysis Services Processing task* enables us

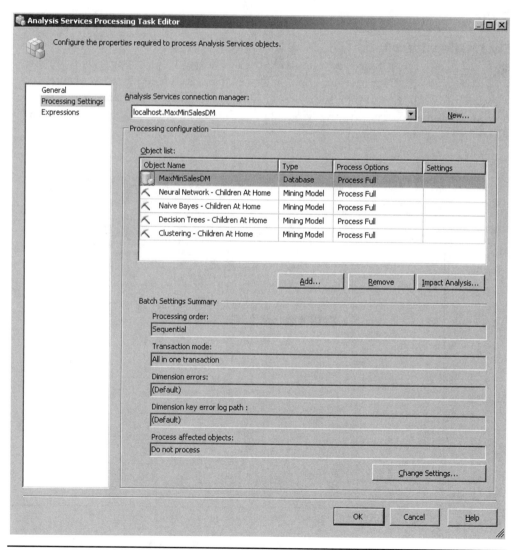

to process objects in Analysis Services. This can include cubes, dimensions, and data mining models. This is important after we have made major data changes that affect any of these objects. The Analysis Services Processing Task Editor dialog box is shown in Figure 7-21.

Bulk Insert Task   The *Bulk Insert task* lets us rapidly copy data from a text file into a SQL Server table or view. This is equivalent to using the bcp utility

Figure 7-21   *The Analysis Services Processing Task Editor dialog box*

program to do a bulk data load. In fact, we can use a bcp format file with the Bulk Insert task. The Bulk Insert Task Editor dialog box is shown in Figure 7-22.

The Bulk Insert task is the fastest way to move large amounts of data into a SQL table. Remember, however, that this data must come from a text file directly and it cannot be transformed as it is being moved. Also, keep in mind that the Bulk Insert task always appends the data to any existing data in the target table.

Data Flow Task   As was stated earlier, the detail of each data flow task is configured using the Data Flow tab. The next section of this chapter contains information about each of the items that may be used on the Data Flow tab.

Data Mining Query Task   The *Data Mining Query task* lets us execute a Data Mining Extensions (DMX) query against an existing data mining structure. The DMX query enables us to feed parameter values to a data mining model, and then have that mining model make predictions for us based on those parameters. The Mining Model tab of the Data Mining Query Task Editor dialog box is shown in Figure 7-23.

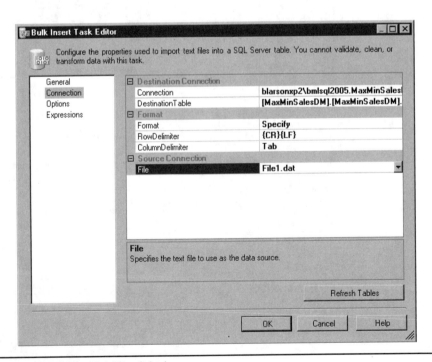

Figure 7-22   *The Bulk Insert Task Editor dialog box*

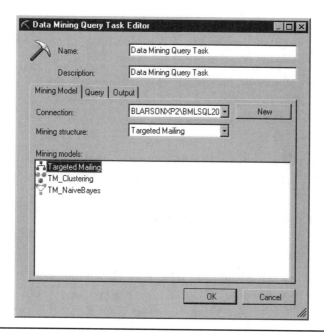

Figure 7-23   *The Mining Model tab of the Data Mining Query Task Editor dialog box*

If the selected data mining structure contains multiple data mining models, our DMX query can be run against more than one of these models. The DMX query results are stored in relational database tables. If the result of the DMX query includes nested tables, those tables are flattened before they are stored in the relational database tables. We discuss data mining in Part IV of this book.

Data Profiling Task   The *Data Profiling task* gathers information about a set of data. This can be used to determine information about a particular set of data we intend to process through an Integration Services package. We can use this information to make intelligent decisions as we design the package that will process this data and the data mart tables that will contain it.

The following profiling operations can be done using this task:

▶ **Candidate Key Profile Request**   Determines whether a column or a set of columns is a unique identifier for the rows in a table. Valid for integer, character, and date/time data types.

▶ **Column Length Distribution Profile Request**   Provides a list of the distinct string lengths present in a column. Valid for character data types.

▶ **Column Null Ratio Profile Request**   Reports the number of NULLS in a column as a percentage of the total number of rows. Valid for all data types.

▶ **Column Pattern Profile Request**   Determines a set of regular expressions that are valid for a specified percentage of the values in a column. Valid for character data types.

▶ **Column Statistics Profile Request**   Finds the maximum, minimum, average, and standard deviation of the data in a numeric column. Finds the maximum and minimum of the data in a date/time column. Valid for numeric and date/time data types.

▶ **Column Value Distribution Profile Request**   Reports the distinct set of values in a column and the number of occurrences of that value as a percentage of the total number of rows. Valid for integer, character, and date/time data types.

▶ **Functional Dependency Profile Request**   Determines how much the value in one column is dependent on the value in another column or set of columns. Valid for integer, character, and date/time data types.

▶ **Value Inclusion Profile Request**   Calculates the commonality of values in two columns or sets of columns. We can use this to determine whether a specific column can be used as a foreign key. Valid for integer, character, and date/time data types.

The Data Profiling Task Editor dialog box is shown in Figure 7-24.

The Data Profiling task outputs its findings to an XML file. This file can be viewed using the Data Profile Viewer. The Data Profile Viewer is run from the Start menu by selecting All Programs | Microsoft SQL Server 2008 | Integration Services | Data Profile Viewer. The Data Profile Viewer is shown in Figure 7-25.

Execute DTS 2000 Package Task

NOTE

In order to have support for SQL Server 2000 DTS packages, you must do the following:

▶ *Select the Client Tools Backward Compatibility option during installation of SQL Server 2008.*

▶ *Run SQLServer2005_BC.msi install from your SQL Server 2008 install media.*

The *Execute DTS 2000 Package task* enables us to execute a DTS package created for SQL Server 2000 as part of an Integration Services package. Using this task, we can continue to use complex DTS 2000 packages without having to re-create them as

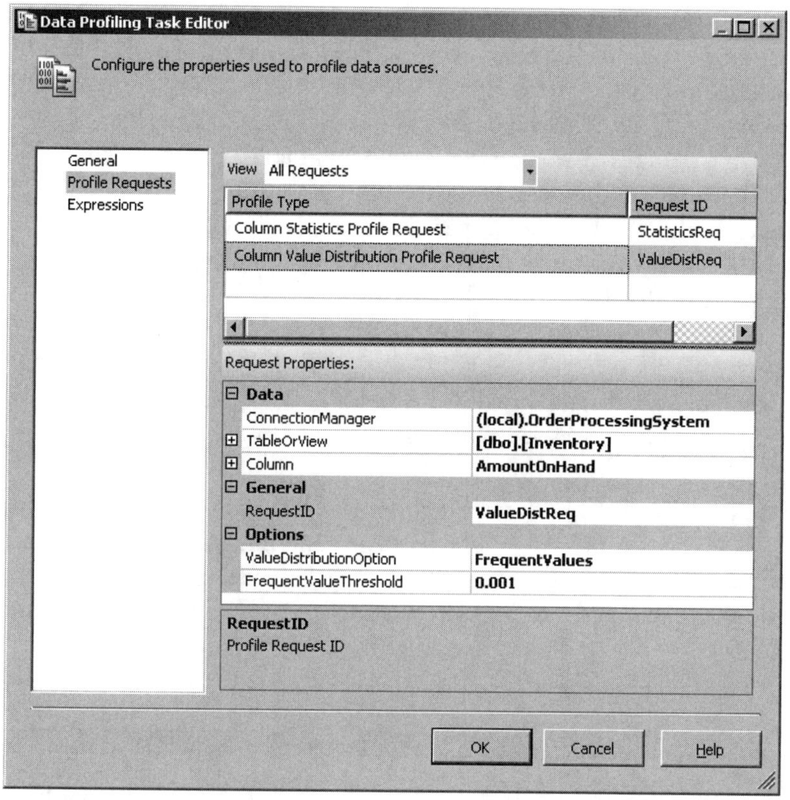

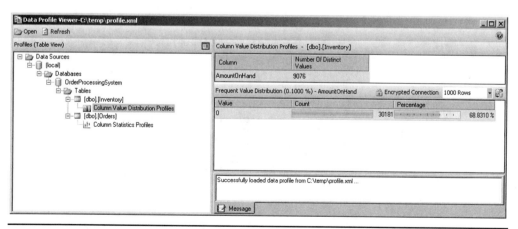

Figure 7-24   *The Data Profiling Task Editor dialog box*

Figure 7-25   *The Data Profile Viewer*

Integration Services packages. To execute this task, the DTS 2000 run-time engine must be installed as part of the SQL Server 2008 installation. The Execute DTS 2000 Package Task Editor dialog box is shown in Figure 7-26.

The Execute DTS 2000 Package task can access DTS 2000 packages stored in SQL Server, in a structured storage file, or in Meta Data Services. If the SQL Server 2000 tools are loaded on the same computer that is running the Business Intelligence Development Studio, the DTS 2000 package can be edited by clicking Edit Package. The DTS 2000 package can be copied and stored in the Integration Services package by clicking Load DTS2000 Package Internally.

We can use two methods to send information to the DTS 2000 package. The Inner Variables page of the Execute DTS 2000 Package Task Editor dialog box lets us pass values to the global variables defined in the DTS 2000 package. The Outer Variables page enables us to create variables, which can be used in the DTS 2000 package.

Execute Package Task   The *Execute Package task* lets us execute a different Integration Services package. The package containing the Execute Package task is the parent package and the package being executed by that task is the child package. The child package can be stored in SQL Server or in a structured storage file.

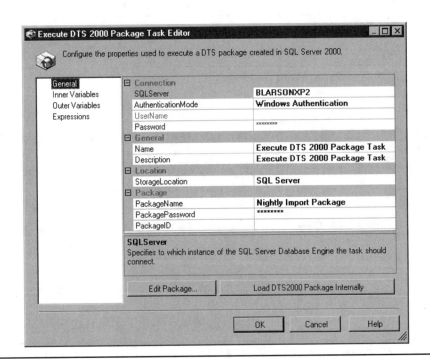

Figure 7-26   *The Execute DTS 2000 Package Task Editor dialog box*

The child package can execute as a separate process by setting the ExecuteOutOfProcess property to true. Otherwise, it executes in the same process as the parent package. Executing a child package as a separate process means an error in the child process cannot crash the parent process. Creating separate processes for each child package does, however, add some overhead each time a child package is launched.

The Execute Package Task Editor dialog box is shown in Figure 7-27.

Execute Process Task The *Execute Process task* enables us to execute a program or 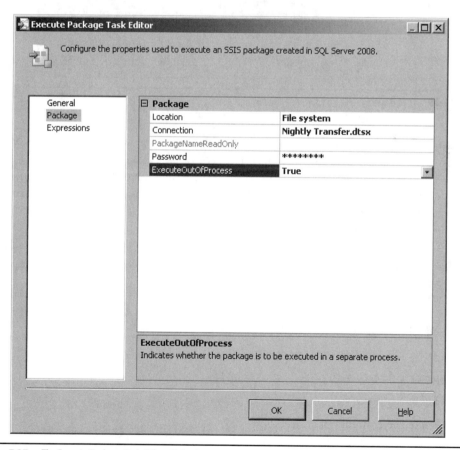 a batch file as part of an Integration Services package. This task can be used to do such things as unzipping compressed files. The Execute Process Task Editor dialog box lets us specify the command-line parameters and working directory, as shown in Figure 7-28. We can also specify variables for the standard input, standard output, and standard error of the process.

Figure 7-27 *The Execute Package Task Editor dialog box*

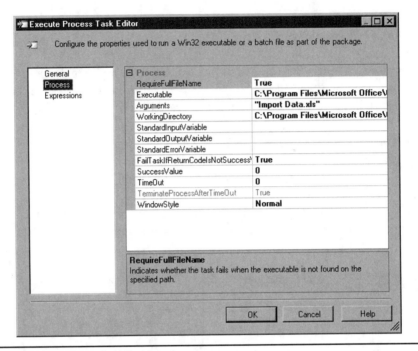

Figure 7-28 *The Execute Process Task Editor dialog box*

Execute SQL Task The *Execute SQL task* enables us to execute SQL statements or stored procedures. The contents of variables can be used for input, output, or input/output parameters and the return value. We can also save the result set from the SQL statements or stored procedure in a package variable. This result set could be a single value, a multirow/multicolumn result set, or an XML document. The Execute SQL Task Editor dialog box is shown in Figure 7-29.

File System Task The *File System task* lets us perform one of the following file system functions:

- ▶ Copy a directory
- ▶ Copy a file
- ▶ Create a directory
- ▶ Delete a directory
- ▶ Delete the contents of a directory

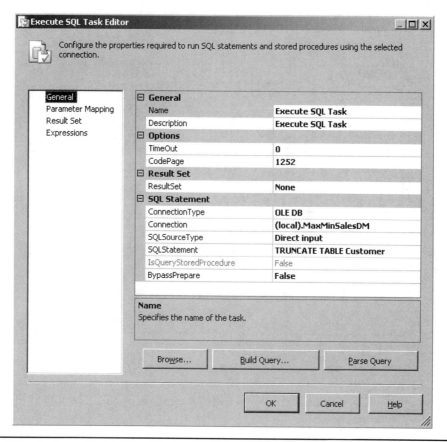

Figure 7-29   *The Execute SQL Task Editor dialog box*

▶ Delete a file

▶ Move a directory

▶ Move a file

▶ Rename a file

▶ Set the attributes of a directory or file

We must create a File Connection Manager in the Connections tray to specify the source and, if necessary, the destination for the file operation. The File System Task Editor dialog box is shown in Figure 7-30.

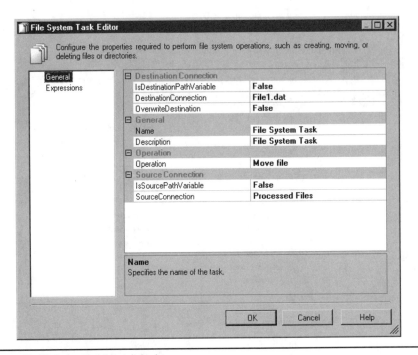

Figure 7-30 *The File System Task Editor dialog box*

FTP Task The *FTP task* enables us to perform the following functions on an FTP site:

► Send files

► Receive files

► Create a local directory

► Create a remote directory

► Remove a local directory

► Remove a remote directory

► Delete local files

► Delete remote files

We must create an FTP Connection Manager in the Connections tray to specify the address and login credentials for the FTP server. In addition, a File Connection Manager or the content of a package variable is used to specify the local path for the transfer. The FTP Task Editor dialog box is shown in Figure 7-31.

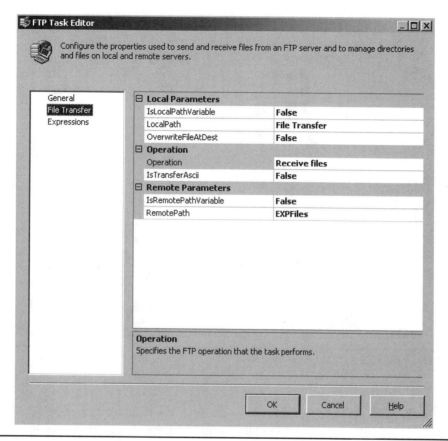

Figure 7-31 *The FTP Task Editor dialog box*

Message Queue Task   The *Message Queue task* lets us send a Microsoft Message Queue (MSMQ) message to a different Integration Services package or to the message queue of another application. This messaging can be used to provide coordinated, but asynchronous, processing between various tasks. A message can be any of the following:

► A data file

► The contents of one or more variables

► A string

We must create an MSMQ Connection Manager in the Connections tray to specify the MSMQ queue to use with this task. The Message Queue Task Editor dialog box is shown in Figure 7-32.

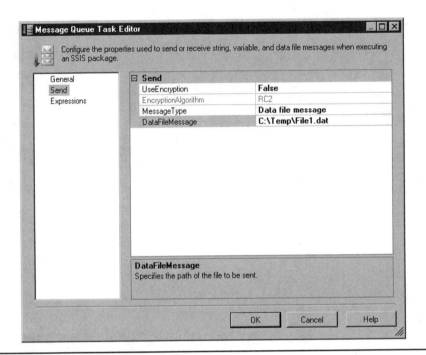

Figure 7-32   *The Message Queue Task Editor dialog box*

Script Task   The *Script task* enables us to create .NET code for execution as part of our Integration Services package. The Script task is similar to the ActiveX Script task in that they can both be used to execute transformations, perform complex calculations, or implement business logic that cannot be created using the other Integration Services tasks. However, the Script task provides a much better code-authoring environment, and the resulting code can be precompiled for superior performance and scalability.

The Script Task Editor dialog box is shown in Figure 7-33. This dialog box is used to specify the .NET language used to create the script, as well as whether the script is precompiled. When a script is precompiled, the code is compiled as soon as the script is saved in the package. The compiled code is then saved in the package as well. This allows for much faster execution when the package is run. The only disadvantage to this approach is this: The size of the package becomes larger because it contains both the source code and the compiled version of that source code.

The EntryPoint property specifies which method is to be executed first when the Script task is run. The ReadOnlyVariables and ReadWriteVariables properties contain

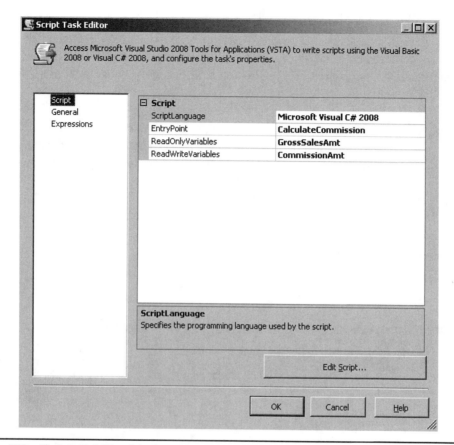

Figure 7-33   *The Script Task Editor dialog box*

comma-separated lists of variables that are to be made available, either as read-only variables or as read-write variables, within the script. These variables are accessed in our script using code similar to the following:

```
Dim GrossSales As Double

Dts.VariableDispenser.LockForRead("GrossSalesAmt")
GrossSales = CDbl(Dts.Variables("GrossSalesAmt").Value)

Dts.VariableDispenser.LockForWrite("CurrentAmt")
Dts.Variables("CurrentAmt").Value = GrossSales

Dts.Variables.Unlock()
```

where "GrossSalesAmt" and "CurrentAmt" are package variables. The variables must be locked before they can be either read or written, and must be unlocked when all variable access is complete. The value of a variable is always returned as a type object and must be cast to the appropriate type. Clicking Edit Script displays the Script Editing window, as shown in Figure 7-34.

Send Mail Task The *Send Mail task* lets us send an e-mail message as part of our Integration Services package. This can be useful for alerting an administrator to an error condition or notifying a key user that a critical process has completed. The Send Mail task uses a Simple Mail Transfer Protocol (SMTP) server to deliver the e-mail. We must create an SMTP Connection Manager in the Connections tray to specify the SMTP server to use with this task. The Send Mail Task Editor dialog box is shown in Figure 7-35.

The content of the e-mail message can come from a file, a package variable, or it can be directly input as a string. If a file is used, we must create a File Connection Manager

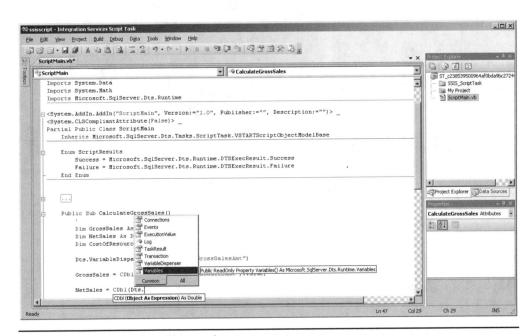

Figure 7-34 *The Script Task Script Editing window*

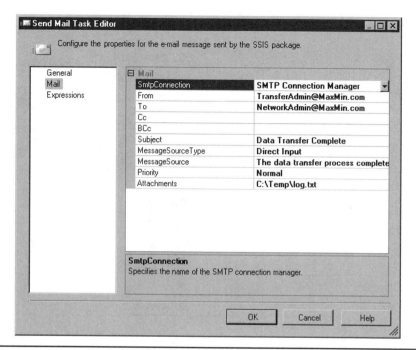

Figure 7-35   *The Send Mail Task Editor dialog box*

in the Connections tray pointing to that file. One or more files can be attached by specifying the path to each file in the Attachments property. If multiple files are attached, the paths are separated by semicolons.

Transfer Database Task, Transfer Error Messages Task, Transfer Jobs Task, Transfer Logins Task, Transfer Master Stored Procedures Task, Transfer SQL Server Objects Task

There are a number of Control Flow items for transferring SQL Server objects from one server to another. The *Transfer Database task* is used to either transfer or move an entire database. Using the *Transfer Error Messages task*, we can copy user-defined error messages. The *Transfer Jobs task* is used to copy SQL Agent Jobs. The *Transfer Logins task* copies one or more SQL logins. Using the *Transfer Master Stored Procedures task*, we can copy user-defined stored procedures between master databases.

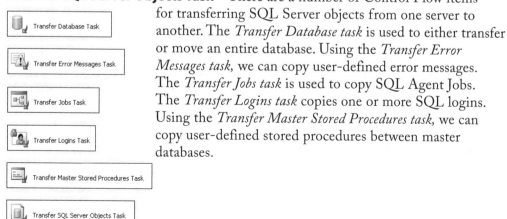

The *Transfer SQL Server Objects task* is used to copy any of the following items:

Object	SQL Server Version
Tables	2000, 2005, or 2008
Views	2000, 2005, or 2008
Stored Procedures	2000, 2005, or 2008
User-Defined Functions	2000, 2005, or 2008
Defaults	2000, 2005, or 2008
User-Defined Data Types	2000, 2005, or 2008
Partition Functions	2005 or 2008
Partition Schemes	2005 or 2008
Schemas	2005 or 2008
Assemblies	2005 or 2008
User-Defined Aggregates	2005 or 2008
User-Defined Types	2005 or 2008
XML Schema Collection	2005 or 2008

Web Service Task   The *Web Service task* lets us execute a web service method as part of our Integration Services package. We must create an HTTP Connection Manager in the Connections tray to specify the connection to the web service. Once a connection has been specified, a Web Services Description Language file must be located to define the web methods that are available. We can then select the web method we want to execute along with the parameters to be passed to that web method. This is shown in the Web Service Task Editor dialog box in Figure 7-36. The result returned by the web method call can be stored in a package variable or a file specified by a File Connection Manager in the Connections tray.

WMI Data Reader Task   The *WMI Data Reader task* enables us to execute a Windows Management Instrumentation (WMI) query to retrieve data about a computer. This could include data from an event log, a list of installed applications and their current versions, or the state of computer hardware. We must create a WMI Connection Manager in the Connections tray to specify the computer that we want to query. The WMI Data Reader Task Editor dialog box is shown in Figure 7-37.

A WMI query is used to select the desired information. The output of the WMI query can be returned as a table, a set of property values, or a set of property name/value pairs. The output can be stored in a file, specified by a File Connection Manager, or in a package variable.

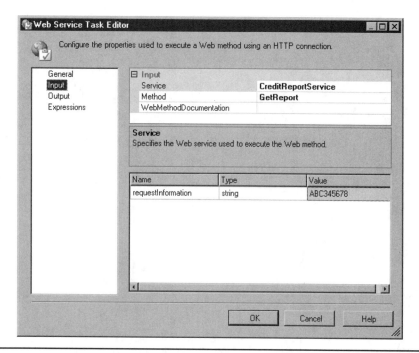

Figure 7-36   *The Web Service Task Editor dialog box*

WMI Event Watcher Task   The *WMI Event Watcher task* lets us wait for a specific computer system event or state before continuing the execution of the Integration Services package. This enables us to do things, such as wait for the server load to drop below a certain level or wait for a file to be copied to a specified folder. We must create a WMI Connection Manager in the Connections tray to specify the computer that we want to watch for the event. The WMI Event Watcher Task Editor dialog box is shown in Figure 7-38.

A *WMI query* is used to specify the event we want to watch for. We can then specify the desired behavior when the event occurs. The ActionAtEvent property determines if the event is simply logged or if it is logged and, at the same time, fires the Integration Services WMIEventWatcherEventOccurred event. If this Integration Services event is being fired, we can then provide an event handler. (This is covered in Chapter 8.) The AfterEvent property determines if this task exits with a success status after the event occurs, exits with a failure status after the event occurs, or waits for another event. If we are waiting for multiple occurrences of the event, the NumberOfEvents property specifies how many occurrences to wait for before exiting the task. The Timeout property lets us specify how many seconds to wait for the event to occur. The ActionAtTimeout and AfterTimeout properties function similarly to their event counterparts.

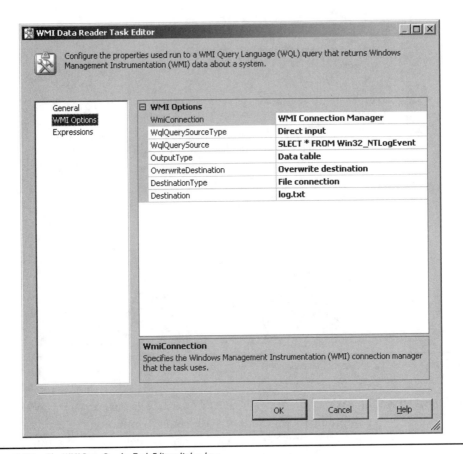

Figure 7-37   *The WMI Data Reader Task Editor dialog box*

XML Task   The *XML task* enables us to manipulate XML documents. Using the XML task, we can perform the following operations:

- ▶ Validate an XML document using an XML Schema Document (XSD) or a Document Type Definition (DTD)
- ▶ Apply an XSL Transformation (XSLT)
- ▶ Apply an XPath query
- ▶ Merge two XML documents
- ▶ Find the difference between two XML documents (Diff operation)
- ▶ Apply the output of a Diff operation

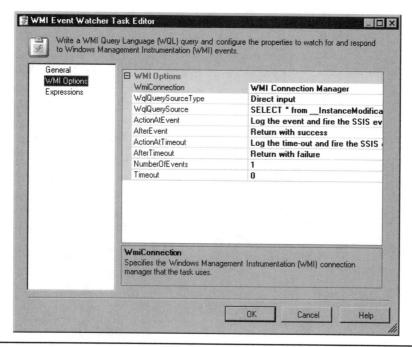

Figure 7-38   *The WMI Event Watcher Task Editor dialog box*

The XML source document can be supplied from a File Connection Manager in the
Connections tray, a package variable, or directly input as a string. The XML document
that results from the operation can be saved in a text file specified by a File Connection
Manager, saved in a package variable, or discarded. The XML Task Editor dialog box is
shown in Figure 7-39.

Maintenance Plan Tasks

In addition to the Control Flow items, the Control Flow tab Toolbox also contains
Maintenance Plan tasks. The Maintenance Plan tasks, as we might guess from the name,
mirror tasks that can be accomplished as part of a database maintenance plan. In fact,
when you create a database maintenance plan through SQL Server Management Studio,
you are actually creating a SQL Server Integration Services package that utilizes these
tasks. The Maintenance Plan tasks can also be used to perform database maintenance
as we are loading data. This can be done to ensure that the database is ready for efficient
operation at the conclusion of the data load.

Each Maintenance Plan task has a View T-SQL button on its dialog box. This
button shows the T-SQL statements that would perform the equivalent operation in
a query window. Looking at these T-SQL statements may be helpful to determine
exactly how a Maintenance Plan task is operating.

We will again examine these items in the order they appear in the Control Flow Toolbox.

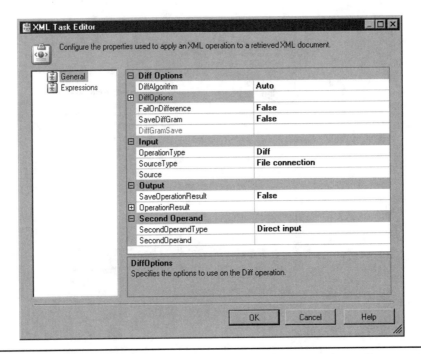

Figure 7-39   *The XML Task Editor dialog box*

Back Up Database Task   The *Back Up Database task* lets us run a database backup
 as part of an Integration Services package. This is a wise thing to
do just before making major changes to the contents of a database.
Often, some type of data load or other operation in an Integration Services package is
responsible for these major changes. By using the Back Up Database task in a package,
we can create the backup within the same process that makes the changes. We may also
find this task useful to create a snapshot of the database contents immediately after a
large data load.

Figure 7-40 shows the Back Up Database Task dialog box used to configure the Back
Up Database task. The dialog box enables us to back up any combination of databases
on a single server. A Full, Differential, or Transaction Log backup can be created. The
backup can be stored in a single file or in multiple files, with one file for each database.

A special type of drop-down box is used to select the databases to be backed up. This
is shown in Figure 7-41. This drop-down box contains predefined choices that let us
select all of the databases on the server, all system databases on the server (master, msdb,
and model), or all user databases on the server. In addition to the predefined choices,
we can use the database list at the bottom of the drop-down box to create our own
selection of databases using the check boxes.

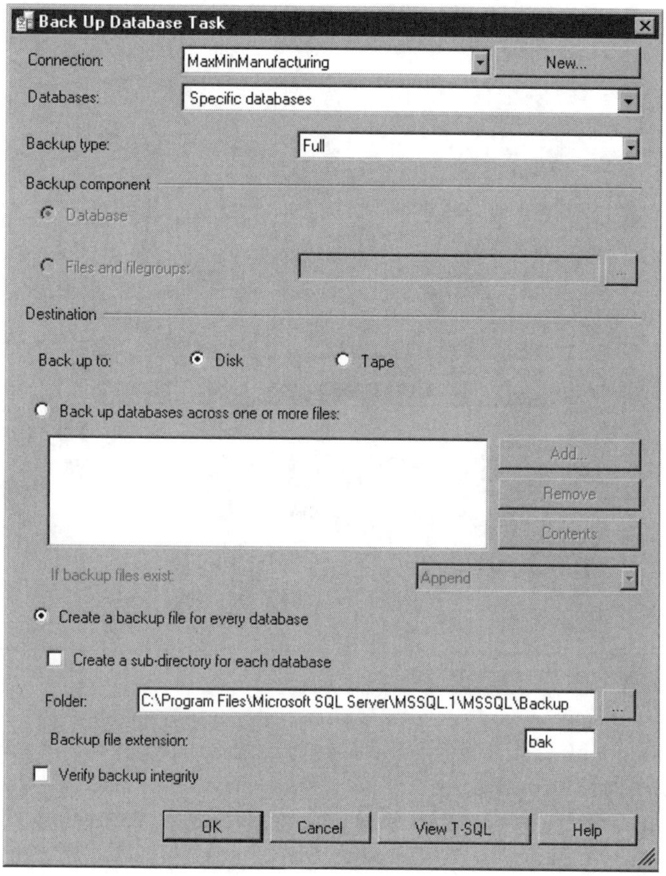

Figure 7-40   *The Back Up Database Task dialog box*

Check Database Integrity Task   The *Check Database Integrity task* lets us check for corruption in one or more databases on a single server. This task executes a

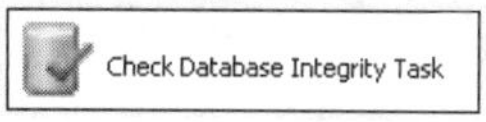

```
DBCC CHECKDB WITH NO_INFOMSGS
```

command against each database specified. This can be a good idea, either right before or right after major changes to the database.

The Check Database Integrity Task dialog box is shown in Figure 7-42. It uses the same database selection drop-down box as the one shown in Figure 7-41 for the selection of the databases to check. We can also specify whether we want indexes included in the integrity check.

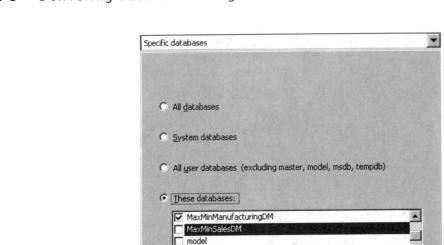

Figure 7-41 *The database selection drop-down box*

If the integrity check is successful, the package execution continues with any tasks linked to the Check Database Integrity task, with either a success or a completion precedence constraint. If the integrity check finds database corruption, the package execution continues with any tasks linked to the Check Database Integrity task, with either a failure or a completion precedence constraint.

Execute SQL Server Agent Job Task The *Execute SQL Server Agent Job task* lets us execute a single SQL Server Agent Job as part of a package. A single job can be selected for execution. The Execute SQL Server Agent Job Task dialog box is shown in Figure 7-43.

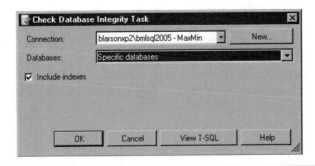

Figure 7-42 *The Check Database Integrity Task dialog box*

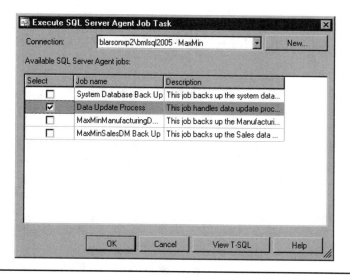

Figure 7-43   *The Execute SQL Server Agent Job Task dialog box*

Execute T-SQL Statement Task   The *Execute T-SQL Statement task* enables us to run
one or more Transact SQL statements on a SQL server. Anything
that can be executed from a query window in the SQL Server
Management Studio can be executed here. The Execute T-SQL Statement Task dialog
box is shown in Figure 7-44.

Notice there is a task called Execute SQL task in the Control Flow items section of
the Toolbox. The Execute T-SQL Statement task that we are looking at here is simple.

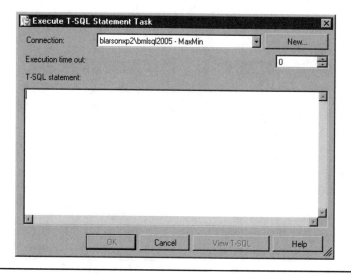

Figure 7-44   *The Execute T-SQL Statement Task dialog box*

It lets us type in T-SQL statements and execute them. The Execute SQL task in the Control Flow items has additional features for creating parameterized statements and dealing with result sets.

History Cleanup Task   The *History Cleanup task* enables us to remove historical
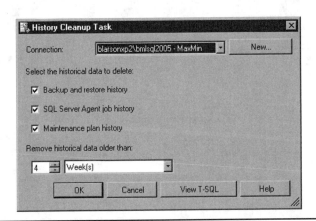
entries from a database. This includes backup history, SQL Agent Job execution history, and database maintenance plan execution history. We can specify the timeframe for the historical entries we want to keep and, therefore, the timeframe for the historical entries we want to remove. The History Cleanup Task dialog box is shown in Figure 7-45.

Maintenance Cleanup Task   The Maintenance Cleanup task allows us to remove files created by database maintenance plans and database backups. Specifically, we can remove maintenance plan text reports and database backups. We can remove a single file based on the filename or a number of files with the same file extension from a folder. We can specify the age of the files we want to remove.

Notify Operator Task   The *Notify Operator task* lets us send an e-mail message to one or more SQL Server operators using SQLiMail. An operator must be set up with an e-mail address in SQL Server before they can be notified using this task. Of course, SQLiMail must be installed and configured for this task to function properly. The Notify Operator task dialog box is shown in Figure 7-46.

Rebuild Index Task   The *Rebuild Index task* enables the rebuilding of indexes in one or more databases. Rebuilding indexes causes SQL Server to drop the existing indexes and rebuild them. The Rebuild Index task uses the same

Figure 7-45   *The History Cleanup Task dialog box*

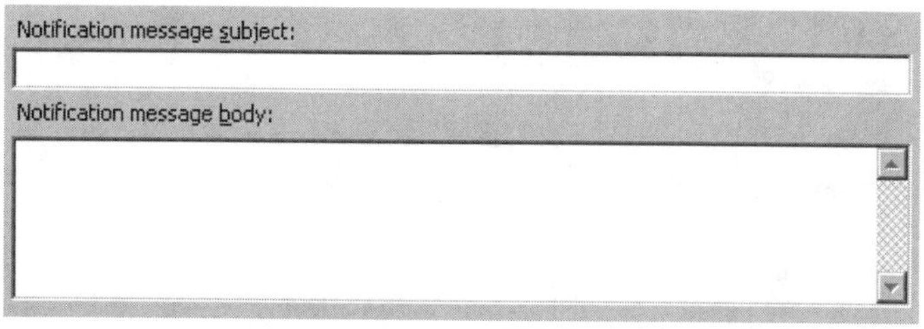

Notification message subject:

Notification message body:

Figure 7-46 *The Notify Operator Task dialog box*

database selection drop-down box as the one shown in Figure 7-41 for the selection of the databases whose indexes are to be rebuilt. We can specify the free space that should be placed into the rebuilt indexes, along with several other advanced indexing options. The Rebuild Index Task dialog box is shown in Figure 7-47.

Reorganize Index Task   The *Reorganize Index task* lets us reorganize the indexes in one or more databases. It uses the same database selection drop-down box as the one shown in Figure 7-41 for the selection of the databases whose indexes are to be reorganized. The Reorganize Index Task dialog box is shown in Figure 7-48.

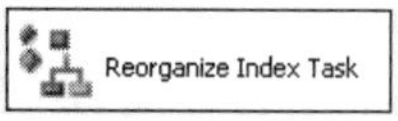

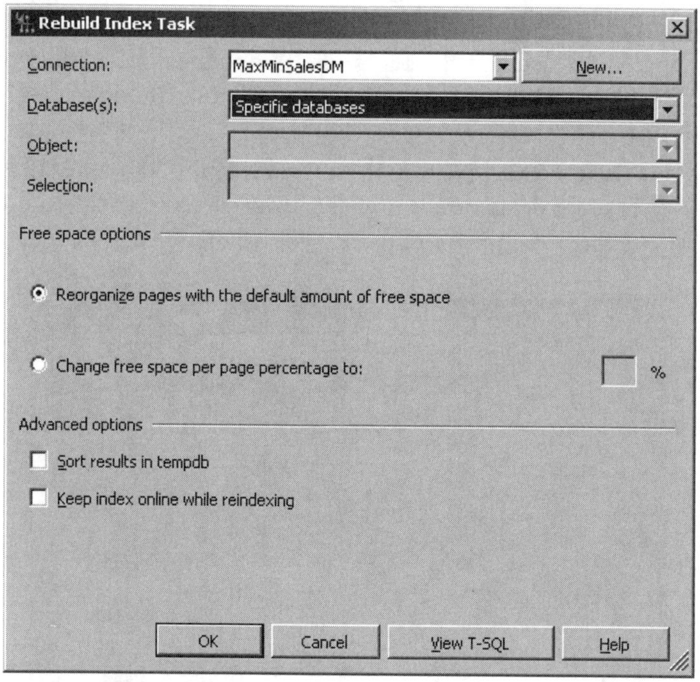

Figure 7-47 *The Rebuild Index Task dialog box*

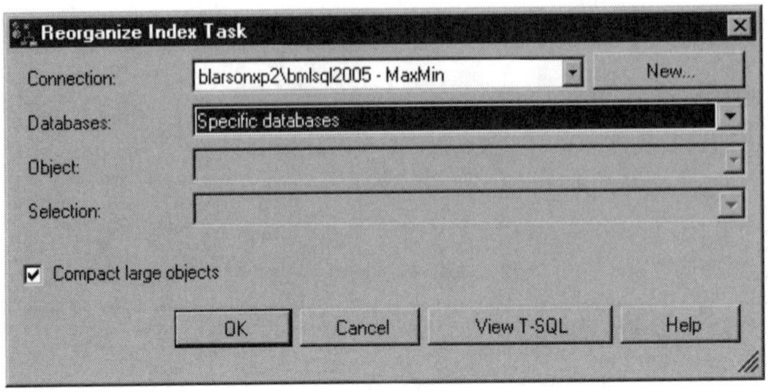

Figure 7-48 *The Reorganize Index Task dialog box*

Reorganizing indexes defragments the leaf-level nodes of both clustered and nonclustered indexes. It does this by reordering the nodes to match the logical order of the leaf nodes. Reorganizing also compacts the indexes. The reorganization process does not, however, drop and re-create the indexes as the rebuild process does.

Shrink Database Task　The *Shrink Database task* enables the recovery of unused pages from tables in one or more databases. It uses the same database selection drop-down box as the one shown in Figure 7-41 for the selection of the databases that are to be shrunk. We can determine whether these recovered pages are to be returned to the operating system or remain allocated to the database. We can also specify how much free space is to be left in the pages allocated to the database to accommodate future growth. The Shrink Database Task dialog box is shown in Figure 7-49.

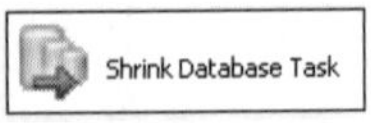

Update Statistics Task　The *Update Statistics task* lets us update the statistics in one or more databases. It uses the same database selection drop-down box as the one shown in Figure 7-41 for the selection of the databases

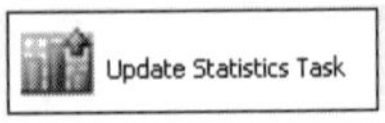

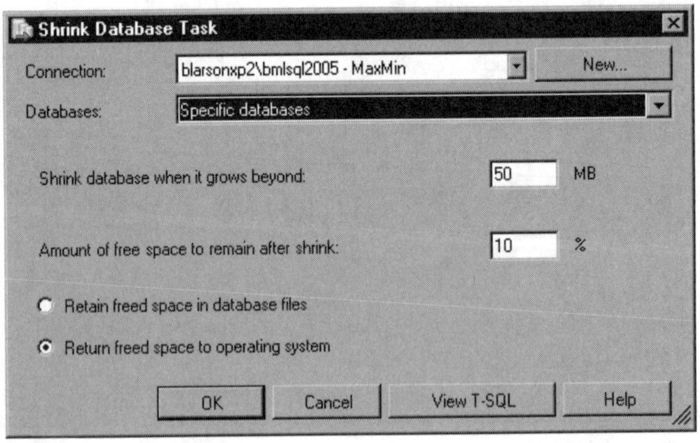

Figure 7-49 *The Shrink Database Task dialog box*

whose statistics are to be updated. Because the database statistics are used by SQL Server to calculate query execution plans, it is important for these statistics to be up-to-date. A large data load can cause the statistics to be inaccurate. Therefore, it is a good idea to use this task to update the database statistics after a major data operation. The Update Statistics Task dialog box is shown in Figure 7-50.

Custom Tasks   If none of the control flow tasks included with Integration Services fits your needs, it is possible to write your own. You can create a .NET assembly that can integrate seamlessly with both Integration Services and the Business Intelligence Development Studio. Creating a custom task requires a solid knowledge of object-oriented programming in the .NET Framework. Consult the SQL Server Books Online "Custom Tasks [SSIS]" topic for more information on developing a custom task.

Data Flow

The Data Flow tab Toolbox is divided into three areas: data flow sources, data flow transformations, and data flow destinations. (We will not be concerned with the General area of the Toolbox, which is empty.) Each Data Flow item—source, transformation, or destination—has an editor dialog box that lets us configure that component in a straightforward manner. The editor dialog box is launched by double-clicking the item

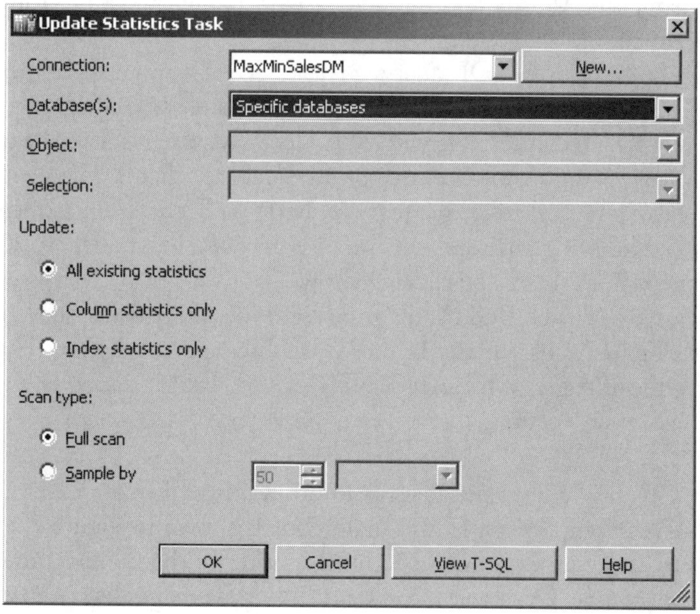

Figure 7-50   *The Update Statistics Task dialog box*

in the design area or right-clicking the item and selecting Edit from the context menu. Each item also has an advanced editor dialog box. Where the editor dialog box enables us to configure the item for use and make most of the necessary property settings for the item, the advanced editor dialog box contains all of the properties of an item. The advanced editor dialog box lets us set any property for the item. The advanced editor dialog box is launched by right-clicking the item and selecting Show Advanced Editor from the context menu.

Data Flow Sources

Data flow sources are the starting point of any data flow. This is where the data comes from. Integration Services allows us to pull data from a wide variety of sources.

ADO.NET Source The *ADO.NET source* lets us use ADO.NET to connect to a data source. We need to create an ADO.NET Connection Manager in the Connections tab for use with this data source. Once the ADO.NET Connection Manager has been created, it can be selected on the Connection Manager page of the ADO.NET Source Editor dialog box. This is shown in Figure 7-51.

The Connection Manager page is also used to specify whether we are getting our data directly from a table or view, or from a SQL query. If the data is coming from a table or a view, the name of the Table or the View property is used to select a table or view in the database. Alternately, the table or view name can come from a package variable at run time.

If the data is coming from a SQL query, we have several ways to specify the content of the query. The simplest method is to type the query into the SQL command text property. This works only if we are comfortable with SQL query syntax and have the database structure memorized or an up-to-date copy of the database schema documentation handy. If this is not the case, we can create the query in the SQL Server Management Studio or some other query-authoring environment and save the completed query to a file. We can then load the query from the file by clicking Browse.

Alternatively, we can click Build Query to create the query using the Query Builder. The Query Builder is discussed later in the "OLE DB Source" section. The Columns and the Error Output pages of the ADO.NET Source Editor dialog box are discussed in the "Flat File Source" section.

Excel Source The *Excel source* enables us to utilize data from an Excel spreadsheet. The Excel Source Editor dialog box is shown in Figure 7-52. We need to create an Excel Connection Manager in the Connections tab for use with this data source. Once the Excel Connection Manager has been created, this Connection Manager can be selected on the Connection Managers page of the Excel

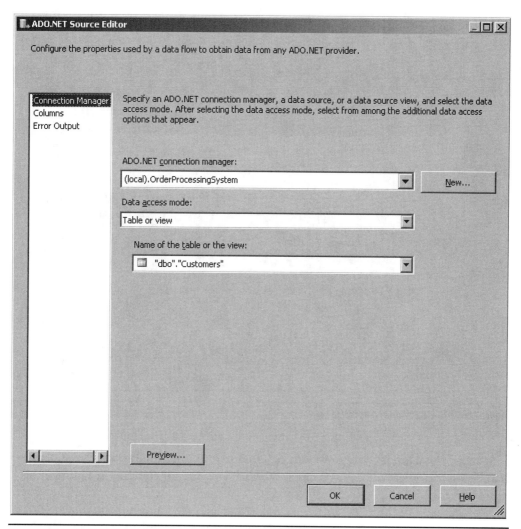

Figure 7-51   *The ADO.NET Source Editor dialog box*

Source Editor dialog box. A spreadsheet is then selected from the Excel file pointed to by this Connection Manager. The columns included in the result set are selected on the Columns page of the Excel Source Editor dialog box.

Flat File Source   The *Flat File source* lets us utilize data from text files. We need to create a Flat File Connection Manager in the Connections tray for use with this data source. The Flat File Connection Manager requires a bit more configuration than the OLE DB Connection Manager and most of the other Connection Managers. The other Connection Managers deal with specific data

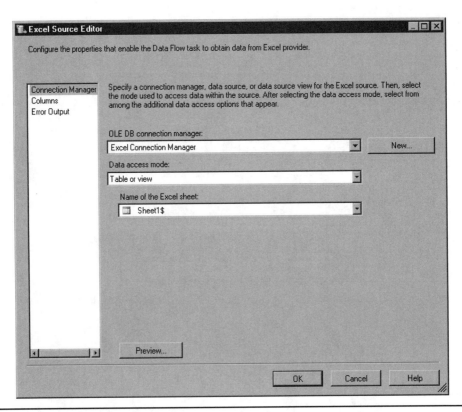

Figure 7-52   *The Excel Source Editor dialog box*

formats, so not a lot of configuration is required beyond the connection information. A flat file, on the other hand, can represent, format, and delimit the data in a number of different ways.

The first page of the Flat File Connection Manager, the General page shown in Figure 7-53, enables us to specify the file location in the File Name text box. In addition, we need to tell the Connection Manager how the data is represented with the Locale and Code Page drop-down lists, along with the Unicode check box. Finally, we need to specify how the data is formatted: whether the data is a fixed-width layout or delimited by a comma, tab, or some other separator (Format); if the text is enclosed in some form of quotation character (Text Qualifier); how the header row is delimited (Header Row Delimiter); if there are header rows to skip (Header Rows to Skip); and if the column names are in the first row (Column Names in the First Data Row).

In this example, we are using the ragged-right format. The *ragged-right format* expects fixed-width columns in the text file. This means, for example, that the first 8 characters of

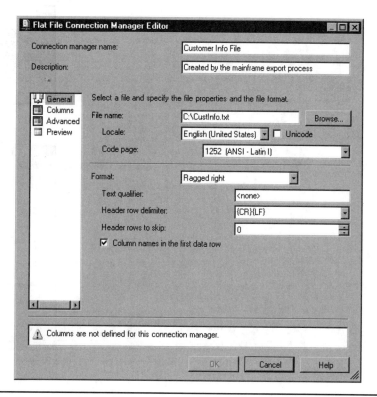

Figure 7-53   *The General page of the Flat File Connection Manager Editor dialog box*

each line are always the first column, the next 34 characters are always the second column, and so on. The ragged-right format expects some type of end-of-line indicator, such as a set of carriage return and line-feed characters. The *fixed-width format* also expects fixed-width columns, but it specifies the exact number of characters in each line, rather than using an end-of-line indicator. The length of the lines in the ragged-right format can vary because the end-of-line indicator tells the parser where to end one line and begin another. The length of the lines in the fixed-width format must be exactly the same for all lines.

The warning at the bottom of the dialog box in Figure 7-53—"Columns are not defined for this connection manager"—tells us that we are not quite done yet. As soon as we select the Columns page, shown in Figure 7-54, the Flat File Connection Manager uses the information from the General page to access the file. When the delimited format is selected on the General page, the Flat File Connection Manager attempts to figure out what the delimiter is and parse the file accordingly. If the wrong delimiter is chosen, you can edit the delimiter information. When the fixed-width format or, as in our example, the ragged-right format is used, we are given the opportunity to graphically specify the width of each column.

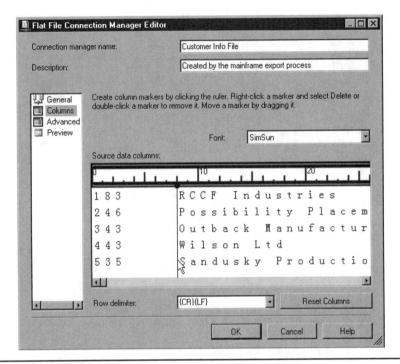

Figure 7-54 *The Columns page of the Flat File Connection Manager Editor dialog box*

We specify column widths by creating column markers in the Source Data Columns area. The column marker is indicated by the mouse pointer in Figure 7-53. *Column markers* are created by clicking along the bottom of the ruler or below the ruler in the sample text area. We can drag the column markers to their appropriate positions, if necessary. We can remove an unneeded column marker by double-clicking it or by right-clicking it and selecting Delete from the context menu.

The Advanced page of the Flat File Connection Manager, shown in Figure 7-55, lets us specify additional information about each column that was defined on the Columns page. We can create, add, and delete column definitions here, as well as on the Columns page. The drop-down list alongside the New button, indicated by the mouse pointer in Figure 7-55, enables us to insert a column definition either before or after the column definition highlighted in the list. We can specify the Name property for each column definition. (If column names are supplied as the first row of the text file, these names appear in the Name property for each column definition.) The *Suggest Types button* instructs the Flat File Connection Manager to suggest a data type for each column definition based on the data in the text file. The final page in the Flat File Connection Manager Editor dialog box lets us preview the data from the text file when it is parsed according to our file layout and column definitions.

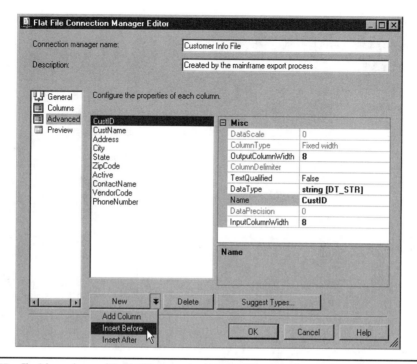

Figure 7-55   *The Advanced page of the Flat File Connection Manager Editor dialog box*

Once the Flat File Connection Manager has been created, this Connection Manager can be selected on the Connection Manager page of the Flat File Source Editor dialog box. We can then use the Columns page to specify which columns should be used in the data flow. The Error output page enables us to specify the behavior of the Flat File source when an error or truncation occurs in any given column. We can ignore the failure, direct the row containing the failure to the error output, or cause the process to fail.

OLE DB Source   The *OLE DB source* lets us utilize data from any source that supports an OLE DB connection. We need to create an OLE DB Connection Manager in the Connections tray for use with this data source. Once the OLE DB Connection Manager is created, it can be selected on the Connection Manager page of the OLE DB Source Editor dialog box. This is shown in Figure 7-56.

The Connection Manager page is also used to specify whether we are getting our data directly from a table or view, or from a SQL query. If the data is coming from a table or a view, the name of the Table or the View property is used to select a table or view in the database. Alternately, the table or view name can come from a package variable at run time.

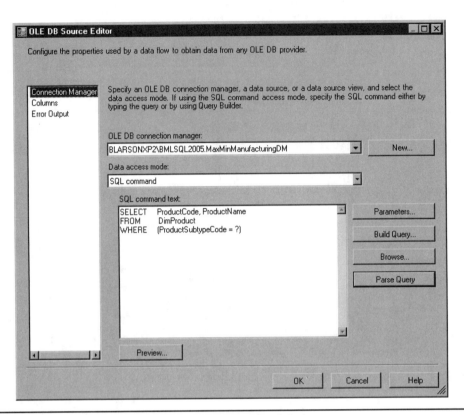

Figure 7-56   *The Connection Manager page of the OLE DB Source Editor dialog box*

If the data is coming from a SQL query, we have several ways to specify the content of the query. The simplest method is to type the query into the SQL Command Text property. This works only if we are comfortable with SQL query syntax and have the database structure memorized or an up-to-date copy of the database schema documentation handy. If this is not the case, we can create the query in the SQL Server Management Studio or some other query-authoring environment and save the completed query to a file. We can then load the query from the file by clicking Browse.

Alternatively, we can click Build Query to create the query using the Query Builder. The Query Builder is shown in Figure 7-57. The top quarter of the Query Builder is the Diagram pane. The *Diagram pane* area is used for selecting tables from the database, creating join conditions between tables, and selecting fields to be used in the query, either in the field list or in the filter conditions. The next quarter of the Query Builder, moving downward, is the Grid pane. The *Grid pane* is used to select the fields to be included in the field list (the Output column), as well as for setting the sort order and filter conditions. The next quarter, again moving downward, is the SQL pane. The *SQL pane* shows the SQL SELECT statement that is equivalent to the contents of the

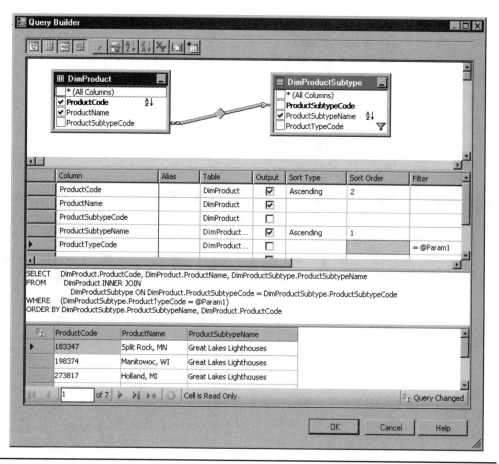

Figure 7-57 *The Query Builder*

Diagram and Grid panes. Changes made directly in the SQL pane are reflected in the Diagram pane and the Grid pane as soon as focus leaves the SQL pane. The bottom quarter of the Query Builder is the *Result pane,* which shows the results of executing the query.

The Columns and the Error Output pages of the OLE DB Source Editor function similarly to their counterparts in the Flat File source.

Raw File Source   The *Raw File source* lets us utilize data that was previously written to a raw data file by a Raw File destination. The *raw file format* is the native format for Integration Services. Because of this, raw files can be written to disk and read from disk rapidly. One of the goals of Integration Services is to improve processing efficiency by moving data from the original source to the ultimate destination without making any stops in between. However, on some occasions, the data must be staged to disk as part of an Extract, Transform, and Load process. When this is necessary, the raw file format provides the most efficient means of accomplishing this task. The Raw File Source Editor dialog box is shown in Figure 7-58. (The Raw File source Editor must be configured through the Advanced Editor.)

XML Source   The *XML source* enables us to utilize the content of an XML document in the data flow. The XML document can come from a file or from the

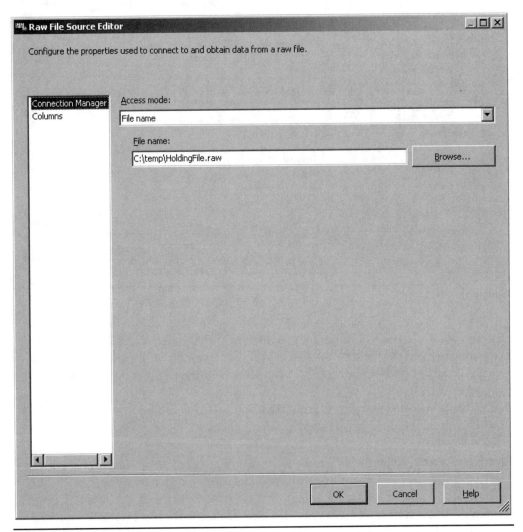

Figure 7-58   *The Raw File Source Editor dialog box*

contents of a package variable. If the XML document is coming from a file, we can specify the file path at design time or obtain the file path from a package variable at run time. We can also specify the location of an XSD that describes the structure of the XML document. If an XSD is unavailable, click Generate XSD to autogenerate an XSD from the XML document structure. The XML Source Editor dialog box is shown in Figure 7-59.

The Columns and the Error Output pages function similarly to their counterparts in the Flat File source.

Data Flow Transformations

The *data flow transformations* are used to modify the data as it moves through the data flow. In most cases, the wide array of data flow transformations makes it possible to change the data into the required format without having to save it to a temporary table or utilize large amounts of custom code. This set of powerful transformations lets us take our data from an ugly duckling to a beautiful swan with just a few drag-and-drop operations.

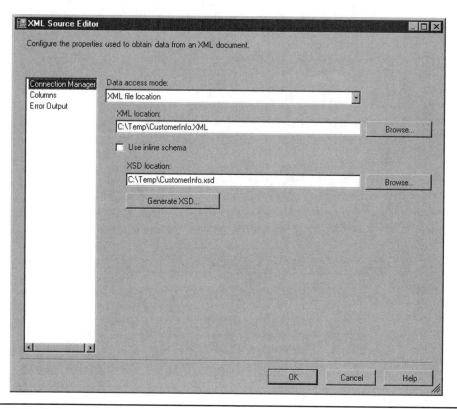

Figure 7-59   *The XML Source Editor dialog box*

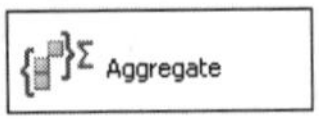

Aggregate   The *Aggregate* transformation enables us to combine information from multiple records in the data flow into a single value. This functions in the same way as aggregation functions and the GROUP BY clause in a SQL statement. The Aggregate Transformation Editor dialog box is shown in Figure 7-60.

We begin by selecting the columns to participate in the aggregation from the Available Input Columns. We then select the Operation that is applied to each of the selected columns. A column can either be used as a group by or it can be aggregated. The following aggregations are available:

▶ Average

▶ Count

▶ Count distinct

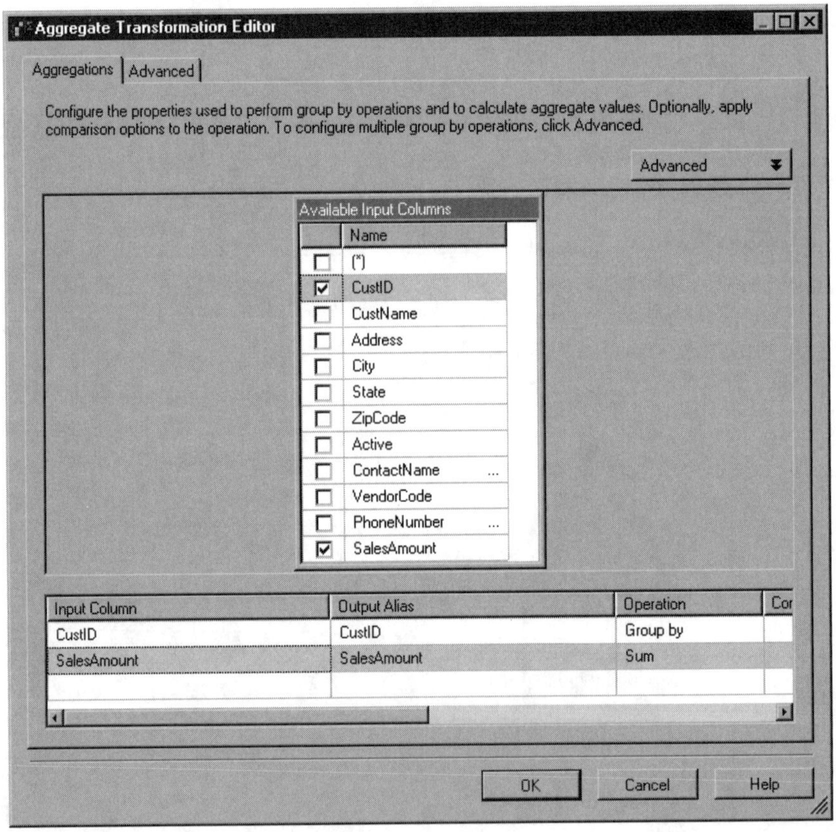

Figure 7-60   *The Aggregate Transformation Editor dialog box*

► Maximum

► Minimum

► Sum

The example in Figure 7-60 calculates the sum of the SalesAmount column for each customer represented by the content of the CustID column.

Audit   The *Audit* transformation lets us add columns that contain information about the package execution to the data flow. These audit columns can be stored in the data destination and used to determine when the package was run, where it was run, and so forth. The following information can be placed in audit columns:

► Execution instance GUID (a globally unique identifier for a given execution of the package)

► Execution start time

► Machine name

► Package ID (a GUID for the package)

► Package name

► Task ID (a GUID for the data flow task)

► Task name (the name of the data flow task)

► User name

► Version ID

The Audit Transformation Editor dialog box is shown in Figure 7-61. The information in the columns defined in this dialog box is duplicated for each row in the data flow. In this example, audit columns are being added to the data flow for machine name, package name, execution start time, and execution instance GUID.

Cache Transform   The *Cache Transform* transformation is an enhancement in SQL Server 2008. It enables us to populate a cache that will be subsequently used by a Lookup transformation. The Cache Transform can be configured to write the cached data to a cache file using a Cache Connection Manager. Only one Cache Transform in a package can write data to a given Cache Connection Manager.

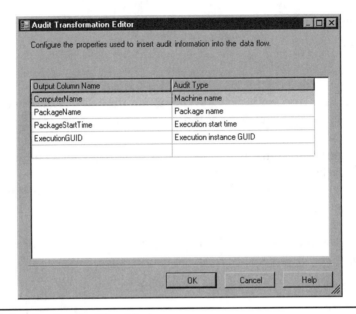

Figure 7-61 *The Audit Transformation Editor dialog box*

With the Cache Transform, we can define an Integration Services data flow to populate a lookup list used by a Lookup transformation. In SQL Server 2005 Integration Services, a Lookup transformation had to use a table, view, or the result set of a query as its lookup data set. The Cache Transform enables us to apply any of the Integration Services data flow transformations to a set of data before using it as the lookup data set.

Character Map   The *Character Map* transformation enables us to modify the contents of character-based columns. The modified column can be placed in the data flow in place of the original column, or it can be added to the data flow as a new column. The following character mappings are available:

- ▶ **Lowercase** changes all characters to lowercase
- ▶ **Uppercase** changes all characters to uppercase
- ▶ **Byte reversal** reverses the byte order of each character
- ▶ **Hiragana** maps Katakana characters to Hiragana characters
- ▶ **Katakana** maps Hiragana characters to Katakana characters
- ▶ **Half width** changes double-byte characters to single-byte characters
- ▶ **Full width** changes single-byte characters to double-byte characters

▶ **Linguistic casing** applies linguistic casing rules instead of system casing rules

▶ **Simplified Chinese** maps traditional Chinese to simplified Chinese

▶ **Traditional Chinese** maps simplified Chinese to traditional Chinese

Multiple character mappings can be applied to a single column at the same time. However, a number of mappings are mutually exclusive. For example, it does not make sense to use both the lowercase and uppercase mappings on the same column. The Character Map Transformation Editor dialog box is shown in Figure 7-62.

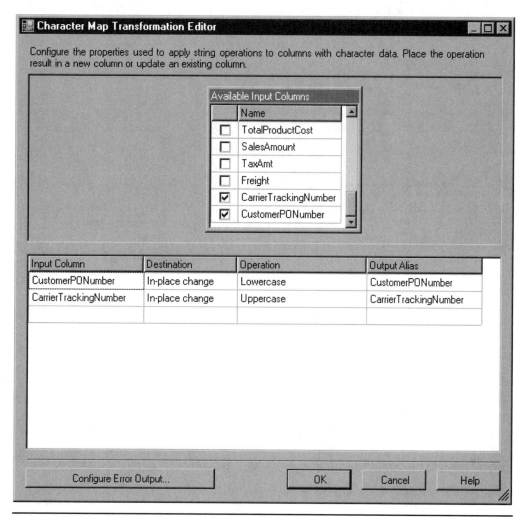

Figure 7-62 *The Character Map Transformation Editor dialog box*

The Configure Error Output button displays the Configure Error Output dialog box, shown in Figure 7-63. The *Configure Error Output dialog box* lets us determine the error behavior of this transformation. For the Character Map transformation, the only error condition we need to worry about is a character truncation caused by one of the mappings. For each character mapping, we can choose to ignore truncation, send the row containing the truncation to the error output, or cause the entire transformation to fail.

Conditional Split   The *Conditional Split* transformation enables us to split the data flow into multiple outputs. In the Conditional Split Transformation Editor dialog box, shown in Figure 7-64, we define conditions for each branch of the split. When the package executes, each row in the data flow is compared against the conditions in order. When the row meets a set of conditions, the row is sent to that branch of the split.

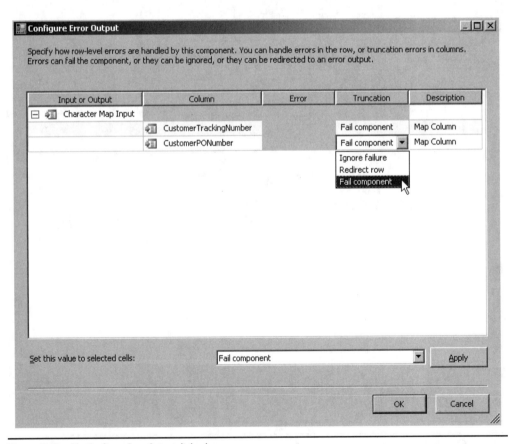

Figure 7-63   *The Configure Error Output dialog box*

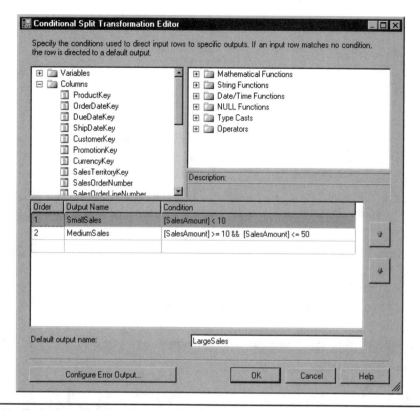

Figure 7-64   *The Conditional Split Transformation Editor dialog box*

In Figure 7-64, the conditional split has been defined with three branches. If the content of the SalesAmount column for a given row is less than $10, that row is sent to the SmallSales output. If the content of the SalesAmount column is between $10 and $50 inclusive, the row is sent to the MediumSales output. If the content of the SalesAmount column does not fit either of these conditions, the row is sent to the default output, named LargeSales. Figure 7-65 shows the three outputs from the Conditional Split Transformation being routed to three different paths through the data flow.

The Configure Error Output button displays the Configure Error Output dialog box, where we determine the error behavior of this transformation. In addition to truncation, we also need to configure the behavior when the condition statement fails during evaluation. For each output column defined, we can choose to ignore an error, send the row containing the error to the error output, or fail the entire transformation.

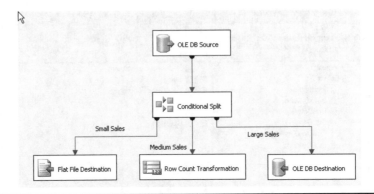

Figure 7-65   *A Conditional Split transformation in a data flow*

Copy Column   The *Copy Column* transformation lets us create new columns in the
 data flow that are copies of existing columns. The new columns can
then be used later in the data flow for calculations, transformations,
or mapping to columns in the data destination. Figure 7-66 shows the Copy Column

Figure 7-66   *The Copy Column Transformation Editor dialog box*

Transformation Editor dialog box with the SalesAmount column being copied to a new column called SalesAmountForTaxCalculation.

Data Conversion   The *Data Conversion* transformation enables us to convert columns from one data type to another. The converted data can either replace the existing column or be added as a new column. The Configure Error Output dialog box functions the same as it does for the Conditional Split transformation.

Figure 7-67 shows the Data Conversion Transformation Editor dialog box with two columns set up for conversion. The Unicode contents of the CustomerPONumber column are replaced by its single-byte equivalent. The currency type contents of the SalesAmount column are converted to a decimal, with two places to the right of the decimal point. The decimal value is placed in a new column called SalesAmountAsDecimal.

Data Mining Query   The *Data Mining Query* transformation lets us execute a DMX query on the data flow. Using the DMX query along with a data mining model, we can make predictions based on the data in each row of the data flow. These predictions can indicate other items that are likely to be associated with

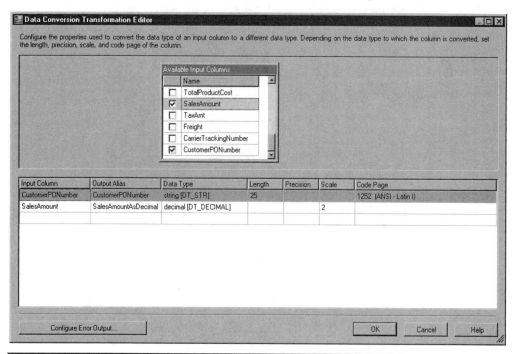

Figure 7-67   *The Data Conversion Transformation Editor dialog box*

the column (that is, other products a customer is likely to purchase based on the current purchase) or the likelihood of a column to fit a certain condition (that is, the likelihood of a prospective client to be interested in a certain service).

The columns that result from the DMX query are added as new columns in the data flow. The new columns can be sent along with the rest of the data to the data destination, or they can be used along with the Conditional Split transformation to send rows to different data destinations based on the prediction. We discuss DMX queries in Part IV of this book. Figure 7-68 shows the Mining Model tab of the Data Mining Query Transformation Editor dialog box.

Derived Column The *Derived Column* transformation enables us to create a value derived from an expression. The expression can use values from variables and the content of columns in the data flow. The value can replace the content of an existing column or be added to the data flow as a new column. Figure 7-69 shows the Derived Column Transformation Editor dialog box defining a new column, AmountWithTax, which contains the sum of the SalesAmount and TaxAmt columns. The Derived Column transformation uses the same Configure Error Output dialog box as the Conditional Split transformation.

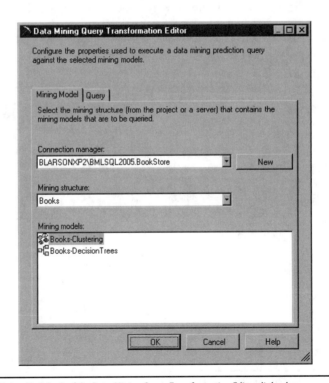

Figure 7-68   *The Mining Model tab of the Data Mining Query Transformation Editor dialog box*

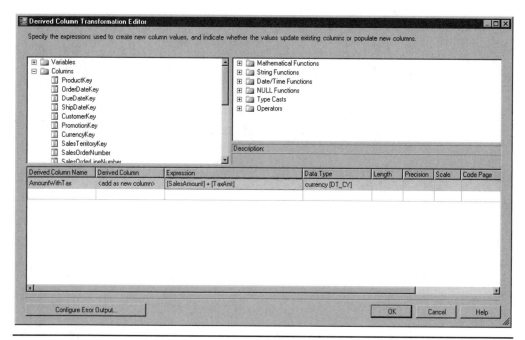

Figure 7-69   *The Derived Column Transformation Editor dialog box*

Export Column   The *Export Column* transformation lets us take the content of a text or image column and write it out to a file. The pathname and filename are specified in a different column in the data flow. In this manner, the content of the text or image column can be written to a different file for each row. The Export Column Transformation Editor dialog box, shown in Figure 7-70, can be used to specify whether to truncate the file or append to it if it already exists.

Fuzzy Grouping   The *Fuzzy Grouping* transformation enables us to find groups of rows in the data flow based on non-exact matches. This is most often used to find possible duplicate rows based on names, addresses, or some other column where the same information may have been entered in different ways. For example, a row for Ms. Kathy Jones, a second row for Ms. Kathryn Jones, and a third row for Ms. Cathy Jones may be three entries for the same person.

The Fuzzy Grouping transformation selects one of the rows in the group as the best candidate for the other rows to be combined into, and this is the *model row*. Once the groups and their model rows have been identified, we can use another transformation to combine any unique information from the non-model rows into the model row and delete the nonmodel rows. This removes the duplication from the data. The Fuzzy

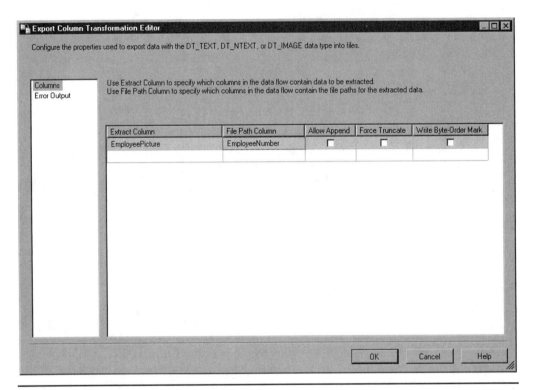

Figure 7-70 *The Export Column Transformation Editor dialog box*

Grouping transformation identifies row groups and model rows; it does not combine any data or delete any nonmodel rows. This must be done as a separate step in the package or as a manual operation.

Fuzzy Grouping transformation creates similarity scores between strings. This is done by considering the edit distance between two strings. In other words, how many character inserts, deletions, and replacements must be made in one string to produce the other string? Kathy and Kathryn have an edit distance of 2, because we need to insert an *r* and an *n* into the first word to get the second. Kathy and Cathy have an edit distance of 1, because we simply need to replace *K* with *C* in the first word to get the second.

In addition to edit distance, Fuzzy Grouping uses information, such as frequency of character occurrence and the positions of the characters, among other things, to increase its accuracy when creating similarity scores. Fuzzy Grouping is great at detecting character transpositions and other common spelling errors. All of the algorithms that create the similarity scores are language-independent, so Fuzzy Grouping can work with any language we care to throw at it.

NOTE

Fuzzy Grouping assumes a string that is all uppercase is an acronym. Because even acronyms that have a close edit distance, say, FTC and FCC, are not likely to be the same thing, it is unlikely that groups will be identified for strings in all uppercase. If your data was entered in all uppercase (this can be especially true for legacy data), it is important to use the Character Map transformation to change the string to lowercase before trying a Fuzzy Grouping transformation.

On the Columns tab of the Fuzzy Grouping Transformation Editor dialog box, shown in Figure 7-71, we select the columns to use when looking for groupings. These columns can be set for fuzzy matching that uses similarity scoring or for exact matching. In the example in Figure 7-71, the content of the Title column—Mr. or Ms.—must match exactly before we want to even think about trying a fuzzy match on the FirstName and LastName columns. In addition to the exact or fuzzy match setting, we can specify whether leading or trailing numerals (0–9) are significant or should be ignored. (Selecting Leading from the Numerals drop-down list indicates that leading numerals are significant, and so forth.)

The columns we select for grouping on the Columns page are automatically passed through to the output of the Fuzzy Grouping transformation. For each of the columns used in the grouping, the Fuzzy Grouping transformation adds a "clean" column to the output. These clean columns contain the values from the row that the Fuzzy Grouping transformation has selected as the model row for that group. In our previous example, if the row containing Ms. Kathy Jones is chosen as the model row for the group, the

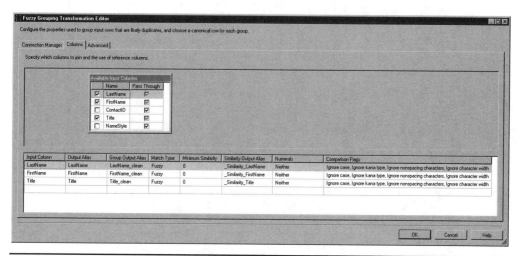

Figure 7-71   *The Columns tab of the Fuzzy Grouping Transformation Editor dialog box*

FirstName_clean column would contain Kathy for the Ms. Kathy Jones row, the Ms. Kathryn Jones row, and the Ms. Cathy Jones row.

We can also select columns to be passed through from the input to the output without participating in the transformation by placing a check mark in the Pass Through column. The Fuzzy Grouping transformation can add three additional columns to the output. The default names for these columns are _key_in, _key_out, and _score. We can change the names of these columns on the Advanced tab of the Fuzzy Grouping Transformation Editor dialog box, shown in Figure 7-72.

The _key_in column contains a unique identifier for each field. This unique identifier is generated by the Fuzzy Grouping transformation. If a row is not grouped with any other rows, or if it is the model row for a group of rows, then it has the same identifier in its _key_out column as it has in its _key_in field. If a row is in a group and it is not the model row for that group, then it has the identifier of the model row in its _key_out column.

The _score column contains the similarity score assigned to the row. The higher the similarity score, the more confidence the Fuzzy Grouping transformation has in the match. A row that is not grouped or that is a model row for a group always has a similarity

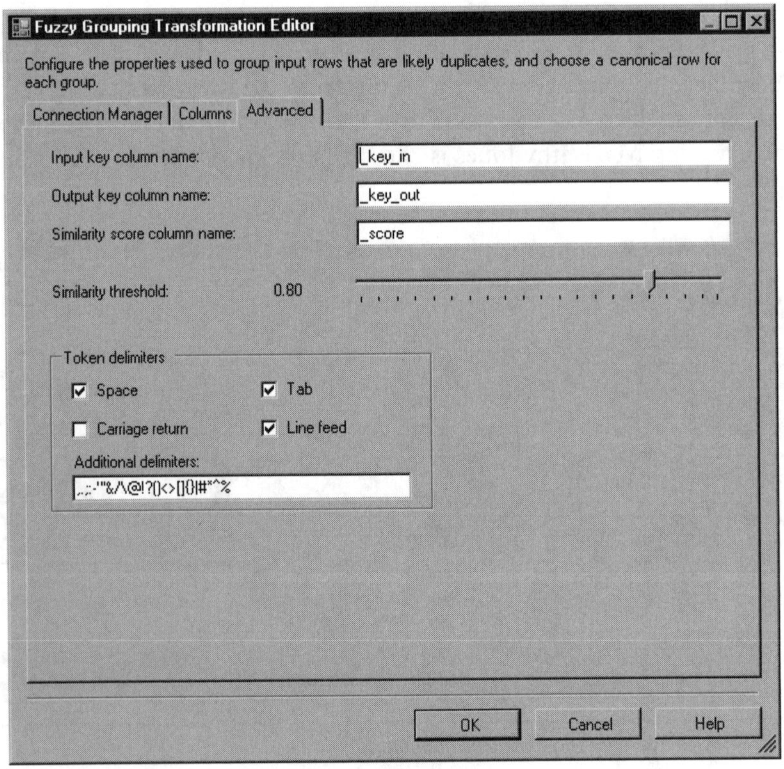

Figure 7-72 *The Advanced tab of the Fuzzy Grouping Transformation Editor dialog box*

score of 1. A row that is in a group and is not a model row has a similarity score between 0 and 1, inclusive.

On the Advanced tab of the Fuzzy Grouping Transformation Editor dialog box, we can set the threshold for the similarity score. Similarity scores that fall below the threshold are not used to create groups. A lower threshold allows the Fuzzy Grouping transformation to find more groups of duplicate rows, but also increases the risk of false positives. A higher threshold makes fewer mistakes, but increases the risk that some actual duplicates will not be found. Some experimenting should be done with your data to determine the best threshold for each Fuzzy Grouping transformation.

The Fuzzy Grouping transformation creates a lookup list of items and does fuzzy matching on that lookup list to create the groupings. If we are dealing with the processing of a data flow with a large number of rows, the Fuzzy Grouping transformation may need to write the lookup list to disk. The OLE DB Connection Manager selected on the Connection Manager tab provides access to a tempdb database where this temporary lookup list can be written. Because of this necessity to create a lookup list, the Fuzzy Grouping task can be rather slow.

Fuzzy Lookup   The *Fuzzy Lookup* transformation lets us look up values using fuzzy matching logic. The Fuzzy Lookup transformation is closely related to the Fuzzy Grouping transformation. In fact, as was noted, the Fuzzy Grouping transformation creates its own lookup list, and then does a fuzzy lookup.

The Fuzzy Lookup transformation is extremely useful when the data is moving from a database where a column was entered as freeform text to another database where that same column uses a lookup table and a foreign key constraint. Without the Fuzzy Lookup transformation, any typos in the freeform data leave us with a situation where we cannot determine the appropriate foreign key value to put in the destination table. However, with the Fuzzy Lookup transformation, we can determine a foreign key value even when typos are present.

The Fuzzy Lookup transformation uses an existing table or view as the source for its lookup operation. The transformation creates a copy of the source lookup table to use during the transformation processing. It then creates a second table that holds the information necessary for calculating the similarity score. This second table is called the *match index*. Don't let the name fool you—this is really a table created in the same database that holds the source lookup table.

The copy of the source lookup table and the match index table can be created as temporary tables each time the package is run. This is a good idea if the package performs a one-time data load operation. However, if the package is going to be run frequently, it is more efficient to create these tables as regular tables in the database. This is done using the Store New Index check box, as shown in Figure 7-73. For the most efficient operation of the package, we can have the database maintain the match index,

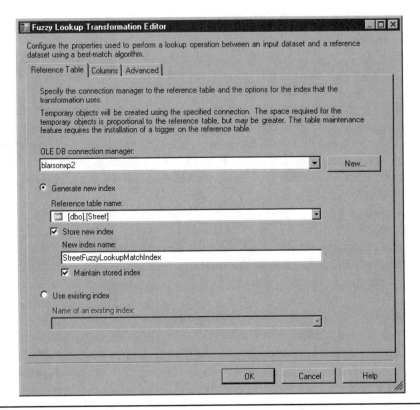

Figure 7-73   *The Reference Table tab of the Fuzzy Lookup Transformation Editor dialog box*

so any changes to the source lookup table cause an update to the match index. If a match index already exists in the database, we can use it directly by selecting Use Existing Index and selecting the name of the index table.

Once the match index is configured, we can use the Columns tab to map one or more columns from the data flow to columns in the source lookup table. This is done by dragging a column from the Available Input Columns and dropping it on the corresponding column in the Available Lookup Columns. We can then set the behavior of the transformation using the Advanced tab. The *Advanced tab* enables us to specify the maximum number of source table records we want the transformation to find for each input row. This is usually one. We can also specify the similarity score threshold for this transformation. This works on the same scale as the Fuzzy Grouping transformation.

The Fuzzy Lookup transformation adds one column to the output for each column from the source lookup table that is used in the lookup. In addition to this, the _Similarity and _Confidence columns are added. The _Similarity column shows the similarity score for the lookup done for that row. The _Confidence column shows how much confidence to place on the lookup that was just completed. Like the similarity score, the confidence figure is a number between 0 and 1, inclusive. A confidence level of 1 represents a near certainty that a value is correct. A confidence level of 0 indicates no confidence in the match at all.

Import Column   The *Import Column* transformation lets us take the content of a 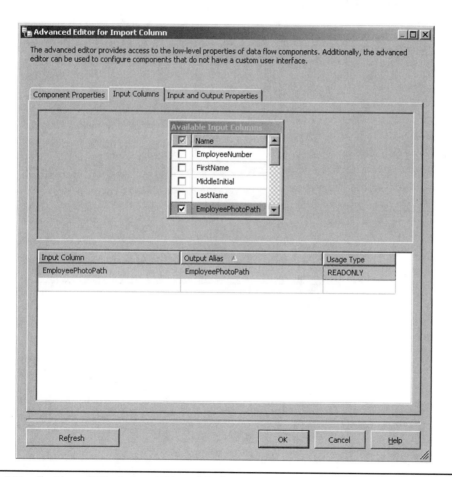set of files and insert it into a text or image column in the data flow. The pathname and filename are specified in a different column in the data flow. In this manner, the content of a different text or image file can be written to each row in the data flow. The Input Columns tab of the Advanced Editor for Import Column dialog box is shown in Figure 7-74.

Figure 7-74   *The Advanced Editor for Import Column dialog box*

Lookup   The *Lookup* transformation works similarly to the Fuzzy Lookup
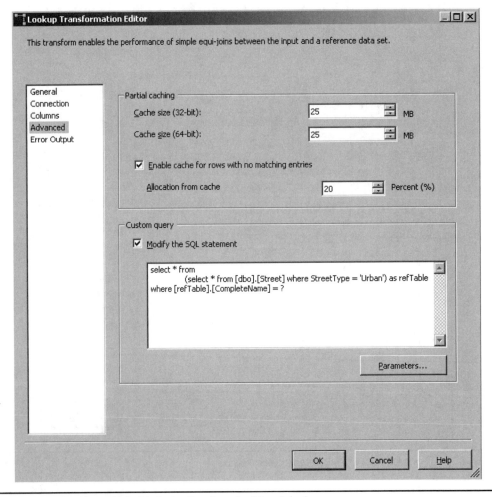
transformation. The difference is the *Lookup transformation* requires
exact matches, rather than using similarity scores. The selection of the
source lookup table and the column mapping is done in much the same way as for the
Fuzzy Lookup transformation.

One difference between the Lookup transformation and the Fuzzy Lookup
transformation is found on the Advanced tab of the Lookup Transformation Editor
dialog box, as shown in Figure 7-75. When the Lookup transformation executes,
by default it loads the entire source lookup table into cache for faster processing. If
the source lookup table is too large to be completely loaded into cache, we can set a
restriction on the amount of memory used. In Figure 7-75, the cache memory usage has
been restricted to 5MB.

Figure 7-75   *The Advanced tab of the Lookup Transformation Editor dialog box*

In addition, if only a portion of the records in the source lookup table are needed to resolve the lookups for a given Lookup transformation, we can load only the required portion of the source lookup table into memory. This is done by modifying the caching SQL statement and adding a WHERE clause. In Figure 7-75, a WHERE clause has been added so only the urban streets in the Street lookup table are loaded into memory. The additional WHERE clause is the highlighted portion of the Caching SQL statement.

The Configure Error Output dialog box lets us determine whether an unresolved lookup is ignored, sent to the error output, or causes the transformation to fail.

Merge   The *Merge* transformation merges two data flows together. For the Merge transformation to work properly, both input data flows must be sorted using the same sort order. This can be done by using the Sort transformation in each data flow prior to the Merge transformation. Alternately, if the rows coming from the data source are already sorted by the data provider, you can set the IsSorted property to true for the output of that data provider. The IsSorted property is only available in the Advanced Editor dialog box for the data source. The two data flows are merged together, so the output is sorted in the same manner as the inputs.

Figure 7-76 shows two lists of street addresses that are being merged together. Each input is sorted first by the street name, and then by the street number. When the records from the two inputs are merged together, the resulting output will also be in street name, street number order.

All of the rows in both of the input data flows are presented in the merged output. For example, say 450 rows are in the first input data flow and 375 rows are in the second input data flow. There will be 825 rows in the output data flow.

Merge Join   The *Merge Join* transformation enables us to merge two data flows together by executing an inner join, a left outer join, or a full outer join. As with the Merge transformation, both of the input data flows must be sorted. With the Merge Join transformation, both of the data flows must be sorted by the columns to be used as the join condition.

Figure 7-77 shows the Merge Join Transformation Editor dialog box. In this example, an inner join is being used to join the Address Table data flow with the Street Lookup List data flow. The *join key* requires the StreetName column from the Address Table to match the CompleteName column from the Street Lookup List. Because an inner join is being used, only those rows that contain a match are included in the output.

If a left outer join were used in the example in Figure 7-77, all of the columns from the Address Table data flow would be included in the output, even if a matching column in the Street Lookup List data flow were not found. (The Address Table data flow was identified as the left input flow when it was connected to the Merge Join transformation.) If a full join were used in the example in Figure 7-77, all of the

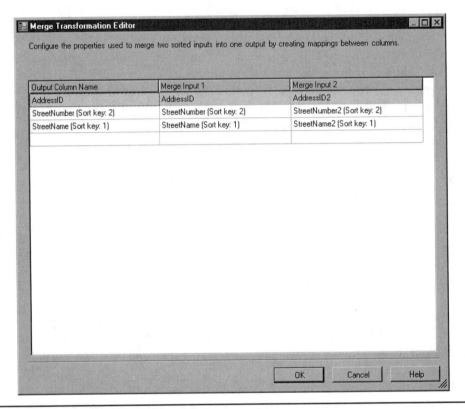

Figure 7-76   *The Merge Transformation Editor dialog box*

columns from both the Address Table data flow and the Street Lookup List data flow would be included in the output. The output of the Merge Join transformation is always sorted on the join key column or columns.

Multicast   The *Multicast* transformation lets us take a single data flow and use it as the input to several data flow transformations or data flow destination items. The Multicast transformation simply copies the data flow and sends it in multiple directions. Figure 7-78 shows the Multicast Transformation Editor dialog box. In this example, a data flow containing product information needs to go to the online store database, to the sales processing system, and to the FTP directory, where it can be picked up by distributed point-of-sale (POS) systems.

OLE DB Command   The *OLE DB Command* transformation enables us to execute a SQL statement for each row in the data flow. We select an OLE DB Connection Manager to determine where the SQL statement is to

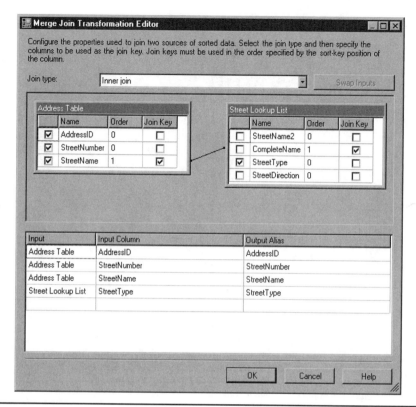

Figure 7-77   *The Merge Join Transformation Editor dialog box*

be executed. We then enter the SQL statement that is to be executed. Question marks can be used to create a parameterized query, as shown in the Advanced Editor for OLE DB Command dialog box in Figure 7-79. Column values from the data flow can then be fed into these parameters as the SQL statement is executed for each data flow. In the example in Figure 7-79, the retail price of existing product records is updated based on information in the data flow.

Percentage Sampling   The *Percentage Sampling* transformation lets us split the data flow into two separate data flows based on a percentage. This can be useful when we want to create a small sample of a larger set of data for testing or for training a data mining model. (We discuss training data mining models in the section "Data Mining Model Training Destination.") Figure 7-80 shows the Percentage Sampling Transformation Editor dialog box.

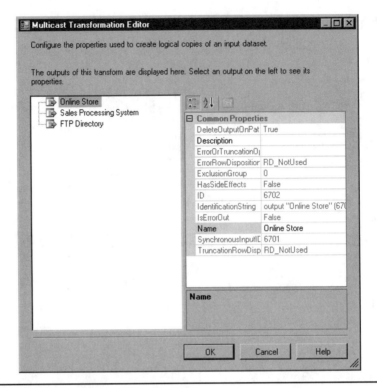

Figure 7-78 *The Multicast Transformation Editor dialog box*

Two outputs are created from the Percentage Sampling Transformation item. The first output contains the rows that were selected to be part of the sample. In the example in Figure 7-80, 10% of the total rows in the input data flow are selected to be part of the sample. These rows are sent to the first output, called Mining Model Training Output in this example. The second output contains the rows that were not selected for the sample. In this case, the remaining 90% of the total rows in the input data flow are to be sent to the second output, called Mining Model Validation Output.

The Percentage Sampling transformation selects rows at random from the input data flow. This random sampling provides a more representative sample of the entire data flow than simply selecting the top *N* rows. Because of the workings of the random sampling algorithm, the number of rows included in the sample is going to be close to the percentage specified, but it may not hit it exactly.

Pivot The *Pivot* transformation enables us to take normalized data and change it into a less normalized structure. This is done by taking the content of one or more columns in the input data flow and using it as column names in the output

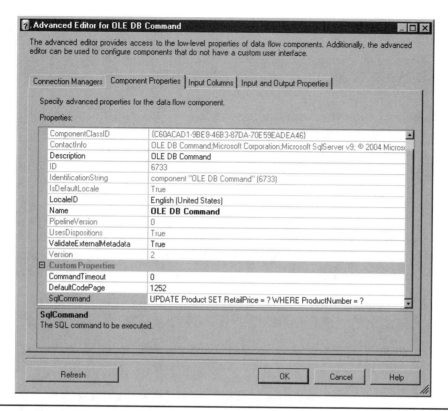

Figure 7-79   *The Advanced Editor for OLE DB Command dialog box*

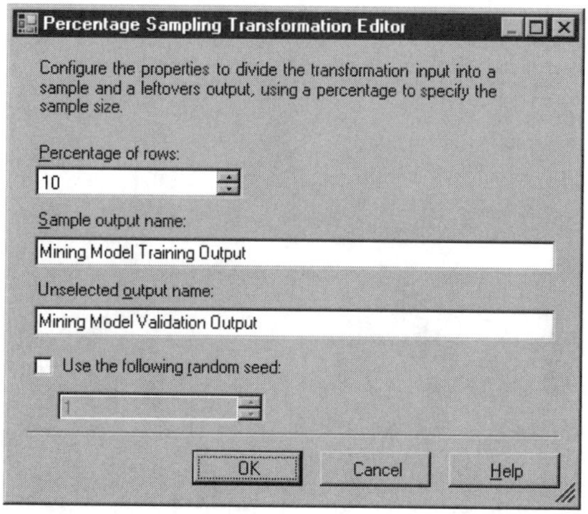

Figure 7-80   *The Percentage Sampling Transformation Editor dialog box*

data flow. The data in these newly created columns is calculated by taking an aggregate of the contents of another column from the input data flow. An aggregate must be used because a number of rows from the input data flow may define a single row in the output data flow. Figure 7-81 shows the Advanced Editor for Pivot dialog box.

Row Count   The *Row Count* transformation lets us determine the number of rows in the data flow. This count is then stored in a package variable. The package variable can then be used in expressions to modify the control flow or the data flow in the package. All of the columns in the Row Count transformation's input flow are simply passed on to the output flow. The Advanced Editor for Row Count dialog box is shown in Figure 7-82.

Row Sampling   The *Row Sampling* transformation enables us to split the data flow into two separate data flows based on the number of rows desired. The Row Sampling transformation works in the same manner as

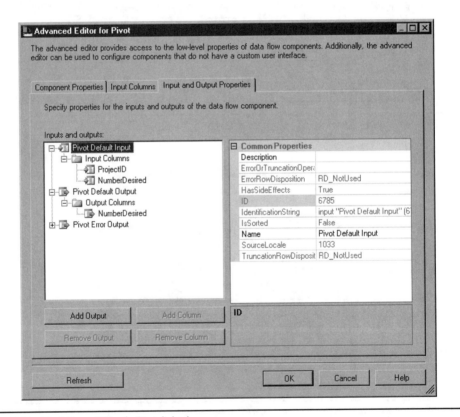

Figure 7-81   *The Advanced Editor for Pivot dialog box*

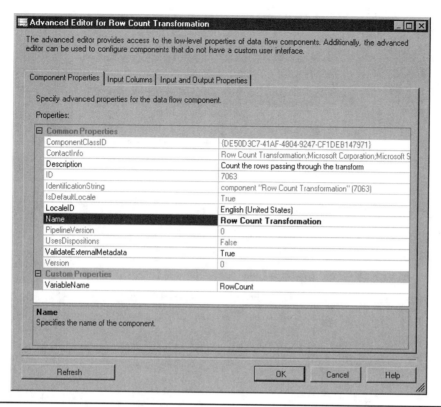

Figure 7-82   *The Advanced Editor for Row Count dialog box*

the Percentage Sampling transformation. The only difference is the Row Sampling transformation determines the number of rows in the sample based on a requested row count, rather than a requested percentage. The Row Sampling Transformation Editor dialog box is shown in Figure 7-83.

Script Component   The *Script Component* transformation lets us create .NET code for execution as part of our data flow. Even though the Script Component transformation is in the Data Flow Transformations section of the Toolbox, it can be used as a data source, a data destination, or a data transformation. Our script code could read data from a file format that is not supported by any of the Connection Managers, and then expose those rows as its output data flow. In this case, the Script Component item functions as a data source. Our script code could take rows from its input data flow and write data to a file format that is not supported by any of the Connection Managers. In this scenario, the Script Component item functions as a data destination. Finally, the script code could take rows from its input data flow, modify

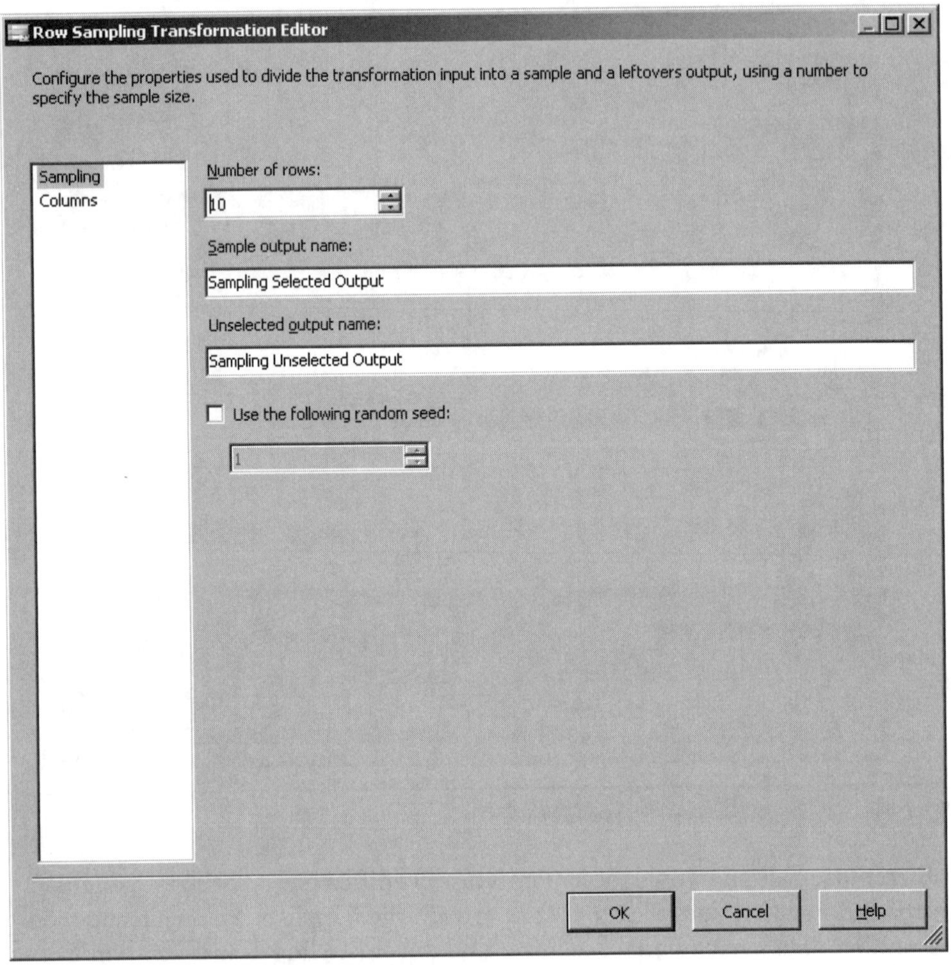

Figure 7-83 *The Row Sampling Transformation Editor dialog box*

the data in a way not supported by the other data transformations, and then expose those rows as its output data flow. Here, the Script Component item functions as a data transformation.

The data inputs and outputs that are going to be used in the script, even if they are just going to be passed through, must be defined on the Inputs and Outputs page of the Script Transformation Editor dialog box. This is shown in Figure 7-84. Make sure to use different names for the input and output columns. If we use the same name for both an input and an output, only the output column will be visible to the script code.

In the example shown in Figure 7-84, we have street names from a legacy system that were entered in uppercase. We want to change these to title case (sometimes

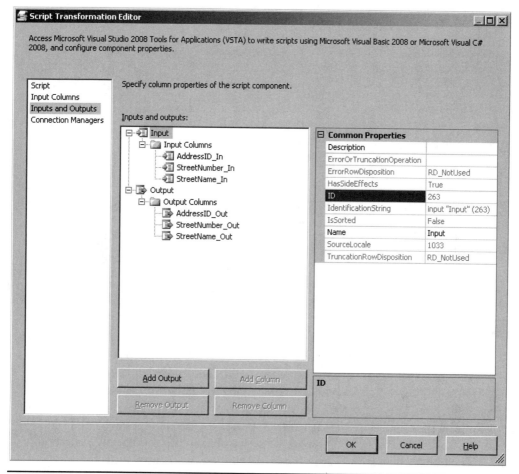

Figure 7-84   *The Inputs and Outputs page of the Script Transformation Editor dialog box*

known as proper case; the first character of each word in uppercase, with the remaining characters in lowercase) as part of our Integration Services package. The Copy Column transformation provides translations to lowercase and uppercase, but not to title case. We need to create a custom script to accomplish this task.

Clicking Edit Script on the Script page of the Script Transformation Editor dialog box displays the Microsoft Visual Studio for Applications dialog box, where we can edit the script. This is shown in Figure 7-85. The Input_ProcessInputRow method is executed once for each row in the input data flow. The Row object parameter, which is passed to this method, contains the properties that provide access to both the input and output columns defined on the Inputs and Outputs page.

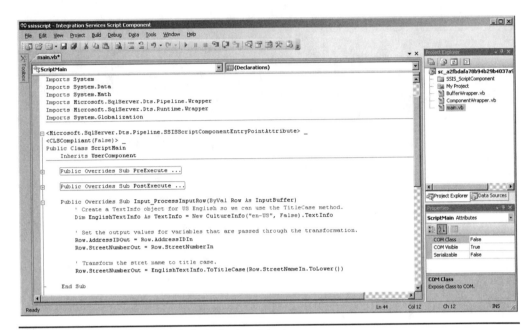

Figure 7-85 *The Microsoft Visual Studio for Applications dialog box*

The sample code simply copies the AddressIDIn and StreetNumberIn values from the input data flow to the AddressIDOut and StreetNumberOut columns in the output data flow. The StreetNameIn column is transformed first to lowercase using the ToLower method, and then to title case using the ToTitleCase method. (ToTitleCase does not work on text that is all uppercase, so we need to use the ToLower method first.) The transformed string is then assigned to the StreetNameOut column.

Slowly Changing Dimension   The *Slowly Changing Dimension* transformation enables us to use a data flow to update the information in a slowly changing dimension of a data mart. This transformation is configured using the Slowly Changing Dimension Wizard. The wizard walks us through the steps necessary to use the input data flow columns to properly update the slowly changing dimension.

The first page of the wizard after the welcome page, the Select a Dimension Table and Keys page, is shown in Figure 7-86. This wizard page requires us to select the Connection Manager that lets us connect to the data mart and to select the table containing the slowly changing dimension. This wizard page also requires us to map the input data flow columns to the fields in the dimension table and to specify which column is the business key column (the unique identifier for the dimension information).

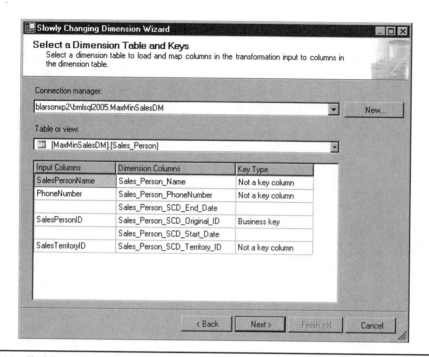

Figure 7-86 *The Select a Dimension Table and Keys page of the Slowly Changing Dimension Wizard*

The next page of the wizard, the Slowly Changing Dimension Columns page, is shown in Figure 7-87. This wizard page enables us to specify how each of the nonkey columns in the dimension table should be treated when it changes. A column such as the Sales_Person_Name column is fixed relative to the salesperson ID. A situation should not occur where a different person assumes the use of this salesperson ID. (Yes, names could change due to marriage or other events, but we will conveniently ignore that fact for this example.) This type of column is marked as a fixed attribute.

A column such as the Sales_Person_PhoneNumber column is changeable. We do not need to track previous phone numbers used by the salespeople. This type of column is marked as a changing attribute. A column such as the Sales_Person_SCD_Territory_ID column is one whose changes we want to track. This type of column is marked as an historical attribute.

The next page of the wizard, the *Fixed and Changing Attribute Options* page, enables us to specify the transformation behavior when a fixed or a changing attribute is modified. We can choose to fail the transformation when a fixed attribute is modified. We can also choose to change all historic occurrences of a changing attribute when that attribute is modified.

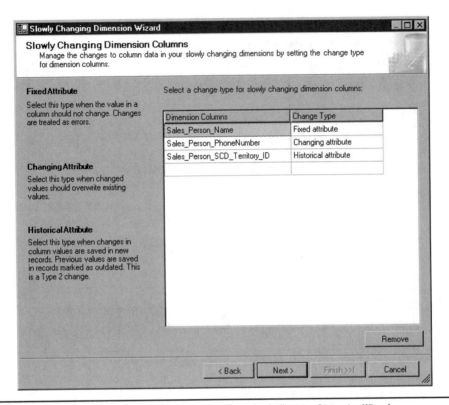

Figure 7-87   *The Slowly Changing Dimension Columns page of the Slowly Changing Dimension Wizard*

The *Historical Attribute Options* page lets us specify the method used to determine which are the historical records and which are the current records. This page is shown in Figure 7-88. The salesperson dimension used in this example has a start date and an end date that determines the current records. We use the system date at the time the new record was created to populate the date fields.

The *Inferred Dimension Members* page lets us specify whether we can infer information for dimension members that do not yet exist. When the wizard completes, it adds a number of transformations to the package, as shown in Figure 7-89. These additional transformations provide the functionality to make the slowly changing dimension update work properly.

Sort   The *Sort* transformation enables us to sort the rows in a data flow. The Sort Transformation Editor dialog box is shown in Figure 7-90. In the example in this figure, the data flow is being sorted first by the StreetType column, and then by the StreetName column. The StreetDirection column is not used as a sort column, but is passed through from the input data flow to the

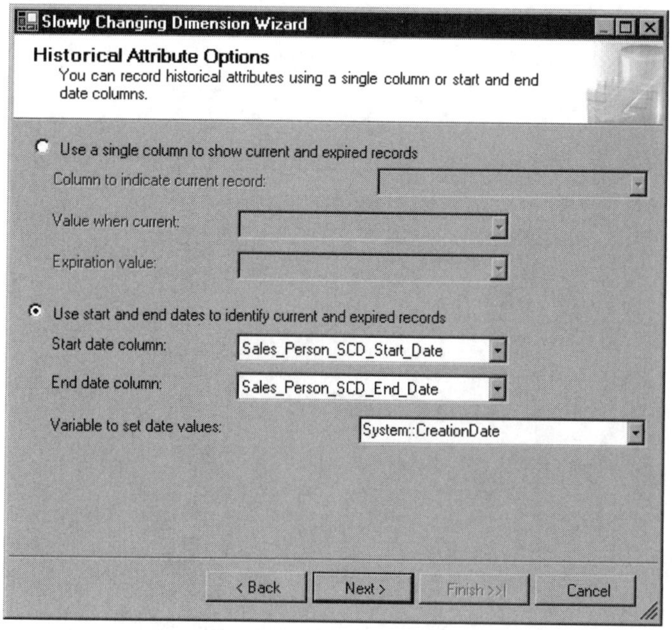

Figure 7-88 *The Historical Attribute Options page of the Slowly Changing Dimension Wizard*

output data flow. The Sort transformation can remove rows with duplicate sort keys if
Remove Rows with Duplicate Sort Values is checked.

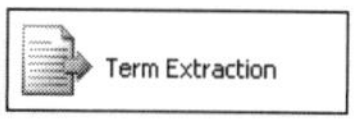

Term Extraction The *Term Extraction* transformation lets us extract a list of words
and phrases from a column containing freeform text. The Term
Extraction transformation identifies recurring nouns and/or noun
phrases in the freeform text, along with a score showing the frequency of occurrence for
each word or phrase. This information can then be used to help discover the content of
unstructured, textual data.

The Term Extraction transformation has two limitations. First, it only works with
Unicode data (the DT_WSTR or DT_NTEXT Integration Services data types). This
limitation is easily overcome by using the Data Conversion transformation to convert
single-byte strings to Unicode. The second limitation is that the Term Extraction
transformation only works with English language text. The term extraction algorithms
require knowledge of the structure and syntax of the language they are parsing.
Currently, this intelligence is only available for English.

On the Term Extraction tab of the Term Extraction Transformation Editor dialog
box, we simply select the column that contains the freeform text, and then specify the

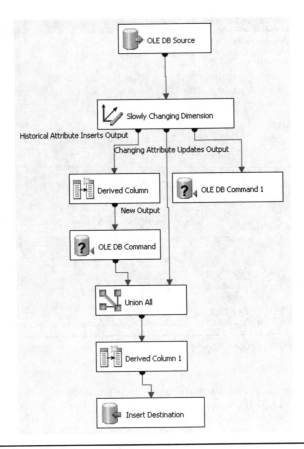

Figure 7-89   *The results of the Slowly Changing Dimension Wizard*

name of the term and score output columns. The Exclusion tab enables us to specify a database table or view that contains a list of words or phrases to exclude from the term list. The Advanced tab, shown in Figure 7-91, lets us configure the operation of the term extraction, including whether nouns, noun phrases, or both are included in the extraction and the number of occurrences that must be found before a word or phrase is added to the list.

Term Lookup   The *Term Lookup* transformation enables us to look for occurrences of a set of words or phrases in a data flow column containing freeform text. The Term Lookup transformation functions almost identically to the Term Extraction transformation. The big difference is this: The Term Lookup transformation starts with a table of terms to look for in the freeform text, whereas the Term Extraction transformation creates its own list on-the-fly.

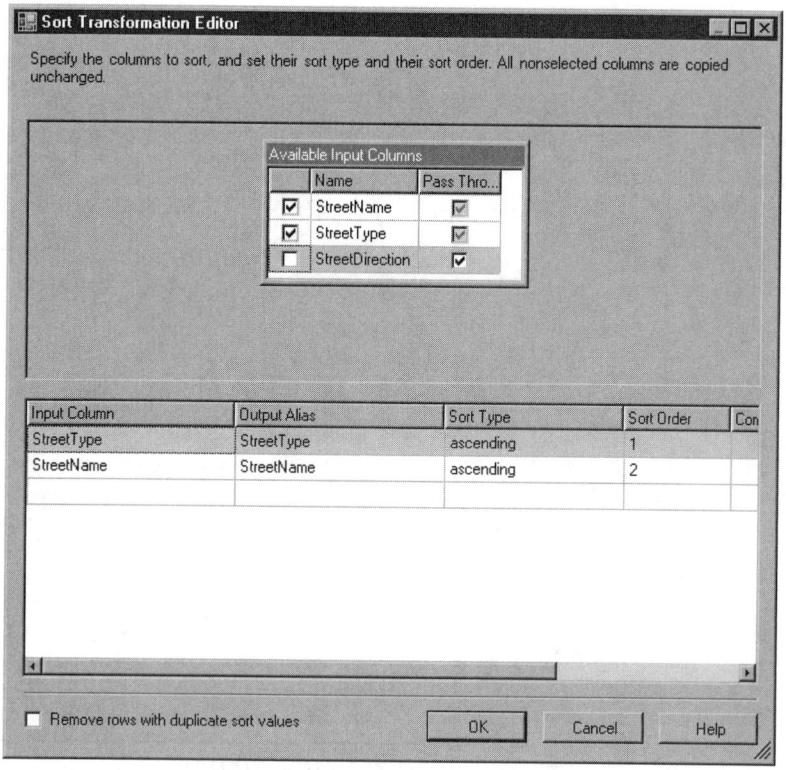

Figure 7-90   *The Sort Transformation Editor dialog box*

The Term Lookup transformation creates one row in the output data flow for each term found in the table of terms and in the text column. If the text column contains more than one term, more than one output row is created. For example, if a text column contains three of the terms from the lookup table, three rows are created in the output data flow. The same restrictions of Unicode text only and English only that applied to the Term Extraction transformation also apply to the Term Lookup transformation. The Term Lookup tab of the Term Lookup Transformation Editor dialog box is shown in Figure 7-92.

Union All   The *Union All* transformation lets us merge several data flows into a single data flow. Any number of data flows can be unioned together. The only limitation is they all must be able to contribute fields to all of the columns defined in the output. The data flows used as inputs to the Union

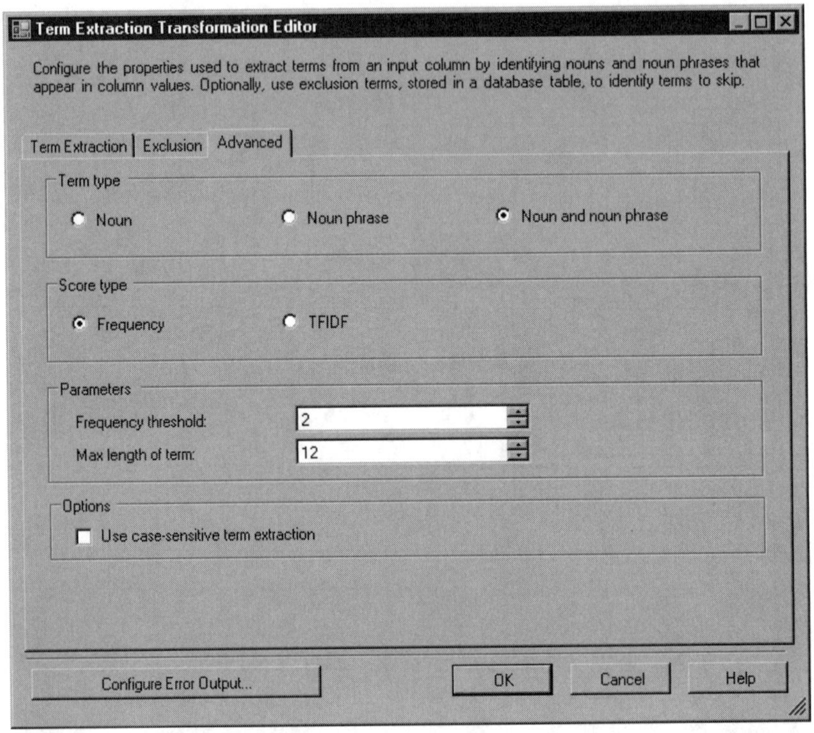

Figure 7-91 *The Advanced tab of the Term Extraction Transformation Editor dialog box*

All transformation do not need to be sorted, as with the Merge and Merge Join transformations. Consequently, the output data flow is not sorted. The Union All Transformation Editor dialog box is shown in Figure 7-93.

Unpivot The *Unpivot* transformation enables us to take a denormalized data flow and turn it into normalized data. The example shown in Figure 7-94 takes a denormalized table that contains several phone number columns—one for home phone, one for work phone, one for cell phone, and so forth—and changes it into a normalized table, with one record for each phone number. If the input data flow for our example contains the following rows:

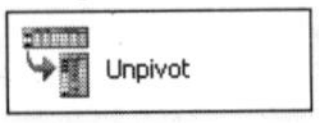

CustomerID	HomePhone	WorkPhone	CellPhone	Fax
3843	891-555-2443	891-555-9384		891-555-2923
4738	891-555-9384		891-555-3045	

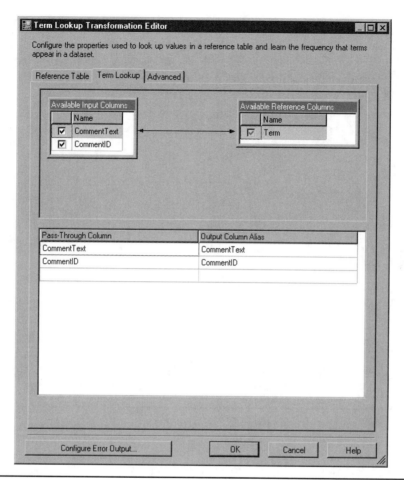

Figure 7-92   *The Term Lookup Transformation Editor dialog box*

Output Column Name	Union All Input 1	Union All Input 2	Union All Input 3
CommentText	CommentText	FeedbackText	ShopperComment
CommentID	CommentID	FeedbackID	ShopperCommentID

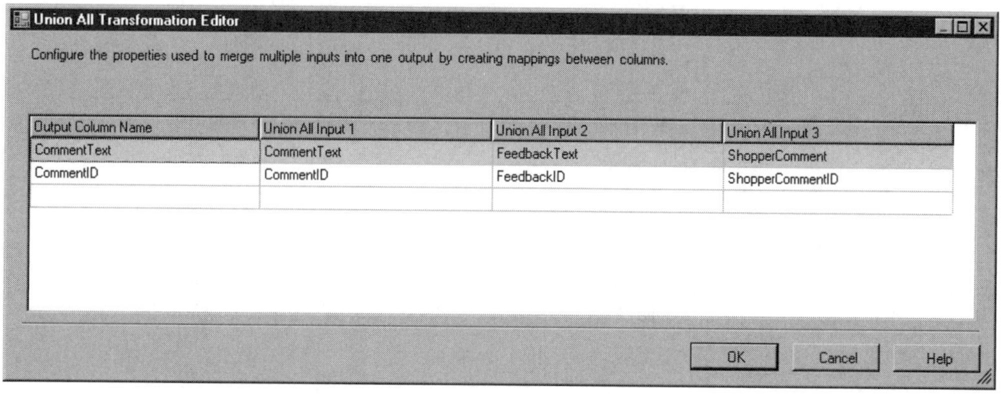

Figure 7-93   *The Union All Transformation Editor dialog box*

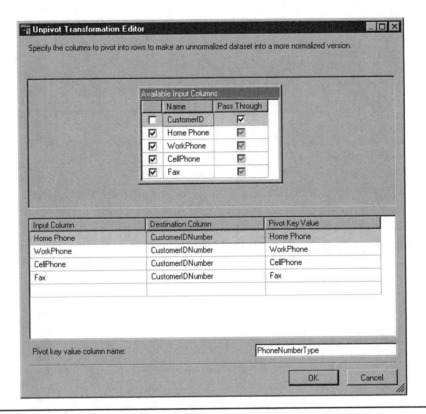

Figure 7-94   *The Unpivot Transformation Editor dialog box*

The output data flow would contain the following rows:

CustomerID	PhoneNumberType	PhoneNumber
3843	HomePhone	891-555-2443
3843	WorkPhone	891-555-9384
3843	Fax	891-555-2923
4738	HomePhone	891-555-9384
4738	CellPhone	891-555-3045

Data Flow Destinations

Now that we have all this data transformed into exactly the right format, we need to do something with it. This is the job of the data flow destinations. Let's take a look at these options for storing our data.

ADO.NET Destination   The *ADO.NET destination* enables us to use ADO.NET to connect to a data destination. We need to create an ADO.NET Connection Manager in the Connections tray for use with this data destination. Once the ADO.NET Connection Manager is created and selected, we can map the columns of the data flow to the fields in the data destination.

Data Mining Model Training Destination   The *Data Mining Model Training destination* lets us use a data flow to train a data mining model. Training a data mining model prepares the model for making predictions by gaining knowledge from a set of sample data. We discuss data mining models and their care, feeding, and training in Part IV of this book.

DataReader Destination   The *DataReader destination* enables us to use ADO.NET to connect to a data destination. We need to create an ADO.NET Connection Manager in the Connections tray for use with this data destination. Once the ADO.NET Connection Manager is created and selected, we can map the columns of the data flow to the fields in the data destination.

Dimension Processing Destination   The *Dimension Processing destination* lets us send a data flow to process a dimension. By using this destination, we can provide new values for a dimension in an Analysis Services cube. Columns from the data flow are mapped to the dimension and its attributes.

Excel Destination   The *Excel destination* enables us to send a data flow to an Excel spreadsheet file. We need to create an Excel Connection Manager in the Connections tray for use with this data destination. Once the Excel Connection Manager is created and selected, we can map the columns of the data flow to the fields in the data destination.

Flat File Destination   The *Flat File destination* lets us send a data flow to a text file. We need to create a Flat File Connection Manager in the Connections tray and define the columns that are in the text file. Once the Flat File Connection Manager is created and selected, we can map the columns of the data flow to the fields in the data destination.

OLE DB Destination   The *OLE DB destination* enables us to send a data flow to an OLE DB–compliant database. We need to create an OLE DB Connection Manager in the Connections tray for use with this data destination. Once the OLE DB Connection Manager is created and selected, we can map the columns of the data flow to the fields in the data destination.

Partition Processing Destination   The *Partition Processing destination* lets us send a data flow to process a partition. By using this destination, we can provide new values for a partition in an Analysis Services cube. Columns from the data flow are mapped to the items in the partition. We discuss Analysis Services partitions in Chapter 10.

Raw File Destination   The *Raw File destination* enables us to write a data flow to a raw data file. The Raw File format is the native format for Integration Services. Because of this, raw files can be written to disk and read from disk rapidly. One of the goals of Integration Services is to improve processing efficiency by moving data from the original source to the ultimate destination without making any stops in between. However, on some occasions, the data must be staged to disk as part of an Extract, Transform, and Load process. When this is necessary, the Raw File format provides the most efficient means of accomplishing this task.

Recordset Destination   The *Recordset destination* lets us send a data flow to a record set. The record set is then stored in a package variable, which is visible outside of the current data flow. This allows the record set to be used by other items within the package.

SQL Server Compact Destination   The *SQL Server Compact destination* enables us to send a data flow to a SQL Server Compact database. We need to create a SQL Server Compact Connection Manager in the Connections tray for use with this data destination. Once the SQL Server Compact Connection Manager is created and selected, we can map the columns of the data flow to the fields in the data destination.

SQL Server Destination   The *SQL Server destination* lets us quickly insert records from a data flow into a SQL Server table or view. The SQL Server destination is the equivalent of using the Bulk Insert task with a data flow, rather than a text file, as the source of the data. Because of this, it results in a shorter load time than is required for the same load into SQL Server using the OLE DB destination.

The Bulk Insert task is extremely fast, but it can only use text files for the data source and it does not allow any transformations to the data. The SQL Server destination enables us to pull data from any of the supported data sources, apply transformations, and then do a fast insert into a SQL Server table or view. We need to create an OLE

DB Connection Manager in the Connections tray for use with this data destination. Once the OLE DB Connection Manager is created and selected, we can map the columns of the data flow to the fields in the data destination.

Getting Under the Sink

This chapter provides a basic understanding of Integration Services package structure and content. In Chapter 8, we will look at how all of this is used to actually get data to flow from one location to another. We will play plumber and get under the sink to connect up these pipes and fittings.

Chapter 8

Fill 'er Up—Using Integration Services for Populating Data Marts

In This Chapter

- ▶ Package Development Features
- ▶ Putting Integration Services Packages into Production
- ▶ Change Data Capture

- ▶ Loading a Fact Table
- ▶ Meanwhile, Back at the Unified Dimensional Model (UDM)

To change and to improve are two different things.

—Anonymous

We have become familiar with the structure and components of Integration Services. Now it is time to begin putting the tool to use. We will take a more in-depth look at Integration Services packages and how they are produced. We will also utilize several Learn By Doing activities to gain experience in Integration Services package development.

Package Development Features

Now you have seen all the wonderful tasks and transformations provided by Integration Services. However, just as with all those gadget commercials on TV, you need to wait, because there's more. Integration Services also provides a number of features to aid in the package development process. In this section, we explore a number of features that make Integration Services packages easy to program and easy to debug.

Give It a Try

Before we begin to discover additional features of Integration Services, let's actually give it a try. We begin with a Learn By Doing exercise.

Learn By Doing—Using Integration Services to Populate the Maximum Miniatures Manufacturing Data Mart Dimensions

Feature Highlighted

▶ Creating an Integration Services package for loading data into a data mart

Business Need In Chapter 6, we created a relational database to hold the information for the Maximum Miniatures Manufacturing data mart. Now it is time to copy information from the Maximum Miniatures online transaction processing (OLTP) systems and load it into the relational database tables. We need to create two processes: one to initially populate all of the dimensional tables and one to add new manufacturing information to the fact table.

NOTE

To complete this Learn By Doing activity, you need the Maximum Miniatures Accounting database. If you have not done so already, go to www.mhprofessional.com and search for the book's page using the ISBN, which is 0071549447. Use the "Code" link to download the zip file containing the book's material. Follow the instruction within the zipped folders in the zip file to install the Maximum Miniatures Accounting database.

Steps to Create the Integration Services Project

1. Open the Business Intelligence Development Studio.
2. Click the New Project button on the toolbar.
3. Make sure Business Intelligence Projects is selected from the Project types, and then select Integration Services Project from the Templates.
4. Enter **MaxMinManufacturingDMDimLoad** for Name and set the Location to the appropriate folder. The Create directory for solution check box should be unchecked.
5. Click OK to create the project.
6. Once the project is open, right-click the Package.dtsx entry in the Solution Explorer window and select Rename from the context menu. Enter **DimensionLoad.dtsx** for the package name and press ENTER.
7. Click Yes when asked if you want to rename the package object as well.

Steps to Create the Data Source for the Load ProductType Data Flow

8. Drag a Data Flow Task item from the Toolbox and drop it on the Control Flow tab.
9. Right-click the Data Flow Task item you just created and select Rename from the context menu. Enter **Load ProductType** and press ENTER. Drag the Data Flow Task item wider so all of the new name can be seen. (You can also single-click the Data Flow Task item to edit the name of the item.)
10. Double-click the Load ProductType item. This takes you to the Data Flow tab.
11. Right-click in the Connections tray and select New ADO.NET Connection from the context menu. Click New in the Configure ADO.NET Connection Manager dialog box to create a new data connection.
12. Enter the name of the server where the MaxMinAccounting database was created in Server name. Select the appropriate method for accessing this server in the Log On to the Server section. Enter credentials if necessary. Select MaxMinAccounting from the Select or enter a database name drop-down list. Click OK to return to the Configure ADO.NET Connection Manager dialog box. Click OK again to exit this dialog box.

13. Drag an ADO.NET Source item from the Data Flow Sources section of the Toolbox and drop it on the Data Flow tab.

14. Double-click the ADO.NET Source item you just created. The ADO.NET Source Editor dialog box appears.

15. Select the MaxMinAccounting data connection that you just created in the ADO. NET connection manager drop-down list. (The server name will be in front of the database name.) Leave the Data access mode drop-down list set to Table or view. Select "dbo". "ProductTypes" from the Name of the table or the view drop-down list. Click OK.

Steps to Create the Data Destination for the Load ProductType Data Flow

16. Right-click in the Connections tray and select New OLE DB Connection from the context menu. Click New in the Configure OLE DB Connection Manager dialog box to create a new data connection.

17. Enter the name of the server where the MaxMinManufacturingDM database was created in Server name. Select the appropriate method for accessing this server in the Log on to the server section. Enter credentials if necessary. Select MaxMinManufacturingDM from the Select or enter a database name drop-down list. Click OK to return to the Configure OLE DB Connection Manager dialog box. Click OK again to exit this dialog box.

18. Drag a SQL Server Destination item from the Data Flow Destinations Section of the Toolbox, and drop it on the Data Flow tab.

19. Click the ADO.NET Source item. Click the green data flow arrow, drag it on top of the SQL Server Destination item, and drop it on this item. This connects the source to the destination.

20. Double-click the SQL Server Destination item. The SQL Destination Editor dialog box appears.

21. Select the MaxMinManufacturingDM data connection that you just created in the Connection manager drop-down list. Select DimProductType from the Use a table or view drop-down list.

22. Click Mappings to view the Mappings page. The columns from the data source (which are Available Input Columns to this data destination item) should be automatically mapped to the columns in the destination (the Available Destination Columns). You see an arrow going from each column name under Available Input Columns to the corresponding column name under Available Destination Columns. The automatic mapping occurs because the column names match. Click OK to exit the SQL Destination Editor dialog box.

Steps to Create the Load ProductSubtype Data Flow

23. Click the Control Flow tab. Drag a second Data Flow Task item on to the Control Flow tab. Rename this new Data Flow Task item Load ProductSubtype.

24. Click the Load ProductType item. Drag the precedence arrow onto the Load ProductSubtype item and drop it there. These two items are now linked by a precedence constraint. The Load ProductType item must complete successfully before the Load ProductSubtype item can execute. This is required because ProductType is a foreign key for ProductSubtype.

25. Double-click the Load ProductSubtype item. This takes you to the Data Flow tab, with Load ProductSubtype selected in the Data Flow Task drop-down list.

26. Drag an ADO.NET Source item from the Toolbox onto the Data Flow tab. Double-click this item. The ADO.NET Source Editor dialog box appears.

27. The MaxMinAccounting data connection will be selected in the ADO.NET connection manager drop-down list. Leave the Data Access Mode drop-down list set to Table or View. Select "dbo"."ProductSubtypes" from the Name of the table or the view drop-down list. Click OK.

28. Drag a SQL Server Destination item from the Toolbox and drop it on the Data Flow tab.

29. Click the ADO.NET Source item. Click the green data flow arrow, drag it on top of the SQL Server Destination item, and drop it on this item. This connects the source to the destination.

30. Double-click the SQL Server Destination item. The SQL Destination Editor dialog box appears.

31. The MaxMinManufacturingDM data connection will be selected in the Connection manager drop-down list. Select DimProductSubtype from the Use a table or view drop-down list.

32. Click Mappings to view the Mappings page. The input columns should be automatically mapped to the columns in the destination. Click OK to exit the SQL Destination Editor dialog box.

Steps to Create Additional Data Flow

33. Repeat Steps 23 through 32 to take data from the AccountingSystem.Products table and copy it to the MaxMinManufacturingDM.DimProduct table. Create the precedence arrow to connect the Load ProductSubtype and Load Product data flow tasks. (The RawMaterial and AmountOfRawMaterial columns in the AccountingSystem.Product table are not mapped to columns in the MaxMinManufacturingDM.DimProduct table.)

34. Repeat Steps 23 through 32 again to take data from the AccountingSystem. Countries table and copy it to the MaxMinManufacturingDM.DimCountry table. Create the precedence arrow to connect the Load Product and Load Country data flow tasks.

Steps to Create the Load Plant Data Flow

35. Click the Control Flow tab. Drag another data flow task item onto the Control Flow tab. Rename this new data flow task item Load Plant.

36. Click the Load Country item. Drag the precedence arrow onto the Load Plant item and drop it there.

37. Double-click the Load Plant item. This takes you to the Data Flow tab, with Load Plant selected in the Data Flow Task drop-down list.

38. Drag an ADO.NET Source item from the Toolbox onto the Data Flow tab. Double-click this item. The ADO.NET Source Editor dialog box appears.

39. We only want plant site records from the Locations table. We will use a query with a WHERE clause to filter out the records we don't want. The MaxMinAccounting data connection will be selected in the ADO.NET connection manager drop-down list. Select SQL command from the Data access mode drop-down list. Enter the following for SQL command text:

```
SELECT LocationCode AS PlantNumber,
       LocationName AS PlantName,
       CountryCode
FROM Locations
WHERE LocationType = 'Plant Site'
```

40. Drag a SQL Server Destination item from the Toolbox and drop it on the Data Flow tab.

41. Click the ADO.NET Source item. Click the green data flow arrow, drag it on top of the SQL Server Destination item, and drop it on this item.

42. Double-click the SQL Server Destination item. The SQL Destination Editor dialog box appears.

43. The MaxMinManufacturingDM data connection will be selected in the Connection manager drop-down list. Select DimPlant from the Use a table or view drop-down list.

44. Click Mappings to view the Mappings page. The input columns should be automatically mapped to the columns in the destination. Click OK to exit the SQL Destination Editor dialog box.

Steps to Create the Load Material - Machine Type - Machine Data Flow

45. Click the Control Flow tab. Drag another data flow task item onto the Control Flow tab. Rename this new data flow task item Load Material—Machine Type— Machine.

46. Click the Load Plant item. Drag the precedence arrow onto the Load Material—Machine Type—Machine item and drop it there.

47. Double-click the Load Material—Machine Type—Machine item.

48. Drag an ADO.NET Source item from the Toolbox onto the Data Flow tab. Double-click this item. The ADO.NET Source Editor dialog box appears.

49. The MaxMinAccounting data connection will be selected in the ADO.NET connection manager drop-down list. Leave the Data Access Mode drop-down list set to Table or View. Select "dbo"."CapitalAssets" from the Name of the table or the view drop-down list.

50. Click OK to exit the ADO.NET Source Editor.

51. Drag a Conditional Split item from the Data Flow Transformation section of the Toolbox, and drop it on the Data Flow tab. Rename this new data flow transformation item Filter For Molding Machines.

52. Click the ADO.NET Source item. Click the green data flow arrow, drag it on top of the Filter For Molding Machines item, and drop it on this item.

53. Double-click the Filter For Molding Machines item. The Conditional Split Transformation Editor dialog box appears.

54. We only want records for molding machines from the CapitalAssets table. We will use the Conditional Split transformation to filter out the records we don't want. Click the cell in the Output Name column and enter **Molding Machine Records**.

55. Expand the Columns folder in the upper-left corner of the dialog box.

56. Click the AssetType column and drag it to the uppermost cell in the Condition column. This will create an "[AssetType]" placeholder for this column.

57. Complete the expression in the Condition cell so it appears as follows:

```
[AssetType] == "Molding Machine"
```

58. Click OK to exit the Conditional Split Transformation Editor dialog box.

59. Drag a Multicast item from the Toolbox and drop it on the Data Flow tab.

60. Click the Filter For Molding Machines item. Click the green data flow arrow, drag it on top of the Multicast item, and drop it on this item. The Input Output Selection dialog box appears. This dialog box appears because the Conditional Split Transformation item has two outputs: one that we created called "Molding Machine Records," containing only those records that satisfy our condition expression, and the "Conditional Split Default Output," containing all other records in the data flow.

61. Select Molding Machine Records from the Output drop-down list. Click OK.

62. Drag an Aggregate item from the Toolbox and drop it on the Data Flow tab. Rename this new aggregate item Aggregate by Material.

63. Click the Multicast item. Click the green data flow arrow, drag it on top of the Aggregate by Material item, and drop it on this item.

64. Double-click the Aggregate by Material item. This opens the Aggregate Transformation Editor dialog box. Check RawMaterial under Available Input Columns. This groups the data by the RawMaterial column to give you a unique list of materials. You can use this unique list to populate the DimMaterial table. Only the RawMaterial column is included in the output of the Aggregate by Material item.

65. In the Output Alias column, change RawMaterial to **Material**.

66. Click OK to exit the Aggregate Transformation Editor dialog box.

67. Drag a SQL Server Destination item from the Toolbox and drop it on the Data Flow tab. Rename this new item SQL Server Destination—DimMaterial.

68. Click the Aggregate by Material item. Click the green data flow arrow, drag it on top of the SQL Server Destination—DimMaterial item, and drop it onto this item.

69. Double-click the SQL Server Destination—DimMaterial item. The SQL Destination Editor dialog box appears.

70. The MaxMinManufacturingDM data connection will be selected in the Connection manager drop-down list. Select DimMaterial from the Use a table or view drop-down list.

71. Click Mappings to view the Mappings page. The single input column should be automatically mapped to the single column in the destination. Click OK to exit the SQL Destination Editor dialog box.

72. Drag another Aggregate item from the Toolbox and drop it on the Data Flow tab. Rename this new Aggregate item Aggregate by Machine Type.

73. Click the Multicast item. Click the unattached green data flow arrow, drag it on top of the Aggregate by Machine Type item, and drop it on this item.

74. Double-click the Aggregate by Machine Type item. This opens the Aggregate Transformation Editor dialog box. Check AssetClass and RawMaterial in the Available Input Columns. This groups the data by the AssetClass and RawMaterial columns to give you a unique list of machine types and their materials. You can use this unique list to populate the DimMachineType table.

75. In the Output Alias column, change AssetClass to MachineType and change RawMaterial to **Material**.

76. Click OK to exit the Aggregate Transformation Editor dialog box.

77. Drag a SQL Server Destination item from the Toolbox and drop it on the Data Flow tab. Rename this new item SQL Server Destination—DimMachineType.

78. Click the Aggregate by Machine Type item. Click the green data flow arrow, drag it on top of the SQL Server Destination—DimMachineType item, and drop it onto this item.

79. Double-click the SQL Server Destination—DimMachineType item. The SQL Destination Editor dialog box appears.

80. Select DimMachineType from the Use a table or view drop-down list.

81. Click Mappings to view the Mappings page. The columns should be mapped automatically. Click OK to exit the SQL Destination Editor dialog box.

82. Drag a SQL Server Destination item from the Toolbox and drop it on the Data Flow tab. Rename this new item SQL Server Destination—DimMachine.

83. Click the Multicast item. Click the unattached green data flow arrow, drag it on top of the SQL Server Destination—DimMachine item, and drop it on this item.

84. Double-click the SQL Server Destination—DimMachine item. The SQL Destination Editor dialog box appears.

85. Select DimMachine from the Use a table or view drop-down list.

86. Click Mappings to view the Mappings page.

87. Drag AssetCode from the Available Input Columns and drop it on MachineNumber in Available Destination Columns.

88. Drag AssetClass from the Available Input Columns and drop it on MachineType in Available Destination Columns.

89. Drag AssetName from the Available Input Columns and drop it on MachineName in Available Destination Columns.

90. Drag LocationCode from the Available Input Columns and drop it on PlantNumber in Available Destination Columns.

91. Click OK to exit the SQL Destination Editor dialog box.

Steps to Save and Execute the Integration Services Package

92. Click the Save All button on the toolbar to save the completed package.

93. Click the Start Debugging button on the toolbar to execute the completed package. When the execution is complete, click Stop Debugging or the Package Execution Completed link to return to design mode.

Executing the DimensionLoad package copies data from the AccountingSystem database tables into the dimension tables of our MaxMinManufacturingDM database.

Programming in Integration Services Packages

In Data Transformation Services (DTS), creating packages was more like creating jobs in SQL Server Agent than it was like creating programs in Visual Studio. We would string together a series of steps that was to execute as a unit. We could do some programming—scripting, actually—inside a DTS package, but it was not elegant and it certainly was not fast.

Integration Services takes us much closer to the program development paradigm. We can now create variables with strong types and scopes. We can use those variables in expressions throughout our Integration Services packages, while still maintaining speed and scalability. In addition, we can define event handlers to react to certain occurrences within a package.

Variables

Variables are used within Integration Services packages to pass information between the various parts of the package. This could be from one data transformation to another, from a control task to a Connection Manager, and so forth. In prior discussions of tasks, data sources, data transformations, and data destinations, we have already seen several examples of variables in use.

Variables are managed using the Variables window, shown in Figure 8-1. (The Variables window can be opened by selecting View | Other Windows | Variables from the Main menu or by right-clicking the designer area and selecting Variables from the context menu.) Variables are added using the Add Variable button in the Variables window toolbar. The variable's name and data type must be specified when the variable is created. In addition, an initial value can be provided, if desired. As opposed to other scripting environments, variables in Integration Services are strongly typed. This allows for memory allocation planning to be done in advance rather than at run time, leading to more efficient operation. A variable's name, data type, and initial value can be edited right in the grid of the Variables window. Variables are deleted using the Delete Variable button in the Variables window toolbar.

Each variable has its own scope, which is displayed in the Scope column in Figure 8-1. The variable's *scope* is the set of locations where the variable can be accessed and utilized.

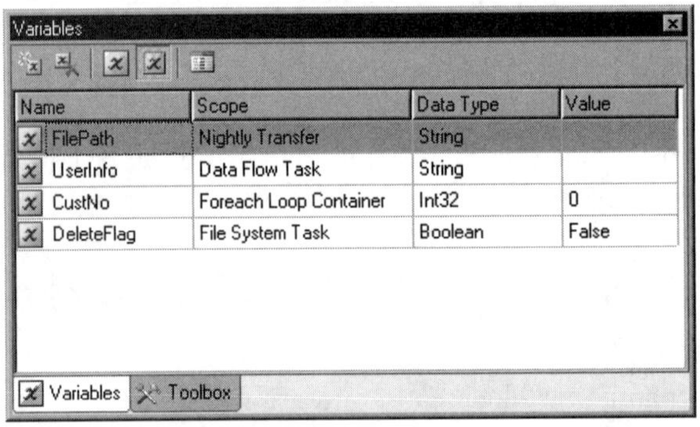

Figure 8-1   *The Variables window*

The Integration Services item that is selected when a variable is created is the item that appears in the Scope column. A variable can be used in expressions and other code that resides in the item specified in the variable's Scope column. The variable can also be used within any items that are contained inside this item. For example, if a For Loop container is selected when a variable called LoopCounter is created, that LoopCounter variable can be used in any task that is placed inside the For Loop container.

The Show System Variables button in the Variables window toolbar toggles the grid between showing and hiding all of the predefined system variables. These system variables let us include information about the package, the user executing the package, and the computer the package is running on in the expressions and code created within the package.

The Choose Variable Columns button in the Variables window toolbar displays the Choose Variables Columns dialog box, which enables us to select the columns displayed in the grid. Two columns are not displayed by default: the Namespace column and the Raise Change Event column. A *namespace* simply provides a way to create logical groupings of variables for easier debugging and maintenance. All of the system variables are in the System namespace. By default, all of the variables we create are in the User namespace. We can change the namespace of these user-defined variables by using the Choose Variables Columns dialog to display the Namespace column, and then editing the namespace in the grid.

Using the Raise Change Event column, we can choose to trigger an event each time the value of a variable changes. We can then configure an event handler that executes each time the value changes. This can be done for both system- and user-defined variables. In fact, this is the only property of the system variables that we can edit in the Variables window grid. We talk more about events and event handlers in the section "Event Handlers."

Expressions

Expressions let us modify the behavior of a package by evaluating conditions and changing properties at run time. Integration Services uses an expression syntax that is similar to that of the C# programming language. This is used to provide strongly typed variables. As was mentioned previously, strong typing is necessary to implement the advanced memory management necessary for top performance.

Literals   *Literals* are used in expressions to represent values that are known at the time the code is written. Literals can be strings, numerics, or Booleans. *String literals* are enclosed in double quotes (""). The following escape sequences can be used in string literals to represent nonprinting characters:

Escape Sequence	Character
\a	Alert
\b	Backspace
\f	Form feed
\n	New line
\r	Carriage return
\t	Horizontal tab
\v	Vertical tab
\"	Double Quote
\\	Backslash
\xhhhh	Unicode character in hexadecimal notation

Numeric literals can be expressed as integers, as decimal numbers, or as scientific notation. They can include a negative sign, but not a digit grouping symbol (the comma is the digit grouping symbol when using U.S. regional settings). Numeric literals may include a suffix that specifies the data type to assign to it.

Integer values may use the following suffixes:

Suffix	Description	Integration Services Data Type
None	Integer	DT_I4
U	Unsigned Integer	DT_UI4
L	Long	DT_I8
UL	Unsigned Long	DT_UI8

Real values and scientific notation may use the following suffixes:

Suffix	Description	Integration Services Data Type
None	Numeric	DT_NUMERIC
F	Float	DT_R4
L	Double-precision float	DT_R8

The suffixes are not case-sensitive.

Boolean literals are simply spelled as true and false. They do not include double quotes. Boolean literals are not case-sensitive.

Identifiers   Identifiers are used in expressions to represent values that are not known until run time. Identifiers can represent variables. For example:

```
@FileName
@_LoopCounter
@PackageName
```

Identifiers that represent variables are always preceded by an at sign (@). Identifiers can also represent data flow columns. For example:

```
Customer#
AmountWith6PercentTax
```

Identifiers that fit the following rules are called regular identifiers:

▶   The first character is a letter or an underscore (_).

▶   The remaining characters are letters, numbers, an underscore (_), an at sign (@), a dollar sign ($), or a pound sign (#).

The at sign that precedes each variable name is not considered part of the variable name when determining if it is a regular identifier. All of the identifiers in the previous paragraph are *regular identifiers*.

If an identifier does not fit these criteria, it is a *qualified identifier*. All this means is it must be enclosed in square brackets. For example:

```
@[Continue Processing Flag]
[Customer Name]
[12MonthTotal]
```

The first two are qualified identifiers because they contain spaces. The third is a qualified identifier because it does not start with a letter or an underscore. If a variable name is a qualified identifier, the at sign is placed outside of the square brackets.

If two identifiers within a given scope have the same name, we must provide additional information to allow the package to determine which identifier to use. When two variables have the same name, they must have different namespaces. We can then include the namespace with the variable name to make the reference unique. The name resolution operator, ::, is placed between the scope and the variable name. Whenever the name resolution operator is used, the identifier is always placed in square brackets, even if it is a regular identifier. For example:

```
@[User::UserName]
@[System::UserName]
```

When two data flow columns have the same name, we can include the name of the data flow source or transformation item where each column was created. A period is placed between the item name and the column name. For example:

```
FlatFileSource.CustomerName
DataConversion.CustomerName
```

If either the item name or the column name is not a regular identifier, they must be enclosed in square brackets. In all cases, the period is not enclosed in the brackets. For example:

```
FlatFileSource.[Customer Number]
[Character Map].ContactName
[Derived Column].[12MonthTotal]
```

Operators   The following operators are supported by expressions:

Operator	Description	Example
(data type)	Data type conversion (Cast)	(DT_WSTR)"Acme"
( )	Grouping	(4+5) * (4+7)
+	Addition	34 + 25
+	(String) Concatenation	"Sally" + " " + "Jones"
–	Subtraction	592–96
–	Negative	–234
*	Multiply	20 * 409
/	Divide	39 / 3
%	Modulo division (provides the remainder of the division)	41 % 4
||	Logical OR	@LoopCount < 5 || @Alldone
&&	Logical AND	@Continue && @ DataIsValid
!	Logical Not	!@InError
|	Bitwise Inclusive OR	@Flags | @MaskVar
^	Bitwise Exclusive OR	@Flags ^ @MaskVar

Operator	Description	Example
&	Bitwise AND	@Flags & @MaskVar
~	Bitwise Not	~@MaskVar
==	Equality	@Quantity == @MaxValue
!=	Inequality	@Quantity != @MaxValue
>	Greater Than	@Quantity > @MaxValue
<	Less Than	@Quantity < @MaxValue
>=	Greater Than or Equal To	@Quantity >= @MaxValue
<=	Less Than or Equal To	@Quantity <= @MaxValue
?:	Conditional	@Counter == @MaxCount? @DoneFlag:@ContinueFlag

Functions   The following mathematical functions are supported by the expressions:

Function	Description	Example	Result
ABS	Returns the absolute value of a numeric expression	ABS(-235)	235
EXP	Returns the exponential of a numeric expression	EXP(4)	54.598150033144236
CEILING	Returns the smallest integer that is greater than or equal to a numeric expression	CEILING(37.483)	38
FLOOR	Returns the largest integer that is less than or equal to a numeric expression	FLOOR(37.483)	37
LN	Returns the natural logarithm of a numeric expression	LN(10)	2.3025850929940459
LOG	Returns the base-10 logarithm of a numeric expression	LOG(20)	1.3010299956639813
POWER	Returns the result of raising a numeric expression to a power	POWER(10,3)	1000
ROUND	Returns the numeric expression rounded to the specified number of decimal places	ROUND(87.3863, 2)	87.39
SIGN	Returns −1 if the number is negative	SIGN(-234)	−1
SQUARE	Returns the square of a numeric expression	SQUARE(5)	25
SQRT	Returns the square root of a given numeric expression	SQRT(25)	5

The following string functions are supported by expressions:

Function	Description	Example	Result
CODEPOINT	Returns the Unicode value of the leftmost character of the string expression	CODEPOINT ("Anderson Co.")	65
FINDSTRING	Returns the one-based index of the first occurrence of a character string within a string expression	FINDSTRING ("ABC XYZ ABC", "ABC", 2)	9
HEX	Returns a string representing the hexadecimal value of an integer expression	HEX(1583)	62F
LEN	Returns the number of characters in a string expression	LEN("ABC XYZ ABC")	11
LOWER	Returns the lowercase version of a string expression	LOWER ("Anderson Co.")	anderson co.
LTRIM	Returns a string expression with all of the leading blanks removed	LTRIM (" ABC XYZ ")	ABC XYZ
REPLACE	Returns a string with a set of characters replaced by another set of characters or with an empty string	REPLACE ("ABC XYZ ABC", "ABC", "DEF")	DEF XYZ DEF
REPLICATE	Returns a string copied a specified number of times	REPLICATE ("XYZ", 3)	XYZXYZXYZ
REVERSE	Returns a string expression in reverse order	REVERSE ("ABC XYZ")	ZYX CBA
RIGHT	Returns the specified number of characters from the end of the string	RIGHT ("Anderson Co.", 7)	son Co.
RTRIM	Returns a string expression with all of the trailing blanks removed	RTRIM (" ABC XYZ ")	ABC XYZ
SUBSTRING	Returns the specified portion of a string expression	SUBSTRING ("Anderson Co.", 3, 6)	derson
TRIM	Returns a string expression with all of the leading and trailing blanks removed	TRIM (" ABC XYZ ")	ABC XYZ
UPPER	Returns the uppercase version of a string expression	UPPER ("Anderson Co.")	ANDERSON CO.

The following date functions are supported by expressions:

Function	Description	Example	Result
DATEADD	Returns a new date based on a set time period added to a specified date	DATEADD, ("day", 100, (DT_ DBTIMESTAMP) "1/1/2008")	2008-04-11 00:00:00
DATEDIFF	Returns the time period between two specified dates	DATEDIFF ("day", (DT_ DBTIMESTAMP) "1/1/2008", (DT_DBTIMESTAMP) "4/10/2008")	100
DATEPART	Returns an integer representing the selected part of the specified date	DATEPART("day",(DT_DBTIMESTAMP) "4/11/2008")	11
DAY	Returns an integer that represents the day portion of the specified date	DAY((DT_DBTIMESTAMP) "4/11/2008")	11
GETDATE	Returns the current system date and time	GETDATE()	2008-04-11 11:39:43
GETUTC DATE	Returns the current system date in Universal Time Coordinate (UTC) time	GETUTCDATE()	2008-04-11 16:39:43
MONTH	Returns an integer that represents the month portion of the specified date	MONTH((DT_DBTIMESTAMP) "4/11/2008")	4
YEAR	Returns an integer that represents the year portion of the specified date	YEAR((DT_DBTIMESTAMP) "4/11/2008")	2008

The following null functions are supported by expressions:

Function	Description	Example
ISNULL	Returns true if the expression is null; otherwise, returns false	ISNULL(@FileName)
NULL	Returns a null value of the requested data type	NULL(DT_WSTR, 50)

Event Handlers

The event handlers within a package enable us to create a control flow that executes in reaction to a certain event. The event could be an error, a warning, or a change to the value of a variable. The event could also be the beginning or the completion of a task within the package.

NOTE

Remember, the Variable Value Changed event is triggered only if you have the Raise Change Event property set to true for one or more variables in the package.

The control flow that we create to respond to an event looks exactly the same as the control flow created for the package as a whole. While the package control flow is executed exactly once each time the package is run, an event handler control flow may be executed many times or not at all. The execution of the event handler control flow depends on what happens during the running of the package. If no error conditions are encountered, the OnError event is never fired. If 20 error conditions are encountered (and this does not terminate the package as a whole), then the OnError event is executed 20 times.

Error handlers are useful for such things as

► Checking the state of the host server to make sure it is appropriate for the Integration Services package to execute

► Sending an e-mail to the administrator when an error occurs

► Doing any necessary cleanup after a process has completed

To create an event handler, click the Event Handlers tab, shown in Figure 8-2. Use the Executable drop-down list to select an item in the Integration Services package. Use the Event Handler drop-down list to select the event. Now drag-and-drop items from the Toolbox to create the functionality for this event handler.

Package Development Tools

The aids to Integration Services package development do not stop with the rich programming environment. Several features help with package creation and testing. These features make Integration Services a truly robust data transformation environment.

Import/Export Wizard

The *Import/Export Wizard* lets us quickly transfer data from one location to another. After we walk through the pages of the wizard to define the data transfer, the wizard creates an Integration Services package and executes it. The package created by the wizard can also be saved for future use.

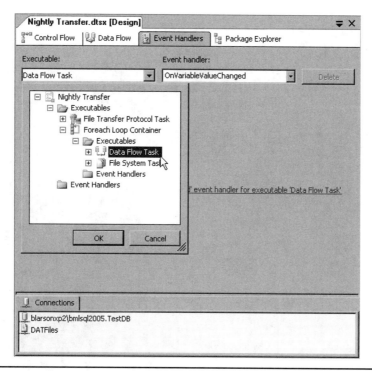

Figure 8-2   *The Event Handlers tab*

To launch the Import/Export Wizard, from the Business Intelligence Development Studio, select Project | SSIS Import and Export Wizard from the Main menu. The Import/Export Wizard can also be launched from the SQL Server Management Studio, as shown in Figure 8-3. To accomplish this, right-click a database entry in the Object Explorer window and select either Tasks | Import Data or Tasks | Export Data from the context menu. The only difference between these two menu items is the fact that the Import Data item defaults the destination to the database that was clicked, while the Export Data item defaults the source to the database that was clicked.

When the wizard is launched from the SQL Server Management Studio, we can choose to save the Integration Services package to a SQL server or to a file for future use. When it is launched from the Business Intelligence Development Studio, the package is automatically saved to the Integration Services project. A saved package can be executed again in the future in its current form, or it can be edited in an Integration Services project to serve as the starting point for a more complex data transformation.

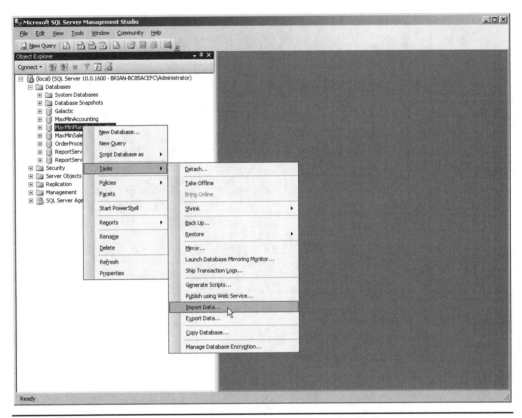

Figure 8-3   *Launching the Import/Export Wizard from the SQL Server Management Studio*

Logging

Because Integration Services packages are, for the most part, designed for unattended operation, it can be extremely important to create a log documenting the execution of the package. This type of execution log can also be helpful for testing and debugging during the creation of the package. We control the logging performed by an Integration Services package using the Configure SSIS Logs dialog box, shown in Figure 8-4.

To display the Configure SSIS Logs dialog box, open an Integration Services package in the Business Intelligence Development Studio and select Logging from the SSIS menu. Use the Providers and Logs tab to determine where the information should be logged. Select the location for the logging from the Provider Type

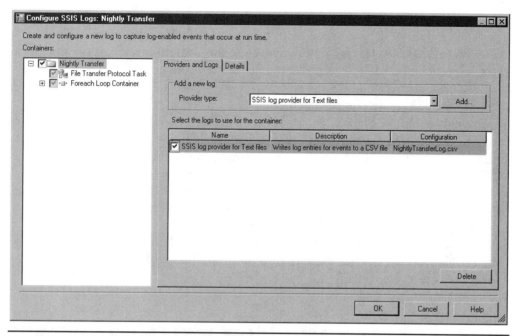

Figure 8-4   *The Providers and Logs tab of the Configure SSIS Logs dialog box*

drop-down list, and then click Add to create a new log. We can create the following types of logs:

- ▶ Comma-separated values text file
- ▶ File to be read by the SQL Profiler
- ▶ SQL Server Table named sysdtslog90
- ▶ Windows Event Log
- ▶ Extensible Markup Language (XML) text file

All of the log types, with the exception of the Windows Event Log, need to be configured to specify exactly where the logged information is to be stored. A Connection Manager is used to determine where each log type will store its entries. Click in the Configuration column to select an existing Connection Manager or create a new one.

In the Containers list, select either the entry for the package itself or an entry for one of the items in the package. Check the check box for an item to enable logging for that item. If a check box is gray, it is being enabled or disabled along with its parent item. You can break this association with the parent by clicking the grayed check box. Once you have enabled logging for an item, click one or more check boxes in the Name column for each of the log types that should be active for that item. Multiple log types can be selected.

Finally, we need to determine which events should be logged for the package or for a package item. On the Details tab, shown in Figure 8-5, check the check boxes for the events that should be logged for this item and any child items that remain associated with it. If no events are checked, only the beginning and ending of an item's execution will be logged.

In addition to the log types discussed, you can also view the log entries for a package by using the Log Events window in the Business Intelligence Development Studio. Logging must be enabled for the package or for one or more items in the package before log events are displayed in the Log Events window. However, you do not need to have any log types enabled for the events to appear in the Log Events window. The Log Events window is cleared each time you run the package.

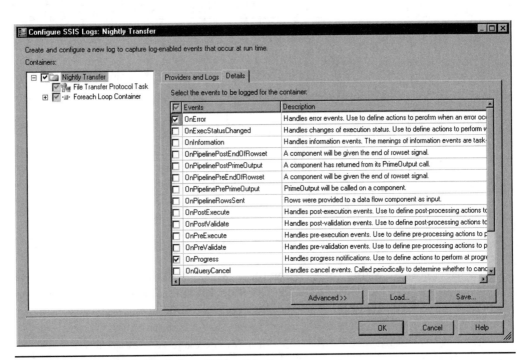

Figure 8-5   *The Details tab of the Configure SSIS Logs dialog box*

Transactions

As with operations in Transact-SQL (T-SQL), we can use transactions in Integration Services packages to ensure that our data remains in a consistent state. By using transactions, we can ensure that a series of items in a package all complete successfully, or the entire process is rolled back to the state where it was prior to the attempted changes. We can even use distributed transactions to commit or roll back changes spread across multiple servers.

Each of the items in the Control Flow Toolbox and the Integration Services package itself has a TransactionOption property that determines how it deals with transactions. This property has three possible settings:

▶ **Supported**   An item with this property setting joins a transaction if one is already active, but it does not initiate a transaction itself. This is the default setting for the property.

▶ **Required**   An item with this property setting joins a transaction if one is already active and will initiate a transaction if one is not currently active.

▶ **NotSupported**   An item with this property setting does not join a transaction if one is already active and does not initiate a transaction if one is not currently active.

The TransactionOption is set by selecting an item, and then modifying this property in the Properties window. This property is not included in the Editor dialog boxes for each item.

Consider the sample Integration Services package with the TransactionOption property settings shown in Figure 8-6. Because the package has its TransactionOption set to Required, a transaction is created when package execution begins. We call this Transaction 1, as shown in Figure 8-7. The File Transfer Protocol task participates in Transaction 1 because its TransactionOption is set to Supported.

The Foreach Loop container does not participate in Transaction 1 because its TransactionOption is set to NotSupported. The data flow task inside the Foreach Loop container cannot participate in Transaction 1, even though its TransactionOption is set to Required. The reason for this is its parent object, the Foreach Loop container, is not participating in Transaction 1. Instead, because its TransactionOption is set to Required, it initiates a second transaction called Transaction 2. All items in the data flow task participate in Transaction 2.

If any of the items in the data flow task should fail, all of the data changes within Transaction 2 are rolled back. Also, because Transaction 2 is nested within Transaction 1, all of the data changes within Transaction 1 are rolled back as well. If, on the other

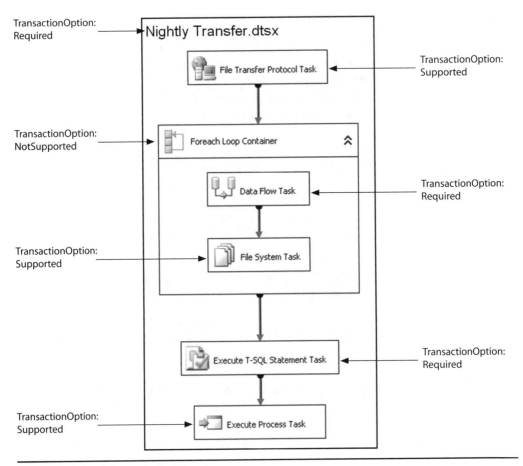

Figure 8-6   *Sample Integration Services package*

hand, all of the items in the data flow task complete successfully, the data changes in Transaction 2 are committed as soon as the data flow task completes. In other words, a rollback of Transaction 2 causes a rollback of Transaction 1, but not the other way around.

The File System task in Figure 8-6 and Figure 8-7 has its TransactionOption set to Supported, but there is no transaction for it to join. It is outside of Transaction 2 and it cannot join Transaction 1, because its parent object is not participating in that transaction. Therefore, the File System task is not a member of any transaction. Its success or failure does not affect either Transaction 1 or Transaction 2.

The Execute T-SQL Statement task has its TransactionOption set to Required. It does not need to create a new transaction, however, because it can join the active

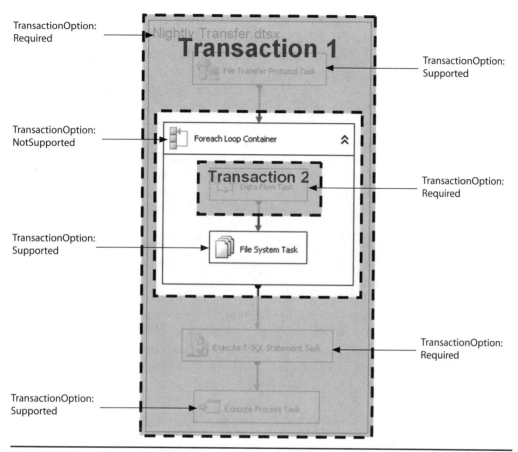

Figure 8-7   *Transactions created when executing the sample Integration Services package*

transaction, Transaction 1. If the Execute T-SQL Statement task should fail, it rolls back all data changes in Transaction 1. As mentioned earlier, the success or failure of the Execute T-SQL Statement task in Transaction 1 has no effect on Transaction 2.

The Execute Process task has its TransactionOption set to Supported. It also joins the active transaction, Transaction 1. Again, its success or failure only affects Transaction 1.

Checkpoints

There are many situations where an Integration Services package could be restarted at some point in the middle of the control flow after a failure, rather than reexecuting the entire package from the beginning. Perhaps the first portion of a package deletes an old import text file and uses File Transfer Protocol (FTP) to download a new copy of this import file. If the package fails at some point later in the process, it is probably not necessary to perform the file deletion and download again. Checkpoints provide a mechanism for performing this restart in the middle of the package.

The package includes three properties that let us enable checkpoint restarting. These are the SaveCheckpoints property, the CheckpointFilename property, and the CheckpointUsage property. The *SaveCheckpoints property* is a Boolean flag that enables or disables the saving of checkpoint information. This property must be set to true for checkpoint information to be saved.

The *CheckpointFilename property* lets us specify the filename where checkpoint information is to be saved. When a package executes, information about each successfully completed task and each committed transaction is saved to this checkpoint file. In the event of a package failure, this file is used to determine where the package can be restarted.

The *CheckpointUsage property* determines how the checkpoint file is used when a package is executed. When the CheckpointUsage property is set to Never, the checkpoint file is not used when executing a package. The package is always run from beginning to end. When the CheckpointUsage property is set to Always, the package always reads the checkpoint file and starts from the last point of failure. When the CheckpointUsage property is set to IfExists, the package looks for a checkpoint file and uses it to restart from the last point of failure, if it exists. If a checkpoint file does not exist, the package is run from beginning to end.

Package Debugging

One of the most helpful tools in program development is the capability to pause program execution at a breakpoint and examine the execution state. This feature makes it much easier to pinpoint a problem and fix it. Fortunately, Integration Services now provides this functionality.

Setting Breakpoints   We can set a breakpoint on any of the control flow tasks in a package. To accomplish this, right-click the task and select Edit Breakpoints from the context menu. The Set Breakpoints dialog box appears as shown in Figure 8-8. A breakpoint can be set on any of the events triggered by that task. We can use the Hit Count Type and Hit Count columns to determine whether execution pauses every time this event is triggered or only after a hit has occurred multiple times.

In addition to these task event breakpoints, breakpoints can be set on any line of code in the Script task. When execution is paused within a script, we may use the Step Into, Step Over, and Step Out features to move through the script code one line at a time. The step features do not function when paused at a task event breakpoint.

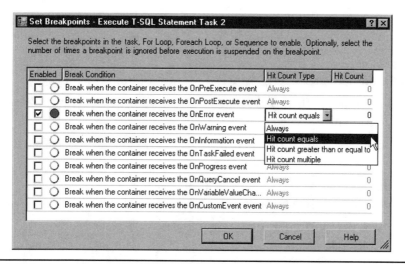

Figure 8-8   *The Set Breakpoints dialog box*

Viewing Package State   While the package execution is paused at a breakpoint, there are several places to see the current execution state of the package. The windows discussed here are opened using the Debug | Windows menu, the View menu, or the Windows Toolbar button.

▶ **Progress Color-coding**   As the tasks of a package execute, their background color changes to show the current execution status: White (waiting to execute), Yellow (currently executing), Green (completed execution successfully), and Red (completed execution with errors). While execution is paused, we can switch between the Control Flow and Data Flow tabs to see the execution status of both.

▶ **Row Counts**   As the data flow tasks of a package execute, the number of rows processed through each data flow are displayed next to the data flow arrows.

▶ **Progress Tab**   We can switch to the Progress tab to see a description of the current execution status in outline form.

▶ **Breakpoints Window**   The Breakpoints window shows all of the breakpoints set in the package and lets us disable or delete breakpoints.

▶ **Output Window**   The Output window displays status messages as the package executes.

▶ **Script Explorer Window**   The Script Explorer window enables us to view the script structure.

▶ **Watch Windows**   The Watch windows enable us to examine and modify variable values. Variable names are entered into a Watch window without a leading "@" sign.

▶ **Autos Window**   The Autos window shows the value of the variables in the current and the previous line of script code.

▶ **Locals Window**   The Locals window displays all of the system and user variables that are currently in scope.

▶ **Immediate Window**   The Immediate window is used for evaluating expressions and displaying the value of variables.

▶ **Call Stack Window**   The Call Stack window shows the hierarchy of containers around the currently executing task.

▶ **Threads Window**   The Threads window shows the threads being used to execute the current package.

▶ **Modules Window**   The Modules window lets us view script modules.

▶ **Processes Window**   The Processes window shows the currently executing processes.

Several of the debug windows are not used for debugging Integration Services packages. These are the Memory window, the Disassembly window, and the Registers window.

Viewing Data Flow   In addition to viewing the doings inside package tasks, it is also helpful (perhaps even more helpful) to see what is happening inside the data flow at various steps along the way. We do this by attaching data viewers to the data flow. The data viewer pauses the package execution and enables us to examine the rows in the data flow as it moves from one item to another.

To attach a data viewer to a data flow, we first need to view the Data Flow Path Editor dialog box. This is done by double-clicking a flow path arrow. The General page of the Data Flow Path Editor dialog box provides general information about this flow path arrow. The Metadata page of this dialog box provides information about the columns in the data flow at that point. This in itself can be helpful when developing and debugging packages. Data viewers are added to the data flow on the Data Viewers page.

Click Add on the Data Viewers page to attach a new data viewer to the data flow path. This displays the Configure Data Viewer dialog box shown in Figure 8-9. On the General tab of this dialog box, we have a choice of using a grid, a histogram, a scatter plot, or a column chart to display the data. The name of the second tab of this dialog box changes, depending on the type of data viewer that is selected. Use that tab to select the data flow columns that should be displayed in the data viewer.

Multiple data viewers can be added to the same flow path arrow to provide different views of the same data. A data viewer icon is placed next to the flow path arrow to show

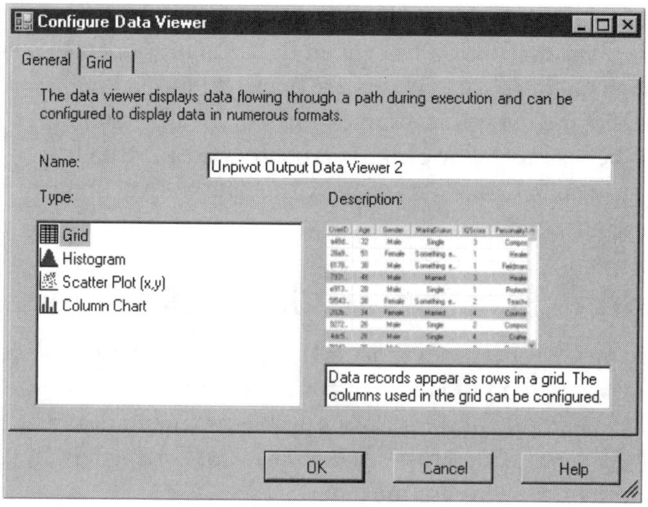

Figure 8-9   *The Configure Data Viewer dialog box*

that one or more data viewers have been attached. When the package executes, the package execution pauses whenever the package reaches a data flow with a data viewer attached. A data viewer window appears for each data viewer, as shown in Figure 8-10.

The data viewers show data one buffer at a time. The number of rows in the buffer depends on the number of columns in the data flow at that point and the width of the data in each column. By default, the buffer will contain either 10,000 rows or 10 MB of data, whichever is less.

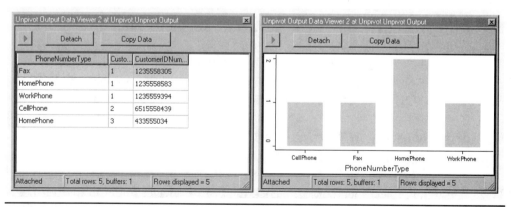

Figure 8-10   *Data Viewer windows*

When one buffer of data is loaded into the data viewer, the package execution pauses until we click the Continue button (the green triangle) or we detach all of the data viewers from that data flow. Data viewers are detached by clicking Detach. When data viewers are detached, the data flow resumes without loading data into the data viewer. Data viewers can be reattached by clicking Attach. We can visually inspect the data in the data viewer or click Copy Data to copy the data to the clipboard for saving or analysis in another application.

Migrating from SQL Server 2000 DTS Packages

It should be clear by now that, even though Integration Services provides all of the functionality that was found in Data Transformation Services in SQL Server 2000, it is a completely different animal. This causes problems when migrating current DTS packages from SQL Server 2000 to SQL Server 2008. Fortunately, SQL Server 2008 gives us several options to help ease the pain.

Executing Without Migration

In order to have support for SQL Server 2000 DTS packages, you must install the SQL Server 2000 DTS run-time engine by doing the following:

▶ Select the Client Tools Backward Compatibility option during installation of SQL Server 2008.

▶ Run the SQLServer2005_BC.msi install from your SQL Server 2008 install media.

The SQL Server 2000 DTS run-time engine lets us schedule and execute SQL Server 2000 DTS packages.

Executing from Within an Integration Services Package

As noted in Chapter 7, we can execute DTS packages as part of an Integration Services package using the Execute DTS 2000 Package task. This enables us to use many of the Integration Services features, such as logging and event handlers, with the DTS packages. The SQL Server 2000 DTS run-time engine must be installed to use this task.

Using the Migration Wizard

SQL Server 2008 also provides a SQL Server Integration Services Migration Wizard for converting DTS packages to Integration Services packages. To launch the Migration Wizard, use the Project menu or right-click the SSIS Packages folder in the Business Intelligence Development Studio Solution Explorer window. Select Migrate DTS 2000

Package from the context menu. The Package Migration Wizard appears and walks you through the migration process.

Custom DTS tasks, some ActiveX Script tasks, and other items in your DTS packages may be unable to be converted by the Migration Wizard. The items that can be converted become tasks in a new Integration Services package. Each item that cannot be converted from DTS is placed into a new DTS package, along with any connections it requires. These intermediate packages are then called from the new Integration Services package using the Execute DTS 2000 Package task.

Putting Integration Services Packages into Production

Integration Services packages can be executed in the Business Intelligence Development Studio. This is convenient for development and debugging, but it probably is not the way you want to use these packages in a production environment. This section looks at how we deploy packages to our servers and execute those packages once they are there.

Deploying Integration Services Packages

In most cases, Integration Services packages are developed on a test or development server and put into regular usage on one or more production servers. This means we need to deploy the package from the test or development environment to the production environment. Fortunately, Integration Services offers several tools to allow this to happen in a convenient and easily maintainable manner.

Package Configurations

The first thing we need as we prepare to deploy a package to a different server is a straightforward means of modifying the server-specific information in the package. Package configurations provide us with just such a tool. We use the package configurations feature to create one or more stores of configuration information that are external to the package. These external stores can be easily modified as the server-specific information changes from server to server.

To create package configurations, open the Integration Services package in the Business Intelligence Development Studio. Select Package Configurations under the SSIS menu. The Package Configurations Organizer dialog box appears. Check Enable Package Configurations to enable package configurations for this package.

Click Add to create a new package configuration. This launches the Package Configuration Wizard. On the Select Configuration Type page of the wizard, select the type of configuration using the Configuration Type drop-down list.

The following types of configurations are supported:

▶ **XML Configuration File** The configuration values for several package items are stored in an XML file. Use Configuration Filename to specify the path and filename of the XML file, or use Environment Variable to specify the name of a Windows environment variable that will contain the path and filename of the XML file.

▶ **Environment Variable** The configuration value for a single package item is stored in a Windows environment variable. Use the Environment Variable dropdown list to select the name of an existing environment variable, or type in the name of a new environment variable.

▶ **Registry Entry** The configuration value for a single package item is stored in a Windows registry entry. Use Registry Entry to specify the name of the registry key, or use Environment Variable to specify the name of a Windows environment variable that will contain the name of the registry key.

▶ **Parent Package Variable** The configuration value for a single package item is stored in a variable in the parent package that is launching this package through the Execute Package task. Use Parent Variable to specify the name of the parent variable, or use Environment Variable to specify the name of a Windows environment variable that will contain the name of the parent variable.

▶ **SQL Server** The configuration values for several package items are stored in a SQL Server table. Use the Connection drop-down list to select an existing OLE DB Connection Manager, or click New to create one. Use the Configuration Table drop-down list to select an existing table to store the configuration information, or click New to create one.

The package configuration can contain values for any or all of the following:

▶ Package-scope variable properties
▶ Task-scope variable properties
▶ Task properties
▶ Connection Manager properties
▶ Package properties

If we select the XML Configuration File or the SQL Server configuration type, we need to place check marks on the Select Properties to Export page for each of the properties we want included in the XML file. If we select the Environment Variable, Registry Entry, or Parent Package Variable configuration types, we need to highlight on the Select Property page the property we want to provide a value for. This completes the SSIS Configuration Wizard.

We may create multiple configurations for the same package. Integration Services attempts to load each configuration in order. The last value loaded in a particular property is the value that is used during package execution. We can change the order in which the configurations are loaded using the up and down arrows in the Package Configuration Organizer dialog box. Any configurations that cannot be found are ignored.

Creating a Package Deployment Utility

To easily deploy the package to another server, we need to create a package deployment utility. The package deployment utility installs the package on a server. In addition, the package deployment utility sets up the necessary package configurations.

To create a package deployment utility, open the package in the Business Intelligence Development Studio. Right-click the project entry in the Solution Explorer window and select Properties from the context menu. This displays the Property Pages dialog box for this project.

On the Deployment Utility page of the Property Pages dialog box, there are three properties to set. The *AllowConfigurationChanges property* determines whether the package configuration settings can be changed at the time the package is installed on another server. The *CreateDeploymentUtility property* determines whether a package installer is created for this project. To create a package deployment utility, this property must be set to True. The *DeploymentOutputPath property* determines the location where the package deployment utility is created. By default, it is set to the binDeployment folder within the project folder.

Once the CreateDeploymentUtility property has been set to true, the package deployment utility can be created by building the project. This is done by right-clicking the project entry in the Solution Explorer and selecting Build from the context menu. The Output window shows us the progress of the build process and whether the build failed or was successful.

NOTE

All of the packages in the Integration Services project are part of the package deployment utility that results from the build.

Installing with a Package Deployment Utility

Once the package deployment utility has been created, copy the entire contents of the Deployment folder to a location that can be accessed by the target server. From the target server, execute the DTSInstall.exe file in the package deployment utility. This launches the SSIS Package Installer. Choose between installing the package as part of the file system or in SQL Server. In most cases, the SQL Server option is used if SQL Server is to be used to share the package between servers. We can also choose whether to have the package validated after installation. The validation lets us know if the package is likely to function properly on the new server, so it is probably a good idea.

If a file system installation is selected, we need to specify the file path for the installation. If a SQL Server installation is selected, we need to specify the SQL Server name and login credentials. We also need to specify a folder for the SQL Server installation. This folder holds the configuration files. If the AllowConfigurationChanges property was set to True, we can change the settings of the configurable properties. If package validation was selected, pay attention to the warnings and error messages that result from the validation process.

NOTE

The DTS Server Windows service must be running before we attempt to do a SQL Server installation.

After we install a package to SQL Server, we can manage that package by creating a connection to that server in the SQL Server Management Studio. To do this, we select Integration Services in the Registered Servers window and connect to an Integration Services server. An Integration Services server is any PC that is running the DTS Server Windows service.

Executing Integration Services Packages

Integration Services packages can be executed in a number of different ways:

- ▶ In the Business Intelligence Development Studio
- ▶ In the SQL Server Management Studio
- ▶ As part of a SQL Server job
- ▶ From the command line using the dtsexec command line utility
- ▶ From .NET code using the Package class in the Microsoft.SqlServer.Dts.Runtime library

The dtutil command line utility can be used to copy, move, delete, or validate the existence of an Integration Services package.

Change Data Capture

One of the biggest challenges of the Extract, Transform, and Load (ETL) process is determining which records need to be extracted from the source data and loaded into the data mart. For smaller dimensional tables that are not used to populate slowly changing dimensions, we may choose to truncate the target table and refill it with all of the data from the source with every load. This won't work for fact tables, large dimensional tables, and slowly changing dimensional tables. In these situations, we need to determine what data has changed since the last extract and only grab those records.

There are several methods for determining which data has changed since the last extract. They include:

▶ Adding create and last update fields to the database table

▶ Adding flag fields to indicate when records have been extracted

▶ Creating triggers or stored procedures to replicate changes to change capture tables

All of these approaches add overhead to the transactional system and can even require changes to the front-end systems that create the transactions.

If our source data is coming from a SQL Server 2008 database, we have a new feature to make this process much easier. That feature is known as *change data capture*. Rather than working from the tables themselves, change data capture uses the SQL transaction log to capture data modifications. These modifications are then written to a set of change data capture tables. Our ETL process can then read data from the change capture tables to update the data mart.

Change Data Capture Architecture

As inserts, updates, and delete transactions occur in a SQL Server database table, they are recorded in both the SQL transaction log and in the table itself. While the table contains the net result of these changes, the SQL transaction log contains a record of the changes themselves. This allows the SQL server to maintain data integrity as the modifications are being made and allows for these modifications to be re-created if a log backup is applied as part of database recovery.

The SQL transaction log, therefore, has just the information we need to determine what data changes need to occur in our data mart. Unfortunately, the SQL transaction

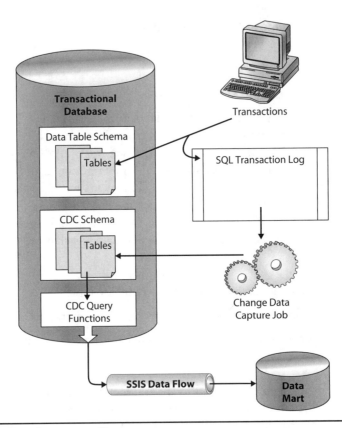

Figure 8-11   *The change data capture architecture*

log is in a format that can only be used internally by the SQL Server database engine. Change data capture provides us with a utility that can harvest the change information from the SQL transaction log and convert it to a format that can be easily understood and used for other purposes. This utility is run as part of a SQL Agent Job, as shown in Figure 8-11.

The transaction information is converted into a more readily usable format and stored in a *change table*. One change table is created for each table that is being tracked by change data capture. The change tables are created in the cdc schema, which is created specifically for that purpose.

Change data tracking also provides a method for creating a set of functions to facilitate easy retrieval of the change information from a change table. These functions return a table-valued result containing all of the changes made to a particular table during a specified period of time. The records in this result set make it possible for a program or an Integration Services package to re-create the changes in another data source, such as a data mart.

Enabling Change Data Capture

Enabling change data capture is a two-step process. This feature must first be enabled for the database as a whole. Once this is done, change data capture must also be enabled for each table individually.

The following system stored procedure will enable change data capture for a specified database:

```
USE OrderProcessingSystem
EXEC sys.sp_cdc_enable_db
```

This example will enable change data capture in the OrderProcessingSystem database.

In addition to enabling change data capture for each database, it must be enabled for a given table. This is done with a command similar to the following:

```
EXECUTE sys.sp_cdc_enable_table
    @source_schema = N'dbo'
  , @source_name = N'Orders'
  , @role_name = N'cdc_Admin'
  , @supports_net_changes = 1
```

This example will enable change data capture on the dbo.Orders table. The @role_ name parameter defines a database role that will be used to establish database rights for the change data capture process. This database role will be created, if it does not already exist in the database.

All Changes versus Net Changes

As stated, change data capture provides a table-valued function that returns all of the changes made to a table in a given time period. If the same record is updated three times during that time period, the function will return three sets of rows: one set for each change. In some cases, we may care only about the current state of a record at the end of the time period. We may not need to know all of the individual changes along the way.

To support this situation, change data capture has an optional setting to support net changes. When the @supports_net_changes function is set to 1, the change data capture for this particular table will support the net changes feature. This feature provides a second function that returns a single record representing the net effect of the changes made to each record over the given time period.

The Change Table

One change table is created for each table where change data capture has been enabled. The table is named for the schema and table name of the source table as follows:

```
cdc.schemaname_tablename_CT
```

The change table has one column that mirrors each column in the source table where changed data is being captured. These columns have the same name and, in most cases, the same data type as the corresponding column in the source table.

The default, as shown in our example of the dbo.sp_cdc_enable_table stored procedure, is to capture changes for all of the columns in a table. The dbo.sp_cdc_enable_table stored procedure has an optional parameter, @captured_column_list, which enables us to capture changes to only selected columns in a table. Enabling change data capture on selected columns would be done as follows:

```
EXECUTE sys.sp_cdc_enable_table
    @source_schema = N'dbo'
  , @source_name = N'Orders'
  , @role_name = N'cdc_Admin'
  , @captured_column_list = N'CustomerAccount, Product, SalesPerson'
```

In addition to the columns that mirror the source table, the change table contains several columns of meta data, as follows:

▶ **__$start_lsn** The log sequence number (LSN) assigned to this change. All changes committed within the same transaction will have the same LSN. The LSN shows the order in which transactions occurred.

▶ **__$end_lsn** This column may be utilized in future versions of SQL Server. In SQL Server 2008, it is always NULL.

▶ **__$seqval** A sequence number used to determine the order of changes that are within the same transaction and thus have the same LSN.

▶ **__$operation** The operation that caused the change as follows:
   1 - delete
   2 - insert
   3 - update (values prior to the update)
   4 - update (values after the update)

▶ **__$update_mask** A bit map indicating which columns were affected by an update.

The Validity Interval

In addition to creating a SQL Agent Job to capture change data from the SQL transaction log, the sys.sp_cdc_enable_db stored procedure creates a SQL Agent Job to remove old change data from the change tables. This prevents the change tables from growing indefinitely. It also means that there is a limited time period during which change data is available. This time period is known as the *validity interval*. By default, the validity interval is three days.

Returning the Change Data

Change data capture provides a method for returning the change data for a given interval for a given table. This takes the form of one or two table-valued functions. Two if the net change option is enabled. One if the net change option is not enabled.

Enabling net change capture for a given table creates the table-valued functions to retrieve change data for that table. These functions are created in cdc schema and are named cdc.fn_cdc_get_all_changes_*schemaname_tablename* and cdc.fn_cdc_get_net_changes_*schemaname_tablename*. These functions take a beginning LSN and an ending LSN as parameters. To save us the trouble of looking up the LSN for a particular date and time, Microsoft has provided a means of generating the source code for wrapper functions that take datetime values rather than LSNs to define the time period. These wrapper functions have the same name as their corresponding functions, but are in the dbo schema rather than the cdc schema.

The following code will generate and execute the source code to create the wrapper functions:

```
CREATE TABLE #WrapperSource (FunctionName sysname, SourceCode
nvarchar(max))


INSERT INTO #WrapperSource
EXEC sys.sp_cdc_generate_wrapper_function

DECLARE @CurrFunctionName sysname
DECLARE @SourceCode nvarchar(max)

SELECT @CurrFunctionName = MIN(FunctionName)
FROM #WrapperSource

WHILE @CurrFunctionName IS NOT NULL
BEGIN
      SELECT @SourceCode = SourceCode
      FROM #WrapperSource
```

```
        WHERE FunctionName = @CurrFunctionName

        EXEC sp_executesql @SourceCode

        SELECT @CurrFunctionName = MIN(FunctionName)
        FROM #WrapperSource
        WHERE FunctionName > @CurrFunctionName
END

DROP TABLE #WrapperSource
```

The call to the wrapper function to return all changes for a given time period is as follows:

```
SELECT *
FROM dbo.fn_all_changes_dbo_Orders('08/09/2008', '08/10/2008', 'all')
```

Both the starting date/time and the ending date/time must fall within the validity interval. If this is not the case, the wrapper function will not be able to find a valid LSN to correspond with the date/time and you will receive the following error message:

```
An insufficient number of arguments were supplied for the procedure or
function cdc.fn_cdc_get_all_changes_ ... .
```

Loading a Data Mart Table from a Change Data Capture Change Table

In order to utilize the data in the change table, we need to create an Integration Services package. This package will use our wrapper function to query data from the change table and then apply those changes to a target table in the data mart. In this section, we will explore the control flow and the data flow of a package that does just that.

Control Flow for Loading Data from Change Data Capture

The control flow for an Integration Services package that loads data from change data capture is shown in Figure 8-12. This control flow has three steps:

1. Finding the start and end dates to use for this data load and creating a query that uses those start and end dates.
2. Load the data from the change data table into the data mart.
3. Save the end date so the package knows where to start from the next time it is run.

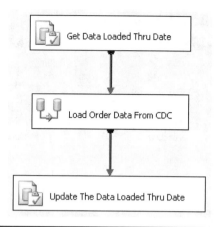

Figure 8-12 *The change data capture data load control flow*

"Get Data Loaded Thru Date" is an Execute SQL task. It runs a query against a table called DataLoadedThru to get the start and end dates for this data load. The query is:

```
SELECT CONVERT(nvarchar(50), OrderDataLoadedThru, 121) AS DataLoadStart,
       CONVERT(nvarchar(50), DATEADD(d, 1, OrderDataLoadedThru), 121)
                                                        AS DataLoadEnd
FROM dbo.DataLoadedThru
```

This query gets the previous end date to use as the new start date. It assumes the Integration Services package is run every 24 hours, so it uses the start date plus one day as the new end date. Care must be taken with this setup to ensure the change data capture has been processed past the calculated end date by the time this package is run.

This Integration Services package uses two variables to hold the dates returned by this query. We tell the Execute SQL task that our query will only return one record in the result set. Then, we set the variable mappings, as shown in Figure 8-13.

A third Integration Services variable uses the DataLoadStart and DataLoadEnd variables to create a query. This variable is called DataLoadQuery. We set the EvaluateAsExpression property of this variable to true and set the Expression property to:

```
"SELECT OrderDate, CustomerAccount, Product, Store, Promotion,
SalesPerson, StoreSales, UnitSales, __CDC_OPERATION AS Operation
FROM dbo.fn_all_changes_dbo_Orders('" + @[User::DataLoadStart]
    + "', '" + @[User::DataLoadEnd]  + "', 'all')
ORDER BY __CDC_STARTLSN, __CDC_SEQVAL"
```

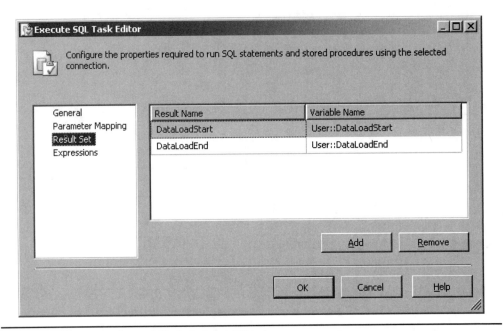

Figure 8-13   *Mapping results to variables in the Execute SQL task*

After this Execute SQL task has run its query and as Integration Services is moving on to the next task, the expression for the DataLoadQuery is reevaluated. This causes the query to be rebuilt using the dates discovered in the DataLoadedThru table. This query string will be utilized in the Load Order Date From CDC data flow.

Skipping the data flow for a moment, we come to the last step in the control flow: Update The Date Loaded Thru Date. This Execute SQL task uses the following query to update the table storing the last date processed. The code is as follows:

```
UPDATE dbo.DataLoadedThru
    SET OrderDataLoadedThru = DATEADD(hh, 24, OrderDataLoadedThru)
```

Data Flow for Loading Data from Change Data Capture

Now let's look at the detail of the data flow. This is shown in Figure 8-14. The control flow in our package used the query created in the control flow to select data from the change table and apply it to the data table. The "Query Data From the Change Table" task executes the query created by the variable expression. This query uses the dbo.fn_all_changes_dbo_Orders function to retrieve data from the change table.

Once we have received the data, we need to separate it by the type of operation that must be performed. This is done with a conditional split transformation. Any record

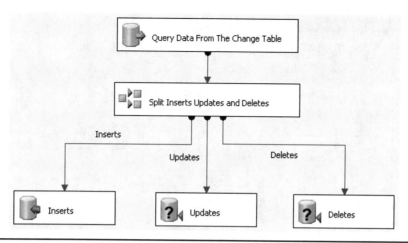

Figure 8-14 *The change data capture data load data flow*

from the change table with an "I" in the operation column goes down the Insert data flow. Any record from the change table with a "U" in the operation column goes down the Updates data flow. Finally, any record from the change table with a "D" in the operation column goes down the Delete flow.

The Inserts portion of the data flow is straightforward. Columns are simply mapped from the data flow to the fact table in the data destination. Updates use the following query to perform operations on the fact table:

```
UPDATE Sales_Information
SET FK_Customer = ?,
FK_Product = ?,
FK_Store = ?,
FK_Promotion = ?,
FK_SalesPerson = ?,
Sales_in_Dollars = ?,
Sales_in_Units = ?
WHERE FK_Time = ?
```

Each question mark serves as a placeholder for a parameter value. They are numbered from the beginning of the query to the end. The parameter mapping is shown in Figure 8-15. (It is assumed for simplicity in this example that the date/time of the sales transaction provides a unique key to the Sales_Information table.)

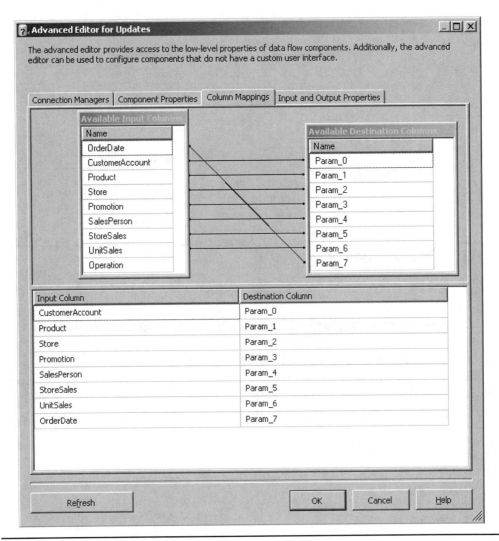

Figure 8-15 *Mapping parameters in the Updates task*

The Delete portion of the data flow is similar to the update data flow. The Delete item uses this SQL:

```
DELETE FROM Sales_Information
WHERE FK_Time = ?
```

This time, the single question mark parameter is mapped to the OrderDate field in the data flow.

Loading a Fact Table

We will wrap up our chapter with two more Learn By Doing exercises. We have populated the dimensional tables in the Manufacturing data mart in a previous Learn By Doing exercise. Now we will populate the fact table in this data mart. In fact, we will add a new wrinkle to the business requirements and populate two fact tables.

Learn By Doing—Adding a Second Fact Table to the Manufacturing Data Mart

Features Highlighted

▶ Modifying the structure of a data mart database

▶ Using Multiple fact tables in a single data mart

Business Need The vice president of production at Maximum Miniatures, Incorporated would like to be able to view the current inventory amount and the number of backorders pending for products while analyzing manufacturing production. The inventory and backorder amounts are available in the order processing system.

The inventory and backorder information is added as a second fact table in the data mart. This is done because the inventory information does not relate to all of the same dimensions as the production information. In addition, because the inventory information is populated from a different data source, loading the data mart is easier with two separate fact tables.

Steps

1. Open the SQL Server Management Studio.
2. Connect to the SQL server where you created the MaxMinManufacturingDM.
3. Expand the Databases folder and expand the MaxMinManufacturingDM database folder. Right-click the Tables folder and select New Table from the context menu. A Table Designer tab appears.
4. If the Properties window is not visible, select Properties Window from the View menu.
5. In the Properties window, enter **InventoryFact** for Name and **Inventory Fact populated from the Order Processing System database** for Description.

6. Add the following columns to the table:

Column Name	Data Type	Allow Nulls
InventoryLevel	Int	No
NumberOnBackorder	Int	No
DateOfInventory	Datetime	No
ProductCode	Int	No
Material	NVarchar(30)	No

7. Select the DateOfInventory, Product Code, and Material entries in the Table Designer. Click the Set Primary Key button on the toolbar.
8. Click the Save toolbar button to save this table design. Click Yes in the dialog box listing the tables to be affected. The InventoryFact table should appear as shown in Figure 8-16.
9. Close the SQL Server Management Studio.

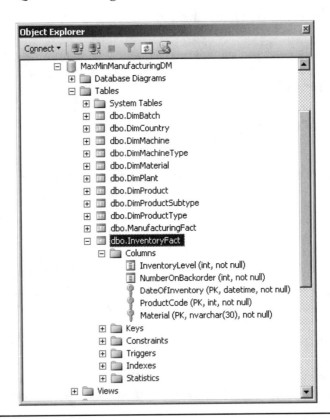

Figure 8-16 *The InventoryFact table*

Learn By Doing—Populating the Fact Tables in the Manufacturing Data Mart

Feature Highlighted

▶   Populating a fact table with Integration Services

Business Need

Obviously, these data marts don't do Maximum Miniatures any good unless they contain facts! Therefore, we need to populate the fact tables. The information for the Manufacturing fact table is in the BatchInfo.csv file. In an actual production environment, this file would probably have the production results for one day or perhaps one week at the most. The Integration Services package that processes this file would be run daily or weekly. However, because we want to have a good deal of sample data to work from, our copy of BatchInfo.csv has three years' worth of data. The design of the Integration Services package used to import this information remains unchanged.

We also have the little issue of one dimension table that has not been populated. This is the DimBatch table. The only source we have for the batch number information is the BatchInfo.csv file. Therefore, we include a data flow in our Integration Services package to populate the dimension table right before the fact table is populated.

We now have a second fact table in this data mart as well: the Inventory fact table. The information for this fact table comes from the order processing database. Our Integration Services package also includes a data flow to handle this.

NOTE

To complete this Learn By Doing activity, you need the BatchInfo.csv file and the Maximum Miniatures Order Processing database. If you have not done so already, go to www.mhprofessional.com and search for the book's page using the ISBN, which is 0071549447. Use the "Code" link to download the zip file containing the book's material. Follow the instructions within the zipped folders in the zip file to install the Maximum Miniatures Order Processing database.

Steps to Create the Integration Services Project

1.   Open the Business Intelligence Development Studio.
2.   Click the New Project button on the toolbar.
3.   Make sure Business Intelligence Projects is selected from the Project Types, and then select Integration Services Project from the templates.
4.   Enter **MaxMinManufacturingDMFactLoad** for the Name and set the Location to the appropriate folder.
5.   Click OK to create the project.

Steps to Create the Load DimBatch Data Flow

6. Once the project is open, right-click the Package.dtsx entry in the Solution Explorer window and select Rename from the context menu. Enter **FactLoad .dtsx** for the package name and press ENTER.

7. Click Yes when asked if you want to rename the package object as well.

8. Drag a Data Flow Task item from the Toolbox and drop it on the Control Flow tab.

9. Right-click the Data Flow Task item you just created and select Rename from the context menu. Enter **Load DimBatch** and press ENTER. Double-click the Load DimBatch item. This takes you to the Data Flow tab.

10. Right-click in the Connections tray and select New Flat File Connection from the context menu. The Flat File Connection Manager Editor dialog box appears.

11. Enter **BatchInfo.CSV File** for Connection Manager Name. Click Browse. The Open dialog box appears.

12. Select CSV Files (*.csv) in the Files of type drop-down list.

13. Browse to the BatchInfo.csv file that you downloaded from the book's web page. Select this file and click Open to exit the Open dialog box.

14. Check Column Names in the first data row.

15. Select Columns in the page selector on the left side of the dialog box. Note the content of the columns being read from the CSV text file.

16. Select Advanced in the page selector.

17. Change the data type for the BatchNumber, MachineNumber, ProductCode, NumberProduced, and NumberRejected columns to four-byte signed integer [DT_I4]. Change the data type for the TimeStarted and TimeStopped columns to database timestamp [DT_DBTIMESTAMP].

18. Click OK to exit the Flat File Connection Manager Editor dialog box.

19. Drag a Flat File Source item from the Data Flow Sources section of the Toolbox, and drop it on the Data Flow tab.

20. Double-click the Flat File Source item you just created. The Flat File Source Editor dialog box appears.

21. The BatchInfo.csv File data connection should be selected in the Flat File Connection Manager drop-down list.

22. Select Columns in the page selector on the left side of the dialog box.

23. Uncheck all of the columns in the Available External Columns list except the BatchNumber column.

24. Click OK to exit the Flat File Source Editor dialog box.

25. Drag a Sort item from the Data Flow Transformation section of the Toolbox, and drop it on the Data Flow tab.
26. Click the Flat File Source item. Click the green data flow arrow, drag it on top of the Sort item, and drop it on this item. This connects the source to the transformation.
27. Double-click the Sort item you just created. The Sort Transformation Editor dialog box appears.
28. Check the box to the left of BatchNumber in the Available Input Columns list.
29. Check Remove Rows with Duplicate Sort Values. This gives us a distinct list of batch numbers that we can use to populate our dimension table.
30. Click OK to exit the Sort Transformation Editor dialog box.
31. Drag a Derived Column item from the Toolbox and drop it on the Data Flow tab.
32. Click the Sort item. Click the green data flow arrow, drag it on top of the Derived Column item, and drop it on this item. This connects the two transformations.
33. Double-click the Derived Column item you just created. The Derived Column Transformation Editor dialog box appears.
34. Enter **BatchName** in the first row under Derived Column Name.
35. Enter the following in the first row under Expression:

```
(DT_WSTR, 50) [BatchNumber]
```

36. Click OK to exit the Derived Column Transformation Editor dialog box.
37. Drag a SQL Server Destination item from the Data Flow Destinations section of the Toolbox, and drop it on the Data Flow tab.
38. Click the Derived Column item. Click the green data flow arrow, drag it on top of the SQL Server Destination item, and drop it on this item. This connects the transformation to the destination.
39. Double-click the SQL Server Destination item. The SQL Destination Editor dialog box appears.
40. Click New to create an OLE DB Connection Manager for use with this SQL Server destination. The Configure OLE DB Connection Manager dialog box appears.
41. Select the connection to the MaxMinManufacturingDM database that you created previously. Click OK to exit the Configure OLE DB Connection Manager dialog box.
42. Select DimBatch from the Use a table or view drop-down list.
43. Click Mappings to view the Mappings page. The columns from the data source (which are Available Input Columns to this data destination item) should be

automatically mapped to the columns in the destination (the Available Destination Columns). The following mappings should be in place:

Available Input Columns		Available Destination Columns
BatchNumber	to	BatchNumber
BatchName	to	BatchName

44. Click OK to exit the SQL Destination Editor dialog box. The Data Flow tab should appear as shown in Figure 8-17.

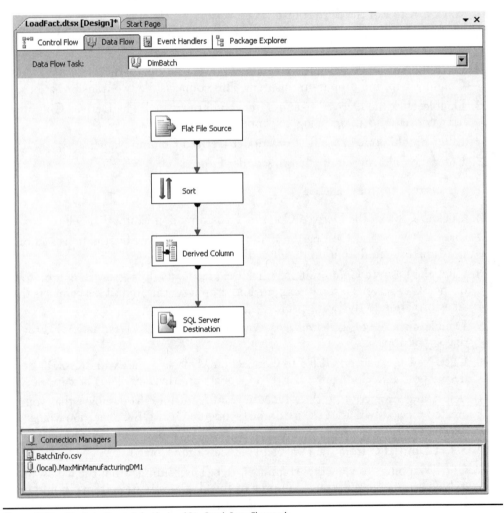

Figure 8-17 *The Data Flow tab for the Load DimBatch Data Flow task*

Steps to Create the Load ManufacturingFact Data Flow

45. Click the Control Flow tab. Drag another Data Flow Task item onto the Control Flow tab. Rename this new Data Flow Task item **Load ManufacturingFact**. Drag the Data Flow Task item wider so all of the new name can be seen.

46. Click the Load DimBatch item. Drag the precedence arrow onto the Load ManufacturingFact item and drop it there. (The DimBatch table must be loaded successfully before the ManufacturingFact table can be loaded.)

47. Double-click the Load ManufacturingFact item. This takes you to the Data Flow tab with Load ManufacturingFact selected in the Data Flow Task drop-down list.

48. Drag a Flat File Source item from the Toolbox and drop it on the Data Flow tab.

49. Double-click the Flat File Source item you just created. The Flat File Source Editor dialog box appears.

50. The BatchInfo.csv File data connection should be selected in the Flat File Connection Manager drop-down list. Click OK to exit the Flat File Source Editor dialog box.

Steps to Create a Derived Column Data Flow Item

51. Drag a Derived Column item from the Toolbox and drop it on the Data Flow tab.

52. Click the Flat File Source item. Click the green data flow arrow, drag it on top of the Derived Column item, and drop it on this item. This connects the source to the transformation.

53. Double-click the Derived Column item you just created. The Derived Column Transformation Editor dialog box appears.

54. Our flat file does not explicitly provide us with the number of products accepted and the elapsed time of production. Instead, we need to calculate this information from the data that is provided in the flat file. The flat file also includes a time portion on TimeStarted. This causes problems when we use this field to build our time dimension. We can solve these issues by adding three derived columns to the data flow. Enter **AcceptedProducts** in the first row under Derived Column Name. Enter the following in the first row under Expression:

```
[NumberProduced] - [NumberRejected]
```

(You can expand the Columns folder in the upper-left corner of the dialog box, and then drag-and-drop the fields onto the expression, if you like.)

55. Enter **ElapsedTimeForManufacture** in the second row under Derived Column Name. Enter the following in the second row under Expression:

```
(DT_NUMERIC,6,2)DATEDIFF("mi", [TimeStarted], [TimeStopped])
```

(You can expand the Date/Time Functions folder in the upper-right corner of the dialog box, and then drag-and-drop the DATEDIFF function onto the expression. You can also drag-and-drop the fields onto the expression.)

56. Enter **DateOfManufacture** in the third row under Derived Column Name. Enter the following in the third row under Expression:

```
(DT_DBTIMESTAMP)SUBSTRING((DT_WSTR,25)[TimeStarted],1,10)
```

This expression converts TimeStarted into a string and selects the first ten characters of that string (the date portion, but not the time portion). This string is then converted back into a datetime, without the time portion, so time defaults to midnight. (You can expand the Type Casts and String Functions folders in the upper-right corner of the dialog box and drag-and-drop the (DT_WSTR) type cast, SUBSTRING function, and (DT_DBTIMESTAMP) type cast onto the expression. You can also drag-and-drop the fields onto the expression.) Click OK to exit the Derived Column Transformation Editor dialog box.

Steps to Create a Lookup Data Flow Item

57. Drag a Lookup item from the Toolbox and drop it on the Data Flow tab.
58. Change the name of this item to Lookup Batch Number.
59. Click the Derived Column item. Click the green data flow arrow, drag it on top of the Lookup Batch Number item, and drop it on this item. This connects the transformation to the destination.
60. Double-click the Lookup Batch Number item. The Lookup Transformation Editor dialog box appears.
61. Select Redirect rows to no match output in the Specify how to handle rows with no matching entries drop-down list.
62. Click Connection to view the Connection page.
63. Select [dbo].[DimBatch] from the Use a table or a view drop-down list.
64. Click Columns to view the Columns page.
65. Click BatchNumber in the Available Input Columns list, and drag-and-drop it on BatchNumber in the Available LookupColumns list.
66. Click OK to exit the Lookup Transformation Editor dialog box.
67. Drag another Lookup item from the Toolbox and drop it on the Data Flow tab.
68. Change the name of this item to **Lookup Machine Number**.
69. Click the Lookup Batch Number item. Click the green data flow arrow, drag it on top of the Lookup Machine Number item, and drop it on this item. The Input Output Selection dialog box appears.
70. Select Lookup Match Output from the Output drop-down list and click OK.
71. Double-click the Lookup Machine Number item. The Lookup Transformation Editor dialog box appears.

72. Select Redirect rows to no match output in the Specify how to handle rows with no matching entries drop-down list.
73. Click Connection to view the Connection page.
74. Select [dbo].[DimMachine] from the Use a table or a view drop-down list.
75. Click Columns to view the Columns page.
76. Click MachineNumber in the Available Input Columns list, and drag-and-drop it on MachineNumber in the Available LookupColumns list.
77. Click OK to exit the Lookup Transformation Editor dialog box.
78. Repeat Steps 67 to 77 to add the following Lookup item to the data flow:

Item Name	Table	Available Input Column	Available Lookup Columns
Lookup Product	[dbo].[DimProduct]	ProductCode	ProductCode

Steps to Create a SQL Server Data Destination Item

79. Drag a SQL Server Destination item from the Toolbox and drop it on the Data Flow tab.
80. Click the Lookup Product item. Click the green data flow arrow, drag it on top of the SQL Server Destination item, and drop it on this item. The Input Output Selection dialog box appears.
81. Select Lookup Match Output from the Output drop-down list and click OK.
82. Double-click the SQL Server Destination item. The SQL Destination Editor dialog box appears.
83. Select ManufacturingFact from the Use a table or view drop-down list.
84. Click Mappings to view the Mappings page. The columns from the data source (which are Available Input Columns to this data destination item) should be automatically mapped to the columns in the destination (the Available Destination Columns). The following mappings should be in place:

Available Input Columns		Available Destination Columns
BatchNumber	to	BatchNumber
MachineNumber	to	MachineNumber
ProductCode	to	ProductCode
AcceptedProducts	to	AcceptedProducts
ElapsedTimeForManufacture	to	ElapsedTimeForManufacture
DateOfManufacture	to	DateOfManufacture

85. Use drag-and-drop to add the following mapping:

Available Input Columns		Available Destination Columns
NumberRejected	to	RejectedProducts

86. Click OK to exit the SQL Destination Editor dialog box.

Steps to Create a Data Destination for the Rows in Error

87. Drag a Union All item from the Toolbox and drop it on the Data Flow tab.
88. Click the Lookup Batch Number item. Click the unattached green data flow arrow, drag it on top of the Union All item, and drop it on this item. Note, the Lookup No Match Output is connected to the Union All item. This means the unmatched records are going to follow this data flow.
89. Click the Lookup Machine Number item. Click the unattached green data flow arrow, drag it on top of the Union All item, and drop it on this item. Drag a Flat File Destination item from the Toolbox and drop it on the Data Flow tab.
90. Repeat this process with the Lookup Product item.
91. Drag a Flat File Destination item from the Toolbox and drop it on the Data Flow tab.
92. Change the name of this item to **Write Error Records To A Text File**.
93. Click the Union All item. Click the green data flow arrow, drag it on top of the Write Error Records item, and drop it on this item.
94. Double-click the Write Error Records item. The Flat File Destination Editor dialog box appears.
95. Click New to create a new Flat File Connection Manager. The Flat File Format dialog box appears.
96. Leave the format set to delimited and click OK. The Flat File Connection Manager Editor appears.
97. Enter **Error Output** for Connection manager name.
98. Click Browse. The Open dialog box appears.
99. Browse to an appropriate location for this error text file. Enter **MfgInfoErrors.txt** for File name.
100. Click Open to exit the Open dialog box.
101. Check the Column names in the first data row check box.
102. Click OK to exit the Flat File Connection Manager Editor.

103. Click Mappings to view the Mappings page of the Flat File Destination Editor dialog box.

104. Click OK to exit the Flat File Destination Editor dialog box. The Data Flow tab should appear as shown in Figure 8-18.

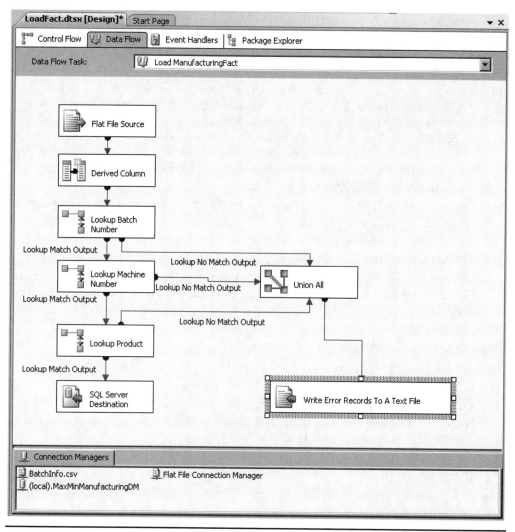

Figure 8-18   *The data flow to load the Manufacturing fact table*

Steps to Create the InventoryFact Data Flow

105. Click the Control Flow tab. Drag a third Data Flow Task item onto the Control Flow tab. Rename this new Data Flow Task item Load InventoryFact. (You do not need to set precedence between the Load InventoryFact item and the other Data Flow Task items. It does not matter when the InventoryFact table is filled relative to the operations being done on the other tables.)

106. Double-click the Load InventoryFact item. This takes you to the Data Flow tab.

107. Right-click in the Connections tray and select New OLE DB Connection from the context menu. Click New in the Configure OLE DB Connection Manager dialog box to create a new data connection.

108. Enter the name of the server where the Maximum Miniatures Order Processing database is installed in Server Name. Select the appropriate method for accessing this server in the Log On to the Server section. Enter credentials if necessary. Select OrderProcessingSystem from the Select or enter a database name drop-down list. (If the drop-down list is empty, either your server name or your login credentials are incorrect.) Click OK to return to the Configure OLE DB Connection Manager dialog box. Click OK again to exit this dialog box.

109. Drag an OLE DB Source item from the Toolbox and drop it on the Data Flow tab.

110. Double-click the OLE DB Source item you just created. The OLE DB Source Editor dialog box appears.

111. Select the OrderProcessingSystem data connection that you just created in the OLE DB connection manager drop-down list. Leave the Data access mode drop-down list set to Table or view. Select Inventory from the Name of the table or the view drop-down list. Click OK.

Steps to Create a Lookup Data Flow Item

112. Drag a Lookup item from the Toolbox and drop it on the Data Flow tab.

113. Change the name of this item to **Lookup Product**.

114. Click the OLE DB Source item. Click the green data flow arrow, drag it on top of the Lookup Product item, and drop it on this item. This connects the transformation to the destination.

115. Double-click the Lookup Product item. The Lookup Transformation Editor dialog box appears.

116. Select Redirect rows to no match output in the Specify how to handle rows with no matching entries drop-down list.

117. Click Connection to view the Connection page.

118. Select [dbo].[DimProduct] from the Use a table or a view drop-down list.

119. Click Columns to view the Columns page.

120. Click Code in the Available Input Columns list and drag-and-drop it on ProductCode in the Available LookupColumns list.

121. Click OK to exit the Lookup Transformation Editor dialog box.

Steps to Create a Data Conversion Data Flow Item

122. Drag a Data Conversion item from the Toolbox and drop it on the Data Flow tab.

123. Click the Lookup Product item. Click the green data flow arrow, drag it on top of the Data Conversion item, and drop it on this item. The Input Output Selection dialog box appears.

124. Select Lookup Match Output from the Output drop-down list. Click OK.

125. Double-click the Date Conversion item. The Data Conversion Transformation Editor dialog box appears.

126. Check the check box next to Material in the Available Input Columns area.

127. Enter **Material-Unicode** in the Output Alias column.

128. Select Unicode string [DT_WSTR] from the drop-down list in the Data Type column.

129. Click OK to exit the Data Conversion Transformation Editor dialog box.

Steps to Create a Data Destination Data Flow Item

130. Drag a SQL Server Destination item from the Toolbox and drop it on the Data Flow tab.

131. Click the Data Conversion item. Click the green data flow arrow, drag it on top of the SQL Server Destination item, and drop it on this item. This connects the transformation to the destination.

132. Double-click the SQL Server Destination item. The SQL Destination Editor dialog box appears.

133. Select the MaxMinManufacturingDM data connection in the OLE DB Connection Manager drop-down list. Select InventoryFact from the Use a table or view drop-down list.

134. Click Mappings to view the Mappings page. Delete the line that joins the Material column in both lists.

135. Use drag-and-drop to add the following mappings:

Available Input Columns		Available Destination Columns
Code	To	ProductCode
InventoryDate	To	DateOfInventory
AmountOnHand	To	InventoryLevel
AmountBackordered	To	NumberOnBackorder
Material-Unicode	to	Material

136. Click OK to exit the SQL Destination Editor dialog box.

Steps to Create a Data Destination for the Rows in Error

137. Drag a Flat File Destination item from the Toolbox and drop it on the Data Flow tab.

138. Change the name of this item to **Write Inventory Error Records To A Text File**.

139. Click the Lookup Product item. Click the green data flow arrow, drag it on top of the Write Inventory Error Records item, and drop it on this item.

140. Double-click the Write Inventory Error Records item. The Flat File Destination Editor dialog box appears.

141. Click New to create a new Flat File Connection Manager. The Flat File Format dialog box appears.

142. Leave the format set to delimited and click OK. The Flat File Connection Manager Editor appears.

143. Enter **Inventory Error Output** for Connection manager name.

144. Click Browse. The Open dialog box appears.

145. Browse to an appropriate location for this error text file. Enter **InvInfoErrors.txt** for File name.

146. Click Open to exit the Open dialog box.

147. Check the Column names in the first data row check box.

148. Click OK to exit the Flat File Connection Manager Editor.

149. Click Mappings to view the Mappings page of the Flat File Destination Editor dialog box.

150. Click OK to exit the Flat File Destination Editor dialog box. The Data Flow tab should appear as shown in Figure 8-19.

151. Click the Save All button on the toolbar to save the completed package.

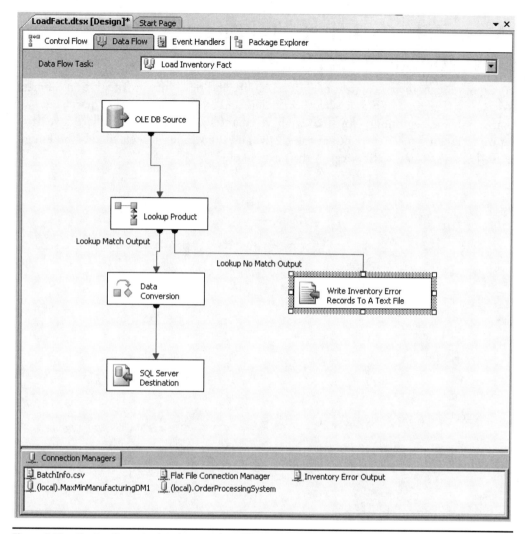

Figure 8-19   *The data flow to load the Inventory fact table*

152. Click the Start Debugging button on the toolbar to execute the completed package. When the execution is complete, click Stop Debugging or the Package Execution Completed link to return to Design mode.

153. Close the project.

Meanwhile, Back at the Unified Dimensional Model (UDM)

As we have seen, there is a great deal of capability and flexibility in Integration Services. We can use Integration Services to cleanse data and load it into our data marts, but that is only the beginning. Now that we have a handle on Integration Services, we can return to looking more in-depth at the UDM and the various aspects of cube building in SQL Server Analysis Services in the next chapter.

Part III

Analyzing Cube Content

Chapter 9

Cubism—Measures and Dimensions

In This Chapter

▶ **Building in Analysis Services**

▶ **Measures**

▶ **Dimensions**

▶ **You Are Special**

There is a fifth dimension beyond those known to man. It is a dimension vast as space and timeless as infinity.

—Rod Serling
Introduction to *The Twilight Zone*

We have looked at the basics of cubes, with their measures, dimensions, and attributes. We also examined the means of getting information from transactional and other data sources into our data marts. Now let's take a closer look at the way measures and dimensions are implemented in Microsoft SQL Server 2008 Analysis Services.

Analysis Services lets us group measures together. It also enables us to create different types of dimensions. This classification and differentiation make it easier for users to analyze the data in our cubes. It also makes the cubes easier for us to manage.

Building in Analysis Services

In Chapter 6, we created two data mart structures for our sample company, Maximum Miniatures, Inc. We called these the Manufacturing data mart and the Sales data mart. These data marts serve as repositories for business information that is not available elsewhere from a single source. We will deal with the Sales data mart later in this chapter. First, we will look at completing the Manufacturing data mart by creating an Analysis Services cube.

Creating a Cube

Now that the Manufacturing data mart contains data, let's go ahead and define an online analytical processing (OLAP) cube on top of the data mart relational database. In Chapter 6, we defined one OLAP cube at the same time we created the Sales data mart relational database. This time around, we approach things from a different direction. We already have the Manufacturing data mart relational database. What we need to do is define our OLAP cube on top of that existing database.

Once the OLAP cube is defined, we use it to help us learn more about measures in the following section of this book.

Learn By Doing—Building an OLAP Cube for the Manufacturing Data Mart

Feature Highlighted

► Creating an OLAP cube on top of an existing data mart

Business Need   The vice president of production wants to perform multidimensional analysis on the information in the Manufacturing data mart. To let him do that, we need to define an OLAP cube on top of that database.

Steps

1. Open the Business Intelligence Development Studio.
2. Click the New Project button on the toolbar.
3. Make sure Business Intelligence Projects is selected from the Project Types, and then select Analysis Services Project from the templates.
4. Enter **MaxMinManufacturingDM** for the Name and set the Location to the appropriate folder.
5. Click OK to create the project.
6. Right-click the Data Sources folder in the Solution Explorer window and select New Data Source from the context menu. The Data Source Wizard appears.
7. Click Next. The Select how to define the connection page appears.
8. Select the data connection to the MaxMinManufacturingDM you previously created. Click Next. The Impersonation Information page appears.

NOTE

Analysis Services needs to access the data mart relational database to populate and update the information in the OLAP cube. This is done using the information in the data connection selected in Step 8. The Analysis Services updates run as a background process. This can be an issue if the data connection specifies Windows Authentication or if the connection is to a file-based database, such as Microsoft Access. In these situations, Analysis Services needs to know what Windows credentials to use when accessing the data source. In other words, Analysis Services needs to impersonate a Windows identity while accessing the data.

9. On the Impersonation Information page, if you are using Windows Authentication in your data connection, select Use a Specific Windows User Name and Password, and then enter a valid Windows user name and password for database access. If you entered a specific SQL Server login in the data connection, you do not need to worry about impersonation. (If you cannot remember how the data connection was configured, select Use a Specific User Name and Password, and then enter valid Windows credentials, just to be on the safe side.) Click Next. The Completing the Wizard page appears.
10. Enter **Max Min Manufacturing DM** for Data Source Name, if it is not already there. Click Finish.

11. Right-click the Data Source Views folder in the Solution Explorer window and select New Data Source View from the context menu. The Data Source View Wizard appears.

NOTE

A data source view enables us to specify the subset of the tables and their fields from the data source that should be included in the OLAP cube. We can also define table relationships and calculated fields that do not exist in the underlying database. In this case, we are accessing a data mart that was architected with the cube in mind. Therefore, we use all of the tables and fields in the data mart database and we do not need to specify additional relationships. However, we do use the data source view to define three calculated fields that let us easily create a time dimension hierarchy from the single datetime field that exists in the fact table.

12. Click Next. The Select a Data Source page appears.
13. The Max Min Manufacturing DM data source that you just created should be selected. Click Next. The Name Matching page appears.
14. This page appears because we do not have foreign key constraints defined in our database. We will allow the wizard to create logical foreign keys in the data source view. Leave the Create logical relationships by matching columns check box checked. Also, leave the Same name as primary key option selected.
15. Click Next. The Select Tables and Views page appears.
16. Move all of the dimension and fact tables to the Included objects list. (Remember, there are two fact tables now.) Click Next. The Completing the Wizard page appears.
17. Enter **Max Min Manufacturing DM** for Name, if it is not already there. Click Finish. The Data Source View Design tab appears.

NOTE

The Data Source View Design tab shows a diagram of the data source view we just created. This looks similar to a database diagram. This is to be expected, because a data source view is simply a view into the underlying database. The data source view gives us the chance to add items that are required by or remove items that are irrelevant to the cube we are creating.

18. Find the ManufacturingFact table in the data source view diagram. Right-click the title bar of this table and select New Named Calculation from the context menu. The Create Named Calculation dialog box appears.
19. Enter **YearOfManufacture** for Column Name.

20. Enter the following for Expression:

```
CONVERT(char(4), YEAR(DateOfManufacture))
```

This creates a character field containing the year corresponding to the date of manufacture.

NOTE

The data source view is interacting with the underlying database to create the named calculation. Therefore, the expression language of that database must be used to define the expression. In this case, the underlying database is SQL Server, so the expression language is T-SQL. The expression is evaluated by sending this SELECT statement to the underlying database:

```
SELECT {Table in Data Source}.*,
{Named Calculation Expression} AS {Named Calculation Name}
FROM {Table in Data Source} AS {Table Name in Data Source View}
```

For the named calculation we are creating here, the SELECT statement would be:

```
SELECT ManufacturingFact.*,
CONVERT (char(4), YEAR(DateOfManufacture))
AS YearOfManufacture
FROM ManufacturingFact AS ManufacturingFact
```

Any T-SQL expression that is valid in this context, including subqueries (when explicitly surrounded by parentheses), is valid as a named calculation.

21. Click OK to exit the Create Named Calculation dialog box.
22. Create a second named calculation called QuarterOfManufacture with the following expression to contain the year and quarter corresponding to the date of manufacture:

```
CONVERT(char(4), YEAR(DateOfManufacture)) +
CASE
WHEN MONTH(DateOfManufacture) BETWEEN 1 AND 3 THEN 'Q1'
WHEN MONTH(DateOfManufacture) BETWEEN 4 AND 6 THEN 'Q2'
WHEN MONTH(DateOfManufacture) BETWEEN 7 AND 9 THEN 'Q3'
ELSE 'Q4'
END
```

23. Create a third named calculation called MonthOfManufacture with the following expression to contain the year and month corresponding to the date of manufacture:

```
CONVERT(char(4), YEAR(DateOfManufacture)) +
RIGHT('0'+CONVERT(varchar(2), MONTH(DateOfManufacture)),2)
```

24. Create YearOfInventory, QuarterOfInventory, and MonthOfInventory named calculations in the InventoryFact table. Use the same T-SQL expressions, substituting DateOfInventory for DateOfManufacture. When completed (and with a little rearranging), the Data Source View Design tab should appear similar to Figure 9-1.

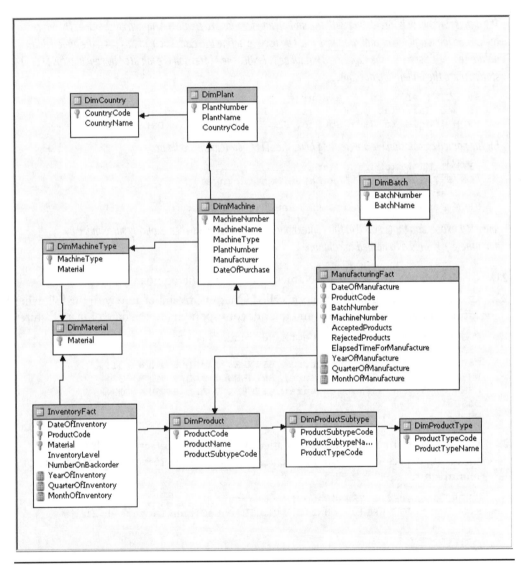

Figure 9-1   *The Data Source View Design tab for the Max Min Manufacturing DM data source view*

25. Right-click the Cubes folder in the Solution Explorer window and select New Cube from the context menu. The Cube Wizard appears.

26. Click Next. The Select Creation Method page appears.

27. Use existing tables should be selected by default. Click Next. The Select Measure Group Tables page appears.

28. The Max Min Manufacturing DM data source view that you just created should be selected. Check ManufacturingFact in the Measure group tables area. We initially leave the measures in the InventoryFact table out of the cube and add them in at a later time.

29. Click Next. The Select Measures page appears.

30. The wizard should have found and checked all of the measure fields in the ManufacturingFact table. The wizard also added a field called Manufacturing Fact Count, which counts the number of records. This does not provide us with any useful information in this data mart, so you should uncheck the Manufacturing Fact Count field.

31. Click Next. The Select New Dimensions page appears.

32. The wizard should have found all of the tables related to the ManufacturingFact table in the data source view. It should also have created hierarchies for the Dim Product and Dim Machine dimensions. Uncheck both ManufacturingFact entries.

33. Click Next. The Completing the Wizard page appears.

34. Enter **Max Min Manufacturing DM** for Cube Name, if it is not already there. Click Finish. The Cube Design tab appears. The Business Intelligence Development Studio windows should appear similar to Figure 9-2.

35. Click the Save All button on the toolbar.

You will notice the wizard did not create our time dimension for us. We will manually create the time dimension later in this chapter.

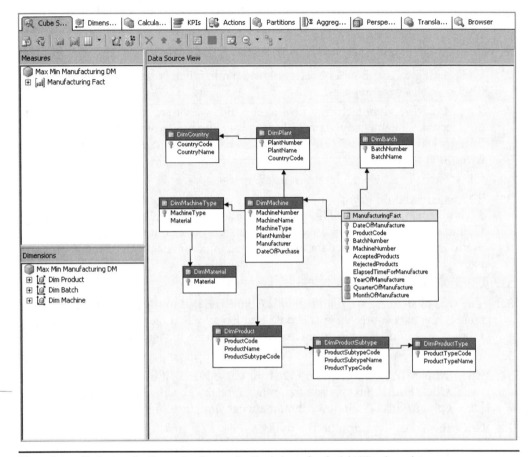

Figure 9-2   *The Business Intelligence Development Studio windows after the Cube Wizard completes*

Measures

Now that we have a real live cube in captivity, we can study its basic parts and look at some of its more advanced features. We begin with measures. Measures provide the actual information that the users of our cubes are interested in. *Measures* are the bits of numerical data that we need to aggregate. As we saw in the Cube Wizard, measures come from the fields in the fact tables in the data mart.

SQL Server 2008 Analysis Services provides us with a number of features for managing measures. We can even create new measures that don't exist in the data mart. We can also control the aggregation of the measures along our dimensions.

Measure Groups

In SQL Server 2008 Analysis Services, measures do not exist on their own inside cubes. Instead, they are clustered together and managed in groupings. These groupings are called measure groups. Each *measure group* in a cube corresponds to a table in the data source view. This table is the measure group's source for its measure data. The measure group is said to be bound to this table. Each record in the table becomes a different member of the measure group.

In the Max Min Manufacturing DM cube created by the Cube Wizard, there is a single measure group called Manufacturing Fact. This measure group contains the Accepted Products, Rejected Products, and Elapsed Time for Manufacture measures. This measure group is bound to the ManufacturingFact table in the data source view.

Measure Groups and Dimensions

Previously, we discussed how dimensions are used to aggregate measures. For this aggregation to take place, the dimensions in a cube must be somehow related to the measures. When we created our data marts, this was done using a foreign key field in the measure or fact table that linked to primary key fields of our dimension tables. In the cube itself, we do the same thing by creating relationships between the measure groups and the dimensions.

At first, this may seem a bit strange. As we have discussed cubes conceptually in previous chapters, we have always talked about measures being related to dimensions, with no talk of measure groups. When we query the data from our cubes, we use dimensions as if they were directly related to measures. However, if you consider the underlying architecture, this makes perfect sense.

In our data mart, we have multiple measures in a single record of our fact table. In the Manufacturing data mart, the Accepted Products, Rejected Products, and Elapsed Time for Manufacture measures are present in each record. The record also contains the foreign key fields linking it to the lowest-level dimension tables in each of the hierarchies. Again, in the Manufacturing data mart, these are DimProduct, DimBatch, and DimMachine (along with the time dimension that will be created virtually from the DateOfManufacture field).

All of the measures in the ManufacturingFact record (a single row of data) depend on all of the foreign key fields in that record. Therefore, if a given Accepted Products measure and Rejected Products measure reside in the same record, it is impossible for them to relate to two different records in the DimProduct table (see Figure 9-3). Only one foreign key field in their record can be used to link to the DimProduct table, so they must both link to the same product. That's the way well-normalized relational databases work.

We just said that measure groups correspond to a table in the data source view. Just as all of the measures in a given record in the fact table must relate to the same

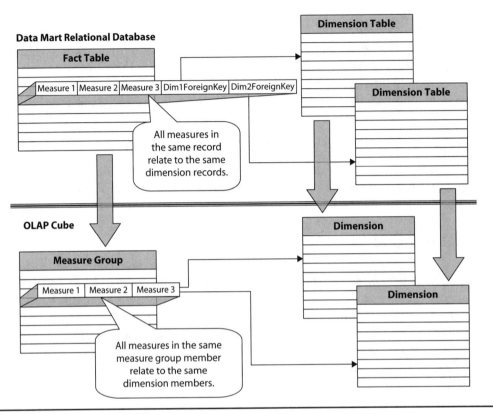

Figure 9-3   *Measure groups and dimensions*

dimension table records, it follows that all of the measures in a given member group must relate to the same members in the cube dimensions.

We look at the technique for creating relationships between measure groups and dimensions in the section "Role Playing Dimensions" when we discuss dimensions.

Granularity

The lowest level of a particular dimension hierarchy that is related to a given measure group determines the granularity of that measure group for that dimension. Analysis can only be done on a measure along a certain dimension down to the granularity of its measure group for that dimension. Because measures are related to dimensions through their measure group, all of the measures in a measure group have the same granularity. Two different measure groups (and their constituent measures) in the same cube can have different granularity.

All of this can sound a bit like double-speak, so let's look at a couple of examples. The Manufacturing Fact measure group is related to the machine dimension at the lowest level, the machine number level. Therefore, the Manufacturing Fact measure group has a granularity of machine number for the machine dimension. We can drill down through the machine hierarchy from material to machine type, all the way to the machine number level, and get information for all of the measures in the Manufacturing Fact measure group.

The Inventory Fact measure group is related to the machine dimension at the material level. The Inventory Fact measure group has a granularity of material for the machine dimension. We can only perform analysis at the material level for measures in the Inventory Fact measure group.

Granularity is important for the analysis, but remember, there will be facts with some values missing or null. Not all materials in the complete list of dimension members are made on all machine types and on all machines in the factory on the same day. SQL Server 2008 Analysis Services continues the tradition of assuring proper handling of null data started by earlier versions of Analysis Services.

Made-up Facts—Calculated Measures

The underlying data sources for our cubes may not contain all of the information we want to make available for our users. In many cases, we need to use the available data to calculate new measures that our users require. Perhaps the list price, discount amount, and sales tax amount need to be added together to determine the actual total of a sale. Perhaps we want to divide the number of rejected products by the total number of products manufactured to get the percentage of rejects produced. We can create this information using calculated measures.

A *calculated measure* is part of a measure group. It functions in the same manner as any other measure in the group. The only difference is this: Instead of coming directly from a field in the underlying data source, a calculated measure is defined by an expression. These expressions are created using a language known as Multidimensional Expression Language (MDX) script. Remember, when we created named calculations in a data source view, we used the language of the underlying data source. In our case, it was T-SQL. It would certainly be easier if we could use the same language here to define calculated measures. Unfortunately, that is not the case. *MDX* is a special language with features designed to handle the advanced mathematics and formulas required by OLAP analysis. MDX also includes features for navigating through the dimensions and hierarchies of OLAP cubes. These features are not found in T-SQL, so we need to use MDX script.

In the "Learn By Doing" section for measures and measure groups, we create some straightforward calculated measures. These calculated measures do not require an in-depth knowledge of the MDX script language. We get into the details of MDX script in Chapter 11.

The definition of a calculated measure is stored in the OLAP cube itself. The actual values that result from a calculated measure are not calculated, however, until a query containing that calculated measure is executed. The results of that calculation are then cached in the cube. The cached value is then delivered to any subsequent users requesting the same calculation.

Creating Calculated Measures

Calculated measures are managed on the Calculations tab of the Cube Design tab. A new calculated measure is created by clicking the New Calculated Member toolbar button, shown in Figure 9-4. This opens the Calculated Member form view, shown in Figure 9-5.

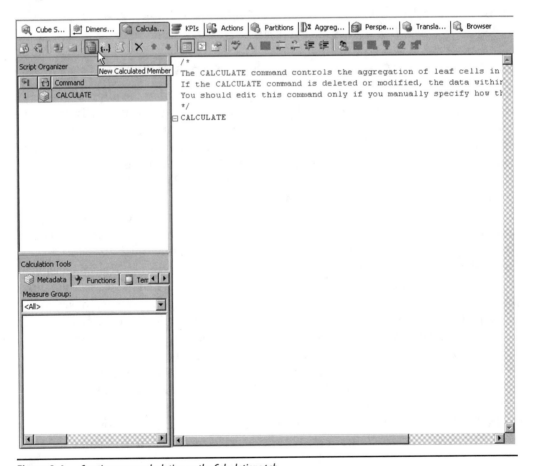

Figure 9-4 *Creating a new calculation on the Calculations tab*

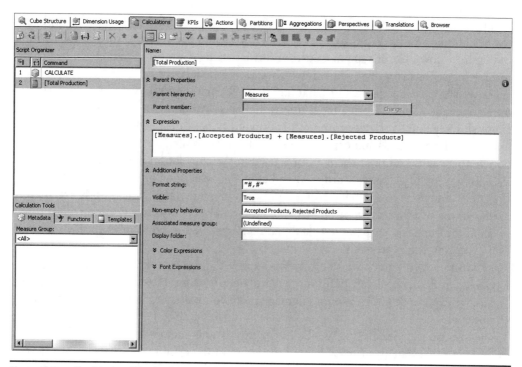

Figure 9-5   *The Calculated Member form view*

The name of the calculated measure is entered in Name. If the name contains one or more spaces, it must be enclosed in square brackets. Likewise, if the name contains one or more of the following characters:

```
! @ # $ % ^ & * ( ) - + = / ? : ; " ' { } \ < >,
```

it must be enclosed in square brackets.

Thus far, we have talked of calculated measures. However, it is possible to calculate members for dimensions as well. In fact, both calculated measures and calculated dimension members are referred to as calculated members, which is why the entry form is called the Calculated Member form. To specify that we are creating a calculated measure, MEASURES must be selected from the Parent hierarchy drop-down list.

The actual definition of the calculated measure is entered in Expression. As mentioned earlier, this expression uses the MDX script language. The expression can be typed by hand or it can be built using the existing measures, MDX script functions, and templates found in the Calculation Tools window. This window can be seen in the lower-left area of Figure 9-5.

The Format string drop-down list enables us to select the formatting to be applied to the calculation results. We can either select from one of the numeric formatting strings in the drop-down list or type in a custom format string. In most cases, one of the formatting strings from the drop-down list can do the job.

As we study MDX queries in Chapter 12, we learn about MDX queries that ask for only non-empty values from a measure. Rather than evaluating a calculated measure expression repeatedly to determine if it is nonempty, we can specify the conditions under which the calculation can produce a nonempty result. In most cases, this depends on whether one or more of the measures used in the calculation is nonempty.

The Non-empty Behavior drop-down list lets us select one or more measures in the cube. If any one of the selected measures is non-empty, the expression is executed to determine whether the resulting calculated measure is non-empty. When all of the selected measures are empty, the calculated measure is assumed to be empty without ever executing the expression.

In addition to the form view shown in Figure 9-5, we can look at the underlying MDX script that completely defines the calculated measure. This is shown in Figure 9-6. Again, we explore the MDX script language more completely to understand this code in Chapter 11.

We can use the measures in a cube in the expressions that define calculated measures in that cube. We can also use calculated measures in the expressions that define other calculated measures. This lets us break up complex calculations into much simpler building blocks that are easier to create and maintain.

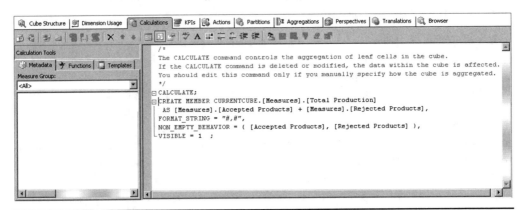

Figure 9-6   *The Script view*

It Doesn't Add Up—Measure Aggregates Other Than Sum

We have already discussed how measures are aggregated along dimension hierarchies. By default, the Sum aggregate function is used for each measure. Measures that use the Sum function for their aggregation are *additive measures*.

In some cases, however, things just don't add up. In other words, there may be some measures that should not be summed along dimension hierarchies. For example, taking the sum of an average results in a number that is total nonsense. Instead, we always want to recalculate the average from the granular data. In other situations, we may want to use the maximum or minimum value for a measure along a dimension, rather than taking the sum. These measures are *nonadditive measures*.

The aggregate function used by a particular measure is controlled by the Aggregate property from that measure. Select the measure in the Measures window, and then use the Properties window to set the Aggregate property for this measure. This is shown in Figure 9-7.

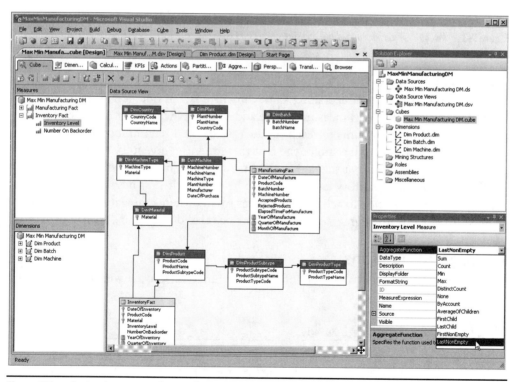

Figure 9-7   *Setting the aggregate function for a measure*

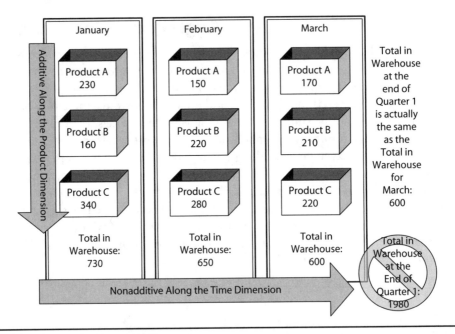

Figure 9-8 *Inventory level is a semiadditive measure*

Semiadditive Measures

Certain measures may be added along some dimensions, but not along others. For example, the inventory level measure can be added along the product dimension. The sum of the inventory amounts for each product yields the total number of products in the warehouse. However, the sum of the first three months' inventory amounts does not give the inventory amount at the end of the first quarter. This is shown in Figure 9-8.

Measures such as inventory level are said to be semiadditive. These measures must use a *semiadditive measure* to achieve the proper results when aggregating. Measures that use a semiadditive aggregate function must be related to a time dimension.

Aggregate Functions

Analysis Services provides a number of aggregate functions for use with measures in an OLAP cube.

Function	Additivity	Result
AverageOfChildren	Semiadditive	The average of all nonempty child members.
ByAccount	Semiadditive	Uses the aggregate function specified by an account dimension in the cube. If the cube does not include an account dimension, this aggregate function works the same as the None aggregate function.

Function	Additivity	Result
Count	Semiadditive	A count of the number of child members.
DistinctCount	Nonadditive	A count of the number of unique child members.
FirstChild	Semiadditive	The value of the first child member.
FirstNonEmpty	Semiadditive	The value of the first nonempty child member.
LastChild	Semiadditive	The value of the last child member.
LastNonEmpty	Semiadditive	The value of the last nonempty child member.
Max	Semiadditive	The greatest value of all child members.
Min	Semiadditive	The least value of all child members.
None	Nonadditive	No aggregation is done.
Sum	Additive	The sum of all child members. This is the default aggregate function for a measure.

Learn By Doing—Working with Measures and Measure Groups

Features Highlighted

▶ Adding formatting to a measure

▶ Adding a measure group to a cube

▶ Setting the aggregation function for a measure

▶ Creating calculated measures

Business Need   We have not yet completed the vice president of production's change request for inventory and backorder information in the Max Min Manufacturing DM cube. We added a table for this information into the data mart and we populated that table from the Order Processing database. We now need to add these measures to the cube in a new measure group.

Once the inventory level measure is added to the cube, we need to specify the correct aggregate function for this measure. As noted earlier, inventory level is not additive. The inventory level for a given period of time is not the sum of the inventory levels within the period. Instead, inventory level is semiadditive. The inventory level for a given period of time is the inventory level at the end of that period.

In addition, the vice president of production has come up with another change. He would like to see not only the number of accepted products produced and the number of rejected products produced, but also the total number of products produced. This, of course, is the sum of the number of accepted products, plus the number of rejected products. He also wants to see the number of rejected products produced as a percentage of the total number of products produced. We can implement these requests using calculated measures.

Steps

1. Open the Business Intelligence Development Studio.
2. Open the MaxMinManufacturingDM project.
3. In the Solution Explorer window, double-click the entry for Max Min Manufacturing DM.cube to display the Cube Design tab, if it is not already visible.
4. Expand the Manufacturing Fact measure group in the Measures window.
5. Select the Accepted Products measure.
6. In the Properties window, select Standard from the Format String drop-down list.
7. Select the Rejected Products measure in the Measures window.
8. In the Properties window, select Standard from the Format String drop-down list.
9. Select the Elapsed Time For Manufacture measure in the Measures window.
10. In the Properties window, select Standard from the Format String drop-down list.
11. Right-click in the Measures window and select New Measure Group from the context menu. The New Measure Group dialog box appears.
12. Select InventoryFact from the Select a table from the data source view list and click OK to exit the New Measure Group dialog box. The InventoryFact table is added to the cube and the Inventory Fact measure group appears in the Measures window.

NOTE

A red, wavy line may appear under the entry for the Inventory Fact measure group in the Measures window. The reason for this error notification is because we have not related this new measure group to any dimensions. We take care of this in the next Learn By Doing exercise titled "Relating Dimensions in the Max Min Manufacturing DM Cube."

13. Expand the Inventory Fact measure group in the Measures window.
14. Select the Inventory Level measure.
15. In the Properties window, select LastNonEmpty from the drop-down list for the AggregateFunction property. The LastNonEmpty aggregate function is now used when aggregating this measure.
16. In the Properties window, select Standard from the Format String drop-down list.
17. Select the Number On Backorder measure in the Measures window.
18. In the Properties window, select LastNonEmpty from the drop-down list for the AggregateFunction property.
19. In the Properties window, select Standard from the Format String drop-down list.
20. Right-click the Inventory Fact Count measure in the Measures window and select Delete from the context menu. The Delete Objects dialog box appears.

21. Click OK to confirm the deletion. The Cube Design tab should appear similar to Figure 9-9.

NOTE

A count of the number of members in the measure group is automatically created when a new measure group is created. In this case, a count of the number of inventory entries is not a helpful measure, so it can be deleted.

22. Select the Calculations tab of the Cube Design tab to create calculated measures.
23. Click the New Calculated Member button on the Calculations tab toolbar. The Calculated Member form view appears.

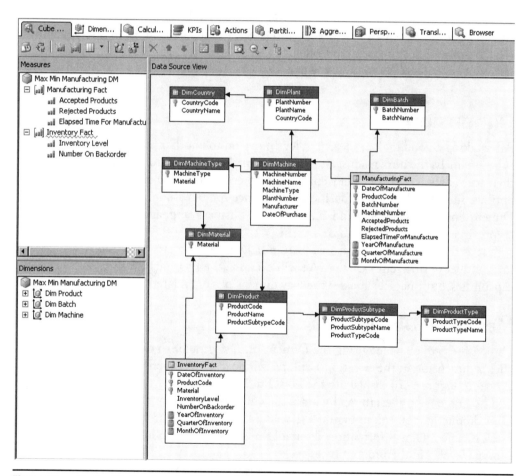

Figure 9-9   *The Max Min Manufacturing DM cube with the Inventory Fact measure group*

24. Enter [**Total Products**] for Name. Enter the following for Expression:

```
[Accepted Products] + [Rejected Products]
```

25. Select Standard from the Format string drop-down list.
26. Check the Accepted Products and Rejected Products measures in the Nonempty Behavior selection window and click OK.
27. Click the New Calculated Member button on the Calculations tab toolbar. The Calculated Member form returns to the default values.
28. Enter [**Percent Rejected**] for Name. Enter the following for Expression:

```
[Rejected Products] / [Total Products]
```

29. Select Percent from the Format String drop-down list.
30. Check the Accepted Products and Rejected Products measures in the Nonempty Behavior selection window and click OK.
31. Click the Save All button on the toolbar.

Dimensions

After taking a good look at measures, let's move on to another part of the OLAP cube—namely, the dimensions. As we have seen, dimensions are what give cubes their true analytical power. They enable us to slice and dice the measures in the cube until we find the meaningful business intelligence hidden among all of the numbers. Dimensions provide understandable phrases in business language to define what may be cryptic in a transactional database system.

Just as there is more to measures than initially meets the eye, dimensions, too, come in a number of different varieties. We will examine their various classifications and capabilities, but first, let's look at the way dimensions are related to measure groups.

Managing Dimensions

Dimensions are managed using the Dimension Design tab. To display this tab, double-click a dimension in the Solution Explorer window. The Dimension Design tab is shown in Figure 9-10 displaying the Dim Product dimension.

The Dimension Design tab includes the entire hierarchy for the dimension. The Dim Product dimension in Figure 9-10 has a three-level hierarchy. The Dimension Design tab contains information about all three levels: the product level, the product subtype level, and the product type level.

The left-hand column of the Dimension Design tab shows all of the attributes for the entire dimension hierarchy. The center column shows the structure of the

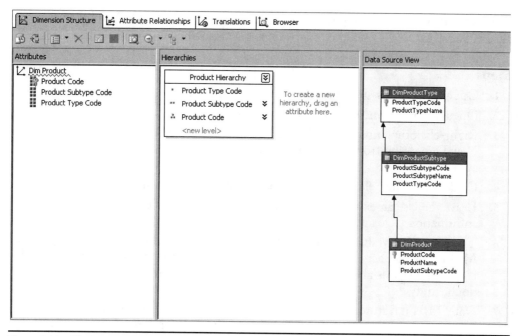

Figure 9-10   *The Dimension Design tab with the Dim Product dimension*

dimension hierarchy. The right-hand column shows the tables from the data source view that define this dimension.

Notice the blue squiggly under the dimension name. This indicates the development environment has some dimensional design suggestions to make. Hover over the squiggle to view these suggestions. We will look at implementing some of this advice in the following Learn By Doing exercise.

We will begin working with dimensions by creating a time dimension in the Max Min Manufacturing DM cube. We will also create hierarchies for two of our dimensions. Finally, we will do some additional clean-up to make our dimensions easier to use when we start to query data from the Max Min Manufacturing DM cube.

Learn By Doing—Cleaning Up the Dimensions in the Max Min Manufacturing DM Cube

Features Highlighted

▶ Creating a time dimension

▶ Creating dimensional hierarchies

▶ Hiding unneeded attribute hierarchies

Business Need We need to have the dimensions in the Max Min Manufacturing DM cube related to the measure groups to perform any meaningful analysis on this cube.

Steps

1. Open the Business Intelligence Development Studio.
2. Open the MaxMinManufacturingDM project.
3. Right-click the Dimensions entry in the Solution Explorer window and select New Dimension from the context menu. The Dimension Wizard dialog box appears.
4. Click Next. The Select Creation Method page of the wizard appears.
5. Leave the Use an existing table item selected and click Next. The Specify Source Information page appears.
6. The Max Min Manufacturing DM data source view is already selected. Make sure ManufacturingFact is selected in the Main table drop-down list. Even though this is a fact table, it is also the table that contains the date information, so it will serve double duty.
7. DateOfManufacture is selected as the first Key column, which is correct. However, the other columns selected in the Key columns area do not apply to our time dimension. Select the blank entry from each of the drop-down lists so DateOfManufacture is the only key column selected.
8. Select DateOfManufacture from the Name column drop-down list. The Specify Source Information page of the wizard should appear as shown in Figure 9-11.
9. Click Next. The Select Related Tables page appears.
10. Uncheck all items in the Related tables area.
11. Click Next. The Select Dimension Attributes page appears.
12. Uncheck Product Code, Batch Number, and Machine Number.
13. Leave Date Of Manufacture checked and also check Year Of Manufacture, Quarter Of Manufacture, and Month Of Manufacture.
14. Click in the Attribute Type column across from Date Of Manufacture.
15. Click the drop-down arrow.
16. Expand the Date entry.
17. Expand the Calendar entry.
18. Select Date and click OK.
19. Click in the Attribute Type column across from Year Of Manufacture.
20. Click the drop-down arrow.
21. Expand the Date entry.
22. Expand the Calendar entry.

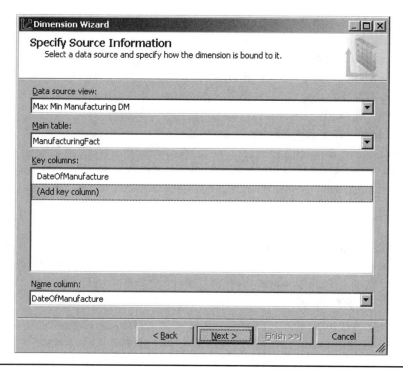

Figure 9-11   *Creating the Time Dimension*

23. Select Year and click OK.

24. Repeat Steps 19–23 for Quarter Of Manufacture, selecting Quarter.

25. Repeat Steps 19–23 for Month Of Manufacture, selecting Month.

26. Click Next. The Completing the Wizard page appears.

27. Change the name to **Dim Time**.

28. Click Finish. The Dimension Design tab appears with the Dim Time dimension.

29. Right-click the entry for Date of Manufacture in the Attributes area and select Rename from the context menu.

30. Enter **Date** for the name of this attribute and press ENTER.

31. Repeat Steps 29 and 30 to rename the other attributes as follows:

Old Name	New Name
Month Of Manufacture	Month
Quarter Of Manufacture	Quarter
Year Of Manufacture	Year

32. Drag the Year item from the Attributes column and drop it in the Hierarchies area.

33. Drag the Quarter item from the Attributes column and drop it on <new level> in the Hierarchies area.

34. Repeat Step 33 for Month and Date.

35. Right-click the word "Hierarchy" in the Hierarchies area and select Rename from the context menu.

36. Enter **Date Hierarchy** and press ENTER.

37. Click Date in the Attributes area. Hold down SHIFT and click Year in the Attributes area. All four attributes should be selected.

38. In the Properties window, change the AttributeHierarchyVisible property to False.

NOTE

These attributes can show up individually in the dimension as their own attribute hierarchies, as well as members of the Date Hierarchy we just created. This gets a bit confusing for the user querying data from the cube. To cut down on this confusion, we told the individual attribute hierarchies to be hidden. Only the Date Hierarchy will be visible to the user.

39. Click the Attribute Relationships tab. Note the Date is related to the other three items, but the relationship structure does not mirror the hierarchy we just created.

40. Select the Month and drop it on the Quarter.

41. Select the Quarter and drop it on the Year.

42. Right-click each of the relationship arrows and select Relationship Type | Rigid from the context menu. The Attribute Relationships tab should appear as shown in Figure 9-12.

NOTE

A flexible attribute relationship may change over time. A rigid attribute relationship does not change. For example, 8/1/2008 will always be in August, 2008. It is a rigid relationship. Attribute relationships default to flexible. They should be set to rigid wherever appropriate.

43. Click the Save All button on the toolbar.

44. Close the Dim Time dimension tab.

45. In the Solution Explorer window, double-click the Dim Machine dimension entry. The Dim Machine dimension tab appears.

46. Create a new hierarchy and name it **Material Hierarchy**. This hierarchy should have the following levels:
Material
Machine Type
Machine Number

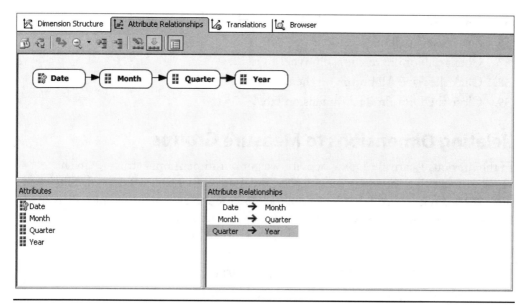

Figure 9-12 *The Attribute Relationships tab*

47. Create a second hierarchy and name it **Plant Hierarchy**. This hierarchy should have the following levels:
    Country Code
    Plant Number
    Machine Number

48. Set the AttributeHierarchyVisible property for all of the attributes to False.

49. Select the Attribute Relationships tab.

50. Change all of the relationship types to rigid.

51. Click the Save All button on the toolbar.

52. Close the Dim Machine dimension tab.

53. In the Solution Explorer window, double-click the Dim Product dimension entry. The Dim Product dimension tab appears.

54. Create a new hierarchy and name it **Product Hierarchy**. This hierarchy should have the following levels:
    Product Type Code
    Product Subtype Code
    Product Code

55. Set the AttributeHierarchyVisible property for all of the attributes to False.
56. Select the Attribute Relationships tab.
57. Change all of the relationship types to rigid.
58. Click the Save All button on the toolbar.
59. Close the Dim Product dimension tab.

Relating Dimensions to Measure Groups

In the previous Learn By Doing activity, we got our dimensional structure in shape. However, we still have one issue with the Dim Time dimension we created. This dimension is not related to either of the measure groups. A dimension must be related to a measure group before we can use it to analyze data from the cube.

We can solve this situation right now with another Learn By Doing activity.

Learn By Doing—Relating Dimensions in the Max Min Manufacturing DM Cube

Feature Highlighted

▶ Relating dimensions to measure groups

Business Need We need to have the Dim Time dimension in the Max Min Manufacturing DM cube related to the measure groups to perform any meaningful analysis on this cube.

Steps
1. Double-click the entry for Max Min Manufacturing DM.cube to display the Cube Design tab.
2. Select the Dimension Usage tab of the Cube Design tab.
3. Right-click in the empty area of the tab and select Add Cube Dimension. The Add Cube Dimension dialog box appears.
4. Select the Dim Time dimension and click OK.
5. The Dim Time dimension is added to the cube. The Business Intelligence Development Studio figures out how to relate the Dim Time dimension to the Manufacturing Fact group. (Not too difficult considering they are both defined from the same table.) We will need to relate the Inventory Fact group ourselves.

6. Click the entry in the Inventory Fact column and the Dim Time row. An ellipsis (…) button appears.

7. Click the ellipsis button. The Define Relationship dialog box appears.

8. Select Regular in the Select relationship type drop-down list. We are specifying that the Dim Time dimension relates to the Inventory Fact measure group as a regular dimension.

9. Select Date from the Granularity attribute drop-down list. This is the attribute in the dimension that defines the granularity of the measure group for this dimension. We can either select the primary key of the table that defines the dimension or we can select one of the attribute fields in this table.

10. In the Relationship grid, select DateOfInventory from the drop-down list under Measure Group Columns. This creates a relationship between the DateOfManufacture column in the table that defines the dimension and the DateOfInventory column in the table that defines the measure group.

11. Click OK to exit the Define Relationship dialog box.

    Once completed, the Dimension Usage tab should appear as shown in Figure 9-13.

12. Click the Save All button on the toolbar.

Types of Dimensions

Dimensions can be placed in a number of classifications. These classifications tell us something about the way a dimension is created and managed. They can also shed some light on how a dimension is utilized.

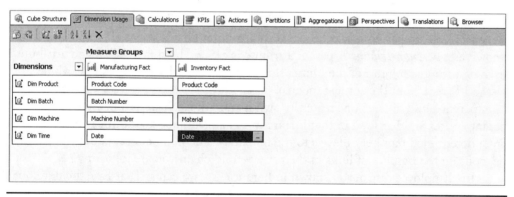

Figure 9-13   *The Dimension Usage tab of the Max Min Manufacturing DM cube*

Fact Dimensions

In most cases, the information used to populate a dimension resides in a dimension table. DimProduct and DimMachine are examples from our Manufacturing data mart. However, when we created the Dim Time dimension, we used data from the DateOfManufacture field and the YearOfManufacture, QuarterOfManufacture, and MonthOfManufacture named calculations in the ManufacturingFact table.

Dimensions created from attributes in a fact table are known as *fact dimensions*. They are also known in the "biz" as degenerate dimensions. (This seems like a highly slanderous name, if you ask me.)

Fact dimensions follow a few simple rules in Analysis Services:

▶   At most, one fact dimension can be in a measure group.

▶   A fact dimension must be defined by one and only one measure group.

▶   A fact dimension can have a fact relationship with only one measure group. It can, however, have a regular relationship with additional measure groups.

The Define Relationship dialog box for a fact dimension is shown in Figure 9-14.

Parent-Child Dimensions

A *parent-child dimension* is built on a table that contains a self-referential relationship. An employee table that contains a supervisor field is a good example. Figure 9-15 shows a table with a Supervisor field. The supervisor field contains the employee number of the person to whom the employee reports. This field is a foreign key field that points back to the same table.

When a table, such as the Employee table in Figure 9-15, is used to define a dimension, the Supervisor field becomes an attribute. This is a special type of attribute known as a *parent attribute*. A parent attribute is created by right-clicking an attribute in the Attributes column of the Dimension Design tab and selecting Set Attribute Usage | Parent from the context menu.

A parent-child dimension creates its own hierarchy. Each step from child to parent creates another level in that hierarchy. What is unique about this is there are an undetermined number of levels to the hierarchy. The number of hierarchy levels depends on the number of links in the parent-child chain you are following.

In the Employee dimension shown in Figure 9-15, we can start at Eva, the developer, and follow the chain of supervisors up to Maya, the CEO. There are six levels to the hierarchy along this path. If, however, we start at Juan, the system administrator, and follow the chain of supervisors up to Maya, there are four levels to the hierarchy.

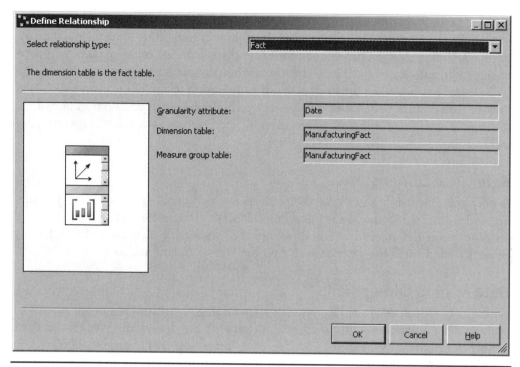

Figure 9-14   *The Define Relationship dialog box for a fact dimension*

Role Playing Dimensions

A *role playing dimension* is a dimension that is related to the same measure group multiple times. Each relationship represents a different role the dimension plays relative to the measure group. One of the best examples of this is a time dimension and a sales

Employees

Emp #	Name	Position	Supervisor
129	Sandra	Team Leader	239
235	Eva	Developer	129
239	Peter	Development Manager	303
293	Maya	CEO	
303	Frank	IT Director	470
470	Tia	CFO	293
487	Juan	System Administrator	303

Figure 9-15   *An employee table with a self-referential field*

measure group. The time dimension is related to the sales measure group once for the date of the sale, another time for the date of shipment, and a third time for the date of payment. In this case, the time dimension plays three different roles—date of sale, date of shipment, and date of payment—relative to the sales measure group.

To create a role playing dimension, add the dimension to the Dimension Usage tab multiple times. Each instance of the dimension should be renamed to reflect one of the roles it is playing for this measure group. Then, create a relationship between each instance of the dimension and the measure group.

Reference Dimensions

A reference dimension is not related directly to the measure group. Instead, a *reference dimension* is related to another regular dimension, which is, in turn, related to the measure group. Reference dimensions are created by selecting Referenced from the Select Relationship Type drop-down list on the Define Relationship dialog box.

Data Mining Dimensions

We can include information discovered by data mining algorithms in our cubes for analysis. This is done through the creation of data mining dimensions. We discuss data mining in Chapters 13, 14, and 15. *Data mining dimensions* are created by selecting Data Mining from the Select Relationship Type drop-down list on the Define Relationship dialog box.

Many-to-Many Dimensions

Many-to-many dimensions, as the name implies, support many-to-many relationships between dimension members and measure group members. For example, if an e-commerce site allows an order to have multiple ship-to addresses, there is a many-to-many relationship. An order can have multiple addresses and, of course, an address can be used by more than one order.

In a relational database, a many-to-many relationship is implemented by creating an intermediate linking table. When a many-to-many relationship is implemented in an Analysis Services cube, the intermediate linking table becomes an intermediate fact table. Many-to-many dimensions are created by selecting Many-to-Many from the Select Relationship Type drop-down list on the Define Relationship dialog box.

Slowly Changing Dimensions

For our cubes to provide meaningful information from year to year, we need to have dimensions whose members are fairly constant. If the dimensions are changing drastically month to month, our analysis across the time dimension becomes worthless. Therefore, we need mainly static dimensions.

Some dimensions, however, change over time. Salespeople move from one sales territory to another. The corporate organizational chart changes as employees are promoted or resign. These are known as Slowly Changing Dimensions (SCD).

SCDs come in three varieties: Type 1, Type 2, and Type 3, as defined by the Business Intelligence community. Not exciting names, but they didn't ask for my input, so it's what we are stuck with! Anyway, let's look at what differentiates each type of SCD.

Type 1 Slowly Changing Dimensions

When a dimension is implemented as a Type 1 SCD, we don't keep track of its history as it changes. The members of the dimension represent the way things are right now. With a *Type 1 SCD*, it is impossible to go back and determine the state of the dimension members at any time in the past.

In actuality, all dimensions in Analysis Services cubes are allowed to change. Some dimensions track that change so a previous state of that dimension's members can be reconstructed during analysis. These are the Type 2 SCD and Type 3 SCD, which we discuss in the sections "Type 2 Slowly Changing Dimensions" and "Type 3 Slowly Changing Dimensions." If a dimension does not track this change, it is a Type 1 SCD. In most cases, the majority of the dimensions in your cubes are going to be Type 1 SCD.

Let's consider a situation where we have four salespeople—Jackie, Andy, Sam, and Mollie—in four sales territories: A, B, C, and D. (All right, so maybe my naming isn't always that creative either!) Figure 9-16 shows the situation in May. Jackie is in sales territory A. Andy is in sales territory B. Sam is in sales territory C, and Mollie is in sales territory D. The figure reflects the fact that the four salespeople are expected to remain in their territories through the rest of the year.

Now, let's suppose at the beginning of August, Mollie is promoted to sales manager. Andy is moved to Mollie's former sales territory (sales territory D) and a new salesperson, Pat, is hired to take over Andy's former territory (sales territory B). The state of the salesperson dimension after the shuffling is shown in Figure 9-17. Because this is a Type 1 SCD, we do not track any history. We just overwrite the previous dimension information with the current dimension information.

If we perform analysis on sales information using this cube, it will look like Andy has always been in sales territory D and Pat has always been in sales territory B. This is true if we look at sales measures for June or if we look at sales information for October. The history is lost.

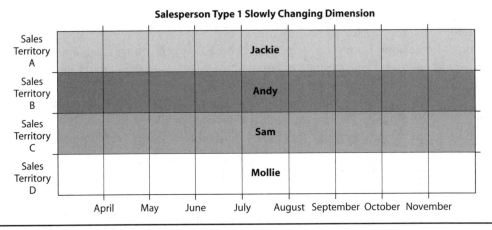

Figure 9-16   *The state of the salesperson Type 1 SCD in May*

Type 2 Slowly Changing Dimensions

When a dimension is implemented as a *Type 2 SCD*, four supplementary attributes are added to the dimension to track the history of that dimension. These four attributes are:

▶ **SCD Original ID**   An alternative primary key for the dimension

▶ **SCD Start Date**   The date this dimension member became active

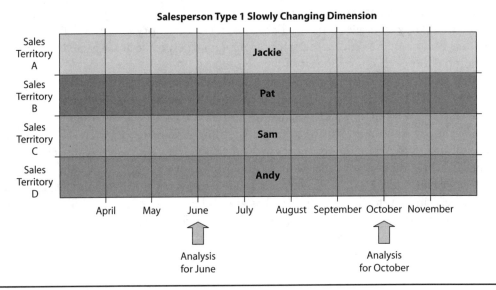

Figure 9-17   *The state of the salesperson Type 1 SCD after August*

▶ **SCD End Date** The date this dimension member ceased being active

▶ **SCD Status** The current state of this dimension member, either active or inactive

Let's return to our salesperson dimension example. Figure 9-18 shows the state of the dimension in May. Three of the four new fields are shown in the figure: Start Date, End Date, and Status. Because none of the dimension members has an end date filled in, they are expected to remain active indefinitely into the future.

After the changes to the sales territories occur at the beginning of August, you can see how the new fields are used to track both the previous state and the current state of the sales territory assignments. This is shown in Figure 9-19. Now, by using the Start Date and End Date attributes, when we perform analysis for May, we see how the salespeople were arranged in May. When we do analysis for October, we see how the salespeople were arranged in October. When we want to find the current state of the dimension, we can use the Status attribute to quickly locate the active members rather than doing a lot of date comparisons.

The Original ID attribute holds a unique identifier that is used as the primary key for this dimension. This alternate key is used in place of the ID field that would normally serve this purpose. In our examples, the Original ID field would be used as the primary key in place of the salesperson's employee number. Because a salesperson can appear in the dimension more than once, this alternate key is necessary to prevent primary key violations.

In the Type 1 SCD example, each employee can only appear once in the Salesperson dimension. Therefore, the salesperson's employee ID can be used as the primary. This is not the case with the Type 2 SCD.

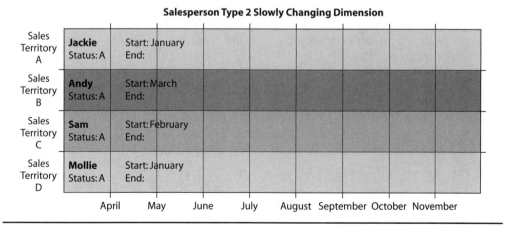

Figure 9-18 *The state of the salesperson Type 2 SCD in May*

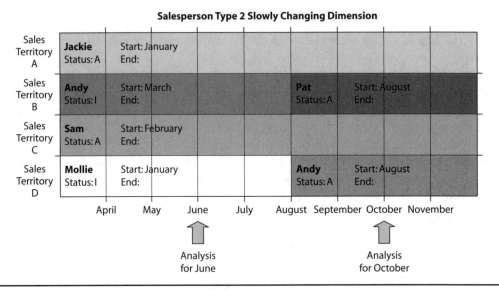

Figure 9-19   *The state of the salesperson Type 2 SCD after August*

In the Type 2 SCD, a salesperson can appear in the dimension more than once. You can see this with Andy in Figure 9-19. Andy has two dimension members: the member with an effective start date in March and the member with the effective start date in August. If we defined a primary key using the employee ID, we would receive an error when we tried to insert the second entry into this dimension. When the Original ID is used as the primary key, there are no run-time errors because the Original ID is unique to each member in the dimension.

When we use the Original ID as the primary key, we also have to use it in the foreign key fields in the fact tables. That way we can tell which measures are linked to Andy when he was in sales territory B and which measures are linked to Andy when he was in sales territory D.

Type 3 Slowly Changing Dimensions

A Type 3 SCD is similar to a Type 2 SCD with one exception. A Type 3 SCD does not track the entire history of the dimension members. Instead, a *Type 3 SCD* tracks only the current state and the original state of a dimension member.

A Type 3 SCD is implemented using two additional attributes:

▶ **SCD Start Date**   The date the current state of this dimension member became active

▶ **SCD Initial Value**   The original state of this attribute

A Slowly Changing Dimension in Action

In addition to the Manufacturing data mart, we created another data mart back in Chapter 6. This is the Sales data mart. You will recall that we created both the database schema for the data mart and the OLAP cube definition at the same time using the Cube Wizard. This data mart may have a cube, but it has even less data than the Manufacturing data mart. It is completely empty. We can remedy this situation as well.

The cube we created for the Sales data mart includes an SCD to track the salespeople as they moved from sales territory to sales territory and from job to job. You can see how we load data into an SCD by using the MaxMinSalesDMDimLoad project to populate the dimension tables in the Sales data mart. You can then use the MaxMinSalesDMDimLoad project to populate the fact table. You need to execute the Integration Services packages in these two projects in order to load data into your copy of the MaxMinSalesDM data mart. Alternately, you can restore the back up of the MaxMinSalesDM database, which has already been loaded with data. It is necessary for you to do one or the other in order to have a populated database to use with Learn By Doing exercises later in this book. The Integration Services projects and the database back up are included in the zip file download for this book. Follow the directions that come along with these projects or with the database backup.

You Are Special

In this chapter, we looked deeper into what makes an OLAP cube tick. We examined the cube's basic parts: measures and dimensions. In Chapter 10, we move from the basics to what makes Microsoft SQL Server Analysis Services such an outstanding tool. We examine many of the special features available to us as we work with our OLAP cubes.

Chapter 10

Bells and Whistles— Special Features of OLAP Cubes

In This Chapter

▶ **Where No Cube Has Gone Before**

▶ **Additional Cube Features**

▶ **More Sophisticated Scripting**

I do not like poems that resemble hay compressed into a geometrically perfect cube.
                                                                —Yevgeny Yevtushenko

Thus far, we have created two data marts for our sample company, Maximum Miniatures, Incorporated. Both data marts are full of data (assuming you used the MaxMinSalesDMDimLoad projects and Max SalesDMFactLoad solutions to populate the Sales data mart). We also have an online analytical processing (OLAP) cube built on top of each of these data marts. You may think our work is almost done. On the contrary, it is just beginning!

We have data sitting in data marts in relational databases. We have cube definitions that exist as Extensible Markup Language (XML) definition documents in our development environments. What we do not have are multidimensional cubes filled with preprocessed aggregates waiting to help us create business intelligence. (In case you forgot after reading the first few chapters, that is why we are here.)

We begin by taking care of this very issue. We can deploy our cubes to SQL Server Analysis Services databases. We can then begin querying aggregates from the cubes and begin to see benefit from our labors.

Once the cubes are deployed, we examine many of the special features available in these OLAP cubes. We move between the Business Intelligence Development Studio and the SQL Server Management Studio to view the data and try out the development tools at our disposal.

Where No Cube Has Gone Before

We begin this chapter by taking our cubes where they have not gone before: to the SQL Server Analysis Services server. Up to this point, when we have worked with dimensions and measures, it has been as definitions in the Business Intelligence Development Studio. This environment is great for creating and refining these objects. Unfortunately, dimensions and measures cannot do much when they only exist here. To put them to work, we must deploy them to an Analysis Services server.

Our Analysis Services projects in the Business Intelligence Development Studio contain several properties that control deployment of the content of a project. Once these properties are set correctly, deploying the project content is a snap. All it takes is one selection from a context menu.

Alternatively, we can turn the entire definition of the project into an XML for Analysis (XML/A) script. This is done using the Analysis Services Deployment Wizard. As the script is generated by the Deployment Wizard, we have the ability to change some of the configuration information, such as server names and credentials, so the scripts function on different servers. Your environment may require slightly different configurations for development, quality assurance, and production. Once the script is generated with the appropriate configuration settings, it can be loaded into a SQL Server Management Studio query window and executed on an Analysis Services server.

Deploying and Processing

We need to complete two steps before our cubes become useful. First, we need to deploy the structures to the Analysis Services database. Second, we need to process those structures in the Analysis Services database.

Deploying

Deploying is the first step to creating a useful Analysis Services structure. When we *deploy* an Analysis Services project, we move that project's definition from the development environment to a server environment. In a development environment, the developer is the only one who has access to the objects in a project. In the server environment, those objects are exposed to any users with the appropriate access rights.

The objects in a project cannot reside on an Analysis Services server on their own. They must be contained within an Analysis Services database. The name of the database is specified in the project definition. If the specified database is not present, it is created as part of the deployment process.

Deploying a project results in an exact copy of that project's measures and dimensions on the server. Deploying a project does not result in any members being placed in those dimensions or any facts being placed in those measures. For this to happen, we need to process the Analysis Services database.

Processing

Processing is the procedure that pumps the database full of the good stuff. When an Analysis Services database is processed, it reads data from its data source. Dimensions are populated with members. Measures are populated with facts. Then the aggregates for all the combinations within the dimensional hierarchy are calculated.

Dimensions are processed first. Data is read from the dimension tables in the data source and used to create dimension members. After all of the dimension members are loaded, map files that contain all of the possible dimension and hierarchy member combinations are created. These map files are used for calculating aggregates.

Measures are processed after the dimension processing is complete. Data is read from the fact tables in the data source and used to create measures. The map files are used to ensure that aggregations are created for the entire cube. Data for calculated members is also determined at this time.

When processing is complete, the Analysis Services database is ready for analysis to begin.

Deploying from the Business Intelligence Development Studio

We first look at the steps necessary to deploy from the Business Intelligence Development Studio. This method is certainly the most straightforward of our two options. However, as we see shortly, it does not provide the flexibility of the Analysis Services Deployment Wizard.

We begin with an Analysis Services project in the Business Intelligence Development Studio. Several properties of this project must be set before the deployment can take place. These properties are found on the Deployment page of the Project Property Pages dialog box, shown in Figure 10-1.

Let's go through the properties starting at the bottom of the dialog box and working our way to the top. The *Database property* is the name of an Analysis Services database. This database is created on the server, if it does not already exist there. The *Server property* contains the name of the SQL Server Analysis Services server where the project is to be deployed.

The *Deployment Mode property* controls how the project is deployed; either all of the project is deployed or only the changed objects are deployed. The *Transactional Deployment property* determines whether the project is deployed as a single transaction or as multiple transactions. If the project is deployed as multiple transactions, the deploying is done in one transaction and each processing operation done as part of the deployment is done in its own transaction.

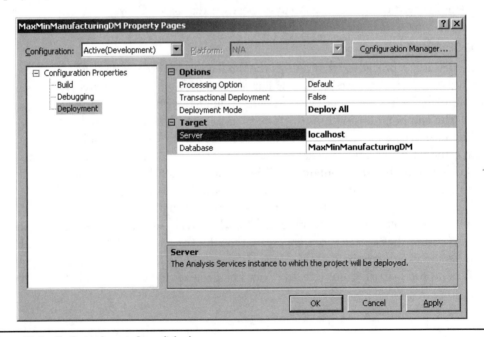

Figure 10-1 *The Project Property Pages dialog box*

The *Processing Option parameter* establishes what cube processing is done as part of the deployment. If Default is selected, the deployment includes whatever processing is necessary to bring the deployed objects to a fully processed state. If Do Not Process is selected, no processing is done. If Full is selected, all of the data is deleted from the deployed objects and all values are reloaded or recalculated.

The information entered on the Deployment page of the Project Property Pages dialog box is stored in two different configuration files. These files are located in the bin folder inside of the folder created for your project. The configuration settings are stored in the {*project name*}.deploymentoptions file. The deployment target settings are stored in the {*projectname*}.deploymenttargets file. Note, the bin folder and these deployment files are created as part of the deployment process, so they will not be present until you have tried to deploy the project.

Once the properties on the Deployment page are set, we can perform the actual deployment. This can be done by selecting Build | Deploy {*project name*} from the Main menu or by right-clicking the project entry in the Solution Explorer window and selecting Deploy from the context menu. The progress of the deployment is displayed in the Output window and the Deployment Progress window, as shown in Figure 10-2.

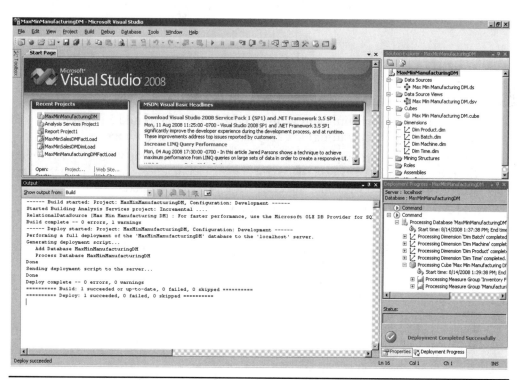

Figure 10-2 *Deploying an Analysis Services project from the Business Intelligence Development Studio*

The Business Intelligence Development Studio begins the deployment by creating a script. This script contains commands to create the specified Analysis Services database, if necessary, and to create each of the objects in the project. If the appropriate processing option is selected for the project, the script also includes commands to process each object. This script is then executed on the specified server. We see what one of these scripts looks like in the next section of this book.

Learn By Doing—Deploying the MaxMinManufacturingDM Project Using the Business Intelligence Development Studio

Features Highlighted

▶   Deploying an Analysis Services project using the Business Intelligence Development Studio

▶   Using the Browse window in the SQL Server Management Studio to browse the content of a cube

Business Need   To have an OLAP cube we can finally put to use, we must deploy and process this project.

Steps

1. Open the Business Intelligence Development Studio.
2. Open the MaxMinManufacturingDM project.
3. Select Project | MaxMinManufacturingDM Properties from the Main menu. The MaxMinManufacturingDM Property Pages dialog box appears.
4. On the Deployment page, enter the name of a test or development server running SQL Server 2008 Analysis Services for Server. (Do *not* perform this or any other Learn By Doing activity on a server used for production operations!)
5. MaxMinManufacturingDM should already be entered for Database.
6. Click OK to exit the MaxMinManufacturingDM Property Pages dialog box.
7. Select Build | Deploy MaxMinManufacturingDM from the Main menu. Provide a set of credentials for completing this deployment, if prompted to do so. Monitor the progress of the deployment in the Output and Deployment Progress windows until the Deployment Completed Successfully message appears.
8. To prove that we actually did something, we use the SQL Server Management Studio to browse the cube in our newly created Analysis Services database. Open the SQL Server Management Studio.
9. Select Analysis Services for Server type and connect to the Analysis Services server where you deployed the project.

10. Expand the Databases folder under this server in the Object Explorer window.

11. Expand the entry for the MaxMinManufacturingDM database, and then expand the Cubes folder under this database.

12. Right-click the Max Min Manufacturing DM cube and select Browse from the context menu. You see a Browse window, as shown in Figure 10-3.

13. Expand the Measures entry in the Browser window. Drag the Total Products calculated member and drop it on Drop Totals or Detail Fields Here. You see the total products calculated for the entire cube.

14. Expand the Dim Product entry in the Browser window. Expand the Product Hierarchy entry beneath it. Drag the Product Type level and drop it on Drop Row Fields Here. You see the total products calculation spread across each of the product types. The product type code numbers are shown. We will modify the cube to display the product type names later in this chapter.

15. Expand the Dim Time entry in the Browser window. Expand the Date Hierarchy entry beneath it. Drag the Month level and drop it on Drop Column Fields Here.

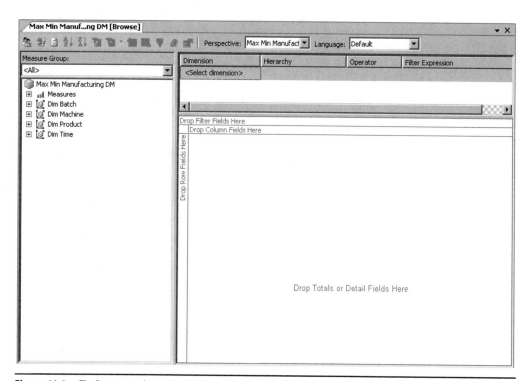

Figure 10-3   *The Browse window in the SQL Server Management Studio*

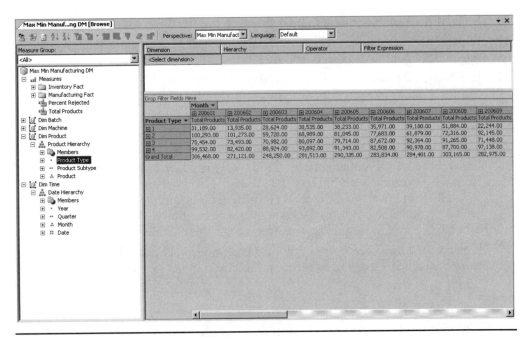

Figure 10-4 *Browsing the Max Min Manufacturing DM cube*

You see the total products calculation spread across the product types and months of the year. You can see now that the Browser is a pivot table. This is shown in Figure 10-4.

16. Expand one of the product type codes to view its product subtype codes. This is shown in Figure 10-5.

17. Drag the Year level and drop it to the left of the Month heading in the pivot table. This is shown in Figure 10-6. This creates a higher level in the pivot table columns. Expand 2006 to view its months. This is shown in Figure 10-7.

NOTE

We are able to skip levels in the hierarchy when we use the Browse window. In this example, we use the year and month levels of the Time dimension without using the Quarter level.

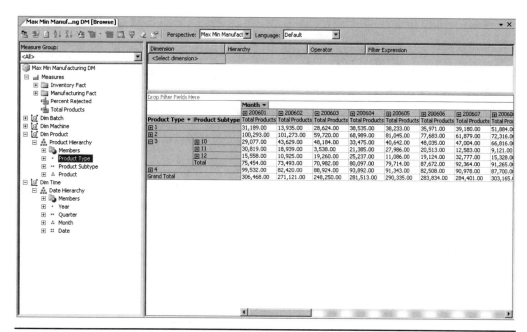

Figure 10-5   *Two levels of rows in the Browse window*

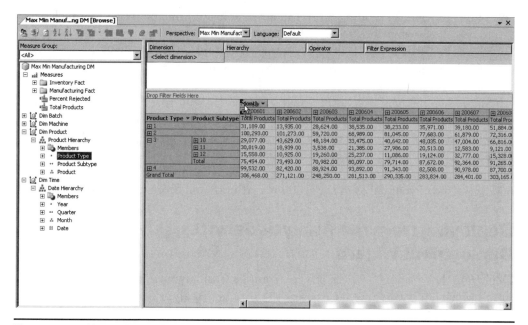

Figure 10-6   *Adding a column level to the Browse window*

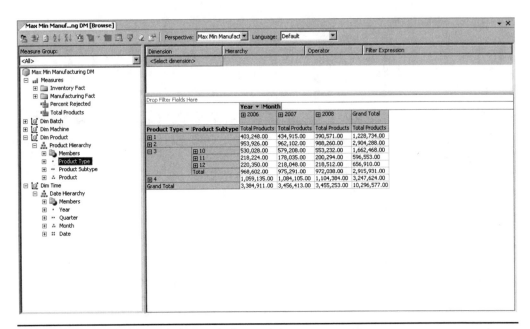

Figure 10-7   *Two levels of rows and columns in the Browse window*

18. Drag the Month heading off of the pivot table until the mouse pointer includes an *X*, as shown in Figure 10-8. Drop the heading any time the mouse pointer includes the *X*, and this dimension is then removed from the pivot table.

19. Continue to experiment with the Browse window as long as you like.

Congratulations, you have just created and browsed your first bit of honest-to-goodness business intelligence (BI). It only took us ten chapters to get here! SQL Server 2008 greatly simplifies the creation of business intelligence, but it still takes some work. Don't worry: This gets easier and goes faster each time you repeat the process from here on. Besides, we look at a shortcut you may be able to use when building some of your cubes in the section "Partitions and Storage Options."

Deploying from the Analysis Services Deployment Wizard

Deploying the Analysis Services project from the Business Intelligence Development Studio works great when we have access to the target Analysis Services server. At times,

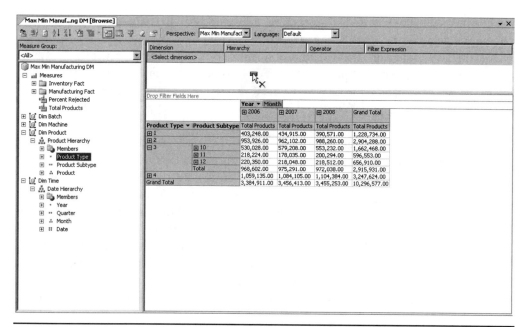

Figure 10-8   *Dragging an item off the pivot table*

however, this may not be the case. And, at other times, we need to make changes to the configuration of the project when it is moved from the development environment into production. Fortunately, we have a second method for deploying that handles both of these needs: deploying from the Analysis Services Deployment Wizard.

The Analysis Services Deployment Wizard can deploy a project directly to a database server, just like the Business Intelligence Development Server. However, it can also examine the definition of a project and create an XML for Analysis (XML/A) script that can re-create the items on a server. The XML/A script is written to a file. It is up to us to execute that file on the server to complete the deployment.

To use the wizard, we need to develop an Analysis Services project in the Business Intelligence Development Studio. Once the project is developed, we need to perform a build operation on the project to create the files necessary for the wizard. This is done by selecting Build | Build {*project name*} from the Main menu. Once the project builds successfully, it is ready to deploy.

The wizard is a stand-alone program, separate from the Business Intelligence Development Studio. The Analysis Services Deployment Wizard is launched from the SQL Server 2008 entry in the Windows Start menu. To launch the wizard, select Start | All Programs | Microsoft SQL Server 2008 | Analysis Services | Deployment Wizard.

After the welcome page, the wizard prompts you for the path and name of an Analysis Services database file on the Specify Source Analysis Services Database page, shown in Figure 10-9. This database file is created when we build the Analysis Services project. It has a file extension of asdatabase and is located in the bin folder inside of the folder created for your project (for example, C:\...\Myproject\bin\MyAnalSrvcsProj.asdatabase).

The Installation Target page, shown in Figure 10-10, asks for the Analysis Services server and Analysis Services database this project is to be deployed to. Remember, the wizard does not perform the deployment; it only creates a script for the deploy step. Therefore, the wizard does not need access to the server you specify.

The Specify Options for Partitions and Roles page enables us to determine how partitions and security entities are to be handled by the deployment. We discuss partitions in the section "Partitions" in this chapter. We discuss security in Chapter 11. This page asks us to specify whether existing objects are overwritten or retained. Therefore, it only applies to situations where we are deploying updates to an existing database. The Specify Options for Partitions and Roles page is shown in Figure 10-11.

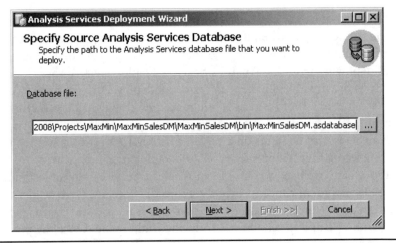

Figure 10-9 *The Specify Source Analysis Services Database page of the Analysis Services Deployment Wizard*

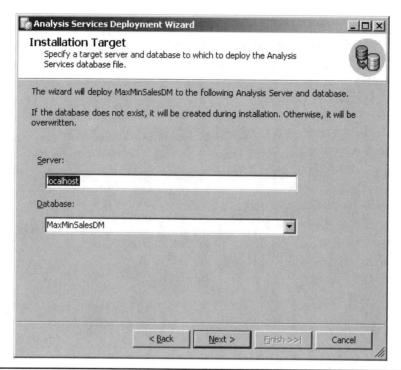

Figure 10-10   *The Installation Target page of the Analysis Services Deployment Wizard*

The Specify Configuration Properties page, shown in Figure 10-12, collects a number of pieces of configuration information. First, it lets us specify whether the configuration and optimization settings for existing objects are retained or overwritten. Next, it enables us to modify the connection strings used by the data sources in this project. This may be necessary as projects are moved from a development environment to a production environment. We can also configure the impersonation settings, error log file locations, and the path to the database file being created.

The Data Source Impersonation Information entry specifies the Windows credentials that are to be impersonated by this data source while accessing the underlying database. The Default Data Source Impersonation Information entry specifies the Windows credentials that are impersonated if the data source's impersonation is set to default. Somewhere in this chain, we need an actual set of credentials to use during data processing. For this reason, you may need to select the

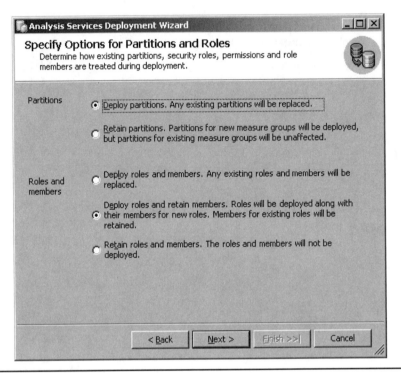

Figure 10-11 *The Specify Options for Partitions and Roles page of the Analysis Services Deployment Wizard*

service account for either the Data Source Impersonation Information or the Default Data Source Impersonation Information to deploy and process the script correctly.

The Select Processing Options page lets us select the type of processing we would like to occur as part of the deployment. It also enables us to configure the writeback options. We discuss writeback in the section "Writeback." This page also lets us choose whether the processing is done in one transaction or in multiple transactions. This page is shown in Figure 10-13.

The Confirm Deployment page, shown in Figure 10-14, is where we start the deployment process, either deploying to a server or creating a deployment script. The Create Deployment Script check box enables us to create a deployment script, rather than having the wizard deploy directly to the server. We need to specify the path and name if the script file option is selected.

Clicking Next on the Confirm Deployment page causes the wizard either to deploy the project to the server or to create the deployment script. Once either of these

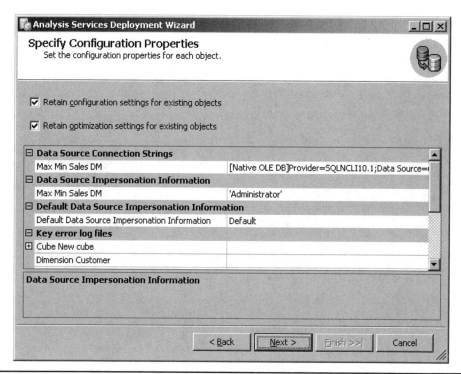

Figure 10-12 *The Specify Configuration Properties page of the Analysis Services Deployment Wizard*

processes is completed, the page appears similar to Figure 10-15. The Deploying Database page is followed by the Deployment Complete page, which confirms the deployment process, or at least the script generation, is complete.

If a script is generated by the wizard, we need to execute that script on the SQL Server 2008 Analysis Services server. If the server is not directly connected to the development environment where it was created, the script file can be copied and transferred as needed. When the script is in a location that can be accessed by the Analysis Services server, it can be opened and executed in the SQL Server Management Studio.

After starting the SQL Server Management Studio, select File | Open | File from the Main menu or use the Open File button on the toolbar to load the deployment script. Loading the script causes the SQL Server Management Studio to open an XML/A query window and to prompt you to connect to an Analysis Services server, if you are not already connected to one. Once the script is loaded

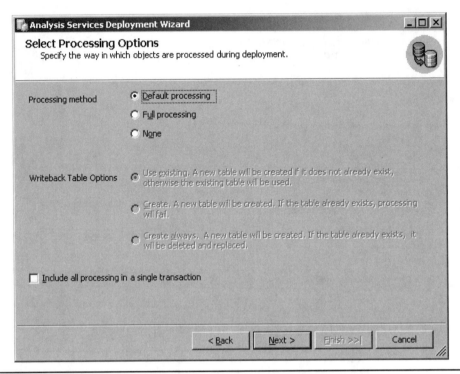

Figure 10-13 *The Select Processing Options page of the Analysis Services Deployment Wizard*

and this connection is made, the SQL Server Management Studio appears similar to Figure 10-16.

Execute the script using the Execute button on the toolbar. The script creates all of the items in your project and performs processing as you instructed in the Deployment Wizard. When the script is completed, you can see the "Query executed successfully" message below the Query window.

Learn By Doing—Deploying the MaxMinSalesDM Project Using the Analysis Services Deployment Wizard

Feature Highlighted

▶ Deploying an Analysis Services project using the Analysis Services Deployment Wizard

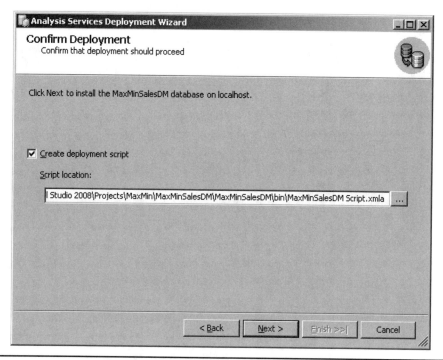

Figure 10-14   *The Confirm Deployment page of the Analysis Services Deployment Wizard*

Business Need   To have a second OLAP cube ready to go, we must deploy and process the MaxMinSalesDM project.

Steps

1. Open the Business Intelligence Development Studio.
2. Open the MaxMinSalesDM project.
3. Open the MaxMinSalesDM.dsv data source view.
4. Right-click anywhere in the unoccupied area of the data source view diagram and select Refresh from the context menu. This will determine the differences between the structures in the data source view and the underlying relational tables. The Refresh Data Source View dialog box appears listing these differences. These are the fields we manually added to the tables near the end of Chapter 6. We need to manually add these changes into the appropriate dimensions.
5. Click OK to incorporate these changes into the data source view. If you receive an error message, click OK.
6. Click the Save All button on the toolbar.
7. Close the data source view design tab.

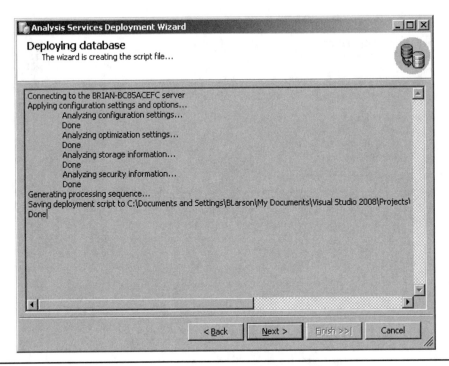

Figure 10-15 *The Deploying Database page of the Analysis Services Deployment Wizard*

8. Open the Customer dimension.

9. In the Data Source View pane of the Customer dimension design tab, select the PK_Customer field.

10. Drag it to the Attributes pane.

11. Repeat this process with the Address, City, State, ZipCode, Homeowner, MaritalStatus, NumCarsOwned, and NumChildrenAtHome fields.

12. In the Attributes Pane, rename the PK Customer attribute to Account Num.

13. With Account Num still selected, change the OrderBy property in the Properties window to Key.

14. Click the Save All button on the toolbar.

15. Close the Customer design tab.

16. Open the Product dimension.

17. Drag the RetailPrice and Weight fields from the Data Source View pane to the Attributes pane.

18. Click the Save All button on the toolbar.

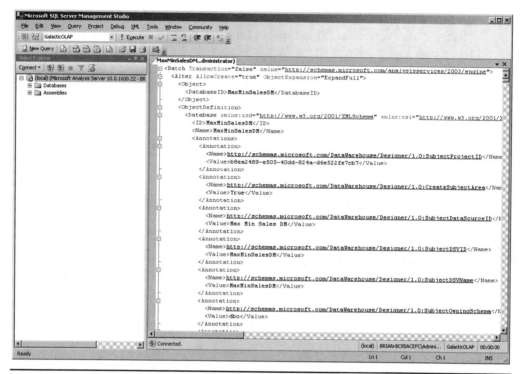

Figure 10-16   *The Deployment Script loaded in a SQL Server Management Studio XML/A Query window*

19. Close the Product design tab.

20. Repeat steps 16-19 to add the SalesPerson_Territory field to the Sales_Person dimension.

21. Repeat steps 16-19 to add the StoreType field to the Sales_Person dimension.

22. Select Build | Build MaxMinSalesDM from the Main menu.

23. Click the Save All button on the toolbar.

24. Close the Business Intelligence Development Studio.

25. From the Windows desktop, select Start | All Programs | Microsoft SQL Server 2008 | Analysis Services | Deployment Wizard. The Analysis Services Deployment Wizard Welcome page appears.

26. Click Next. The Specify Source Analysis Services Database page of the wizard appears.

27. Click the ellipsis button (...). The Open dialog box appears.

28. Browse to the location of the bin directory under the MaxMinSalesDM project. Select the MaxMinSalesDM.asdatabase file and click Open. Click Next. The Installation Target page of the wizard appears.

29. Enter the name of a test or development server running SQL Server 2008 Analysis Services for Server. (Do *not* perform this or any other Learn By Doing activity on a server used for production operations!)

30. MaxMinSalesDM should already be entered for Database. Click Next. The Specify Options for Partitions and Roles page of the wizard appears.

31. Leave the default settings on this page. Click Next. The Specify Configuration Properties page of the wizard appears.

32. Click the word "Default" under Default Data Source Impersonation Information. An ellipsis (...) button appears. Click the ellipsis button. The Impersonation Information dialog box appears.

33. Select Use a specific Windows user name and password. Enter the User name and Password for an account that has administrative rights on the selected Analysis Services server. Click OK.

34. Click Next. The Select Processing Options page of the wizard appears.

35. Leave the default settings on this page. Click Next. The Confirm Deployment page of the wizard appears.

36. Check Create Deployment Script. Click the ellipsis (...) button. The Save As dialog box appears. Browse to a folder that is accessible from the test or development Analysis Services server you are using. Enter **MaxMinSalesDM Script.xmla** for the filename. Click Save, and then click Next. The Deploying Database page of the wizard appears as the wizard creates the deployment script.

37. When the script creation is done, click Next. The Deployment Complete page of the wizard appears. Click Finish.

38. Open the SQL Server Management Studio and connect to the Analysis Services server.

39. Click the Open File button on the toolbar. The Open File dialog box appears.

40. Browse to the location where you created the MaxMinSalesDM Script.xmla file. Select this file and click Open. The script is loaded into an XML/A Query window.

41. Enter the server name and appropriate credentials for the Analysis Services server, and then click Connect.

42. Click the Execute button on the toolbar.

43. The SQL Server Management Studio executes the script and creates the MaxMinSalesDM Analysis Services database.

44. When the Query Executed Successfully message appears below the Query window, right-click the Databases folder entry in the Object Explorer

window and select Refresh from the context menu. The MaxMinSalesDM database appears in the Object Explorer window.

45. Expand the MaxMinSalesDM database and the Data Sources folder.

46. Double-click the Max Min Sales DM data source. The Data Source Properties dialog box appears.

47. Click the Impersonation Info item to select it. Click the elipsis (...) button. The Impersonation Information dialog box appears.

48. Enter the password for this user name and click OK.

49. Click OK to exit the Data Source Properties dialog box.

50. Right-click the MaxMinSalesDM database and select Process from the context menu. The Process Database dialog box appears.

51. Click OK to begin processing the database.

52. Click Close when processing is complete. Feel free to browse the MaxMinSales cube, just as we did with the Max Min Manufacturing DM cube.

Additional Cube Features

Throughout the past few chapters, we have learned how to create and, most recently, deploy Analysis Services cubes. I know you are all ready to rush off and create data marts and cubes to start analyzing your own data. This is when I need to be like the knife salesperson on late-night TV and say, "But wait, there's more!"

SQL Server 2008 offers a number of special features in its OLAP cubes. These features enable us to provide our users with more meaningful, better organized, and more secure business intelligence. Space does not permit a detailed examination of each of these features. Instead, the goal here is to give you a basic understanding of each item so you can do additional exploration on your own. SQL Server 2008 has online documentation called Books Online. Refer to this documentation for a more detailed explanation.

Linked Objects

Depending on the intricacy of your organization and its data processing structure, you may end up creating a number of different Analysis Services cubes from a number of different data sources. Odds are there will be measures in two or three different cubes that a user wants to analyze together. We could solve this problem by duplicating the measures in several cubes. Duplicating data is not a great option, especially if we are preprocessing hundreds of thousands, or even millions, of aggregate values in each cube. Fortunately, we have a better alternative: using linked objects.

By linking objects, we can take measures and their related dimensions from one cube and allow them to be referenced through another cube. This solves our problem without creating maintenance nightmares. Once created, these linked measures and dimensions look to the end user like any other measure or dimension in the cube.

Creating a Linked Measure

Linked objects are created on the Cube Structure tab of the Cube Design tab in the Business Intelligence Development Studio. We open the project for the cube that will contain the linked objects. Right-click in the Measures or Dimensions area and select New Linked Object from the context menu, as shown in Figure 10-17, to launch the Linked Object Wizard.

After the introductory page, the Select a Data Source page of the wizard is displayed. Here, we can select an existing Analysis Service data source, if one exists, or create a new data source using the New Data Source button. If the New Data Source button is clicked, the Data Source Wizard appears. This wizard walks us through the creation of a new data source as we have done previously. The only difference is we are creating a connection to an Analysis Services database, rather than to a transactional database.

Once a data source is created, we are returned to the Linked Object Wizard. Clicking Next takes us to the Select Objects page of the wizard. On this page, we can select the dimensions and measures we want to utilize from this cube to link back into the cube open in the Business Intelligence Development Studio. This is shown in Figure 10-18.

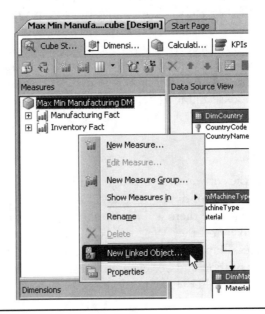

Figure 10-17   *Creating a linked object*

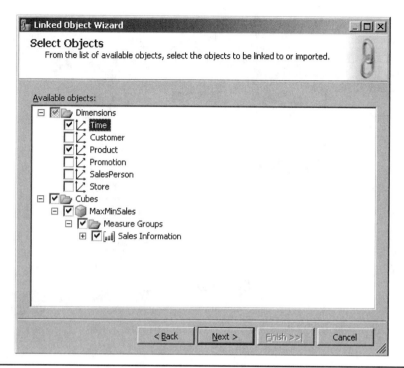

Figure 10-18   *The Select Objects page of the Linked Object Wizard*

The next page of the wizard lets us review our selections and complete the process. After we click Finish, the selected items are added to the cube definition open in the Business Intelligence Development Studio, as shown in Figure 10-19. The linked items appear in the Measures and Dimensions areas with a chain link added to their icons. These items must still be maintained through their original cube. This is why the source tables for these dimensions are not added to the Data Source View in this cube.

The Business Intelligence Wizard

A number of complex business intelligence concepts can be applied to cubes in SQL Server 2008 Analysis Services. The Business Intelligence Development Studio wraps a number of these concepts into the Business Intelligence Wizard. You can think of this as being nine wizards wrapped into one.

The Business Intelligence Wizard enables us to do any of the following:

▶ **Define time intelligence**   Adds time-related calculated measures to the cube. This includes period-to-date calculations, rolling averages, and period over period growth.

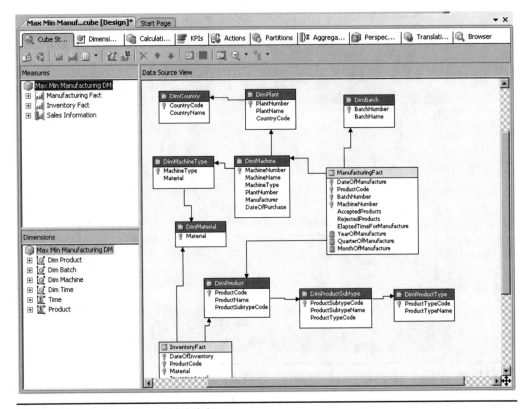

Figure 10-19   *A cube definition with linked objects*

- ▶ **Define account intelligence**   Identifies a dimension and its attributes that define a chart of accounts. Once the chart of accounts is defined, additional calculated values can be created using the account definition.

- ▶ **Define dimension intelligence**   Identifies a dimension and its attributes as being of a certain type, such as products, customers, rates, time, and so forth. Once the dimension type is defined, additional calculated values can be created using the dimension definition.

- ▶ **Specify a unary operator**   Specifies the operator to be used instead of the default aggregation in a dimension with a parent-child hierarchy.

- ▶ **Create a custom member formula**   Creates a calculation to be used instead of the default aggregation in a hierarchy.

- ▶ **Specify attribute ordering**   Specifies how the members of a particular attribute are to be sorted. The default order is by name.

▶ **Enable dimension writeback** Allows the members and their attributes to be updated through the cube.

▶ **Define semiadditive behavior** Defines the semiadditive behavior of a measure.

▶ **Define currency conversion** Defines the rules for converting currency and analyzing other multinational information.

The Business Intelligence Wizard is launched by clicking the Add Business Intelligence button in the Cube Design tab toolbar or by right-clicking a cube or a dimension in the Solution Explorer window and selecting Add Business Intelligence from the context menu. This is shown in Figure 10-20.

Key Performance Indicators

A Key Performance Indicator (KPI) lets us define a simple, graphic method for analyzing business intelligence that is important to our organization. *KPIs* are meant to enable a decision maker to monitor a number of key aspects of the organization's operations at a single glance. KPIs are often used as part of a concept called a digital dashboard.

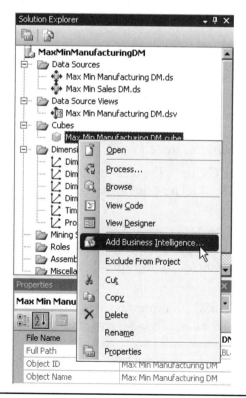

Figure 10-20 *Launching the Business Intelligence Wizard*

The *digital dashboard* is modeled after the dashboard in your car: On the car's dashboard, a number of gauges and lights enable you to easily monitor the status of your car's operation. When you want to know what speed you are traveling at, you don't need to wade through an output of the tire's rotational speed over the past few minutes or perform a calculation to determine the tire's circumference. All of the intelligence is built into the dashboard. You simply look down at the speedometer, and the needle tells you what your speed is.

The same is true with the digital dashboard. The decision maker doesn't need to plow though voluminous reports or crunch numbers in a spreadsheet to determine how the organization is doing against specified goals. This business intelligence is in the digital dashboard. A set of electronic gauges and other symbols provides the necessary status information at a single glance.

In SQL Server 2008 Analysis Services, a KPI can reflect five different status levels:

▶ Very Good

▶ Good

▶ Fair

▶ Bad

▶ Very Bad

Creating a Key Performance Indicator

Key Performance Indicators are created using the KPIs tab on the Cube Design tab shown in Figure 10-21. On this tab, we define each property of the KPI.

▶ **Name**   A unique name for this KPI.

▶ **Associated Measure Group**   The measure group being used to calculate the values for this KPI. This can be a single measure group in the cube or all measure groups in the cube.

▶ **Value Expression**   An MDX expression used to calculate the current value of the KPI. This may be as simple as a single measure or a calculated member from the cube, or it may be a complex MDX expression looking at the interaction of several measures.

▶ **Goal Expression**   An MDX expression used to express the current goal for the KPI. If the goal is a set value, this is a constant value. In other cases, the goal may need to reflect cyclic trends or it may need to vary, depending on dimensional members. The goal could even come from a dimensional attribute. For example, the production goal for each product could be an attribute in the product dimension.

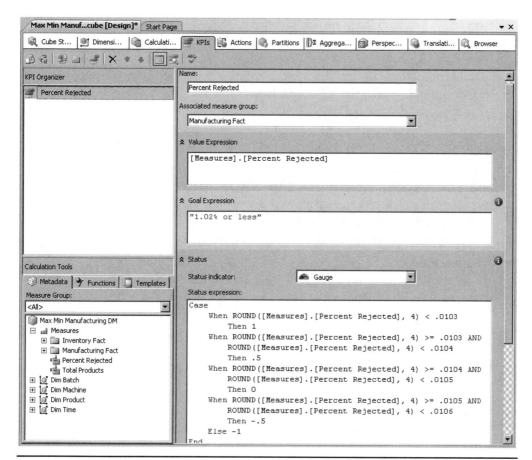

Figure 10-21   *The KPIs tab on the Cube Design tab*

▶ **Status Indicator**   The graphical representation to be used with this KPI. The
Business Intelligence Development Studio and its KPI viewer support eight
different graphics. Be aware, however: The graphics available to the user depend
heavily on the client tool being used to browse and analyze the cube.

▶ **Status Expression**   An MDX expression used to translate the current value of
the KPI into a graphic representation. As noted previously, the KPI can support
five different status levels. These equate to five different numeric values: 1 for Very
Good, 0.5 for Good, 0 for Fair, –0.5 for Bad, and –1 for Very Bad. The MDX
expression must calculate the appropriate value for each status.

Beyond these required items, we can define the following to give the KPI additional functionality:

▶ **Trend Indicator**   The graphical representation to be used when expressing the direction in which the KPI value is trending. The Business Intelligence Development Studio and its KPI viewer support four different graphics. As with the Status Indicator, the graphics available to the user depend heavily on the client tool being used to browse and analyze the cube.

▶ **Trend Expression**   An MDX expression used to translate the trend of the KPI value into a graphic representation. The KPI supports five trend states: 1 for an upward trend, 0.5 for a mildly upward trend, 0 for a flat trend, –0.5 for a mildly downward trend, and –1 for a downward trend. The MDX expression must calculate the appropriate value for each trend situation.

▶ **Display Folder**   The grouping folder for this KPI. This property can be used to collect KPIs into groupings. KPIs that are related can be placed in the same display folder. The client tool used to browse and analyze the cube should then present all of the KPIs in a display folder as a single grouping.

▶ **Parent KPI**   The KPI that serves as a rollup for this and other child KPIs. KPIs can be created in a hierarchical structure where one KPI displays the status of a rollup value and its child KPIs display the status of the more detailed indicators that make up this value.

▶ **Current Time Member**   An MDX expression defining the current time member. We discuss the concept of a current member of a dimension in Chapter 11.

▶ **Weight**   An MDX expression that expresses the emphasis given to this KPI relative to other KPIs in the group. This expression usually returns a numeric value.

▶ **Description**   A textual description of the KPI.

Key Performance Indicators and Client Software

We can define KPIs in our cubes and even suggest the graphics we would like used to present those KPIs. However, it is up to the client software used to browse and analyze the cube to display the KPI. Therefore, the client software must not only have the same graphics available, but also honor our suggested graphic for each KPI for the KPIs to appear as we designed them.

You should look at the capabilities of the client tools being used in your organization before spending a lot of time defining KPIs. Make sure KPIs are supported and determine which parts of the KPI definition the client tools can utilize.

Learn By Doing—Adding a KPI to the Max Min Manufacturing DM Cube

Feature Highlighted

▶ Defining a Key Performance Indicator

Business Need   Maximum Miniatures is contemplating the creation of a digital dashboard using KPIs. An initial KPI should be created showing the status of the Percent Rejected calculated measure. This KPI will be used as part of a proof-of-concept project.

The Percent Rejected KPI should reflect status as follows:

▶ Values less than 1.03 percent should get a Very Good status.

▶ Values greater than or equal to 1.03 percent but less than 1.04 percent should get a Good status.

▶ Values greater than or equal to 1.04 percent but less than 1.05 percent should get a Fair status.

▶ Values greater than or equal to 1.05 percent but less than 1.06 percent should get a Bad status.

▶ Values greater than or equal to 1.06 percent should get a Very Bad status.

Steps

1. Open the Business Intelligence Development Studio.
2. Open the MaxMinManufacturingDM project.
3. Double-click the entry for Max Min Manufacturing DM.cube in the Solution Explorer window. The Cube Design tab appears.
4. Select the KPIs tab. Click the New KPI button on the KPIs tab toolbar.
5. Enter **Percent Rejected** for Name.
6. Select Manufacturing Fact from the Associated Measure Group drop-down list.
7. Enter the following for Value Expression:

   ```
   [Measures].[Percent Rejected]
   ```

8. Enter the following for Goal Expression:

   ```
   "1.02% or less"
   ```

9. Leave Status Graphic set to the default of Gauge.

10. Enter the following MDX expression for Status Expression:

```
Case
    When ROUND([Measures].[Percent Rejected],4) <.0103
        Then 1
    When ROUND([Measures].[Percent Rejected],4) >= .0103 AND
        ROUND([Measures].[Percent Rejected],4) < .0104
        Then .5
    When ROUND([Measures].[Percent Rejected],4) >= .0104 AND
        ROUND([Measures].[Percent Rejected],4) < .0105
        Then 0
    When ROUND([Measures].[Percent Rejected],4) >= .0105 AND
        ROUND([Measures].[Percent Rejected],4) < .0106
        Then -.5
    Else -1
End
```

We discuss MDX expressions in detail in Chapter 11.

11. Click the Save All button on the toolbar. The KPIs tab should appear similar to Figure 10-21.

12. We now want to use the Business Intelligence Development Studio's KPI browser to look at the result of our efforts. To do this, we need to deploy these modifications to the Analysis Services database. Select Build | Deploy MaxMinManufacturingDM from the Main menu.

13. When the Deployment Completed Successfully message appears in the Deployment Progress window, click the Browser View button on the KPIs tab toolbar, as shown in Figure 10-22. The KPI browser appears.

The KPI browser shows us the Percent Rejected KPI we just created, as shown in Figure 10-23. The value shown represents the value for the Percent Rejected calculated measure across the entire cube. Our KPI translates this value to a status of Bad (between the red and yellow areas on the gauge).

The upper portion of the KPI browser allows us to filter the information we are sending to the KPI. We use the filter to look at the KPI for some specific dates of production, rather than across the entire cube.

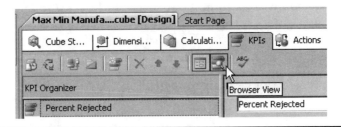

Figure 10-22   *The Browser View toolbar button*

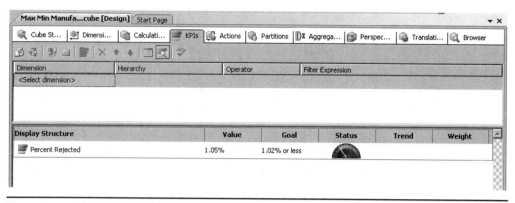

Figure 10-23   *The KPI browser with the Percent Rejected KPI for the entire cube*

14. Click the cell containing <Select dimension> in the upper portion of the KPI browser. A dimension drop-down list appears. Select Dim Time from this drop-down list. (If <Select dimension> does not appear in the upper portion of the KPI browser, click the Reconnect button on the toolbar of the KPIs tab.)

15. Click the cell immediately below the Hierarchy heading. The hierarchy drop-down list appears. Select Date Hierarchy from this drop-down list.

16. Click the cell immediately below the Filter Expression heading. The Filter Expression drop-down window control appears. Click the down arrow to display the drop-down window.

17. Expand the All entry on the drop-down window. Next expand the 2006 entry, the 2006Q1 entry, and the 200601 entry. Check 1/2/2006 and click OK.

18. Click anywhere on the KPI browser so the Filter Expression cell loses focus. This causes the KPI to refresh. The KPI browser now has a value of 1.04 percent, which translates to a status of Fair (straight up in the yellow), as shown in Figure 10-24.

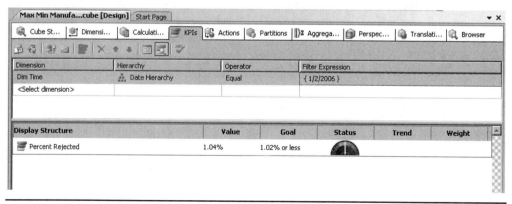

Figure 10-24   *The KPI browser with the Percent Rejected KPI for January 2, 2006*

19. Try this process again for the following dates:

Date	Value	Status
1/7/2006	1.06%	Very Bad
1/17/2006	1.03%	Good
1/29/2006	1.02%	Very Good

Be sure to uncheck one date before checking another to see the figures described here.

20. You can experiment with additional analysis. Try adding a second filter to see the KPI for a single product or a single product type.

Actions

Actions allow the OLAP cubes to "reach out and touch someone." They enable us to define commands, statements, and directives that are to be executed outside of the cube. In fact, Actions are designed to be executed outside of the Analysis Services environment altogether.

Actions are instructions that are defined and stored inside the cube itself. They are linked to certain objects in the cube. When the user is browsing a certain object in the client software, that software can look for any Actions related to the object. These Actions are then displayed to the user as menu items or Action buttons on the client screen. The user can select one of these Actions to launch separate, but related, applications or interfaces to accomplish related tasks.

For example, suppose a user is browsing a cube that analyzes changing stock prices. This cube may include an action for navigating to a website that contains up-to-the-minute market analysis. If the stock symbol for the company is stored as an attribute in the cube, the Action could pass this along as a parameter in the Uniform Resource Locator (URL).

In another case, a user may be browsing a cube that contains information on purchasing. The cube could include an Action that would launch the organization's document management system and take the user to the folder containing scanned copies of the hardcopy purchase orders. Then, when a questionable purchase is spotted, the user can launch the document management program and examine the paper trail for the purchase.

Types of Actions

Three different types of Actions are available:

► **Action** The generic Action type, which has a number of subtypes:

  ► **Dataset** Retrieves a dataset.

  ► **Proprietary** A proprietary action defined by the client software.

- ▶ **Rowset**   Retrieves a rowset.
- ▶ **Statement**   Runs an OLE DB command.
- ▶ **URL**   Displays a page in a browser.
- ▶ **Drillthrough Action**   Defines a dataset to be returned as a drillthrough to a more detailed level.
- ▶ **Reporting Action**   Launches a SQL Server 2008 Reporting Services report.

Creating an Action

Actions are created on the Actions tab on the Cube Design tab shown in Figure 10-25. On this tab, we define each property of the action.

- ▶ **Name**   A unique name for this Action.
- ▶ **Target type**   The type of object with which this Action is associated.
- ▶ **Target object**   The specific objects of the selected Target type to which this Action is associated.

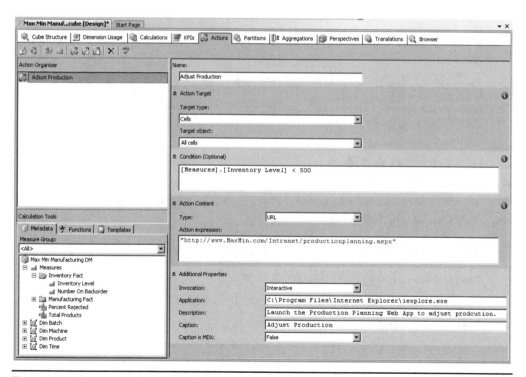

Figure 10-25   *The Actions tab on the Cube Design tab*

- ▶ **Condition**   An MDX expression defining a condition that would further limit the objects to which this Action is associated.

- ▶ **Type**   The type of Action (Dataset, Proprietary, Rowset, Statement, or URL).

- ▶ **Action expression**   The command that is executed to carry out the Action.

- ▶ **Invocation**   How the command is executed: Batch, Interactive, On Open.

- ▶ **Application**   The application used to carry out the Action.

- ▶ **Description**   A description of the Action.

- ▶ **Caption**   A caption for this Action.

- ▶ **Caption is MDX**   A flag showing whether the caption is a string constant or an MDX expression to be evaluated.

Creating Drillthrough Actions

For the most part, Drillthrough Actions have the same properties as Actions. *Drillthrough Actions* do not have Target Type or Target Object properties. In their place, the Drillthrough Action has the following:

- ▶ **Drillthrough Columns**   Defines the objects to be included in the drillthrough dataset.

- ▶ **Default**   A flag showing whether this is the default Drillthrough Action.

- ▶ **Maximum Rows**   The maximum number of rows to be included in the drillthrough dataset.

Creating Report Actions

For the most part, Report Actions have the same properties as Actions. *Report Actions* do not have Type or Action expression Target Object properties. In their place, the Report Action has the following:

- ▶ **Server name**   The name of the report server.

- ▶ **Server path**   The path to the report sever.

- ▶ **Report format**   The format of the report to be returned (HTML, Excel, PDF).

- ▶ **Parameters**   The parameter values to be passed to the report.

Actions and Client Software

We can define Actions in our cubes. However, it is up to the client software used to browse and analyze the cube to display and implement the Action. You should look at the capabilities of the client tools being used in your organization before spending a lot of time defining Actions. Make sure Actions are supported and determine which parts of the Action definition the client tools can utilize.

Partitions

We have deployed and processed our cubes to databases on the SQL Server Analysis Services server. We now have, as we have seen, cubes full of information that can be browsed and analyzed. What we have not discussed up to this point is exactly how and where the information in the databases is stored. Let's take care of that deficiency right now.

Measure Groups and Partitions

When we created the measure groups in our cubes, the Business Intelligence Development Studio created something else for us behind the scenes. It created one partition for each of our measure groups. These partitions are where all of the measure group information is stored. We can view the partitions defined in a cube by using the Partitions tab on the Cube Design tab, as shown in Figure 10-26.

In Figure 10-26, you can see the partitions that were created for each of the measure groups in the Max Min Manufacturing DM cube. The partitions were given the same name as the measure group they are tied to. The *Source column* on this tab tells us where

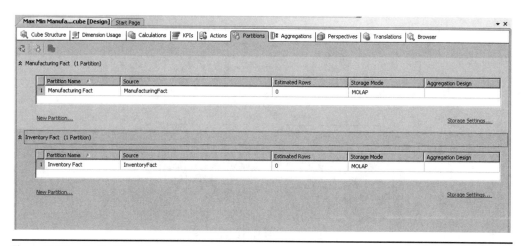

Figure 10-26   *The Partitions tab on the Cube Design tab*

each partition and, therefore, each measure group gets its fact data. Each partition is tied to a fact table in the data mart. The *Aggregations column* tells us how each partition is configured for storing aggregate data.

Multiple Partitions for a Measure Group

Although we start out with one partition for each measure group, that does not mean we have to keep it that way. We can assign a number of partitions to a single measure group. Each partition has its own data source table.

This is similar to the concept of partitioned views on the relational side of SQL Server. With partitioned views, we distribute the data from what would be a large table among a number of smaller tables, as shown in Figure 10-27. Sales data from 2005 is in one table. Sales data from 2006 is in another table, and so on. These tables are presented to the client application as if they were a single table by combining them together in a partitioned view. This is done for ease of management and for better performance.

We can essentially do the same thing with partitions and measure groups, as shown in Figure 10-28. Our data can be divided among a number of tables. These tables could be in the same data source or in different data sources. Because they can be in different data sources, the tables could even be on different database servers. We can define multiple partitions, each one pulling data from one of the data source tables. These multiple partitions are then brought together in a single measure group.

As with a partitioned view in a relational database, all of the partitions combined in a single measure group must have the same structure. They must have the same measures and the same relationships to dimensions. If the measures and dimensional relationships don't match, we cannot make the partitions into a single measure group.

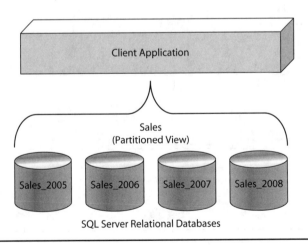

Figure 10-27   *A partitioned view*

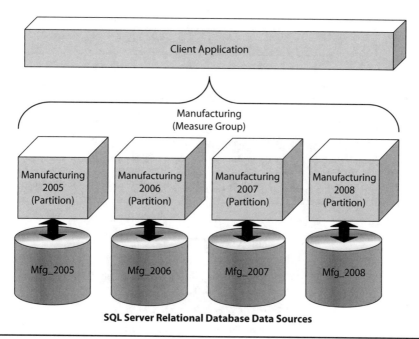

Figure 10-28   *A measure group with multiple partitions from multiple relational tables*

It is also possible to create multiple partitions from a single table. We may want to do this because our source data works just fine in a single table, but we can better manage it as a number of separate partitions in Analysis Services. This is shown in Figure 10-29.

We do this by creating a number of views in the relational database or named queries in the data source view. You can think of named queries as equivalent to views. They are defined in the data source view of a cube. We try creating a few named queries in the section "Learn By Doing—Creating Multiple Partitions from a Single Table." Each view or named query becomes the data source for a single partition. The partitions are joined together again by the measure group.

Any time we use multiple partitions in a single measure group, but especially when using named queries with a single table, we must be careful not to get the same data in two partitions. If this occurs, the information in our measure group will be incorrect. To prevent this, it is important to strictly define the criteria for membership in each view or named query. In many cases, dividing data by time is wise, as is shown in Figure 10-27, Figure 10-28, and Figure 10-29.

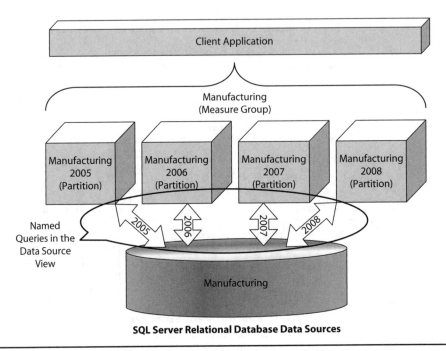

Figure 10-29   *A measure group with multiple partitions from a single relational table*

Learn By Doing—Creating Multiple Partitions from a Single Table

Features Highlighted

▶ Creating named queries in a data source view

▶ Creating multiple partitions for a single measure group

Business Need   To better manage the Manufacturing Fact information in Analysis Services, this measure group should utilize three partitions. One partition should contain data from 2006, one partition should contain data from 2007, and one partition should contain data from 2008.

Steps

1. Open the Business Intelligence Development Studio.
2. Open the MaxMinManufacturingDM project.
3. Double-click the entry for the Max Min Manufacturing DM.dsv data source view. The Data Source View Design tab appears.

4. Right-click any place there isn't a table in the data source diagram area. Select New Named Query from the context menu. The Create Named Query dialog box appears, as shown in Figure 10-30.

5. Enter **ManufacturingFact_2006** for Name.

6. Enter the following query in the SQL pane:

```
SELECT *
FROM ManufacturingFact
WHERE YEAR(DateOfManufacture) = 2006
```

The Create Named Query dialog box appears, as shown in Figure 10-31.

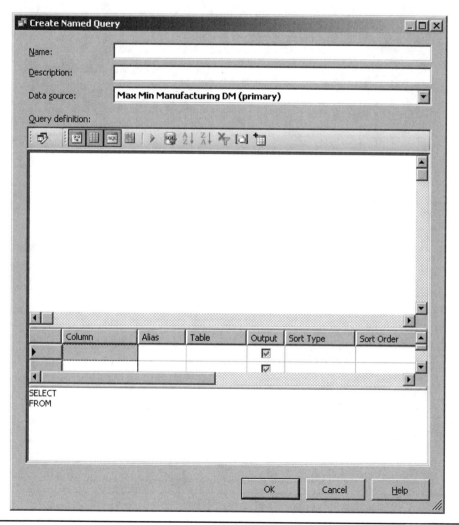

Figure 10-30 *Creating a new named query*

7. Click OK.

8. Create a second named query called ManufacturingFact_2007, which includes only 2007 data.

9. Create a third named query called ManufacturingFact_Current using the following query:

```
SELECT *
FROM ManufacturingFact
WHERE YEAR(DateOfManufacture) > 2007
```

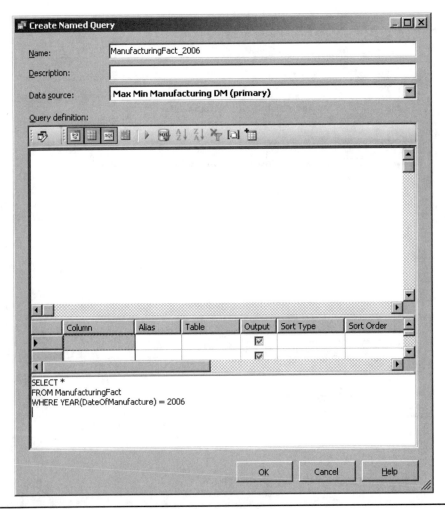

Figure 10-31   *The ManufacturingFact_2006 Named Query definition*

Obviously, some annual maintenance is required at the beginning of each year. At least, by keeping our final named query open-ended, using > 2007 rather than = 2008, we do not run the risk of leaving out data.

10. Click the Save All button on the toolbar and close the Data Source View Design tab.

11. Double-click the entry for Max Min Manufacturing DM.cube in the Solution Explorer window. The Cube Design tab appears.

12. Select the Partitions tab.

13. Click the New Partition link or the New Partition button on the Partitions tab toolbar. The Welcome page of the Partition Wizard dialog box appears.

14. Click Next. The Specify Source Information page of the wizard appears. Select the Manufacturing Fact measure group and the Max Min Manufacturing DM data source view if they are not already selected. Click the Find Tables button and check ManufacturingFact_2006 in the Available tables list.

15. Click Next. The Restrict Rows page of the wizard appears. Here, we can further filter the rows in the selected table or named query to ensure no overlap exists between partitions. Our named queries are structured such that no overlap occurs, so we do not need to specify a filter here.

16. Click Next. The Processing and Storage Locations page of the wizard appears. This page enables us to specify which Analysis Services server is to be used to calculate the aggregates and where the resulting data should be stored. You can see, if we needed a great deal of computing power to calculate a large set of aggregates, we could have a separate server for calculating each partition! If we needed a large amount of storage space, we could have a separate drive system to store the data from each partition! We don't have those types of requirements, so we can leave the defaults.

17. Click Next. The Completing the Wizard page appears. This page lets us choose when and how to design aggregations. We execute the Aggregation Design Wizard manually in the next Learn By Doing exercise. For now, select Design aggregations later.

18. Click Finish. The new partition appears under the Manufacturing Fact measure group.

19. Repeat Step 13 through Step 18 for the Manufacturing_2007 named query and again for the Manufacturing_Current named query.

20. Right-click the original Manufacturing Fact partition and select Delete from the context menu. The Delete Objects dialog box appears.

21. Click OK to confirm the deletion. Click the Save All button on the toolbar. The Partitions tab should appear as shown in Figure 10-32.

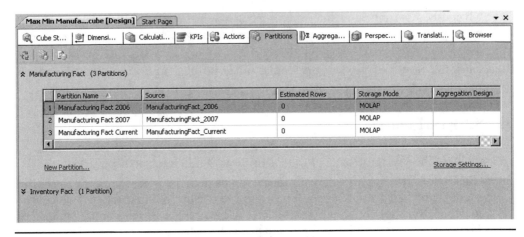

Figure 10-32   *The Manufacturing Fact measure group with three partitions*

Partitions and Storage Options

In Chapter 4 of this book, we discussed the different types of OLAP architectures: Relational OLAP (ROLAP), Multidimensional OLAP (MOLAP), and Hybrid OLAP (HOLAP). Refer to Figure 4-4, if you need a refresher. We are now going to discuss these storage options with regard to our partitions.

As we have said, the aggregates in our partitions are going to be preprocessed. Once the preprocessing is completed, all of that data needs to be stored somewhere. SQL Server 2008 Analysis Services provides us with a number of options here, enabling us to select the best mix of query speed versus data latency.

If we click the Storage Settings link or the Storage Settings button on the Partitions tab toolbar, we see the Partition Storage Settings dialog box, as shown in Figure 10-33. This dialog box presents a continuum of storage choices on the Standard Setting slider. These are preconfigured storage options that Analysis Services makes available to us. You can also create your own custom storage settings, but leave that alone for the moment.

The options on the left side of the slider represent the lowest latency but the slowest query speed. The options on the right side of the slider represent the highest latency but the fastest query speed. We need to determine the best choice for each partition.

The predefined options control the following characteristics:

▶ **Storage location for the detail data and the preprocessed aggregates**   The detail data and preprocessed aggregates can be stored in one of the following three ways:

  ▶ **ROLAP**   The detail data and the preprocessed aggregates are both stored in a relational format.

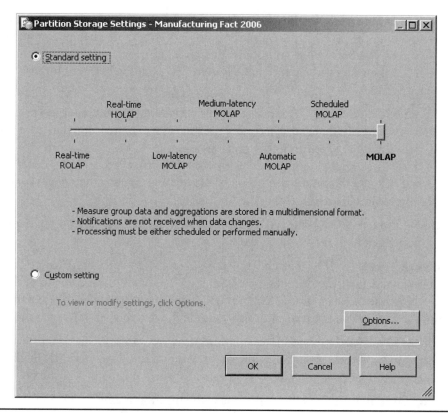

Figure 10-33   *The Partition Storage Settings dialog box*

▶ **HOLAP**   The detail data is stored in a relational format and the aggregates
are stored in a multidimensional format.

▶ **MOLAP**   The detail data and the preprocessed aggregates are both stored in
a multidimensional format.

▶ **How Analysis Services finds out a data source has changed**   Analysis Services
can discover data source changes in the following ways:

▶ **SQL Server Notification**   The SQL Server relational database engine notifies
Analysis Services when changes are made to a data source table. When the
partition is linked to a view or a named query, we must specify a SQL table that
will cause the notification when it is changed. This is known as a *tracking table*.

▶ **Client Initiated Notification** The client software that is responsible for updating the relational data source sends a NotifyTableChangeCommand to Analysis Services to let it know that data has been changed. Of course, this only works if the data source is modified exclusively through this client software.

▶ **Scheduled Polling** Analysis Services periodically runs a query to determine if the data has changed. This query must return a single value that is compared with the value saved from the previous query execution. This value could be the MAX() of an identity field in the fact table that catches adds, but not edits and deletes. This could also be a MAX() of a last updated date/time stamp, which would catch inserts and edits, but still miss deletes.

▶ **Enable Proactive Caching** Whether proactive caching is used. (See Chapter 4 for more information on proactive caching.)

▶ **Silence Interval** The length of time the data must go without a change before processing begins. The thinking here is that data updates often come in bursts. We don't want to start processing the cube if another ten data changes are coming down the pike. We can wait until things settle down and then start processing.

▶ **Silence Override Interval** The length of time we wait for a silence interval before we go ahead and initiate processing without one. This prevents the data in the cube from getting too old while waiting for the data changes to die down.

▶ **Drop Outdated Cache Latency** This is the maximum amount of time we permit outdated aggregates to live in proactive cache while we are waiting for processing to complete. When this time period is reached, the cache is dropped and querying is directed to the relational data source.

▶ **Update Cache Periodically** This is a schedule for updating the proactive cache, even if we have not received a notification that it is out-of-date. This is often used when no notification mechanism is in place.

Let's look at each of the predefined settings in a bit more detail.

Real-Time ROLAP All detail data and aggregates are queried directly from the relational data source. No notification is necessary. No proactive caching is used. This may result in slow query performance, but data is always current.

This setting is best for data that is changing frequently, leaving no time for cube processing, but which must always be up-to-date.

Real-Time HOLAP   Detail data remains in the relational data source. Aggregates are in multidimensional storage. When Analysis Services is notified that the aggregates are out-of-date, it processes the cube. It does not wait for a silence interval. While the aggregates are out-of-date or being processed, queries are sent directly to the relational data source. No proactive cache is used. This provides better performance for queries when the aggregates are up-to-date, but reverts to slow performance while processing.

This setting is best for data that is also changing frequently, but provides some intervals for processing.

Low-Latency MOLAP   Detail data and aggregates are in multidimensional storage. When Analysis Services is notified that the aggregates are out-of-date, it waits for a silence interval of ten seconds before beginning processing. It uses a silence override interval of ten minutes. While the cube is processing, queries are sent to a proactive cache. If processing takes longer than 30 minutes, the proactive cache is dropped and queries are sent directly to the relational data source. This provides fast query response, unless processing takes longer than 30 minutes. Maximum latency is 30 minutes.

This setting is best in situations where query performance is important but data must remain fairly current.

Medium-Latency MOLAP   Detail data and aggregates are in multidimensional storage. When Analysis Services is notified that the aggregates are out-of-date, it waits for a silence interval of ten seconds before it starts processing. It uses a silence override interval of ten minutes. While the cube is processing, queries are sent to a proactive cache. If processing takes longer than four hours, the proactive cache is dropped and queries are sent directly to the relational data source. This provides fast query response, unless processing takes longer than four hours. Maximum latency is four hours.

This setting is best in situations where query performance is important and a bit more latency can be tolerated.

Automatic MOLAP   Detail data and aggregates are in multidimensional storage. When Analysis Services is notified that the aggregates are out-of-date, it waits for a silence interval of ten seconds before it starts processing. It uses a silence override interval of ten minutes. While the cube is processing, queries are sent to a proactive cache. The proactive cache is not dropped, no matter how long processing takes. This provides fast query response at all times, but it can lead to a large latency if processing is long-running.

This setting is best in situations where query performance is the most important factor and a potentially large latency can be tolerated.

Scheduled MOLAP   Detail data and aggregates are in multidimensional storage. Analysis Services does not receive notification of data source changes. Instead, it processes automatically every 24 hours. While the cube is processing, queries are sent to a proactive cache. The proactive cache is not dropped, no matter how long processing takes. This provides fast query response at all times, but it has a maximum latency of 24 hours, plus the time required for processing.

This setting is typically used in situations where a notification mechanism is not available or where data updates occur nightly.

MOLAP   Detail data and aggregates are in multidimensional storage. Analysis Services does not receive notification of data source changes. Instead, processing is initiated manually by an administrator. No proactive caching is used, so queries cannot be run while processing is occurring.

This setting is typically used in situations where data is changing rarely or for development and testing environments.

Learn By Doing—Setting Storage Options for a Cube Partition

Features Highlighted

► Setting storage options for a cube

► Enabling SQL Notification when using named queries

Business Need   Before we put the Max Min Manufacturing DM cube into production, we need to revise the storage settings so it keeps itself up-to-date without having to be manually processed. The vice president of production at Maximum Miniatures has asked that this cube have a maximum latency of four hours.

Steps

1. Open the Business Intelligence Development Studio.
2. Open the MaxMinManufacturingDM project.
3. Double-click the entry for Max Min Manufacturing DM.cube in the Solution Explorer window. The Cube Design tab appears.
4. Select the Partitions tab.
5. Select the Manufacturing Fact 2006 partition.
6. Click the Storage Settings link or the Storage Settings button on the Partitions tab toolbar. The Partition Storage Settings – Manufacturing Fact 2006 dialog box appears.

7. Move the slider to the Medium-latency MOLAP setting. Note the warning message at the bottom of the screen telling us that the default notification method does not work with a named query as a data source.

8. Click the Options button. The Storage Options dialog box appears, as shown in Figure 10-34.

9. Select the Notifications tab.

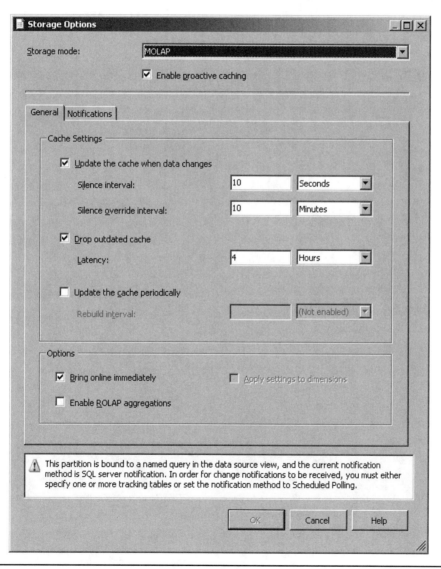

Figure 10-34   *The General tab of the Storage Options dialog box*

10. Check Specify tracking tables. This lets us specify a table whose changes cause changes to our named queries. In other words, when this table changes, the data in our named queries changes and the cube needs to be processed.

11. Click the ellipsis (...) button to the right. The Relational Objects dialog box appears.

12. Check the box next to the ManufacturingFact table. Changes to this table cause the SQL Server relational database engine to notify Analysis Services that the cube must be processed.

13. Click OK to exit the Relational Objects dialog box. The Notifications tab of the Storage Options dialog box should appear as shown in Figure 10-35.

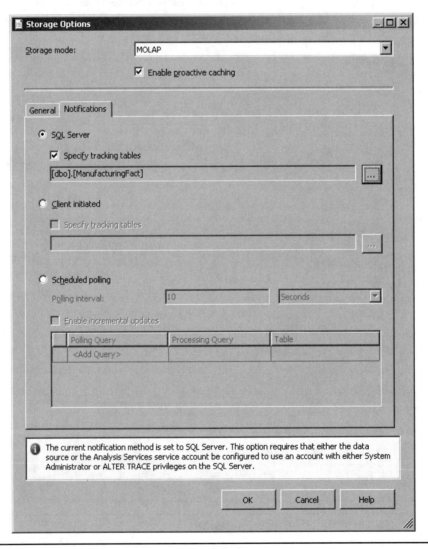

Figure 10-35   *The Notifications tab of the Storage Options dialog box*

14. Click OK to exit the Storage Options dialog box. Click OK to exit the Partition Storage Settings dialog box.

15. Repeat Step 5 through Step 14 for the Manufacturing Fact 2007 partition and the Manufacturing Fact Current partition.

16. Click the Save All button on the toolbar.

17. Select Build | Deploy MaxMinManufacturingDM from the Main menu. The cube is deployed to the server and processed.

18. Now let's test our notification mechanism. Select the Browser tab on the Cube Design tab.

19. Expand the Measures entry, drag the Total Products calculated member and drop it on Drop Totals or Detail Fields Here. The total should be 10,296,577.

20. Open the SQL Server Management Studio (leave the Business Intelligence Development Studio open as well) and connect to the SQL Server database engine hosting the MaxMinManufacturingDM relational database.

21. Expand the items in the Object Explorer window until you can see the ManufacturingFact table in the MaxMinManufacturingDM database.

22. Right-click the ManufacturingFact table and select Edit Top 200 Rows from the context menu.

23. Change the AcceptedProducts field at the top of the grid from 3875 to 4875.

24. Move your cursor off of the modified row and wait about a minute.

25. Return to the Business Intelligence Development Studio.

26. Click the Refresh button on the Browser tab toolbar. If everything is working properly, the total should change to 10,297,577.

27. Go back to the SQL Server Management Studio and change the AcceptedProducts field back to 3875.

28. Move your cursor off of the modified row, and then close the SQL Server Management Studio.

Writeback

Many times, while a user is analyzing data in a cube, they discover data that needs to be adjusted for one reason or another. It may be too time-consuming to make the change in the data source, and then wait for it to be processed into the cube. Also, in some situations, it may not be possible, for business reasons, to make the adjustment in the data source. This is where writeback comes in.

Writeback enables us to make adjusting entries to the cube data. These entries are stored in a special table that is added to the data source. This table then shows up as an additional partition in the measure group. The adjusting entries are incorporated into queries from this measure group in the same way that data from all of the other partitions is combined.

Writeback is enabled by right-clicking a partition on the Partitions tab and selecting Writeback Settings on the context menu. This displays the Enable Writeback dialog box shown in Figure 10-36. We can specify the name of the writeback table being created and the data source it is created in. We can also specify the storage mode used for the writeback data.

Once writeback is enabled, the writeback partition can be seen on the Partitions tab, as shown in Figure 10-37. Clicking Writeback Settings on the context menu when writeback is enabled lets you disable this feature.

As with a number of other cube features, the client software used to browse and analyze the cube must support writeback for this feature to be put to use. Microsoft's Office Tools, Excel 2000, XP, 2003, and 2007 all support this writeback function.

Aggregation Design

Previously, we discussed preprocessing all of the aggregates in a cube and putting the results in a multidimensional storage. This is a bit of an overstatement. In fact, Analysis Services determines a pattern of aggregates within the partition that strikes a balance between storage requirements and query speed. This is called an *aggregation design*. This process determines key aggregates, and then calculates and stores them. Other aggregations are calculated from the key aggregates at the time a query is submitted.

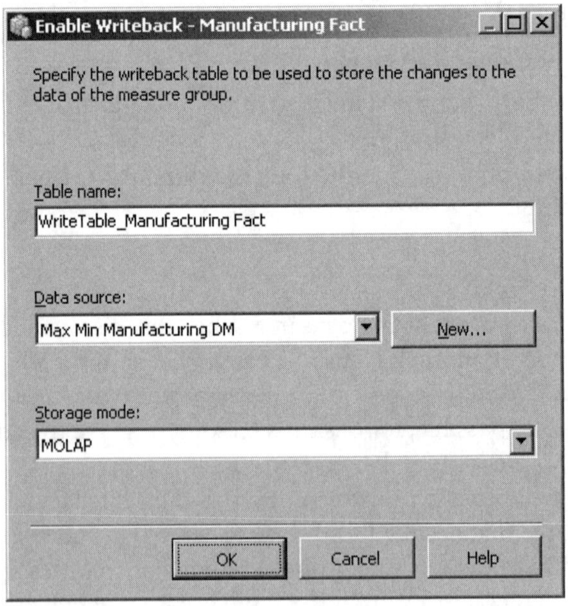

Figure 10-36   *The Enable Writeback dialog box*

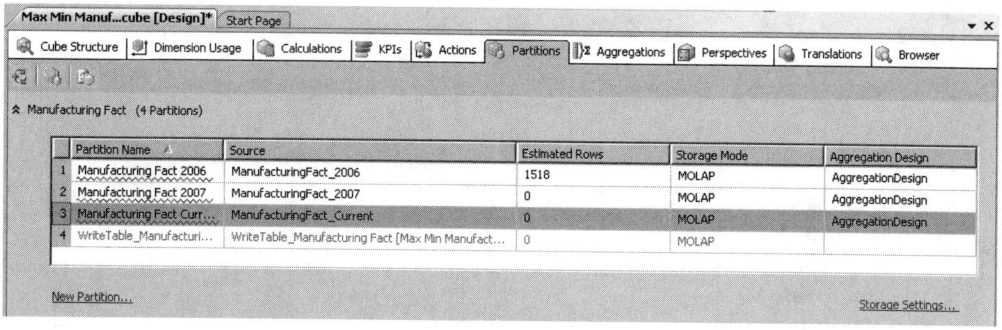

Figure 10-37   *The Partition tab with a writeback partition*

Aggregations can be designed in two different ways: based on usage or manually. With usage-based aggregation design, the Usage-Based Optimization Wizard uses information from the Analysis Services query log to determine the best aggregation design for a partition. When aggregations are designed manually, the Aggregation Design Wizard guides us through the manual design process. Both wizards are launched from the Aggregations tab on the Cube Design tab.

Manual Aggregation Design

Here, we look at a few of the screens from the Aggregation Design Wizard. After the Welcome page, the wizard allows you to select which partitions within a measure group you wish to work with. The next page of the wizard is the Review Aggregation Usage page, shown in Figure 10-38.

As we have discussed previously, the dimensional attributes in the cube are used to slice and dice the fact data during analysis. It is the various combinations of these attributes that define the multitude of aggregations that could be created in advance. The aggregation designer looks at each attribute in the cube and makes a determination on how it should be used for preprocessed aggregations. The Review Aggregation Usage page of the wizard allows us to make that determination for the aggregation designer by selecting one of the following:

▸ **Default**   The default aggregation rule is used for this dimensional attribute.

▸ **Full**   Every preprocessed aggregate must include either this attribute or a lower attribute in the same hierarchy. This forces every precalculated aggregate to be sliced by this dimensional attribute. This should not be selected for dimensional attributes that have a large number of members.

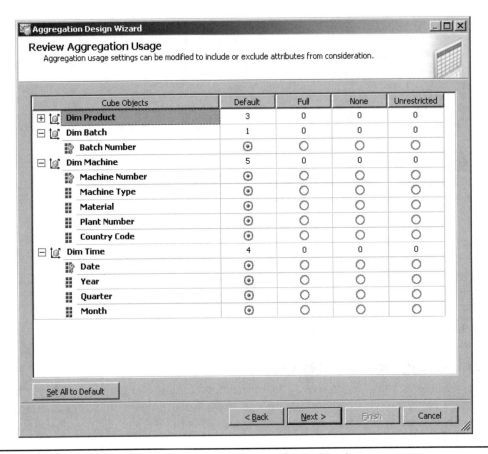

Figure 10-38 *The Review Aggregation Usage page of the Aggregation Design Wizard*

▶ **None** None of the preprocessed aggregates will include this attribute. It will be ignored when designing preprocessed aggregates.

▶ **Unrestricted** No restrictions are placed on the consideration of this attribute for use when designing preprocessed aggregates.

The next page of the wizard is the Specify Object Counts page, shown in Figure 10-39. When the Count button is clicked, the wizard counts the number of members in each of the dimensions, including the fact dimension. If you are working with a large cube and do not want to wait for the wizard to do all of this counting, you can enter the member counts manually. You may also want to manually enter counts if you have a small set of data in the cube for testing, but know that a much larger set of data with a different count distribution will be processed into the cube at a later date.

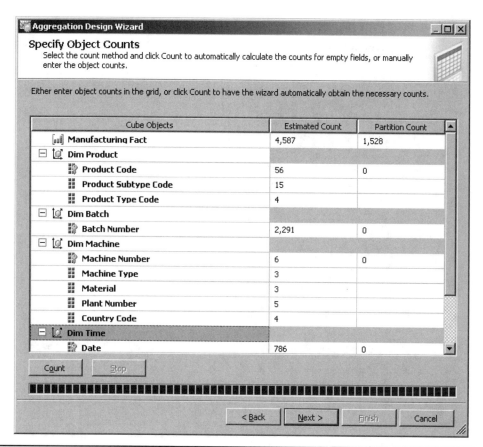

Cube Objects	Estimated Count	Partition Count
Manufacturing Fact	4,587	1,528
⊟ Dim Product		
Product Code	56	0
Product Subtype Code	15	
Product Type Code	4	
⊟ Dim Batch		
Batch Number	2,291	0
⊟ Dim Machine		
Machine Number	6	0
Machine Type	3	
Material	3	
Plant Number	5	
Country Code	4	
⊟ Dim Time		
Date	786	0

Figure 10-39   *The Specify Object Counts page of the Aggregation Design Wizard*

The following page is the Set Aggregation Options page. This is shown in Figure 10-40. On this page, we tell the wizard how to optimize the aggregation design. We can specify a maximum amount of storage we want to allow for aggregates, a maximum performance gain we require, or choose not to design aggregations at all. A fourth option allows the optimization process to run until we tell it to stop. With this last option, the optimizer continues running until it has the best solution or until you get tired of waiting for it and stop it manually. As the optimizer runs, it shows you a graph of its progress.

The last page of the wizard enables us to either deploy and process the changes immediately or save them for later processing. Once the aggregation design has been completed, the Aggregations tab displays the number of aggregations being preprocessed for each partition. This is shown in Figure 10-41.

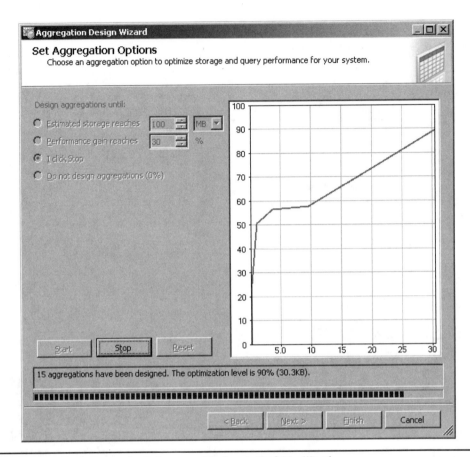

Figure 10-40   *The Set Aggregation Options page of the Aggregation Design Wizard*

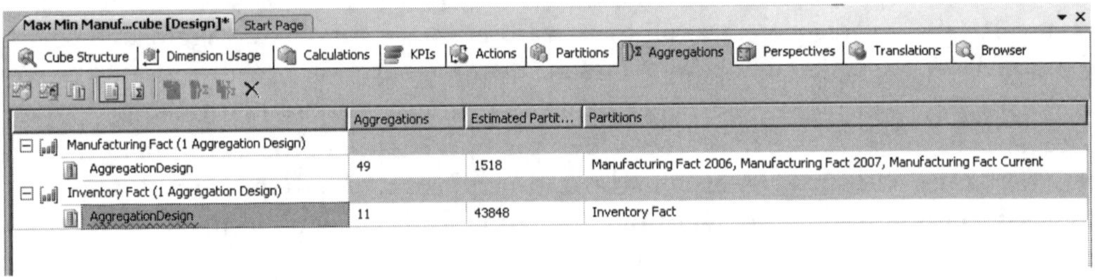

Figure 10-41   *The Aggregations tab with aggregation design completed*

Be sure to complete the aggregation design before putting your cubes into production to ensure you get the query performance you expect.

Perspectives

In real life, many objects look different, depending on how you look at them—depending on your perspective. In the same way, we can define different perspectives so our cubes look different to different users. By using perspectives, we can provide our users with what they need and not overwhelm them with things they don't.

Creating Perspectives

Perspectives are created on the *Perspectives tab*. This tab lists all of the items in our cube, as shown in Figure 10-42. We can then determine which items are visible in each perspective.

New perspectives are added by clicking the New Perspective button on the Perspectives tab toolbar. Each perspective is given a unique name to identify it. When the perspective is first created, it includes all of the items in the cube. We can remove (uncheck) the items

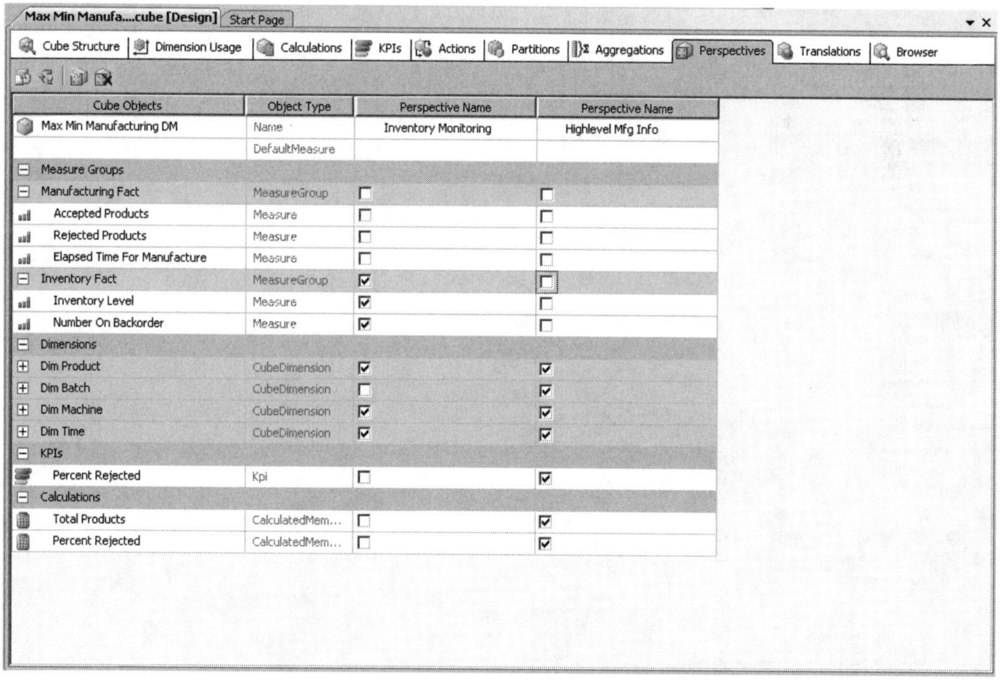

Figure 10-42 *The Perspectives tab*

that are not needed or that should not be viewed by people who are going to use that perspective to access the cube.

In Figure 10-42, we created two perspectives in our Max Min Manufacturing DM cube. The Inventory Monitoring perspective is for users who will be looking at the Inventory Fact measures. They do not need access to the Manufacturing Fact measures or other items that apply only to those measures. The Highlevel Mfg Info perspective is for users who are only interested in the KPI and the two calculated members we have created in our cube. Therefore, only those items and the dimensions are included in this perspective.

Translations

We live in a global society. More and more, we are required to work internationally to get things done. Business intelligence is certainly no exception to this trend.

To help this along, Analysis Services provides us with the means to localize the metadata contained in our cubes. This is done using the *Translations tab*. The Translations tab is shown in Figure 10-43.

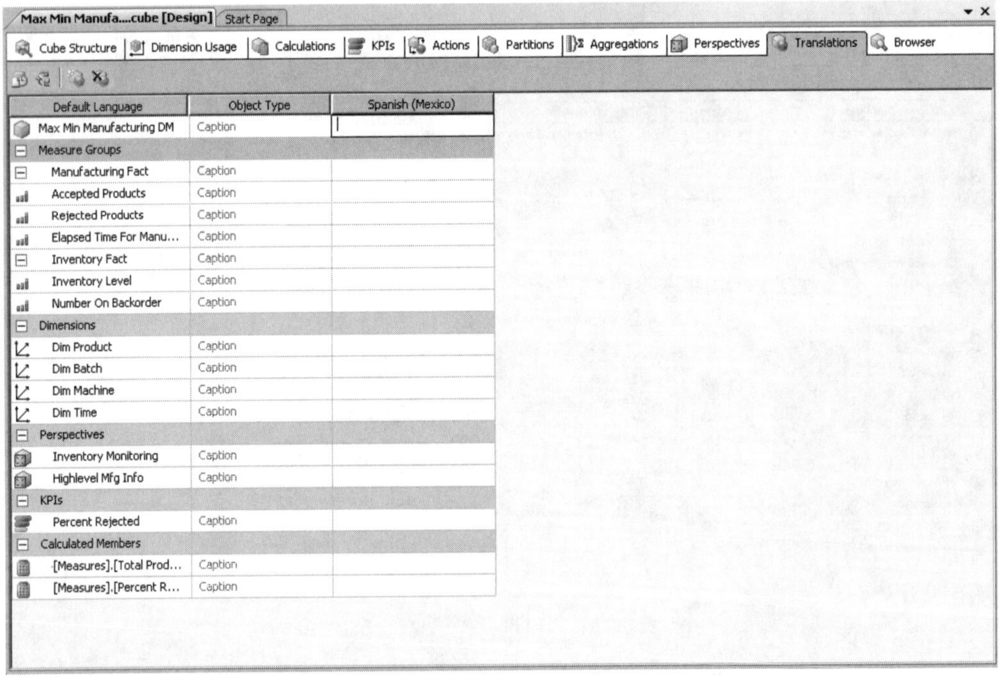

Figure 10-43   *The Translations tab*

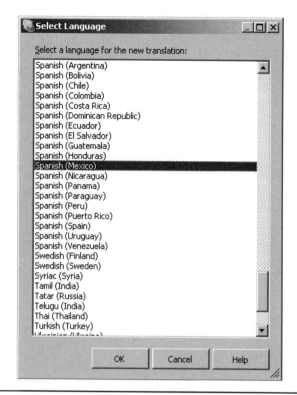

Figure 10-44   *The Select Language dialog box*

Creating Translations

New translations are created by clicking the New Translation button on the Translations tab toolbar. First, we must pick the language for the translation. The Select Language dialog box, shown in Figure 10-44, enables us to select the language and country designation for this translation. Next, we can fill in the appropriate translation for each of the metadata items in the cube.

The translations entered in the Translations tab only apply to metadata in the cubes, not to the data in each of the dimensions. To implement multilingual support for the dimensional members, each dimension must have an attribute for each language supported. These attributes then contain the appropriate translations for each member.

More Sophisticated Scripting

We have used some basic scripting to define objects in Chapters 9 and 10. In Chapter 11, we add to your ability to write MDX script expressions. As a result, we enhance your ability to manipulate and analyze the information in your OLAP cubes.

Chapter 11

Writing a New Script— MDX Scripting

In This Chapter

- ▶ **Terms and Concepts**
- ▶ **Putting MDX Scripting to Work**
- ▶ **Extracting Data from Cubes**

The world is a stage and most of us are desperately unrehearsed.

—Sean O'Casey,
Playwright

We have already used some basic MDX script expressions to create calculated members in Chapter 9 and to define Key Performance Indicators (KPIs) and Actions in Chapter 10. To complete these tasks, we used the basics of MDX scripting. You probably need to employ more complex MDX scripts to meet the needs of your organization. Thus, we have Chapter 11.

In this chapter, we work to get a handle on the power of MDX scripts. We see how they can be used to perform powerful analysis on your organization's information. In addition to data analysis, we use MDX scripts to set up security restrictions on a cube.

Terms and Concepts

Before we begin doing all of this good stuff, we need to cover some basics. Up to this point, we have looked at cube concepts and definitions, with the goal of cube creation and population. Now, we need to shift gears a bit and look at the concepts and definitions required for extracting and analyzing the information residing in our cubes.

Let's use an analogy from the relational database world. When we are defining and populating a relational database, we need to know about normalization, constraints, and foreign keys. When we are querying data from a relational database, we need to know about INNER and OUTER JOINS, ORDER BY, and GROUP BY.

As we move to extracting and analyzing information in the cube, we need to learn how to move through our dimensional hierarchies to address a particular location or set of locations in the cube. We need to know how to select a particular measure and combine that with other measures in complex calculations. In short, we need to know how to navigate our cubes without getting lost or, worse yet, without returning utter nonsense to our users.

Where Are We?

We live in an age of many electronic wonders: computers, of course, but also cell phones, digital cameras, and global positioning satellite (GPS) receivers. With a GPS receiver, we can tell exactly where we are on the planet to within a few feet, perhaps even to within a few inches! The question is this: Will we men now be too stubborn to consult our GPS receivers for directions?

In the world of online analytical processing (OLAP) cubes, we need the equivalent of a GPS system. We need a means to uniquely specify any location within a cube. Fortunately, MDX scripting provides just such a mechanism.

Cells

The first question might be: Just what are we trying to locate? The answer is: We are trying to locate cells. Fortunately, we do not need a microscope to find these cells. (I never was very good at biology.) These cells are located right inside of our cubes.

Figure 11-1 shows a simplified version of our Max Min Manufacturing DM cube with three dimensions: Dim Machine, Dim Product, and Dim Time. The dimensions divide the cube up into smaller sections. These are cells.

In our cubes, cells contain the values for our measures. In Figure 11-1, the highlighted cell contains the measures for the Woodland Creatures product type produced on the Clay Molder machine type for all of 2007. We can see that 951,959 products were produced while 10,143 products were rejected and 89,720 minutes were spent in this manufacturing process. If cells contain the measures in a cube, then it is important that we know how to properly address them.

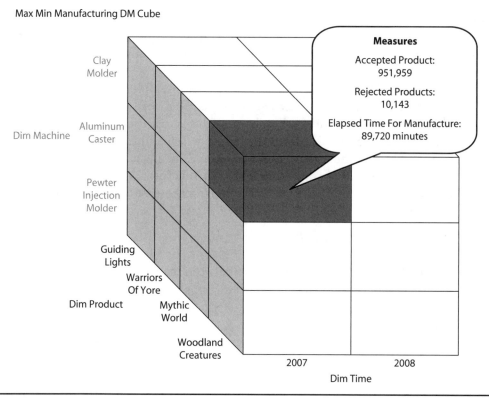

Figure 11-1 *A simplified Max Min Manufacturing DM cube*

Identifying the location of a cell in a cube is similar to identifying the location of a point on a three-dimensional graph. On a 3-D graph, we specify the value from each axis (or dimension) that corresponds to the point's location along that axis. Our cube works the same way. We specify the member from each dimension that identifies the cell's location along that dimension. So the cell in Figure 11-1 has a location of

```
[Clay Molder], [Woodland Creatures], [2007]
```

NOTE

Identifiers in MDX—member names, dimension names, hierarchy levels, and so forth—must be enclosed in square brackets ([ ]) when they contain a space or other special character or start with a numeral. Because we often have one or more spaces in our identifiers and they often start with numerals, it is a good idea to always enclose identifiers in square brackets, whether they need them or not. This saves trouble down the road.

Tuples

The cell location we came up with from Figure 11-1 has a special name. It is a tuple (pronounced *to pull*). A *tuple* is a list of dimension members with one member present from each dimension.

In our example from Figure 11-1 and in most of the examples in this chapter, we are going to look at examples with three dimensions. Therefore, our tuples have three members. We are using three dimensions because this is easier for you to grasp and for me to illustrate. (I haven't yet mastered drawing in four-dimensional space!) Just don't fall into the trap of thinking all tuples have three members. A cube with 100 dimensions would have a tuple that includes 100 members.

In MDX expressions, tuples are enclosed in parentheses. So our tuple from Figure 11-1 becomes

```
([Clay Molder], [Woodland Creatures], [2007])
```

You can think of it this way: The information between the parentheses, no matter if it is three members or a hundred members, points to a single cell.

NOTE

MDX expressions are not case-sensitive. The tuple

```
([clay molder], [woodland creatures], [2007])
```

is also valid.

Levels

You are probably thinking: What's the big deal about locating cells? Creating tuples seems pretty straightforward. Well, it would be except for one little detail. Many of our dimensions contain hierarchies. We have to take those hierarchies into account as we create our tuples.

Figure 11-2 shows the structure and the members of the Dim Product hierarchy in the Max Min Manufacturing DM cube. In this hierarchy, we created three levels: the product type, the product subtype, and the product. In addition to the levels we defined, Analysis Services automatically adds another level at the top of the dimension. In Figure 11-2, this upper level is given the same name as the dimension itself: Dim Product. The upper level always contains a single element called All. This element contains all of the dimension members from the lower levels.

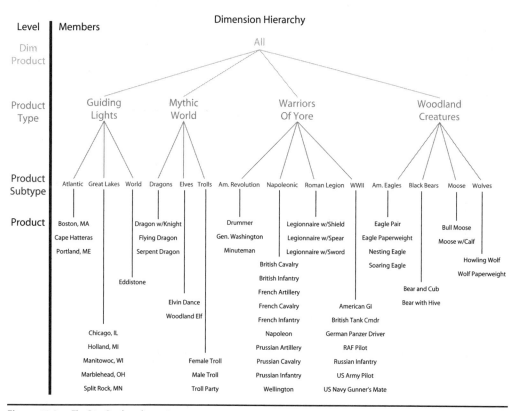

Figure 11-2   *The Dim Product dimension*

Suppose we want to specify the location of the cell containing measures for the Dragon w/Knight product. Figure 11-3 shows the path we must follow from the highest level of the dimension to reach this product at the lowest level. To specify this location in a tuple, start with the name of the dimension. Then follow the path from the top of the hierarchy to the bottom, including every member we pass along the way.

What we end up with is this:

```
[Dim Product].[All].[Mythic World].[Dragons].[Dragon w/Knight]
```

If you look at this expression in Figure 11-3, you can see by the gray shading which level of the hierarchy provided each piece of the path. Of course, dimensions with more hierarchies are going to have longer expressions.

We do not always want to retrieve measures at the lowest level of a hierarchy. We may want to see figures for a product subtype or even a product type. Figure 11-4 shows this situation. Here, we want measures for the WWII product subtype. Again, we start with

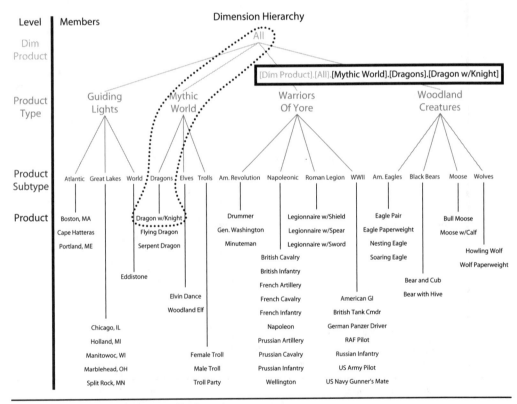

Figure 11-3   *The path to the Dragon w/Knight product*

the name of the dimension, and then follow the path until we get to the desired member. We do not have to go all the way to the bottom of the tree. The correct expression from Figure 11-4 is:

```
[Dim Product].[All].[Warriors Of Yore].[WWII]
```

Shortcuts

You can see these expressions tend to get long rather quickly. Fortunately, MDX scripting provides some shortcuts for us. Figure 11-5 illustrates one of these shortcuts. Instead of following the chain of members all the way down, we specify the name of the dimension, as before, but then add the name of the hierarchy level we are interested in and, finally, the member of that hierarchy. So, the expression becomes

```
[Dim Product].[Product Subtype].[WWII]
```

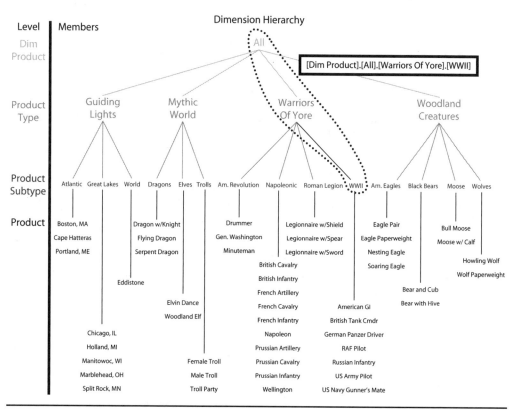

Figure 11-4 *The path to the WWII product subtype*

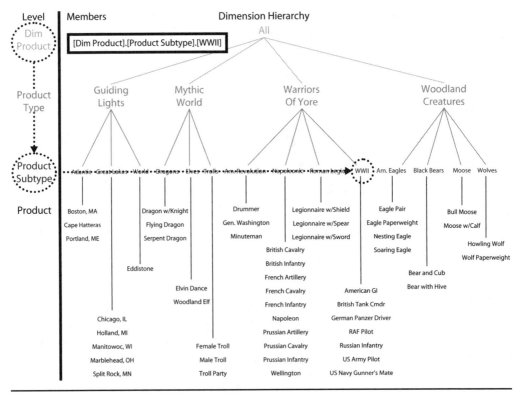

Figure 11-5   *A shortcut path to the WWII product subtype*

Using this shortcut, it is possible to specify any dimension member with only three items. In a hierarchy with a large number of levels, this can save a lot of typing. However, this is not the only way we can save keystrokes.

It is possible to leave out additional pieces of this path. We can drop the name of the dimension, the dimension level, or both. The key is this: We always have to end up with a nonambiguous location in the dimension. In our Max Min Manufacturing DM cube, any of the following expressions are valid references to the WWII member:

```
[Product Subtype].[WWII]
[Dim Product].[WWII]
[WWII]
```

Because WWII is a unique member name across all levels of all dimensions in our cube, that's all we need to uniquely identify the dimension member.

Even if we are using our original method from Figure 11-3 and Figure 11-4, we can take some shortcuts. First, we can leave out the All member. Thus, our expression from Figure 11-3 becomes

```
[Dim Product].[Mythic World].[Dragons].[Dragon w/Knight]
```

The name of the dimension can be removed as well:

```
[Mythic World].[Dragons].[Dragon w/Knight]
```

We can also trim off members from the top of the hierarchy, so this still works:

```
[Dragons].[Dragon w/Knight]
```

The one thing we cannot do is drop members out of the middle of the path. Therefore, this expression will not work:

```
[Mythic World].[Dragon w/Knight]
```

Expression Errors

If we inadvertently enter an expression for a dimension member that is incorrect, we do not receive an error message. Instead, we end up with nothing for this dimension. The tuple that included the errant dimension is not included in the final result.

This is both a benefit and a problem. It is a benefit because an invalid path expression does not bring everything to a screeching halt. It is a problem because our expression may return information that appears good, but is missing something we expected!

Default Members

Now that we know how to specify expressions for hierarchical dimensions, let's go back to building tuples. Figure 11-6 shows a more complex, but still watered-down, representation of the Max Min Manufacturing DM cube. This cube includes two-level hierarchies on all three of its dimensions.

Figure 11-6 has one cell highlighted in the cube. The tuple identifying this location is also shown in the figure. Here we are using a shortcut and omitting the dimension names from our path expressions. We could even shorten this up a bit more:

```
([Machine #1], [Wolves], [2007].[Q1])
```

As the dimension members are shown in the figure, we could *not* use the following:

```
([Machine #1], [Wolves], [Q1])
```

Max Min Manufacturing DM Cube

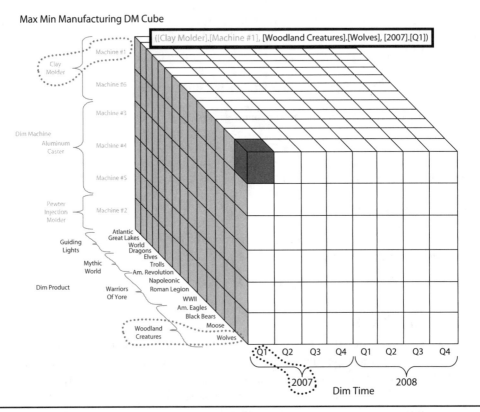

Figure 11-6 *A more complex version of the Max Min Manufacturing DM cube*

There is a Q1 member under 2007 and under 2008, so this last path expression would result in an ambiguous reference.

NOTE

In the actual Max Min Manufacturing DM cube we created, we use the form 2007Q1 for quarters and 200701 for months, so there is no problem with ambiguous references, even if we use only a single member name.

What happens if we leave one of the dimensions out of a tuple? Figure 11-7 shows the result. The tuple in this figure includes a member from the Dim Product dimension and the Dim Time dimension. It does not include a member from the Dim Machine dimension.

In this situation, Analysis Services supplies the member for the missing dimension. It does this by using the default member. In this case, the *default member* for the Dim Machine dimension is All. (The All member is not shown in the dimensional hierarchies in Figure 11-7, but is there at the top of each hierarchy by default.) The path expression shown in Figure 11-7 is the equivalent of

```
([All], [Woodland Creatures].[Wolves], [2007].[Q1])
```

Each dimension in the cube has a default member. In almost all cases, the All member is most appropriate for the default member. For some dimensions, however, a different member makes more sense. For instance, it may be reasonable to have the Dim Time dimension default to the current year or current quarter. We set the default member of the Dim Time dimension in the Max Min Manufacturing DM cube to 2008 in our next Learn By Doing activity.

The result of this tuple in Figure 11-7 is not six cells. Instead, it is a single cell. This cell contains aggregates of each measure for the first quarter of 2007 for Wolves that were produced on any of the machines. The cell is an aggregate, but it is still a single cell—a single number for each measure in the cube.

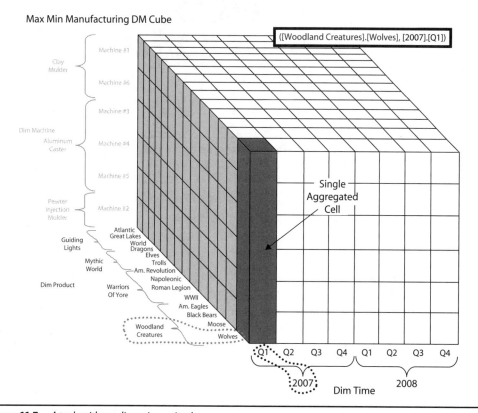

Figure 11-7   *A tuple with one dimension omitted*

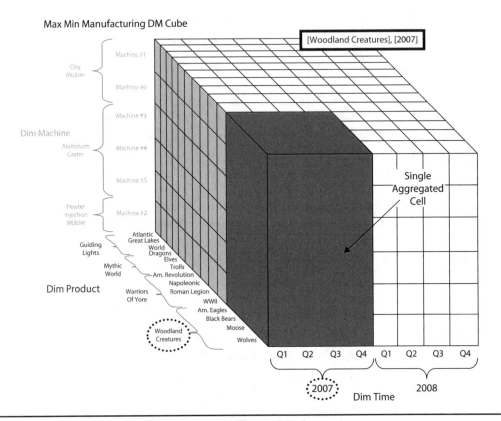

Figure 11-8   *Another aggregate cell in the Max Min Manufacturing DM cube*

Indeed, tuples, as we have seen them expressed so far, can only return a single cell from the cube. Next, we see how to return multiple cells.

Sets

Figure 11-8 shows another aggregate cell in our simplified Max Min Manufacturing DM cube. This cell contains aggregates of each measure for 2007 for Woodland Creatures produced on any of the machines. Suppose, instead of a single aggregate cell, we want to see the measures from all of the individual cells at the lower levels of the hierarchy.

What we want is the *set* of cells shown in Figure 11-9. To do this, we need to use a group of tuples to specify each of the cells in our set. We express this set of tuples as follows:

```
{([Am. Eagles], [2007].[Q1]), ([Am. Eagles], [2007].[Q2]),
([Am. Eagles], [2007].[Q3]), ([Am. Eagles], [2007].[Q4]),
```

```
([Black Bears], [2007].[Q1]), ([Black Bears], [2007].[Q2]),
([Black Bears], [2007].[Q3]), ([Black Bears], [2007].[Q4]),
([Wolves], [2007].[Q1]), ([Wolves], [2007].[Q2])
([Wolves], [2007].[Q3]), ([Wolves], [2007].[Q4]),
([Moose], [2007].[Q1]), ([Moose], [2007].[Q2]),
([Moose], [2007].[Q3]), ([Moose], [2007].[Q4])}
```

Note the curly brackets ({ }) surrounding the entire set in addition to the parentheses around each tuple.

This notation gets the job done, but it is inefficient. Let's look at another way to specify a set that requires fewer keystrokes.

Range Operator

Excel is another Microsoft product that deals with cells. This program has a special syntax for specifying a range of cells. This is the colon (:) operator. To specify cells A1 through A15, for example, we enter **A1:A15** in an Excel expression.

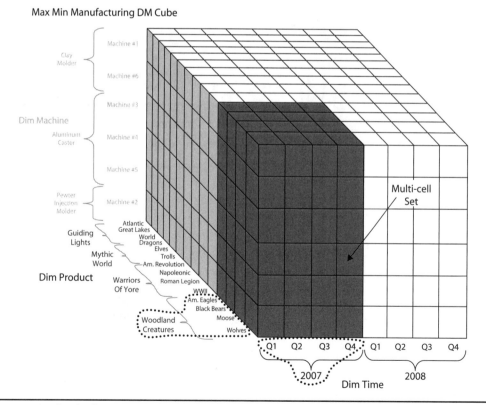

Figure 11-9   *A multicell set*

The same is true in Analysis Services. We can use the colon operator to specify a range of members in a tuple. To specify the set shown in Figure 11-9, we can use the range operator as follows:

```
([American Eagles]:[Wolves], [2007].[Q1]:[2007].[Q4])
```

This may not be quite as self-documenting as the set notation, but it is more efficient.

Of course, some groupings cannot be specified by a range. One such grouping is shown in Figure 11-10. Because these cells are not contiguous, we cannot use a range. We can also combine ranges and sets, as shown in Figure 11-11.

Name Attributes

When we set up the MaxMinManufacturingDM data mart relational database, we used integer key fields to identify members in the dimensions. The foreign key relationships we created in the data mart are all based on these integer keys. When the OLAP cube

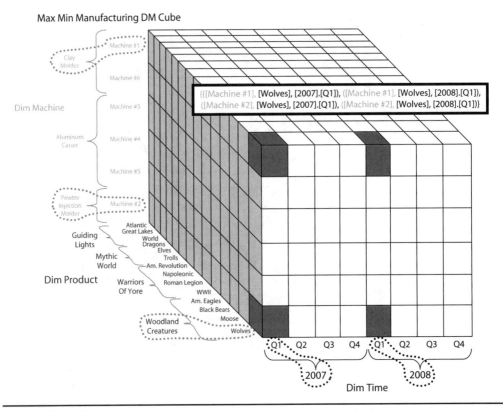

Figure 11-10 *A cell group requiring a set*

Max Min Manufacturing DM Cube

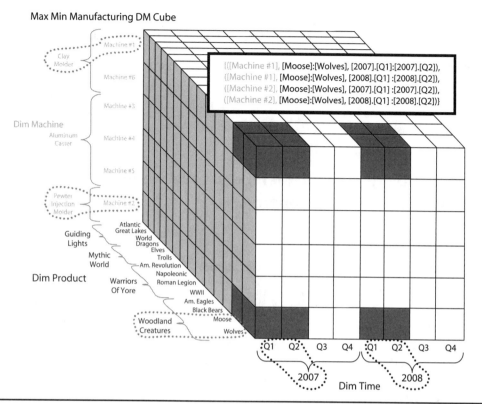

Figure 11-11 *A cell group using a set with ranges*

was created on top of this data mart, the integer keys were used as the unique identifiers for our members.

This is not convenient. We don't want our users to have to remember that the Wolf Paperweight is product 21 and the plant in Mumbai is plant 6. As a matter of fact, we would not like to have to remember this stuff either. Fortunately, we and our users don't have to.

In addition to having integer key fields in our relational data mart, we have text fields that contain names for each member value. The text fields became attributes in our OLAP cube. If we tell Analysis Services which attribute contains the name for each dimension hierarchy, we can use those names in our MDX expressions. In fact, we have anticipated this by using names rather than key values in all of the examples in this chapter. We see how to specify the name attributes using the NameColumn property in the section "Learn By Doing—Default Members, Level Names, and the NameColumn Property."

At times, we may need to reference a member by its key value rather than its name. We can do this by putting an ampersand (&) in front of the member key. For example:

```
[Dim Product].[Product].&[21]
```

is the same as

```
[Dim Product].[Product].[Wolf Paperweight]
```

Learn By Doing—Default Members, Level Names, and the NameColumn Property

Features Highlighted

▶ Providing user-friendly hierarchy level names

▶ Specifying a name column for hierarchy levels

Business Need   To make it easier for our users to query the Max Min Manufacturing DM cube, we need to provide more user-friendly names for our hierarchy levels. We should also specify which attribute holds the name for each hierarchy level. In addition, we can set the sort order of the hierarchies. Finally, we can set the default member for our Dim Time dimension to 2008.

Steps

1. Open the Business Intelligence Development Studio.
2. Open the MaxMinManufacturingDM.sln solution.
3. Double-click the Dim Time.dim dimension in the Solution Explorer. The Dimension Design tab appears.
4. Select the Year entry in the Attributes area.
5. In the Properties Window, click the DefaultMember property. An ellipsis (…) button appears. Click the ellipsis button. The Set Default Member dialog box appears.
6. Select Enter an MDX expression that specifies the default member.
7. Enter **[Dim Time].&[2008]**. The Set Default Member dialog box appears, as shown in Figure 11-12.
8. Click OK to exit the Set Default Member dialog box.
9. Click the Save All button on the toolbar.

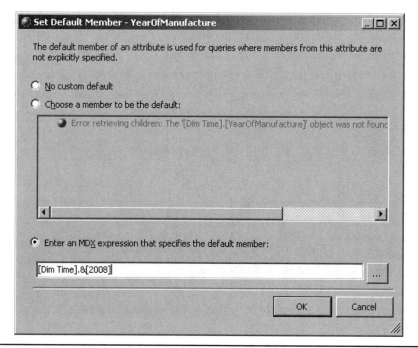

Figure 11-12 *The Set Default Member dialog box*

10. Close the Dimension Design tab.
11. Double-click the Dim Product.dim dimension in the Solution Explorer. The Dimension Design tab appears.
12. Select the Product Subtype Code entry in the Attributes area.
13. In the Properties window, click the elipsis (...) button for the NameColumn property. The Name Column dialog box appears.
14. Select ProductSubtypeName in the Source column list.
15. Click OK to exit the Name Column dialog box.
16. In the Properties window, select Name from the OrderBy drop-down list.
17. Select the Product Type Code entry in the Attributes area.
18. In the Properties window, click the elipsis (...) button for the NameColumn property. The Name Column dialog box appears.
19. Select ProductTypeName in the Source column list.
20. Click OK to exit the Name Column dialog box.
21. Select the Product Code entry in the Attributes area.

22. In the Properties window, click the ellipsis (...) button for the NameColumn property. The NameColumn dialog box appears.

23. Select ProductName in the Source column list.

24. Click OK to exit the NameColumn dialog box.

25. Again, in the Properties window, select Name from the OrderBy drop-down list.

26. Rename the items in both the Attributes and the Hierarchies areas as follows:

Old Name	New Name
Product Type Code	Product Type
Product Subtype Code	Product Subtype
Product Code	Product

The Dimension Design tab should appear as shown in Figure 11-13.

27. Click the Save All button on the toolbar.

28. Close the Dimension Design tab.

29. Double-click the Dim Machine.dim dimension in the Solution Explorer. The Dimension Design tab appears.

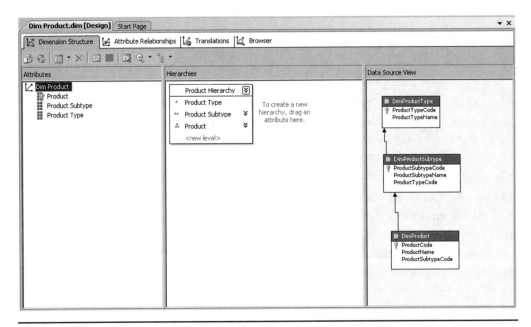

Figure 11-13 *The Dim Product dimension with revised hierarchy level names*

30. Set the NameColumn property and the OrderBy property for the following items in the Attributes area:

Item	NameColumn	OrderBy
Country Code	CountryName	Name
Machine Number	MachineName	Name
Plant Number	PlantName	Name

31. Rename the items in the Hierarchies and Levels area as follows:

Old Name	New Name
Machine Number (under the Material Hierarchy)	Machine
Country Code	Country
Plant Number	Plant
Machine Number (under the Plant Hierarchy)	Machine

The Dimension Design tab should appear as shown in Figure 11-14.

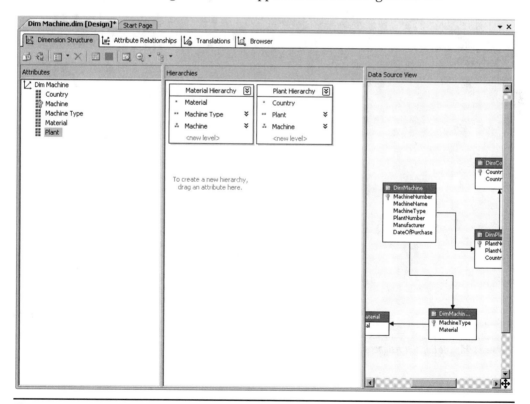

Figure 11-14   *The Dim Machine dimension with revised hierarchy level names*

32. Click the Save All button on the toolbar.
33. Close the Dimension Design tab.
34. Double-click the Dim Batch.dim dimension in the Solution Explorer. The Dimension Design tab appears.
35. Set the NameColumn property and the OrderBy property for the following item in the Attributes area:

Item	NameColumn	OrderBy
Batch Number	BatchName	Name

The Dimension Design tab should appear as shown in Figure 11-15.

36. Click the Save All button on the toolbar.
37. Close the Dimension Design tab.
38. Select Build | Deploy MaxMinManufacturingDM from the Main menu.

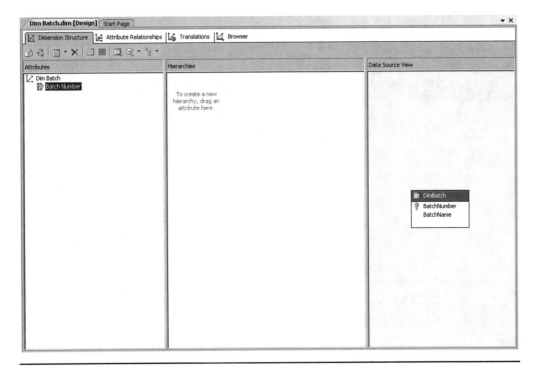

Figure 11-15 *The Dim Batch dimension*

Getting There from Here

We now know how to address any cell or group of cells in the cube. This type of absolute navigation is important as we move toward being able to manipulate and extract information from our cubes. We need to master one other skill, which is the skill of relative navigation. *Relative navigation* is the capability to start from a given location and move to another location based on that starting point.

For example, suppose we are examining measures for Wolves produced on Machine #6 in Q1, 2008. This is the Current Cell in Figure 11-16. We may want to look at those same measures from one year ago. This is designated as the Comparison Cell in the figure. We need to know how to find the position of the Comparison Cell relative to the Current Cell.

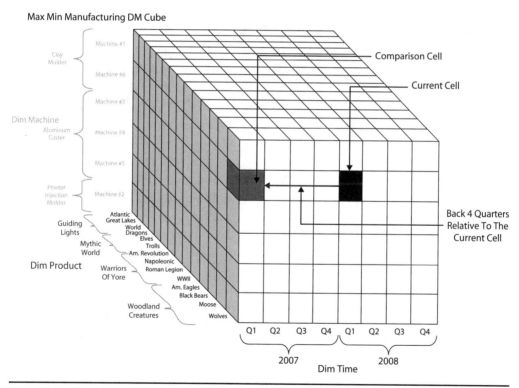

Figure 11-16 *Comparing measures from two cells using relative location*

Of course, we could do this using the absolute navigation we already know. We know the tuple for the Comparison Cell is

```
([Machine #6], [Wolves], [2007].[Q1])
```

This works fine until we move on to look at the measures for Q2, 2008. Now we have to figure out the tuple for the Comparison Cell all over again. Perhaps we are looking at measures in a set of cells—say Q1, 2008 through Q4, 2008. Now it becomes even more tedious to manually determine the tuples for all of the Comparison Cells.

Even more helpful would be a way to identify one cell by its relative position to another cell. Fortunately, MDX scripting provides a way for us to do this: through the use of MDX functions. But, before we look at functions that help us determine the tuple for the Comparison Cell, we need a function that helps us determine the tuple for the Current Cell.

The Starting Point—The CurrentMember Function

Like any other cell, the Current Cell can be identified by a tuple. This tuple contains the current member from each hierarchy in the cube. But how can we determine what those current members are?

The answer is through the use of the CurrentMember function. For example, we can use the following expression to find out the current member of the Time Hierarchy dimension:

```
[Dim Time].CurrentMember
```

In the example in Figure 11-16, this expression would return the [2008].[Q1] member.

As with any function, the CurrentMember function takes input and returns output. In MDX expressions, the function's input is whatever precedes the function. In this case, that input is the [Dim Time] hierarchy. In fact, the Current Member function requires either a hierarchy or a dimension as its input. This makes sense because only hierarchies and dimensions have members.

The *CurrentMember function* returns a member. The CurrentMember function does not return a string containing the name of the member. Instead, it returns a reference to the member itself. This distinction is important as we begin to apply other MDX functions to the result returned by the CurrentMember function.

Function	Input	Output	Description
CurrentMember	Hierarchy or Dimension	Member	Returns the current member of the specified hierarchy or dimension

Relative Position Within a Hierarchy Level—The Lag, Lead, NextMember, and PrevMember Functions

A number of MDX functions enable us to select a member relative to a specified member within the same hierarchy. These are shown in Figure 11-17. Assuming the [Dim Time].CurrentMember is [2008].[Q1], the expressions corresponding to the figure are shown here:

Expression	Resulting Member
[Dim Time].CurrentMember.Lag(4)	[2007].[Q1]
[Dim Time].CurrentMember.Lead(-4)	[2007].[Q1]
[Dim Time].CurrentMember.PrevMember	[2007].[Q4]
[Dim Time].CurrentMember.NextMember	[2008].[Q2]
[Dim Time].CurrentMember.Lead(3)	[2008].[Q4]
[Dim Time].CurrentMember.Lag(-3)	[2008].[Q4]

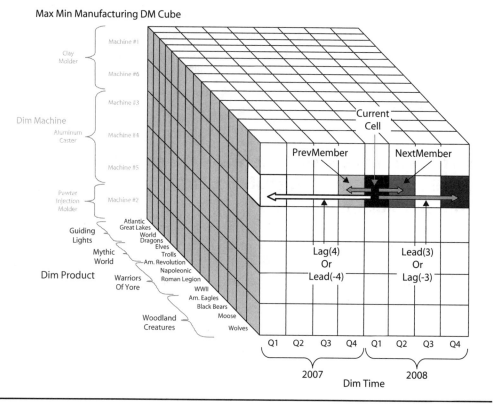

Figure 11-17 *Comparing measures from two cells using relative location*

As you can see, the PrevMember function takes us to the member immediately preceding the current member. The NextMember function takes us to the member immediately after the current member. These functions are useful for looking at the way measures are trending from one period to the next.

The Lag and Lead functions require an additional parameter. This is an integer representing the number of members to lag or lead. This second parameter is passed in parentheses immediately after the function name.

The *Lag function* moves us backward by the specified number of members. The *Lead function* moves us forward by the specified number of members. Using a negative integer for the number of members parameter reverses the natural direction of each function.

Function	Input	Output	Description
Lag(N)	Member, N = number of members	Member	Returns the member that is N *before* the specified member. (A negative value for N reverses the direction of the function.)
Lead(N)	Member, N = number of members	Member	Returns the member that is N *after* the specified member. (A negative value for N reverses the direction of the function.)
NextMember	Member	Member	Returns the member that is immediately after the specified member.
PrevMember	Member	Member	Returns the member that is immediately before the specified member.

Immediate Relative Position Between Hierarchy Levels— The Children, FirstChild, FirstSibling, LastChild, LastSibling, Parent, and Siblings Functions

Just as we may want to move across a hierarchy level, we may want to move up and down between hierarchy levels. A number of MDX functions can help us here as well. We begin by looking at the functions that deal with the immediate family in the hierarchy, and then look at functions that return more distant relations.

The functions dealing with immediate relatives are shown in Figure 11-18. Assuming the [Dim Product].CurrentMember is [Roman Legion], the expressions corresponding to the figure are shown here:

Expression	Resulting Member(s)
[Dim Product].CurrentMember.Children	[Legionnaire w/Shield], [Legionnaire w/Spear], [Legionnaire w/Sword]
[Dim Product].CurrentMember.FirstChild	[Legionnaire w/Shield]
[Dim Product].CurrentMember.FirstSibling	[Am. Revolution]
[Dim Product].CurrentMember.LastChild	[Legionnaire w/Sword]
[Dim Product].CurrentMember.LastSibling	[WWII]
[Dim Product].CurrentMember.Parent	[Warriors Of Yore]
[Dim Product].CurrentMember.Siblings	[Am. Revolution], [Napoleonic], [Roman Legion], [WWII]

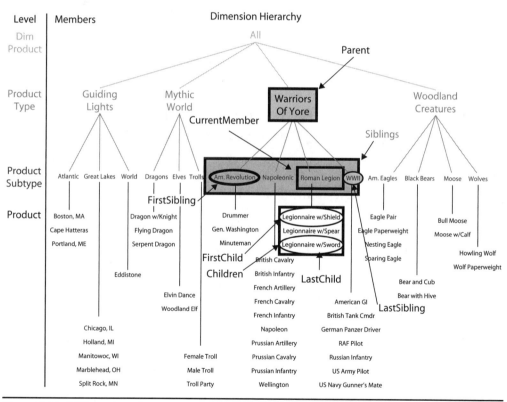

Figure 11-18 *MDX immediate relative position functions within the same hierarchy*

Most of the functions are self-explanatory, but a word about the Siblings functions may be helpful. If you look at the list of members returned by the Siblings function, you see that the Roman Legion member is included. This is true even though Roman Legion is the current member when we call the function. The member itself is always included in a list of its siblings.

Function	Input	Output	Description
Children	Member	Set	Returns the set of members from the hierarchy level immediately below the specified member that is related directly to the specified member
FirstChild	Member	Member	Returns the first member from the hierarchy level immediately below the specified member that is related directly to the specified member
FirstSibling	Member	Member	Returns the first member that shares the same parent with the specified member
LastChild	Member	Member	Returns the last member from the hierarchy level immediately below the specified member that is related directly to the specified member
LastSibling	Member	Member	Returns the last member that shares the same parent with the specified member
Parent	Member	Member	Returns the members from the hierarchy level immediately above the specified member that is related directly to the specified member
Siblings	Member	Set	Returns the set of members that shares the same parent with the specified member

Distant Relative Position Between Hierarchy Levels— The Ancestor, Cousin, and Descendants Functions

In addition to the functions that return the close relatives of a member, a number of MDX functions let us select more distant relatives. These are shown in Figure 11-19. The expressions corresponding to the figure are shown here:

Expression	Resulting Member
Ancestor([2006].[Q3].[Jul], [Dim Time] .[YearOfManufacture]) or Ancestor ([2006].[Q3].[Jul], 2)	[2006]
Cousin([2006].[Q2].[Apr], [2006].[Q4])	[2006].[Q4].[Oct]
Descendants([2008], [MonthOfManufacture]) or Descendants([2008], [2])	[2008].[Q1].[Jan], [2008].[Q1].[Feb], [2008].[Q1].[Mar], [2008].[Q2].[Apr], [2008].[Q2].[May], [2008].[Q2].[Jun], [2008].[Q3].[Jul], [2008].[Q3].[Aug], [2008].[Q3].[Sep], [2008].[Q4].[Oct], [2008].[Q4].[Nov], [2008].[Q4].[Dec]

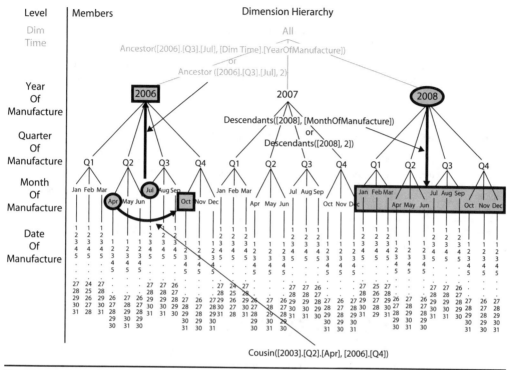

Figure 11-19 *MDX distant relative position functions within the same hierarchy*

The Ancestor function returns the parent, grandparent, great-grandparent, and so forth of the specified member. The Ancestor function requires two parameters, both of which must be placed within the parentheses. The first parameter is the member that serves as the starting point for the function. The second parameter is either the hierarchy level where the ancestor is to be found or an integer specifying the number of levels to move upward to find the ancestor.

The Cousin function finds the equivalent member at the same level of the hierarchy, but down a different branch of the hierarchy structure. For example, January is the first month of Q1. Its cousins would be the first months in the other three quarters of the year—namely, April, July, and October. Likewise, Q2 is the second quarter in 2006. Its cousins would be Q2, 2007 and Q2, 2008. Obviously, this is extremely helpful when we are trying to compare like periods in the time dimension.

The Cousin function requires two parameters, both of which must be placed within the parentheses. The first parameter is the member whose cousin is to be found. The second parameter is a member at a higher level in the hierarchy under which the cousin is to be found.

The Descendants function returns the children, grandchildren, greatgrandchildren, and so forth of the specified member. The Descendants function requires two parameters, both of which must be placed within the parentheses. The first parameter is the member that serves as the starting point for the function. The second parameter is either the hierarchy level where the descendants are to be found or an integer specifying the number of levels to move downward to find the descendants.

Function	Input	Output	Description
Ancestor	Member, Hierarchy Level, or number of levels to go up	Member	Returns the member that is a parent, grandparent, and so forth of the specified member at the specified level
Cousin	Member, Member	Member	Returns the member that is in the same sibling position as the specified member
Descendants	Member, Hierarchy Level, or number of levels to go down	Set	Returns a set of members that are the children, grandchildren, and so forth of the specified member

Putting MDX Scripting to Work

Now that you have a basic understanding of MDX scripting, we can take a look at some of the places it is used in Analysis Services. We do this by completing two Learn By Doing exercises. First, we define a security role in an Analysis Services database. Second, we create additional calculated members in the Max Min Manufacturing DM cube. Along the way, we utilize three additional MDX functions to get the job done.

Cube Security

In Chapter 10, we saw how to create perspectives that can divide a cube into more manageable pieces for our users. Perspectives are helpful for organizing information in a cube, but they do not limit users' access to only those items in a particular perspective. To secure portions of a cube from unwanted access, we need to use security roles.

Security roles enable us to restrict or permit access to items within the cube, measures, dimensions, and dimensional members. We can also allow or prevent users from doing certain administrative tasks, such as processing the cube or viewing the definition of its structure. The roles are associated with Windows logins and Windows groups to provide access to the cube information.

Learn By Doing—Setting Security Within an OLAP Cube

Features Highlighted

▶ Creating a security role

▶ Using an MDX expression to limit access to cube members

Business Need Maximum Miniatures would like to provide access to the Max Min Manufacturing DM cube to the plant manager at the Kawaguchi plant. The plant manager should be given access to the Total Products and Percent Rejected calculated members, but none of the other measures in the cube. This plant only produces products from the Guiding Lights and Woodland Creatures product types. Therefore, access should be limited to these two product types.

Steps

1. Open the Business Intelligence Development Studio.
2. Open the MaxMinManufacturingDM project.
3. Right-click the Roles entry in the Solution Explorer window and select New Role from the context menu. The Role Design tab and a Role.role entry in the Solution Explorer window appears.
4. Double-click the Role.role entry in the Solution Explorer window.
5. In the Properties window, enter **Kawaguchi Plant** for Name. On the General tab on the Role Design tab, enter an appropriate description for Role Description.
6. The items under Set the database permissions for this role determine whether members of this role can perform these administrative tasks or read the definition of the cube. Do not check any of these items for this role. The General page of the Role Design tab is shown in Figure 11-20.
7. Select the Membership tab. This is the place where the Kawaguchi plant manager's Windows login would be added to this role. If you have a test Windows login that you can use for testing this role, click Add and add the login to the role. Otherwise, move on to Step 8. The Membership page of the Role Design tab is shown in Figure 11-21.
8. Select the Data Sources tab. Here, we control the access to each data source. Select Read from the Access drop-down list for the Max Min Manufacturing DM data source. We do not want this role to be able to read the definition of the data source, so leave Read Definition unchecked. The Data Sources page of the Role Design tab is shown in Figure 11-22.

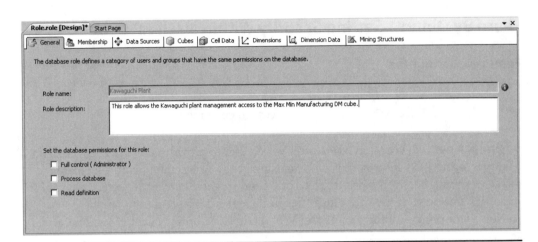

Figure 11-20 *The General page of the Role Design tab*

9. Select the Cubes tab. Select Read from the Access drop-down list for the Max Min Manufacturing DM cube. We do not need to allow drillthrough or rights to process this cube, so do not make any changes to these two items. The Cubes page of the Role Design tab is shown in Figure 11-23.

10. Select the Cell Data tab. This is where we restrict access to the measures in the cube cells. Make sure the Max Min Manufacturing DM cube is selected at the top of the page.

11. Check Enable read permissions.

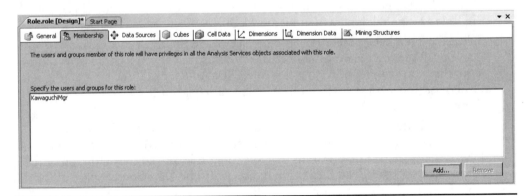

Figure 11-21 *The Membership page of the Role Design tab*

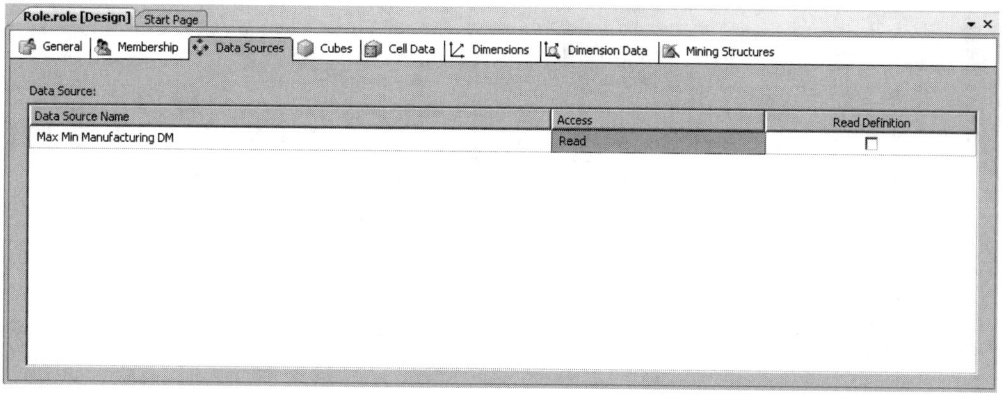

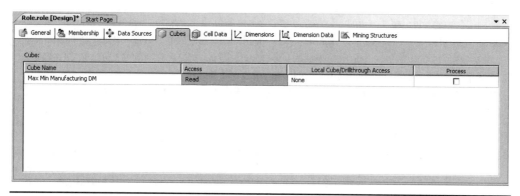

Figure 11-22 *The Data Sources page of the Role Design tab*

12. Enter the following MDX expression for Allow reading of cube content:

```
[Measures].CurrentMember IS [Measures].[Total Products] OR
[Measures].CurrentMember IS [Measures].[Percent Rejected]
```

When creating expressions here, you can click the button next to Edit MDX to use the MDX Builder dialog box for assistance in building your MDX expressions. The Cell Data page of the Role Design tab should appear as shown in Figure 11-24.

Figure 11-23 *The Cubes page of the Role Design tab*

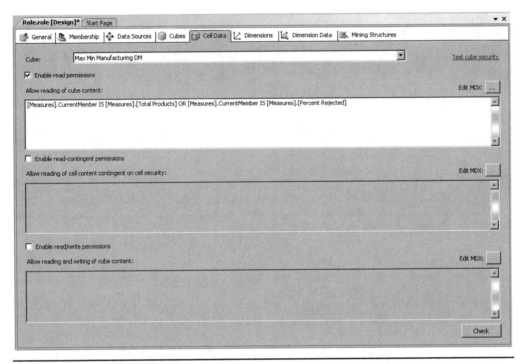

Figure 11-24 *The Cell Data page of the Role Design tab*

NOTE

This MDX expression used the CurrentMember function along with Measures. This syntax uses Measures as a pseudodimension in the cube. The current member of the Measures pseudodimension is whatever measure we are trying to query information from. We are also using the IS operator to determine if the current member is the specified member. The expression here will return true and, thus, allow access only if we are querying information from the Total Products measure or the Percent Rejected measure. If any other measure is queried, the current member of the measure will not be equal to either of the two we have specified and the MDX expression will return false. When the MDX expression is false, access is denied.

13. Select the Dimensions tab. On this page, we set the access rights for the dimensions. Leave the Access drop-down list set to Read for all of the dimensions. Do not allow this role to read the definitions or process any of the dimensions. The Dimensions page of the Role Design tab is shown in Figure 11-25.

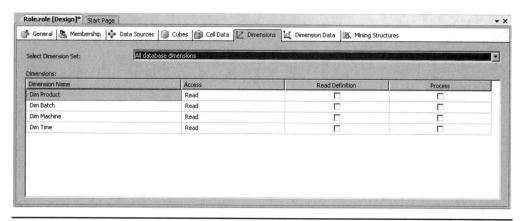

Figure 11-25 *The Dimensions page of the Role Design tab*

14. Select the Dimension Data tab. Here is the place to limit access to members of a particular dimension. The Basic tab enables us to use the brute force method and check or uncheck dimension members to determine access. Expand the Dimension drop-down window at the top of the tab. Select the Dim Machine dimension under the Max Min Manufacturing DM cube and click OK. (Select the Dim Machine dimension in the cube, not the Dim Machine dimension definition in the project. The dimension you want is probably the second occurrence of Dim Machine in the drop-down window.)

15. Select Plant from the Attribute hierarchy drop-down list. Click the Deselect all members radio button on the left side of the tab. Check the Maximum Miniatures—Kawaguchi member. The Basic tab of the Dimension Data tab is shown in Figure 11-26.

16. Expand the Dimension drop-down window at the top of the tab. Select the Dim Product dimension under the Max Min Manufacturing DM cube and click OK.

17. Select the Advanced tab on the Dimension Data page. Here, we can create MDX expressions to determine access.

18. Select Product Type from the Attribute drop-down list.

19. Enter the following expression for Allowed Member Set:

```
{[Dim Product].[Product Type].[Guiding Lights],
[Dim Product].[Product Type].[Woodland Creatures]}
```

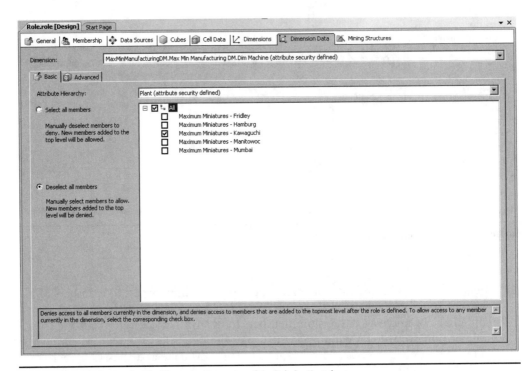

Figure 11-26 *The Basic tab of the Dimension Data page of the Role Design tab*

Here, we have created a set containing the two allowed members. The Advanced tab of the Dimension Data tab should now appear as shown in Figure 11-27.

20. Select the Mining Structures tab. We do not have any data mining structures defined in this cube, so we do not need to make any entries here. Click the Save All button on the toolbar. Close the Role Design tab.

21. Select Build | Deploy MaxMinManufacturingDM from the Main menu to deploy the changes to the Analysis Services server.

22. Next, we use the Browser tab to test our security settings. Double-click the entry for Max Min Manufacturing DM.cube in the Solution Explorer window. The Cube Design tab appears.

23. Select the Browser tab on the Cube Design tab. You are browsing the cube with your credentials, which have administration rights.

24. Drag the Dim Product dimension and drop it on the Drop Row Fields Here target. Notice all four product types are present.

25. Expand the Dim Machine dimension, and then expand the Plant Hierarchy.

26. Drag the Plant entry and drop it on the Drop Column Fields Here target. Notice there are three plants present.

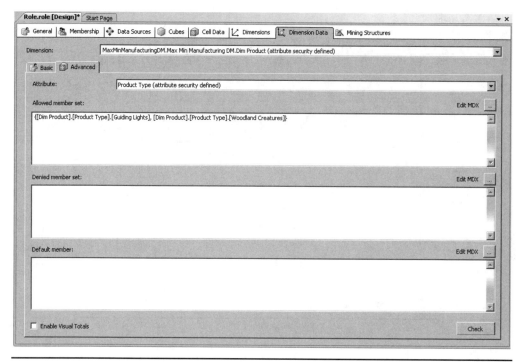

Figure 11-27 *The Advanced tab of the Dimension Data page for the Dim Product dimension*

27. Expand Measures, and then expand the Manufacturing Fact measure group.

28. Drag the Accepted Products measure and drop it on the Drop Total or Detail Fields Here target.

29. Drag the Total Products calculated member and drop it next to the Accepted Products measures. The Browser tab appears as shown in Figure 11-28.

30. Click the Change User button on the Browser tab toolbar.

31. Select the Roles radio button. In the Roles drop-down window, check the Kawaguchi Plant Role. (The All Roles item is also checked.) Click OK to exit the drop-down window. The Security Context dialog box appears as shown in Figure 11-29.

32. Click OK to exit the Security Context dialog box. The Browser tab resets. A message under the Browser tab toolbar informs us that we are browsing while using the credentials of the Kawaguchi Plant security role.

33. We can build the same query as we did before. Drag the Dim Product dimension and drop it on the Drop Row Fields Here target. As our security role stipulates, only two product types are present.

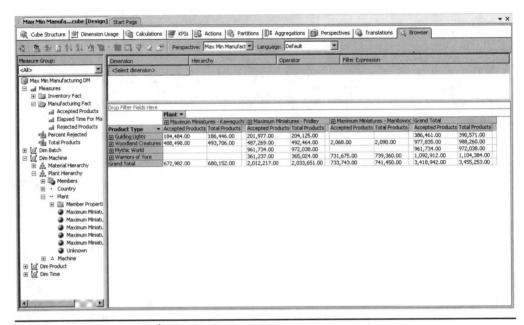

Figure 11-28 *The Browser tab using administrative credentials*

34. Expand the Dim Machine dimension, and then expand the Plant Hierarchy. Drag the Plant entry and drop it on the Drop Column Fields Here target. Again, as expected, only one plant is present.

35. Expand Measures, and then expand the Manufacturing Fact measure group. All of the measures still appear in this list. However, watch what happens when we try to query from a restricted measure.

36. Drag the Accepted Products measure and drop it on the Drop Total or Detail Fields Here target. We receive # N/A for each cell because our security role does not allow querying from this measure.

37. Drag the Total Products calculated member and drop it next to the Accepted Products measures. Our security role does allow querying from this calculated member, so we do receive our results. The Browser tab appears as shown in Figure 11-30.

NOTE

You may recall that the Total Products calculated member is the sum of the Accepted Products measure and the Rejected Products measure. Even though our security role does not provide access to these two measures, the calculated member still works. This lets us provide a user with calculated members without having to expose the underlying data.

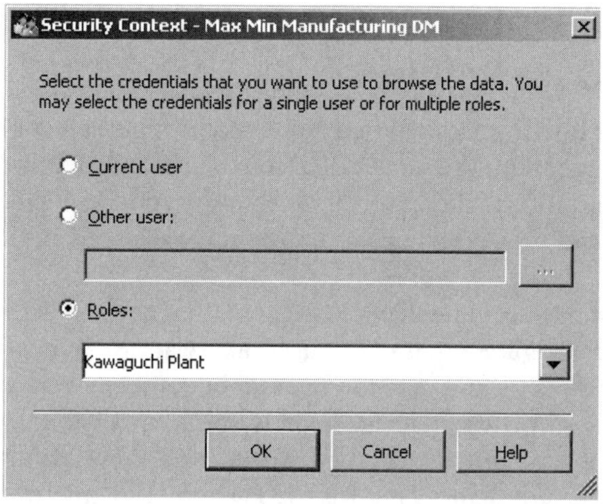

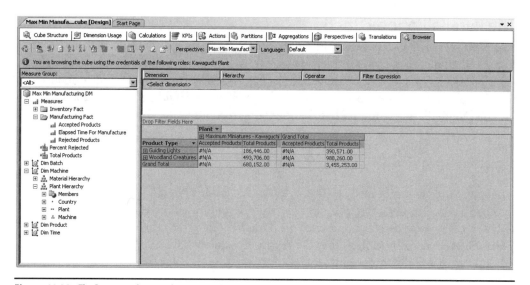

Figure 11-29   *The Security Context dialog box*

Figure 11-30   *The Browser tab using the Kawaguchi Plant security role*

This Year to Last Year Comparisons and Year-to-Date Rollups

Two bits of business intelligence are often requested by users. The first is the comparison of a value from this year with the same value from one year ago. It is a natural desire to know how the organization is doing versus where it was one year ago. In many cases, this is also a telling statistic, providing beneficial insight into the organization's health and performance.

The second bit of business intelligence that is often requested is the year-to-date total. Monthly and quarterly figures are fine, but users also want to know the grand totals as we move through the year. If the year-to-date numbers are not monitored, the year-end figures could be a big surprise to management, which is usually not a good thing!

In this section, we add two calculated members to the Max Min Manufacturing DM cube. One calculated member returns the Percent Rejected from the previous year. The other calculated member returns the year-to-date amount for the Total Products calculated member. To create these calculated members, we use three new functions: ParallelPeriod, YTD, and SUM.

The ParallelPeriod Function

The *ParallelPeriod function* returns the member from the time dimension that corresponds to a specified member. For example, if we ask for the time dimension member parallel to Q1 2008 from one year earlier, we would get Q1 2007. If we ask for the time dimension member parallel to August 2007 from one year earlier, we would get August 2006.

The ParallelPeriod function has the following format:

ParallelPeriod(TimeHierarchyLevel, NumberOfPeriodsBack, TimeDimensionMember)

TimeHierarchyLevel is the level in the Time Dimension Hierarchy that we are using to move backward. The most common hierarchy level to use here is the year level. *NumberOfPeriodsBack* is the number of the TimeHierarchyLevels to move backward. *TimeDimensionMember* is the Time Dimension Member that serves as the starting point.

Consider the following example:

```
ParallelPeriod([Year], 1, [Time Hierarchy].[Month].[200803]
```

This function starts at the March 2008 member and moves backward one year to return the March 2007 member. In this example:

```
ParallelPeriod([Quarter], 1, [Time Hierarchy].[Month].[200809]
```

the function starts at the September 2008 member and moves backward one quarter to return the June 2008 member.

The YTD Function

The *YTD function* returns a set of members from a time hierarchy level that represents the beginning of the year, up to and including the specified member. If the specified member is Q3 2008, the members Q1 2008, Q2 2008, and Q3 2008 are returned in the set. If the specified member is April 2008, the members January 2008, February 2008, March 2008, and April 2008 are returned in the set.

The YTD function has the following format:

YTD(TimeDimensionMember)

TimeDimensionMember is a member from the time dimension. For example:

```
YTD([Time Hierarchy].[Month].[200803])
```

returns a set of [200801], [200802], and [200803].

The SUM Function

The *SUM function* adds together the values in a set of measures to create an aggregate value. The SUM function has the following format:

SUM(SetOfMeasures)

SetOfMeasures is a set of measures. For example:

```
SUM({([200804], [Measure].[Total Products]),
                    [200805], [Measure].[Total Products])})
```

adds the total products produced in April 2008 to the total products produced in May 2008.

Learn By Doing—Time-Based Analytics

Features Highlighted

▶ Creating a calculated member to return a value from the previous year

▶ Creating a calculated member to return a year-to-date value

Business Need   To make analysis easier, the vice president of production would like to have calculated members for the Percent Rejected in the parallel period of the previous year and for the Year-To-Date Total Products produced.

Steps

1. Open the Business Intelligence Development Studio.
2. Open the MaxMinManufacturingDM project.
3. Double-click the Max Min Manufacturing DM.cube in the Solution Explorer. The Cube Design tab appears.
4. Select the Calculations tab.
5. Click the New Calculated Member button on the Calculations tab toolbar. A blank Calculated Members form appears.
6. Enter **[Prev Year Percent Rejected]** for Name.
7. Enter the following for Expression:

   ```
   (ParallelPeriod([Date Hierarchy].[Year], 1, [Date Hierarchy].
   CurrentMember), [Measures].[Percent Rejected])
   ```

8. Select Percent from the Format String drop-down list.
9. Check the Accepted Products and Rejected Products measures in the Non-empty Behavior selection window and click OK. The Calculations tab should appear as shown in Figure 11-31.

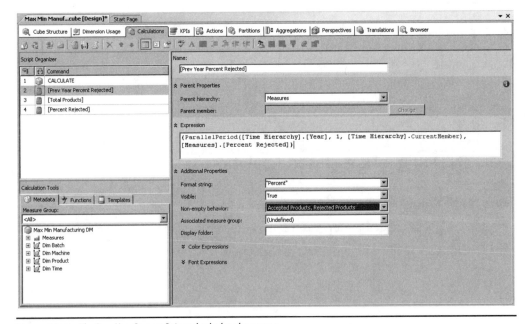

Figure 11-31   *The Prev Year Percent Rejected calculated measure*

10. Click the New Calculated Member button on the Calculations tab toolbar to add a second calculated member.

11. Enter [**Year-To-Date Total Products**] for Name.

12. Enter the following for Expression:

```
SUM(YTD([Date Hierarchy].CurrentMember), [Measures] . [Total Products])
```

13. Select Standard from the Format String drop-down list.

14. Check the Accepted Products and Rejected Products measures in the Non-empty behavior selection window and click OK. The Calculations tab will appear as shown in Figure 11-32.

15. Click the Save All button on the toolbar.

16. Select Build | Deploy MaxMinManufacturingDM from the Main menu. The cube definition is deployed to the Analysis Services server.

17. When the deploy is complete, select the Browser tab.

18. If dimensions and measures are still on the browser from the previous Learn By Doing exercise, click the Reconnect button on the Browser tab toolbar.

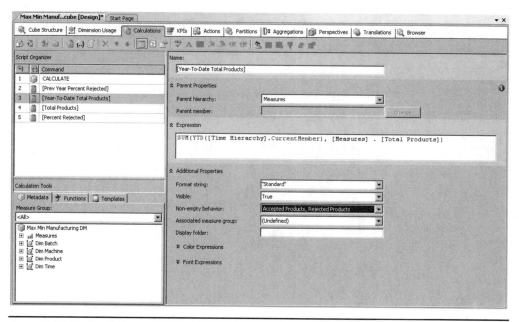

Figure 11-32 *The Year-To-Date Total Products calculated measure*

19. Click the Change User button on the Browser tab toolbar. The Security Context dialog box appears.

20. Select Current User and click OK.

21. Drag the Dim Time dimension and drop it on the Drop Row Fields Here target.

22. Expand Measures. Drag the Percent Rejected calculated member and drop it on the Drop Totals or Detail Fields Here target.

23. Drag the Prev Year Percent Rejected calculated member and drop it next to the Percent Rejected calculated member.

24. Drag the Total Products calculated member and drop it next to the two calculated members already in the browser.

25. Drag the Year-To-Date Total Products calculated member and drop it with the other three.

26. Drill down in the Date dimension hierarchy to confirm that the calculated members are functioning properly. Be patient. Browsing can take a few moments as you drill down to the month and day levels. The Browser tab appears similar to Figure 11-33.

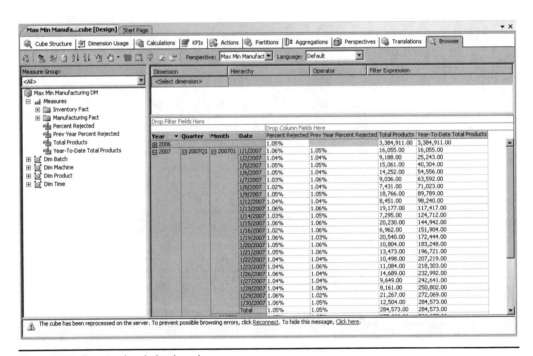

Figure 11-33 *Browsing the calculated members*

Extracting Data from Cubes

Up to this point, we have been concentrating on building our OLAP cubes. Here, at the end of this last Learn By Doing exercise, we can begin to see some of the potential for getting data out of these cubes and analyzing it to gain business intelligence. In the next chapter, we concentrate on this aspect of Analysis Services as we explore MDX queries.

Chapter 12

Pulling It Out and Building It Up— MDX Queries

In This Chapter

▶ **The MDX SELECT Statement**

▶ **Additional MDX Syntax**

▶ **Can You Dig It?**

I've never been convinced that experience is linear, circular, or even random. It just is. I try to put it in some kind of order to extract meaning from it, to bring meaning to it.

—Toni Cade Bambara

U.S. fiction writer

We now turn our attention from building and maintaining online analytical processing (OLAP) cubes to extracting the information resting within them. After all, this is the whole reason these cubes exist. To do this extraction, we utilize MDX queries. As a reminder, the acronym MDX stands for Multidimensional Expression Language.

We have been looking at MDX expressions since Chapter 9. In this chapter, we look at MDX statements. An MDX statement, specifically the *SELECT statement,* provides the mechanism for querying information. We look at other MDX statements in addition to the SELECT statement. These statements enable us to manipulate the data in an OLAP cube. They also let us build a cube from scratch.

Many visual tools are available for extracting information from a cube. We worked with one of these when we used the Browser tab in the Business Intelligence Development Studio in Chapter 10. This tool enables us to drag-and-drop dimensions and measures to pull data from the cube. Of course, the Business Intelligence Development Studio is one big visual tool for defining and managing OLAP cubes.

Why, when we have such capable tools for defining cubes and extracting their information, do we need to learn anything about MDX statements? The answer is this: It creates character, and helps build strong bones and muscles. Well, perhaps not. The real answer is: It gives us a deeper understanding of how these visual tools operate. After all, the Business Intelligence Development Tool creates MDX statements behind the scenes to perform the information extraction and cube management activities we ask of it.

In addition, at times, it is more convenient and, perhaps, even faster to use an MDX statement to accomplish a goal, rather than using a visual interface. When we are first creating or deploying a cube, we need to verify that everything is set up correctly. At these times, we want to look at the raw information and not have a visual tool adding layers between us and the cube.

With that in mind, let's begin with the MDX SELECT statement.

The MDX SELECT Statement

The MDX SELECT statement is our means of extracting information from OLAP cubes. In the same way the T-SQL SELECT statement produces a result set from a relational database, the MDX SELECT statement produces a result set from a multidimensional database. The first major difference between the two statements is the *T-SQL SELECT statement* returns rows and columns, while the *MDX SELECT statement* returns a multidimensional result set that can contain rows and columns, but it also can contain things called pages, sections, and chapters. More on that in the "Additional Dimensions" section of this chapter.

The other difference between the T-SQL SELECT statement and the MDX SELECT statement is the MDX SELECT statement is easier. That may be hard for many of you relational database jockeys to believe, but it is true. Just work through this section and see if you don't agree.

When I say "work through this section," I mean it. This section is not labeled "Learn By Doing," but it might as well be. You can gain a better understanding if you read this in front of a running copy of the SQL Server Management Studio and try out each query as you go. By the time you're done, you'll agree this multidimensional analysis is no trouble at all.

The Basic MDX SELECT Statement

We begin with the most basic MDX SELECT statement and gradually add complexity. When we are done, you should have a good understanding of the statement and be ready for almost any data analysis challenge. We begin with some brief instructions for opening an MDX Query window so you can play along at home.

Opening a SQL Server Management Studio MDX Query Window

To open a SQL Server Management Studio MDX Query window pointing to the Max Min Manufacturing DM cube, do the following:

1. Open the SQL Server Management Studio.
2. Connect to the Analysis Services server hosting the MaxMinManufacturingDM database.
3. Expand the entry for this server in the Object Explorer window, and then expand the Databases Folder under this server.
4. Right-click the entry for the MaxMinManufacturingDM database and select New Query | MDX from the context menu. The MDX Query window displays, as shown in Figure 12-1.
5. The Cube drop-down list shows the cubes and perspectives available in the MaxMinManufacturingDM database. This database contains one cube.

NOTE

You can save your entries in the SQL Server Management Studio Query window by selecting the Save button on the toolbar or by selecting File | Save filename from the Main menu.

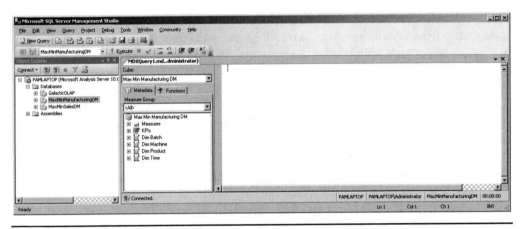

Figure 12-1 *The SQL Server Management Studio with an MDX Query window*

The Very Basics

We begin with the most basic MDX SELECT statement possible:

```
SELECT FROM [Cube Name]
```

For example:

```
SELECT FROM [Max Min Manufacturing DM]
```

SELECT identifies this as a SELECT statement. The FROM clause identifies the cube or partition the information is selected from. This is known as the cube context for the SELECT statement. The result of this SELECT statement is shown in Figure 12-2.

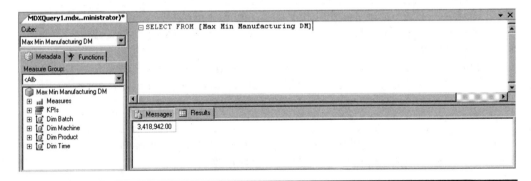

Figure 12-2 *The most basic MDX SELECT statement*

NOTE

*You can type **SELECT FROM** in the Query window, and then drag the name of the cube from the Metadata tab and drop it after the word "FROM" in the Query window. If you do this, make sure you un-highlight the cube name before executing the query. If any text is highlighted in the Query window, only that text is executed. This means you can have several query statements in the Query window at the same time and highlight the single query you want to execute. To execute the query, click the Execute button on the toolbar or press F5.*

When a SELECT statement executes, it creates a set of tuples, and then returns the value of one or more measures for each of those tuples. Remember, a tuple must contain one member from each dimension in the cube. This includes one of the measures in the cube that is considered part of the Measures dimension. A tuple from the Max Min Manufacturing DM cube includes the following dimensions:

```
(Dim Batch Hierarchy Member,
Dim Machine Hierarchy Member,
Dim Product Hierarchy Member,
Dim Time Hierarchy Member,
Measures Member)
```

In our basic MDX SELECT statement, we are not specifying the members of any dimensions to be included in the result. As we learned in Chapter 11, when a member is not explicitly specified for a dimension, the default member is used. Therefore, our query must be using the default members for all of the dimensions, including the Measures dimension, to get the result.

The tuple that defines our result is

```
([Dim Batch].[Dim Batch].DefaultMember,
[Dim Machine].[Material Hierarchy].DefaultMember,
[Dim Product].[Product Hierarchy].DefaultMember,
[Dim Time].[Time Hierarchy].DefaultMember,
[Measures].DefaultMember)
```

The default member for most of the dimensions is All. Recall we set the default member for the Time dimension to 2008. The default member for the Measures dimension is the first measure we defined—namely, the Accepted Products measure. So, the equivalent tuple is

```
([Dim Batch].[Dim Batch].[All],
[Dim Machine].[Material Hierarchy].[All],
[Dim Product].[Product Hierarchy].[All],
[Dim Time].[Time Hierarchy].[2008],
[Measures].[Accepted Products])
```

By executing our basic MDX SELECT statement, we learned that for all batches, all materials, and all products for the year 2008, a total of 3,418,942 products were accepted.

Query Dimensions

As you might expect, we need to be able to specify members other than the default members in our MDX SELECT statements for those statements to be of much interest. We do this by including query dimensions. An MDX SELECT statement with one query dimension has the following format:

```
SELECT {set of dimension members} ON COLUMNS
FROM [Cube Name]
```

For example:

```
SELECT {[Guiding Lights],
        [Mythic World],
        [Warriors Of Yore],
        [Woodland Creatures]} ON COLUMNS
FROM [Max Min Manufacturing DM]
```

Remember, a set is enclosed in curly brackets ({ }). The results of this statement are shown in Figure 12-3.

NOTE

As with the cube name, you can locate the dimension members in the Metadata tab, and then drag-and-drop them into the query. Spaces, tabs, and new lines can be used interchangeably in MDX queries. The new lines are used in the code listing and figures to display the SELECT statements conveniently in the space allowed. Also, the query editor does syntax checking via Intellisense to give you cues if your query is not in proper form.

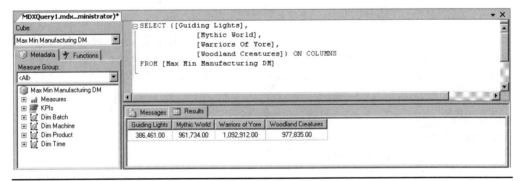

Figure 12-3 *An MDX SELECT statement with a query dimension*

If you are paying attention, you realize we can save ourselves some typing and enter this query as follows:

```
SELECT [Product Type].Members ON COLUMNS
FROM [Max Min Manufacturing DM]
```

When a set of members is specified in this manner, the curly brackets are optional.

Figure 12-4 illustrates how the COLUMNS query dimension is used to create the result set of the SELECT statement. A tuple is created using each member of the COLUMNS query dimension. A value is then retrieved for the member of the Measures dimension in each tuple.

Let's add a second query dimension to our MDX SELECT statement. With two query dimensions, the MDX SELECT statement has the following format:

```
SELECT {set of dimension members} ON COLUMNS,
       {set of dimension members} ON ROWS
FROM [Cube Name]
```

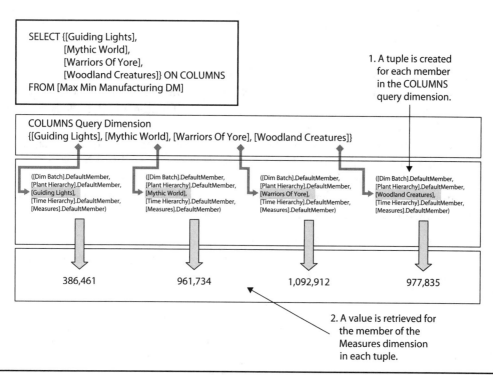

Figure 12-4   *Creating a result with a COLUMNS query dimension*

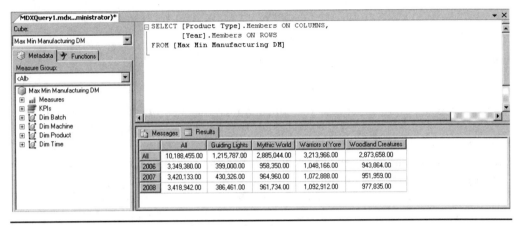

Figure 12-5   *An MDX SELECT statement with two query dimensions*

For example:

```
SELECT [Product Type].Members ON COLUMNS,
       [Year].Members ON ROWS
FROM [Max Min Manufacturing DM]
```

The results of this statement are shown in Figure 12-5.

Figure 12-6 illustrates how the COLUMNS query dimension and the ROWS query dimension are used to create the result set of the SELECT statement. A tuple is created combining each member of the COLUMNS query dimension with each member of the ROWS query dimension. A value is then retrieved for the member of the Measures dimension in each tuple. We can go beyond two query dimensions in an MDX SELECT statement, but we save that discussion for the section "Additional Dimensions."

Because Measures is considered another dimension of our cube, we can use a set of dimension members for a query dimension. For example:

```
SELECT {[Measures].[Accepted Products], [Measures].[Total Products]}
                                                              ON COLUMNS,
       [Year].Members ON ROWS
FROM [Max Min Manufacturing DM]
```

This MDX SELECT statement uses a set containing the Accepted Products measure and the Total Products calculated member for the COLUMNS query dimension. The result is shown in Figure 12-7. We end up with the total of all accepted products and the total of all products for each year.

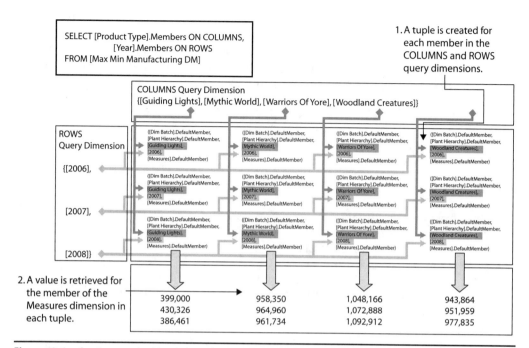

SELECT [Product Type].Members ON COLUMNS,
        [Year].Members ON ROWS
FROM [Max Min Manufacturing DM]

1. A tuple is created for each member in the COLUMNS and ROWS query dimensions.

COLUMNS Query Dimension
{[Guiding Lights], [Mythic World], [Warriors Of Yore], [Woodland Creatures]}

ROWS Query Dimension
{[2006], [2007], [2008]}

([Dim Batch].DefaultMember, [Plant Hierarchy].DefaultMember, [Guiding Lights], [2006], [Measures].DefaultMember)	([Dim Batch].DefaultMember, [Plant Hierarchy].DefaultMember, [Mythic World], [2006], [Measures].DefaultMember)	([Dim Batch].DefaultMember, [Plant Hierarchy].DefaultMember, [Warriors Of Yore], [2006], [Measures].DefaultMember)	([Dim Batch].DefaultMember, [Plant Hierarchy].DefaultMember, [Woodland Creatures], [2006], [Measures].DefaultMember)
([Dim Batch].DefaultMember, [Plant Hierarchy].DefaultMember, [Guiding Lights], [2007], [Measures].DefaultMember)	([Dim Batch].DefaultMember, [Plant Hierarchy].DefaultMember, [Mythic World], [2007], [Measures].DefaultMember)	([Dim Batch].DefaultMember, [Plant Hierarchy].DefaultMember, [Warriors Of Yore], [2007], [Measures].DefaultMember)	([Dim Batch].DefaultMember, [Plant Hierarchy].DefaultMember, [Woodland Creatures], [2007], [Measures].DefaultMember)
([Dim Batch].DefaultMember, [Plant Hierarchy].DefaultMember, [Guiding Lights], [2008], [Measures].DefaultMember)	([Dim Batch].DefaultMember, [Plant Hierarchy].DefaultMember, [Mythic World], [2008], [Measures].DefaultMember)	([Dim Batch].DefaultMember, [Plant Hierarchy].DefaultMember, [Warriors Of Yore], [2008], [Measures].DefaultMember)	([Dim Batch].DefaultMember, [Plant Hierarchy].DefaultMember, [Woodland Creatures], [2008], [Measures].DefaultMember)

2. A value is retrieved for the member of the Measures dimension in each tuple.

399,000	958,350	1,048,166	943,864
430,326	964,960	1,072,888	951,959
386,461	961,734	1,092,912	977,835

Figure 12-6 *Creating a result with two query dimensions*

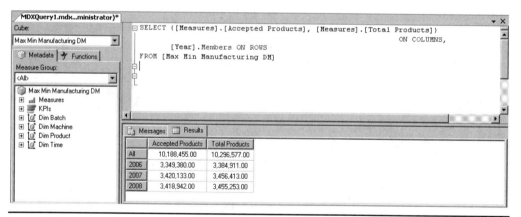

Figure 12-7 *Measures dimension members in the COLUMNS query dimension*

Slicer Dimension

Using members of the Measures dimension in a query dimension is one way to view different measures in the result set. Using a slicer dimension is another. When using a *slicer dimension*, the MDX SELECT statement has the following format:

```
SELECT {set of dimension members} ON COLUMNS,
       {set of dimension members} ON ROWS
FROM [Cube Name]
WHERE [Measures dimension member]
```

For example:

```
SELECT [Product Type].Members ON COLUMNS,
       [Year].Members ON ROWS
FROM [Max Min Manufacturing DM]
WHERE [Measures].[Total Products]
```

The results of this statement are shown in Figure 12-8. Remember, the default measure is Accepted Products. Now in this result set, we get the total products for each product type for each year.

In addition to specifying the measure used in the result set, we can use the slicer dimension to do a bit more. We can specify dimension members to use in place of our default members for dimensions not included in the query dimensions. The format for this type of MDX SELECT statement is

```
SELECT {set of dimension members} ON COLUMNS,
       {set of dimension members} ON ROWS
FROM [Cube Name]
WHERE ([Measures dimension member], [dimension member])
```

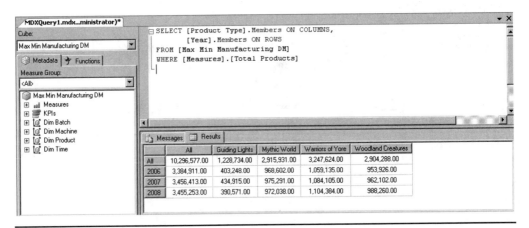

Figure 12-8   *An MDX SELECT statement with a slicer dimension*

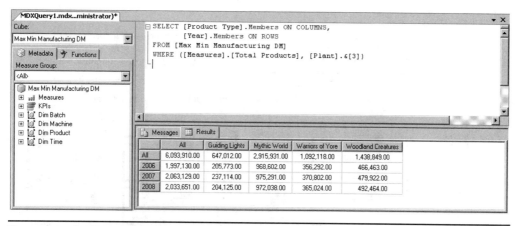

Figure 12-9   *An MDX SELECT statement with a tuple in the slicer dimension*

The WHERE clause now contains a tuple, rather than a single Measures dimension member. This tuple can include as many dimension members as you like. The rule is this: A dimension can only appear in one place in the MDX SELECT statement: either on one of the query dimensions or in the slicer dimension.

This sounds confusing, but an example clears things up. Suppose we want to see the total products for our product types for each of the years in the cube, but we only want to see those numbers as they pertain to the Maximum Miniatures plant in Fridley (Plant #3). We can use the following MDX SELECT statement to get this information:

```
SELECT [Product Type].Members ON COLUMNS,
       [Year].Members ON ROWS
FROM [Max Min Manufacturing DM]
WHERE ([Measures].[Total Products], [Plant].&[3])
```

The result of this query is shown in Figure 12-9.

Figure 12-10 illustrates how the tuple in the slicer dimension affects the result set. Each member of the COLUMNS query dimension is combined with each member of the ROWS query dimension. These combinations are then combined with the members of the slicer dimension tuple. The default member is used for any dimension not represented in the COLUMNS query dimension, the ROWS query dimension, or the slicer dimension tuple.

Filtering with the FILTER Function

Many times, as we are creating MDX SELECT statements, the set of members we want to see on a dimension is dependent on the content of the data. For example, the production manager at Maximum Miniatures may want to see the number of accepted

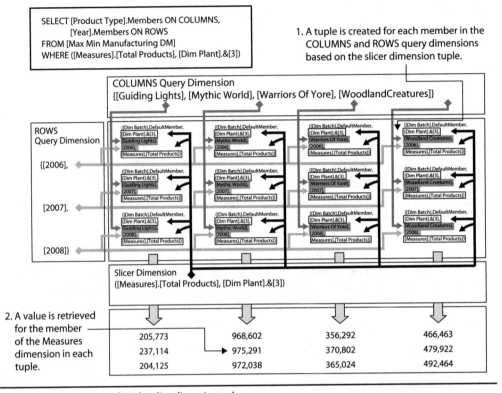

Figure 12-10 *Creating a result with a slicer dimension tuple*

products produced for those products that had an increase in their backorder amounts during the month. The production manager does not want to see all of the products in the dimension, only those with a higher amount on backorder. It is not possible to manually type a set of products to satisfy this query from month to month. A product that may have an increasing backorder from May to June may not be in that same state from June to July. It all depends on the data.

Fortunately, the *FILTER function*, which is an MDX function, lets us determine the content of a set using a condition expression. The FILTER function starts with a set of members as a parameter. Then it removes members from the set that do not satisfy the condition expression. Let's see if we can come up with a FILTER condition that can satisfy the production manager. We can compare the backorder amounts for November 2008 and December 2008.

If you switch to the Functions tab, you find the FILTER function in the Set folder because it returns a set. Drag the FILTER function and drop it on the Query window to use it as the content of one of the query dimensions. You see the following:

```
FILTER ( «Set», «Search Condition» )
```

The syntax tells us we need to supply the FILTER function with two parameters: a set and a search condition.

The set should be all members of the Product dimension at the product level. The FILTER function then removes those products that do not meet the search condition. The expression [Product] provides a list of all products.

For the search condition, we use an expression comparing two values with a Boolean operator. The values we are creating come from two tuples. The first tuple is composed of the December 2008 member of the MonthofManufacture hierarchy along with the Accepted Products measure. The second tuple is composed of the November 2008 member of the MonthofManufacture hierarchy along with the Accepted Products measure.

These two tuples are evaluated by including each member of the set of Products (the first parameter of the function) one at a time. The function evaluates

```
([Product].[American GI],  [Month].[200812],
                      [Measures].[Number On Backorder])> <
([Product].[American GI],  [Month].[200811],
                      [Measures].[Number On Backorder])
```

and then it evaluates

```
([Product].[Bear and Cub],  [Month].[200812],
                      [Measures].[Number On Backorder])> <
([Product].[Bear and Cub],  [Month].[200811],
                      [Measures].[Number On Backorder])
```

Any members of the set of products that result in an expression evaluating to true are included in the set returned as the FILTER function's result. The result is then used by the SELECT statement to create columns. The MDX SELECT statement and its result are shown in Figure 12-11.

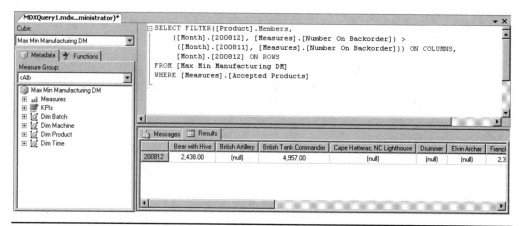

Figure 12-11 *An MDX SELECT statement using the FILTER function*

Note, a number of products show "(null)" for the number of accepted products in December 2008. This occurs because this product was not manufactured in December 2008. No data exists to report for this measure in this timeframe, which probably explains why the number of backorders increased for these products!

The NON EMPTY Statement

In the sample query in Figure 12-11, the data for many of the products was (null). These cells in our results set are really empty. The "(null)" string is put there as a placeholder so we can tell the difference between an empty cell and a cell that might happen to contain an empty string ("").

In many situations, we are only interested in the items that actually have data. We only want to see the non-empty cells in our result. We can achieve this by adding the NON EMPTY statement at the beginning of any query dimension statement. This is shown in Figure 12-12.

Additional Tools for Querying

We have now covered the basics of the MDX SELECT statement. You've seen how to quickly assemble dimensions, hierarchies, and measures to analyze the cube data and discover business intelligence (BI). However, a few more tools can help take the query process one step further.

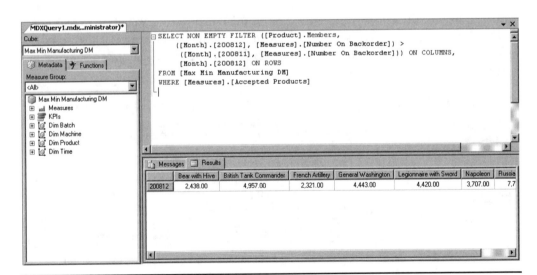

Figure 12-12 *An MDX SELECT statement with a NON EMPTY statement*

The WITH Statement

In the previous section, we used the FILTER function to create the desired set for one of our query dimensions. But there may be times when the desired set cannot be defined by an expression in a FILTER function. Perhaps we want to look at the production of American WWII figures. There is nothing that lets us create this set using a filter (at least, not a straightforward filter). We need to build this set manually.

Rather than putting this manually created set in the MDX SELECT statement itself, we can use the WITH statement to define a *named set*. Once the named set is defined, it can be used in the MDX SELECT statement. The format for a WITH statement creating a named set is

```
WITH SET [named set name] AS
'{set definition}'
```

Here is the WITH statement and an MDX SELECT statement that uses it:

```
WITH SET [American WWII Figures] AS
'{[American GI], [US Army Pilot], [US Navy Gunner''s Mate]}'

SELECT {[American WWII Figures]} ON COLUMNS,
       [Year].Members ON ROWS
FROM [Max Min Manufacturing DM]
WHERE [Measures].[Total Products]
```

The results are shown in Figure 12-13.

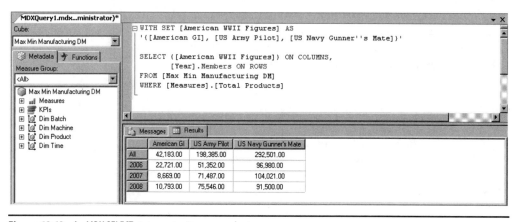

Figure 12-13 *An MDX SELECT statement using a named set*

NOTE

We must enclose the string defining the set in single quotes. This poses a bit of a challenge because one of the member names contains a single quote, or more accurately, an apostrophe. To make this work, we need to double the single quote contained within the string.

The main advantage of the named set is to keep your MDX SELECT statements neat, easily understandable, and self-documenting. The named set is also reusable. As we saw in Figure 12-3, even a simple query can look rather complex when a large set is specified right in one of the query dimensions. Named sets provide a way to avoid these complex statements by splitting things up.

We can also use the WITH statement to define temporary calculated members. These can be members of one of our dimensional hierarchies or members of the Measures dimension. The format for a WITH statement that defines a temporary calculated member is

```
WITH
    MEMBER [parent member].[calculated member name] AS
      '{member definition}'
```

Let's expand on our American WWII Figures set and create calculated members that create rollups for each nationality in the WWII product subtype.

Here is the code:

```
WITH
    MEMBER [World War II].[American Figures] AS
      '[American GI]+[US Army Pilot]+[US Navy Gunner''s Mate]'
    MEMBER [World War II].[British Figures] AS
      '[British Tank Commander]+[RAF Pilot]'
    MEMBER [World War II].[Russian Figures] AS
      '[Russian Infantry]+[Russian Tank Commander]'
    MEMBER [World War II].[German Figures] AS
      '[German Panzer Driver]'

SELECT {[American Figures],
         [British Figures],
         [Russian Figures],
         [German Figures]} ON COLUMNS,
       [Year].Members ON ROWS
FROM [Max Min Manufacturing DM]
WHERE [Measures].[Total Products]
```

The results are shown in Figure 12-14.

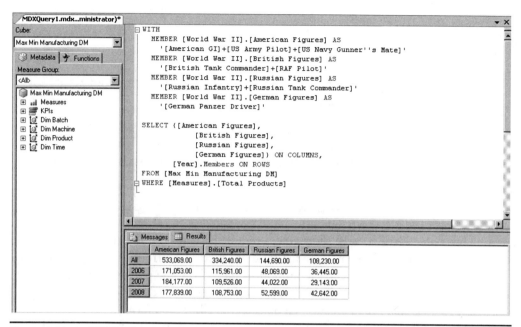

Figure 12-14 *An MDX SELECT statement using temporary calculated members*

The difference between the named set and the calculated member can seem a bit subtle at first glance. The named set is just that—a set of individual members. When we used the set in Figure 12-13, each of the individual members appeared in the result set.

Each calculated member is a new individual member that is composed of the aggregation of information from other members. When the calculated members are used in Figure 12-14, only the newly defined calculated members, not their constituent parts, appear in the result set.

While we are at it, let's define a temporary member of the Measures dimension. Suppose we want to know what percentage of total production our members of the product hierarchy accounted for. We can define a temporary calculated member of the Measures dimension and use it as follows:

```
WITH
    MEMBER [Measures].[Percent Of Parent] AS
        'CStr(ROUND(([Product Hierarchy].CurrentMember,
                        [Measures].[Total Products])*100/
            ([Product Hierarchy].CurrentMember.Parent,
                        [Measures].[Total Products]),2) )+"%"'
SELECT {[Product Type].Members} ON COLUMNS,
```

```
[Year].Members ON ROWS
FROM [Max Min Manufacturing DM]
WHERE [Measures].[Percent Of Parent]
```

The expression used to define the temporary calculated member is somewhat complex: It consists of two tuples. The first tuple:

```
([Product Hierarchy].CurrentMember, [Measures].[Total Products])
```

returns the value of the total products measure for the current member of the product dimension. The second tuple:

```
([Product Hierarchy].CurrentMember.Parent,[Measures].[Total Products])
```

returns the value of the total products measure for the parent of the current member of the product dimension. We multiply the total products value from the current member by 100, and then divide it by the total products value from the parent member. The resulting decimal number is rounded to two decimal places and converted to a string. Finally, we concatenate the percent sign on the end. There you have it.

The results are shown in Figure 12-15. Note, we get a divide-by-zero error for the All products column, but we can ignore this and analyze the valid data for each product.

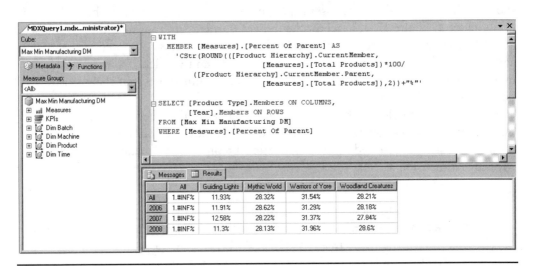

Figure 12-15   *An MDX SELECT statement using a temporary calculated member of the Measures dimension*

NOTE

If you are working through these examples on your computer, you will notice the color coding on the Query window gets a bit confused with the new lines in the middle of the string defining the calculated member. Despite this, the query executes without a problem.

CROSSJOIN

Up to this point, our MDX SELECT statements have been limited to one dimension on each query dimension. Given that they are called query dimensions, it does make sense that would be the case. However, at times, we would like to break what seems an obvious correlation and put two dimensions on a single query dimension. Fortunately, MDX provides a way to do just that. (Of course it does; otherwise, I wouldn't have brought it up!)

We use the *CROSSJOIN function* to combine sets from two dimensions into a single joined set. This joined set can then be placed on a query dimension. If you are familiar with the cross join in T-SQL, you have a pretty good idea how this is going to work. Our new set is going to be made out of tuples, which combine every member of one set with every member of the other set.

If you switch to the Functions tab, you find the CROSSJOIN function in the Set folder because it returns a set. Drag the CROSSJOIN function and drop it on the Query window. You see the following:

```
CROSSJOIN( <<Set1>>, <<Set2>> )
```

The syntax tells us we need to supply the CROSSJOIN function with two parameters: both sets. Let's look at an example.

Suppose we want to see the total products by product type, by plant, by year. We have three dimensions to work with. Here is what it looks like using the CROSSJOIN function:

```
SELECT CROSSJOIN({[Product Type].Members},
                        {[Plant].Members}) ON COLUMNS,
     {[Year].Members} ON ROWS
FROM [Max Min Manufacturing DM]
WHERE [Measures].[Total Products]
```

In this query, we are taking all of the members of the product type hierarchy and cross-joining them to all of the members in the plant hierarchy. With four product types and five plants, we end up with 20 tuples in the cross-joined set and 20 columns in the result set. The result is shown in Figure 12-16.

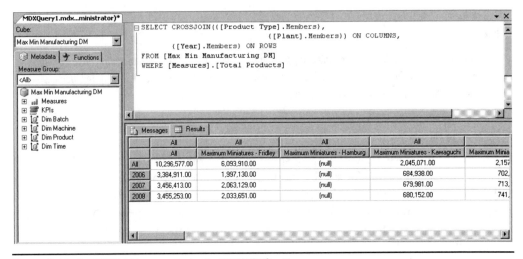

Figure 12-16 *An MDX SELECT statement using the CROSSJOIN function*

If you look at the result set in Figure 12-16, you see a number of (null) entries. This indicates a particular product type was not manufactured at a particular plant during that year. For example, there have never been any products from the Guiding Lights product type manufactured at the Hamburg plant.

Let's make our result set easier to analyze by eliminating columns with null values in every row. Again, we do that by adding the NON EMPTY statement to the MDX SELECT statement. With the NON EMPTY keyword included, our query looks like this:

```
SELECT NON EMPTY CROSSJOIN({[Product Type].Members},
                           {[Plant].Members}) ON COLUMNS,
     {[Year].Members} ON ROWS
FROM [Max Min Manufacturing DM]
WHERE [Measures].[Total Products]
```

The results, with the empty columns removed, are shown in Figure 12-17.

TOPCOUNT/BOTTOMCOUNT

Often during analysis, we want to see the highest or the lowest values for a given measure. Of course, we can manually scan the rows and columns of numbers to make this determination. However, the more information we need to sift through, the more this becomes an arduous and error-prone task. Instead, we should have our MDX SELECT query do this analysis for us.

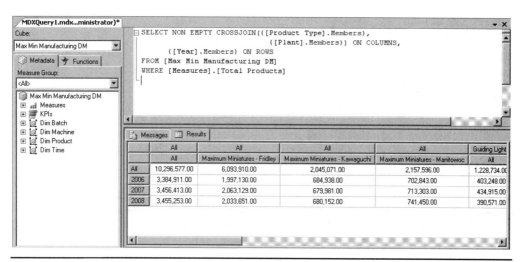

Figure 12-17 *An MDX SELECT statement using the NON EMPTY keyword*

This is where the TOPCOUNT and BOTTOMCOUNT functions come in. These functions return the select set of the members with the highest or lowest values for a specified measure. The TOPCOUNT and BOTTOMCOUNT functions are found in the Set folder because they each return a set. Drag the TOPCOUNT function and drop it on the Query window. You see the following:

```
TOPCOUNT( <<Set>>, <<Count>>[, <<Numeric Expression>>])
```

The first parameter is the set we are to select from. The second parameter is the number of members to include in our result set. The third parameter is the numeric expression, usually a measure, which is used to rank the set members before taking the requested number of members off the top. The syntax of the BOTTOMCOUNT function is identical to that of the TOPCOUNT function. The only difference, of course, is the BOTTOMCOUNT function is pulling from the bottom of the ranking rather than the top.

Let's begin by looking for the five products we have manufactured the most in 2008. To accomplish this, we use the TOPCOUNT function in the following query:

```
SELECT TOPCOUNT([Product].Members, 5,
      [Measures].[Total Products]) ON COLUMNS
FROM [Max Min Manufacturing DM]
```

The results are shown in Figure 12-18. Note, we now only have five products in the result set, including the All member, but the products are in their ranking order.

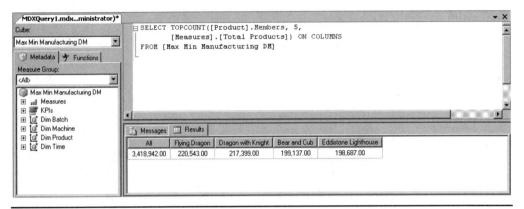

Figure 12-18 *An MDX SELECT statement using the TOPCOUNT function*

To find the three machines that have manufactured the least amount of product in 2008, we can use the following query:

```
SELECT BOTTOMCOUNT([Machine].Members, 3,
        [Measures].[Total Products]) ON COLUMNS
FROM [Max Min Manufacturing DM]
```

The results are shown in Figure 12-19.

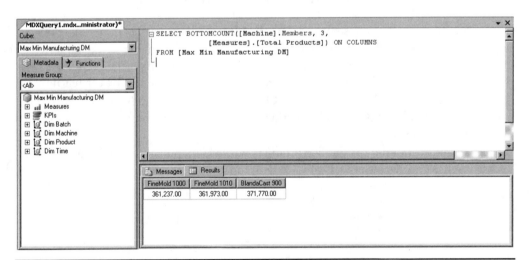

Figure 12-19 *An MDX SELECT statement using the BOTTOMCOUNT function*

Remember, the TOPCOUNT and BOTTOMCOUNT functions simply create a set to use in one of the query dimensions. Let's look at another example to illustrate this point:

```
SELECT TOPCOUNT([Product].Members, 5,
                [Measures].[Total Products]) ON COLUMNS,
       {[Year].[2007]} ON ROWS
FROM [Max Min Manufacturing DM]
```

The results are shown in Figure 12-20.

At first, a problem seems to exist with the result set shown in Figure 12-20. The products do not appear in the proper rank order. Maximum Miniatures made more Bear and Cub than Dragon with Knight, yet Dragon with Knight is second in the result set and Bear and Cub is third. We need to look at exactly what our MDX SELECT statement is doing.

The TOPCOUNT function executes first to create the set for the COLUMNS query dimension. Because we have not specified a member of the Time dimension, the function uses the default member of 2008. It finds the five products with the largest production in 2008. Using this set of five products for the COLUMNS query dimension, the SELECT statement combines it with the 2007 member from the ROWS query dimension to get the total production for our five products in 2007. Dragon with Knight production may have exceeded Bear and Cub production in 2008, but it did not in 2007. As with most computer code, you usually get exactly what you ask for. The trick is asking for the correct thing!

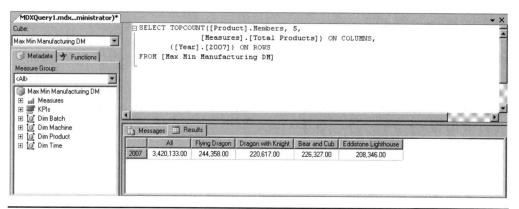

Figure 12-20 *An MDX SELECT statement using the TOPCOUNT function along with a ROWS query dimension*

Aggregates

We have looked at aggregate functions with respect to the rollup done for hierarchy members in the cube. MDX also offers aggregation functions that may be used for creating calculations in MDX SELECT statements. We examine two of these functions here.

First, the SUM function adds the values of a numeric expression for all of the members in a set. The format of the SUM function is

```
SUM( <<Set>> [, <<Numeric Expression>>] )
```

Second, the COUNT function counts the number of items in a set. The COUNT function has the following format:

```
COUNT( <<Set>> [, EXCLUDEEMPTY | INCLUDEEMPTY] )
```

The optional second parameter to the COUNT function determines whether empty cells are counted.

Let's use these two aggregate functions to calculate the average amount produced per month for each product. We use the following query:

```
WITH
        MEMBER [Measures].[Avg per Month] AS
        'ROUND(Sum(Descendants([Date Hierarchy].CurrentMember, [Date]),
                                     [Measures].[Total Products]) /
        Count(Descendants([Date Hierarchy].CurrentMember, [Date])),0)'

SELECT [Year].Members ON COLUMNS,
        [Product Type].Members ON ROWS
FROM [Max Min Manufacturing DM]
WHERE [Measures].[Avg per Month]
```

In our temporary calculated member, we first find the descendants of the current time hierarchy member at the day level. We then take the SUM of the Total Products measure to determine the number produced for this time period. We also take the COUNT of the number of days in the current time hierarchy member. We can then divide the sum of the total products produced by the sum of the number of days in the time period to get the average. Add a Round function to get rid of the fraction amount, and we are done. The results are shown in Figure 12-21.

NOTE

MDX also includes a DISTINCTCOUNT function that has the same structure and function as the COUNT function. The only difference is the DISTINCTCOUNT function counts multiple occurrences of a member in the set only once.

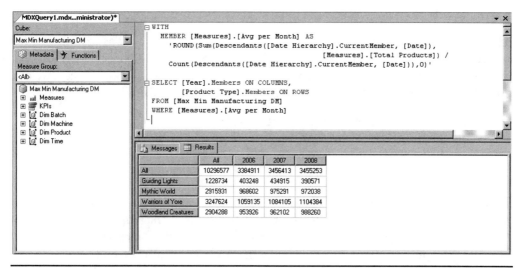

Figure 12-21 *An MDX SELECT statement using SUM and COUNT aggregates*

Additional Dimensions

To this point, we have worked only with the COLUMNS and ROWS query dimensions. We did hint that more dimensions were possible. Indeed, though it is hard for our brains to visualize in more than three dimensions, Analysis Services can provide many more.

Pages, Sections, and Chapters

Five named query dimensions are supported by the MDX SELECT statement. They are

- COLUMNS
- ROWS
- PAGES
- SECTIONS
- CHAPTERS

These query dimensions must be used in the order they are presented here. You cannot have a ROWS query dimension in your MDX SELECT statement unless a COLUMNS query dimension is also present. You cannot have a PAGES query dimension in your MDX SELECT statement unless ROWS and COLUMNS query dimensions are also present, and so on.

AXIS(*n*)

The MDX SELECT statement supports a number of query dimensions beyond the five named query dimensions. Indeed, it is possible to define up to 128 query dimensions. Once we move beyond five, we refer to the query dimensions as AXIS(*n*). In fact, we can use AXIS(0) in place of COLUMNS and AXIS(1) in place of ROWS, like so:

```
SELECT [Product Type].Members ON AXIS(0),
       [Year].Members ON AXIS(1)
FROM [Max Min Manufacturing DM]
WHERE [Measures].[Total Products]
```

The results are shown in Figure 12-22.

Unfortunately, the Query window in the SQL Server Management Studio does not display more than two query dimensions. When we try, we receive an error message, as shown in Figure 12-23. This is an error from the front-end Query window, not from the Analysis Services server. Other front-end tools allow for more dimensions in our queries.

Additional MDX Syntax

Up to this point in the chapter, we have looked at the ins and outs of the MDX SELECT statement. This statement is extremely important to cube analysis. For the remainder of this chapter, we touch on some additional MDX that is useful in both the MDX SELECT statement and in MDX syntax scripts.

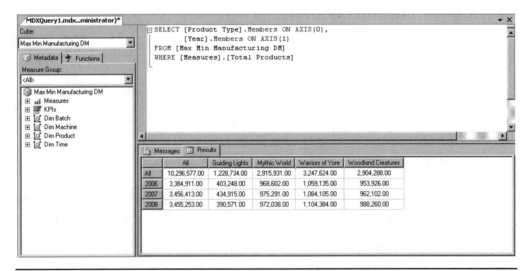

Figure 12-22 *An MDX SELECT statement using AXIS(0) and AXIS(1)*

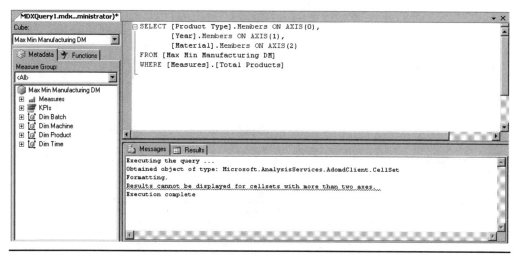

Figure 12-23 *A front-end Query window error when trying to use three query dimensions*

Operators

First, we take a look at the operators available in MDX.

Comment

Item	Description
/*...*/	Multiline comment
--	Single-line comment
//	Single-line comment

If you save your MDX queries for use by others or for your own reuse later, documenting what the query is for and exactly what it returns is important. With some of the more intricate MDX statements, it is not always easy to decipher the statement's purpose. A comment or two can be a lifesaver in these situations.

Multiline comments can span several lines and are not terminated until a */ is encountered. Single-line comments are terminated at the end of the line. Any of the comment types can begin at the beginning or in the middle of a line. Comments are completely ignored during MDX processing.

Here is an example of all three types of comments.

```
/* This is an MDX SELECT statement from the
   "Delivering Business Intelligence with SQL
   Server 2008" book. */
```

```
SELECT [Product Type].Members ON COLUMNS, -- the COLUMNS dimension
       [Year].Members ON ROWS              // the ROWS dimension
FROM [Max Min Manufacturing DM]
WHERE [Measures].[Total Products]          /* The slicer dimension */
```

Numeric

Item	Description
+	Positive
+	Addition
–	Negative
–	Subtraction
*	Multiplication
/	Division

The numeric operators function as we would expect.

String

Item	Description
+	Concatenation

String concatenation is performed with the plus (+) sign, as in T-SQL.

Logical

Item	Description
<	Less Than
<=	Less Than or Equal To
<>	Not Equal To
=	Equal
>	Greater Than
>=	Greater Than or Equal To
AND	Logical And
IS	Tuple Equality
NOT	Logical Not
OR	Logical Or
XOR	Logical Exclusive Or

The logical operators perform as expected.

Set

Item	Description
–	Except
*	Crossjoin
+	Union

The except (–) and union (+) operators only work with sets from the same dimension. The crossjoin (*) operator requires two sets from different dimensions. The Range operator was covered in Chapter 11. The crossjoin operator functions in the same manner as the CROSSJOIN function covered in the section "CROSSJOIN" in this chapter.

If Set 1 is

```
{[Bear and Cub], [Bear with Hive], [Bull Moose]}
```

and Set 2 is

```
{[Bull Moose], [Eagle Pair], [Howling Wolf]}
```

then

```
[Set 1] - [Set 2]
```

is

```
{[Bear and Cub], [Bear with Hive]}
```

In other words, it is the members in Set 1 that are not in Set 2.

```
[Set 1] + [Set 2]
```

is

```
{[Bear and Cub], [Bear with Hive], [Bull Moose],
                  [Eagle Pair], [Howling Wolf]}
```

Items found in both sets appear only once in the resulting concatenated set.

Functions

We look at some additional MDX functions that may be of use.

Dimensional

These functions return a dimension, a hierarchy, or a level.

Dimension   Returns the dimension to which the given object belongs.

```
[Bear and Cub].Dimension
```

returns

```
[Dim Product]
```

Hierarchy   Returns the hierarchy to which the given object belongs.

```
[Bear and Cub].Hierarchy
```

returns

```
[Product Hierarchy]
```

Level   Returns the level to which the given object belongs.

```
[Bear and Cub].Level
```

returns

```
[Product]
```

Logical

These functions return either true or false.

IsAncestor(member1, member2)   Returns true if *member1* is an ancestor of *member2*.

```
IsAncestor([Woodland Creatures], [Bear and Cub])
```

returns true.

IsEmpty(MDXexpression)   Returns true if *MDXexpression* results in an empty cell.

```
IsEmpty(([Warriors Of Yore],[Maximum Miniatures—Mumbai]))
```

returns true because the cell represented by this tuple has no data.

IsGeneration(member1, numeric expression)   Returns true if *member1* is a member of the generation represented by *numeric expression*. The lowest level, or leaf level, of a hierarchy is level 0.

```
IsGeneration([Black Bears],1)
```

returns true.

IsLeaf(member1)   Returns true if *member1* is at the lowest level of its hierarchy.

```
IsLeaf ([Bear and Cub])
```

returns true.

IsSibling(member1, member2)   Returns true if *member1* is a sibling of *member2*.

```
IsSibling ([Bear and Cub], [Bear with Hive])
```

returns true.

IIF(logical expression, expression1, expression2)   The IIF function may return true or false. The reason the IIF function is here is because it requires a logical expression as its first parameter. Therefore, the IIF function is a likely place to find one of these other logical expressions.

If the *logical expression* evaluates to true, *expression1*, the second parameter, is evaluated and the result returned by the IIF function. If the *logical expression* evaluates to false, *expression2*, the third parameter, is evaluated and the result returned. For example:

```
IIF(IsLeaf([Product Hierarchy].CurrentMember),
    [Product Hierarchy].CurrentMember,
    [Product Hierarchy].CurrentMember.FirstChild)
```

In this example, if the current member of the product hierarchy is a leaf member, the current member of the product hierarchy is returned. This is the content of the second parameter passed to the IIF function. If the current member of the product hierarchy is not a leaf member, the first child of the current member of the product hierarchy is returned. This is the content of the third parameter passed to the IIF function.

Member

These functions return a member.

ClosingPeriod(level, member)   Returns the member at the level of *level* that represents the last item in the period occupied by *member.*

```
ClosingPeriod([Month], [2008Q3])
```

returns [200809], the last month member in Q3, 2008.

Item(n)   Returns the *n*th member of the tuple. Note, the index is zero-based.

```
([2007], [Bear and Cub], [Clay]).Item(1)
```

returns [Bear and Cub].

OpeningPeriod(level, member)   Returns the member at the level of *level* that represents the first item in the period occupied by *member.*

```
OpeningPeriod([Month], [2008Q3])
```

returns [200807], the first month member in Q3, 2008.

The AGGREGATE Function

When we used the SUM function to aggregate values to calculate the average production per month, we forced an aggregation on the rollup. All of the items were added together to create the aggregate. In some cases, this may not have been appropriate.

If we were working with sales figures, we could have inadvertently added in return amounts that should have been subtracted. If we were working with financial data, we could have added in credits that should have been subtracted. (In these days of Sarbanes-Oxley, that can get a company in real trouble, real fast!)

Instead of forcing an aggregation by using a function like the SUM function, we can use the AGGREGATE function. The AGGREGATE function works just like the SUM function, with one major exception. The *AGGREGATE function* uses the default aggregation operator for a measure, rather than forcing one on it. This helps ensure the data resulting from an aggregation is correct.

Data Analysis

MDX provides a number of numerical functions to assist in the analysis of OLAP cube data. We do not have space here to treat each in detail. We'll provide a list of these functions here to make you aware of their existence. Then, if you or one of your users has need of a particular type of data or statistical analysis, you can track down the details for the function or functions that fit the bill.

Function	Description
Covariance	Returns the population covariance of two series evaluated over a set, using the biased population formula.
CovarianceN	Returns the sample covariance of two series evaluated over a set, using the unbiased population formula.
LinRegIntercept	Calculates the linear regression of a set and returns the value of b in the regression line $y = ax + b$.
LinRegPoint	Calculates the linear regression of a set and returns the value of y in the regression line $y = ax + b$.
LinRegR2	Calculates the linear regression of a set and returns R2 (the coefficient of determination).
LinRegSlope	Calculates the linear regression of a set and returns the value of a in the regression line $y = ax + b$.
LinRegVariance	Calculates the linear regression of a set and returns the variance associated with the regression line $y = ax + b$.
LookupCube	Returns the value of an MDX expression evaluated over another specified cube in the same database.
Max	Returns the maximum value of a numeric expression evaluated over a set.
Median	Returns the median value of a numeric expression evaluated over a set.
Min	Returns the minimum value of a numeric expression evaluated over a set.
Stddev, Stdev	Returns the sample standard deviation of a numeric expression evaluated over a set, using the unbiased population formula.
StddevP, StdevP	Returns the population standard deviation of a numeric expression evaluated over a set, using the biased population formula.
Var, Variance	Returns the sample variance of a numeric expression evaluated over a set, using the unbiased population formula.
VarP, VarianceP	Returns the population variance of a numeric expression evaluated over a set, using the biased population formula.

Can You Dig It?

With our cube definitions solid and our ability to query information developed, it is time to move on to another aspect of business intelligence. We are moving on to data mining. We dig in (pun intended) to the topic to learn how to set up structures that enable us to unlock secrets buried deep within our data.

So, don your hard hat and grab your pick. We're off to the mines!

Part IV

Mining

Chapter 13

Panning for Gold— Introduction to Data Mining

In This Chapter

- ▶ **What Is Data Mining?**
- ▶ **Data Mining Algorithms**
- ▶ **Grab a Pick Axe**

*People who want milk shouldn't sit on a stool in the middle of a field in the hopes that a cow
will back up to them.*

—Curtis Grant, author

As the previous quote states so vividly, we should not sit around and wait for
good things to drop into our milk pails. However, in Part IV of this book, we
are talking about a technique that can, at first blush, sound like sitting and
waiting for good things to drop out of your data and into your milk p…er, into your lap.
We are talking about a technique called data mining.

In Chapter 2, we defined *data mining* as the use of a complex mathematical
algorithm to sift through detail data to identify patterns, correlations, and clustering
within the data. Does that mean we simply turn one of these complex mathematical
algorithms loose on our data and nuggets of business intelligence (BI) wisdom will pour
forth? Not exactly.

In this chapter, we learn more about what data mining is and how it is used. We
look at the work we have to do to gain business intelligence using data mining and
what things the data mining algorithms can do for us. Finally, we look at the nine data
mining algorithms provided in SQL Server 2008 and discover what each one is good at.

What Is Data Mining?

If data mining is not something akin to magic, just what is it and why should we care?
Data mining enables us to put computing power to work, combing through mounds of
data to find meaningful bits of information. Data mining takes this number-crunching
responsibility out of our hands. We do, however, need to follow a number of steps to
prepare the data and the algorithm for the mining process. We also need to evaluate the
result to find the gold among the rock produced.

Order from Chaos

Relational database systems are great at piling up mounds of data as they record day-
to-day business transactions. Multidimensional systems summarize that data with their
aggregations, but they also multiply it along a myriad of dimensions and hierarchies. All
this data can be a bit overwhelming. In many cases, this much data is so overwhelming,
it is dumped onto backup tapes or placed in archives and forgotten.

The problem, from a business perspective, is that this data is the life story of your
organization. It contains the entire record of where your organization has been and,
more importantly, it may be able to provide some clues as to where your organization
is going. This information could be helpful in your organization's management. The
problem lies in making sense from all this data.

798	799	799	799	799	799	799	800	800	800	800	799	799	799	798	798	798	798	797	797	797	797	797	796
799	800	800	800	800	800	800	800	803	803	800	800	800	799	798	800	800	800	800	800	800	800	797	796
799	800	803	805	805	805	805	805	805	805	805	805	805	800	800	805	805	805	805	805	805	803	800	798
800	801	803	805	808	808	808	808	808	808	808	808	807	805	805	805	808	808	808	807	806	805	800	800
800	802	804	805	806	809	810	810	810	810	810	810	810	810	810	810	810	810	810	807	805	804	802	800
800	802	804	805	806	808	810	811	811	812	812	812	812	811	811	811	811	810	808	806	805	803	800	800
800	803	804	805	806	808	809	810	810	810	810	810	810	810	810	811	811	810	808	806	805	803	800	798
799	800	803	804	805	806	808	809	809	809	809	809	809	809	809	810	810	810	808	806	805	803	800	798
799	800	803	804	805	806	807	808	808	808	808	808	808	808	808	809	809	809	807	806	805	803	800	798
799	800	802	803	804	805	805	806	805	805	805	805	805	805	807	808	808	807	806	806	805	803	800	798
799	800	802	802	803	804	804	805	804	804	803	803	803	804	805	805	805	805	805	805	805	802	800	798
799	800	801	801	802	803	804	804	803	803	802	802	802	803	804	804	804	804	804	804	804	802	800	798
799	800	800	801	802	802	803	803	802	802	801	801	801	802	803	803	803	803	803	803	802	801	800	798
799	799	799	800	801	801	801	801	800	800	800	800	800	801	802	802	802	802	802	802	802	801	800	798
798	798	798	799	800	800	800	800	799	799	798	799	799	800	800	801	801	801	801	801	801	801	800	798
797	797	797	798	799	799	799	799	798	798	797	798	798	799	800	800	800	800	800	800	800	800	800	798

Figure 13-1 *Topographic information data overload*

We can compare the task of comprehending these mounds of data with understanding the topography of a patch of land we are preparing to hike across. Each point has a certain elevation above sea level. We could print the elevation of each of these points on our map, as shown in Figure 13-1. The result would, indeed, represent the topography of the land, but it would be nearly incomprehensible. This is the same problem we face when we are overwhelmed by transactional and multidimensional data.

Making Connections

In the world of topography, we have the simple, yet powerful, tool of contour lines to help us distill the data down to something understandable. One contour line connects all the points at 800 feet above sea level. Another line connects all the points at 805 feet above sea level. And, yet another, at 810 feet. The remaining values are removed from the map, as shown in Figure 13-2.

The resulting contour map, with its concentric curves, provides almost as much information as the printout of the elevation for every point. The advantage is the contour map is immediately understandable with a little training and experience. With the topographic map, we can plan our route in a matter of minutes, as shown in Figure 13-3, and still have confidence we will not walk off a cliff. With the printout of

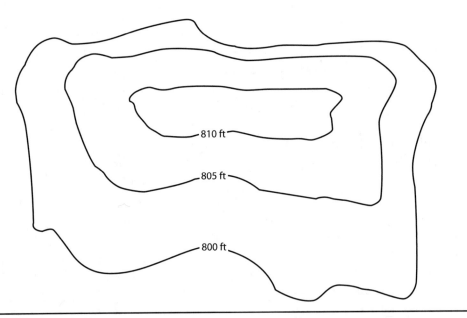

Figure 13-2 *A topographic map*

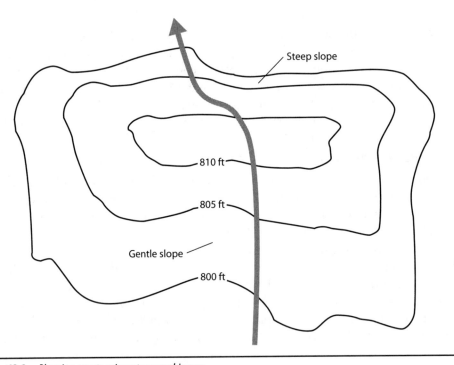

Figure 13-3 *Planning a route using a topographic map*

elevations shown in Figure 13-4, darkness would probably fall before we could figure out which way to go!

Data mining works in a manner similar to our topographic map. It makes connections within the data that may not be readily apparent to the human observer. These connections make the data easier to understand. Using this new understanding, we can efficiently analyze the data and set direction so our organizations do not tumble over a cliff.

Making Predictions

The topographic map holds another advantage for us. Looking at the data shown on the map, we can make predictions of what lies beyond. Judging from the patterns appearing in the contour lines of the map, we can extrapolate to infer the topography of areas beyond the map. This is shown in Figure 13-5.

With any prediction of the unknown, we have a risk of being incorrect. Still, we have a much better chance of being correct when we work with the patterns provided by the topographic map. Of course, the more data we have to extrapolate from, the better chance we have of making the correct prediction.

Data mining provides us with a similar capability. We can use the patterns found in our data to make predictions of what will happen next. Data mining may find patterns in the way our clients make use of our services. Based on these patterns, we can predict

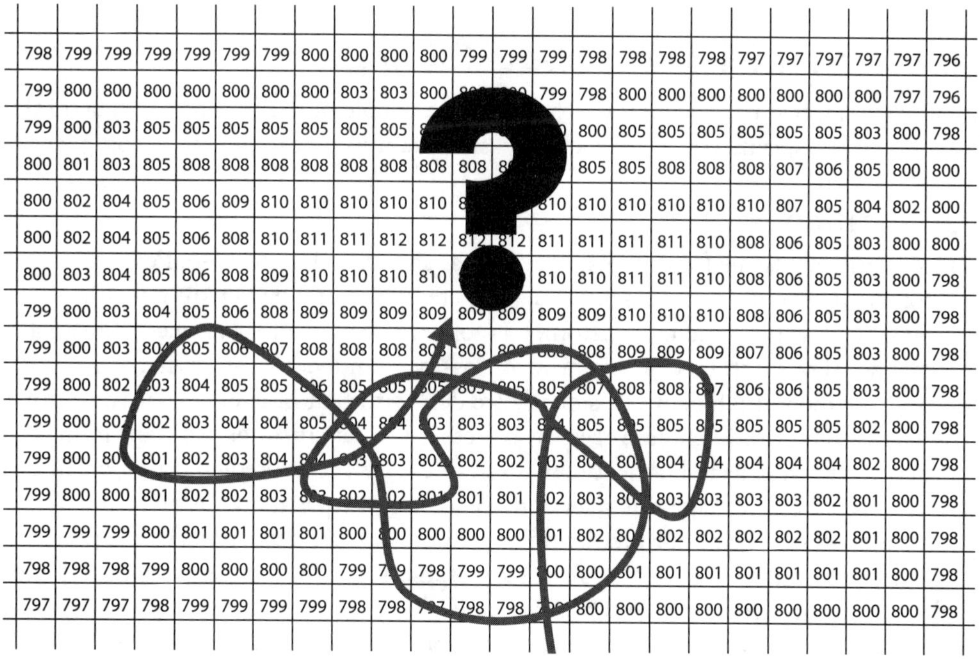

Figure 13-4 *Data overload leads to confusion*

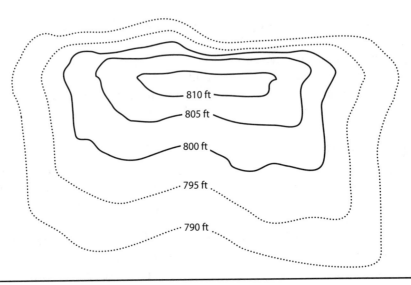

Figure 13-5 *Making predictions from the topographic map*

which clients may need additional services in the future. Data mining may find patterns in the valid data entered for a particular screen. Based on these patterns, we can predict whether a newly entered set of data is accurate or contains a data entry error.

Tasks Accomplished by Data Mining

In our topographic map analogy, we touched on a couple of the benefits of data mining. Let's look more specifically at the various tasks data mining can help us accomplish.

Classification

Classification enables us to fit items into slots, as shown in Figure 13-6. Perhaps we have a customer we would like to classify as a good credit risk or a bad credit risk. Or, we may need to classify a potential customer as someone who is likely to need our services or someone who is not. If we know how to classify an individual, an entity, or a thing, we can make more intelligent decisions as we deal with that individual, entity, or thing.

We begin our classification process by selecting the classification we want to make. In other words, we select an attribute whose value we want to predict as part of future transactions. Once we make this selection, we look at the past data. In this data, we already know the value of our prediction attribute. Next, we determine, in the past data, which attributes most distinguish the customers with one value for our prediction attribute from customers with a different value. These distinguishing attributes are then used to forecast the value of the prediction attribute in future transactions.

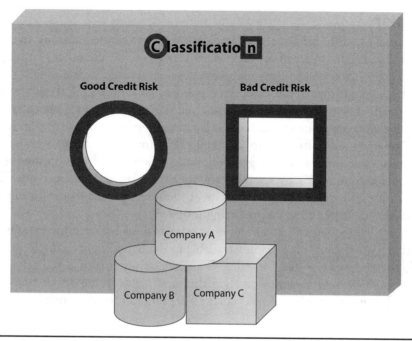

Figure 13-6 *Classification*

Let's look at an example. Maximum Miniatures is having a problem with some wholesale customers not paying their invoices in a timely manner. Therefore, we want a way to predict the credit risk of prospective customers. Credit risk is our prediction attribute. We look at the past data, where we already know the value of the credit risk attribute. We know who paid their bills on time and who had to be taken to collections. We can examine the past data and determine the attributes that most distinguish the customers that were good credit risks from those that were bad credit risks. These are the distinguishing attributes. This sounds like an easy thing to do, but if we have millions of records in our past data, it can be a daunting task.

This is where data mining proves its worth. Data mining is excellent at plowing through millions of records to find correlations. It can process the past data and determine whether it is net assets, annual revenue, invoice payment history, or a CEO's favorite color that is a distinguishing attribute for credit risk.

Perhaps customers with over ten million dollars in assets and three million dollars in annual revenue are almost always good credit risks, while customers that don't meet these criteria are almost always bad credit risks. These become our distinguishing attributes: the measures we can apply to prospective customers to determine what their credit risk is likely to be. Using the distinguishing attributes, we can identify bad credit-risk prospects and ask for cash in advance, before they have thousands of dollars' worth of overdue invoices.

Regression

Classification is used to predict the value for a discrete attribute, meaning an attribute that has one of a set number of distinct values. *Regression,* on the other hand, is used to predict a continuous value. (It would seem the opposite of discrete values would be indiscreet values, but that doesn't sound too good, so we will use the term "continuous values" instead.) The measures that we have been talking about since the beginning of this book are all continuous values. Sales is a good example, as shown in Figure 13-7. Sales can be any number from $0 to $1,000,000,000 (or maybe more).

To predict a continuous value, regression looks at trends likely to continue and repeat over time. Perhaps our sales are seasonal, with peaks in August and December. The regression algorithm discovers these peaks while looking at sales figures from past years and continues those trends when predicting future years.

Like classification, regression also looks at relationships between the value being predicted and other continuous values available in the data. In our example, perhaps the price of gasoline has a big effect on sales. (This is certainly true of anyone trying to sell sport utility vehicles!) Our regression algorithm may factor in the price of gasoline at the beginning of the month as it predicts the sales amount for that month.

Figure 13-7   *Regression*

Segmentation

Segmentation is the "divide and conquer" approach to data analysis. *Segmentation* divides data into groups with similar characteristics. We can then analyze the characteristics of each group for insights. This is shown in Figure 13-8.

For example, a service company can apply segmentation to divide its clients into groups. One group might be companies with over 1,000 employees. Another group might be companies with 500 to 999 employees, and so on. The analyst for the service company can then look at each group to see how much revenue they have generated, what types of needs they have, how much management time they have required, and other factors.

When looking at groups of companies, insights can be gained that would not have been apparent when looking at one company at a time. Using this information, the service company can determine which types of companies should be the focus of its sales and marketing efforts. The service company can also create policies on project management approaches at various types of companies.

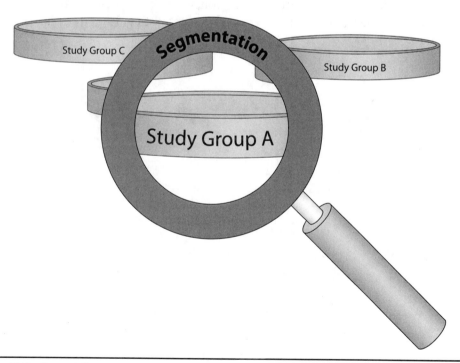

Figure 13-8 *Segmentation*

Association

Association requires we have some type of grouping in our data. Multiple items could be grouped together in a single sales transaction. Multiple services could be provided to a single family unit. Multiple classes could be taken by a student. This is shown in Figure 13-9.

The association algorithm examines the groups found in past data to find patterns in the group membership. For example, items *A, B,* and *C* may occur together in a large number of groupings. Based on the patterns found, predictions can be made on the makeup of future groups. If items *A* and *B* are in a group, there is a strong possibility that item *C* will be added as well.

We are all familiar with the buying suggestions generated by association. When I have *Delivering Business Intelligence with Microsoft SQL Server 2008* from McGraw-Hill in my online shopping cart, the website informs me that a number of people who bought this book also purchased *Microsoft SQL Server 2008 Reporting Services* from McGraw-Hill. (How's that for a subtle product plug?)

Classification, segmentation, and association can sometimes run together. They seem similar. The difference is this: With classification, we pick the attribute that defines the grouping and the algorithm determines what most distinguishes those groupings.

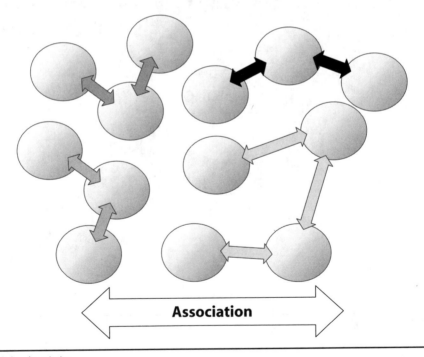

Figure 13-9 *Association*

With segmentation, the algorithm itself creates the grouping, based on what it determines as distinguishing characteristics. With association, the underlying data already contains some type of grouping. The algorithm makes determinations about items likely to be in the group, rather than attributes they are likely to have in common.

Sequence Analysis

Sequence analysis is used to examine ordered stops along a route, as shown in Figure 13-10. Data on past routes is processed by the algorithm. Then, the algorithm can predict future routes. Given the current stop, the algorithm can determine the probability of navigating a given route.

Sequence analysis is often applied to navigation on a website. A user is on Page *A*. The user is then most likely to navigate to Page *B*, with a somewhat smaller probability of navigating to Page *C*.

Of course, sequence analysis can be applied to other types of events occurring in a sequence. Customers may buy products or utilize services in a particular sequence. We can analyze this data and determine the likely products or services the customer will be interested in next.

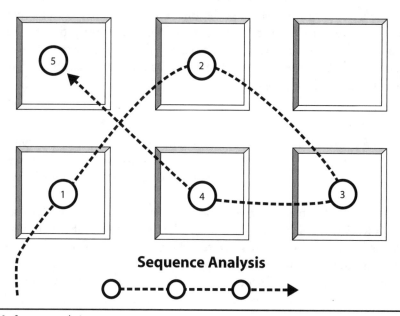

Sequence Analysis

Figure 13-10 *Sequence analysis*

Probability Predictions

As stated earlier, data mining is not magic. It cannot see into the future to predict events. Instead, it mathematically analyzes what has occurred in the past and determines what is most probable to occur if present trends continue. A chance always exists that some outside force could cause present trends not to continue. The user, buyer, or prospect we are trying to analyze may be the anomaly that doesn't follow the present trends, even when everyone else does.

At least with data mining, we can determine, with some confidence, what the present trends are. We can then make intelligent decisions based on those trends. Without data mining, we don't know what the trends and associations are, so we are left operating on gut feelings alone.

Steps for Data Mining

Now that you know what data mining can do for you, the next logical question is this: How do I make data mining do all that great stuff for me? Data mining is a multistep process. As with all of the business intelligence approaches we cover in this book, it takes some time and preparation. Despite the complex mathematics data mining algorithms bring to the table, utilizing data mining is not all that complex. This is especially true in SQL Server 2008 and the Business Intelligence Development Studio.

In this section, we introduce the steps required for data mining in the abstract. This lets you gain some familiarity with the general process, without being overwhelmed by the specifics. In Chapter 14, we work through the specific tasks that must be accomplished in the Business Intelligence Development Studio.

Problem Definition

The first step for a data mining solution is to define the problem we are trying to solve. Data mining is great at finding patterns and relationships that are not apparent to human eyes. However, it cannot solve problems unless we point that analytical power in a specific direction.

We need to define the business goal we are working toward. Perhaps we want to do a better job at identifying perspective customers who are a bad credit risk. Perhaps we want to identify customers who are likely to switch to our competitor's products or services. Perhaps we want to predict future sales to put in place the capacity to meet those needs.

Once the business goal is defined, we determine what we need data mining to do for us. We select which of the five data mining tasks we are looking to accomplish:

▶ Classification
▶ Regression

- ▶ Segmentation
- ▶ Association
- ▶ Sequence Analysis

Our choice of task influences our choice of data mining algorithm.

SQL Server 2008 provides several algorithms to perform each task. Often, we try several algorithms capable of accomplishing our selected task. We can determine which algorithm proves most accurate for our purpose. We discuss the algorithms provided by SQL Server 2008 and their appropriate tasks in the section "Data Mining Algorithms." With one or more algorithms selected, we determine what data we need to feed into those algorithms.

Data Preparation

When we learned about online analytical processing (OLAP) cube design, one of our main concerns was where the data to populate the cube was going to come from. With data mining, we have the same concern: Where are we going to get the data to be fed into our data mining algorithms?

Data mining in SQL Server 2008 uses the same data sources and data source views we used in our Analysis Services cube projects in the Business Intelligence Development Studio. This gives us great flexibility in where we get our data for data mining. The data source may be tables in a relational database or an OLAP cube in an Analysis Services database. It can also come from one of the OLE DB or other data sources supported by the Business Intelligence Development Studio.

If the data is not readily accessible, we can use the power of SQL Server Integration Services to extract the data, cleanse it, and put it in a location where it can be utilized. You may recall from Chapter 7 a special data flow destination called Data Mining Model Training, which loads data from an Integration Services package directly into a data mining model. We talk about data mining models in Chapter 14.

Training

With algorithms selected and our data in place, we begin the process of working with the data mining model. You can think of a data mining model as the combination of one or more data mining algorithms with some real, live data. The model applies the algorithms to the data and creates the classifications, associations, regression formulas, and so forth that we use to solve our business problem.

This step is known as *training the data mining model*. We provide our data to the data mining algorithms so they can be trained on a particular aspect of our organization. They "learn" what is unique about our data, as well as the operations and entities, customers, products, and sales transactions that produced that data.

Validation

We spoke previously in this chapter about providing a data mining algorithm with past data so it could find the classifications, associations, and so forth contained within. In actuality, we often divide our past data into two sets. One set of data is used to train the data model. The second set is used to validate the model after it is trained. Let's return to our credit risk example for an illustration.

We have historical data containing a number of attributes for our customers, including whether they turned out to be a good credit risk or a bad credit risk. To create and test a data mining model, we divide this data into two sets. One serves to train the model, as we discussed. The second set is used to test each of the data mining algorithms.

The data in the second set is fed into the data mining model, and we ask the model to predict which customers will be good credit risks and which will be bad credit risks. Remember, this is historical data, so we already know whether the customers in this set of data were good or bad credit risks.

Each algorithm makes a prediction for each customer in the training data set. Next, we compare the predictions against the known reality for each customer. We can then select the data mining algorithm to use in our production solution based on which had the highest percentage of correct predictions. This algorithm should do the best job of predicting which customers will be good or bad credit risks in the future.

As we separate data into training and testing data sets, it is important we do not do the separation in such a way as to skew the results. For example, taking the first 100,000 records is not a good way to separate the data, especially if we are dealing with transactional records in chronological order. Some event or circumstance may have affected the data during the time the first 100,000 records were generated, which was not present when the rest of the data was generated or as future records are generated. For example, your business may be seasonal. Using a training data set from a time when the seasonal cycle is at its peak can make the data model a poor predictor of outcomes during those times when the cycle is at its nadir.

A random sampling is often a good way to ensure impartiality. Data selected from across business cycles can provide the best training for the model. The SQL Server Integration Services row sampling data flow task is excellent for creating random samples for training and testing data mining models.

Deployment

Once we test the data mining model and determine which data mining algorithm gives us the most accurate information, we can put it to work. We place the model where it can be accessed by the front-end tools that will put it to work. We use the Data Mining Extensions (DMX) query language to feed new records to our algorithm and have it generate information. We discuss the DMX query language in Chapter 15.

Data Mining Algorithms

SQL Server 2008 provides us with nine data mining algorithms. Most of these algorithms perform several different tasks. Having a detailed understanding of the inner workings of each algorithm is unnecessary. Instead, this section provides a brief explanation of each to give you some background information. More important is the knowledge of what each can be used to accomplish.

Microsoft Decision Trees

The *Microsoft Decision Trees algorithm* is one of the easiest algorithms to understand because it creates a tree structure during its training process. (You probably already guessed that from the name.) The tree structure is then used to provide predictions and analysis.

Function

Figure 13-11 shows a sample decision tree created by the Microsoft Decision Trees algorithm. In this tree, we are analyzing the relationship between various product attributes and likelihood to be a high seller. Each new attribute the algorithm processes

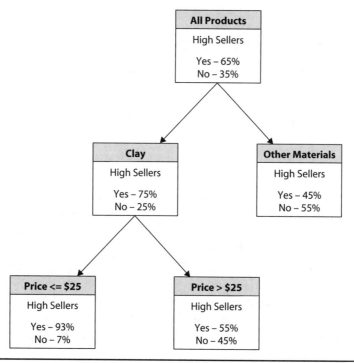

Figure 13-11 *The Microsoft Decision Trees algorithm*

adds a new branch to the tree. In the diagram, we have a binary tree. But, using an attribute with more than two values, it is possible to have a fork with more than two branches—an *N*-ary tree, if you like the lingo.

As each node in the tree is created, the attribute we will be predicting is examined in the training data set. In Figure 13-11, 75% of products made from clay were high sellers in the training data. Further down the tree, 93% of clay products costing $25 or less were top sellers. If you were a member of the Maximum Miniatures planning team, what types of new products would you emphasize? (If you said clay products costing under $25, all this talk about mathematical algorithms has not yet put you in a stupor and you are definitely catching on.)

Tasks

The main purpose of the Microsoft Decision Trees algorithm is

▶   Classification

It can also be used for

▶   Regression
▶   Association

Microsoft Linear Regression

The *Microsoft Linear Regression algorithm* is a specialized implementation of the Microsoft Decision Trees algorithm. As the name suggests, this algorithm is used to model a linear relationship between two numeric variables. Using that linear relationship, if we know the value of one variable, called the *independent variable*, we can predict the value of the other variable, called the *dependent variable*.

Function

The Microsoft Linear Regression algorithm begins with a set of known points, as shown in Figure 13-12. The algorithm works to find the line that will best model these known points. The distance of any given point from the line is the error of that point in the current model. The sum of the errors for all of the points is the error of the model. The model is adjusted by changing both the position and the angle of the line until the model with the smallest error is found.

Once we have a established a linear model, we can use that model to make predictions. Let's assume the line shown in Figure 13-12 represents the model with the smallest error. Then, using that model we can predict the value of the dependent variable for any value of the independent value.

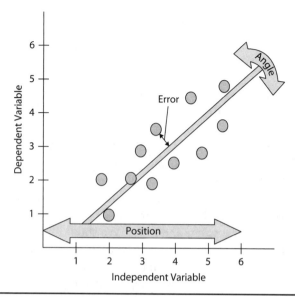

Figure 13-12 *Creating a linear model with the Microsoft Linear Regression algorithm*

If we have an independent value of 5, we move straight up from 5 on the independent axis until we intersect the linear model. Next, we move to the left until we reach the dependent axis. Using this method, our linear model predicts the dependent value will be 4 when the independent value is 5.

Obviously, this is a very simplified view of how the Microsoft Linear Regression algorithm functions. A decision tree structure is created to assist in the development of the linear model. Also, the predictions are done algebraically rather than in the graphical manner just described. Still, you get the idea of the basic concepts.

The Microsoft Linear Regression algorithm requires that both the independent and the dependent variables are continuous, numeric data types.

Tasks

As the name implies, the Microsoft Linear Regression algorithm can only be used for

▶   Regression

Microsoft Naïve Bayes

Donald Farmer, Principal Program Manager for Microsoft Data Mining, claims because there is a Naïve Bayes algorithm, there must be a "deeply cynical" Bayes algorithm out there somewhere in data mining land. I guess it is needed to bring balance to data mining's version of the "force." We will try not to be too naïve as we explore the benefits and shortcomings of this algorithm.

Function

The *Naïve Bayes algorithm* looks at each attribute of the entity in question and determines how that attribute, on its own, affects the attribute we are looking to predict. Figure 13-13 shows a Naïve Bayes algorithm being used to predict whether a customer is a good credit risk. One by one, the Naïve Bayes algorithm takes a single attribute of a customer, size of company, annual revenue, and so forth and looks at the training data to determine its effect on credit risk.

In our diagram, 57% of companies with a size attribute of small are bad credit risks. Only 14% of companies with a size attribute of large are bad credit risks. In this particular example, it looks pretty cut and dried: We should never extend credit to small companies and we should always extend credit to large companies.

What the Naïve Bayes algorithm does not tell us is what the results might be if we consider more than one attribute at a time. Are small companies with annual profits of more than $500,000 a bad credit risk? Are large companies with annual profits in the negative a good credit risk? The Naïve Bayes does not consider combinations of attributes, so it simply doesn't know. This is why our Naïve Bayes algorithm is so naïve!

Tasks

The Naïve Bayes algorithm can only be used for

▶   Classification

Customer Attributes

Name	Values
Size of Company	Small Medium Large
Revenue	< $1M $1M to $3M $3M to $5M > $5M
Profit	<= $0 $1 to $100K $100K to $500K > $500K

Credit Risk

Attribute	% Bad Credit
Small Company	57%
Medium Company	38%
Large Company	14%
Revenue < $1M	41%
Revenue $1M to $3M	33%
Revenue $3M to $5M	21%
Revenue > $5M	9%
Profit <= $0	72%
Profit $1 to $100K	64%
Profit $100K to $500K	28%
Profit > $500K	6%

Figure 13-13 *The Naïve Bayes algorithm*

Microsoft Clustering

Next on our list is the Microsoft Clustering algorithm.

Function

The *Microsoft Clustering algorithm* builds clusters of entities as it processes the training data set. This is shown in Figure 13-14. Once the clusters are created, the algorithm analyzes the makeup of each cluster. It looks at the values of each attribute for the entities in the cluster.

When we view the Microsoft Clustering algorithm in the Business Intelligence Development Studio, we see a diagram similar to Figure 13-14. By entering the attribute value we want, we can have the clusters color-coded according to the concentration of our desired value.

For example, say we are trying to determine the distinguishing characteristics of customers who are likely to go to the competition in the next two months. We create our clusters of customers from the training data. Next, we ask the Business Intelligence

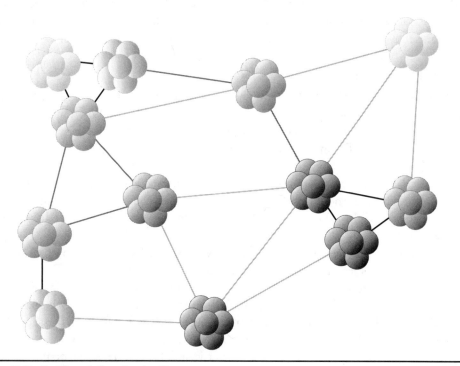

Figure 13-14 *The Microsoft Clustering algorithm*

Development Studio to show us the concentration of customers from the training data set who did leave within two months. The darker the cluster, the more departed customers it contains. Finally, we can examine what attributes most distinguish the high-concentration clusters from the others.

Tasks

The main purpose of the Microsoft Clustering algorithm is

▶   Segmentation

It can also be used for

▶   Regression
▶   Classification

Microsoft Association Rules

As the name suggests, the *Microsoft Association Rules algorithm* is used for association. Therefore, to use this algorithm, we must have entities that are grouped into sets within our data. Refer to the section "Association" if you need more information.

Function

The Microsoft Association Rules algorithm creates its own sets of entities and then determines how often those sets occur in the test data set. This is shown in Figure 13-15. In this set, we are looking at groupings of products purchased together in a single purchase transaction. To simplify our example, we are only looking at products in the World War II product subtype.

The Microsoft Association Rules algorithm begins by creating one-item sets. You may think it takes more than one item to make a set, but just set that aside for a moment. This algorithm then looks at how many times a purchase included the item in each one-item set.

Next, the algorithm determines which sets were popular enough to go on to the next level of analysis. For this, a particular threshold, or *minimum support,* is used. In Figure 13-15, the minimum support required is 15,000. In other words, a particular set must be present in at least 15,000 purchases in the test data set to move on. In our example, British Tank Commander, German Panzer Driver, RAF Pilot, Russian Tank Commander, and U.S. Army Pilot have the minimum support required.

The algorithm now repeats the process with two-item sets. The 5 one-item sets that had the minimum support at the previous level are combined to create 10 two-item sets.

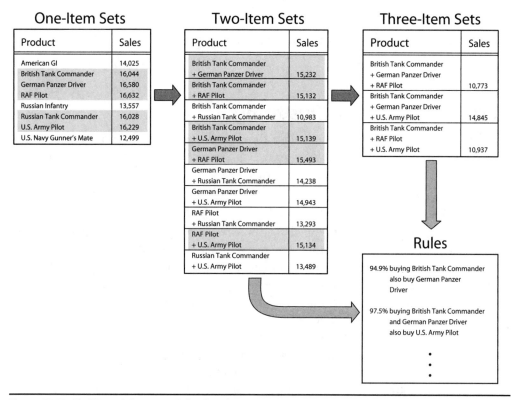

One-Item Sets

Product	Sales
American GI	14,025
British Tank Commander	16,044
German Panzer Driver	16,580
RAF Pilot	16,632
Russian Infantry	13,557
Russian Tank Commander	16,028
U.S. Army Pilot	16,229
U.S. Navy Gunner's Mate	12,499

Two-Item Sets

Product	Sales
British Tank Commander + German Panzer Driver	15,232
British Tank Commander + RAF Pilot	15,132
British Tank Commander + Russian Tank Commander	10,983
British Tank Commander + U.S. Army Pilot	15,139
German Panzer Driver + RAF Pilot	15,493
German Panzer Driver + Russian Tank Commander	14,238
German Panzer Driver + U.S. Army Pilot	14,943
RAF Pilot + Russian Tank Commander	13,293
RAF Pilot + U.S. Army Pilot	15,134
Russian Tank Commander + U.S. Army Pilot	13,489

Three-Item Sets

Product	Sales
British Tank Commander + German Panzer Driver + RAF Pilot	10,773
British Tank Commander + German Panzer Driver + U.S. Army Pilot	14,845
British Tank Commander + RAF Pilot + U.S. Army Pilot	10,937

Rules

94.9% buying British Tank Commander also buy German Panzer Driver

97.5% buying British Tank Commander and German Panzer Driver also buy U.S. Army Pilot

•
•
•

Figure 13-15 *The Microsoft Association Rules algorithm*

Now, the algorithm examines the test data set to determine how many purchases included both items in each two-item set. Again, a minimum level of support is required. In Figure 13-15, you can see we have 5 two-item sets with the minimum support required.

Items from the two-item sets are now combined to form three-item sets. This process continues until there is either one or zero sets with the minimum support. In Figure 13-15, no three-item sets have the minimum support required so, in this case, the algorithm does not continue with four-item sets.

Once the sets are created, the algorithm creates membership rules based on the result. The algorithm determined that 16,044 purchases included the British Tank Commander. Of those purchases, 15,232, or 94.9%, also included the German Panzer Driver. This becomes a rule for predicting future associations. In the future, when someone puts the British Tank Commander in their shopping cart, 95 times out of 100, they will also include the German Panzer Driver in the same purchase.

Tasks

The Microsoft Association Rules algorithm can only be used for

▶ Association

Microsoft Sequence Clustering

The Microsoft Sequence Clustering algorithm was developed by Microsoft Research. As the name implies, the *Microsoft Sequence Clustering algorithm* is primarily used for sequence analysis, but it has other uses as well.

Function

The Microsoft Sequence Clustering algorithm examines the test data set to identify transitions from one state to another. The test data set contains data, such as a web log showing navigation from one page to another, or perhaps routing and approval data showing the path taken to approve each request. The algorithm uses the test data set to determine, as a ratio, how many times each of the possible paths is taken.

Figure 13-16 shows an example of the sequence cluster diagram that results. In the diagram, we can see that if in state *A*, 35 times out of 100 there will be a transition to state *B*, 30 times out of 100 there will be a transition to state *C*, and 15 times out of 100 there will be a transition to state *D*. The remaining 20 times out of 100, it remains in state *A*. These ratios discovered by the algorithm can be used to predict and model behavior.

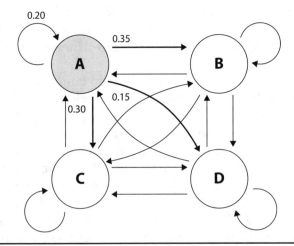

Figure 13-16 *The Microsoft Sequence Clustering algorithm*

Tasks

The main purposes of the Microsoft Sequence Clustering algorithm are

► Sequence Analysis

► Segmentation

It can also be used for

► Regression

► Classification

Microsoft Time Series

The *Microsoft Time Series algorithm* is used for analyzing and predicting time-dependent data. It is actually a combination of two algorithms in one: the ARTxp algorithm developed by Microsoft and the industry-standard ARIMA algorithm, which was developed by Box and Jenkins.

Function

The ARTxp algorithm has proved to be very good at short-term prediction. The ARIMA algorithm is much better at longer-term prediction. By default, the Microsoft Time Series algorithm blends the results of the two algorithms to produce the best prediction for both the short and long term.

The Microsoft Time Series algorithm starts with time-related data in the test data set. In Figure 13-17, this is sales data for each month. To simplify things, we are only looking at data for two products in our example.

The sales data is pivoted to create the table at the bottom of Figure 13-17. The data for case 1 is for March 2008. The sales amounts in the (t0) columns for this case come from the March 2008 sales figures. The sales amounts in the (t-1), or time minus one month, columns come from February 2008, and the sales amounts in the (t-2) columns come from January 2008. Case 2 shifts the months ahead one, so (t0) becomes April, (t-1) becomes March, and (t-2) becomes February.

The algorithm then uses the data in this pivot table to come up with mathematical formulas that use the numbers from the (t-1) and (t-2) columns to calculate the number in the (t0) column for each product. In fact, it uses both the ARTxp and ARIMA algorithms to do this calculation and comes up with a blended result. Using these formulas, we can predict the sales values for a product into the future.

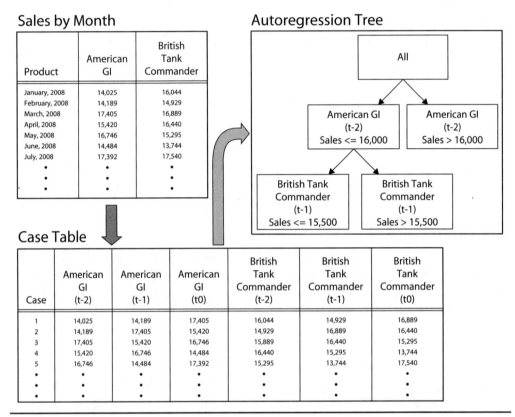

Figure 13-17 *The Microsoft Time Series algorithm*

With something as complex as predicting the future, you can understand that a single formula for each product is probably not going to do the trick. This is where the autoregression tree comes into play. The autoregression tree is shown in the upper-right corner of Figure 13-17. The *autoregression tree* allows the algorithm to set up conditions for choosing between multiple formulas for making a prediction. Each node in the autoregression tree has its own formula for making a prediction. In the figure, we have one formula when sales for the American GI at (t-2) are less than or equal to 16,000 and another formula where sales are over 16,000.

Don't worry; we don't need to know how to create autoregression trees or the formulas they contain. All we need to know is how to use them. We will see how to do this in Chapter 14 and Chapter 15.

Tasks

The Microsoft Time Series algorithm can only be used for

▶   Regression

Microsoft Neural Network

Neural networks were developed in the 1960s to model the way human neurons function. Microsoft has created the *Microsoft Neural Network algorithm* so we can use neural networks for such mundane activities as predicting product sales. Of course, predicting product sales might not seem so mundane if your future employment is dependent on being correct.

Function

The Microsoft Neural Network algorithm creates a web of nodes that connect inputs derived from attribute values to a final output. This is shown in Figure 13-18. Each node contains two functions. The *combination function* determines how to combine the inputs coming into the node. Certain inputs might get more weight than others when it comes to affecting the output from this node.

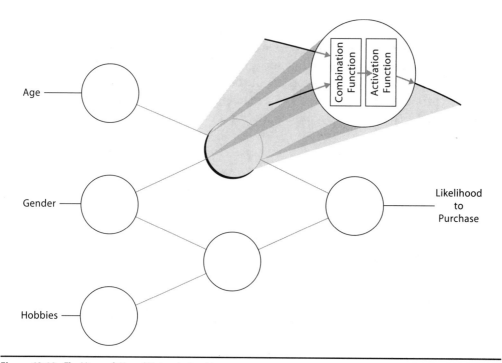

Figure 13-18 *The Microsoft Neural Network algorithm*

The second function in each node is the activation function. The *activation function* takes input from the combination function and comes up with the output from this node to be sent to the next node in the network.

Again, don't ask me how the algorithm comes up with the functions for each node. Some very smart people at Microsoft and elsewhere figured that out for us already. All we need to do is use the algorithm and reap the rewards.

Tasks

The main purposes of the Microsoft Neural Network algorithm are

► Classification

► Regression

Microsoft Logistic Regression Algorithm

The Microsoft Logistic Regression algorithm is a special form of the Microsoft Neural Network algorithm. Logistic regression is used to model situations where there are one of two possible outcomes. A customer will or will not buy a given product. A person will or will not develop a certain medical condition.

Function

The *Microsoft Logistic Regression algorithm* uses a neural network to model the influence of a number of factors on a true/false outcome. The magnitude of the various influences is weighed to determine which factors are the best predictors of a given outcome. The "logistical" part of the name comes from a mathematical transformation, called a logistic transformation, that is used to minimize the effect of extreme values in the model.

Tasks

The Microsoft Logistic Regression algorithm can be used for

► Regression

Grab a Pick Axe

Now that you are familiar with data mining procedures, tasks, and algorithms, it's time to put all of this to work. In the next chapter, we create data mining models and go through the process of creating, training, and testing data mining solutions. Let's see what we can dig up!

Chapter 14

Building the Mine—Working with the Data Mining Model

In This Chapter

- ▶ **Data Mining Structure**
- ▶ **Mining Model Viewer**
- ▶ **Reading the Tea Leaves**

We shall not cease from exploration
And the end of all our exploring
Will be to arrive where we started
And know the place for the first time.

—Little Gidding
T. S. Eliot

You have learned some of the basics of data mining in Chapter 13. Now it is time to dive into the specifics of the data mining process in SQL Server 2008. We use the Business Intelligence Development Studio to create and train data mining models. This tool provides all we need to quickly get the job done.

The examples in this chapter utilize the Max Min Sales DM cube in the Analysis Services database with the same name. You should have created and populated these items as part of the Learn By Doing exercises earlier in this book. If you have not done this, you may download the cube definition and its underlying relational data mart from the book's website.

Data Mining Structure

As we work with data mining in the Business Intelligence Development Studio, we use a data mining structure to contain everything we develop. The data mining structure enables us to define the data we will use, either from a relational database or from an online analytical processing (OLAP) cube, as the source for the mining. It also lets us define one or more data mining algorithms to apply to that data.

Data Columns

The first step in doing any mining is to select the data being mined. We select a data source: either relational data or an OLAP cube. Once this is done, we need to select a table, if this is a relational data source, or a dimension, if this is an OLAP data source. Finally, we must select the table columns or dimension attributes to be used as the data columns for our data mining.

Although an initial table or dimension must be selected for data mining, it is possible to select additional related tables or dimensions for inclusion. These are known as *nested tables*. If a relational database is being used, the initial table and the nested table must be linked by a foreign key relationship (or a chain of foreign key relationships). If a cube is being used, the initial dimension and the nested dimension must be linked through the fact table.

Data Mining Model

The data mining model combines the data columns with a data mining algorithm. In addition, we must determine how each data column should be used by the data mining algorithm. This process determines how the data mining algorithm functions and what it predicts.

Data Column Usage

Each column in the data mining structure must have one of the following usages:

▶ **Key** The *key* is the unique identifier for a table or a dimension. The key is not used to uniquely identify records or members, and it is not used by the data mining algorithm to predict values.

▶ **Input** *Input columns* are used by the data mining algorithm when making a prediction. The *input values* are the values that influence the prediction made by the algorithm.

▶ **Predict** A *predict* is a data column whose value is being predicted by the data mining algorithm. This column can also be used as an input column. If data column *A* and data column *B* are both predict, then data column *A* will serve as an input when the algorithm is predicting data column *B,* and vice versa.

▶ **Predict Only** A *predict only* is a data column whose value is being predicted by the data mining algorithm. This column cannot be used as an input column when predicting other columns.

▶ **Ignore** This data column is not used by the data mining algorithm.

Training Data Set

In Chapter 13, we discussed the fact that data must be divided into training and testing data sets. For the exercises in this book, we will use an OLAP cube as our data source. If we were to use a relational data source, the data would need to be split up elsewhere. It is a bit more challenging to divide the data when it resides in a single OLAP cube. To accomplish this division, we use the cube slice.

Cube Slice

The *cube slice* enables us to specify an expression that divides the cube into two parts. The portion of the data that satisfies the expression is fed into the data mining algorithm for training. The rest of the data will be the testing data set.

Learn By Doing—Defining a Data Mining Model

Features Highlighted

▶ Creating a data mining structure based on an OLAP cube

▶ Defining data mining models

▶ Slicing the source cube

Business Need   The Maximum Miniatures Marketing Department wants to do a targeted mailing promoting the Mythic World line of figurines. Previous research has shown that the buyers of the Mythic World line of products do not have any children living at home. Unfortunately, the list purchased for the Mythic World mailing does not include the statistic on the number of children living at home for each household, but it does include the following facts about each household:

▶ Number of cars owned

▶ Marital status

▶ Whether the address is a rental property or occupied by the owner

The marketing department would like to find a way, using the three facts included in the mailing list data and the information known about current customers, to predict which households have no children living at home. The mailing will then be sent only to those households likely to have no children living at home.

Wholesale customers have customer numbers below 5000. Retail customers have customer numbers of 5000 and above. Of course, we should only use retail customers as our data for this mining operation.

Steps

1. Look at the business requirements and determine which data mining task we need to accomplish. In this case, we want to classify the households in the new mailing list as either having no children living at home or having children living at home.

2. Select the data mining algorithms to perform this task. Four algorithms perform classification: Microsoft Decision Trees, Microsoft Naïve Bayes, Microsoft Clustering, and Microsoft Neural Network.

3. Determine where the data for the mining operation will come from. We have an OLAP cube full of customer data. This can provide an efficient source for our mining operation.

4. Open the Business Intelligence Development Studio.

5. Open the MaxMinSalesDM project. In Chapter 10, we deployed this cube using the Deployment Wizard. Now, we will deploy it directly from the Business Intelligence Development Studio.

6. Select Project | Properties from the main menu. The MaxMinSalesDM Property Pages dialog box appears.

7. On the Deployment page, enter the name of the Analysis Services server where the MaxMinSalesDM database resides, for the Server property. Click OK.

8. Select Build | Deploy MaxMinSalesDM from the main menu to deploy the latest version of the cube to the server. If you receive a prompt concerning overwriting the existing MaxMinSalesDM, go ahead and overwrite it.

9. When the deployment is complete, right-click the entry for the MaxMinSalesDM project in the Solution Explorer window. Select Process from the context menu. The Process Database—MaxMinSalesDM dialog box appears.

10. Click Run. The Process Progress dialog box appears.

11. When the process has succeeded, click Close to close the Process Progress dialog box. Click Close to close the Process Database—MaxMinSalesDM dialog box.

12. Right-click the Mining Structures folder in the Solution Explorer window and select New Mining Structure from the context menu. The Data Mining Wizard appears.

13. Click Next. The Select the Definition Method page of the wizard appears, as shown in Figure 14-1.

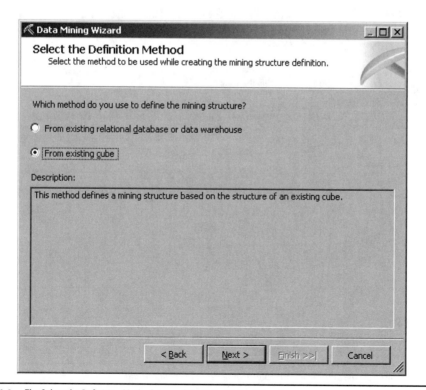

Figure 14-1 *The Select the Definition Method page of the Data Mining Wizard*

NOTE

Data mining structures can use both relational databases and OLAP cubes for data. We could just as easily have used the MaxMinSalesDM relational database as the source for this cube. Relational databases designed for transactional operations, rather than for a data mart, can also be used.

14. Select the From Existing Cube radio button. Click Next. The Create the Data Mining Structure page of the wizard appears as shown in Figure 14-2.

15. Select Microsoft Decision Trees from the drop-down list. Click Next. The Select the Source Cube Dimension page of the wizard appears, as shown in Figure 14-3.

16. Select the Customer Dimension. This is the main source of information for this mining operation. Click Next. The Select the Case Key page appears as shown in Figure 14-4.

17. Leave the Customer attribute selected. This attribute serves as the primary key for the mining operation. Click Next. The Select Case Level Columns page of the wizard appears.

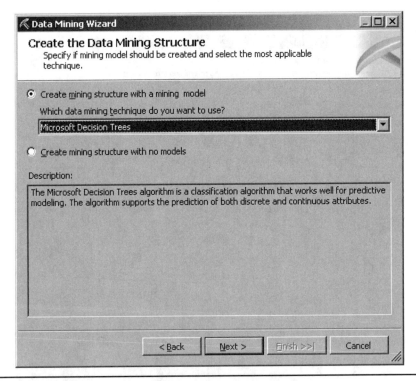

Figure 14-2   *The Create the Data Mining Structure page of the Data Mining Wizard*

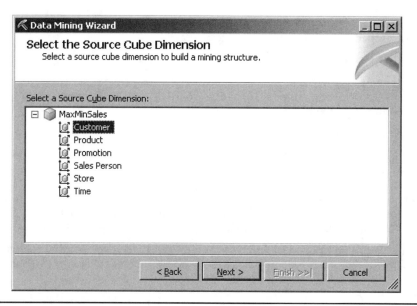

Figure 14-3   *The Select the Source Cube Dimension page of the Data Mining Wizard*

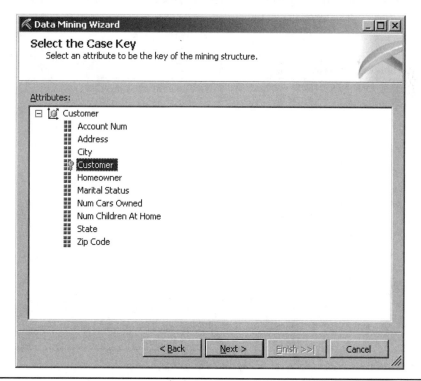

Figure 14-4   *The Select the Case Key page of the Data Mining Wizard*

18. The columns selected here serve as the input and predictable columns in our model. Check the following attributes:

   ► Homeowner

   ► Marital Status

   ► Num Cars Owned

   ► Num Children At Home

   The Select Case Level Columns wizard page appears as shown in Figure 14-5.

19. Click Next. The Specify Mining Model Column Usage page of the wizard appears.

20. Uncheck the check box in the Input column for Num Children At Home. Check the check box in the Predictable column for Num Children At Home. The Specify Mining Model Column Usage page appears as shown in Figure 14-6.

21. Click Next. The Specify Columns' Content and Data Type page of the wizard appears.

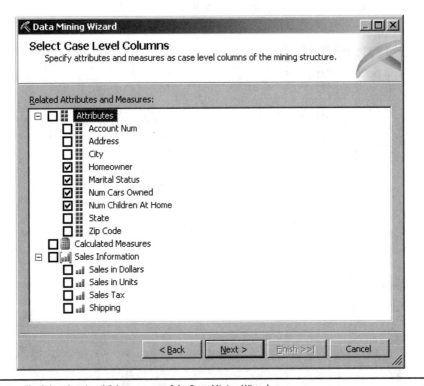

Figure 14-5 *The Select Case Level Columns page of the Data Mining Wizard*

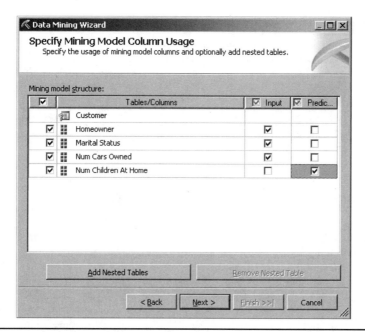

Figure 14-6   *The Specify Mining Model Column Usage page of the Data Mining Wizard*

22. Change the Content Type for Num Cars Owned to Discrete. Change the Content Type for Num Children At Home to Discrete. The Specify Columns' Content and Data Type page appears as shown in Figure 14-7.

NOTE

In Chapter 13, we said that some data mining algorithms can predict discrete values, while others can predict continuous values. In this case, we are using algorithms that require discrete values. Even though the Num Cars Owned and Num Children At Home have long integer data types, we know, in reality, that they have only a few discrete values. Therefore, we can change their content type to discrete. It is possible to force a continuous set of values to be discrete. We do this by choosing Discretized as the Content Type, and then selecting a method that groups continuous values into a discrete number of buckets (that is, ages 11–15, ages 16–20, and so on). Often, it is much easier to do analysis on discretized values than on continuous values. For the purposes of a given analysis, the buying habits of 16–20-year-olds may be similar enough so that we can study them as a group in one discretized bucket.

23. Click Next. The Slice Source Cube page of the wizard appears.

24. We need to use only retail customers for our data mining (Account Num attribute of 5000 and above). Select Customer from the drop-down list in the first row of the Dimension column.

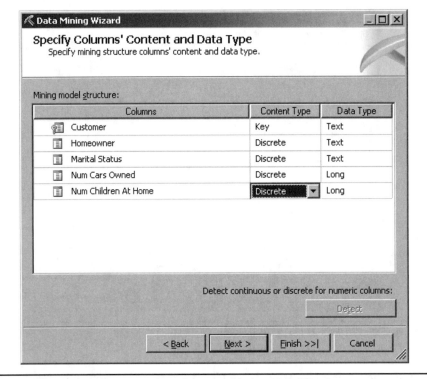

Figure 14-7   *The Specify Columns' Content and Data Type page of the Data Mining Wizard*

25. Select Account Num from the drop-down list in the first row of the Hierarchy column.

26. Select Range (Inclusive) from the drop-down list in the first row of the Operator column.

27. Click in the first row of the Filter Expression column. Two drop-down lists appear. Activate the drop-down list on the left.

28. Select 5000 from the list and click OK.

29. Activate the drop-down list on the right. Scroll to the bottom of the list.

30. Click the Filter Members link. The Filter Members dialog box appears.

31. Select Name in the drop-down list under Property.

32. Select Begins with in the drop-down list under Operator.

33. In the Value area, enter **444**.

34. Click Test. The Filter Members dialog box appears, as shown in Figure 14-8.

35. Click OK to exit the Filter Members dialog box.

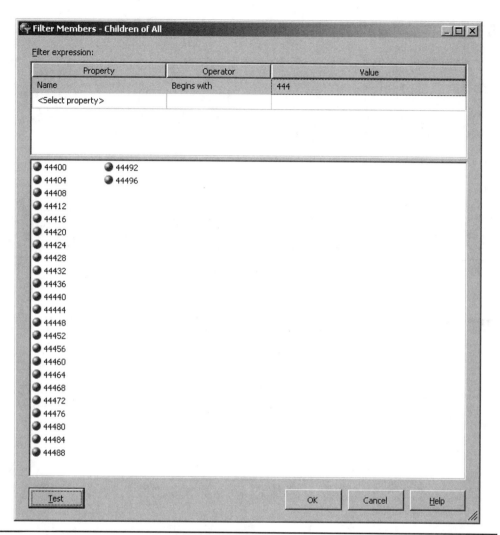

Figure 14-8 *The Filter Members dialog box*

36. Select 44496 in the list and click OK. The Slice Source Cube page appears, as shown in Figure 14-9.

37. Click Next. The Create Testing Set page appears. We need to split our data into a training data set and a testing data set. We will split our data down the middle.

38. Change the Percentage of data from testing to **50%**. The Create Testing Set page appears as shown in Figure 14-10.

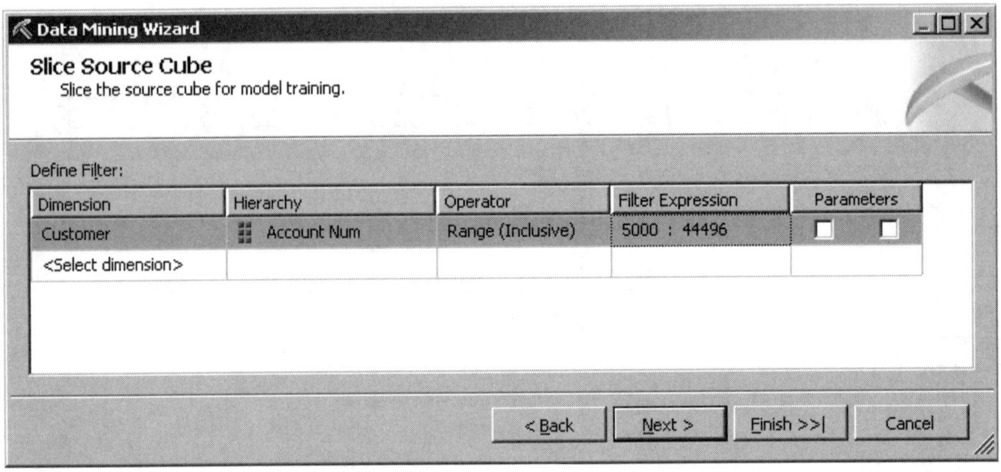

Figure 14-9 *The Slice Source Cube page of the Data Mining Wizard*

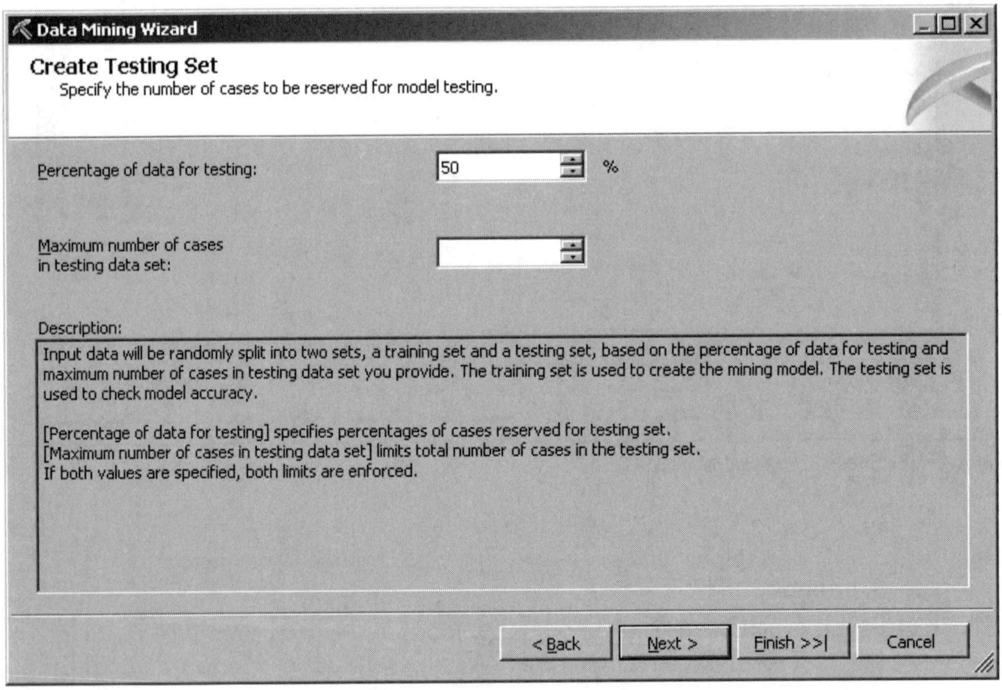

Figure 14-10 *The Create Testing Set page of the Data Mining Wizard*

39. Click Next. The Completing the Wizard page appears.
40. Enter **Classification—Children At Home** for Mining structure name.
41. Enter **Decision Trees—Children At Home** for Mining model name. The wizard page appears as shown in Figure 14-11.
42. Click Finish. The data mining structure containing our new data mining model is created and the Data Mining Design tab appears as shown in Figure 14-12.
43. Select the Mining Models tab on the Data Mining Design tab.

NOTE

If needed, we can change the column usage right on the Mining Models tab, as shown in Figure 14-13. However, we do not need to make any changes here for our model.

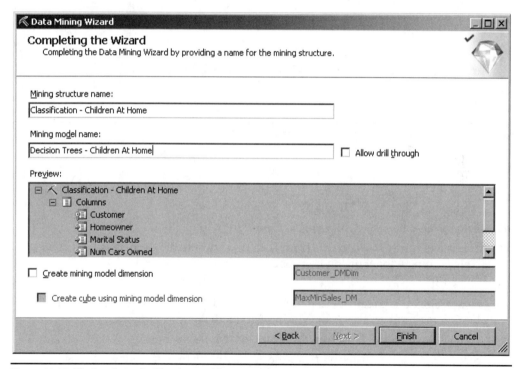

Figure 14-11 *The Completing the Wizard page of the Data Mining Wizard*

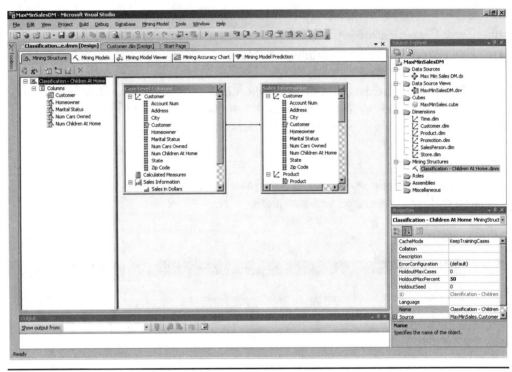

Figure 14-12   *The Mining Structure tab on the Data Mining Design tab*

44. Click the Create a related mining model button on the Mining Models Design tab toolbar. The New Mining Model dialog box appears.

45. Enter **Naive Bayes—Children At Home** for Model Name.

46. Select Microsoft Naive Bayes from the Algorithm name drop-down list. The New Mining Model dialog box appears as shown in Figure 14-14.

47. Click OK.

48. Again, click the Create a Related Mining Model button on the Mining Models Design tab toolbar. The New Mining Model dialog box appears.

49. Enter **Clustering—Children At Home** for Model Name.

50. Select Microsoft Clustering from the Algorithm name drop-down list.

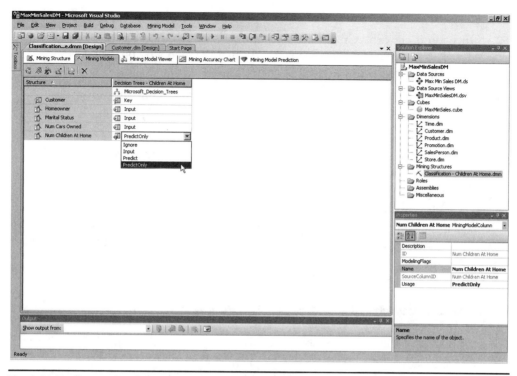

Figure 14-13 *Changing the column usage*

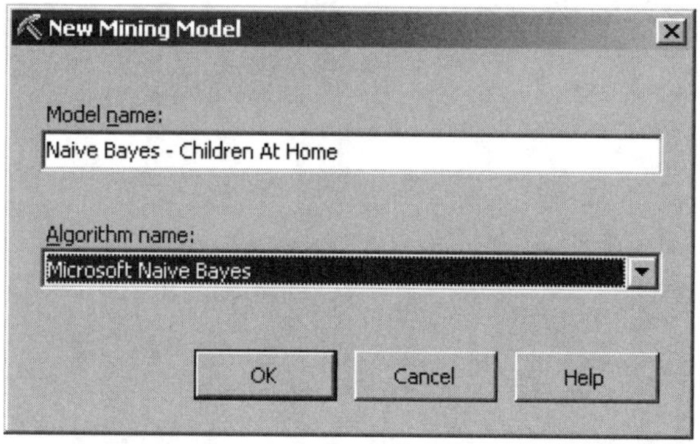

Figure 14-14 *The New Mining Model dialog box*

51. Click OK.

52. Once more, click the Create a related mining model button on the Mining Models Design tab toolbar. The New Mining Model dialog box appears.

53. Enter **Neural Network—Children At Home** for Model Name.

54. Select Microsoft Neural Network from the Algorithm name drop-down list.

55. Click OK. The Mining Models tab appears as shown in Figure 14-15.

56. Click the Save All button on the toolbar.

57. Click the Process the mining structure and all its related models button on the Mining Models tab toolbar. A dialog box informs you the server content appears to be out-of-date.

58. Click Yes to deploy the project.

59. When the deployment is complete, the Process Mining Structure dialog box appears, as shown in Figure 14-16. Click Run. The Process Progress dialog box appears.

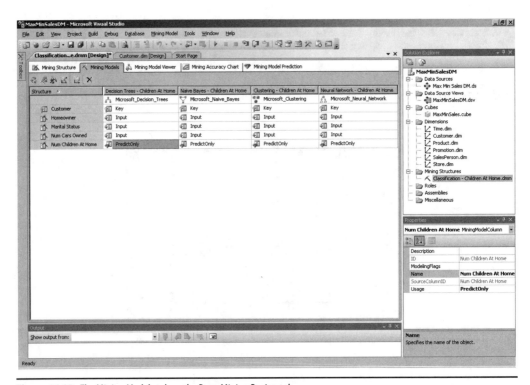

Figure 14-15   *The Mining Models tab on the Data Mining Design tab*

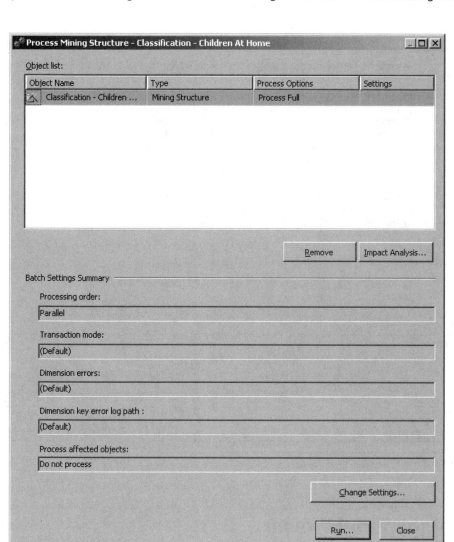

Figure 14-16 *The Process Mining Structure dialog box*

60. When the models have all been trained and the process has been completed successfully, the Process Progress dialog box appears as shown in Figure 14-17. Click Close to exit the Process Progress dialog box.

61. Click Close to exit the Process Mining Structure dialog box.

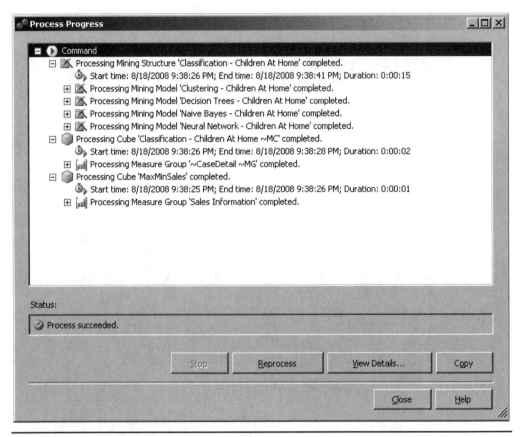

Figure 14-17 *The Process Progress dialog box*

Mining Model Viewer

Now that we have several data mining models created and trained, let's look at how we begin to analyze the information. We do this by using the data mining model viewers, which are found on the Mining Model Viewer tab on the Data Mining Design tab.

Each data mining algorithm has its own set of viewers, enabling us to examine the trained data mining algorithm. These viewers present the mining information graphically for ease of understanding. If desired, we can also use the Microsoft Mining Content Viewer to look at the raw data underlying the graphical presentations.

We will not do a specific Learn By Doing activity in this section. Really, the whole section is a Learn By Doing exercise. Please feel free to follow along on your PC as we explore the data models created in the previous Learn By Doing activity.

Microsoft Decision Trees

Recall, from Chapter 13, the Microsoft Decision Trees algorithm creates a tree structure. It would make sense, then, to view the result graphically as a tree structure. This is exactly what is provided by the Decision Tree tab of the Microsoft Tree Viewer. We can also determine how much each input attribute affects the result using the Dependency Network tab of the Microsoft Tree Viewer.

Microsoft Tree Viewer—Decision Tree Tab

To use the Decision Tree tab of the Microsoft Tree Viewer, select the Mining Model Viewer tab on the Data Mining Design tab. (I know this "tab on tab within tabs" stuff sounds rather confusing. As strange as it sounds, the description here is correct!) Select Decision Trees—Children At Home from the Mining Model drop-down list. The Microsoft Tree Viewer appears with the Decision Tree tab selected, as shown in Figure 14-18. To duplicate this figure on your PC, adjust the following settings *after*

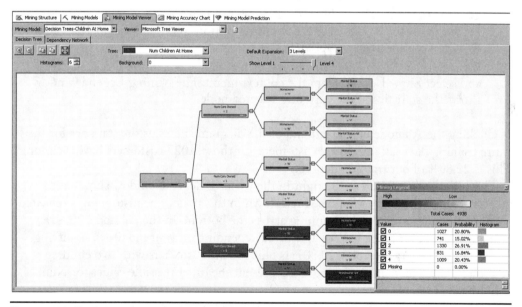

Figure 14-18 *The decision tree view for the Microsoft Decision Tree algorithm*

you reach the Decision Tree tab and have the Decision Trees - Children At Home mining model selected:

1. The Tree drop-down list lets us select the predictable column to view. In this case, there is only one predictable column, Num Children At Home, so it is already selected for us.

2. By default, the background color of the tree nodes reflects the distribution of the cases throughout the tree. In our example, 4938 customers are in our training data. Nodes representing a larger percentage of those 4938 customers are darker than those representing a smaller percentage. The All node represents all 4938 customers, so it is the darkest. We can change the meaning of the node shading using the Background drop-down list. From the Background drop-down list, select 0. The background color now represents the percentage of customers with 0 children in each node. In other words, the color now represents how many customers with no children are represented by each group.

3. The Default Expansion drop-down list and the Show Level slider control work together to determine the number of nodes that are expanded and visible in the viewer. Move the Show Level slider to Level 4 to show all levels of the decision tree.

4. The decision tree is probably too large for your window. You can click the Size to Fit button or the Zoom In and Zoom Out buttons on the Decision Tree tab to size the decision tree appropriately.

5. If the Mining Legend window is not visible, right-click in the Decision Tree tab and select Show Legend from the context menu. The Mining Legend window shows the statistics of the currently selected node.

Clicking the All node on the left end of the diagram shows us the statistics for the entire training data set: 4938 total customers. Of those, 1027 customers have 0 children. This is 20.80% of our training data set.

The Histogram column at the right in the Mining Legend window shows us a graphical representation of the case breakdown in this node. The histogram is repeated inside each node as a rectangle running across the bottom. In the All node, 20.80% of the histogram is orange (or possibly pink, depending on your monitor), signifying no children. The largest group, 20.80% is blue for the customers with two children at home. Other colors in the histogram represent the other possible values for Num Children At Home.

Judging by the background color and the histograms, we can see two leaf nodes contain the most customers with no children at home. These are the Homeowner = *N* node under Marital Status = *N* and the Homeowner not = *N* node under Marital Status = *Y*. In Figure 14-18, one of these two nodes is highlighted. This is the node with the most customers with no children at home. The bottom of the Mining Legend window shows the path through the decision tree to get to this node. This can also be thought of as the rule that defines this decision tree node. From this, we can see that someone who owns no cars, is unmarried, and does not own a home is likely to have no children at home.

Microsoft Tree Viewer—Dependency Network Tab

Switching to the Dependency Network tab brings up a screen similar to Figure 14-19. This screen shows how each of the attributes included in the data mining model affect the other attributes. We can see which attributes predict other attributes. We can also see the strength of these interactions.

Clicking an attribute activates the color coding on the diagram. The selected node is highlighted with aqua green. The attributes predicted by the selected attribute are blue. The attributes that predict the selected attribute are light brown. If an attribute is predicted by the selected attribute but also can predict that attribute, it is shown in purple. The key for these colors is shown below the diagram.

The arrows in Figure 14-19 also show us which attributes predict other attributes. The arrow goes from an attribute that is a predictor to an attribute it predicts. Num Cars Owned, Marital Status, and Houseowner all predict Num Children At Home.

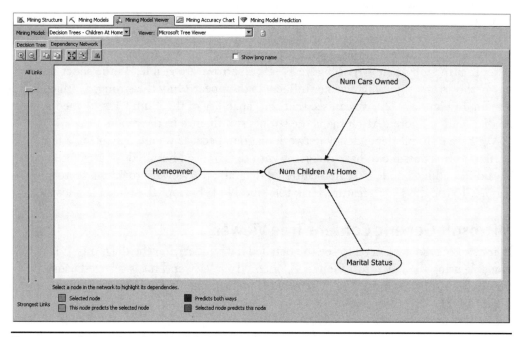

Figure 14-19 *The Dependency Network tab for the Microsoft Decision Tree algorithm*

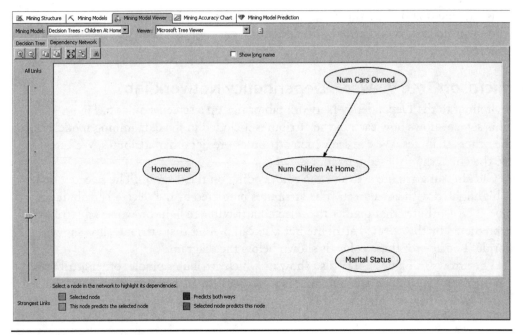

Figure 14-20 *The strongest influence in this data mining model*

The slider to the left of the diagram controls which arrows are displayed. When the slider is at the top, as shown in Figure 14-19, all arrows are visible. As the slider moves down, the arrows signifying weaker influences disappear. Only the stronger influences remain. In Figure 14-20, we can see that the capability of the Num Cars Owned to predict Num Children At Home is the strongest influence in the model.

We have a simple dependency network diagram because we are only using a few attributes. It is possible to have diagrams with tens or even hundreds of attribute nodes. To aid in finding a node in such a cluttered diagram, the viewer provides a search feature. To use the search feature, click the Find Node button (the binoculars icon).

Microsoft Generic Content Tree Viewer

If, for some reason, we need to see the detailed data underlying the diagrams, it is available using the Microsoft Generic Content Tree Viewer. This is selected using the Viewer drop-down list. The Microsoft Generic Content Tree Viewer is shown in Figure 14-21.

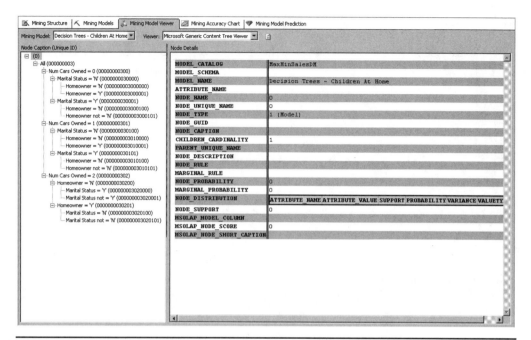

Figure 14-21 *The Microsoft Generic Content Tree Viewer*

Microsoft Naïve Bayes

We look next at the tools available for reviewing the results of the Naïve Bayes algorithm. Recall, from Chapter 13, the Naïve Bayes algorithm deals only with the influence of each individual attribute on the predictable value. Let's see how this is represented graphically.

Microsoft Naïve Bayes Viewer—Dependency Network

Selecting the Naïve Bayes—Children At Home mining model from the Mining Model drop-down list displays the Microsoft Naïve Bayes Viewer—Dependency Network. This looks a lot like the Dependency Network Viewer we just looked at for the Decision Trees algorithm, as shown in Figure 14-22. (Does this look like a Klingon starship to you, too?) In fact, it functions in an identical manner. Using the slider to the left of the diagram, we can see the Num Cars Owned attribute is also the best predictor of Num Children At Home for this model. This is shown in Figure 14-23.

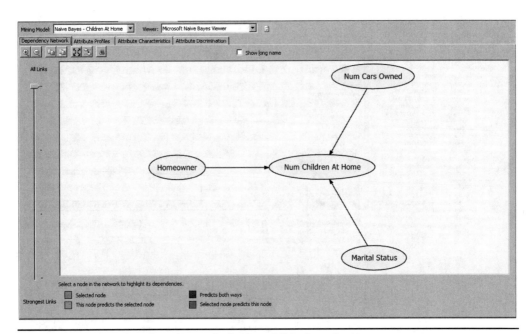

Figure 14-22 *The Dependency Network Viewer for the Microsoft Naïve Bayes algorithm*

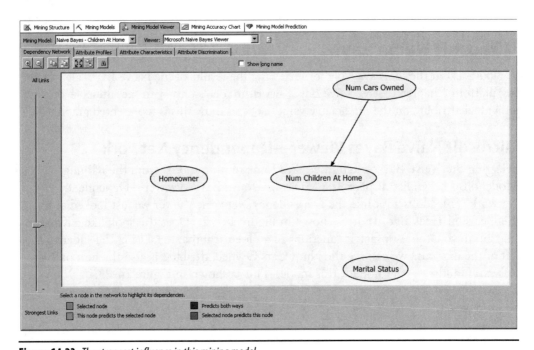

Figure 14-23 *The strongest influence in this mining model*

Attribute Profiles

Next, select the Attribute Profiles tab. We can select the predictable we want to analyze using the Predictable drop-down list. Num Children At Home is our only predictable in this model, so it is already selected. The diagram shows the distribution of each attribute value for the various predictable values. This is shown in Figure 14-24.

Again, we have a Mining Legend window to provide more detailed information. Selecting a cell in the Attribute Profiles grid shows, in the Mining Legend, the numbers that underlie the histogram for that cell. The cell for the Num Cars Owned where Num Children At Home is 0 is selected and pointed to by the mouse cursor in Figure 14-24.

Attribute Characteristics

Select the Attribute Characteristics tab. Num Children At Home is already selected in the Attribute drop-down list and 0 is already selected in the Value drop-down list. We can see the attribute characteristics for the model. In other words, we can see the probability of a particular attribute value being present along with our predictable value. This is shown in Figure 14-25.

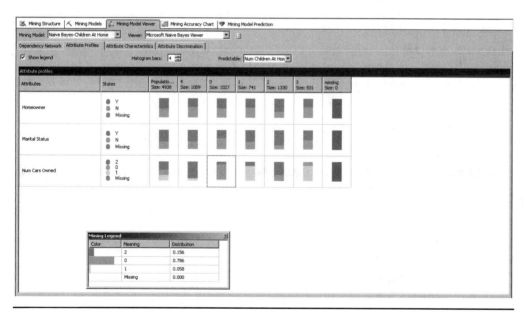

Figure 14-24 *The Attribute Profiles Viewer for the Microsoft Naïve Bayes algorithm*

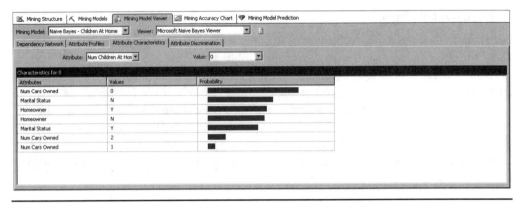

Figure 14-25 *The Attribute Characteristics Viewer for the Microsoft Naïve Bayes algorithm*

In this figure, we can see a customer with no cars has a high probability of having no children at home. We can also see a high probability exists that a customer who is not married does not have any children at home. There is a low probability that a person with one car has no children at home.

Attribute Discrimination

Select the Attribute Discrimination tab. Num Children At Home is already selected in the Attribute drop-down list and 0 is already selected in the Value 1 drop-down list. All other states is selected in the Value 2 drop-down list. This diagram lets us determine what attribute values most differentiate nodes favoring our desired predictable state from those disfavoring our predictable state. This is shown in Figure 14-26.

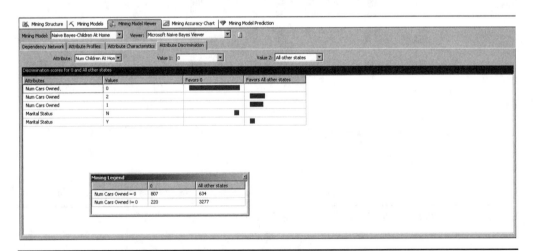

Figure 14-26 *The Attribute Discrimination Viewer for the Microsoft Naïve Bayes algorithm*

From the figure, we can see that not owning a car favors having no children at home. Being married favors having children at home. As with the other diagrams, selecting a cell displays the detail for that cell in the Mining Legend.

Microsoft Clustering

We move from Naïve Bayes to the Microsoft Clustering algorithm. In Chapter 13, we learned the Clustering algorithm creates groupings, or clusters. We examine the clusters to determine which ones have the most occurrences of the predictable value we are looking for. Then we can look at the attribute values that differentiate that cluster from the others.

Cluster Diagram

Selecting the Clustering—Children At Home mining model from the Mining Model drop-down list displays the Microsoft Cluster Viewer - Cluster Diagram. We can see the algorithm came up with eight different clusters. The lines on the diagram show how closely related one cluster is to another. A dark gray line signifies two clusters that are strongly related. A light gray line signifies two clusters that are weakly related.

Select Num Children At Home from the Shading Variable drop-down list. The State drop-down list should have the 0 value selected. The shading of the clusters now represents the number of customers with 0 children at home in each cluster. This is shown in Figure 14-27.

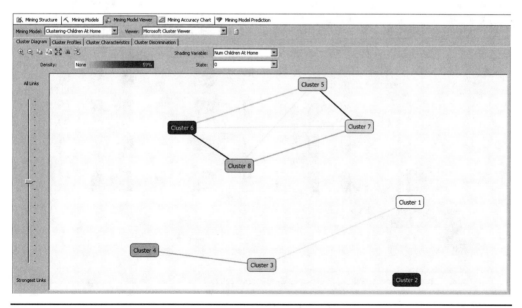

Figure 14-27 *The Cluster Diagram Viewer for the Microsoft Clustering algorithm*

In the diagram, Cluster 7 has the highest concentration of customers with no children at home. To make analysis easier on the other tabs, let's rename this cluster. Right-click Cluster 7 and select Rename Cluster from the context menu. The Rename Cluster dialog box appears. Enter **No Children At Home** and click OK.

Cluster Profiles

Selecting the Cluster Profiles tab displays a grid of cluster profiles, as shown in Figure 14-28. This functions exactly the same as the Naïve Bayes Attribute Profiles tab. We use this tab to examine the characteristics of the clusters that most interest us. In this case, it is easy to pick out the cluster of interest because we named it No Children At Home.

Cluster Characteristics

We next select the Cluster Characteristics tab to display the grid of cluster characteristics. Select No Children At Home from the Cluster drop-down list to view the characteristics of this cluster. The Cluster Characteristics tab functions in the same manner as the Attribute Characteristics tab we encountered with the Microsoft Naïve Bayes algorithm. The Cluster Characteristics tab is shown in Figure 14-29.

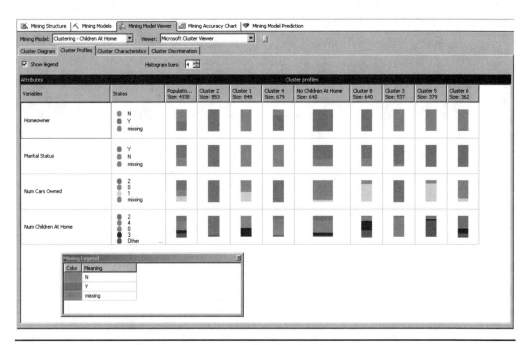

Figure 14-28 *The Cluster Profiles Viewer for the Microsoft Clustering algorithm*

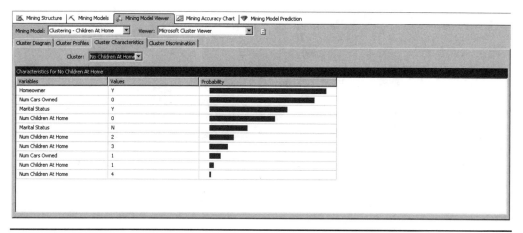

Figure 14-29 *The Cluster Characteristics Viewer for the Microsoft Clustering algorithm*

Cluster Discrimination

Select the Cluster Discrimination tab, and then select No Children At Home from the Cluster 1 drop-down list. This diagram enables us to determine what attribute values most differentiate our selected cluster from all the others. This is shown in Figure 14-30.

Microsoft Neural Network

Selecting the Neural Network—Children At Home mining model from the Mining Model drop-down list displays the Microsoft Neural Network Viewer. The Microsoft Neural Network algorithm uses a Discrimination Viewer similar to those we have seen

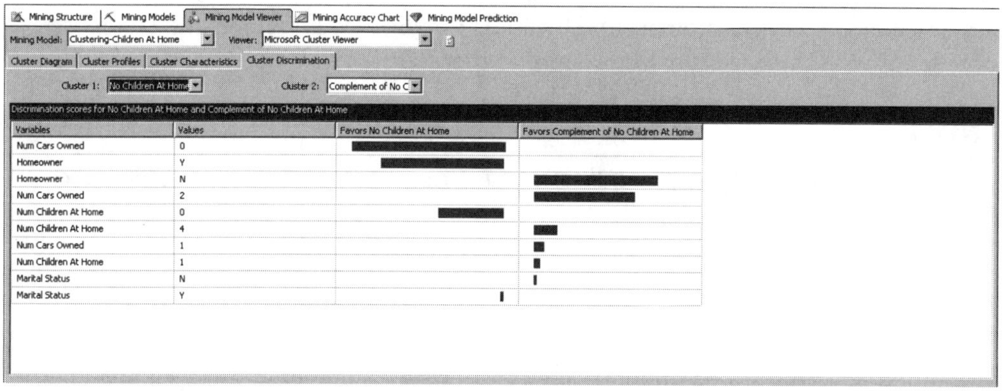

Figure 14-30 *The Cluster Discrimination Viewer for the Microsoft Clustering algorithm*

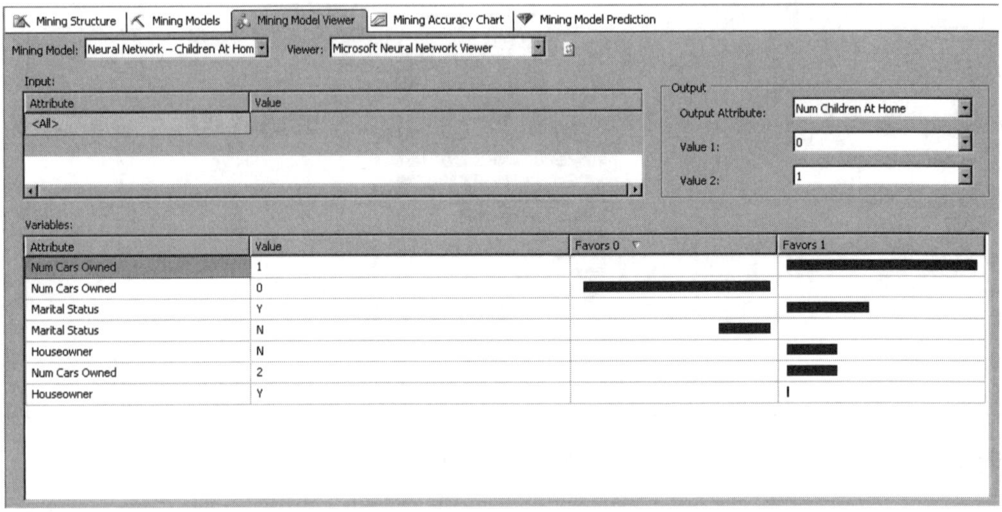

Figure 14-31 *The Discrimination Viewer for the Microsoft Neural Network algorithm*

with other algorithms. This lets us determine the characteristics that best predict our predictable value.

Num Children At Home is already selected in the Output Attribute drop-down list. Select 0 in the Value 1 drop-down list. Select 1 in the Value 2 drop-down list. We can now see what differentiates customers with no children at home from customers with one child at home. The Discrimination Viewer is shown in Figure 14-31.

Microsoft Association Rules

The Microsoft Association Rules algorithm deals with items that have been formed into sets within the data. In the example here, we look at sets of products that were purchased by the same customer. The Business Intelligence Development Studio provides us with three viewers for examining these sets.

NOTE

We did not use the Microsoft Association or the other algorithms that follow in the remainder of this section in our mining structure.

Itemsets

The Itemsets Viewer is shown in Figure 14-32. The *Itemsets Viewer* shows a textual description of each set. The Support column shows the number of cases supporting the set. For clarity of analysis, we set Minimum Support to require at least 300 occurrences for a set to be displayed. The Size column tells us the number of members in the set.

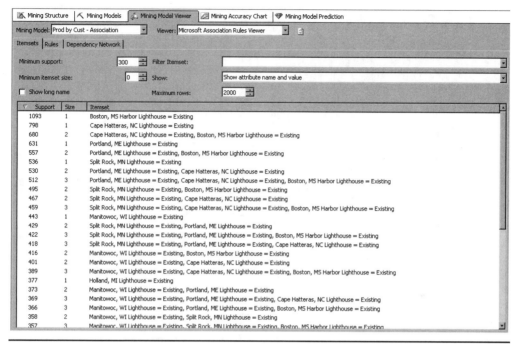

Figure 14-32 *The Itemsets Viewer for the Microsoft Association Rules algorithm*

Rules

The Rules Viewer displays the rules the algorithm created from the sets. This is shown in Figure 14-33. The Probability column shows the probability of a rule being true. In Figure 14-33, we have a number of rules with a 100% (1.000) probability—a sure thing! This means we do not have a single case in our training data set where this rule is not true.

The *Importance column* tells us how useful the rule may be in making predictions. For example, if every set contained a particular attribute state, a rule that predicts this attribute state is not helpful; it is of low importance. The *Rule column,* of course, describes the rule. The rule at the top of Figure 14-33 says a set that contains a British Infantry figure and a Flying Dragon figure also contains a Cape Hatteras, NC Lighthouse.

Dependency Network

The Dependency Network Viewer functions in the same manner as we have seen with other algorithms. There is a node for each predictable state. In our example, there is a node for each member of the Product dimension. Selecting a product node shows

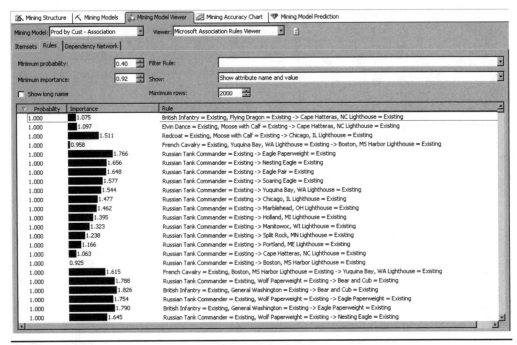

Figure 14-33 *The Rules Viewer for the Microsoft Association Rules algorithm*

which products it predicts will be in the set and which products predict it will be in the set. The Dependency Network Viewer is shown in Figure 14-34.

Microsoft Sequence Clustering

The Microsoft Sequence Clustering algorithm is similar to the Microsoft Clustering algorithm. Consequently, these two algorithms use the same viewers. The only difference is the addition of the State Transitions Viewer. This viewer shows the probability of moving from one state in the sequence to another.

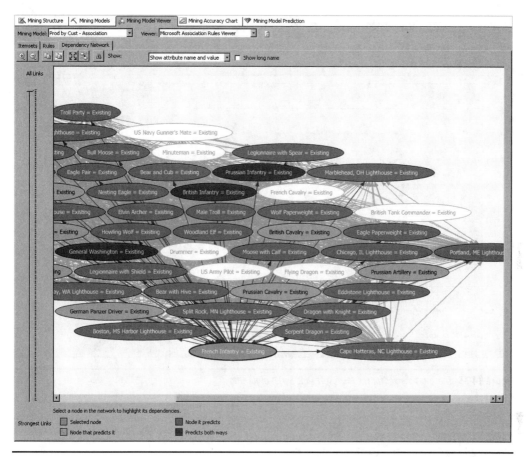

Figure 14-34 *The Dependency Network Viewer for the Microsoft Association Rules algorithm*

Microsoft Time Series

The Microsoft Time Series algorithm uses a Decision Tree Viewer, as we have seen with other algorithms. Recall, from Chapter 13, each node in the decision tree contains a regression formula that is used to forecast future continuous values. The Microsoft Time Series also uses a Chart Viewer, shown in Figure 14-35, to chart these forecast values.

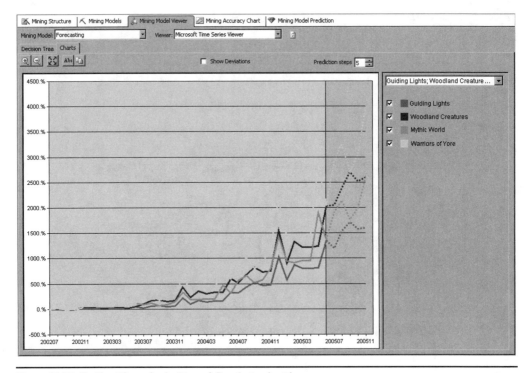

Figure 14-35 *The Chart Viewer for the Microsoft Time Series algorithm*

Reading the Tea Leaves

Now that we have built a data mining model and done some preliminary analysis, it is time to put data mining to work. In Chapter 15, we look at ways to combine data mining with applications. This combination can add immense value and functionality to business solutions.

Spelunking—Exploration Using Data Mining

In This Chapter

- ► **Mining Accuracy Chart**
- ► **Mining Model Prediction**
- ► **Data Mining Extensions**
- ► **Special Delivery**

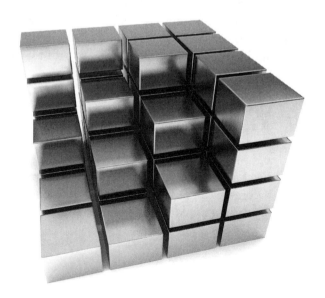

All we discover has been with us since the sun began to roll.

—Herman Melville

In Chapter 13, we learned the five steps for data mining:

- ► Problem Definition
- ► Data Preparation
- ► Training
- ► Validation
- ► Deployment

In Chapter 14, we worked through the first three steps. Now it is time to work on the final two.

In this chapter, we use the Mining Accuracy Chart in the Business Intelligence Development Studio to validate the data mining models we created in Chapter 14. Then, we use the Mining Model Prediction tab to make predictions with our mining models. Finally, we look at the Data Mining Extensions (DMX), which enable us to create data mining queries.

Mining Accuracy Chart

Before we put a data mining model to use in a production environment, we need to ensure the model is making predictions with the desired accuracy. This is done using the Mining Accuracy Chart tab in the Business Intelligence Development Studio. The *Mining Accuracy Chart tab* provides four tools for determining the accuracy of our mining models: the Lift Chart, the Profit Chart, the Classification Matrix, and Cross Validation.

The *Lift Chart* is a line graph showing the performance of our mining models using a test data set. The *Profit Chart* is a line graph showing the projected profitability of a marketing campaign as it relates to the accuracy of our mining models. The *Classification Matrix* provides a chart showing the number of correct predictions and the number of each type of error made by our models. *Cross Validation* provides a technical analysis of the model's performance when making a specified prediction. Before we can use any of these tools, we need to use the Input Selection tab to specify the data to use for testing our models.

Column Mapping

The *Input Selection tab* lets us determine which models to include in our tests. It also lets us select which prediction we are testing. Finally, it allows us to determine the source for the data we use to do the model validation. The Input Selection tab is shown in Figure 15-1.

Select the Mining Models and Prediction

The upper portion of the tab is where we select which of the models in the mining structure to include in our accuracy charts. We do this by placing a check mark next to each mining model. We can select from any of the mining models we included in our mining structure.

Our mining models may include more than one predictable column. If that is the case, we need to select which predictable to use for testing. We can test our model on the prediction of all values for the predictable or on its accuracy at predicting a selected value.

We can choose to test the same prediction for all of the selected models by checking the Synchronize Prediction Columns and Values check box. When this box is checked, whatever predictable column and predict value we select for one model is automatically copied to the other models.

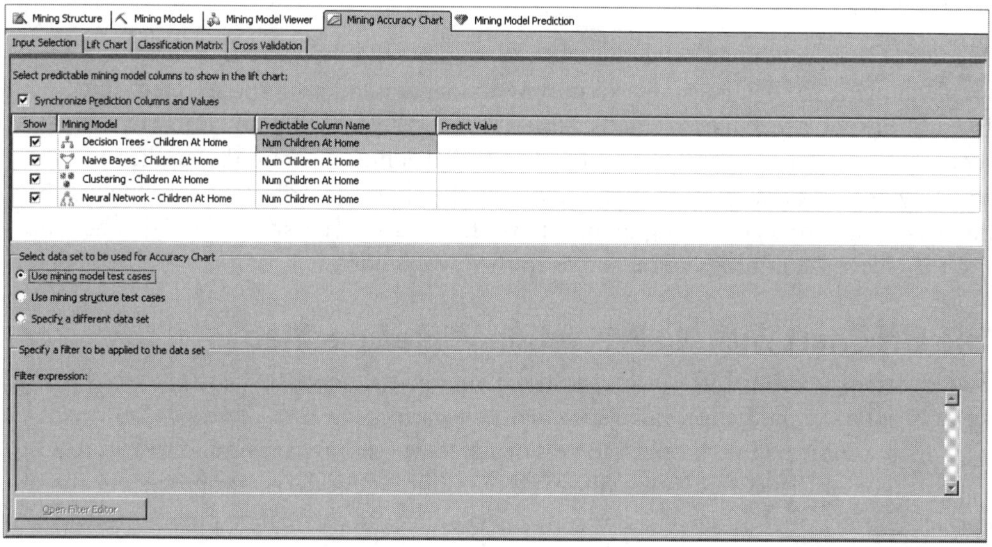

Figure 15-1 *The Input Selection tab*

Select the Test Data

The lower portion of the tab is where we select which data to use when testing our model. We have three options: mining model test cases, mining structure test cases, or another data source. Mining model test cases are created as part of defining the training data for a mining model. Mining structure test cases are created as part of defining the mining model structure.

Viewing the Mining Accuracy Charts

In order to view the mining accuracy charts described in the next section of this chapter, we actually do not need to make any changes on the Input Selection tab. All of the mining models in the mining structure are selected by default, which is exactly what we want. Our models have only one predictable column, so there is nothing to change there. We will begin by looking at all predictable values, so that can also remain at its default setting.

Recall, when we created the mining structure in Chapter 14, we specified retail customers (customers with account numbers of 5000 and above) from the customer dimension were to be used to train the mining models. Actually, we said 50% of those customers should be used to train the models. The other 50% was to be set aside for testing the models. This mining model test case is selected for us by default.

Lift Chart

The Lift Chart is used to judge the effectiveness of a mining model. It creates a line graph showing the accuracy of each mining model at predicting the selected value. In addition, the Lift Chart contains a line showing the perfect prediction of an ideal model. Finally, when a prediction value is specified, a line showing the prediction accuracy of a random-guess model is added to the chart. Any distance that the graph line has for a particular mining model above the random-guess model is *lift*. The more lift, the closer the mining model comes to the ideal model.

The Lift Chart with No Prediction Value Specified

Two different types of Lift Charts are available to use. The first type is produced when we do not have a prediction value specified. If we select the Lift Chart tab, and then wait a few moments for the chart to be calculated, we see a chart similar to Figure 15-2.

This type of Lift Chart shows how well each mining model did at predicting the correct number of children at home for each customer in the testing data set. The X axis represents the percentage of the testing data set that was processed. The Y axis represents the percentage of the testing data set that was predicted correctly. The blue

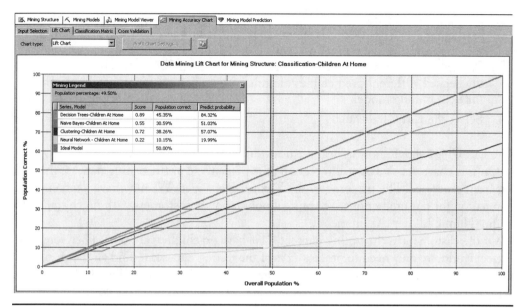

Figure 15-2   *The Lift Chart with no prediction value specified*

line shows the ideal prediction model. If 50% of the testing data set has been processed, then 50% of the testing data set has been predicted correctly. This type of Lift Chart does not include a line for a random-guess model.

The *Mining Legend* gives the statistics for each mining model at a certain overall population percentage. This percentage is shown at the top of the Mining Legend window and is represented on the graph by the dark gray line. This line can be moved to different positions by clicking the desired location on the graph. In Figure 15-2, the Mining Legend contains information for an overall population percentage of 49.50%. We can see when 49.50% of the population is processed, the Decision Trees mining model will have predicted 45.35% of the values correctly. The Neural Network mining model will have predicted only 10.15% correctly.

The Lift Chart with a Prediction Value Specified

To view the second type of Lift Chart, we need to specify the prediction value we are looking for. To view this type of Lift Chart, do the following:

1.   Select the Input Selection tab.
2.   Click the first row in the Predict Value column to activate the drop-down list.

3. Select 0 from the drop-down list. This means we are testing the accuracy of predicting a value of 0 for the Num Children At Home column. Selecting 0 in this first row places a 0 in all the rows. This happens because the Synchronize Prediction Columns and Values check box is checked. When this box is unchecked, different predictable columns and prediction values may be selected for each mining model.

4. Select the Lift Chart tab.

The Lift Chart should now appear as shown in Figure 15-3.

On this chart, the X axis still represents the percentage of the testing data set that has been processed. The meaning of the Y axis has changed. We now have a target population for our predictions. That target population is customers with no children at home (Num Children At Home = 0).

Of the customers in the testing data set, 21% have no children at home. Therefore, in a perfect world, we only need to process 21% of the testing data set to find all the customers with no children at home. This is why the line for the ideal model reaches 100% on the Y axis at 21% on the X axis. Using the random-guess model, when 50% of the testing data set has been processed, 50% of the target population will have been found.

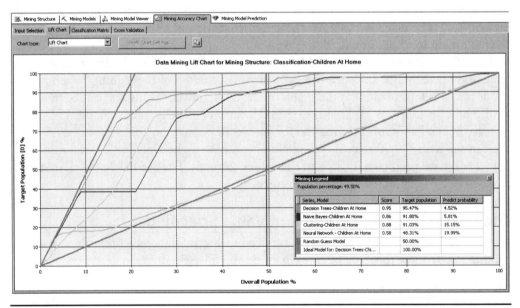

Figure 15-3 *The Lift Chart with a predict value of 0*

On this Lift Chart, it is hard to see where some of the lines are because they overlap. This is where the Mining Legend window comes in handy. If we click at about 6% on the *X* axis, we can see where these overlapping lines are located. This is shown in Figure 15-4. Using the figures in the Mining Legend, we can see the Decision Trees mining model is found at 6.90% and the Naïve Bayes mining model is found at 26.42% of the target population.

If we jump up to near 20%, as shown in Figure 15-5, we can see things have changed. The Decision Trees mining model has now found 78.30% of the target population. The Naïve Bayes mining model is at 38.42%, hardly any progress over where it was at 6%.

Moving to about 60%, we can see that most of the other mining models have finally caught up to the Decision Trees mining model. This is shown in Figure 15-6. All the models except the Neural Network have found at least 95% of the target population. Some differentiation occurs between the mining models as we move higher than 35%, but the spread is small and we have already identified the vast majority of the target population at this point.

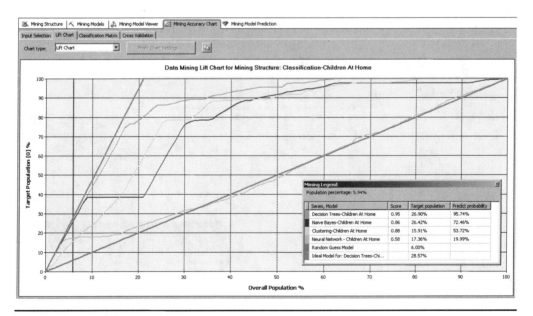

Figure 15-4   *The Lift Chart at 6%*

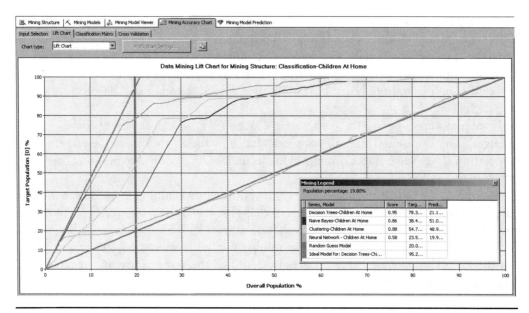

Figure 15-5   *The Lift Chart at 20%*

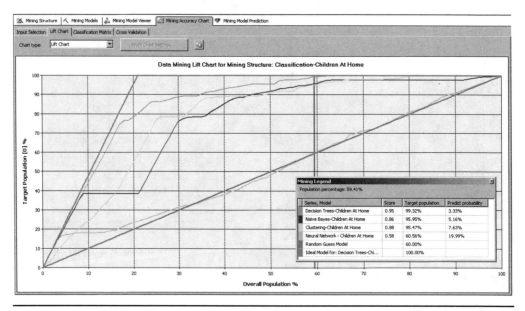

Figure 15-6   *The Lift Chart at 60%*

Profit Chart

The Profit Chart lets us analyze financial aspects of a campaign that depend on the predictive capabilities of our mining models. The information in the Profit Chart can help us determine the size of campaign we should undertake. It can also provide a prediction of the profit we should expect from a campaign (hence, the name).

Creating a Profit Chart

To create a Profit Chart, select Profit Chart from the Chart type drop-down list. This displays the Profit Chart Settings dialog box, shown in Figure 15-7. We need to enter the population and financial aspects of the campaign we are modeling. In our case, let's suppose Maximum Miniatures has purchased a mailing list with 100,000 names. Enter **50000** for Population in the dialog box. This mailing will have $5,000 of fixed costs— costs that do not change no matter how many items we mail—and $3 per mailing sent. Enter **5000** for Fixed Cost and **3** for Individual Cost. Finally, for each person who receives the mailing and makes a purchase, we are going to receive, on average, $15. Enter **15** for Revenue per individual. Click OK to produce the Profit Chart.

The resulting Profit Chart is shown in Figure 15-8. We can see from this graph, the maximum profit will come if Maximum Miniatures sends the mailing to 24% of the names in the mailing list it purchased. At least, that is the case if the Decision Trees mining model is used to select that 24%. We use this mining model to predict which customers have no children at home. (Remember, previous research has shown Maximum Miniatures that these are the most likely buyers of the Mythic World figurines.) Given this mining model's capability to predict, we should make about

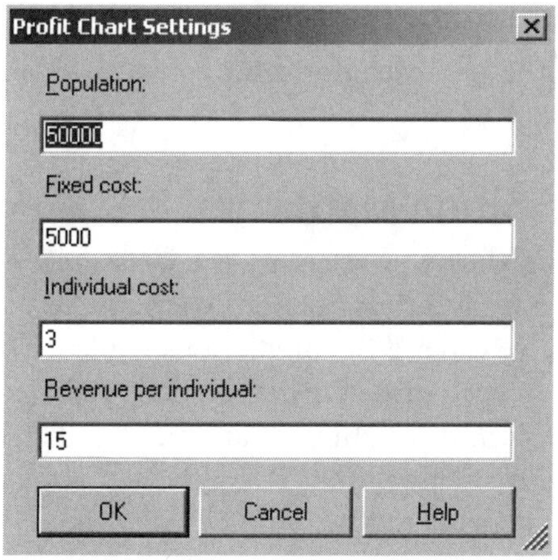

Figure 15-7   *The Profit Chart Settings dialog box*

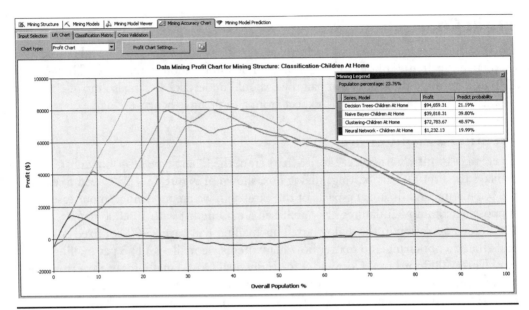

Figure 15-8   *The Profit Chart*

$393,376 in profit after the cost of the mailing. Mailing to more people does not significantly improve our chances of getting sales, but it does increase our costs. Because of this, our expected profit goes down if we mail to more people.

Classification Matrix

We know our mining models are not going to do a perfect job of predicting. They are going to make mistakes. The Classification Matrix lets us see exactly what mistakes our models have made.

Viewing the Classification Matrix

We view the Classification Matrix by selecting the Classification Matrix tab on the Mining Accuracy Chart tab. The Classification Matrix is shown in Figure 15-9. Using the Classification Matrix, we can see the predictions made by each mining model.

The left-hand column in each grid shows the value predicted by the mining model. In Figure 15-9, this is the number of children at home predicted for each customer in the training data set. The other columns show the actual value for the number of children at home for each customer.

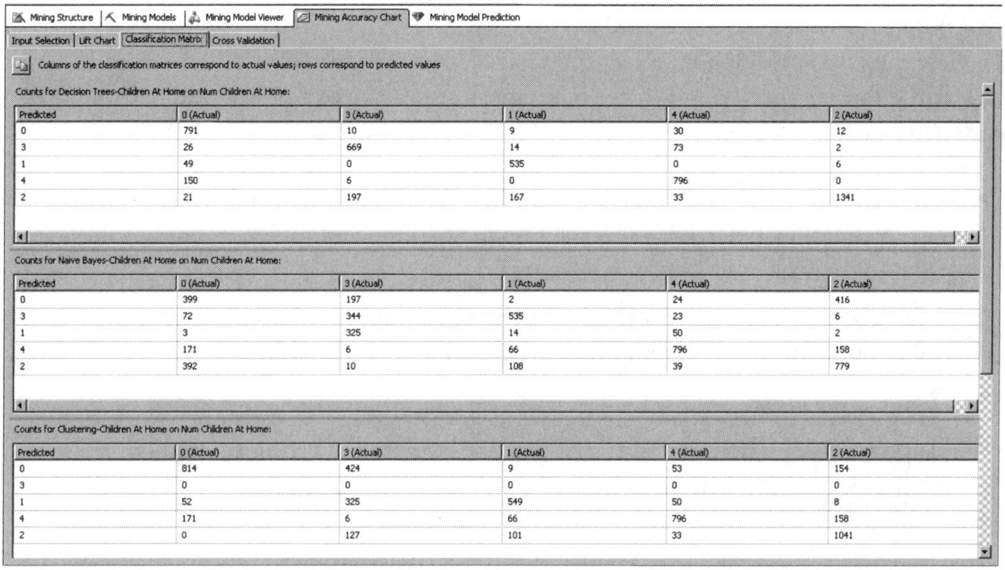

Figure 15-9   *The Classification Matrix*

In Figure 15-9, the top grid shows the result for the Decision Trees mining model. Looking at the top row in the grid, we can see that in 791 cases, the Decision Trees mining model predicted zero children at home when there were actually zero children at home. These were correct predictions. In ten cases, the Decision Trees mining model predicted zero children at home when there were actually three children at home. These predictions were in error.

The diagonal of the grid shows the correct predictions: predicted zero with actual zero, predicted three with actual three, predicted one with actual one, and so on. We want to have the largest numbers along the diagonal. This is the case for the Decision Trees mining model. We already know this model is accurate. The Naïve Bayes mining model, shown second from the top in Figure 15-9, does not always have the largest numbers along the diagonal. This mining model had a tendency to predict two children at home when there were actually zero children at home. This mistake occurred 392 times during the processing of our testing data set.

Cross Validation

The final tab on the Mining Accuracy Chart tab provides access to the Cross Validation analysis tool. This tool provides one more method for comparing the accuracy of several mining models within a mining structure. Cross Validation provides a grid of technical figures for each mining method tested.

Viewing the Cross Validation

To view the Cross Validation, select the Cross Validation tab. This tab provides an area at the top for specifying the various parameters required for cross validation. The parameters are as follows:

▶ **Fold Count** The fold count divides the validation data into distinct sets. For each validation, one fold is used to test the model, while the remaining folds are used to first train the model before testing.

▶ **Max Cases** The max cases signifies the maximum number of cases to use for validation. The cases are then divided evenly among the folds.

▶ **Target Attribute** The attribute we are trying to predict.

▶ **Target State** The value of the target attribute we are trying to predict.

▶ **Target Threshold** The required probability that a prediction is correct. This is a number between 0.0 and 1.0. A number closer to 1.0 represents a higher prediction probability.

The Cross Validation tab is shown in Figure 15-10. Analysis of the cross validation results is beyond the scope of this book. For further information, consult SQL Books Online.

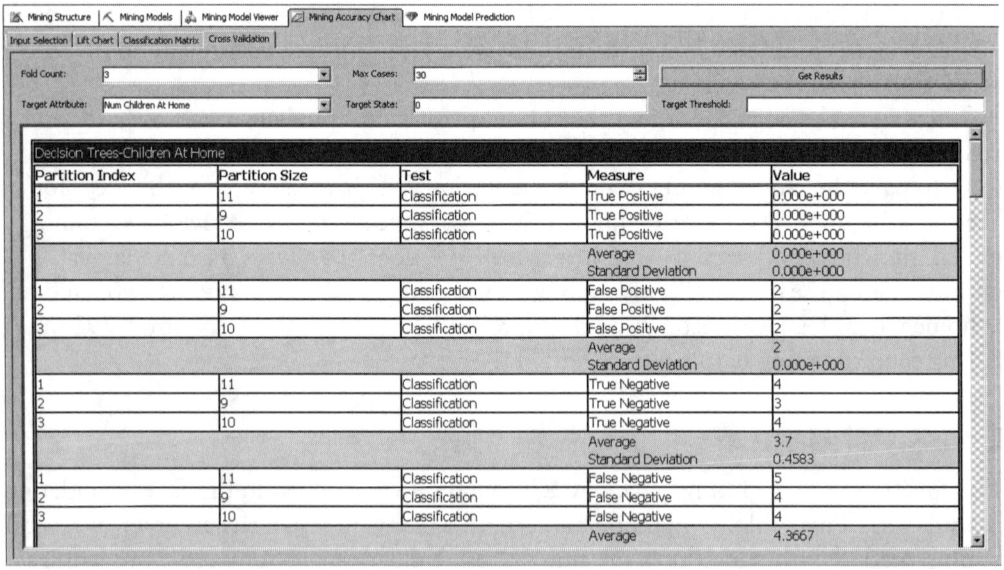

Figure 15-10 *The Cross Validation tab*

Mining Model Prediction

All this training and testing has finally gotten us to a place where we have a mining model ready to make real-world predictions. We have seen how each of the mining models does at making predictions; now, we can pick one and put it to work. The Mining Model Prediction tab enables us to do just that.

Using the Mining Model Prediction tab, we can create queries that use a mining model to make predictions. Two types of prediction queries are supported: a singleton query and a prediction join. We look at the singleton query first.

A Singleton Query

A *singleton query* lets us feed a single set of input values to the mining model. We receive a single value for the predictable based on these values. This enables us to manually enter a scenario to see what the mining model will predict.

Creating a Singleton Query

For both the singleton query and the prediction join, we must first select the mining model to use. When the model is selected, the Singleton Query Input dialog box contains an input field for each input column in the mining model. We can then enter values for each of these input columns.

We then select the columns we would like in the result set. The predictable column should be included in the result set; otherwise, the query isn't doing much for us. We can also include our own custom expressions, as desired.

When the query is designed, we switch to the result view to see the result set. We can also switch to the SQL view to see the DMX query being created for us behind the scenes—more on that in the section "Data Mining Extensions." Queries can be saved to be re-run at a later time.

Learn By Doing—Creating a Singleton Query

Feature Highlighted

▶   Creating a singleton query using the Mining Model Prediction tab

Business Need   Our business need is simple. We will try out the mining model we have worked so hard to create.

Steps
1.   Open the Business Intelligence Development Studio.
2.   Open the MaxMinSalesDM project.

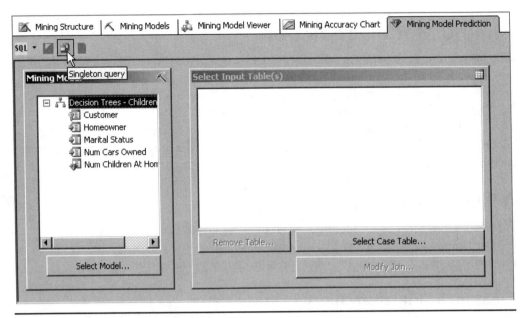

Figure 15-11 *The Singleton Query toolbar button*

3. If the Data Mining Design tab for the Classification - Children At Home data mining structure is not displayed, double-click the entry for this data mining structure in the Solution Explorer window.

4. Select the Mining Model Prediction tab on the Data Mining Design tab.

5. Click the Singleton Query button on the Mining Model Prediction tab toolbar. This is shown in Figure 15-11.

6. Click Select Model in the Mining Model window. The Select Mining Model dialog box appears, as shown in Figure 15-12.

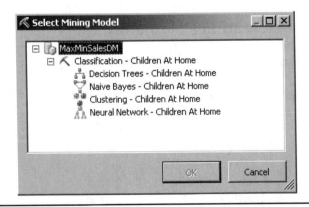

Figure 15-12 *The Select Mining Model dialog box*

7. Select the Decision Trees - Children At Home mining model and click OK.

8. In the Singleton Query Input window, select Y from the Homeowner drop-down list in the Value column. Select N from the Marital Status drop-down list. Select 2 from the Num Cars Owned drop-down list.

9. Now select the columns in the result set. In the first row under the Source column, select Decision Trees - Children At Home mining model from the drop-down list. This is shown in Figure 15-13. Num Children At Home is selected by default in the Field column because it is the only predictable in the mining model.

10. In the second row under the Source column, select Custom Expression from the drop-down list.

11. In the second row under the Field column, enter the following:

    ```
    'Homeowner = Y; Marital Status = N; Num Cars Owned = 2'
    ```

12. In the second row under the Alias column, enter **InputCriteria**. The Mining Model Prediction tab appears as shown in Figure 15-14.

13. Select Result from the View drop-down list on the Mining Model Prediction tab toolbar, as shown in Figure 15-15.

14. The result view is displayed, as shown in Figure 15-16. The model predicts that someone who is a homeowner, is not married, and owns two cars will most likely have four children at home.

15. Select Design from the View drop-down list on the Mining Model Prediction tab toolbar to return to the design view.

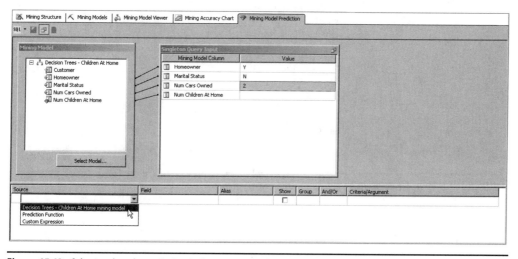

Figure 15-13 *Selecting the columns in the singleton query result set*

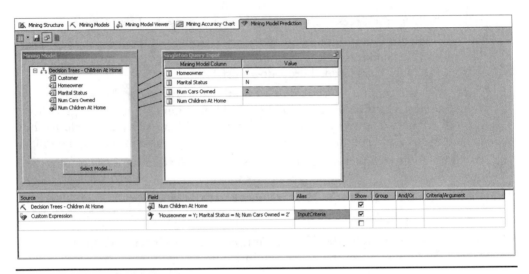

Figure 15-14   *The completed singleton query*

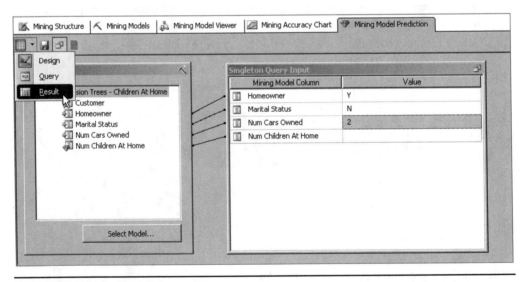

Figure 15-15   *Selecting the result view*

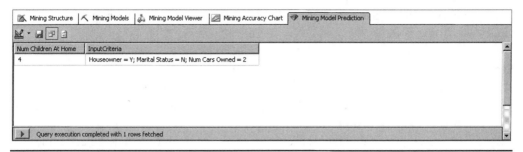

Figure 15-16 *The singleton query result set in the result view*

A Prediction Join Query

The singleton query lets us use a single set of inputs to generate a single row result set. The prediction join query enables us to use a tableful of inputs to generate a multiple row result set. We feed multiple records to the mining model and it creates a prediction for each of these records.

Creating a Prediction Join Query

The *prediction join query* functions similarly to the singleton query: The difference is that the Singleton Query Input window is replaced by the Select Input Table(s) window. This window lets us select the table or joined set of tables that will serve as the record source for the prediction join.

Learn By Doing—Creating a Prediction Join Query

Feature Highlighted

▶ Creating a prediction join query using the Mining Model Prediction tab

Business Need   In a previous Learn By Doing exercise, we discussed a scenario where the Maximum Miniatures marketing department purchased a mailing list that they wanted classified into those households likely to have no children at home and those that have one or more children at home. We now have a trained and tested mining model ready to perform that classification.

To keep things simple, we can use the same customer table and a little imagination to pretend this is the newly purchased list. Remember, the whole reason we had to do this classification was because the newly purchased list did not include the number of children at home. Therefore, if we are having our existing customer table play the role of the newly purchased list, we must ignore the fact that it already has a number of children at home field.

Steps

1. Click the Singleton Query button on the Mining Model Prediction tab toolbar to toggle back to the Prediction Join Query mode. Click Yes to continue when warned about losing your query.
2. Click Select Case Table in the Select Input Table(s) window. The Select Table dialog box appears.
3. Select the Customer (dbo) table and click OK. The fields are automatically mapped, based on field names.
4. We are not supposed to have a Num Children At Home field in this table, so we need to delete this mapping and predict this value instead. Click the mapping line going from Num Children At Home to NumChildrenAtHome so it is highlighted.
5. Right-click the mapping line and select Delete from the context menu.
6. In the first row under the Source column, select Decision Trees - Children At Home mining model from the drop-down list. Again, Num Children At Home is selected by default in the Field column because it is the only predictable in the mining model.
7. In the second row under the Source column, select Customer Table from the drop-down list.
8. In the second row under the Field column, select CustomerName from the drop-down list.
9. In the third row under the Source column, select Customer Table from the drop-down list.
10. In the third row under the Field column, select Address from the drop-down list.
11. Continue this process to include City, State, and ZipCode in the result set. The Mining Model Prediction tab appears as shown in Figure 15-17.
12. Select Result from the View drop-down list on the Mining Model Prediction tab toolbar. The result view is displayed, as shown in Figure 15-18.
13. One issue remains. The marketing department only wants to mail to households that are predicted to have no children at home. All of the others should be eliminated from the list. Select Design from the View drop-down list on the Mining Model Prediction tab toolbar to return to the design view.
14. In the first row under the Criteria/Argument column, enter = **0**.

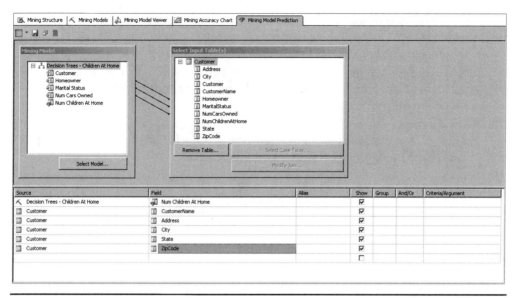

Figure 15-17 *The completed prediction join query*

Num Children At...	CustomerName	Address	City	State	ZipCode
4	Stanley R Johnson	135 Waymore Blvd.	Edgeview	ND	56293
4	Henry D Cramer	9483 49th St.	Appleford	ME	03904
4	Owen N Von Brocken	2843 Drummin Lane	Foggyville	AK	99302
4	Wilhelm A Hoover	135 Poplar St.	Parkside	ND	56293
4	Vern Z Von Stubben	2839 5th Ave.	Yankton	MD	21201
4	Terry K Anthony	2932 50th St.	Diffley	KS	58239
4	Marian W Smith	27391 Overton Dr.	Lipton	TX	75201
4	Jennifer N Ali	3489 Waverly St.	Templeton	VA	23607
4	Ramona C Pearl	2384 Park Ct.	Ivers	OR	97205
4	Walter R Hederson	2932 Waverly St.	Quincy	KY	42718
4	Winifred S Pearl	8293 Polar Ave	Karlstown	NM	88044
4	Arun J Anthony	135 Wicker Way	Lipton	ND	56293
4	Jennifer W Mueller	4839 73rd Ave.	Foggyville	SD	57049
4	Ralph M Pearl	283 Highview Blvd.	Lipton	PA	19107
4	Brad R Taft	2838 Becker Way	Venice	CT	06032
4	Xia F Goldbloom	3838 Mortimer Ct.	Appleford	NJ	09483
4	Melissa V Wellington	2839 Seasame Ln.	Hillburg	CT	06032
4	Henry N Sipulski	3489 45th St.	Diffley	AK	99302
4	Walter D Winstrom	2833 39th Ave.	Parkside	IL	60610
4	Douglas E Alvarez	2843 Waverly St.	Big Fork	MS	38804
4	Cassie N Petrov	2939 73rd Ave.	Parkside	RI	02892
4	Zeb Y Hoover	7472 Anchor St.	Lowry	NC	27412
4	Nels E Roosevelt	135 23rd St.	Orville	MN	55802
4	Nels L Allens	2839 Hwy 45	Crawley	WA	98011
4	Ralph J Popovich	828 Seasame Ln.	Yankton	MI	48226
4	Ramona V Sipulski	8232 Baker Ave.	Jonesbourgh	OK	59304
4	Edward K Roberts	2843 Birch St.	Watertown	CA	94109
4	Xia W Popovich	2843 5th Ave.	Stapleton	AK	99302

Query execution completed with 10000 rows fetched

Figure 15-18 *The prediction join query result set in the result view*

15. We do not need to see the predictable value in our result set, especially now that it will be 0 for every row. Uncheck the check box in the first row of the Show column. The Mining Model Prediction tab appears as shown in Figure 15-19.

16. Select Result from the View drop-down list on the Mining Model Prediction tab toolbar. Now only those households predicted to have no children at home are included in our result set, as shown in Figure 15-20.

17. Now we need to place this result set somewhere where it can be used for the mailing. Click the Save button on the Mining Model Prediction tab toolbar. The Save Data Mining Query Result dialog box appears.

18. We save the query result set to a table in the Max Min Sales DM data source. Enter **MythicWorldMailing** for Table Name. We can choose to add the table to a data source view, if desired, but we do not need to do that here. The Save Data Mining Query Result dialog box appears as shown in Figure 15-21.

NOTE

Saving a table such as this one to a data mart database is probably not a great idea, because it is being created for a one-time mailing, not for ongoing analysis. We do this here for demonstration purposes only!

19. Click Save. A table called MythicWorldMailing is created in the MaxMinSalesDM database and all the rows of the result set are inserted into that table.

20. Select Query from the View drop-down list on the Mining Model Prediction tab toolbar. The query appears as shown in Figure 15-22. This is the DMX query you created using the graphical tools. We learn more about DMX in the following section.

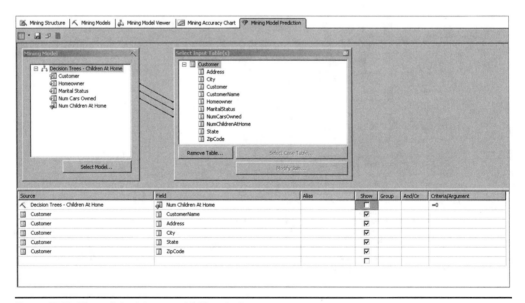

Figure 15-19   *The prediction join query with filter criteria*

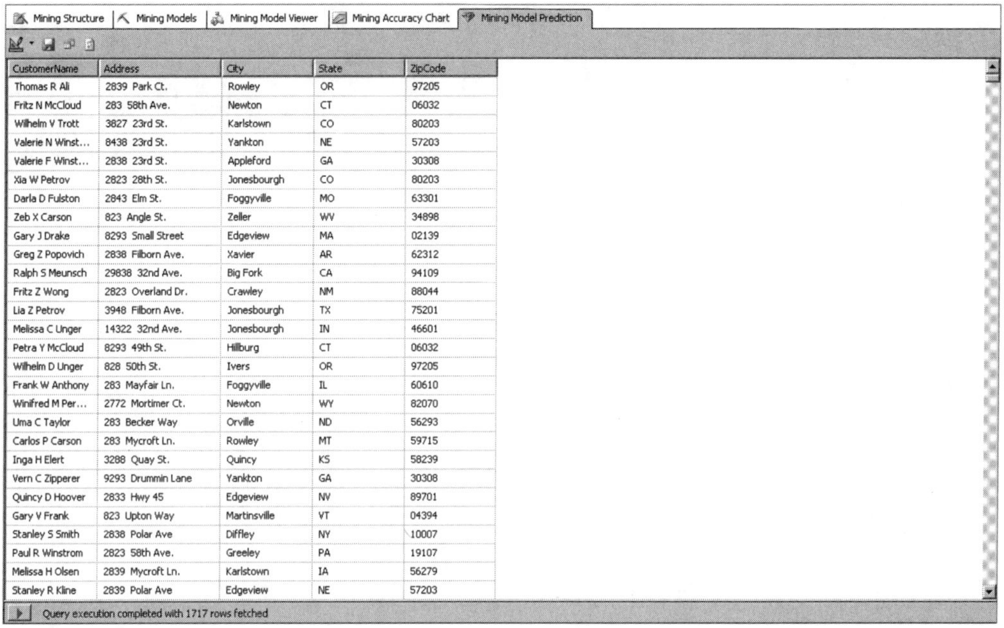

Figure 15-20 *The prediction join query result set with filter criteria*

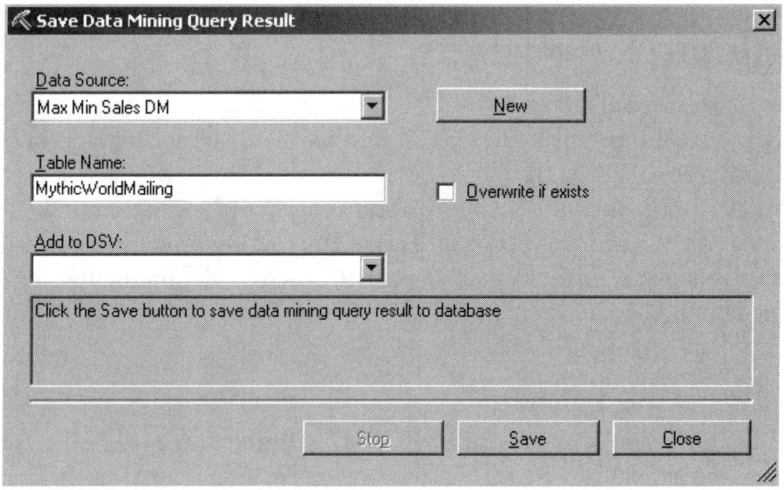

Figure 15-21 *The Save Data Mining Query Result dialog box*

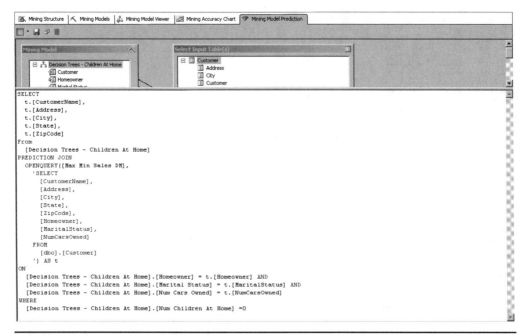

```
SELECT
    t.[CustomerName],
    t.[Address],
    t.[City],
    t.[State],
    t.[ZipCode]
From
    [Decision Trees - Children At Home]
PREDICTION JOIN
    OPENQUERY([Max Min Sales DM],
        'SELECT
            [CustomerName],
            [Address],
            [City],
            [State],
            [ZipCode],
            [Homeowner],
            [MaritalStatus],
            [NumCarsOwned]
        FROM
            [dbo].[Customer]
        ') AS t
ON
    [Decision Trees - Children At Home].[Homeowner] = t.[Homeowner] AND
    [Decision Trees - Children At Home].[Marital Status] = t.[MaritalStatus] AND
    [Decision Trees - Children At Home].[Num Cars Owned] = t.[NumCarsOwned]
WHERE
    [Decision Trees - Children At Home].[Num Children At Home] =0
```

Figure 15-22   *A DMX prediction join query*

Data Mining Extensions

In Chapter 12, we learned about the MDX query language and its use in querying
OLAP cubes. Data mining structures also have their own query language, known as
Data Mining Extensions (DMX).

In this section, we look at the most prominent aspect of DMX, the prediction query.
The *prediction query* provides a means to have a data mining model create predictions
based on rows in another table. In fact, you already used DMX prediction queries when
you used the Mining Model Prediction tab.

Prediction Query Syntax

The prediction query looks much like a SELECT statement in T-SQL. In fact, it has
many of the same clauses as a SELECT statement. We look at each of those clauses
and how they are used.

SELECT Clause

The SELECT clause in a DMX query serves the same function as the SELECT clause in a T-SQL statement. The *SELECT clause* specifies what fields or calculations are going to be included as columns in the result set. This is done by placing a field list following the word "SELECT." For example:

```
SELECT Fname, Lname, Address1, City, State_Province, Postal_Code
```

The SELECT statement has two special keywords that may precede the field list: FLATTENED and TOP *n*. The *FLATTENED keyword* causes the prediction query to return a flattened result set of rows and columns. When the FLATTENED keyword is not used, the SELECT statement may return a hierarchical result set.

The *TOP* n *keyword* works the same here as it does in the T-SQL SELECT statement: It limits the number of rows in the result set to the number specified for *n*. We can order the result set, perhaps by a probability in descending order, and then use the TOP *n* keywords to include only the rows with the highest probability.

FROM Clause

The *FROM clause* specifies the mining model being used in the query. For example:

```
FROM [Decision Trees-Children At Home]
```

PREDICTION JOIN Clause

The *PREDICTION JOIN clause* lets us feed information into the inputs of the mining model. The content or the absence of this clause determines the type of prediction query being run. See the section "Types of Prediction Queries" for details on the syntax of the PREDICTION JOIN clause.

WHERE Clause

The *WHERE clause* enables us to filter the result of the SELECT statement. The filter conditions in the WHERE clause are applied after the predictions are made by the mining model. Therefore, we can use the prediction result as part of the filter. For example, if the Decision Trees-Children At Home mining model is predicting Num Children At Home, we can create a filter to give us only those records where Num Children At Home was predicted to be 0:

```
WHERE [Decision Trees-Children At Home].[Num Children At Home] = 0
```

ORDER BY Clause

The *ORDER BY clause* lets us sort the result set: We can sort in either ascending or descending order. Adding DESC to the clause provides a descending sort. Adding ASC to the clause provides an ascending sort. ASC is the default sort order when neither ASC nor DESC is specified.

The ORDER BY clause in T-SQL includes a comma-separated list of fields to provide the sort columns. The ORDER BY clause in DMX is a bit different. It allows only a single expression. If we want to sort by more than one column, we need to create an expression concatenating these two columns, as follows:

```
ORDER BY [Lname] + [Fname] ASC
```

Types of Prediction Queries

Several types of prediction queries are available to us. As stated earlier, the format or absence of the PREDICTION JOIN clause determines the type of prediction query being created. Let's look at the format and operation of each type.

PREDICTION JOIN

The standard prediction join query enables us to take records from another data source and feed those results into our mining model to create predictions. For this to happen, we must specify where the joined data is coming from. We also need to specify how the columns in the data source are mapped to the input columns of the mining model.

A typical PREDICTION JOIN clause looks like this:

```
PREDICTION JOIN
  OPENQUERY([Max Min Sales DM],
    'SELECT
      [Fname],
      [Lname],
      [Address1],
      [City],
      [State_Province],
      [Postal_Code],
      [Num_Cars_Owned],
      [Homeowner],
      [Marital_Status]
    FROM
      [MaxMinSalesDM].[Customer]
    ') AS t
ON
  [Decision Trees-Children At Home].[Num Cars Owned] = t.[Num_Cars_Owned]
```

```
AND
  [Decision Trees-Children At Home].[Homeowner] = t.[Homeowner]
AND
  [Decision Trees-Children At Home].[Marital Status] = t.[Marital_Status]
```

Remember, the DMX query is running on an Analysis Services server. If we want to include data from a relational table in the prediction join, we need to use the appropriate syntax for utilizing data from another server. This is the OPENQUERY() function.

The OPENQUERY() function executes the specified statement on the server indicated. The OPENQUERY() function requires two parameters. The first is the name of the server where the query is to be executed. In the prediction join, this will probably be the name of a data source defined in the Analysis Services database. In the example code, we are using the Max Min Sales DM data source. This data source points to the MaxMinSalesDM relational database.

The second parameter contains the query to be executed. The query is enclosed in single quotes. In our example, we are selecting fields from the Customer table in the MaxMinSalesDM database. The result set from the OPENQUERY() function is given an alias so it can be referred to elsewhere in the prediction join query. The alias is provided by the "AS t" portion of the PREDICTION JOIN clause.

The lines following the ON keyword map columns from the joined data to the input columns of the mining model. This tells the mining model what input values it should use for each prediction. In our example, the Num_Cars_Owned field from the Customer table is used as the Num Cars Owned input column in the mining model. The Homeowner field is used as the Homeowner input, and the Marital_Status field is used as the Marital Status input.

NATURAL PREDICTION JOIN

The NATURAL PREDICTION JOIN clause works exactly like the PREDICTION JOIN clause, with one convenient exception: It does not include the ON portion. Instead, the *NATURAL PREDICTION JOIN clause* does its mapping of fields to input columns based on the names of each. This can be convenient when working with mining models with a large number of input columns. As you might guess, for this to work, the names of the fields must exactly match the names of the input columns.

We can make our PREDICTION JOIN example work as a NATURAL PREDICTION JOIN, with a slight modification to the query inside the OPENQUERY() function, as follows:

```
NATURAL PREDICTION JOIN
  OPENQUERY([Max Min Sales DM],
    'SELECT
      [Fname],
        [Lname],
```

```
        [Address1],
        [City],
        [State_Province],
        [Postal_Code],
        [Num_Cars_Owned] AS [Num Cars Owned],
        [Homeowner],
        [Marital_Status] AS [Marital Status]
    FROM
        [MaxMinSalesDM].[Customer]
    ') AS t
```

By applying aliases to the Num_Cars_Owned and Marital_Status fields, we can make the field names in the OPENQUERY() result exactly match the input column names. Now, no mapping is necessary.

Empty Prediction Join

The empty prediction join is not a join at all. With an *empty prediction join,* we do not pass any information to the mining model input columns. When we do this, the mining model returns the most likely prediction.

Here is a sample of an empty prediction join:

```
SELECT
    [Num Children At Home]
From
    [Decision Trees-Children At Home]
```

Singleton Query

Where the prediction join and the natural prediction join enabled us to feed data from another data source into the mining model, the singleton query lets us enter hardcoded values for each input column. For example:

```
SELECT
    [Decision Trees-Children At Home].[Num Children At Home]
From
    [Decision Trees-Children At Home]
NATURAL PREDICTION JOIN
(SELECT 'Y' AS [Homeowner],
    'N' AS [Marital Status],
    '2' AS [Num Cars Owned]) AS t
```

To create our singleton query, we are using a NATURAL PREDICTION JOIN clause and hardcoding the content of the inner SELECT statement. Of course, to make this work with a natural prediction join, we must alias each column in the inner SELECT statement to match the names of the mining model input columns.

Learn By Doing—Creating a Query in the SQL Server Management Studio

Feature Highlighted

▶   Creating a DMX query in the SQL Server Management Studio

Business Need   One of the power users in the marketing department is familiar with DMX queries and wants to be able to create DMX queries against the mining models without the graphical interface. Entering DMX queries into the query view of the Mining Model Prediction tab is possible. However, if we switch back to the design view, we lose everything entered in the query view.

   The SQL Server Management Studio provides a better alternative.

NOTE

Always take care when giving users, even power users who seem to know what they are doing, access to tools such as SQL Server Management Studio. Make sure security is set appropriately so the users do not do catastrophic damage, either maliciously or by accident. SQL Server 2008 has expanded its security model. See SQL Books Online for more information.

Steps

1. Open the SQL Server Management Studio.
2. Connect to the Analysis Services server hosting the MaxMinSalesDM database.
3. Expand the Databases folder in the Object Explorer window.
4. Right-click the MaxMinSalesDM database entry in the Object Explorer window and select New Query | DMX from the context menu. A DMX Query window appears.
5. Select Decision Trees - Children At Home from the Mining Model drop-down list.

6. Enter the following in the query area to create an empty prediction query:

```
SELECT
    [Num Children At Home]
From
    [Decision Trees-Children At Home]
```

7. Click the Execute button on the toolbar. The SQL Server Management Studio appears as shown in Figure 15-23.

8. Replace the empty prediction query with the following singleton query:

```
SELECT
    [Decision Trees-Children At Home].[Num Children At Home]
From
    [Decision Trees-Children At Home]
NATURAL PREDICTION JOIN
(SELECT 'Y' AS [Homeowner],
 'N' AS [Marital Status],
 '2' AS [Num Cars Owned]) AS t
```

9. Click the Execute button on the toolbar. The SQL Server Management Studio appears as shown in Figure 15-24.

10. If you want to give your fingers a workout, try entering and executing the prediction join query shown in Figure 15-25.

Figure 15-23   *An empty prediction query in the SQL Server Management Studio*

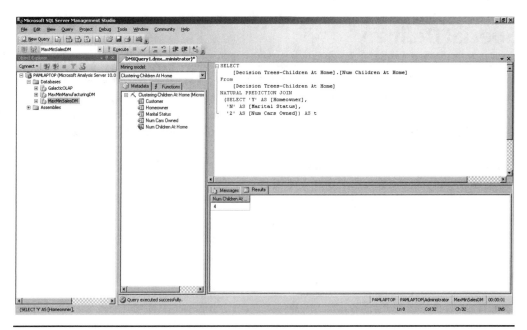

Figure 15-24 *A singleton query in the SQL Server Management Studio*

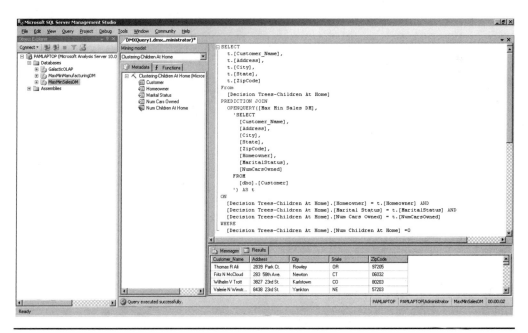

Figure 15-25 *Prediction join query*

Special Delivery

We created OLAP cubes and mining models, and we used MDX and DMX queries to extract data from these items. However, unlike the power user in our last Learn By Doing exercise, most users will not want to jump into the Business Intelligence Development Studio or the SQL Server Management Studio and start cranking out queries. Most users want the data delivered to them in a polished, prepackaged format that is easy to understand and easy to use.

Fortunately, SQL Server 2008 has just the tool for the job: Reporting Services. We cover Reporting Services in Chapters 16 and 17.

Part V

Delivering

Chapter 16

On Report—Delivering Business Intelligence with Reporting Services

In This Chapter

- ▶ Reporting Services
- ▶ Report Serving Architecture
- ▶ Creating Reports using the Tablix Data Region
- ▶ Get Me the Manager

The two most engaging powers of an author are to make new things familiar, and familiar things new.

—Samuel Johnson

In the preceding chapters of this book, we discovered ways to create business intelligence (BI). We saw how online analytical processing (OLAP) cubes and data mining algorithms dissect and analyze data. The result of this dissection and analysis is the foundational and feedback information needed for business intelligence.

Creating this information is only half the battle. As we discussed in Chapter 1, delivering business intelligence to decision makers in a timely manner is as important as creating that intelligence in the first place. The name of this book begins with the word "delivering" for just that reason.

Beginning with this chapter and through to the end of the book, we now examine the tools provided by SQL Server 2008 for delivering business intelligence. In this chapter and in Chapter 17, we learn to use the many capabilities of Reporting Services. In Chapter 18, we work at ways to integrate business intelligence with other applications. Finally, in Chapter 19, we review other Microsoft tools that put business intelligence into the hands of decision makers.

Reporting Services

Since before the invention of computers, the primary method for sharing business intelligence has been the report. This is slowly changing as BI tools become easier to use and more widely available. In fact, some of the tools and capabilities of SQL Server 2008 encourage that process.

Still, in the business intelligence world, the report is king. That being the case, it is important to have a capable and easy-to-use reporting environment at our disposal. Reporting Services fits that bill.

If Reporting Services were simply a report authoring environment, it would be a good tool. However, Reporting Services has much more to offer beyond just report creation. In fact, *Reporting Services* is a complete, enterprise-wide report management and distribution service. Reporting Services enables us to securely distribute reports throughout an organization using an existing intranet infrastructure, and it provides for the integration of reports with both desktop and web-based applications.

Reporting Services also is a bridge between static, paper reports and interactive business intelligence tools. In addition to creating reports for printing, Reporting Services permits users to interact with reports, drilling down from summary to detail information, navigating to related reports, and even jumping to related websites. To use Reporting Services to its fullest extent, we need to create reports that encourage user interaction.

Reporting Services enables both developers and users to create reports. It offers two report authoring tools: the Report Builder and the Report Designer. The *Report Builder* is geared toward those power users and analysts who want to do their own ad hoc reporting, without having to learn all the details of database structure and query creation. The Report Builder presents report authors with a simplified model of a database, so these authors do not need to know the details of querying databases to create reports. Once the Report Builder creates a report, that report can be deployed to the report server and function exactly like a report created with the Report Designer.

The Report Builder is an outstanding tool for these types of users, but to be easy to use, it must remain fairly simple. Therefore, Report Builder cannot support all the many wonderful features of Reporting Services reports. The *Report Designer* offers far greater capabilities for creating interesting and highly functional reports used to convey business intelligence to report users. The Report Designer contains everything necessary to create a wide variety of reports for Reporting Services. Everything we need to select information from data sources, create a report layout, and test our creation is right at our fingertips. Best of all, the Report Designer is found in both the Business Intelligence Development Studio and in Visual Studio 2008.

Report Structure

A report project can contain a number of reports. Each report contains two distinct sets of instructions that determine what the report will contain. The first is the *data definition,* which controls where the data for the report comes from and what information is to be selected from that data. The second set of instructions is the *report layout,* which controls how the information is presented on the screen or on paper. Both of these sets of instructions are stored using the Report Definition Language (RDL).

Figure 16-1 shows this report structure in a little more detail.

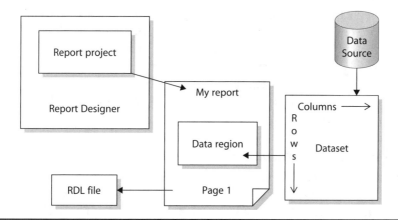

Figure 16-1 *Report structure*

Data Definition

The data definition contains two parts: the data source and the dataset. The *data source* is the same as we have seen used in OLAP projects: It is the set of instructions the report needs to gain access to a data source that provides data for the report. The *data source definition* can be created right inside the report definition, or it can be created externally and shared by a number of reports. In most cases, report management is easier when we use external shared data sources.

When the report is executing, it uses the data source instructions to gain access to the data source. It then extracts information from the data source into a new format that can be used by the report. This new format is called a *dataset.*

The content of the dataset is defined using a tool called the Query Designer. The *Query Designer* helps us build a database query. The database query may be in T-SQL for querying relational data, MDX for querying multidimensional data, or DMX for querying data-mining data. The query provides instructions to the data source, telling it what data we want selected for our report. The query is stored in the report as part of the data definition.

The data selected by the query into the dataset consists of rows and columns. The rows correspond to the records the query selects from the data source. The columns correspond to the fields the query selects from the data source. (Reporting Services does not support hierarchical result sets, so MDX and DMX query results are flattened into a single table of rows and columns.) Information on the fields to be selected into the dataset is stored in the report as part of the data definition. Only the information on what the fields are to be called and the type of data they are to hold is stored in the report definition. The actual data is not stored in the report definition, but instead, is selected from the data source each time the report is run.

Report Layout

The data the report has extracted into a dataset is not of much use to us unless we have some way of presenting it to the user. We need to specify which fields go in which locations on the screen or on paper. We also need to add things such as titles, headings, and page numbers. All of this forms the report layout.

In most cases, our report layout will include a special area that interacts with the dataset. This special area is known as a data region. A *data region* displays all the rows in the dataset by repeating a section of the report layout for each row.

Report Definition Language

The information in the data definition and the report layout is stored using the Report Definition Language (RDL). *RDL* is an Extensible Markup Language (XML) standard designed by Microsoft specifically for storing report definitions. This includes the data source instructions, the query information that defines the dataset, and the report layout. When we create a report in the Report Designer, it is saved in a file with a .rdl extension.

Report Delivery

We have discussed how a report is created by the report server. What we have not discussed is where that report is going after it is created. The report may be sent to a user through the Report Manager website. It may be sent in response to a web service request that came, not from a user, but from another program. It may also be e-mailed to a user who has a subscription to that report.

Report Manager Website

One way for users to request a report from the report server is through the Report Manager website. The Report Manager website organizes reports into folders. Users can browse through these folders to find the report they need. They can also search the report titles and descriptions to locate a report.

The Report Manager also includes security that can be applied to folders and reports. With this security, the site administrator can create security roles for the users who will be accessing the site. These security roles control which folders and reports a user is allowed to access.

In the Report Manager, reports are always displayed using the Hypertext Markup Language (HTML) format. Once a report has been displayed as an HTML page, the user can then export it into any of the other available formats.

Subscription Delivery

If the users do not want to go to the report, Reporting Services can make the report go to them. In other words, users do not necessarily need to come to the Report Manager website to receive a report. They can have the report delivered to them through a subscription service. The Report Manager enables users to locate a report on the site, and then subscribe to it so it will be delivered to them in the future.

When users subscribe to a report, they provide an e-mail address to which the report is to be delivered, either as the body of the e-mail or as an e-mail attachment, depending on the requested format. Users can specify the format for the report at the time they create their subscription.

The site administrator can also set up report subscriptions. These function like a mass mailing, using a list of e-mail addresses. Rather than requiring each user to access the Report Manager to create their own subscription, the site administrator can create one subscription that is delivered to every user in the list.

Web Service Interface

In addition to delivering reports to humans, either at their request or on a subscription basis, the request handler can deliver reports to other software applications. This is done through a series of web services. A program calls a web service on the report server, requesting a particular report in a particular format. The completed report is returned to the program that originated the request as the response to the web service request.

Report Serving Architecture

After a report has been developed, it is time to share that report with our users. This is when our report moves from its safe childhood life inside a report project to its adult life on a report server. This is known as *deploying* the report. Let me assure you, reports pass through deployment much easier than you and I passed through adolescence!

Report Server

The report server is the piece of the puzzle that makes Reporting Services the product it is. This is the software environment that enables us to share our report with the masses, at least those masses who have rights to the server. Figure 16-2 shows the functional structure of the report server.

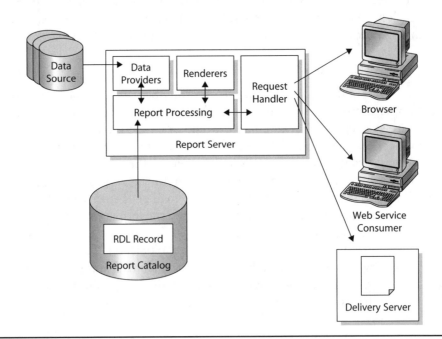

Figure 16-2   *Report server functional structure*

Report Catalog

When a report is deployed to a report server, a copy of the report's RDL definition is put in that server's Report Catalog. The *Report Catalog* is a set of databases used to store the definitions for all the reports available on a particular report server. It also stores the configuration, security, and caching information necessary for the operation of that report server.

Even though we may use any ODBC- or OLE DB–compliant data source to supply data to our reports, the Report Catalog database can only exist in SQL Server 2005 or SQL Server 2008. The Report Catalog database is created as part of the Reporting Services installation process.

Report Processor

When a report needs to be executed, the report processor component of the report server directs the show. The report processor retrieves the RDL for the report from the Report Catalog. It then reads through this RDL to determine what is needed for the report.

The report processor orchestrates the operation of the other components of the report server as the report is produced. It takes the output from each of the other components and combines them to create the completed report.

Data Providers

As the report processor encounters dataset definitions in the report RDL, it retrieves the data to populate that dataset. It does this by first following the instructions in the report's data source for connecting to the database server or file that contains the data. The report processor selects a data provider that knows how to retrieve information from this type of data source.

The data provider then connects to the source of the data and selects the information required for the report. The data provider returns this information to the report processor, where it is turned into a dataset for use by the report.

Renderers

Once all the data for the report has been collected, the report processor is ready to begin processing the report's layout. To do this, the report processor looks at the format requested. This might be HTML, Portable Document Format (PDF), Tagged Image File Format (TIFF), or one of several other possible formats. The report processor then uses the renderer that knows how to produce that format.

The *renderer* works with the report processor to read through the report layout. The report layout is combined with the dataset, and any repeating sections of the report are duplicated for each row in the dataset. This expanded report layout is then translated into the requested output format. The result is a report ready to be sent to the user.

Request Handler

The *request handler* is responsible for receiving requests for reports and passing those requests on to the report processor. Once the report processor has created the requested report, the report handler is also responsible for delivering the completed report.

The Parts of the Whole

Reporting Services is not a single program that runs on a computer to produce reports. Instead, it is a series of services, web applications, and databases that work together to create a report management environment. As you plan your Reporting Services installation, it is important that you understand a little bit about each piece of the puzzle and how all these pieces work together to create a complete system.

Figure 16-3 shows all the parts that make up a complete Reporting Services installation. Each part has a specific role to play in the development, management, and

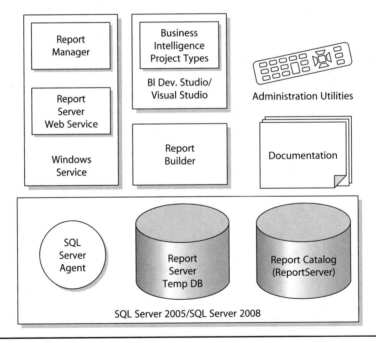

Figure 16-3 *Reporting Services component parts*

delivery of reports or in the management of the Reporting Services environment itself. Let's take a look at each part and see how it fits into the whole.

The Report Server Service

The Report Server service is the heart of Reporting Services. This service is responsible for the two main interfaces with the report server. First, it contains the application that implements the Report Manager website. Second, it provides a web service interface for programmatic interaction with the report server. In past versions of Reporting Services, these two interfaces were hosted by Internet Information Services (IIS). In SQL Server 2008, the Report Server Service uses the Hypertext Transfer Protocol (HTTP) library in Windows to serve as its own HTTP request handler, so IIS is not needed.

As discussed earlier, the Report Manager website provides a user interface for requesting reports and managing the report server. The Report Server web service provides a programmatic interface for requesting reports. It also provides an interface for report server administration.

In addition to these two interfaces, the Reporting Services Windows service provides the engine responsible for report rendering. This is true whether the report is requested through the Report Manager website, the Report Server web service, or subscription delivery. This includes fetching the report definition, retrieving the data used in the report, and rendering the report in the desired format. By default, the Report Manager is accessed through a website called Reports.

The Reporting Services Windows service needs to have a valid user name and password that it can use to access the Report Catalog. This login information, along with other information that determines how the report server operates, is stored in the RSReportServer.config file. Most of the information in the RSReportServer.config file is stored as plain text and can be modified using Notepad or a similar text editor. The login information, however, is encrypted when it is stored in this file. It cannot be changed except through the administration utilities.

The Administration Utilities

The *administration utilities* are tools for managing the Reporting Services Windows service and for making changes to its configuration. These utilities take care of tasks such as manually starting the Reporting Services Windows service if it fails to start automatically. The utilities can also be used to change the login information used by the service.

Most of these utility programs are run in a command window. The one administration utility that does have a Windows user interface is the *Report Server Configuration Manager*, which provides a convenient method for examining and modifying the configuration settings of a Reporting Services installation.

The administration utilities can be run on the computer that is hosting the Reporting Services Windows service to manage the configuration on that computer. Most of the administrative utilities can also be used to manage a Reporting Services Windows service that is running on another computer. This is called *remote administration*.

SQL Server 2005/SQL Server 2008 and SQL Server Agent

SQL Server 2005 or SQL Server 2008 is required to hold the database where Reporting Services stores its Report Catalog database. Reporting Services also uses the SQL Server Agent as its task scheduler. When a user creates a subscription, Reporting Services creates a SQL Server Agent job to handle that subscription.

The Report Server and Report Server Temp DB Databases

Reporting Services uses two databases within SQL Server: the Report Server and the Report Server Temp DB. The *Report Server database* is used to store the Report Catalog. The Report Server database also holds information about the Report Manager website. This includes such things as the folder structure of the website and the security settings for each folder and report.

As the name implies, the *Report Server Temp DB database* is used as temporary storage for Reporting Services operations. Information can be stored here to track the current users on the Report Manager website. Short-term copies of some of the most recently executed reports are also stored here in what is known as the *execution cache*.

Report Designer

As previously discussed, Reporting Services reports are created using the Report Designer, either in the Business Intelligence Development Studio or in Visual Studio 2008. The Report Designer functions exactly the same in either development tool. No difference exists between a report created in the Business Intelligence Development Studio and in Visual Studio 2008. The Report Designer uses Business Intelligence Project Types to create reports.

Documentation

The final piece of Reporting Services is the documentation. The bulk of this documentation is found in the SQL Server Books Online. After Reporting Services is installed, you can view the SQL Server Books Online through your Start menu. You can find it under Programs | Microsoft SQL Server 2008 | Documentation and Tutorials | SQL Server Books Online. In addition to this is a set of help screens for the Report Manager interface that can be accessed through the Reports website.

Reporting Services Installation Considerations

We may install both the Reporting Services Windows service and the Report Catalog on the same server. However, some organizations may choose to place these items on separate servers. This can be done through either a distributed installation or a scale-out installation.

The Distributed Installation

In a distributed installation, the Reporting Services items discussed are not installed on a single computer. Instead, they are split between two computers that work together to create a complete Reporting Services system. One computer runs SQL Server 2005 or SQL Server 2008 and hosts the databases that make up the Report Catalog. This is the database server. The other computer runs the Reporting Services Windows service. This is the report server.

Figure 16-4 shows a distributed installation. Note, this figure shows the servers and the report designer workstations. It does not show computers used for viewing reports.

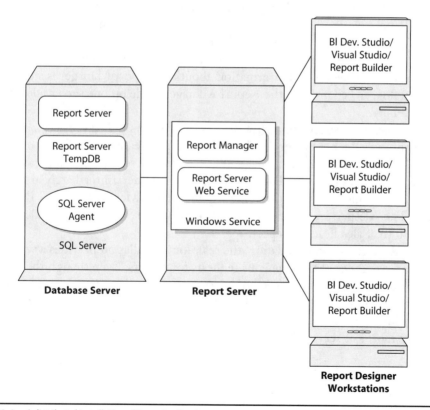

Figure 16-4   *A distributed installation of Reporting Services*

The distributed installation has advantages when it comes to scalability. Because the workload of the Reporting Services Windows service and the SQL Server database engine is divided between two servers, a distributed installation can serve reports to a larger number of simultaneous users. The disadvantage of this type of installation is that it is more complex to install and administer. However, if we need a high-volume solution, it is certainly worth the effort to obtain a solution that can provide satisfactory response times under a heavy workload.

The Scale-Out Installation

The *scale-out installation* is a specialized form of the distributed installation, as shown in Figure 16-5. In a scale-out installation, a single database server interacts with several report servers. Each of the report servers uses the same set of Report Catalog databases for its information. By using additional report servers, we can handle even more simultaneous users with the scale-out installation than we could with the distributed installation.

Again, note that Figure 16-5 shows only the servers and the report designer workstations. It does not show computers used for viewing reports.

When Report Designers create reports, they can deploy them to any of the report servers. No matter which server is used, the reports end up in the single Report Catalog. Once the reports are in the Report Catalog, they can be delivered by any of the report servers. In addition, because all information about the Report Manager is stored in the Report Catalog, any changes to the Report Manager made on one server take effect on all the servers.

For example, suppose an administrator uses the Reports website to access the Report Manager through Report Server A. The administrator creates a new folder in Report Manager—called Sales Forecasts 2008—sets the security so the sales staff can access this folder, and places the Sales Forecast report in the folder. Immediately after the administrator is finished, a salesperson brings up Report Manager through Report Server C. The salesperson can browse the contents of the Sales Forecasts 2008 folder and can run the Sales Forecast report.

As with the distributed installation, the scale-out installation provides a way to handle a large number of simultaneous requests for reports. Even though the scale-out installation uses a number of servers to deliver reports, it allows the Report Manager interface to be administered without duplication of effort. The scale-out installation may take additional effort to get up and running, but once it is ready to go, it provides an efficient means of serving a large number of users.

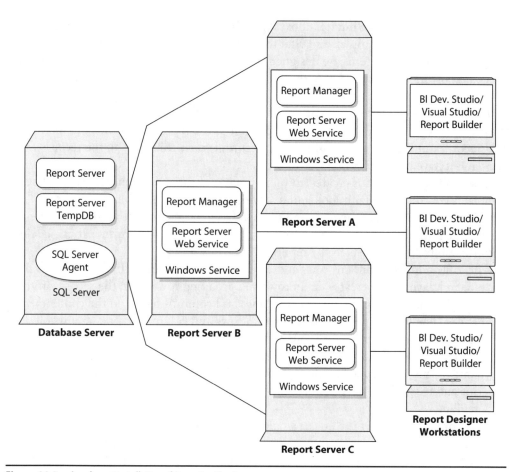

Figure 16-5   *A scale-out installation of Reporting Services*

Creating Reports Using the Tablix Data Region

We begin working with Reporting Services by using the Report Designer to create several reports. In Chapter 17, we deploy these reports to the report server and explore the report administration and distribution features offered by Reporting Services. Also in Chapter 17, we look at the capabilities that enable power users to create their own ad hoc reports.

Reports are created using a drag-and-drop approach. Report items are taken from the Toolbox window and placed on the report. The function of some of these report items is not hard to figure out: text boxes contain text, images display image files. Other report items are more complex and vital to the workings of Reporting Services reports.

Three special report items are designed specifically for working with datasets. These special report items are called data regions. The three data regions are the tablix, the chart, and the gauge.

Data regions are able to work with multiple records from a dataset. The data region reads a record from the dataset, creates a portion of the report using the data found in that record, and then moves on to the next record. It does this until all the records from the dataset have been processed.

The tablix data region is created through the use of three different templates. These templates control the default look and behavior of the resulting tablix. The three templates are the table, the matrix, and the list. It should be noted that the templates specify the initial state of a tablix added to a report. They do not limit what can be done with the tablix after it exists in the report layout.

The table template contains rows and columns. A tablix created by the table template has a default layout that creates detail rows and grouping rows from the records in the dataset. The matrix template creates both rows and columns based on the contents of the dataset. The list template is not limited to rows and columns. It creates a whole section, perhaps a whole page or more, for each record in the dataset.

Each data region item has a property called DataSetName. This property contains the name of the dataset used by the data region. In most cases, the Report Designer sets this automatically. This property is set to the dataset of the first field placed in the data region.

In many cases, a report includes a single data region to create the body of the report. In other cases, multiple data regions are combined on a single report. This mix and match has no limit. Perhaps a chart data region containing a line graph and a tablix containing the detail information from the chart are placed in the same report. We can mix and match to our hearts' content.

A Tablix Data Region Created with the Table Template

The *table template* creates the traditional-style report with rows and columns. *Rows* are created from the records in the dataset. *Columns* are created from the fields in the dataset.

The table template creates what is called a *banded report* in some other report authoring environments. The *detail bands* in these reports correspond to the detail rows in the table. The *summary bands* in these reports correspond to the header and footer rows in the table.

The tablix that results from the table template includes a tablix header and footer. The tablix header often contains column headings for the tablix. The tablix footer often contains the grand totals for the entire tablix.

In addition to the tablix header and footer, the tablix data region can include multiple group headers and footers. The group headers often contain the information to identify a grouping. The group footers usually contain totals for the group.

Learn By Doing—Creating a Tablix Report Using the Table Template

Features Highlighted

▶ Creating a Reporting Services report using the Report Wizard

▶ Using the tablix report item

▶ Using query parameters

Business Need   Back in Chapter 6, the vice president (VP) of production for Maximum Miniatures, Incorporated asked for statistics on the number of products accepted and the number of products rejected as they come off the production line. He also asked for information on the amount of time it took to produce these items. We created a data mart to hold this information, as well as an OLAP cube on top of that data mart. Now it is time to take this information and put it into a format the VP is comfortable with, namely a report.

The VP has asked to see these three statistics for each product. The products should be grouped by the machine where they were manufactured. The VP would like to see this information for a single year, which will be specified when the report is run.

We could use either the MaxMinManufacturingDM relational database or the Max Min Manufacturing DM OLAP cube as the source for this data. For the sake of demonstrating a number of data sources, we use the relational database for this report. We create this report using the Report Wizard. The remainder of the reports created in this chapter are going to be created from scratch.

Steps

1. Open the Business Intelligence Development Studio.
2. Click the New Project button on the toolbar.
3. Make sure Business Intelligence Projects is selected from the Project Types, and then select Report Server Project from the Templates.
4. Enter **MaxMinReports** for Name and set the Location to the appropriate folder. Leave Create directory for solution unchecked.
5. Click OK to create the project.
6. Right-click the Reports folder in the Solution Explorer window and select Add New Report from the context menu. The Welcome page of the Report Wizard appears.

7. Click Next. The Select the Data Source page of the wizard appears.

8. Enter **MaxMinManufacturingDM** for Name. Click Edit. The Connection Properties dialog box appears.

9. Enter the name of the server hosting the MaxMinManufacturingDM relational database for Server Name. Enter the appropriate credentials to access this server.

10. From the Select or enter a database name drop-down list, select MaxMinManufacturingDM.

11. Click OK to exit the Connection Properties dialog box.

12. Check the Make this a shared data source check box.

13. Click Next. The Design the Query page of the wizard appears.

14. Click the Query Builder button. The Query Designer dialog box appears.

NOTE

If you prefer additional assistance while building queries, you can use the Graphical Query Designer. As the name implies, this query designer allows you to graphically create T-SQL queries. To streamline the report-authoring process, we will use the Generic Query Designer.

15. Click the Edit As Text toolbar button to switch to the Generic Query Designer.

16. Enter the following query:

```
SELECT
    DimMachine.MachineName,
    DimProduct.ProductName,
    SUM (ManufacturingFact.AcceptedProducts) AS AcceptedProducts,
    SUM (ManufacturingFact.RejectedProducts) AS RejectedProduct,
    SUM (ManufacturingFact.ElapsedTimeForManufacture) AS
    ElapsedTimeForManufacture
FROM
    DimMachine
INNER JOIN
    ManufacturingFact ON DimMachine.MachineNumber =
    ManufacturingFact.MachineNumber
INNER JOIN
    DimProduct ON ManufacturingFact.ProductCode =
    DimProduct.ProductCode
GROUP BY
    DimMachine.MachineName,
    DimProduct.ProductName,
    DimMachine.MachineNumber,
    DimProduct.ProductCode,
    YEAR(ManufacturingFact.DateOfManufacture)
HAVING
    (YEAR(ManufacturingFact.DateOfManufacture) = @Year)
ORDER BY
    DimMachine.MachineNumber,
    DimProduct.ProductCode
```

17. Click the Execute button (the red exclamation point). The Define Query Parameters dialog box appears. This dialog box appears because we included the @Year parameter in our query. This parameter enables us to specify which year's data we want to see in the report. We need to specify a value for this parameter before the query can execute. Enter **2008** for the parameter value and click OK. The Query Designer screen should appear as shown in Figure 16-6.

NOTE

The @Year in our query is a query parameter. A value must be specified for this parameter at the time the report is run. To facilitate this, query parameters are automatically mapped to report parameters with the same name. A report parameter named Year has been automatically created for us.

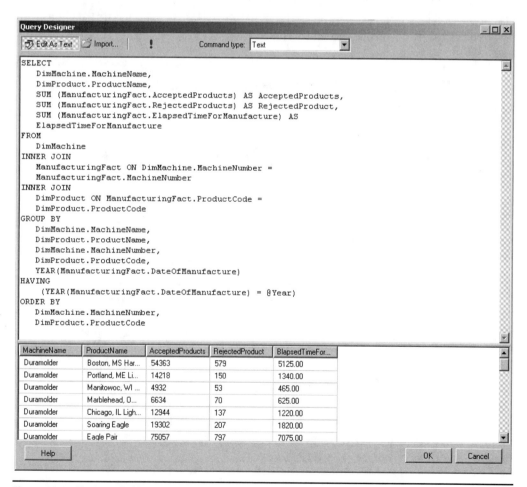

Figure 16-6   *The Query Builder screen*

18. Click OK to exit the Query Designer. You return to the Design the Query page of the wizard.

19. Click Next. The Select the Report Type page of the wizard appears.

20. Leave Tabular selected to produce a report using the table template to create a tablix data region. (We can create reports using the matrix template from the Report Wizard as well. We cannot create reports using the list template, the chart data region, or the gauge data region from the Report Wizard.)

21. Click Next. The Design the Table page appears. On this page, we specify how each field is to be used in the table.

22. With the MachineName field selected in the Available fields list, click Group. The MachineName field is placed in the Group list for Displayed fields. Data is grouped by MachineName in the table.

23. Click Details four times to place the remaining fields in the Details list. The wizard page appears as shown in Figure 16-7.

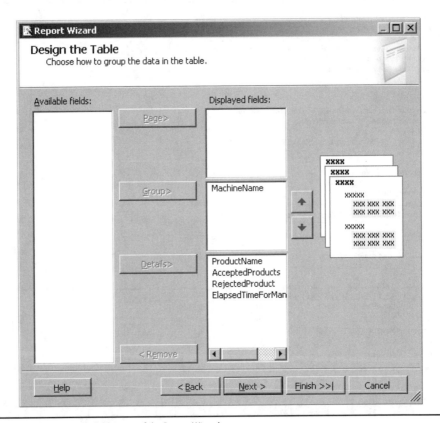

Figure 16-7   *The Design the Table page of the Report Wizard*

24. Click Next. The Choose the Table Layout page appears.
25. Leave the Stepped radio button selected. Check both the Include subtotals and Enable drilldown check boxes. The wizard page appears as shown in Figure 16-8.

NOTE

Include subtotals places totals in the footer for each group and in the footer at the end of the tablix. Enable drilldown causes the report to start out at a summary or group level. We can drill down to the detail level by clicking the plus (+) sign next to a grouping.

26. Click Next. The Choose the Table Style page of the wizard appears.
27. Select the Corporate style and click Next. The Completing the Wizard page appears.
28. Enter **Manufacturing By Machine Report** for Report name. The wizard page appears as shown in Figure 16-9.

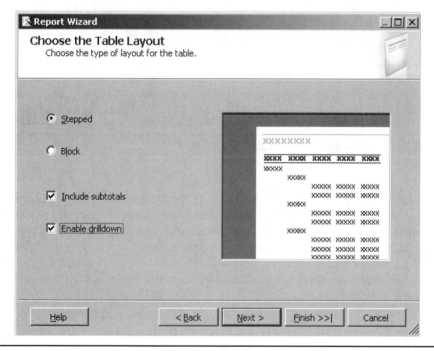

Figure 16-8   *The Choose the Table Layout page of the Report Wizard*

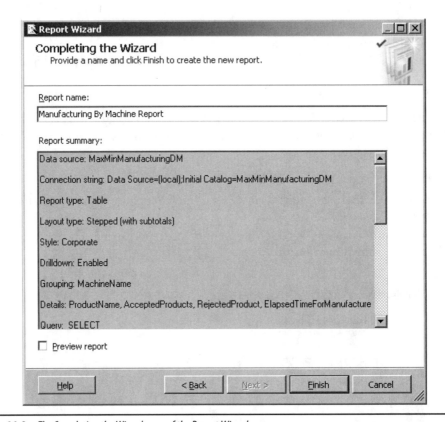

Figure 16-9 *The Completing the Wizard page of the Report Wizard*

29. Click Finish. The report design appears in the Design tab on the Report Design tab. The Report Wizard placed two report items in the body of the report it created for us. The first is a text box containing the report title: Manufacturing By Machine Report. The second is a tablix data region. Click any of the cells in the table. This displays the gray column and row handles, as shown in Figure 16-10. The table contains three rows: a table header row, a group header row, and a detail row.

30. Grab the divider between the Machine Name column and the Product Name column handles, and then drag the Machine Name column wider. This is shown in Figure 16-11.

31. Repeat this process to widen the Product Name column and the Elapsed Time For Manufacture column.

Table Header

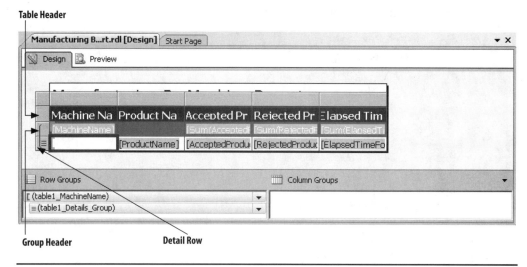

Group Header   **Detail Row**

Figure 16-10 *The tablix data region created by the Report Wizard*

32. Right-click the table cell directly under the Accepted Products heading (it contains "[Sum(AcceptedProducts)]"). This is the group header cell in the Accepted Products column. Select Text Box Properties from the context menu. The Textbox Properties dialog box appears, as shown in Figure 16-12.

NOTE

Each type of report item has its own custom properties dialog box. These properties dialog boxes are used to control the appearance and behavior of each item on the report. In addition to the properties dialog boxes, we can modify the properties of a report item using the Properties window. Some of the formatting properties of the report items can also be modified using buttons and drop-down lists on the toolbar.

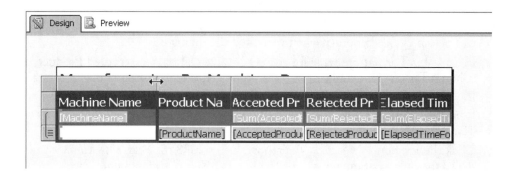

Figure 16-11 *Widening a tablix column*

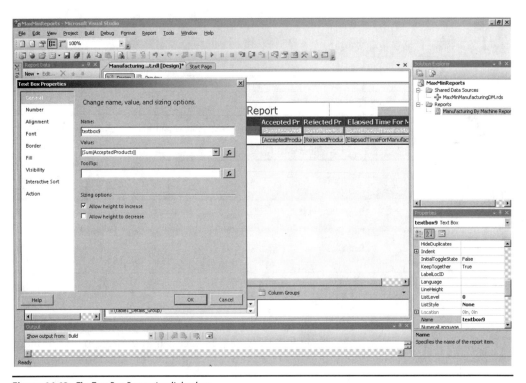

Figure 16-12 *The Text Box Properties dialog box*

33. Select the Number page from the list on the left side of the dialog box.
34. Select Number in the Category list.
35. Change Decimal places to **0**.
36. Check the Use 1000 separator (,) check box.
37. Select -12,345 in the Negative numbers list.
38. Click OK to exit the Text Properties dialog box.
39. Find the Format property in the Properties window. The formatting string "#,0" was placed in this property when we exited the dialog box.
40. Place **#,0** in Format property for the other table cell in the Accepted Products column. This is the detail cell in the Accepted Products column.
41. Repeat Step 40 for the group header cell and the detail cell in the Rejected Products column and for the group header cell and the detail cell in the Elapsed Time For Manufacture column.
42. Click the Preview tab to view the report. Enter **2008** for Year. This value is then fed to the query parameter we created in our SELECT statement.
43. Click View Report. The report is rendered on the Preview tab. Note, only the group headers for our grouping on Machine Name are visible. This occurs because

we checked Enable Drilldown in the Report Wizard. When we enable drilldown, a report starts at a summary or group level and lets the user selectively drill down to the detail level.

44. Click the plus sign next to Duramolder to see all of the products created on this machine in 2008. This is shown in Figure 16-13.

45. Let's examine a few more of the properties that make this report work. Select the Design tab.

46. Click the Elapsed Time For Manufacture cell in the tablix heading row.

NOTE

It is likely that only some of the words of this heading are visible. However, when we previewed the report, the entire heading is visible. The cell grows taller when the report is rendered. The cell can grow because the CanGrow property of the text box is set to True. If the CanGrow property is set to False, the text box cannot change size when it is rendered. Text boxes can grow vertically, but they cannot grow horizontally when the report is rendered.

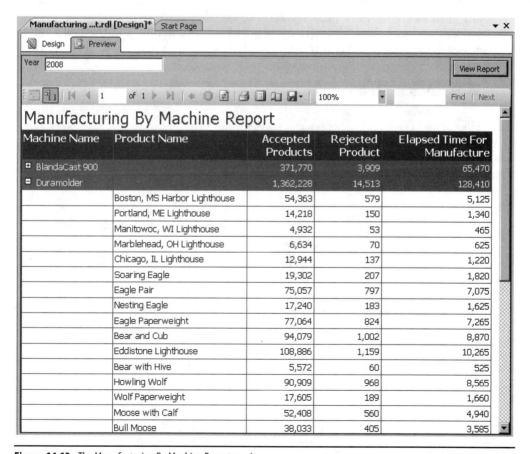

Machine Name	Product Name	Accepted Products	Rejected Product	Elapsed Time For Manufacture
⊞ BlandaCast 900		371,770	3,909	65,470
⊟ Duramolder		1,362,228	14,513	128,410
	Boston, MS Harbor Lighthouse	54,363	579	5,125
	Portland, ME Lighthouse	14,218	150	1,340
	Manitowoc, WI Lighthouse	4,932	53	465
	Marblehead, OH Lighthouse	6,634	70	625
	Chicago, IL Lighthouse	12,944	137	1,220
	Soaring Eagle	19,302	207	1,820
	Eagle Pair	75,057	797	7,075
	Nesting Eagle	17,240	183	1,625
	Eagle Paperweight	77,064	824	7,265
	Bear and Cub	94,079	1,002	8,870
	Eddistone Lighthouse	108,886	1,159	10,265
	Bear with Hive	5,572	60	525
	Howling Wolf	90,909	968	8,565
	Wolf Paperweight	17,605	189	1,660
	Moose with Calf	52,408	560	4,940
	Bull Moose	38,033	405	3,585

Figure 16-13 *The Manufacturing By Machine Report preview*

47. Right-click the detail cell in the Elapsed Time For Manufacture column. Select Expression from the Context menu. The Expression dialog box appears, as shown in Figure 16-14. The expression shown in the dialog box returns the value of the ElapsedTimeForManufacture field. Click Cancel to exit the Edit Expression dialog box. When you look at this cell in the tablix grid, you do not see the same expression. Instead, you see "[ElapsedTimeForManufacture]" in this cell. This is a placeholder for the expression.

NOTE

The expressions in Reporting Services use Visual Basic.NET. Access to dataset information is provided through a collection called Fields, which contains a member called ElapsedTimeForManufacture. The ElapsedTimeForManufacture member has a property called Value that contains the value of this field.

48. Right-click the group header cell in the Elapsed Time For Manufacture column. Select Expression from the context menu. The Expression dialog box again appears, this time with the Sum aggregate function around the field expression, as shown in Figure 16-15. Click Cancel to exit the Expression dialog box. Again, we see the placeholder "[Sum(ElapsedTimeForManufacture)]" in the tablix cell rather than the complete expression.

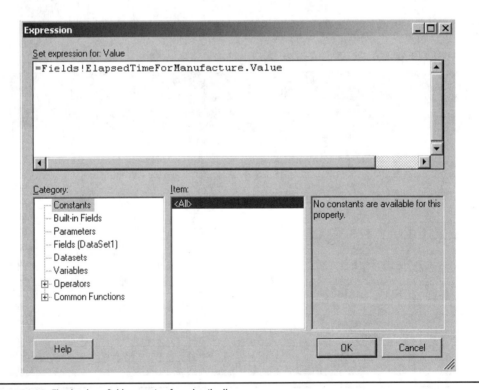

Figure 16-14 *The database field expression for a detail cell*

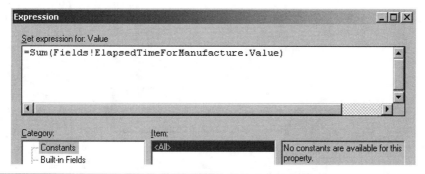

Figure 16-15 *The database field expression with an aggregate function for a group header cell*

NOTE

The Sum aggregate function is used here because we are looking at a cell in a group header. Group headers (and footers, for that matter) must, by definition, group together a number of records to get a single value for each column. To do that, we use aggregate functions. Here, the Sum aggregate function is used to add all detail values together to get group totals. We can use aggregates in both headers and footers. In some reporting environments, aggregates are calculated as the detail rows are processed and can only be placed in the footers. That is not the case with Reporting Services. Aggregates are calculated separately and can be placed anywhere in the report.

49. The drop-down box on the top of the Properties window shows the name of the selected report item. The currently selected table cell contains a text box called textbox11. Click the detail cell in the Elapsed Time For Manufacture column. This cell is named for the dataset field placed in the cell. Click the group header cell in the Machine Name column. The text box in this cell, MachineName, is also named for the dataset field placed here.

NOTE

Each cell in a tablix must contain another report item. There is no such thing as an empty tablix cell. If no other report item has been placed in a tablix cell, a text box is automatically created and placed there by default. Report item names are only important when one report item is referenced by another item. In all other cases, the default names, such as table1 or textbox2, work just fine.

50. Click the gray square in the upper-left corner of the tablix. This is how we select the tablix itself. Click in any of the cells to unselect the tablix, and then right-click that same gray square. The context menu that appears is the context menu for the tablix itself. Select Tablix Properties from the context menu. The Tablix Properties dialog box appears. The General page, shown in Figure 16-16, controls several properties of the tablix, including whether the header and footer rows should be displayed and whether the report should begin a new page either before or after the tablix.

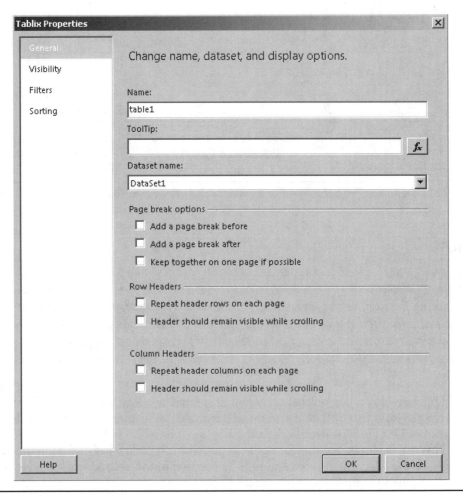

Figure 16-16 *The General page of the Tablix Properties dialog box*

51. Select the Visibility page. This is shown in Figure 16-17. The Visibility page controls whether a report item is seen or is hidden. We explore the workings of the Visibility page more in a moment.

52. Select the Filters page. This is shown in Figure 16-18. The Filters page enables us to specify an expression for filtering the rows in the dataset. No filtering expression is specified in this report.

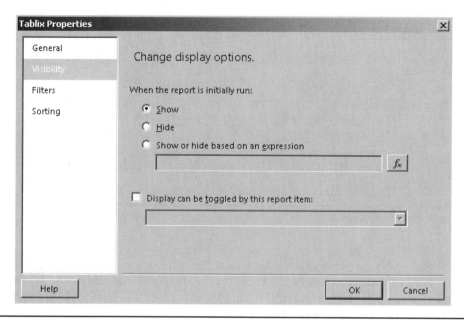

Figure 16-17 *The Visibility page of the Tablix Properties dialog box*

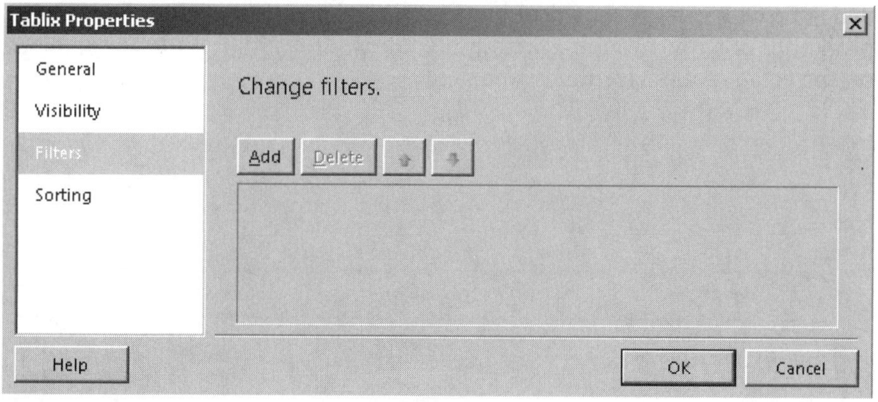

Figure 16-18 *The Filters page of the Tablix Properties dialog box*

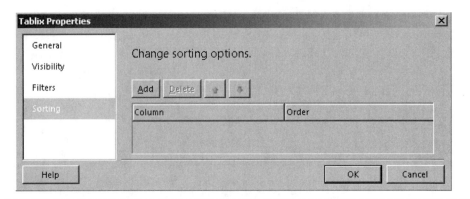

Figure 16-19 *The Sorting page of the Tablix Properties dialog box*

53. Select the Sorting page. This is shown in Figure 16-19. The Sorting page enables us to specify an expression for sorting the detail rows in the table. Any sorting expression specified here overrides the sort in the SELECT statement. No sorting expression is specified here in this report.

54. Click OK to exit the Tablix Properties dialog box.

55. In the Row Groups area at the bottom of the screen, click the drop-down arrow. You will see a menu, as shown in Figure 16-20.

56. Select Group Properties from the Row Groups menu. The Group Properties dialog box appears, as shown in Figure 16-21. This dialog box defines the properties of a row grouping within the tablix. This group is grouping data based on the value of the MachineName field.

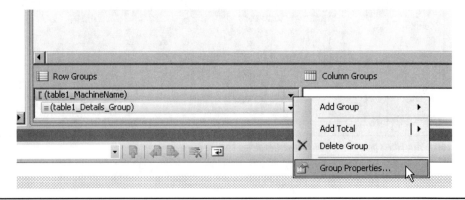

Figure 16-20 *The Row Groups menu*

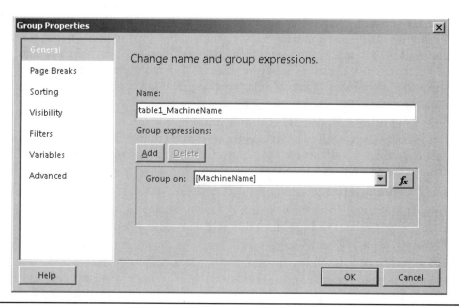

Figure 16-21 *The General page of the Group Properties dialog box*

57. Select the Page Breaks page. This is shown in Figure 16-22. Using the Page Breaks page, we can specify whether the report should place a page break in between each grouping, as well as at the start of the set of groups, or at the end of the set of groups.

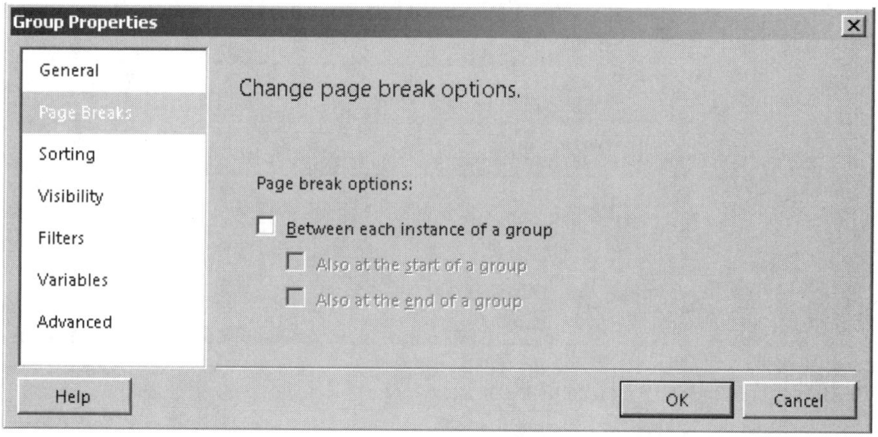

Figure 16-22 *The Page Breaks page of the Group Properties dialog box*

58. Select the Sorting page. This appears similar to the Sorting page of the Tablix Properties dialog box shown in Figure 16-19. This Sorting page enables us to control the sort order of the groups themselves. The detail data within each group is still sorted according to the settings on the Tablix Properties dialog box or, if no sort order is set in the Tablix Properties dialog box, according to the sorting in the database query itself.

59. Select the Advanced page. This is shown in Figure 16-23. The Document map item on this page enables us to assign expressions to the Document map label—sort of a table of contents for the report. Currently, a document map is not being created for this report.

60. Click Cancel to exit the Group Properties dialog box.

61. In addition to the entry for our table1_MachineName group, you can see there is an entry for the details group. The detail records in a tablix can be considered their own grouping.

62. Click the drop-down arrow for the table1_Details_Group and select Group Properties from the menu.

63. Select the Visibility page. The Visibility page has been changed from the default settings, as shown in Figure 16-24.

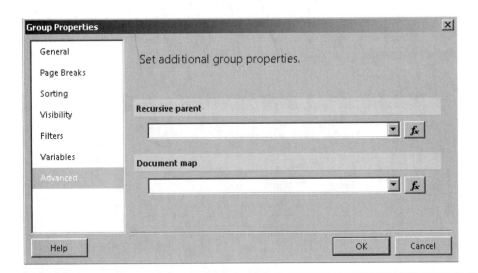

Figure 16-23   *The Advanced page of the Group Properties dialog box*

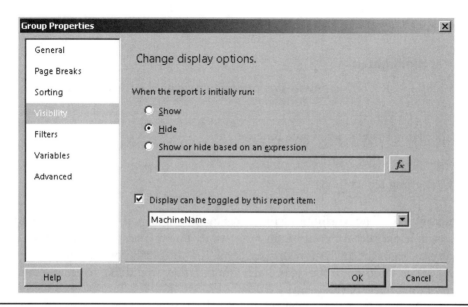

Figure 16-24 *The Visibility page of the Group Properties dialog box for the details group*

NOTE

The settings on the Visibility page can be used to implement the drilldown feature in our report. To implement drilldown, the initial visibility of the report item (the detail group in this report) is set to Hide. In addition, the properties on the Visibility page are set so the visibility of the item is toggled by another report item (in this report, the MachineName text box). This setting places a plus sign next to the toggling report item and causes the display of the previously hidden report item when the plus sign is clicked.

64. Click Cancel to exit the Group Properties dialog box.
65. Click the Save All button on the toolbar.

A Tablix Data Region Created with the Matrix Template

The *matrix template* does not create a banded report, but it does create what is known as a pivot table or a crosstab report. The table template produces a predefined set of columns and an unknown number of rows; the number of rows depends on the content of the dataset. The matrix template creates both rows and columns based on the content of the dataset. The resulting tablix has groupings on both rows and columns. Drilldown can be defined for both rows and columns as well.

The data cells created by the matrix template always contain aggregate data. Therefore, the data in the cells is numeric. Because of this, the matrix mirrors the fact and dimension structure of an OLAP cube and works well for displaying cube data.

Learn By Doing—Creating a Matrix Report

Features Highlighted

▶ Creating a Reporting Services report without using the Report Wizard

▶ Using the matrix template

▶ Specifying scope in aggregate functions

▶ Manually enabling drilldown

▶ Formatting report items

Business Need   The Maximum Miniatures marketing department would like to analyze wholesale sales for each product over time. The marketing department wants to be able to begin the analysis at the year level, and then drill down to the quarter and month level. In addition to the sales dollar amount, they would like to see the sales as a percent of total sales for the year.

We use the Max Min Sales DM cube as the data source for this report.

Steps

1. Open the Business Intelligence Development Studio, if it is not already open.

2. Open the MaxMinReports project, if it is not already open.

3. Close the Report Design tab containing the Manufacturing By Machine Report, if it is open.

4. Right-click the Shared Data Sources folder in the Solution Explorer window and select Add New Data Source from the context menu. The Shared Data Source Properties dialog box appears.

5. Enter **MaxMinSalesDMCube** for Name.

6. Select Microsoft SQL Server Analysis Services from the Type drop-down list.

7. Click Edit. The Connection Properties dialog box appears.

8. Enter the name of the Analysis Services server hosting the Max Min Sales DM OLAP cube for Server Name.

9. From the Select or enter a database name drop-down list, select MaxMinSalesDM.

10. Click OK to exit the Connection Properties dialog box. Click OK to exit the Shared Data Source Properties dialog box. The shared data source is created.

11. Right-click the Reports folder in the Solution Explorer window and select Add | New Item. (Selecting Add New Report launches the Report Wizard, which we are not using for this report.) The Add New Item dialog box appears.

12. Select Report in the Templates area. Enter **Wholesale Sales By Month Report** for Name.

13. Click Add. The Report Design tab appears.
14. In the Report Data window, select New | Data Source from the toolbar. The Data Source Properties dialog box appears.
15. Enter **MaxMinSalesDMCube** for Name.
16. Select the Use shared data source reference option.
17. Select the MaxMinSalesDMCube shared data source from the drop-down list.
18. Click OK to exit the Data Source Properties dialog box.
19. Right-click the MaxMinSalesDMCube data source you just created in the Report Data window and select Add Dataset from the context menu. The Dataset Properties dialog box appears.
20. Enter **WholesaleSales** for Name.
21. Click Query Designer. The MDX Query Designer window appears.
22. Expand the Time dimension, and then expand the Year—Quarter—Month—Date hierarchy. Drag the Year, Quarter, and Month members of this hierarchy onto the query area. (The area labeled Drag levels or measures here to add to the query.)
23. Expand the Product dimension and drag the Product attribute onto the query area.
24. Expand Measures and the Sales Information measure group and drag the Sales in Dollars measure onto the query area. The query executes.
25. Because our business requirements were for wholesale sales only, we need to add a filter to the query to include only wholesale customers (customer numbers below 5000). In the Filter pane (directly above the query pane), click the cell labeled <Select Dimension>. From the drop-down list, select Customer.
26. For Hierarchy, select Account Num.
27. For Operator, select Range (Inclusive).
28. For Filter Expression, create a range from 4500 to 4996.
29. The query executes again. The MDX Query Builder appears as shown in Figure 16-25.
30. Click OK to exit the Query Designer window. Click OK to exit the Dataset Properties dialog box.
31. Drag a text box from the Toolbox and drop it on the report body layout area. Using the Properties window, modify the properties of the text box as follows:

Property	Value
Font: FontSize	16pt
Font: FontWeight	Bold
Location: Left	0in
Location: Top	0in
Size: Width	4in
Size: Height	0.375in

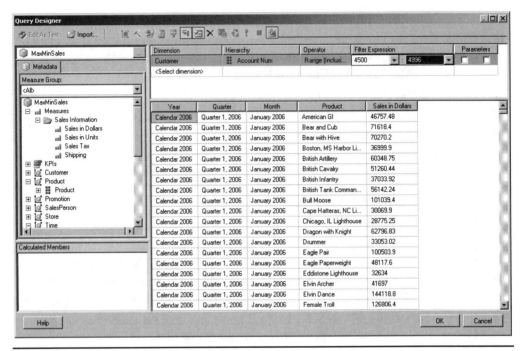

Figure 16-25 *The MDX Query Builder with the query for the Wholesale Sales By Month Report*

NOTE

Several properties, such as the Font property, contain subproperties. The property must be expanded to view the subproperties. These are referred to with the following format: Property: Subproperty.

32. In the text box, enter **Wholesale Sales By Month Report**.
33. Drag a matrix from the Toolbox and drop it on the report body layout area below the text box. This will create a tablix data region using the matrix template.
34. From the Report Data window, drag the Month field and drop it in the Columns cell.
35. Drag the Product field and drop it in the Rows cell.
36. Drag the Sales_in_Dollars field and drop it in the Data cell.
37. Drag the Quarter field and drop it on the line forming the top of the Month cell.
38. Drag the Year field and drop it on the line forming the top of the Quarter cell. The report layout should appear as shown in Figure 16-26.

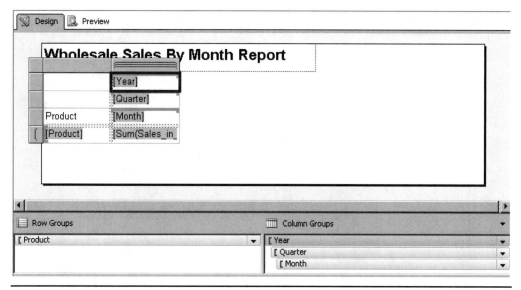

Figure 16-26 *The report layout for the Wholesale Sales By Month Report*

39. To prevent the user from being overwhelmed with information, we are going to manually enable drilldown in this report. Click the drop-down arrow for the Month group in the Column Groups area. Select Group Properties from the menu. The Group Properties dialog box appears.

40. Select the Visibility page.

41. Select the Hide option under the When the report is initially run prompt.

42. Check the Display can be toggled by this report item check box.

43. Select Quarter from the drop-down list. The Group Properties dialog box appears as shown in Figure 16-27.

44. Click OK to exit the Group Properties dialog box.

45. Click the drop-down arrow for the Quarter group in the Column Groups area. Select Group Properties from the menu. The Group Properties dialog box appears.

46. Select the Visibility page.

47. Select the Hide option under the When the report is initially run prompt.

48. Check the Display can be toggled by this report item check box.

49. Select Year from the drop-down list.

50. Click OK to exit the Group Properties dialog box.

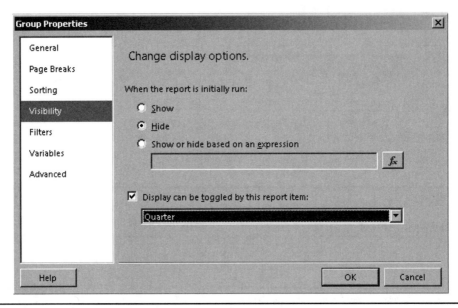

51. Click the Preview tab. The report appears as shown in Figure 16-28.
52. Click the Design tab. Let's make a few changes to improve the looks and readability of the matrix.
53. Select the cell containing the Sum of the Sales_in_Dollars field (the detail cell for the matrix). Set the following properties in the Properties window:

Property	Value
Format	C
Size: Width	1.5 in

The "C" value provides currency formatting for the number in this cell.

54. Select the cell containing the Year field. Set the following properties in the Properties window:

Property	Value
BackgroundColor	MediumBlue
Color	White
Font: FontWeight	Bold

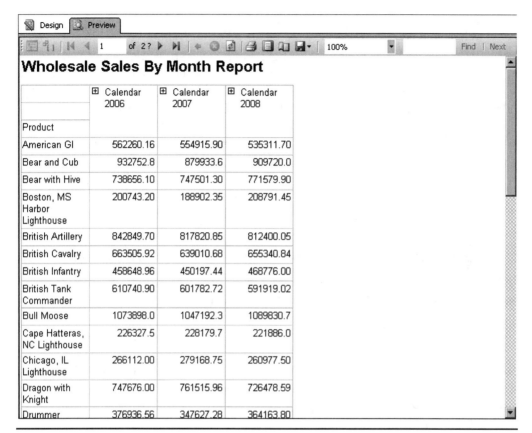

Figure 16-28 *The Wholesale Sales By Month Report preview*

55. Select the cell containing the Quarter field. Set the following properties in the Properties window:

Property	Value
BackgroundColor	CornflowerBlue
Font: FontWeight	Bold
TextAlign	Right

56. Select the cell containing the Month field. Use the toolbar buttons to set the font weight to bold, the background color to PowderBlue, and the alignment to align right. (Hint: Click the More colors link to select the color by name.)

57. Select the cell containing the Product field. Use the toolbar buttons to set the font weight to bold and the background color to PowderBlue.

58. Select the cell containing the Year field. Hold down SHIFT and click the detail cell. Hold down CTRL and click the cell containing the Product field. The selected cells appear as shown in Figure 16-29.

59. With these cells selected, set the following properties in the Properties window:

Property	Value
BorderColor	MediumBlue
BorderWidth	2pt

NOTE

The border properties can be either set at the default level to affect all four sides of the report item or expanded and set for each side individually.

60. Click the Preview tab. Expand Calendar 2007. Expand Quarter 1, 2007. The report should appear similar to Figure 16-30.

61. We have one business goal left to fulfill: percent of sales for the year. Click the Design tab.

62. Right-click the detail cell. Select Tablix: Insert Row | Inside Group - Below. A new detail cell is created below the existing detail cell.

63. Right-click the new detail cell and select Textbox: Expression from the context menu. The Expression dialog box appears.

64. Enter the following expression:

```
=Sum(Fields!Sales_in_Dollars.Value) /
             Sum(Fields!Sales_in_Dollars.Value, "Year")
```

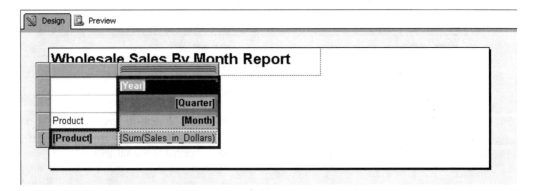

Figure 16-29 *The matrix layout with multiple cells selected*

| | Design | Preview |

| ≡ | | ◁◁ | ◁ | 1 | of 2? | ▷ | ▷▷ | | ○ | | | | | | | 100% | ▾ | Find | Next |

Wholesale Sales By Month Report

	⊟ Calendar 2006	⊟ Calendar 2007					
		⊟			Quarter 1, 2007 ⊞	Quarter 2, 2007 ⊞	Quarter
Product		January 2007	February 2007	March 2007			
American GI	$562,260.16	$52,931.34	$50,473.50	$50,766.10	$146,153.70	$128
Bear and Cub	$932,752.80	$88,401.60	$66,729.60	$82,857.60	$219,844.80	$222
Bear with Hive	$738,656.10	$72,768.15	$68,017.95	$68,673.15	$195,700.05	$166
Boston, MS Harbor Lighthouse	$200,743.20	$31,729.95	$22,733.55	$24,894.45	$58,432.50	$34
British Artillery	$842,849.70	$73,265.50	$69,919.85	$68,649.35	$210,225.40	$200
British Cavalry	$663,505.92	$64,778.56	$41,401.36	$63,016.80	$156,085.16	$155
British Infantry	$458,648.96	$35,703.36	$31,095.68	$39,079.04	$119,035.84	$116
British Tank Commander	$610,740.90	$52,875.90	$35,671.02	$57,015.42	$146,823.60	$143
Bull Moose	$1,073,898.00	$87,431.40	$84,879.90	$86,467.50	$274,654.80	$254
Cape Hatteras, NC Lighthouse	$226,327.50	$30,901.50	$27,310.50	$25,174.80	$55,188.00	$52

Figure 16-30 *The Wholesale Sales By Month Report preview with additional formatting*

NOTE

The first Sum aggregate function in this expression adds all the sales for the current detail cell. This aggregate function determines what items to add based on the scope of the cell it is in. When no items are expanded in the matrix, the scope of each cell is the year column and product row the cell is in. When we pass a second parameter to the aggregate function, we explicitly specify the scope of the function. In this case, we require the second Sum aggregate function to always add sales for the current year column grouping. This enables us to calculate the total for the column to complete the percent of total calculation.

65. Click OK to exit the Expression dialog box. You will see "<<Expr>>" as a placeholder for the expression.

66. Click in the new detail cell to the right of the <<Expr>> placeholder until you see the blinking edit cursor in the cell.

67. Enter a space followed by **of annual** in the cell after the placeholder.

68. Click the <<Expr>> placeholder until it is highlighted.

69. Right-click the <<Expr>> placeholder and select Placeholder Properties from the context menu. The Placeholder Properties dialog box appears.

70. Select the Number page.

71. Select Percentage from the Category list.

72. Select the Font page.
73. Check the Bold check box.
74. Click OK to exit the Placeholder Properties dialog box.

NOTE

We changed the numeric formatting and the font weight for just the expression portion of the cell content as represented by the placeholder. We did not change the formatting of the text after the placeholder.

75. Click elsewhere to unselect this cell, and then click this cell again. Now the entire cell is selected, rather than just one portion of the content.
76. Set the following properties of this cell in the Properties window:

Property	Value
BorderStyle: Left	Solid
BorderStyle: Right	Solid
BorderStyle: Top	None
BorderStyle: Bottom	Solid
TextAlign	Right

77. Select the original detail cell and set the following properties in the Properties window:

Property	Value
BorderStyle: Left	Solid
BorderStyle: Right	Solid
BorderStyle: Top	Solid
BorderStyle: Bottom	None
Font: FontWeight	Bold
TextAlign	Right

78. Let's also create totals for our rows and columns. Right-click the product cell and select Tablix: Add Total | After.
79. Select the Preview tab. Your report appears as shown in Figure 16-31. Everything looks great, except for the background color of our total row; it is still white with black text. We only changed the background for the cell containing the Total label, not for the total cells themselves.
80. Click the Save All button on the toolbar.

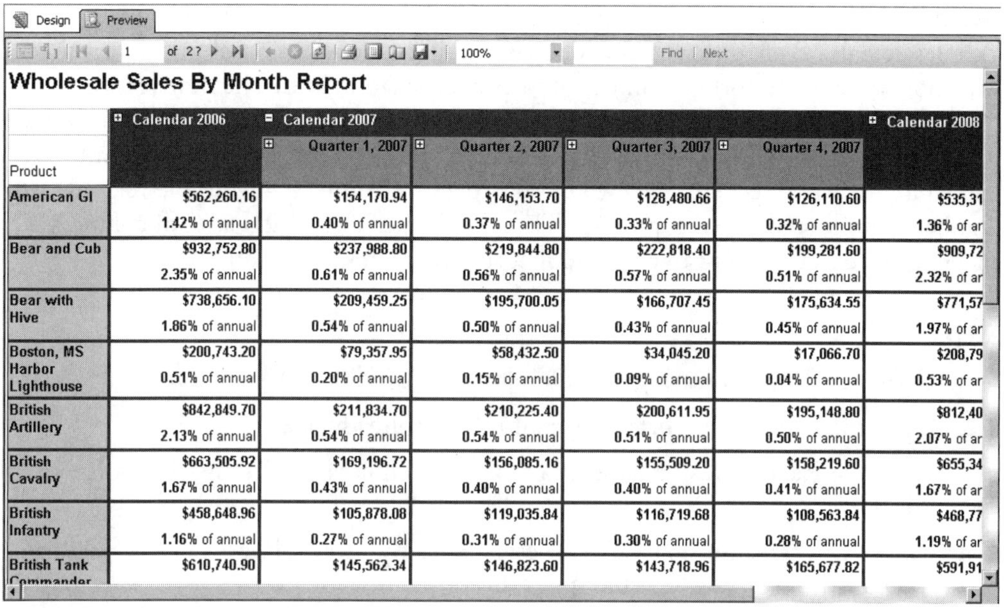

Figure 16-31 *The Wholesale Sales By Month Report preview—completed*

Combining Static and Dynamic Columns in a Tablix

In the previous two Learn By Doing exercises, we have used the table template to create a tablix with a static set of columns and the matrix template to create a tablix with a dynamic set of columns. One of the strengths of the tablix data region is its ability to combine both static and dynamic columns in the same object. In the next Learn By Doing exercise, we will modify the report we just created to add static and dynamic columns to our existing tablix.

Learn By Doing—Creating the Sales Analysis Report

Features Highlighted

- ▶ Creating a calculated column in an MDX query
- ▶ Using the YTD() function in an MDX query
- ▶ Adding a static column to an existing tablix
- ▶ Adding dynamic columns to an existing tablix
- ▶ Freezing header rows and columns in a tablix

Business Need   The Maximum Miniatures marketing department really likes the Wholesale Sales By Month Report. They would like a new version of this report that will allow them to perform a number of sales analysis functions. The new version of the report should only show information for 2008. Because of this change, data should display at the month level without the drilldown functionality. Also, the percent of annual figure is not needed. They would like to add a column showing the year-to-date number of units sold for each product. They would also like to add a set of columns showing the dollar amount of each product sold by each salesperson.

Steps

1. Open the Business Intelligence Development Studio, if it is not already open.

2. Open the MaxMinReports project, if it is not already open.

3. Close the Report Design tab containing the Wholesale Sales By Month Report, if it is open.

4. Right-click the entry for the Wholesale Sales By Month Report in the Solution Explorer window and select Copy from the context menu.

5. Right-click the entry for the MaxMinReports project in the Solution Explorer window and select Paste from the context menu. A copy of the Wholesale Sales By Month Report is created in the project.

6. Right-click the new copy of the report and select Rename from the context menu. Name the report **Sales Analysis Report** and press ENTER.

7. Double-click the Sales Analysis Report in the Solution Explorer window to open this report.

8. Right-click the WholesaleSales dataset entry in the Report Data window and select Query from the context menu. The Query Designer window appears.

9. In the filter area along the top of the Query Designer window, click in the second row of the Dimension column. Select Time from the drop-down list.

10. In the second row of the Hierarchy column, select Year - Quarter - Month - Date from the drop-down list.

11. In the second row of the Operator column, select Equal from the drop-down list.

12. In the second row of the Filter Expression column, expand the All entry and place a check mark next to the Calendar 2008 entry. Click OK to exit the drop-down window.

13. Drag the Year and Quarter attributes off of the query area to remove them from the query.

14. Right-click the Calculated Members area in the lower-left portion of the window and select New Calculated Member from the context menu. The Calculated Member Builder dialog box appears.

15. Enter **YTD Unit Sales** for Name.

16. In the Functions area of the screen, expand the Statistical folder.

17. Scroll down to the entry for the SUM function and double-click this entry. The SUM function template is added to the Expression area.

18. Highlight the <<Set>> placeholder and the left square bracket in the Expression area, as shown in Figure 16-32.

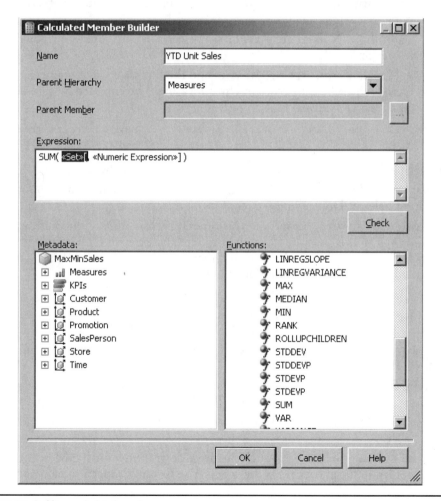

Figure 16-32 *Building a calculated member*

19. In the Functions area, expand the Time folder and double-click the YTD function entry. The YTD() function template takes the place of the <<Set>> placeholder. We will use the YTD() function to create the set required by the SUM function.

20. Highlight the [<<Member>>] placeholder. Be sure to include the square brackets when you highlight.

21. In the Metadata area, expand the Time Dimension, and then double-click the Year—Quarter—Month—Date hierarchy. This will add a reference to the time hierarchy ([Time].[Year—Quarter—Month—Date]) to the expression in place of the [<<Member>>] placeholder.

22. Add **.currentmember** to the expression immediately after the time hierarchy without a space in between.

23. Highlight the <<Numeric Expression>>] placeholder. Be sure to include the right square bracket.

24. In the Metadata area, expand Measures and the Sales Information measure group, and then double-click the Sales in Units measure. The completed expression should appear as follows:

```
SUM( YTD([Time].[Year -  Quarter -  Month -  Date].currentmember ),
                                        [Measures].[Sales in Units])
```

25. Click OK to exit the Calculated Member Builder dialog box.

26. Drag the YTD Unit Sales calculated member you just created and drop it to the right of Sales in Dollars in the query.

27. In the Metadata area, expand the Customer dimension. Drag the State attribute and drop it in the query between the Product and Sales in Dollars columns. In addition, expand the Sales Person dimension. Drag the Sales Person attribute and drop it in between the Product and the Store columns.

28. Click OK to exit the Query Designer window.

29. In the Column Groups area, click the drop-down arrow for the Year group. Select Delete Group from the menu. The Delete Group dialog box appears.

30. Leave the Delete group and related rows and columns items selected, and click OK.

31. In the Column Groups area, click the drop-down arrow for the Quarter group. Select Delete Group from the menu. The Delete Group dialog box appears.

32. Leave the Delete group and related rows and columns items selected, and click OK.

33. In the Column Groups area, click the drop-down arrow for the Month group. Select Group Properties from the menu. The Group Properties dialog box appears.

34. Select the Visibility page.

35. Select the Show item under the When the report is initially run prompt.

36. Uncheck the Display can be toggled by this report item check box.

37. Click OK to exit the Group Properties dialog box.

38. Right-click the cell containing <<Expr>> of annual and select Delete Rows from the context menu.

39. Right-click the cell containing the [Month] placeholder in the tablix and select Tablix: Insert Column | Outside Group - Right from the context menu. This will add a static column to the right of the group of dynamic columns.

40. Drag the YTD_Unit_Sales field from the Report Data window and drop it in the detail cell in the new column.

41. In the heading cell in the new column, enter **YTD Units**.

42. Right-click the YTD Units heading and select Tablix: Add Group | Adjacent Right. The Tablix group dialog box appears.

43. Select [Sales_Person] from the Group by drop-down list.

44. Click OK to exit the Tablix group dialog box. A new column is created for this column group.

45. Drag the Sales_in_Dollars field from the Report Data window and drop it in the detail cell in the new column.

46. Right-click the gray square in the upper-left corner of the tablix. Select Tablix Properties from the context menu. The Tablix Properties dialog box appears.

47. In the Row Headers area, check the Header should remain visible while scrolling check box.

48. In the Column Headers area, check the Header should remain visible while scrolling check box.

49. Click OK to exit the Tablix Properties dialog box.

50. Select the cell containing the Product heading. (This is the cell with the white background.) Press DELETE.

51. Change the title text box to Sales Analysis Report. Your report design should appear as shown in Figure 16-33.

52. Click the Preview tab. After scrolling right and down, the report appears as shown in Figure 16-34.

53. Click the Save All button on the toolbar.

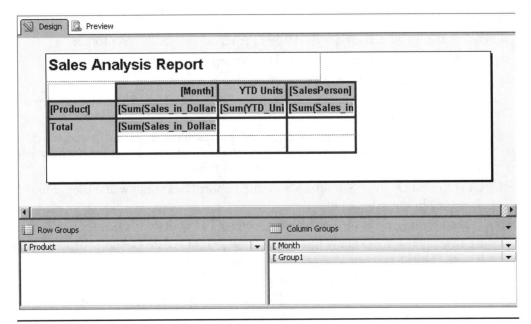

Figure 16-33 *The Sales Analysis Report design*

Knight	October 2008	November 2008	December 2008	YTD Units	Anne	Briggette	Dari
Drummer	$28,728.70	$27,487.46	$29,989.96	121269	9349.34	72112.04	14714.7
Eagle Pair	$78,021.30	$64,943.55	$68,338.20	113785	25821.60	178525.20	29828.4
Eagle Paperweight	$44,575.20	$38,818.80	$35,453.52	116278	12929.76	104323.68	15084.7
Eddistone Lighthouse	$31,707.90	$29,370.60	$32,215.05	118291	13737.15	78299.55	12965.4
Elvin Archer	$32,472.00	$41,549.40	$31,069.80	116522	9446.4	86370.6	15399.
Elvin Dance	$126,149.10	$158,566.80	$147,821.10	127645	42711.9	355511.1	62758.
Female Troll	$106,449.00	$99,922.20	$118,881.00	118147	39627.0	277155.9	54234.
Flying Dragon	$52,805.54	$46,808.88	$43,257.46	120201	13798.14	110879.99	17844.4
French Artillery	$58,125.76	$70,846.16	$55,926.64	127775	17377.36	165020.24	33116.1
French Cavalry	$59,632.65	$54,088.65	$62,231.40	124391	14691.60	129244.50	25502.4
French Infantry	$46,246.20	$36,514.17	$37,962.54	121802	7775.46	92517.81	19946.8
General Washington	$58,688.63	$47,544.42	$55,058.08	124022	14743.19	123312.42	21246.6
German Panzer Driver	$43,428.00	$37,668.40	$51,189.60	115255	13613.6	109709.6	22884.
Holland, MI Lighthouse	$20,807.85	$21,645.75	$22,144.50	104082	7620.90	57296.40	6483.7
Howling Wolf	$44,658.60	$38,955.00	$37,514.40	122778	16758.0	107045.4	18404.

Figure 16-34 *The Sales Analysis Report preview*

A Tablix Data Region Created with the List Template

The *list template* does not deal in columns and rows at all. Instead, the list template provides a freeform layout area that is repeated for each record in the dataset. This makes it a good choice for creating a report that is meant to resemble a form.

Learn By Doing—Creating a Report Using the List Template

Features Highlighted

▶ Creating a tablix using the list template

▶ Adding an image to a report

▶ Using rectangles and lines in a report

▶ Controlling report item formatting with expressions

Business Need   The Maximum Miniatures marketing department would like a list of information from its newly purchased mailing list, discussed in Chapter 15. The list should include the name and address of each household, along with homeowner status, marital status, number of cars owned, and the predicted number of children at home. The marketing department also wants a graphic to appear with entries predicted to have no children at home, indicating these are likely Mythic World buyers.

We can use the Decision Trees-Children At Home mining model and the Customer dimension from the Max Min Sales DM cube as the data source for this report.

Steps

1. Open the Business Intelligence Development Studio, if it is not already open.

2. Open the MaxMinReports project, if it is not already open.

3. Close the Report Design tab containing the Sales Analysis Report, if it is open.

4. Right-click the Reports folder in the Solution Explorer window and select Add | New Item. The Add New Item dialog box appears.

5. Select Report in the Templates area. Enter **Customer List With Prediction Report** for Name.

6. Click Add. The Report Design tab appears.

7. In the Report Data window, select New | Data Source from the toolbar. The Data Source Properties dialog box appears.

8. Enter **MaxMinSalesDMCube** for Name.

9. Select the Use shared data source reference option.

10. Select the MaxMinSalesDMCube shared data source from the drop-down list.

11. Click OK to exit the Data Source Properties dialog box.

12. Right-click the MaxMinSalesDMCube data source you just created in the Report Data window and select Add Dataset from the context menu. The Dataset Properties dialog box appears.

13. Enter **MailingListPrediction** for Name.

14. Click Query Designer. The MDX Query Builder appears.

15. Click the Command Type DMX button on the MDX Query Designer toolbar to switch to the DMX Query Builder.

16. Click Yes when asked if you want to proceed with the switch. The DMX Query Designer appears.

17. Click Select Model. The Select Mining Model dialog box appears.

18. Expand Classification - Children At Home.

19. Select Decision Trees - Children At Home and click OK to exit the Select Mining Model dialog box.

20. Click Select Case Table. The Select Table dialog box appears.

21. Select Customer (dbo) and click OK to exit the Select Table dialog box.

22. Highlight the mapping of the Num Children At Home predictable to the Num_Children_At_Home field. Press DELETE to remove this mapping.

23. Click the Source column of the grid in the DMX Query Builder to activate the drop-down list.

24. Select Customer Table from the drop-down list.

25. Activate the drop-down list in the Field column and select Customer_Name.

26. Repeat Steps 23 through 25 to add the following fields to the query output:

   ▶ Address

   ▶ City

   ▶ State

   ▶ ZipCode

   ▶ NumCarsOwned

   ▶ Homeowner

   ▶ MaritalStatus

27. In the next available row, select Decision Trees—Children At Home from the Source drop-down list. Num Children At Home is selected in the Field column by default.

28. When completed, the DMX Query Builder appears as shown in Figure 16-35.
29. Click OK to exit the Query Designer window. Click OK to exit the Dataset Properties dialog box.
30. Right-click the report body layout area and select View | Ruler from the context menu. The horizontal and vertical rulers appear.
31. Drag the right edge of the report body layout area so it is ten inches wide.
32. Drag a list from the toolbox and drop it on the layout area. Size the resulting tablix so it takes up almost the entire layout area.

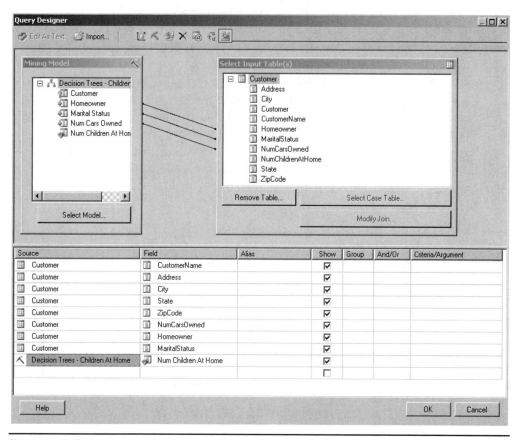

Figure 16-35 *The DMX Query Builder*

33. Set the properties of the tablix as follows:

Property	Value
BorderStyle	Double
BorderWidth	5pt
DataSetName	MailingListPrediction

34. Drag fields from the MailingListPrediction dataset in the Report Data window onto the rectangle to create the layout shown in Figure 16-36. The text boxes have been expanded to show the entire field placeholders in each text box.

35. Click the text box containing the [City] field to select it. Right-click this text box and select Expression from the context menu. The Expression dialog box appears.

36. Type & ", " & at the end of the existing field expression. Put a space before the first ampersand, after the comma, and after the second ampersand.

37. Select Fields (MailingListPrediction) from the Category area. The fields in this dataset appear in the Value area. Double-click the State field to add it to the expression. It will be inserted at the point of your cursor. If you have text selected, the double-clicked field is inserted in place of that text.

38. Type & " " & at the end of the existing field expression. Put a space before the first ampersand, between the quotes, and after the second ampersand.

39. Double-click the ZipCode field in the Value area to add this field to the end of the expression.

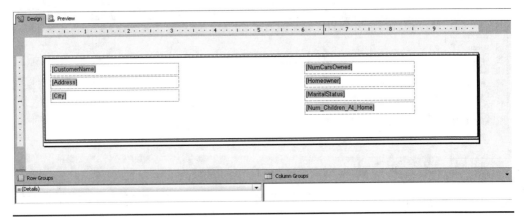

Figure 16-36 *The initial field layout for the Customer List With Prediction Report*

40. Click OK to exit the Edit Expression dialog box.

41. Increase the length of the three address fields.

42. Decrease the length of the four numeric value fields.

43. Add text boxes to create labels for the numeric value fields, as shown in Figure 16-37. The labels should be right-aligned.

44. Add a line report item to separate the address section from the numeric value section of the layout.

45. Add a second line across the bottom of the tablix to separate one record from another.

46. Add an image report item to the upper-right corner of the rectangle. The Image Properties dialog box appears as shown in Figure 16-38.

47. Leave Embedded selected. Click Import.

> **NOTE**
>
> The images we use in reports can be stored in four different locations. Embedded images are placed right in the RDL file for the report. This ensures the image is always available to the report, but it makes the RDL file larger and it makes the image hard to update. Project images are stored within the report project and deployed with the report to the report server. Project images cannot be shared between projects. Database images are stored as binary large objects (BLOBs) in the database itself. Database images can be hard to manage and can put a strain on database server resources. They do have an advantage in situations where each record in a dataset should reference a different image. Web images are pulled from a URL each time the report is rendered. Web images offer the most flexibility for updating and sharing images among reports. Of course, web images require that the URL be available for report rendering.

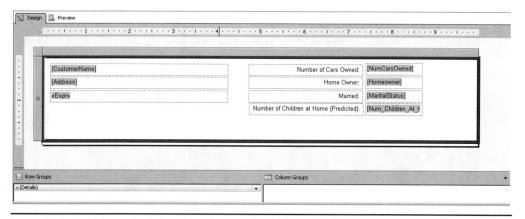

Figure 16-37 *The Customer List With Prediction Report layout with labels added*

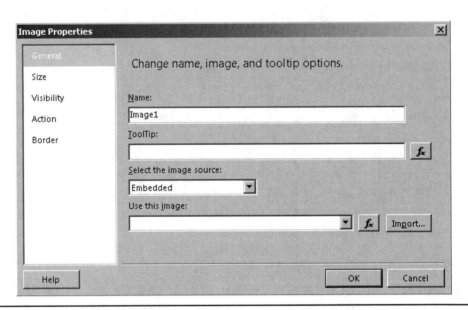

Figure 16-38 *The Image Properties dialog box*

48. Browse to the copy of Mythic World Buyer.gif you downloaded from the book's website. Select this image file and click Open.

49. Select the Size page of the Image Properties dialog box.

50. Select the Original size option.

51. Select the Visibility page.

52. Select the Show or hide based on an expression option.

53. Click the *fx* button. The Expression dialog box appears.

54. Enter the following expression to control whether the image is visible or hidden for each record:

    ```
    =IIF(Fields!Num_Children_At_Home.Value = 0, False, True)
    ```

    This expression displays the graphic, set Hidden to False, when the predicted number of children at home is 0. Recall this was the criterion for a Mythic World product type buyer.

55. Click OK to exit the Edit Expression dialog box.

56. Click OK to exit the Image Properties dialog box. You return to the report layout, which appears as shown in Figure 16-39.

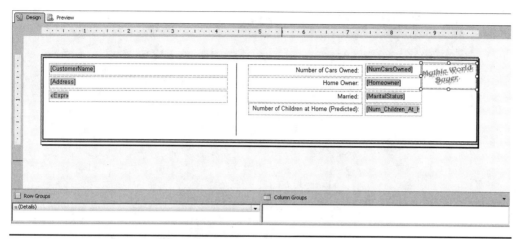

Figure 16-39 *The Customer List With Prediction Report with the Mythic World Buyer image*

NOTE

You can manage embedded images in the Report Data window in the Images folder.

57. We created a report body that is ten inches wide to accommodate our layout. If we print this report, we need to use a landscape orientation. We set the report properties for landscape printing. Select Report | Report Properties from the Main menu. The Report Properties dialog box appears.

58. Set the following properties:

Property	Value
Orientation	Landscape
Left margin	0.5in
Right margin	0.5in

The Report Properties dialog box appears as shown in Figure 16-40.

NOTE

For a report to print properly, the width of the report body plus the width of the left and right margins must be less than or equal to the page width. If this is not the case, the rightmost portion of the report will be cut off and printed on a separate page.

59. Click OK to exit the Report Properties dialog box.

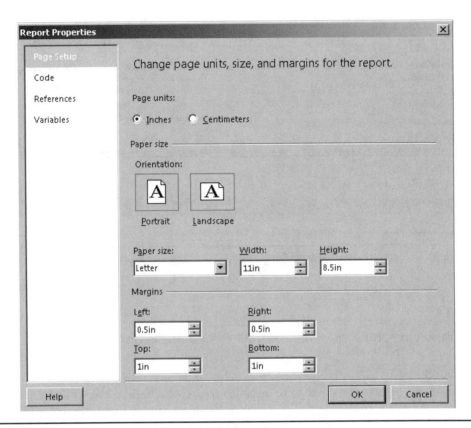

Figure 16-40 *The Design tab of the Report Properties dialog box*

60. We seem to have left no room for a report heading on our layout. We can remedy this by using special layout areas: the page header and the page footer. The content of the page header and page footer layout areas will appear on each page of the report. Select Report | Add Page Header from the Main menu to toggle on the page header layout area.

61. Place a text box in the page header and set the properties as follows:

Property	Value
Font: FontSize	16pt
Font: FontWeight	Bold
Location: Left	0in
Location: Top	0in
Size: Width	4.5in
Size: Height	0.5in

62. Type **Customer List With Prediction Report** in the text box.

63. Size the page header appropriately.

64. Select Report | Add Page Footer from the Main menu to toggle on the page footer layout area.

65. Place a text box in the page footer and set the properties as follows:

Property	Value
Location: Left	4in
Location: Top	0in
Size: Width	1.9in
Size: Height	0.25in
TextAlign	Center

66. Right-click the text box and select Expression from the context menu. The Expression dialog box appears.

67. Select Built-in Fields in the Category area. The built-in or global fields are displayed in the center list.

68. Type **=CStr(** in the expression area.

69. Double-click PageNumber in the center list.

70. In the expression, after page number, type **) & " out of " & CStr(**.

71. Double-click TotalPages in the center list.

72. Type **)**. The Edit Expression dialog box appears as shown in Figure 16-41.

73. Click OK to exit the Edit Expression dialog box.

74. Size the page footer appropriately.

75. The data in the dataset is not sorted, so let's add sorting in the tablix data region itself. Click the tablix, and then right-click the square in the upper-left corner of the tablix. Select Tablix Properties from the context menu. The Tablix Properties dialog box appears.

76. Select the Sorting page.

77. Click Add.

78. Select [Customer_Name] from the Sort by drop-down list.

79. Click OK to exit the Tablix Properties dialog box.

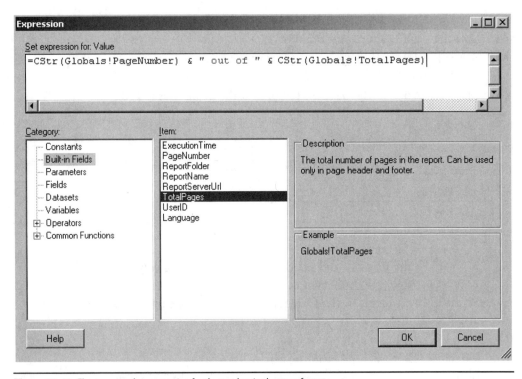

Figure 16-41 *The page number expression for the text box in the page footer*

80. Let's use one of the navigation features of Reporting Services to make it easier to find a person in this report. In the Row Groups area, click the drop-down arrow for the Details group. Select Group Properties from the menu. The Group Properties dialog box appears.

81. Select the Advanced page.

82. Select [Customer_Name] from the Document map drop-down list.

83. Click OK to exit the Group Properties dialog box.

NOTE

In addition to the document map we are creating here, Reporting Services provides three actions that can occur when a user clicks a text box or image. These actions are all configured using the Action page of the Textbox Properties dialog box. The user can jump to another report. The user can jump to a predefined bookmark within the current report. And the user can jump to a website through a URL.

84. Select the Preview tab. The Document Map appears on the left. Expand the Customer List With Prediction Report entry. Click the entry for Anders C Carson in the document map. This takes us to the entry for Anders C Carson in the report. Note, the Mythic World Buyer graphic appears when the number of children at home is predicted to be 0. This page of the report appears as shown in Figure 16-42.

85. Scroll up and down the pages, and note the page header and page footer on every page.

86. Click the Save All button on the toolbar.

87. Click the Print Layout button on the Preview tab toolbar. A print preview of the report is created. This takes a minute or so to complete. The print preview appears as shown in Figure 16-43.

The Chart Data Region

The *chart report item* is a data region like the tablix, which means the chart can process multiple records from a dataset. The tablix enables you to place other report items in a row, a column, or a list area that is repeated for every record in the dataset. The chart, on the other hand, uses the records in a dataset to create bars, lines, or pie wedges. You cannot place other report items inside a chart item.

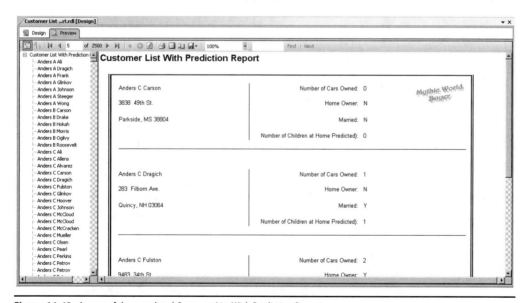

Figure 16-42 *A page of the completed Customer List With Prediction Report*

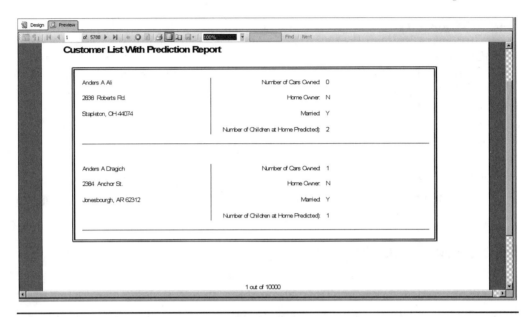

Figure 16-43 *A page from the Customer List With Prediction Report print preview*

Learn By Doing—Creating a Chart Report

Features Highlighted

▶ Creating a chart report item

▶ Working with report parameters

▶ Using a subreport

Business Need The Maximum Miniatures production department would like a line graph showing the inventory levels of each product type at the end of each month for a selected year. The production department wants to select that year from a drop-down list showing which years have data available. In addition, they would like to see the number of each product type manufactured on each machine for the same year.

NOTE

This report requires the stp_InventoryByTypeByMonth stored procedure. Download the Create InventoryByTypeByMonth Stored Proc.sql file from this book's website and execute this script in a Query window for the MaxMinManufacturingDB relational database.

Steps

1. Open the Business Intelligence Development Studio, if it is not already open.

2. Open the MaxMinReports project, if it is not already open.

3. Close the Report Design tab containing the Customer List With Prediction Report, if it is open.

4. Right-click the Reports folder in the Solution Explorer window and select Add | New Item. The Add New Item dialog box appears.

5. Select Report in the Templates area. Enter **Inventory Levels By Month Report** for Name.

6. Click Add. The Report Design tab appears.

7. In the Report Data window, select New | Data Source from the toolbar. The Data Source Properties dialog box appears.

8. Enter **MaxMinManufacturingDM** for Name.

9. Select the Use shared data source reference option.

10. Select the MaxMinManufacturingDM shared data source from the drop-down list.

11. Click OK to exit the Data Source Properties dialog box.

12. Right-click the MaxMinManufacturingDM data source you just created in the Report Data window and select Add Dataset from the context menu. The Dataset Properties dialog box appears.

13. Enter **InventoryLevels** for Name.

14. Under Query type, select the Stored Procedure option.

15. From the Select or enter stored procedure name drop-down list, select stp_InventoryByTypeByMonth.

16. Click OK. The Report Designer determines that a parameter called @Year is required by the stored procedure and prompts for it. This is necessary to determine the structure of the stored procedure's output. It also creates a report parameter to correspond to the stored procedure parameter. You are asked to supply a value for the @Year parameter. Enter **2008** and click OK.

17. The business goals state that the user should select a year from a drop-down list. To do this, we need a dataset that can serve to populate this drop-down list. We create that dataset now. Right-click the MaxMinManufacturingDM data source in the Report Data window and select Add Dataset from the context menu. The Dataset Properties dialog box appears.

18. Enter **YearList** for Name.

19. Enter the following for Query:

```
SELECT DISTINCT YEAR (DateOfInventory) AS Year FROM InventoryFact
ORDER BY YEAR(DateOfInventory) DESC
```

This query puts the most recent year at the top of the list. This is probably the year selected most often by the users.

20. Click OK to exit the Dataset Properties dialog box.

21. In the Report Data window, expand the Parameters folder.

22. Right-click the Year parameter entry and select Parameter Properties from the context menu. The Report Parameters Properties dialog box appears.

23. The Year report parameter was created to match the @Year stored procedure parameter. We can provide a more user-friendly prompt and set up the drop-down list for selecting a year. Enter **Select a Year:** for Prompt, as shown in Figure 16-44.

24. Select the Available Values page of the dialog box.

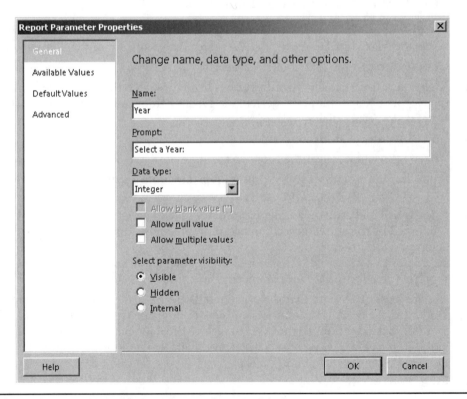

Figure 16-44 *The General Page of the Report Parameter Properties dialog box*

25. Select the Get values from a query option.

26. Select the YearList dataset from the Dataset drop-down list.

27. Select Year from the Value field drop-down list. This is the value passed to the report parameter when an item is selected from the drop-down list.

28. Select Year from the Label field drop-down list. This determines what is displayed in the drop-down list for the user. This page of the dialog box is shown in Figure 16-45.

29. Select the Default Values page of the dialog box. Here we can create a default value for this parameter. We will use the same dataset. The default will be the value in the first record in the dataset.

30. Select the Get values from a query option.

31. Select the YearList dataset from the Dataset drop-down list.

32. Select Year from the Value field drop-down list. This page of the Report Parameter Properties dialog box appears as shown in Figure 16-46.

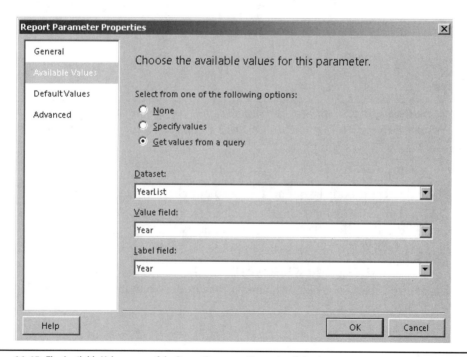

Figure 16-45 *The Available Values page of the Report Parameter Properties dialog box*

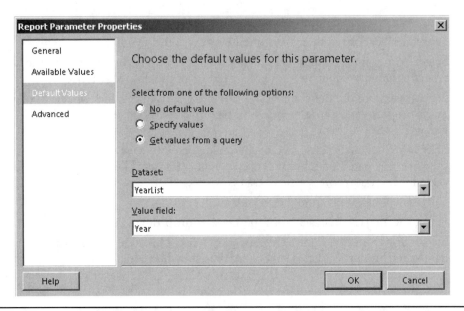

Figure 16-46 *The Default Values Page of the Report Parameter Properties dialog box*

NOTE

In addition to creating a drop-down list and a default value from a dataset, we can create a drop-down list and a default value from a set of hard-coded values. This is done with the Specify values options on the Report Parameter Properties dialog box pages.

33. Click OK to exit the Report Parameter Properties dialog box.
34. Make the report body layout area large so our chart will be easy to read.
35. Drag a chart data region from the Toolbox and drop it on the report body layout area. The Select Chart Type dialog box appears.
36. Select the 3-D Line chart, as shown in Figure 16-47.
37. Click OK to exit the Select Chart Type dialog box.
38. Expand the chart so it takes up almost the entire layout area. Charts look better when they are bigger.

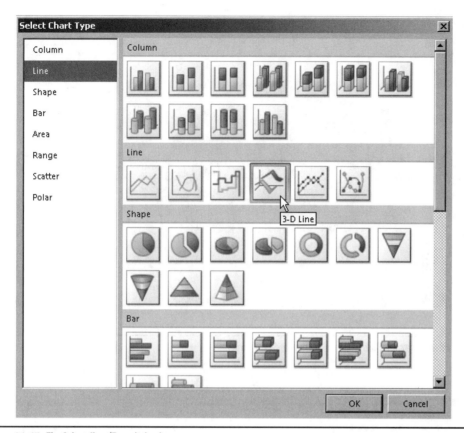

Figure 16-47 *The Select Chart Type dialog box*

39. Click the chart. This displays three drag-and-drop targets, as shown in Figure 16-48. If these drag-and-drop targets are not visible, click the chart again and they will appear.

40. Drag the InventoryLevel field from the Report Data window and drop it on the Drop data fields here target. This is the value to be charted.

41. Drag the ProductTypeName field and drop it on the Drop series fields here target. This creates the series of lines or bars on the chart.

42. As an alternative to dragging-and-dropping, we can select fields from the field selector. Hover your mouse cursor over the Drop category fields here target. A small icon appears in the upper-right corner of the target area. Click this icon and a list of fields appears. This is shown in Figure 16-49.

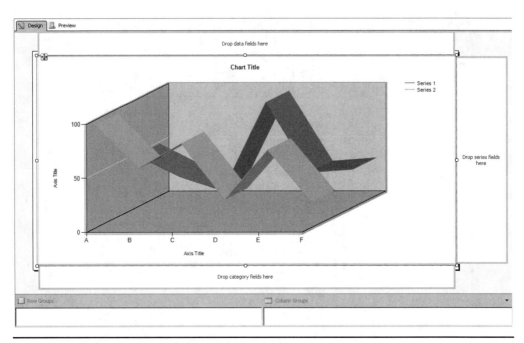

Figure 16-48 *The chart data region with drag-and-drop targets*

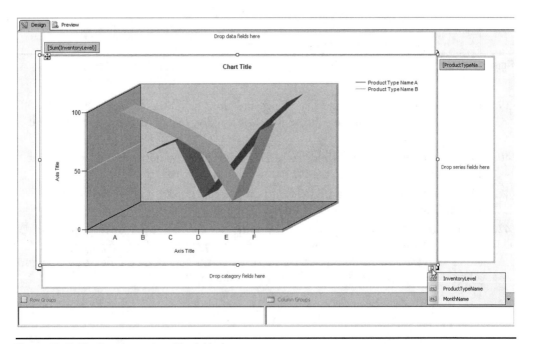

Figure 16-49 *The Chart data region with a field selector*

43. Select the MonthName field from this list. This field will create the items on the *X* axis.

44. Select the Preview tab. The report appears as shown in Figure 16-50. The report did not wait for a parameter value to be selected. Instead, it rendered the report using the default value of 2008. Select 2007 from the Select a Year drop-down list and click View Report. The chart for the year 2007 is displayed.

45. Let's modify our chart a bit. Select the Design tab.

46. Double-click the Chart Title. Replace the current title with **Inventory Levels By Month** and press ENTER.

47. Right-click the chart title and select Title Properties from the context menu. The Chart Title Properties dialog appears.

48. Select the Font page of the dialog box.

49. Set Size to 16pt, and then click OK to exit the Chart Title Properties dialog box.

50. Right-click one of the sample data lines, as shown in Figure 16-51.

51. Select Series Properties from the context menu. The Series Properties dialog box appears.

52. Select the Markers page of the dialog box.

53. Select Circle from the Marker type drop-down list.

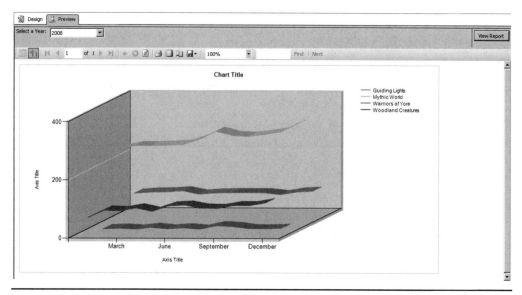

Figure 16-50 *The first version of the Inventory Levels By Month Report*

Figure 16-51 *Modifying the series properties*

54. Change Marker size to **10pt**. The Markers page of the Series Properties dialog box appears as shown in Figure 16-52.

55. Click OK to exit the Series Properties dialog box.

56. Double-click the Axis Title for the *X* axis.

57. Replace the current title with **Months** and press ENTER.

58. Right-click this title and select Axis Title Properties from the context menu. The Axis Title Properties dialog box appears.

59. Select the Font page of the dialog box.

60. Set Size to 12pt and check the Bold check box. Click OK to exit the Axis Title Properties dialog box.

61. Double-click the Axis Title for the *Y* axis.

62. Replace the current title with **Sales ($)** and press ENTER.

63. Right-click this title and select Axis Title Properties from the context menu. The Axis Title Properties dialog box appears.

64. Select the Font page of the dialog box.

65. Set Size to 12pt and check the Bold check box. Click OK to exit the Axis Title Properties dialog box.

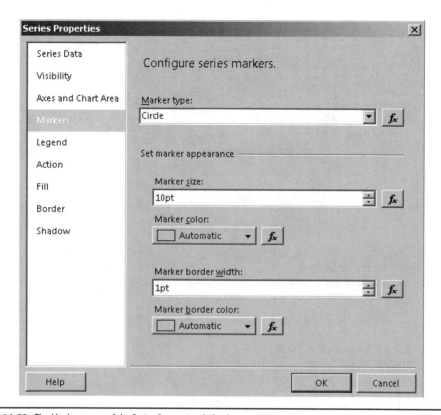

Figure 16-52 *The Markers page of the Series Properties dialog box*

66. Right-click the *Y* axis and select Axis Properties from the context menu. The Value Axis Properties dialog box appears.

67. Select the Number page of the dialog box.

68. Select Custom from the Category list.

69. Enter **#,0K** for Custom format, as shown in Figure 16-53. The stored procedure divides the sales values by 1,000, so our graph scale should read thousands of dollars, thus the K on the end.

70. Click OK to exit the Value Axis Properties dialog box.

71. Right-click the chart legend in the upper-right corner of the chart and select Legend Properties from the context menu. The Legend Properties dialog box appears.

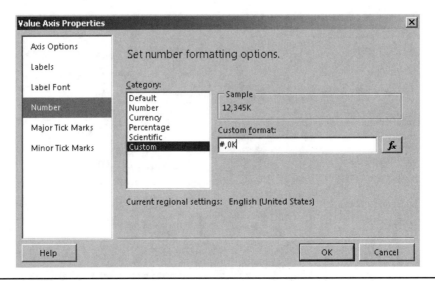

Figure 16-53 *The custom format for the Y axis labels*

72. Move the legend to the center bottom of the chart by selecting the center-bottom option button, as shown in Figure 16-54.

73. Click OK to exit the Legend Properties dialog box.

74. Right-click anywhere in the background of the charting area (the gray area of the chart). Select Chart Area Properties from the context menu. The Chart Area Properties dialog box appears.

75. Change the Rotation to **10**.

76. Change Inclination to **15**. The 3D Options tab appears as shown in Figure 16-55.

77. Click OK to exit the Chart Area Properties dialog box.

78. Select the Preview tab. The chart appears as shown in Figure 16-56.

79. Select the Design tab. The business needs stated we need to include the content of the Manufacturing By Machine Report at the bottom of this report. Instead of duplicating this report design in our current report, we can use the subreport report item to place one entire report inside another.

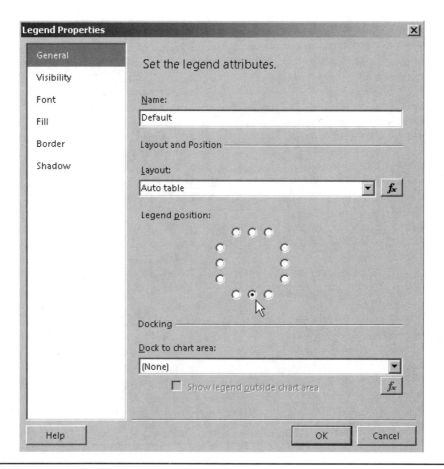

Figure 16-54 *Positioning the chart legend*

80. Lengthen the report body so there is room below the chart.

81. Place a subreport report item in the report body below the chart. Drag the subreport larger so it nearly fills the space.

82. Right-click the subreport and select Subreport Properties from the context menu. The Subreport Properties dialog box appears.

83. The Use this report as a subreport drop-down list enables us to select another report from this report project that should appear inside the report we are editing. Select Manufacturing By Machine Report from this drop-down list. The General page of the Subreport Properties dialog box appears, as shown in Figure 16-57.

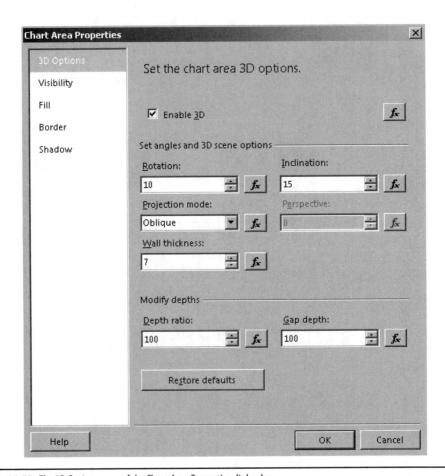

Figure 16-55 *The 3D Options page of the Chart Area Properties dialog box*

NOTE

There is nothing special about a particular report that allows it to be used as a subreport. Any report in the project can be placed inside another report using the subreport report item.

84. Select the Parameters page of the dialog box.

85. Click Add.

86. View the content of the drop-down list in the Name column. This list includes all of the report parameters defined in the report selected as the subreport. In this case, the Manufacturing By Machine Report we selected has only one report parameter, namely Year. Select Year from the drop-down list.

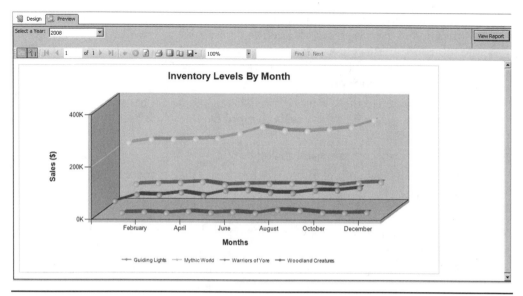

Figure 16-56 *The completed chart in the Inventory Levels By Month Report*

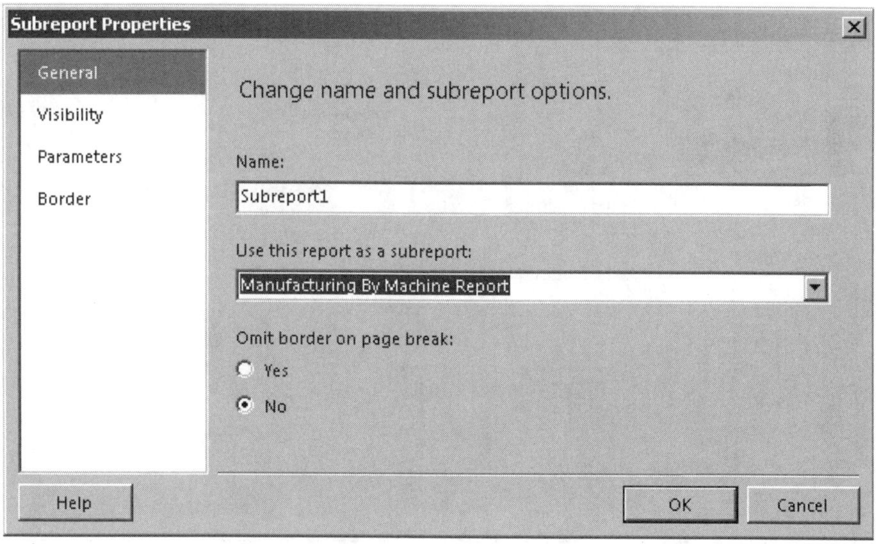

Figure 16-57 *The General page of the Subreport Properties dialog box*

87. We need to pass values to the parameters in the subreport so it has enough information to execute. Here, we need to pass a value to the Year parameter in the subreport. In this report, we want to pass the Year report parameter in the Inventory Levels By Month Report to the subreport. Click the *fx* button. The Expression dialog box appears.

88. Select Parameters in the Category list. A list of the report parameters defined in this report is shown in the Values column. Double-click Year to add it to the expression.

89. Click OK to exit the Expression dialog box.

90. The Parameters page of the Subreport Properties dialog box appears as shown in Figure 16-58.

91. Click OK to exit the Subreport Properties dialog box.

92. The subreport report item appears in the report layout, as shown in Figure 16-59.

93. Click the Preview tab. The report appears as shown in Figure 16-60.

94. Select 2007 from the Select a Year drop-down list and click View Report. Notice the values in the subreport change to 2007 values as well.

95. Click the Save All button on the toolbar.

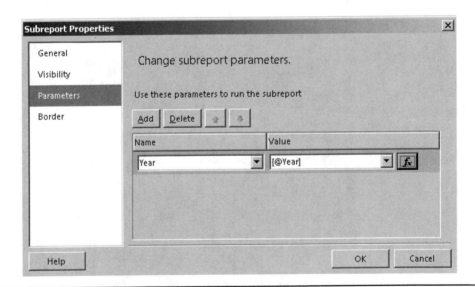

Figure 16-58 *The Parameters page of the Subreport Properties dialog box*

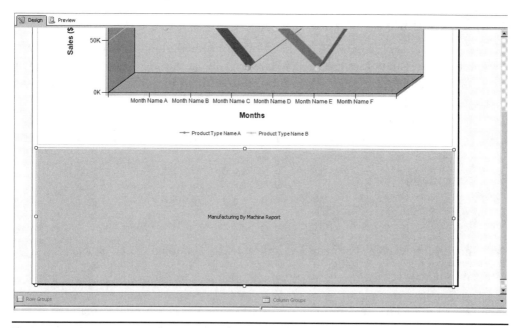

Figure 16-59 *The Inventory Levels By Month Report layout with a subreport*

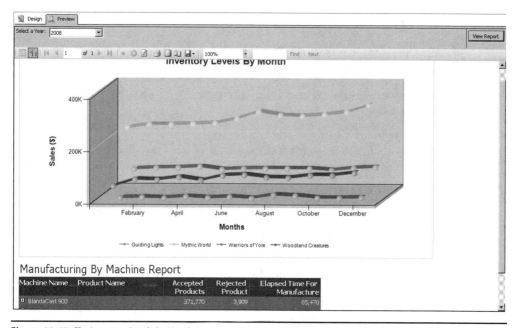

Figure 16-60 *The Inventory Levels By Month Report preview with a subreport*

The Gauge Data Region

The *gauge report item* is a data region that functions something like the chart. It creates a graphical representation of report data. However, where the chart can present multiple pieces of information, the gauge represents one or perhaps two data items. Also, like the chart, you cannot place other report items inside a gauge item.

Learn By Doing—Using the Gauge to Create a Dashboard Report

Features Highlighted

▶ Creating a gauge report item

▶ Parameterizing an MDX query

▶ Incorporating a Key Performance Indicator (KPI) into an MDX query

▶ Nesting data regions

Business Need   The vice president of manufacturing at Maximum Miniatures would like to have a quick way to monitor the percentage of each product subtype that is rejected for a given month. The percentage should be represented graphically and should include a color code to indicate how the percentage is doing against the goal.

Steps

1. Open the Business Intelligence Development Studio, if it is not already open.
2. Open the MaxMinReports project, if it is not already open.
3. Close the Report Design tab containing the Inventory Levels By Month Report, if it is open.
4. Right-click the Shared Data Sources folder in the Solution Explorer window and select Add New Data Source from the context menu. The Shared Data Source Properties dialog box appears.
5. Enter **MaxMinManufacturingDMCube** for Name.
6. Select Microsoft SQL Server Analysis Services from the Type drop-down list.
7. Click Edit. The Connection Properties dialog box appears.
8. Enter the name of the Analysis Services server hosting the Max Min Manufacturing DM OLAP cube for Server Name.
9. From the Select or enter a database name drop-down list, select MaxMinManufacturingDM.

10. Click OK to exit the Connection Properties dialog box. Click OK to exit the Shared Data Source Properties dialog box. The shared data source is created.

11. Right-click the Reports folder in the Solution Explorer window and select Add | New Item. The Add New Item dialog box appears.

12. Select Report in the Templates area. Enter **Percent Rejected Dashboard Report** for Name.

13. Click Add. The Report Design tab appears.

14. Drag a table template from the Toolbox and drop it on the report body layout area. The Data Source Properties dialog box appears.

15. Enter **MaxMinManufacturingDMCube** for Name.

16. Select the Use shared data source reference option.

17. Select MaxMinManufacturingDMCube from the drop-down list.

18. Click Next. The MDX Query Designer window appears.

19. In the Metadata area, expand the Dim Product dimension entry.

20. Expand the Product Hierarchy entry.

21. Drag the Product Type hierarchy level and drop it in the query area.

22. Drag the Product Subtype hierarchy level and drop it in the query area as well.

23. In the Metadata area, expand the KPIs entry.

24. Expand the Percent Rejected KPI.

25. Select Value and drop it in the query area.

26. Select Status and drop it in the query area.

27. At the top of the Query Designer window, click the cell in the Dimension column to activate the drop-down list.

28. Select Dim Time from this drop-down list.

29. Activate the drop-down list in the Hierarchy column and select Date Hierarchy.

30. Activate the drop-down list in the Operator column and select Equal.

31. Activate the drop-down window in the Filter Expression column.

32. Expand the All entry, followed by the 2008 entry, and the 2008Q4 entry.

33. Check the entry for 200810 and click OK.

34. A Parameters column appears to the right. (You may need to expand the Query Designer window or scroll right to see the Parameters column.) Check the check box in the Parameters column. The Query Designer window appears as shown in Figure 16-61.

35. Click Finish to exit the Query Designer window. The tablix appears in the report body.

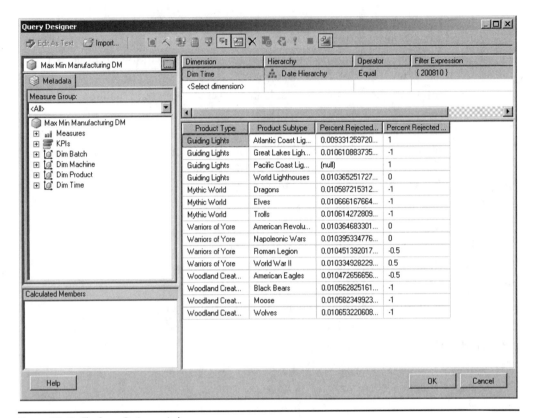

Figure 16-61 *The Query Designer window*

36. Click the tablix so the gray row and column handles are visible. Click the gray column handle above the middle column and hold down the mouse button.

37. Drag the mouse pointer over the column handle above the right column. Both columns should be selected.

38. Right-click either of the selected column handles and select Delete Columns from the context menu.

39. Right-click the row handle for the header row and select Delete Rows from the context menu.

40. Click the gray square in the upper-left corner to select the tablix. Set the following properties in the Properties window:

Property	Value
Size: Width	2in
Size: Height	1.5in

41. In the Row Groups area, click the drop-down arrow for the Details group. Select Group Properties from the menu. The Group Properties dialog box appears.
42. Click the Add button to add a grouping expression to the details group.
43. Select [Product_Type] from the Group on drop-down list. The detail level of this tablix will now actually be a grouping of records based on product type.
44. Click OK to exit the Group Properties dialog box.
45. Drag a matrix template from the Toolbox and drop it on the existing tablix. A new tablix is created.
46. Drag the Product_Type field from the Report Data window and drop it in the Rows cell.
47. Set the following properties in the Properties Window:

Property	Value
Font: FontWeight	Bold
Size: Width	0.25in
WritingMode	Vertical

48. Click the upper-left cell and press DELETE to remove the heading in this cell.
49. Drag the Product_Subtype field from the Report Data window and drop it in the Columns cell.
50. Set the following property in the Properties window:

Property	Value
Size: Width	1.75in

51. Right-click the row handle for the top row and select Delete Rows from the context menu. The Delete Rows dialog box appears.
52. Select the Delete rows only option and click OK. This will delete the row but leave the column grouping on product subtype. The report layout appears as shown in Figure 16-62.
53. Drag a gauge report item from the Toolbox and drop it in the large empty cell. The Select Gauge Type dialog box appears.
54. Select the 180 Degrees North Radial gauge type, as shown in Figure 16-63.
55. Click OK to exit the Select Gauge Type dialog box.
56. Click the gauge to activate the Drop data fields here area.
57. Hover the mouse pointer over the RadialPointer1 entry. A field selector appears.

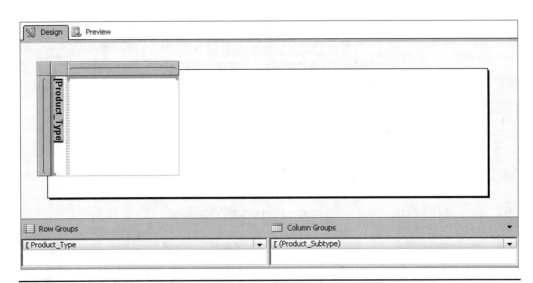

Figure 16-62 *The Percent Rejected Dashboard Report layout in progress*

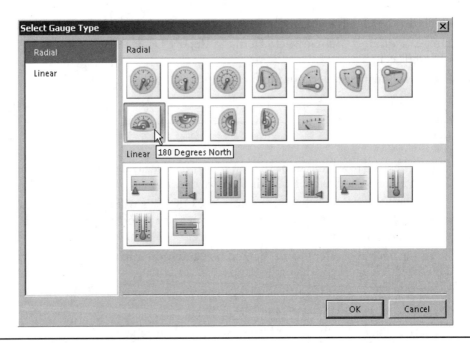

Figure 16-63 *The Select Gauge Type dialog box*

58. Click the field selector, and then click the Percent_Rejected_Value field, as shown in Figure 16-64.

59. Click the range on the gauge to select it. Right-click the range and select Range Properties, as shown in Figure 16-65. The Radial Scale Range Properties dialog box appears.

60. Set the following properties on the General page of the dialog box:

Property	Value
Start range at scale value	0.009
End range at scale value	0.011
Placement relative to scale	Cross
Distance from scale	0
End width	15

61. Select the Fill page of the dialog box.

62. Select the Solid option.

63. Click the *fx* button. The Expression dialog box appears.

64. Enter the following expression:

```
=Switch(Fields!Percent_Rejected_Status_.Value = 1, "GreenYellow",
        Fields!Percent_Rejected_Status_.Value = 0.5, "DarkKhaki",
        Fields!Percent_Rejected_Status_.Value = 0, "PaleGoldenrod",
        Fields!Percent_Rejected_Status_.Value = -0.5, "DarkSalmon",
        Fields!Percent_Rejected_Status_.Value = -1, "IndianRed")
```

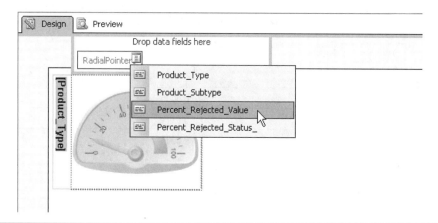

Figure 16-64 *Selecting the field for the gauge pointer*

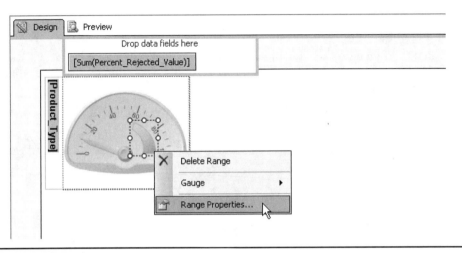

Figure 16-65 *Selecting the gauge range*

NOTE

This expression causes the range to change color relative to the status of the Percent Rejected KPI. Recall, when the KPI status value is 1, it is excellent. When the KPI status value is 0, it is so-so. When the KPI status value is -1, it is bad. The color scale reflects these statuses.

65. Click OK to exit the Expression dialog box. Click OK to exit the Radial Scale Range Properties dialog box.

66. Click the scale on the gauge to select it. Right-click the scale and select Scale Properties from the context menu. The Radial Scale Properties dialog box appears.

67. Set the following properties on the General page of the dialog box:

Property	Value
Minimum	0.009
Maximum	0.011
Interval	0.0005

68. Select the Number page of the dialog box.

69. Select Percentage from the Category list.

70. Click OK to exit the Radial Scale Properties dialog box.

71. Right-click just above the gauge and select Add Label from the context menu. A label is added to the gauge.

72. Right-click the label and select Label Properties from the context menu.

73. Click the top *fx* button next to the Text entry area. The Expression dialog box appears.
74. Select Fields (DataSet1) in the Category area.
75. Double-click the Product_Subtype entry in the Values area.
76. Click OK to exit the Expression dialog box.
77. Set the following properties on the General page of the Label Properties dialog box:

Property	Value
Text alignment	Center
Top	3
Left	3
Width	100
Height	9

78. Select the Font page of the dialog box.
79. Check the Bold check box.
80. Click OK to exit the Label Properties dialog box. The report layout should appear as shown in Figure 16-66.
81. Click the Preview tab. The report preview is shown in Figure 16-67.
82. Click the Save All button on the toolbar.

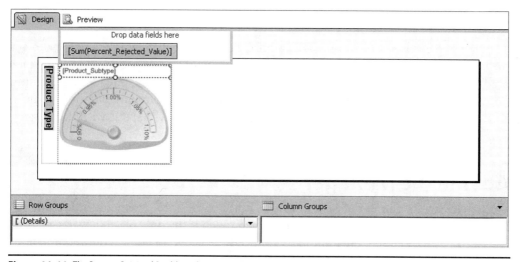

Figure 16-66 *The Percent Rejected Dashboard Report layout—final version*

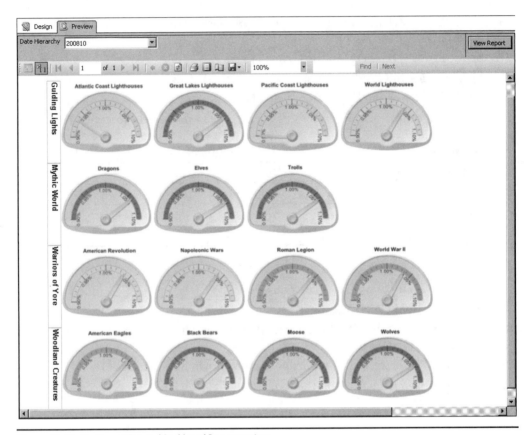

Figure 16-67 *The Percent Rejected Dashboard Report preview*

In the Percent Rejected Dashboard Report, we use three different data regions to get the job done. The first tablix, created from the table template, provides one row for each product type. The second tablix, created from the matrix template, provides one column for each product subtype. Finally, the gauge provides a graphical representation of the KPI, showing the KPI value with the gauge needle and the KPI status with the gauge range color.

Get Me the Manager

We have created a number of nice reports to fulfill business requirements at Maximum Miniatures. However, these reports aren't worth much if the only place they can be run is inside our development environment. We need to be able to publish our reports in a secure, yet accessible environment. We explore that environment in the next chapter.

Chapter 17

Falling into Place—Managing Reporting Services Reports

In This Chapter

▶ **Report Manager**

▶ **Managing Reports on the Report Server**

▶ **Ad Hoc Reporting**

▶ **Putting It All Together**

A place for everything and everything in its place.
          —From *The Book of Household Management* by Isabella Mary Beeton

I n the previous section, we learned how to create wonderful reports from our relational, online analytical processing (OLAP), and data mining data. Creating the report, however, is only half the battle. We need to place these reports where they can be put to use and, once they are there, we need to manage them.

In Chapter 16, we discussed the structure of Reporting Services, including the report server. We saw that the report server provides a user interface for both viewing reports and managing the server. This is the Report Manager.

Report Manager

First, we need to know how to deploy our report to the report server. This can be done from the Business Intelligence Development Studio or Visual Studio 2008. It can also be done from the Report Manager application.

Once on the report server, we can organize our reports to assist users in finding what they need. We can set up security to control access to the reports. We can also define caching schemes to make the most efficient use of the computing resources we have available.

Folders

Before we deploy reports to the report server, we need to have an understanding of the way the report server organizes reports in the Report Catalog. In the *Report Catalog,* reports are arranged into a system of folders similar to the Windows file system. Folders can contain reports, supporting files (such as external images and shared data sources), and even other folders. The easiest way to create, view, and maintain these folders is through the Report Manager.

Although the Report Catalog folders look and act like Windows file system folders, they are not actual file system folders. You cannot find them anywhere in the file system on the computer running the report server. *Report Catalog folders* are screen representations of records in the Report Catalog database.

The Report Manager

The *Report Manager* application provides a straightforward method for creating and navigating folders in the Report Catalog. When we initially install Reporting Services, the Home folder is created by default. This is the only folder that exists at first.

By default, the Report Manager site is installed in the default website on the server. It is located in a virtual directory called Reports. Therefore, the default URL for the Report Manager is as follows, where *ComputerName* is the name of the computer hosting Reporting Services.

```
http://ComputerName/reports
```

No matter how we get there, the Report Manager appears similar to Figure 17-1.

NOTE

Figure 17-1 shows the Report Manager as it appears for a user with content manager privileges. If you do not see the New Folder, New Data Source, Upload File, and Report Builder buttons on the toolbar on the Contents tab, you do not have content manager privileges and will be unable to complete the exercises in this section of the chapter. If possible, log out and then log in with a Windows login that has local administration privileges on the computer running the report server.

To use the Report Manager, we must be using Microsoft Internet Explorer 7.0, Internet Explorer 6.0 with Service Pack 1 (SP1), or Internet Explorer 5.5 with Service Pack 2 (SP2). For all of these, scripting must be enabled.

Deploying Reports Using the Report Designer

The most common method of moving reports to the report server is by using the Report Designer. Once we are satisfied with a report, we can make it available to our users without leaving the development environment. This capability to create, preview, and deploy a report from a single authoring tool is a real plus.

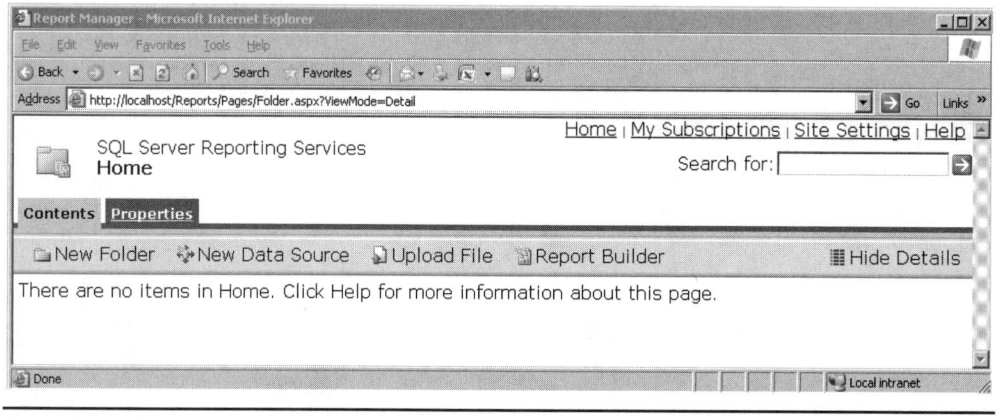

Figure 17-1   *The Report Manager with no folders defined*

NOTE

As we have done in other chapters, we are not going to do a specific Learn By Doing exercise here. Instead, you are encouraged to follow along and try each of these activities.

Deploying Reports in the MaxMinReports Project Using the Report Designer

Let's try deploying the reports in our report project:

1. Start the Business Intelligence Development Studio and open the MaxMinReports project, if it is not already open.
2. Select Project | MaxMinReports Properties from the Main menu. The MaxMinReports Property Pages dialog box appears.
3. Enter **MaxMinReports/DataSources** for TargetDataSourceFolder.
4. Enter **MaxMinReports/BIStudioDeploy** for TargetReportFolder.
5. Type **http://ComputerName/ReportServer** for TargetServerURL, where ComputerName is the name of the computer where the report server is installed. If you are using a secure connection, you should replace http: with https:. The MaxMinReports Property Pages dialog box appears, as shown in Figure 17-2.

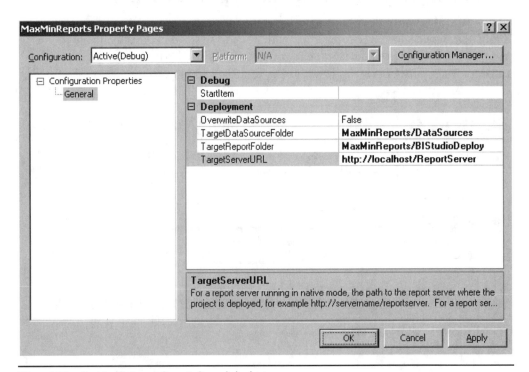

Figure 17-2 *The MaxMinReports Property Pages dialog box*

6. Click OK to exit the MaxMinReports Property Pages dialog box.

7. Right-click the MaxMinReports project entry in the Solution Explorer window and select Deploy from the context menu.

8. The Report Designer builds all the reports in the project and then deploys all the reports, along with their supporting files, to the report server. (During the build process, the Report Designer checks each report for any errors that would prevent it from executing properly on the report server.) The results of the build and deploy are shown in the Output window.

9. Open the Report Manager in your browser. Click the MaxMinReports folder to view its content. Click the BIStudioDeploy folder to view its content. All the items in the MaxMinReports project—six reports and three shared data sources—were deployed.

10. Click the Wholesale Sales By Month report. You see the Hypertext Markup Language (HTML) version of the report.

NOTE

You can also deploy the contents of a project by selecting Build | Deploy {Project Name} from the Main menu.

Deploying a Single Report

In Step 7, you used the project's context menu to deploy all the items in the project. Alternatively, you could have right-clicked a report and selected Deploy from the report's context menu. This would have deployed only this report, not the entire project.

On some occasions, you might want to deploy a single report, rather than the entire project. At times, one report is going to be completed and ready for deployment, while the other reports in the project are still under construction. At other times, one report is revised after the entire project has already been deployed. In these situations, it is only necessary to redeploy the single revised report.

Uploading Reports Using Report Manager

Another common method of moving a report to the report server is by using the Report Manager. This is known as *uploading* the report. Deploying reports from the Report Designer can be thought of as pushing the reports from the development environment to the report server, whereas uploading reports from the Report Manager can be thought of as pulling the reports from the development environment to the report server.

You may need to use the Report Manager upload in situations where your report authors do not have rights to deploy reports on the report server. The report authors create their reports and test them within the Report Designer. When a report is completed, the report author can place the Report Definition Language (RDL) file for the report in a shared directory or send it as an e-mail attachment to the report server administrator. The report server administrator can upload the RDL file to a quality assurance report server and test the report for clarity, accuracy, and proper use of database resources. Once the report has passed this review, the report server administrator can upload the report to the production report server.

Uploading Reports in the MaxMinReports Project Using the Report Manager

Let's try uploading the Manufacturing By Machine Report to a different folder:

1. Open the Report Manager in your browser. Click the MaxMinReports folder to view its content.
2. Click New Folder on the toolbar of the Contents tab.
3. Enter **RMUpload** for Name.
4. Enter **Uploaded Reports** for Description.
5. Click OK to create the new folder.
6. Select the new folder to view its contents.
7. Click the Upload File button on the toolbar on the Contents tab. The Upload File page appears, as shown in Figure 17-3.
8. Click Browse. The Choose File dialog box appears. Navigate to the folder where you created the MaxMinReports project.
9. Select the RDL file for the Manufacturing By Machine Report and click Open to exit the Choose File dialog box.

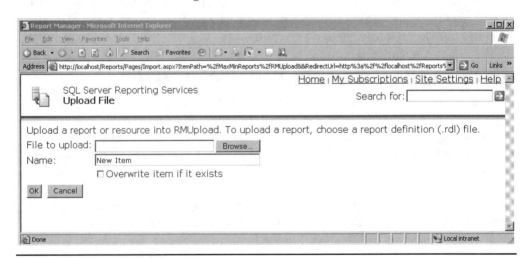

Figure 17-3   *The Upload File page*

10. Click OK to upload the file.

11. The Manufacturing By Machine Report has been uploaded to the RMUpload folder.

12. Click the Manufacturing By Machine Report to execute it. You see an error similar to the one in Figure 17-4. You received this because, unlike the deployment from the Report Designer, the upload in Report Manager did not bring the shared data source along with the report.

13. Click the link to the RMUpload folder at the top of the page.

Creating a Shared Data Source in the Report Manager

To get the Manufacturing By Machine Report functioning, you need to provide it with a shared data source. One way to do this is to create a new shared data source using the Report Manager. Follow these steps:

1. Click the New Data Source button on the toolbar on the Contents tab. The New Data Source page for a shared data source appears, as shown in Figure 17-5.

2. Type **MaxMinManufacturingDM** for Name.

3. Type **Connection to the MaxMinManufacturing Database** for Description.

4. Make sure Microsoft SQL Server is selected in Data Source Type. Other options here are OLE DB, Microsoft SQL Server Analysis Services, Oracle, ODBC, XML, SAP NetWeaver BI, and Hyperion Essbase.

5. Type **Data Source=(local); initial catalog=MaxMinManufacturingDM** for Connection String. If the MaxMinManufacturingDM database is not on the report server but is on a different computer, put the name of that computer in place of (local) in the connection string.

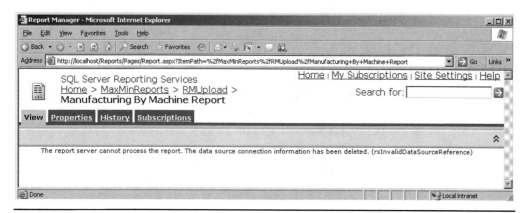

Figure 17-4   *The Reporting Services Error page*

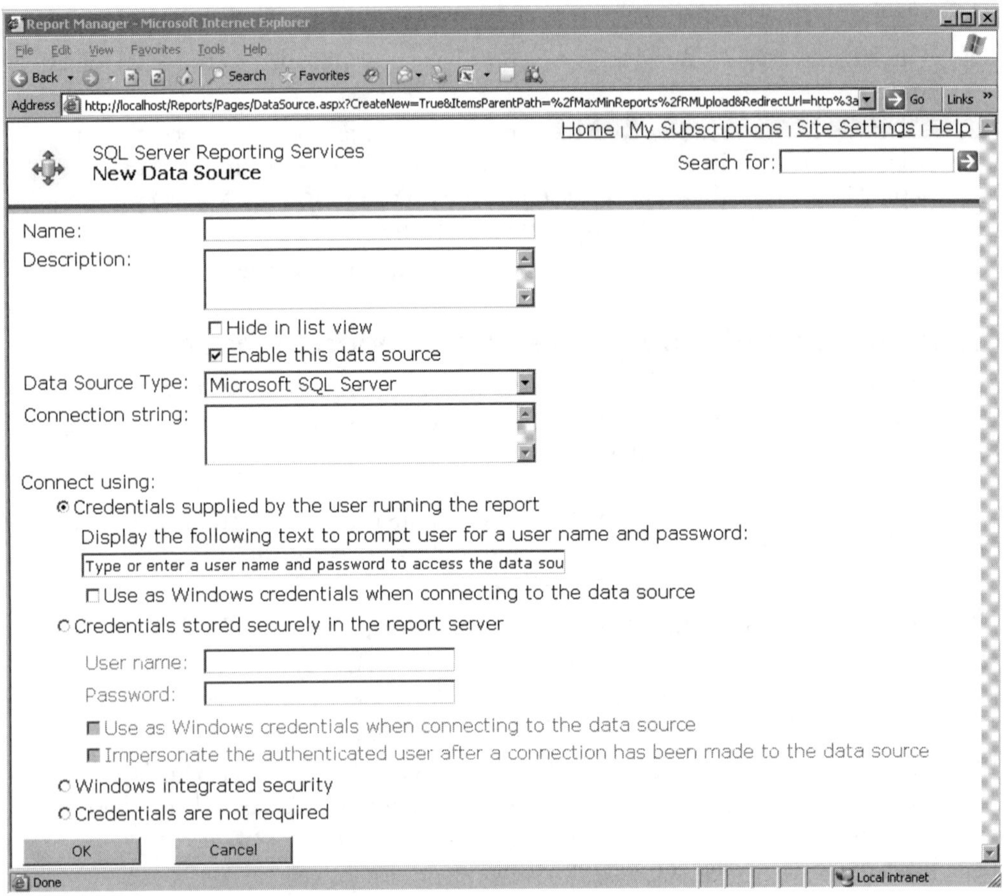

Figure 17-5   *The New Data Source page*

NOTE

Do not include the parentheses if you use a computer name in place of (local).

6. Select the Credentials stored securely in the report server option.

7. Enter a user name and password that has rights to access the MaxMinManufacturing data.

8. Check the box next to Use as Windows credentials when connecting to the data source.

9. Click OK to save the data source and return to the RMUpload folder.

10. Click the Manufacturing By Machine Report to execute it. You receive the same error message page because we have not yet told the report to use our new data source.

11. Select the Properties tab. The Properties page for the Manufacturing By Machine Report appears.

12. Click the Data Sources link on the left side of the screen. The Data Sources page for an individual report appears.

13. A shared data source should be selected. Click Browse. The Select a Shared Data Source page appears.

14. Expand each folder in the tree view under Location until you can see the MaxMinManufacturingDM shared data source in the RMUpload folder. Click the MaxMinManufacturingDM shared data source. The path to the MaxMinManufacturingDM shared data source is filled in Location. (You can also type this path into Location if you do not want to use the tree view.)

15. Click OK to exit the Select a Shared Data Source page.

16. Click Apply at the bottom of the page.

NOTE

It is easy to forget to click Apply when making changes to a report's data sources. If you do not click Apply, none of your changes are saved. This can lead to confusion, frustration, and wasted troubleshooting time. At least, that is what I have been told.

17. Select the View tab. Enter 2008 for Year and click View Report. The report now generates using the new shared data source.

18. Once the report has completed generating, click the RMUpload link at the top of the page.

Hiding an Item

The MaxMinManufacturingDM shared data source we just created can be seen when browsing through folders using the Report Manager. We may not want these types of items to be readily visible to the user. It makes more sense to have the shared data sources out of sight of the users. Fortunately, Report Manager provides a way to do just that:

1. Click the MaxMinManufacturingDM data source. The Data Source Edit page appears.

2. Check the Hide in List View check box.

3. Click Apply to save this change.

4. Click the RMUpload link at the top of the page.

The MaxMinManufacturingDM data source is no longer visible in the list view. You can use this same technique to hide reports you do not want to have generally available to users browsing through the folders.

If you do need to edit the MaxMinManufacturingDM data source, you can view it by using the detail view of the folder. Follow these steps:

1. Click the Show Details button on the toolbar on the Contents tab. The MaxMinManufacturingDM data source is now visible in this detail view, as shown in Figure 17-6. By default, the detail view is in alphabetical order by name.
2. Click the Type column heading. The detail view is now sorted by type in ascending order. (In an ascending sort by type, the reports are at the top of the list, with supporting items, such as shared data sources, at the bottom.) Note, the downward, black arrow is now next to the Type column heading on your screen.
3. Click the Type column heading again. The detail view is now sorted by type in descending order. Now the black arrow is pointing upward next to the column heading.

NOTE

The name of the sort order (ascending or descending) and the direction of the black arrow may seem opposite to one another. Remember this: In an ascending sort, you move from smaller values (A, B, C . . .) to larger values (. . . X, Y, Z). When you move through the list in the direction of the arrow, you also move from smaller values to larger values.

Uploading Other Items Using Report Manager

In addition to reports and shared data sources, other items can be uploaded to report server folders. External images needed as part of the reports can be uploaded, for example, as well as documentation and other supporting materials. Anything

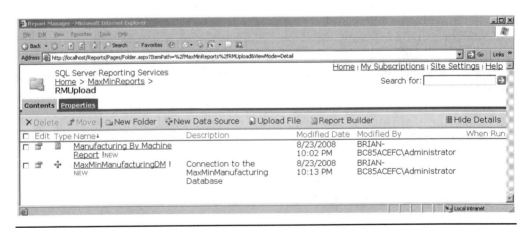

Figure 17-6 *RMUpload folder detail view*

that can be viewed in Internet Explorer—even Word documents and PowerPoint presentations—can be uploaded to the report server and accessed by the users.

Printing from Report Manager

No matter how convenient you make it for your users to access reports in a browser, and no matter how many interactive drilldown and drillthrough features you provide, your users always want to print their reports on paper. You can explain all the wonders of the multiple, cascading parameters you have created until you are blue in the face, but some users always need to touch and feel the numbers on paper. They need to be able to put something in a briefcase and take it home with them at night. It doesn't matter that they could receive up-to-date numbers through their virtual private network (VPN) at home. They want ink on paper.

Reporting Services provides several options for printing a report from Report Manager. Each provides some advantages and disadvantages for the user.

HTML Printing

These users could just click the Print button in their browser and get whatever type of printout HTML printing provides. As you are probably aware, HTML printing is not a good choice when formatting is important, as it usually is for reports. Lines of text can wrap in unusual ways or simply be cut off. A line of text at the bottom of the page can even be cut right in half, with the top half on one page and the bottom half on the next page.

Fortunately, the Report Manager provides a couple of alternatives to HTML printing.

Printing from a PDF Document or a TIFF File

A Portable Document Format (PDF) document or a Tagged Image File Format (TIFF) file does an excellent job of maintaining the report format when a report is printed. Therefore, when users want to have a high-quality report printout, they can export the report to a PDF document or a TIFF file. Once this is complete, they can view the exported report using the appropriate viewer: Adobe Acrobat Reader for the PDF document and the Windows Picture and Fax Viewer for a TIFF file. The report can then be printed using the viewer.

This process provides the user with a quality printout. However, not all users are comfortable saving a file to a local disk, finding that file and opening it in the appropriate viewer, and then printing the report. There is another printing alternative, which is even more straightforward.

Client-Side Printing

You may have noticed a button with a printer icon on the report toolbar. This button is for the client-side printing feature of Reporting Services. *Client-side printing* works through an ActiveX object downloaded to the user's computer. From then on, whenever the Client-Side Printing button is clicked, this ActiveX object provides the user interface and controls the printing.

The first time a user activates the client-side printing feature, they may be prompted with a security warning about the ActiveX download. After taking the appropriate precautions, such as making sure the ActiveX object is signed by Microsoft, the user should approve the download to enable client-side printing. Once the ActiveX control has been downloaded by this first use, it does not need to be downloaded again.

If a user has trouble downloading the ActiveX control, they may need to set the Report Manager as a trusted site in their browser. This is done on the Security tab of the Internet Options dialog box. The user should not lower their security setting for all sites in general to accomplish the ActiveX download.

Once downloaded, client-side printing enables users to set various report attributes. These include margins, page size, and even page orientation. Users can also preview a report before putting it on paper.

Managing Reports on the Report Server

Now that we have moved some of our reports to the report server, you may be thinking our job is about done, but it is just beginning. Now we need to manage the reports and supporting materials to ensure the reports can be utilized properly by our users.

Two of the biggest concerns when it comes to managing reports are security and performance. Reports containing sensitive data must be secured so they are only accessed by the appropriate people. Reports must return information to users in a reasonable amount of time, without putting undue stress on database resources. Fortunately, Reporting Services provides tools for managing both of these concerns. Security roles and item-level security give you extremely fine control over who has access to each report and resource. Caching, snapshots, and history let us control how and when reports are executed.

Security

In Reporting Services, security was designed with both flexibility and ease of management in mind. Flexibility is provided by the fact that individual access rights can be assigned to each folder and to each item within a folder. An *item* is either a report or a resource. We can specify exactly who has rights to each item and exactly what those rights are. Ease of management is provided by security inheritance, security roles, and integration with Windows security. We begin our discussion with the last entry in this list.

NOTE

Remember, although we are creating and maintaining these role assignments using the Report Manager, the security rights apply to Reporting Services as a whole. No matter how you access folders and items—through the Report Manager or through the web service—these security rights are enforced.

Integration with Windows Security

Reporting Services does not maintain its own list of users and passwords. Instead, it depends entirely on integration with Windows security. When a user accesses either the Report Manager application or the web service, that user must authenticate with the report server. In other words, the user must have a valid domain user name and password, or a local user name and password, to log on to the report server. Both the Report Manager application and the web service are set up requiring integrated Windows authentication to ensure this logon takes place.

NOTE

If it is impossible for each report user to have their own credentials on the report server, it is possible to create your own custom security. You can create a security scheme, such as forms-based security, to enable the users to authenticate and access reports. However, this is not a trivial process.

Once this logon occurs, Reporting Services utilizes the user name and the user's group memberships to determine what rights the user possesses. The user can access only those folders and items they have rights to. In Report Manager, users do not even see the folders they cannot browse and the reports they cannot run. There is no temptation for the user to try and figure out how to get into places they are not supposed to go because they do not even know these places exist.

Local Administrator Privileges

In most cases, rights must be explicitly assigned to folders and items. One exception to this rule, however, is local administrator privileges. Any user who is a member of the local administrators group on the computer hosting the report server has content manager rights to all folders and all items. These automatic rights cannot be modified or removed.

Let's look at the Security page:

1. Open the Report Manager in your browser and navigate to the Home folder.
2. Select the Properties tab. You see the Security page for the Home folder, as shown in Figure 17-7.

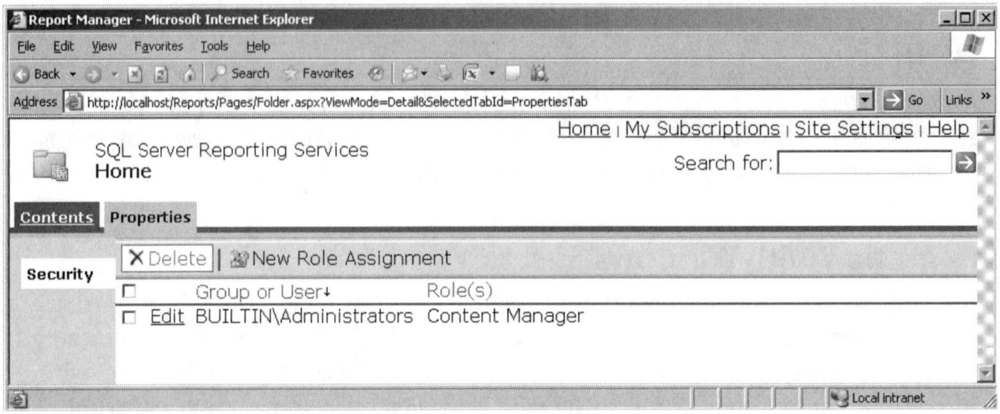

Figure 17-7   *The Security page for the Home folder*

The report server maintains a Security page for each item in the Report Catalog—every folder, every report, and every supporting item. The Security page lists all the role assignments for an item. Each *role assignment* is made up of two things: a Windows user or group and a security role. The rights associated with the security role are assigned to the Windows user or group.

Initially, one role assignment is on the Security page for each item. This entry assigns the Content Manager security role to the BUILTIN\Administrators group. This entry is a reminder that any user who is a member of the local administrators group has rights to manage the contents of this folder.

NOTE

You could delete the role assignment for BUILTIN\Administrators, and the members of the local administrators group would still have rights to manage the contents of this folder. These rights are hardwired into Reporting Services. The BUILTIN\Administrators assignment on the Security page is, in most cases, just a reminder of the rights held by anyone in the local administrators group.

Tasks and Rights

We can perform a number of tasks in Reporting Services. Each task has a corresponding right to perform that task. For example, we can view reports. Therefore, a corresponding right exists to view reports. The tasks within Reporting Services are shown in Table 17-1.

In addition to the tasks listed in Table 17-1 are system-wide tasks with associated rights. These system-wide tasks deal with the management and operation of Reporting Services as a whole. The system-wide tasks within Reporting Services are shown in Table 17-2.

Task	Description
Consume reports	Read report definitions.
Create linked reports	Create linked reports and publish them to a folder.
Manage all subscriptions	View, modify, and delete any subscription, regardless of who owns it.
Manage data sources	Create, modify, and delete shared data sources.
Manage folders	Create, view, and delete folders. View and modify folder properties.
Manage individual subscriptions	Create, view, modify, and delete your own subscriptions.
Manage models	Create, view, and delete models. Modify model properties.
Manage report history	Create, view, and delete report history snapshots. Modify report history properties.
Manage reports	Create, view, and delete reports. Modify report properties.
Manage resources	Create, modify, and delete resources. View and modify resource properties.
Set security for individual items	View and modify security settings for reports, folders, resources, and shared data sources.
View data sources	View shared data sources and their properties.
View folders	View folders and their properties.
View models	View models. Use models as report data sources. Query models for data.
View reports	View reports and linked reports, along with their report history snapshots and properties.
View resources	View resources and their properties.

Table 17-1   *Security Tasks Within Reporting Services*

Task	Description
Execute Report Definitions	Start execution of a report from a report definition without deploying it to the report server.
Generate events	Provide an application with the capability to generate events within the report server.
Manage jobs	View and cancel running report server jobs.
Manage Report Server properties	View and modify configuration properties for the report server.
Manage Report Server security	View and modify system-wide role assignments.
Manage roles	Create, view, modify, and delete role definitions.
Manage shared schedules	Create, view, modify, and delete shared schedules used for snapshots and subscriptions.
View Report Server properties	View properties that apply to the report server.
View shared schedules	View a shared schedule.

Table 17-2   *System-wide Security Tasks Within Reporting Services*

Roles

The rights to perform tasks are grouped together to create *roles*. Reporting Services includes several predefined roles to help us with security management. In addition, we can create our own custom roles, grouping together any combination of rights we like. The predefined roles and their corresponding rights are listed here.

The Browser Role   The *Browser* role is the basic role assigned to users who are going to view reports but who are not going to create folders or upload new reports. The Browser role has rights to perform the following tasks:

- ▶ Manage individual subscriptions
- ▶ View folders
- ▶ View models
- ▶ View reports
- ▶ View resources

The Publisher Role   The *Publisher* role is assigned to users who are going to create folders and upload reports. The Publisher role does not have rights to change security settings or manage subscriptions and report history. The Publisher role has rights to perform the following tasks:

- ▶ Create linked reports
- ▶ Manage data sources
- ▶ Manage folders
- ▶ Manage models
- ▶ Manage reports
- ▶ Manage resources

The My Reports Role   The *My Reports* role is designed to be used only with a special folder called the My Reports folder. Within this folder, the My Reports role gives the user rights to do everything except change security settings. The My Reports role has rights to perform the following tasks:

- ▶ Create linked reports
- ▶ Manage data sources
- ▶ Manage folders

- Manage individual subscriptions
- Manage report history
- Manage reports
- Manage resources
- View data source
- View folders
- View reports
- View resources

The Content Manager Role   The *Content Manager* role is assigned to users who are managing the folders, reports, and resources. All members of the Windows local administrators group on the computer hosting the report server are automatically members of the Content Manager role for all folders, reports, and resources. The Content Manager has rights to perform all tasks, excluding system-wide tasks.

The System User Role   The system-wide security tasks have two predefined roles. The *System User* role has rights to perform the following system-wide tasks:

- Execute Report Definitions
- View Report Server properties
- View shared schedules

The System Administrator Role   The *System Administrator* role provides the user with rights to complete any of the tasks necessary to manage the report server. All members of the Windows local administrators group on the computer hosting the report server are automatically members of the System Administrator role. This role has rights to perform the following system-wide tasks:

- Execute Report Definitions
- Manage jobs
- Manage Report Server properties
- Manage Report Server security
- Manage roles
- Manage shared schedules

Creating Role Assignments

Role assignments are created when a Windows user or a Windows group is assigned a role for a folder, a report, or a resource. Role assignments are created on the Security page for each item. These role assignments control what the user can see within a folder and what tasks the user can perform on the folder, report, or resource.

Let's try creating role assignments for some of our folders and reports.

NOTE

To complete the next set of activities, you need a user who has rights to log onto the report server but who is not a member of the local administrators group on that computer. You should know the password for this user so you can log on as that user and view the results of your security settings.

Creating a Role Assignment for a Folder   Let's try creating a new role assignment for the Home folder:

1. Open the Report Manager in your browser. You should be viewing the contents of the Home folder.

2. Select the Properties tab. You see the Security page for this folder.

3. Click New Role Assignment. The New Role Assignment page appears, as shown in Figure 17-8.

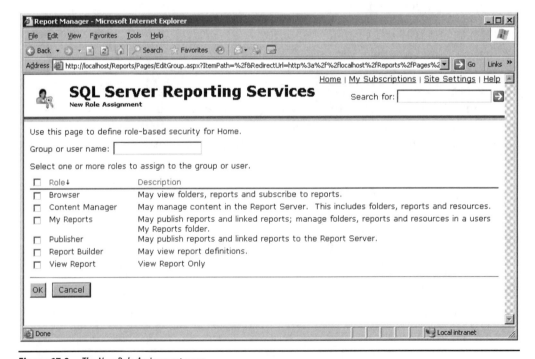

Figure 17-8   *The New Role Assignment page*

4. Type the name of a valid user for Group or User Name. If you are using a domain user or domain group, this must be in the format DomainName\UserName or DomainName\GroupName. If you are using a local user or local group, this must be in the format ComputerName\UserName or ComputerName\GroupName.

5. Check the check box for the Browser role.

6. Click OK to save your role assignment and return to the Security page. Reporting Services checks to ensure you entered a valid user or group for the role assignment. If this is not a valid user or group, you receive an error message and your role assignment is not saved.

NOTE

A user needs to have viewing rights at least in the Home folder to view other folders and navigate to them.

Inherited Role Assignments   By default, folders (other than the Home folder), reports, and resources inherit their role assignments from the folder that contains them. We can think of the nested folders as branches of a tree, with the reports and resources as the leaves. *Inherited security* means we can make security changes to one folder and have those changes take effect for all the branches and leaves further along the tree.

This makes managing security easy. We can maintain security for all the reports and resources within a folder simply by modifying the role assignments for the folder itself. We can maintain security for an entire branch of the tree structure by modifying the role assignments for the folder that forms the base of that branch.

The first time we make a role assignment for a folder, we first need to break the security inheritance that was in effect. A dialog box warns us that the inherited security structure will be broken. We need to confirm our decision to break inheritance before continuing with the role assignment.

Giving users only the rights they need is important. This prevents users from viewing data they should not see or from making modifications or deletions they should not be allowed to make. On the other hand, providing users with enough rights is important so their reports function properly.

Role Assignments Using Windows Groups

As mentioned previously, role assignments can be made to Windows users or to Windows groups. If we create our role assignments using Windows users, we need to create a new set of role assignments every time a new user needs to access Reporting Services. This can be extremely tedious if we have a complex set of role assignments for various folders, reports, and resources.

In most cases, creating role assignments using Windows groups is better. Then, as new users come along, we simply need to add them to the Windows group that has the appropriate rights in Reporting Services. This is much easier!

Linked Reports

In many cases, the security set up within Reporting Services restricts the folders a user can access. The sales department may be allowed to access one set of folders. The personnel department may be allowed to access another set of folders. The personnel department doesn't want to see sales reports and, certainly, some personnel reports should not be seen by everyone in the sales department.

This works well—a place for everything and everything in its place—until we come to the report that needs to be used by both the sales department and the personnel department. We could put a copy of the report in both places, but this gets to be a nightmare as new versions of reports need to be deployed to multiple locations on the report server. We could put the report in a third folder accessed by both the sales department and the personnel department, but that can make navigation in the Report Manager difficult and confusing.

Fortunately, Reporting Services provides a third alternative: the linked report. With a *linked report*, our report is deployed to one folder. It is then pointed to by links placed elsewhere within the Report Catalog, as shown in Figure 17-9. To the user, the links look just like a report. Because of these links, the report appears to be in many places. The sales department sees it in their folder. The personnel department sees it in their folder. The fact of the matter is the report is only deployed to one location, so it is easy to administer and maintain. Use the Create Linked Reports button on a report's General Properties page to create a linked report.

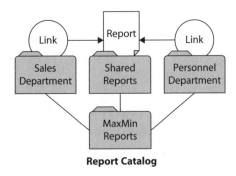

Report Catalog

Figure 17-9   *A linked report*

Report Caching

One of the best features of Reporting Services is that the data is requeried each time the report is executed. The user is not viewing information from a static web page that is weeks or months old. Reporting Services reports include data accurate up to the second the report was run.

This feature can also be the source of one of the drawbacks of Reporting Services. The user is required to wait for the data to be requeried each time a report is run. If our query or stored procedure runs quickly, this may not be a problem. However, even fairly quick queries can slow down a server if enough of them are running at the same time. Fortunately, Reporting Services has a solution to this problem. The solution is report caching.

With many reports, it is not essential to have up-to-the-second data. We may be reporting from a data source that is only updated once or twice a day. The business needs of our users may only require data that is accurate as of the end of the previous business period, perhaps a month or a quarter. In these types of situations, it does not make sense to have the data requeried every time a user requests a report. Report caching is the answer.

Report caching is an option that can be turned on individually for each report on the report server. When this option is turned on, the report server saves a copy, or *instance*, of the report in a temporary location the first time the report is executed. On subsequent executions, with the same parameter values chosen, the report server pulls the information necessary to render the report from the report cache, rather than requerying data from the database. Because these subsequent executions do not need to requery data, they are, in most cases, faster than the report execution without caching.

Cached Report Expiration

Once an instance of the report is stored in the report cache, it is assigned an expiration date and time. The expiration date and time can be calculated in one of two ways. The expiration date can be calculated based on a certain number of minutes after the creation of the cached instance. For example, the cached instance of the report exists for 30 minutes, and then it is deleted. Or, the expiration date can be determined by a set schedule. For example, the cached instance of the report is deleted at 2:00 A.M. every Sunday morning.

The first type of expiration calculation is appropriate for a report that requires a large amount of database resources and is run often but does not require up-to-the-second data. We can decrease the workload on the database server by fulfilling most of the requests for the report from the report cache. Every 30 minutes, we throw the cached report away. The next person who requests the report causes a new instance of the report, with updated data, to be placed in the report cache.

The second type of expiration calculation is appropriate for reports run against data that changes on a scheduled basis. Perhaps you have a report being run from your data mart. The data mart is updated from your transactional database each Sunday at 12:30 A.M. The data in the warehouse remains static in between these loads. The cached report is scheduled to expire right after the data load is completed. The next time the user requests the report after the expiration, a new instance of the report, with the updated data, is placed in the cache. This cached report contains up-to-date data until the next data load.

Cached Reports and Data Source Credentials

To create a cached instance of a report, the report must be using stored credentials. These can be credentials for either a Windows logon or a database logon, but they must be stored with the data source. If you think about this from a security standpoint, this is how it has to be.

Suppose for a minute that Reporting Services allowed a cached report to be created with Windows Integrated Security. The Windows credentials of the first person to run the report would be used to create a cached instance of the report. Subsequent users who request this report would receive this cached instance. However, this would mean the subsequent users are receiving data in the report created using the credentials from another user.

If the results of the database query or stored procedure that populates this report vary based on the rights of the database logon, we have the potential for a big problem. If the vice president (VP) of sales is the first person to run the report and create the cached instance, all subsequent users would receive information meant only for the VP! Conversely, if a sales representative is the first person to run the report and create the cached instance, when the VP comes along later and requests the report, he will not receive all the information he needs.

The same problem exists if the report prompts for credentials. The first person who runs the report and creates the cached instance is the one who supplies the credentials. Everyone who views the cached instance is essentially using someone else's logon to see this data.

The only way that caching works without creating the potential for a security problem is with credentials stored with the report. In this situation, the same credentials are used to access the database—whether it is the VP or a lowly sales representative running the report. There is no risk that the cached instance of the report will create a breach in database security.

Enabling Report Caching

Let's try enabling caching for the Manufacturing By Machine Report. (The database credentials must be stored in the shared data source to complete the following exercise.)

1. Open the Report Manager and navigate to the BIStudioDeploy folder.

2. Click Show Details.

3. Click the icon in the Edit column for the Manufacturing By Machine Report. The Properties page for the Manufacturing By Machine Report appears.

4. Select Execution from the left side of the screen. The Execution Properties page appears, as shown in Figure 17-10.

5. Select the option "Cache a temporary copy of the report. Expire copy of report after a number of minutes."

6. Set the number of minutes to 45.

7. Click Apply.

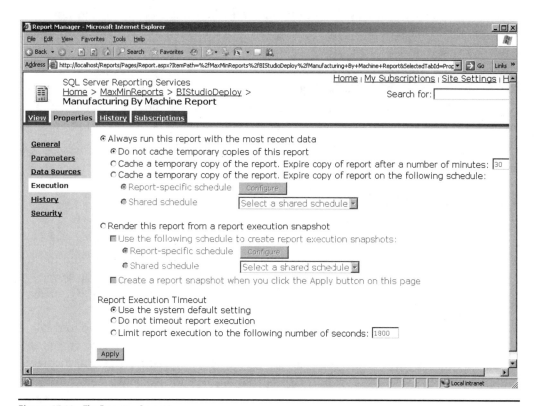

Figure 17-10   *The Execution Properties page*

The first time the Manufacturing By Machine Report runs after caching is turned on, the report needs to perform its regular execution process to gather the data for the intermediate format. This intermediate format is then copied to the report cache before it is rendered for you in the browser.

Report Cache and Deploying

When a cached report instance expires, either because of a schedule or because it has existed for its maximum length of time, it is removed from the report cache. One other circumstance can cause a cached report instance to be removed from the report cache. If a new copy of a report is deployed from the Report Designer or uploaded using the Report Manager, any cached instances of that report are removed from the report cache.

Report Caching and Report Parameters

What happens with our report caching if different users enter different parameters when the report is executed? Fortunately, the report server is smart enough to handle this situation. As part of the instance of the report in the report cache, the report server stores any parameter values used to create that cached instance. The cached instance is used to satisfy requests made by a subsequent user only if all the parameters used to create the cached instance match the parameters entered by the subsequent user.

Report Caching and Security

Not all users can change report-caching properties. To change the report-caching properties for a report, you must have rights to the Manage Reports task. Of the four predefined security roles, the Content Manager, My Reports, and Publisher roles have rights to this task.

Execution Snapshots

Report caching is a great tool for improving the performance of reports with long execution times, but one problem still exists. The first user who requests the report after the cached instance has expired must wait for the report to be created from the underlying data. It would be nice if there were a way to have cached report instances created automatically so no user has to endure these wait times. Fortunately, Reporting Services can do this as well.

An *execution snapshot* is another way to create a cached report instance. Up to this point, we have discussed situations where cached report instances are created as the result of a user action. A user requests a report, and a copy of that report's intermediate format is placed in the report cache. With execution snapshots, a cached report instance is created automatically.

Execution snapshots can create cached report instances on a scheduled basis, or they can be created as soon as this feature is turned on for a particular report. If a schedule is used, each time the schedule is run, it replaces the current cached instance with a new one. Cached report instances created by an execution snapshot are used to satisfy user report requests the same as any other cached report instance. Execution snapshots can be either created manually or created automatically on a scheduled basis.

Execution Snapshots and Security

Not all users can change execution snapshots. To change the execution snapshot properties for a report, you must have rights to the Manage Reports task. Of the four predefined security roles, the Content Manager, My Reports, and Publisher roles have rights to this task.

Report History

The *report history* feature of the Report Manager enables us to keep copies of a report's past execution. This lets us save the state of our data without having to save copies of the data itself. We can keep documentation of inventory levels, production schedules, or financial records. We can look back in time, using the report history to do trend analysis or to verify past information.

Report History Snapshots and Report Parameters

To make a report work with report history snapshots, we have to provide a default value for each report parameter. These parameters cannot be changed when each snapshot is created. (They can be changed, however, if the report is run normally through the Report Manager.) Essentially, we are saving report history snapshots for one set of parameters. To save report history snapshots for other sets of parameters, we need to create linked reports with different sets of default parameters for each report. Report history snapshots can then be set up for each linked report.

Managing Report History Snapshots

Report history snapshots can start to pile up if we are not careful. Making business decisions about the number of history snapshots to save for each report is important. Even more important, then, is to implement those business decisions and manage the number of history snapshots being saved on the report server.

Updating Report Definitions and Report History Snapshots

One of the best features of report history snapshots is this: They are not lost if the definition of the underlying report is changed. Just like the cached report instance, the report history snapshot contains both the report definition and the dataset. Therefore, it is unaffected by subsequent changes to the report definition.

Standard Subscriptions

Reporting Services supports several types of *subscriptions*. The first is the *standard* subscription, which is a request to push a particular report to a particular user or set of users. The standard subscription is usually a self-serve operation. A user logs on to the Report Manager site and finds the report they want. The user then creates the subscription by specifying the schedule for the push delivery and the delivery options.

Standard subscriptions have two delivery options: e-mail and file share. The *e-mail delivery* option, of course, sends an e-mail to the specified e-mail addresses with a link to the report or with the report itself either embedded as HTML or as an attached document. The *file share* option creates a file containing the report in a specified folder on a file share. The file share option can be used to place the report into a document store managed and/or indexed by another application, such as Microsoft's SharePoint Portal Services.

Multiple Subscriptions on One Report

Nothing prevents a user from creating more than one subscription on the same report. Perhaps the user wants a report delivered every Friday and on the last day of the month. We can't do this with one subscription, but we can certainly do it with two—a weekly subscription for the Friday delivery and a monthly subscription for delivery on the last day of the month.

Another reason for multiple subscriptions is to receive a report run for multiple sets of parameters. It is possible to specify parameter values as part of the subscription properties. Using this feature, we can have one subscription send us a report with one set of parameters and another subscription send us the same report with a different set of parameters.

Standard Subscriptions and Security

Not all users can create standard subscriptions. In fact, it is possible to view a report but not be able to subscribe to it. To subscribe to a report or create a subscription for delivery to others, you must have rights to the Manage Individual Subscriptions task. Of the four predefined security roles, the Browser, Content Manager, and My Reports roles have rights to manage individual subscriptions.

Data-Driven Subscriptions

A better name for a data-driven subscription might be "mass mailing." The data-driven subscription enables us to take a report and e-mail it to a number of people on a mailing list. The mailing list can be queried from any valid Reporting Services data source.

The mailing list can contain fields in addition to the recipient's e-mail address, which are used to control the content of the e-mail sent to each recipient.

Data-Driven Subscriptions and Security

Not all users can create data-driven subscriptions. To create a data-driven subscription for a report, you must have rights to the Manage All Subscriptions task. Of the four predefined security roles, only the Content Manager role has rights to this task.

Data-Driven Subscriptions and Event-Driven Behavior

We can do a couple of tricks with data-driven subscriptions that make them even more powerful. For instance, we might not want a subscription sent out until after a certain event has occurred. We may also want to e-mail a report to a number of recipients after a specific data update process has completed. While a data-driven subscription is a scheduled process rather than triggered by a particular event, we can make it behave almost as if it were event-driven.

We need a field in a status table that contains the completion date and time of the last data load. We also need a field in a status table that contains the date and time when the report was last distributed. With these two flag fields in place, we can simulate event-driven behavior for our data-driven subscription.

First, we need to build a stored procedure that returns the mailing list for the report distribution. To this stored procedure, add logic that checks the date and time of the last data load and the date and time of the last report distribution. If the data load is complete and the report has not yet been distributed today, the stored procedure returns the mailing list result set. If the data load is incomplete, or if the report has already been distributed today, the stored procedure returns an empty result set.

Now we create a series of data-driven subscriptions based on this stored procedure. If the data load completes sometime between 1:00 A.M. and 3:00 A.M., we might schedule one data-driven subscription to execute at 1:00 A.M., another at 1:30 A.M., another at 2:00 A.M., and so on. When each data-driven subscription executes, the stored procedure determines whether the data load is complete and whether the report was already distributed. If the stored procedure returns a result set, the data-driven subscription e-mails the report to the mailing list. If the stored procedure returns an empty result set, the data-driven subscription terminates without sending any e-mails.

This same approach can be used to e-mail reports only when the report data has changed. We create a stored procedure that only returns a mailing list result set if the data has changed since the last time the report was e-mailed. This stored procedure is used to create a data-driven subscription. Now the data-driven subscription only sends out reports when the data has changed; otherwise, it sends nothing.

Ad Hoc Reporting

Thus far, we have looked at tools available in Reporting Services for developers to create and manage reports for users. At times, however, users need direct access to the reporting capability. Perhaps the need for information is immediate and no time exists to involve a report developer. Perhaps it is a one-time need and, thus, does not justify development time.

Fortunately, Reporting Services provides tools to meet this user's reporting need. The Report Builder, along with the Report Models, provides a means for end users to explore their data without having to learn the ins and outs of SELECT statements and query builders. Best of all, the data stays in a managed and secure environment.

Here are the basic features of the two report authoring environments:

Report Builder	Report Designer (in Visual Studio 2008 or Business Intelligence Development Studio)
Targeted at business users	Targeted at IT pros and developers
Ad hoc reports	Managed reports
Autogenerates queries using Report Model layer on top of the source	Native queries (SQL, OLE DB, XML/A, ODBC, Oracle)
Reports built on templates	Freeform (nested, banded) reports
Click-once application, easy to deploy and manage	Integrated into Visual Studio
Cannot import Report Designer reports	Can work with reports built in Report Builder

Report Model

The Report Model provides a nontechnical user with a view of database content without requiring an intimate knowledge of relational theory and practice. It hides all of the complexity of primary keys and foreign key constraints. In other words, the Report Model hides the technical nature of the database and enables the users to concern themselves with the data.

Once created, the Report Model serves as the basis for report creation with the Report Builder. First, we need to have one or more Report Models built over the top of our database. Once these have been created and deployed to the report server, we can turn a select number of users loose to create ad hoc reports and do data analysis on the fly.

Creating a Report Model

Like reports, Report Models are created in the Business Intelligence Development Studio and then deployed to a report server. Unlike reports, Report Models can have security rights assigned to different pieces of their structure to provide the fine-grained security that is often required in ad hoc reporting situations.

We use the Report Model Wizard to create the Report Model, and then do some manual tweaking to make it more usable. We then deploy the Report Model to the report server. Finally, we set security within the model itself.

NOTE

Before defining a Report Model from a relational database, it is important that the database exhibit good design and implementation practices. Tables should have explicitly declared primary keys. Also, all foreign keys should be maintained by foreign key constraints.

Learn By Doing—Creating a Table Report

Features Highlighted

▶ Creating a Report Model

▶ Deploying the Report Model to the Report Server

Business Need   Maximum Miniatures has decided to set up an ad hoc reporting environment for its employees. The SQL Server 2008 Reporting Services Report Model and Report Builder are to be used to implement this ad hoc reporting. The MaxMinManufacturingDM serves as the pilot database for the project.

Steps

1. Open the Business Intelligence Development Studio.
2. Click the New Project button on the toolbar.
3. Make sure Business Intelligence Projects is selected from the Project Types, and then select Report Model Project from the Templates.
4. Enter **ManufacturingModel** for Name and set the Location to the appropriate folder. Leave Create Directory for Solution unchecked.
5. Click OK to create the project.
6. Right-click the Data Sources folder in the Solution Explorer window and select Add New Data Source from the context menu. The Data Source Wizard dialog box appears.
7. Click Next. The Select how to define the connection page appears.
8. If a connection to the MaxMinManufacturingDM database already exists in the Data Connections list, select this connection and go to Step 13. If there is no connection, click New. The Connection Manager dialog box appears.

9.   Type the name of the Microsoft SQL Server database server that is hosting the MaxMinManufacturingDM database or select it from the drop-down list. If the MaxMinManufacturingDM database is hosted by the computer you are currently working on, you may type **(local)** for the server name.

10. Select and complete the appropriate authentication method.

11. Select MaxMinManufacturingDM from the Select or enter a database name drop-down list.

12. Click Test Connection. If a Test Connection Succeeded message appears, click OK. If an error message appears, make sure the name of your database server, the user name, the password, and the database have been entered properly. Click OK. You return to the Data Source Wizard dialog box.

13. Click Next. The Completing the Wizard page appears.

14. Enter **MaxMinManufacturingDM** for the Data Source Name.

15. Click Finish.

16. Right-click the Data Source Views folder in the Solution Explorer window and select Add New Data Source View from the context menu. The Data Source View Wizard dialog box appears.

17. Click Next. The Select a Data Source page appears.

18. Select the MaxMinManufacturingDM data source and click Next. The Name Matching page appears. This page appears because we do not have any foreign key relationships defined in the MaxMinManufacturingDM database. The report model depends on these relationships, so it will define logical foreign key relationships in the data source view.

19. Leave the default settings and click Next. The Select Tables and Views page appears.

20. Move all of the tables into the Included objects list.

21. Click Next. The Completing the Wizard page appears.

22. Enter **Manufacturing Data Mart** for the Data Source View Name.

23. Click Finish.

24. Right-click the Report Models folder in the Solution Explorer window and select Add New Report Model from the context menu. The Report Model Wizard appears.

25. Click Next. The Select Data Source View page appears.

26. Select the Manufacturing Data Mart data source view and click Next. The Select report model generation rules page appears, as shown in Figure 17-11. This page lets us select the rules to be applied during the first pass and the second pass through the tables in the data source view. The default settings work for most data models, so we can leave the default settings. You can also select the language to use when creating your data model. The figures here use a data model generated in English.

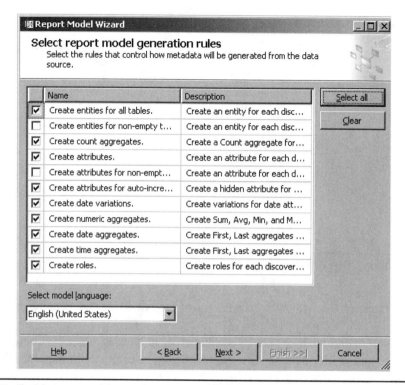

Figure 17-11 *The Select report model generation rules page of the Report Model Wizard*

27. Click Next. The Collect Model Statistics page appears.

28. The data model generation process uses the database statistics in the data source view. To create a data model that best reflects the current database and how it is used, it is recommended that you select the Update model statistics before generating option. Therefore, we leave this option selected. Click Next. The Completing the Wizard page appears.

29. Make sure the Name is Manufacturing Data Mart. Click Run. The wizard creates the model. The wizard page shows the actions taken during each pass of the model generation process.

30. Click Finish. If you receive a message saying the file has been modified outside of the source editor, simply click "Yes to All" and continue.

The Report Data Model Parts and Pieces

Let's first take a look at the model that resulted from the wizard. Double-click the Manufacturing Data Mart.smdl file entry in the Solution Explorer window to open it, if it is not already open. The model appears as shown in Figure 17-12. You can see that

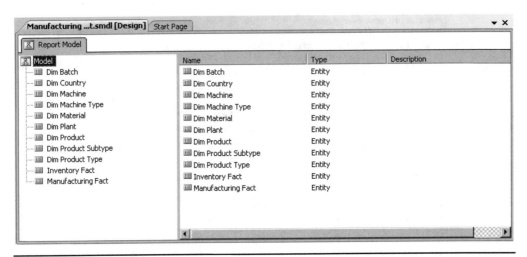

Figure 17-12 *Entities in the Manufacturing Data Mart Report Model*

each of the tables in the MaxMinManufacturingDM database has become an entity in the model.

The fields from our database become attributes of our entities, as shown in Figure 17-13. The attribute type is identified by the icon to the left of each attribute name. The # denotes a numeric attribute. The *a* denotes an alphanumeric attribute. The calendar identifies a date/time attribute. The check box identifies a bit or Boolean attribute. Numeric attributes also include sum, average, minimum, and maximum aggregates. Date/time attributes also include the date parts of day, month, year, and quarter, along with aggregates for the first and last date.

NOTE

The Report Model contains some attributes that provide a count of the number of instances of an entity. For example, Figure 17-13 shows an attribute called #Dim Machines, which provides a count of the number of machine entities. Do not confuse the # icon, which indicates the attribute type, with the # that is used at the beginning of the attribute name.

Finally, in the model, entities can have various roles. Roles are created by the foreign key constraints in the database. The roles link one entity to other entities in the model. A role can be a one-to-many, many-to-one, or one-to-one relationship. For example, in Figure 17-13, a machine may have many manufacturing facts associated with it. This is a one-to-many relationship. On the other hand, a machine may be associated with only one plant. Note the differing icons associated with each of these types of relationships.

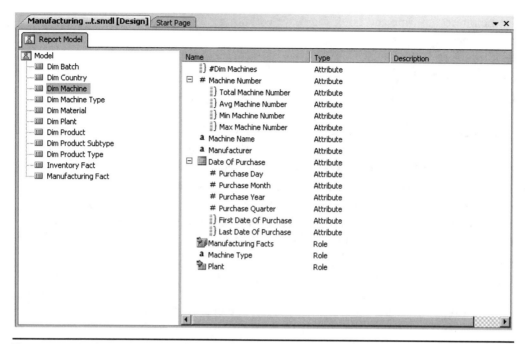

Figure 17-13 *Attributes and roles of the Dim Machine entity in the Manufacturing Data Mart*

Cleaning Up the Report Model

Creating the Report Model using the Report Model Wizard is only half the battle. The wizard does a great job of creating the model for us. However, a number of refinements still need to be made to the model by hand to get it ready for users.

Here are the tasks that should be accomplished to clean up the Report Model:

► Remove any numeric aggregates that don't make sense

► Remove attributes that should not be present

► Rename entities that have cryptic names

► Put the proper items in the Lookup folder

► Use folders to organize entities, attributes, and roles

► Rearrange the entity, attribute, and role order

► Manually create calculated attributes

► Add descriptions

► Create perspectives coinciding with business areas

In the interest of time and book pages, we will not go through these cleanup tasks as part of these exercises.

Deploy the Model

Continuing with our process, it is time to deploy the model.

1. Right-click the entry for the ManufacturingModel Project and select Properties from the context menu. The ManufacturingModel Property Pages dialog box appears.
2. Enter **MaxMinReports/DataSources** for the TargetDataSourceFolder.
3. Enter **MaxMinReports/Models** for the TargetModelFolder. This creates a new folder to contain the Report Model itself.
4. Enter **http://{ReportServer}/ReportServer** for the TargetServerURL, where {ReportServer} is the name of the report server.
5. Click OK to exit the dialog box.
6. Right-click the entry for the ManufacturingModel Project and select Deploy from the context menu. The model deploys to the server. You receive one warning stating that the shared data source cannot be deployed because it already exists.

Secure the Model

The number of people who have access to the Report Model for ad hoc reporting will probably be larger than the number of people who have access to the database for report authoring. This wider audience and increased exposure makes security doubly important. Personal information, such as Social Security numbers, pay rates, and employee's healthcare information, must be protected. In addition, there may be important financial information in the data that should not be widely disbursed.

Let's first take a look at the Report Model using the Report Manager. Open the Report Manager and browse to the /MaxMinReports/Models folder where the model was deployed. As you can see in Figure 17-14, the entry in the folder for the Manufacturing Data Mart model looks very much like the entries we have seen for reports and shared data sources. Clicking the Manufacturing Data Mart model opens the Properties tab for the model.

The General page, the Data Sources page, and the Security page on the Properties tab for the Report Model look and function almost identically to their counterparts for a report. This means we can use the Report Manager to make security role assignments on the Report Model as a whole.

The Model Item Security page provides us with a means to make security role assignments at a more granular level. The Model Item Security page is shown in Figure 17-15. Once the Secure individual model items independently for this model check box is checked, you can assign read permissions for individual entities or attributes to individual users or groups.

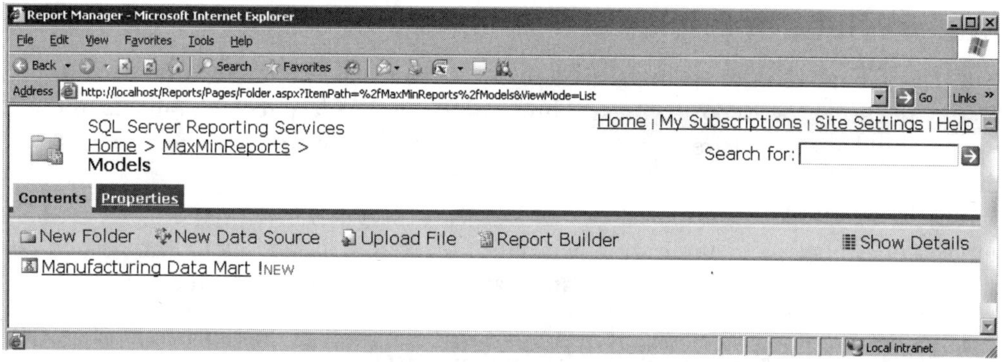

Figure 17-14 *The Manufacturing Data Mart Report Model deployed to the report server*

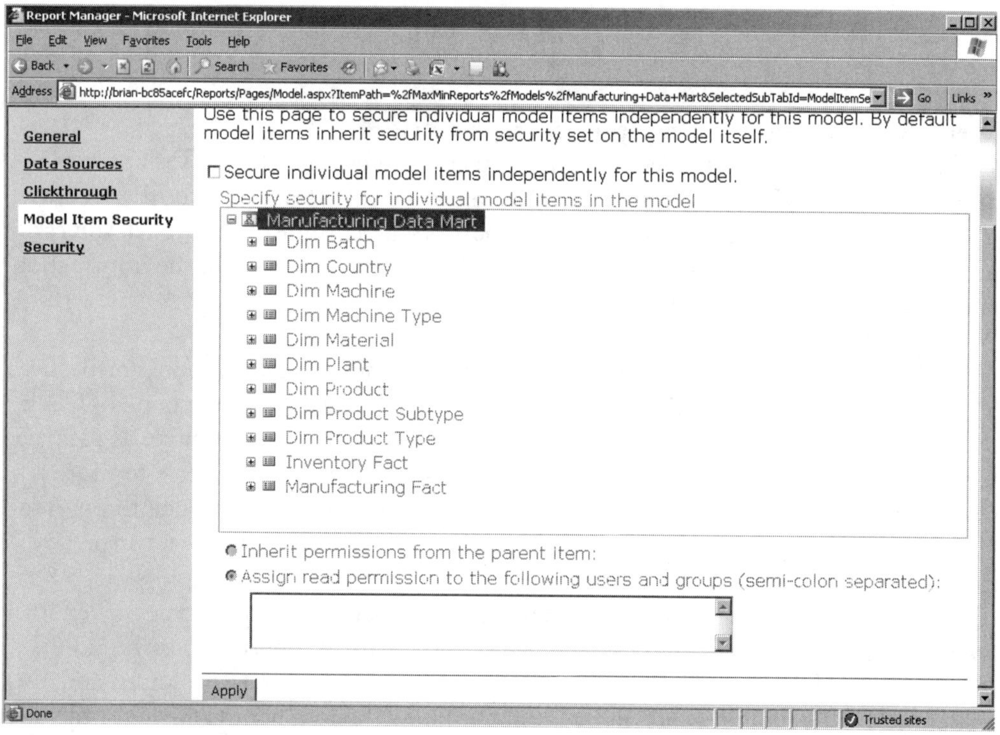

Figure 17-15 *The Item Model Security page*

Report Builder Basics

Now that a Report Model is in place on the server, users can create reports based on that model using the Report Builder. Three types of report layouts are available in the Report Builder: the table report, the matrix report, and the chart. Let's go over some of the basics.

The Report Builder is a special type of Windows program known as a ClickOnce application. This type of application is installed on your computer by following a link or clicking a button on a web form. The application is launched in the same way.

Launching the Report Builder Application

You launch the Report Builder by bringing up Report Manager in a browser and then clicking the Report Builder button on the toolbar. You can also launch the Report Builder without first going to the Report Manager. This is done by using the following URL:

```
http://{ReportServer}/ReportServer/ReportBuilder/ReportBuilder.
application
```

where {ReportServer} is the name of your report server.

The Report Builder launches and begins creating a new report. The Task pane is displayed on the right side of the screen. You must select a data source for the report (see Figure 17-16). Instead of basing your report on the entire Report Model, you can select a perspective from within the model. A perspective is a subset of the information in the model. Usually, a perspective coincides with a particular job or work area within an organization.

If a plus sign is to the left of the model, the model contains one or more perspectives. (Our Manufacturing Data Mart model does not have any perspectives defined.) Click the plus sign to view the perspectives. If you select one of these perspectives as the data source for your report, only the entities in that perspective will be available to your report. Because perspectives reduce the number of entities you have to look through to find the data you need on your report, it is usually a good idea to choose a perspective, rather than using the entire Report Model.

You must also select a report layout. The Task pane shows the three types of report layouts available in Report Builder. The *table report* creates a report with rows and columns. This is the most familiar report layout. In a table report, the columns are predefined by the report layout, and we will not know the number of rows until the data is selected at run time.

The *matrix report* creates a report containing what is known as either a crosstab or a pivot table. We do not know how many columns or rows will be in the matrix in advance because it uses data selected at run time to define both. The matrix report can

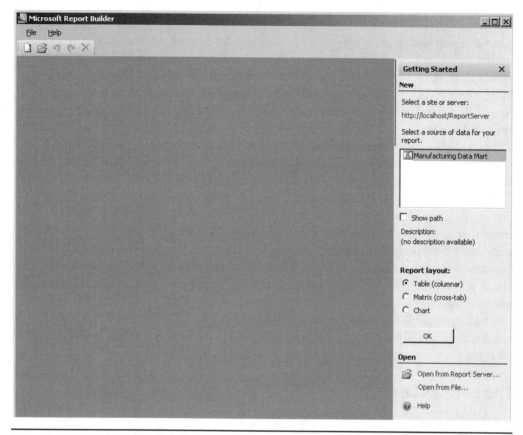

Figure 17-16 *Selecting a source of data from a Report Model*

be somewhat confusing the first time you encounter it, but an example usually helps. If you are fuzzy on how a matrix works, be sure to check out the sample matrix report in Chapter 16.

The *chart* creates a business graphic from the data. This can be a line graph, a bar chart, or a pie chart, among other things. While you can create a basic chart with a few mouse clicks, the chart report itself has a large number of options that enable you to format the chart just the way you want it.

If you are creating a new report, select the Report Model or the perspective that should serve as the data source, along with the report layout, and click OK. If you want to edit an existing report, click the Open button on the toolbar. You can then navigate the report server folder structure to find the Report Builder report you want to edit. You cannot use the Report Builder to edit reports that were created or edited using the Report Designer in Visual Studio 2008 or the Business Intelligence Development Studio.

Entities, Roles, and Fields

Reports are created in the Report Builder using entities, roles, and fields. *Entities* are simply the objects or processes that our data knows something about. Dim Product, Dim Machine, and Dim Batch are all examples of entities in the Manufacturing Data Mart Report Model used in these examples. A single report may contain information from a single entity or from several related entities. Entities can be grouped together in entity folders within the Report Model or in perspectives to help keep things organized.

Roles show us how one entity relates to another entity. For example, a product is related to a product subtype through its role as a member of that subtype. A machine is related to a plant through its role as a machine in that plant.

Roles enable us to show information from multiple entities together on a single report in a meaningful manner. This may seem a bit confusing as you read about it, but remember, the roles are already defined for you by the Report Model. If the model has been created properly, you should find they are natural to the way you think about your business processes. Information from different entities should combine on your reports just as you expect, without having to get caught up in the technical structure behind the relationships.

The information about the entities is stored in fields. A *field* is simply one bit of information: a product name, a machine number, or a date of manufacture. Fields are what we place on our reports to spit out these bits of information.

The Entities List

Once a Report Model has been selected for your data source, or an existing report has been chosen for editing, the main Report Builder opens. When creating a new report, the Report Builder appears similar to Figure 17-17. Let's take a look at each of the windows that make up this screen.

The Entities list, in the upper-left corner, shows the entities and entity folders in the selected Report Model or perspective. All of the data in a Report Builder report comes from the entities displayed in this window. Once an entity has been selected and placed on the report, the Entities list shows that entity along with its roles.

The Fields List

The Fields list, in the lower-left corner, shows the fields available for the selected entity. Some of these fields contain information coming directly from the database, while others contain information that is calculated by the report. The icon to the left of the field identifies the type of data being stored in the field. A pound sign (#) indicates that a field contains numeric data. A small *a* indicates a field containing alphanumeric data. A check box indicates a field that contains yes or no, true or false data. A calendar

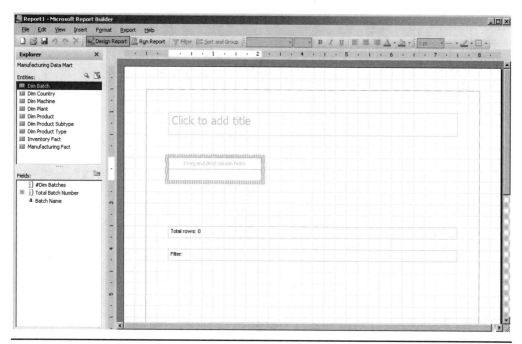

Figure 17-17   *The Report Builder screen*

indicates a date and time. A grouping of three yellow boxes indicates a calculated field that combines values from a number of items into one value, for example, the number of machines in the Machine dimension.

You can create your own calculated fields by clicking the New Field button at the upper-right corner of the Fields list. This displays the Define Formula dialog box, shown in Figure 17-18. Use this dialog box to define your calculated field. You can create expressions by dragging existing fields onto the Formula area. The fields' values can be combined using the arithmetic and string operator buttons below the Formula area. You can also use the Functions tab to reference a large number of functions that can be used in your expressions. Once you click OK to create the calculated field, it is displayed in the Fields window of the Report Builder.

Clickthrough Reports

As we discussed earlier, entities are related through roles in our data model. Sometimes it can be helpful, as you are analyzing your data, to follow these role relationships through your data. The Report Builder enables you to do this by using clickthrough reports.

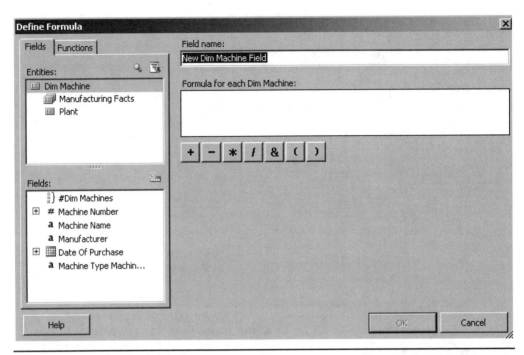

Figure 17-18 *The Define Formula dialog box*

Clickthrough reports are automatically created when you click a role relationship to move from one entity to another. The clickthrough reports are defined on-the-fly according to the data that is in the model for the entity being reported on. Each clickthrough report can lead to other clickthrough reports. Using clickthrough reports, you can continue to follow your data wherever it may lead to perform in-depth analysis.

Putting It All Together

Business intelligence that simply sits on a relational or OLAP server without ever getting to the users does no good for anyone. To make a difference, this information must reach its target audience. In many cases, the target audience is too busy with other commitments to seek out the information. It is up to us to put business intelligence at their fingertips.

In this chapter, we saw how Reporting Services is part of the solution for getting information to the decision makers. In the next chapter, we look at ways developers can integrate business intelligence right into their applications.

Chapter 18

Let's Get Together—
Integrating OLAP
with Your Applications

In This Chapter

▶ **ADOMD.NET**

▶ **Using Reporting Services Without the Report Manager**

▶ **Ready-Made Solution**

If you want to make beautiful music, you must play the black and the white notes together.
—Richard Milhous Nixon

Reporting Services provides us with a capable tool for delivering business intelligence (BI) to decision makers. In some situations, however, our business intelligence solution must be more than a paper report—even more than an interactive report available in a browser. At times, our business intelligence must integrate tightly with other programs and solutions.

Once again, SQL Server 2008 provides us with the tools to fulfill this need. The ADOMD.NET data provider enables us to execute Multidimensional Expression (MDX) queries against online analytical processing (OLAP) cubes on Analysis Services servers. Analysis Management Objects (AMO) provides a programming interface for the management of an Analysis Services server and the objects residing on that server. Reporting Services offers a number of methods for integrating reports with applications.

With these features, we can provide our users with the complete package, the integrated solution, the all-in-one application, the tightly coupled, well-oiled …well, you get the picture.

ADOMD.NET

ADOMD.NET, the multidimensional counterpart to ADO.NET, is our means to programmatically access the wealth of business intelligence we have been creating on the Analysis Services server. With ADOMD.NET, our client applications can query databases on an Analysis Services server. ADOMD.NET also allows these applications to programmatically view and manipulate the structures residing in Analysis Services databases.

ADOMD.NET uses XML for Analysis (XML/A) to interact with the Analysis Services server.

ADOMD.NET Structure

The structure of ADOMD.NET is similar to the structure of ADO.NET. Both use a connection object to manage the connection string and set up access to the server. Both use a command object to execute queries against a database. And both provide structures for connected and disconnected access to data.

AdomdConnection

The *AdomdConnection* manages the connection between the client application and the multidimensional data server. A connection string similar to the following is used to initiate the connection to a server:

```
Data Source=ServerName;Catalog=AnalSvcsDB;Provider=msolap;
```

The connection to the server is made using either Transmission Control Protocol/Internet Protocol (TCP/IP) or Hypertext Transfer Protocol (HTTP). This enables connections to be made with a minimum of firewall and network interference.

Once the connection is open, an AdomdCommand object can be used to interact with the Analysis Services database. When the session has concluded, the connection must be explicitly closed with the Close method. An AdomdCommand object does not automatically close the connection when it goes out-of-scope in your code. (This is done to facilitate connection sharing.)

AdomdCommand

The *AdomdCommand* manages the execution of queries against a multidimensional server. The query is set using either the CommandText property or CommandStream property. The query itself must be an MDX command or an XML/A-compliant command that is valid on the target server.

AdomdCommand offers the following methods for executing the query:

- ▶ **Execute**   The Execute method returns the result of the command either as a CellSet or as an AdomdDataReader, depending on the format of the results themselves.

- ▶ **ExecuteCellSet**   The ExecuteCellSet method returns the result of the command as a CellSet.

- ▶ **ExecuteNonQuery**   The ExecuteNonQuery method executes a command that does not return a result.

- ▶ **ExecuteReader**   The ExecuteReader method returns the result of the command as an AdomdDataReader.

- ▶ **ExecuteXMLReader**   The ExecuteXMLReader method returns the result of the command in the native XML/A format using an XMLReader.

AdomdDataReader

The *AdomdDataReader* provides a means for reading a forward-only result set from a query. While this result set is being read, the connection to the data source remains busy. This is a connected result set. Connected access requires more server overhead to maintain the active connection.

CellSet

Unlike the AdomdDataReader, the *CellSet* facilitates a disconnected result set. The CellSet contains the entire structure of the multidimensional result set. Therefore, an application can interact with this result set without having to maintain a connection to the server.

A portion of the CellSet structure is shown in Figure 18-1. The CellSet contains one or more axis objects. These represent the query dimensions: Column, Row, Page, and so on. Review Chapter 12 if you need a refresher on query dimensions in an MDX query. Each axis contains a set of tuples. A set can have zero, one, or many tuples. As we discussed in Chapter 11, tuples are made up of dimension and hierarchy members.

In addition to the items shown in Figure 18-1, the CellSet contains a collection of cells called Cells. These *cells* contain the measures that are included in the MDX query. The cell collection contains one index for each dimension in the MDX query. For example, if the MDX query contains Column, Row, and Page dimensions, the cell collection will have three indexes and an individual cell would be addressed as shown:

```
CellSet.Cells(x, y, z)
```

The measure calculated for an individual cell is accessed through the Value property, as shown:

```
CellSet.Cells(x, y, z).Value
```

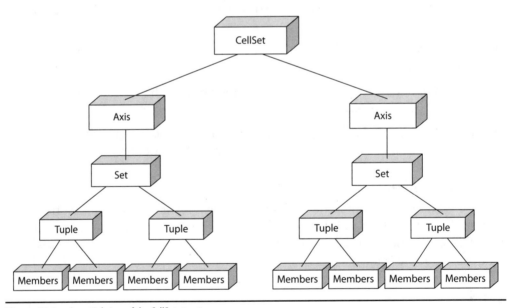

Figure 18-1   *A partial view of the CellSet structure*

ADOMD.NET Example

Let's look at an example using ADOMD.NET to incorporate an MDX query result into an application. A Maximum Miniatures developer has created a Windows program for analyzing prospective customers called *Prospect Analyzer*. The method of analysis being used by this program is to take a prospective customer's city of residence and display the buying habits of other residents of that city for the past three years. Many of Max Min's products have regional appeal, so this type of analysis can be helpful when planning a sales approach to a prospective customer.

The program displays the number of product sales by store by year. Because we have three dimensions in the result set, a bit of creativity was required. Two of the three dimensions are represented by the rows and columns of a data grid. Multiple data grids are placed on a set of tab pages to represent the third dimension. The user interface for the Prospect Analyzer is shown in Figure 18-2.

Recall the MDX Query window in SQL Server Management Studio only allows two dimensions in query results. Here, we have an MDX query result viewer that allows three. Your homework is to design your own MDX query result viewer that will display four dimensions.

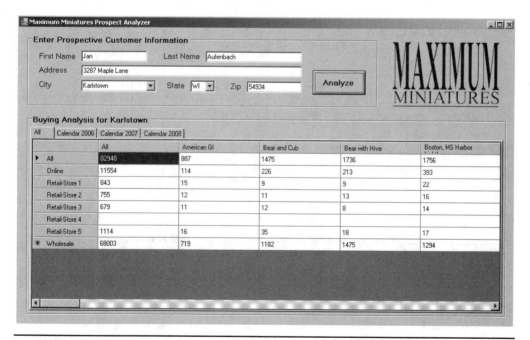

Figure 18-2   *The Prospect Analyzer sample application with a three-dimensional MDX query result viewer*

NOTE

The Prospect Analyzer sample application can be downloaded from the website for this book.

Setting a Reference

We can use ADOMD.NET in a number of different .NET project types. But before we can use ADOMD.NET in the project, we must first set a reference to the assembly that implements it. That reference is set by doing the following:

1. Right-click the project entry in the Solution Explorer window and select Add Reference from the Context menu. The Add Reference dialog box appears.
2. Scroll down and select the entry for Microsoft.AnalysisServices.AdomdClient, as shown in Figure 18-3.
3. Click OK to exit the Add Reference dialog box and add a reference to this assembly in your project.

If you need to view the references currently set for a project to determine if the ADOMD.NET client has already been referenced, use the following steps:

1. Double-click the MyProject entry in the Solution Explorer window. The Project Properties tab appears. (This tab will have the name of the project you are working with.)
2. Select the References page of the Project Properties tab. This page appears as shown in Figure 18-4. Notice the entry for Microsoft.AnalysisServices. AdomdClient at the top of the list of References.

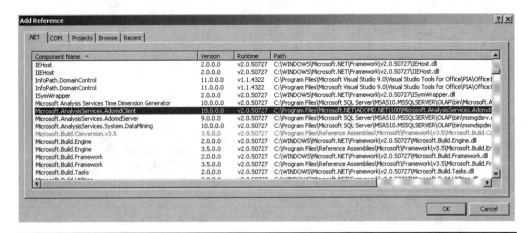

Figure 18-3   *The Add Reference dialog box with the entry for the ADOMD.NET client highlighted*

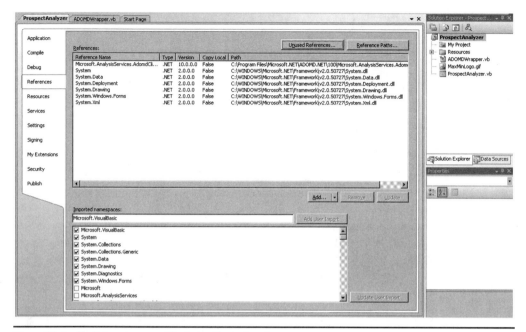

Figure 18-4   *The References page of the Project Properties tab*

We also need to import AdomdClient. The following line of code must be at or near the beginning of each program:

```
Imports Microsoft.AnalysisServices.AdomdClient
```

Retrieving a CellSet

The code to retrieve the CellSet is shown here. This code should look familiar to anyone who has used ADO.NET because it has the same format. We connect to the database server, we create and execute the query on this server, and then we pick up the query result and pass it back.

```
Imports Microsoft.AnalysisServices.AdomdClient

Public Class ADOMDWrapper
    Public Function BuyingByProductByStoreByYearMDX( _
                    ByRef CityName As String) As CellSet
        Dim conn As AdomdConnection
        Dim cmd As AdomdCommand
        Dim cst As CellSet
```

```vbnet
Dim strServer As String = "local"
Dim strDatabase As String = "MaxMinSalesDM"
Dim strMDXQuery As String

strMDXQuery = "SELECT [Time].[Year].members ON PAGES, " & _
              "[Store].[Store].members ON ROWS, " & _
              "[Product].[Product].members ON COLUMNS " & _
              "FROM [MaxMinSales] " & _
              "WHERE ([Measures].[Sales in Units], " & _
                     " [Customer].[City].[" & CityName & "])"

' Open the connection to the Analysis Services server
Try
    ' Create a new AdomdConnection object, providing the
    ' connection string.
    conn = New AdomdConnection("Data Source=" & strServer & _
    ";Catalog=" & strDatabase & ";Provider=msolap;")
    ' Open the connection.
    conn.Open ()
Catch ex As Exception
    Throw New ApplicationException( _
        "An error occurred while connecting.")
End Try

' Execute the MDX Query
Try
    ' Create a new AdomdCommand object,
    ' providing the MDX query string.
    cmd = New AdomdCommand(strMDXQuery, conn)
    ' Run the command and return a CellSet object.
    cst = cmd.ExecuteCellSet()

    ' Return the CellSet object
    Return cst

Catch ex As Exception
    Throw New ApplicationException( _
        "An error occurred while opening the cellset.")
End Try

' Release resources.
Try
    conn.Close ()
```

```
        Catch ex As Exception
            ' Ignore errors
        Finally
            cst = Nothing
            cmd = Nothing
            conn = Nothing
        End Try


    End Function
End Class
```

The next code listing shows how to parse the information into our fancy three-dimensional viewer. First, we loop through the content of Axis(2), the Pages dimension, to create a tab page for each one. Each tab page has a DataGridView control for displaying columns and rows on that tab. Second, we loop through the content of Axis(0), the Column dimension, to create columns in the DataGridView. Third, we loop through the content of Axis(1), the Row dimension, to create row labels in the DataGridView. Finally, we loop through the cells in the CellSet to populate the content of the DataGridView on each tab page.

```
Imports Microsoft.AnalysisServices.AdomdClient

Public Class ProspectAnalyzer

    Private Sub cmdAnalyze_Click(ByVal sender As System.Object, _
            ByVal e As System.EventArgs) Handles cmdAnalyze.Click
        Dim ADOMDBWpr As New ADOMDWrapper
        Dim CSet As CellSet
        Dim i, j, k As Integer
        Dim DataGridView As System.Windows.Forms.DataGridView
        Dim DataGridViewColumn As _
            System.Windows.Forms.DataGridViewTextBoxColumn

        ' Don't do any analysis if there is no city selected
        If String.IsNullOrEmpty(cboCity.Text) Then
            Return
        End If

        ' Set the label on the buying analysis group box
        gbxBuyingAnalysis.Text = "Buying Analysis for " & cboCity.Text

        ' Call the function to get a CellSet
```

```
' with the results for the specified city
CSet = ADOMDBWpr.BuyingByProductByStoreByYearMDX(cboCity.Text)

' Create a tab for each Page in the resulting CellSet
TabForPages.TabPages.Clear()

For i = 0 To CSet.Axes(2).Set.Tuples.Count - 1
    ' Label the tab using the caption for
    ' each Page in the CellSet

    TabForPages.TabPages.Add( _
        CSet.Axes(2).Set.Tuples(i).Members(0).Caption)

    ' Place a DataGridView on the new tab
    DataGridView = New System.Windows.Forms.DataGridView
    DataGridView.ReadOnly = True
    DataGridView.Width = TabForPages.TabPages(i).Width
    DataGridView.Height = TabForPages.TabPages(i).Height
    DataGridView.RowHeadersVisible = True
    DataGridView.RowHeadersWidth = 123

    ' Create a column in the DataGridView for
    ' each Column in the CellSet
    For j = 0 To CSet.Axes(0).Set.Tuples.Count - 1
        DataGridViewColumn = New _
            System.Windows.Forms.DataGridViewTextBoxColumn

        ' The headers for the column is the caption
        ' for each Column in the CellSet
        DataGridViewColumn.HeaderText = _
            CSet.Axes(0).Set.Tuples(j).Members(0).Caption

        DataGridViewColumn.Width = 150

        DataGridView.Columns.Add(DataGridViewColumn)
    Next

    ' Create an empty row in the DataGridView
    ' for each Row in the CellSet
    DataGridView.RowCount = CSet.Axes(1).Set.Tuples.Count

    ' The headers for each row is the caption
    ' for each Row in the CellSet
```

```
        For k = 0 To CSet.Axes(1).Set.Tuples.Count - 1
            DataGridView.Rows(k).HeaderCell.Value = _
                CSet.Axes(1).Set.Tuples(k).Members(0).Caption
        Next

        ' Place the values from the CellSet in the DataGridView
        ' cells
        For j = 0 To CSet.Axes(0).Set.Tuples.Count - 1
            For k = 0 To CSet.Axes(1).Set.Tuples.Count - 1
                DataGridView(j, k).Value = CSet.Cells(j, k, i).Value
            Next
        Next

        ' Place the DataGridView on the tab page
        TabForPages.TabPages(i).Controls.Add(DataGridView)
    Next

    ' Set the Buying Analysis group box visible
    gbxBuyingAnalysis.Visible = True

    End Sub
End Class
```

Using Reporting Services Without the Report Manager

The *Report Manager* provides a nice interface for finding and executing reports, but sometimes, the Report Manager is not the best way to deliver a report to your users. Perhaps the user is browsing your website or using a custom application and needs to view a report. In these situations, we want to provide an integrated approach with reporting available within the application. We want to deliver the report to the user right where they are.

URL Access

One way to execute a report without using Report Manager is through URL access. *URL access* allows a browser or a program capable of issuing HTTP requests to specify a URL and receive a report in the HTML report viewer. This URL can be built into a standard HTML anchor tag to allow a report to be displayed with one mouse click.

Basic URL Access

The basic URL used to access a report has two parts. The first part is the URL of the Report Server web service. In a default installation, this is

```
http://ComputerName/ReportServer
```

where *ComputerName* is the name of the computer hosting the Report Server. This is followed by a question mark and the path through the Reporting Services virtual folders to the report you want to execute. The Home folder is the root of this path, but it's not included in the path itself. The path must begin with a forward slash (/).

Let's try an example. We can execute the Inventory Levels By Month Report. This report is in the BIStudioDeploy folder inside of the MaxMinReports folder.

NOTE

In the examples used throughout the rest of this chapter, we assume Reporting Services is installed on your computer. If you have Reporting Services installed on a different computer, substitute the name of that computer in place of localhost in the following examples.

1. Start Internet Explorer.
2. Enter the following URL in the address bar:
   ```
   http://localhost/ReportServer?/MaxMinReports/BIStudioDeploy/
                                  Inventory Levels By Month Report
   ```
3. Click Go. The Inventory Levels By Month Report appears in the browser, as shown in Figure 18-5. Note the parameters area and the report toolbar in the browser above the report.

NOTE

When your URL is submitted, it is URL-encoded. Some of the characters in your URL may be replaced by other characters or by hexadecimal strings, such as %20. This ensures the URL can be interpreted correctly when it is sent to the web server.

As with the Report Manager, Windows Integrated Security is being used when a user executes a report through URL access. The user must have rights to execute the report; otherwise, an error results. However, because the user is not browsing through the folder structure to get to the report, the user does not need to have any rights to the folder containing the report. You can use this fact to hide a report from nonadministrative users who are browsing through folders in the Report Manager, while still making the report accessible to someone using URL access.

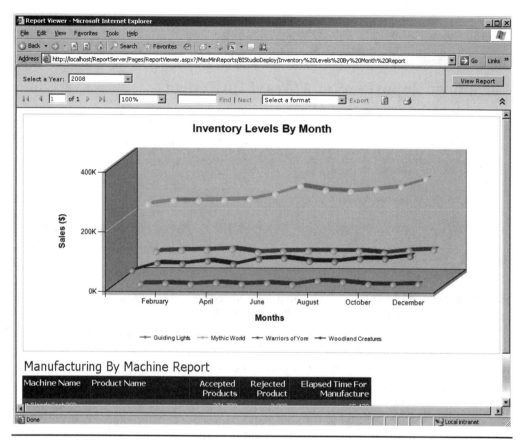

Figure 18-5   *A URL-rendered report*

In addition to executing reports, you can view the contents of folders, resources, and shared data sources. Try the following:

1. Enter this URL in the address bar:

    ```
    http://localhost/ReportServer?/MaxMinReports
    ```

2. Click Go. The contents of the MaxMinReports folder appears, as shown in Figure 18-6.

Command Parameters

Look at the URL in the address bar. You see something has been added to the URL, namely &rs:Command=ListChildren. This is called a *command parameter* and it tells

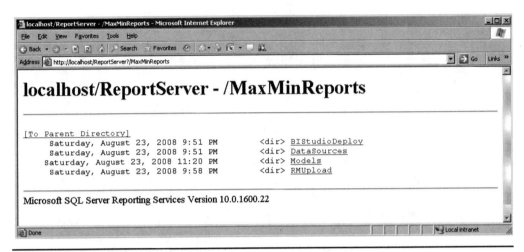

Figure 18-6 *Browsing folder contents using URL access*

Reporting Services what to do with the item pointed to by the URL. The four possible values for the command parameter are listed in Table 18-1.

Looking at this table, you quickly realize that only one command parameter value applies to each type of item you can encounter in the Reporting Services virtual folders. Attempting to use a command parameter with the wrong type of item results in an error. If you do not include the command parameter, Reporting Services simply performs the one and only command that applies to the type of item you are targeting in your URL. Because specifying the command parameter is completely unnecessary, we can only assume this was put in place to allow for future growth.

Passing Parameters

When you executed the Inventory Levels By Month Report through URL access, you received the default value for the Year report parameter. You can change the year in the Report Viewer, but only after waiting for the report to execute with the default value. It would be much better to get exactly what you want the first time around.

Command Parameter	Applies To	Result
GetDataSourceContents	Data Source	Displays the data source definition as an XML structure.
GetResourceContents	Resource Item	Displays the contents of the resource item in the browser.
ListChildren	Folder	Lists the contents of the folder with links to each content item.
Render	Report	Displays the report in the Report Viewer.

Table 18-1 *Values for the Command Parameter*

Fortunately, you have a way to do just that. You can pass the values for report parameters as part of the URL. On the URL, include an ampersand (&) followed by the name of the report parameter, an equal sign, and the parameter value.

Try the following:

1. Enter the following URL in the address bar:

```
http://localhost/ReportServer?/MaxMinReports/BIStudioDeploy/
                 Inventory Levels By Month Report&Year=2007
```

2. Click Go. The Inventory Levels By Month Report appears with data for 2007, as shown in Figure 18-7.

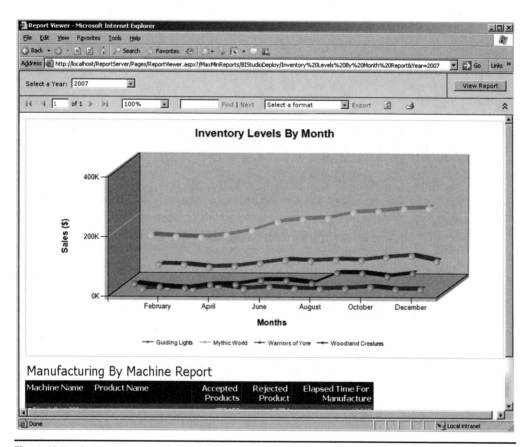

Figure 18-7   *A report parameter passed in the URL*

Hiding parameters from interactive report users is possible, while still allowing values to be passed to those parameters through the URL or web service access. This is done through the Hide option for each parameter. (Note that we are changing from the Inventory Levels By Month Report to the Manufacturing By Machine Report for this example.) Let's try the following:

1. Open the Report Manager and navigate to the /MaxMinReports/BIStudioDeploy folder.
2. Click Show Details.
3. Click the icon in the Edit column next to the Manufacturing By Machine Report.
4. Click Parameters on the left side of the screen. The Parameter management page appears.
5. Check the Has Default check box for the Year parameter.
6. Enter 2008 as the Default Value for the Year parameter.
7. Check the Hide check box for the Year parameter. The Parameter management page appears as shown in Figure 18-8.
8. Click Apply.
9. Select the View tab. Notice the Year prompt no longer appears in the parameter area. In fact, because this was the only parameter for the report, the entire parameter area is gone, as shown in Figure 18-9. The data for 2008 appears.
10. Enter the following URL in the address bar:

```
http://localhost/ReportServer?/MaxMinReports/BIStudioDeploy/
                        Manufacturing By Machine Report&Year=2006
```

11. Click Go. The Manufacturing By Machine Report appears with data for 2006.

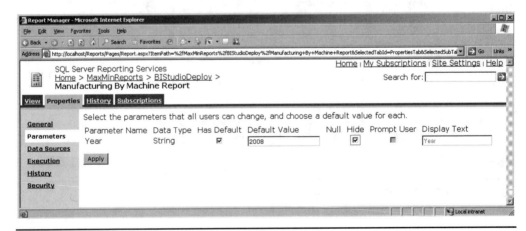

Figure 18-8   *The Parameter management page with a hidden parameter*

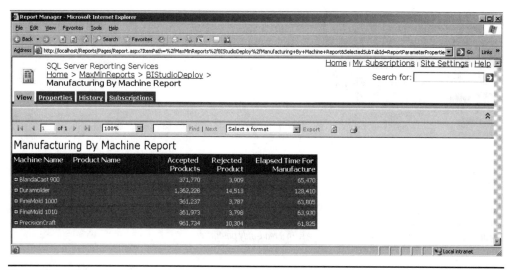

Figure 18-9 *The report without a parameter area*

Even though the Year parameter does not appear, we can still specify a value for it other than the default value. This is not the case, however, if the Hide check box is not checked. Give this a try:

1. Return to the BIStudioDeploy folder so you are viewing the folder contents.
2. Click the icon in the Edit column next to the Manufacturing By Machine Report.
3. Click Parameters on the left side of the screen. The Parameter management page appears.
4. Uncheck the Hide check box for the Year parameter.
5. Uncheck the Prompt User check box for the Year parameter. The Year parameter is now a read-only parameter. The Parameter management page appears as shown in Figure 18-10.
6. Click Apply.
7. Enter the same URL as before in the address bar:

```
http://localhost/ReportServer?/MaxMinReports/BIStudioDeploy/
                        Manufacturing By Machine Report&Year=2006
```

8. Click Go. You receive an error stating, "The report parameter 'Year' is read-only and cannot be modified." If you do not receive this error message, the report is probably pinned in cache. Click your browser's refresh button.
9. Enter the same URL without the value for the Year parameter:

```
http://localhost/ReportServer?/MaxMinReports/BIStudioDeploy/
                        Manufacturing By Machine Report
```

10. Click Go. The Manufacturing By Machine Report appears with data for 2008, the default value.

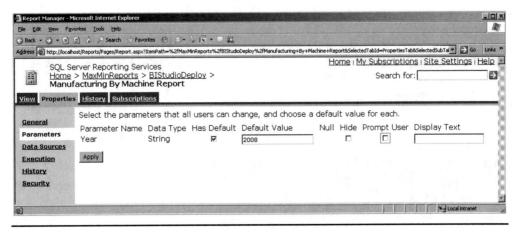

Figure 18-10   *The Parameter management page with a read-only parameter*

When Hide is checked for a report parameter, we can pass a value for the parameter, even though it is not displayed at the top of the report. When both Hide and Prompt User are unchecked, we cannot pass a value for the parameter. The default value must be used.

Let's return the parameter back to its default setting:

1. Return to the BIStudioDeploy folder so you are viewing the folder contents.
2. Click the icon in the Edit column next to the Manufacturing By Machine Report.
3. Click Parameters on the left side of the screen. The Parameter management page appears.
4. Check the Prompt User check box for the Year parameter.
5. Click Apply.

Controlling the Report Viewer

In addition to specifying report parameters in the URL, you can include parameters to control the format of the response from Reporting Services. You can specify which rendering format should be used for the report. Rather than using the Export drop-down list in the Report Viewer to export the report to a particular format, you can have it delivered in that format straight from Reporting Services. Give this a try:

1. Enter the following URL in the address bar:

```
http://localhost/ReportServer?/MaxMinReports/BIStudioDeploy/
                    Manufacturing By Machine Report&rs:Format=PDF
```

2. Click Go.

3. If you are prompted whether to open or save the file, click Open.

4. The Manufacturing By Machine Report appears in Portable Document Format (PDF) in Adobe Acrobat Reader.

NOTE

If the report fails to open as a PDF, save the file to your hard drive first and then open the newly created PDF file.

5. Close Adobe Acrobat Reader.

The valid format parameters are as follows:

► CSV

► EXCEL

► HTML4.0

► IMAGE

► MHTML

► NULL

► PDF

► WORD

► XML

In addition to the rs:Command and rs:Format parameters, several other Report Server parameters use the rs: prefix. Table 18-2 shows these.

Device information parameters can also be passed as part of the URL. These *device information parameters* are specific to the format being used to render the report. Because they are rendering-format–specific, device information parameters can also be thought of as *renderer control parameters*. Therefore, they use an rc: prefix.

Let's look at a couple of examples using device information parameters. When you receive a report rendered as HTML, you also receive the Report Viewer controls. This may not always be desirable. Several device information parameters enable you to specify what portion of the Report Viewer interface you want visible. For example:

1. Enter the following URL in the address bar:

```
http://localhost/ReportServer?/MaxMinReports/BIStudioDeploy/
                    Manufacturing By Machine Report&rc:Parameters=false
```

Parameter	Valid Values	Function
rs:ClearSession	True False	When true, this parameter prevents a report from being pinned in cache by forcing the report to be re-rendered.
rs:ParameterLanguage	A valid culture identifier, such as en-us.	Used to specify a language for the parameters passed in the URL that is different from the browser's language setting. This defaults to the browser's language setting when it is not specified.
rs:SessionID	A unique session identifier.	Used to maintain session state when the Report Server has been configured not to use session cookies.
rs:Snapshot	The data and time of a valid snapshot for the specified report.	Used to render the requested report from a history snapshot.

Table 18-2   *Report Server (rs) URL Parameters and Their Possible Values*

2. Click Go. The Manufacturing By Machine Report appears. The parameter portion of the Report Viewer is invisible, as shown in Figure 18-11, so the user cannot change the parameter values.

You can get rid of the entire Report Viewer interface as follows:

1. Enter the following URL in the address bar:

```
http://localhost/ReportServer?/MaxMinReports/BIStudioDeploy/
                    Manufacturing By Machine Report&rc:Toolbar=false
```

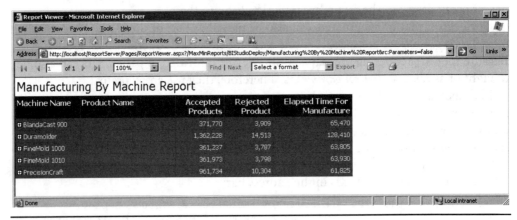

Figure 18-11   *The parameters are suppressed.*

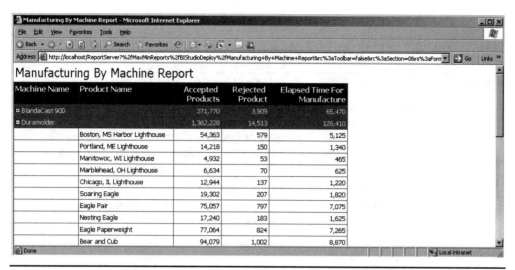

Figure 18-12 *The suppressed toolbar*

2. Click Go. The Manufacturing By Machine Report appears.
3. Expand the Duramolder group. The report is shown in Figure 18-12.

Even when we expand the group, causing a new page to be sent from the Report Server, the toolbar does not reappear.

Table 18-3 shows the device information parameters for the comma-separated value (CSV) format.

Setting	Valid Values	Function
rc:Encoding	ASCII UTF-7 UTF-8 Unicode	The character-encoding scheme to use. The default is Unicode.
rc:Extension		The file extension for the file. The default is .csv.
rc:FieldDelimiter		The field delimiter to use in the file. The default is a comma.
rc:NoHeader	True False	If true, no header is written with the data in the file. The default is false.
rc:Qualifier		The string qualifier to put around fields that contain the field delimiter. The default is a quotation mark.
rc:RecordDelimiter		The record delimiter to use in the file. The default is a carriage return and linefeed.
rc:SupressLineBreaks	True False	If true, line breaks in the data are not included in the file. The default is false.

Table 18-3 *CSV-Format Device Information (rc) URL Parameters and Their Possible Values*

Setting	Valid Values	Function
rc:OmitDocumentMap	True False	If true, the document map for the rendered report is not included in the Excel file. The default is false.
rc:OmitFormulas	True False	If true, formulas are not included in the Excel file. The default is false.
rc:RemoveSpace	An integer or decimal followed by in (the abbreviation for inches)	When this parameter is included, rows and columns that do not contain data and are smaller than the size specified are not included in the Excel file. This parameter is used to exclude extra rows or columns that do not contain report items. The default is 0.125in.
rc:SimplePageHeader	True False	If true, the report page header is placed in the Excel page header. Otherwise, the report page header is placed in the first row of the worksheet. The default value is false.

Table 18-4   *Excel-Format Device Information (rc) URL Parameters and Their Possible Values*

Table 18-4 shows the device information parameters for the Excel format. The device information parameters for the HTML format are shown in Table 18-5. Table 18-6 shows the device information parameters for the image format.

Table 18-7 shows the device information parameters for the MIME HTML (MHTML) format.

Setting	Valid Values	Function
rc:BookmarkID	{BookmarkID}	Jumps to the specified Bookmark ID in the report.
rc:DocMap	True False	Specifies whether the document map is shown.
rc:DocMapID	{DocMapID}	Jumps to the specified Document Map ID.
rc:EndFind	{PageNumber}	The last report page to be searched when executing a Find from the URL (*see* FindString).
rc:FallbackPage	{PageNumber}	The report page to go to if the Find is unsuccessful or a jump to a Document Map ID fails.
rc:FindString	{TextToFind}	Searches for this text in the report and jumps to its first location.
rc:HTMLFragment	True False	When this is set to true, the report is returned as a table rather than a complete HTML page. This table can then be placed inside your own HTML page. The default value is false.
rc:JavaScript	True False	If true, JavaScript is supported in the rendered report.

Table 18-5   *HTML-Format Device Information (rc) URL Parameters and Their Possible Values*

Setting	Valid Values	Function
rc:LinkTarget	{TargetWindowName} _blank _self _parent _top	Specifies the target window to use for any links in the report.
rc:Parameters	True False	Specifies whether to show the parameters section of the Report Viewer.
rc:ReplacementRoot		The path used to prefix any hyperlinks created in the report.
rc:Section	{PageNumber}	The page number of the report to render.
rc:StartFind	{PageNumber}	The first report page to be searched when executing a Find from the URL (*see* FindString).
rc:StreamRoot	{URL}	The path used to prefix the value of the src attribute of any IMG tags in an HTML rendering of the report.
rc:StyleSheet		The name of a cascading style sheet in the Report Server Styles folder to be applied to the Report Viewer. The name should not include the .css extension. The default location of the Styles folder is C:\Program Files\Microsoft SQL Server\MSRS10 .MSSQLSERVER\ Reporting Services\ReportServer\Styles.
rc:StyleStream	True False	If true, styles and scripts are created as separate streams, rather than in the document. The default is false.
rc:Toolbar	True False	Specifies whether the Report Viewer toolbar is visible.
rc:Type		The short name of the browser type, as defined in browsercap. ini.
rc:Zoom	Page Width Whole Page 500 200 150 100 75 50 25 10	The zoom percentage to use when displaying the report.

Table 18-5 *HTML-Format Device Information (rc) URL Parameters and Their Possible Values (Continued)*

Setting	Valid Values	Function
rc:ColorDepth	1 4 8 24 32	The color depth of the image created. The default is 24. This is only valid for the Tagged Image File Format (TIFF) image type.
rc:Columns		The number of columns to use when creating the image.
rc:ColumnSpacing		The column spacing to use when creating the image.
rc:DpiX		The number of dots per inch in the x-direction. The default is 96.
rc:DpiY		The number of dots per inch in the y-direction. The default is 96.
rc:EndPage		The last page to render. The default value is the value for the StartPage parameter.
rc:MarginBottom	An integer or decimal followed by in (the abbreviation for inches).	The bottom margin to use when creating the image.
rc:MarginLeft	An integer or decimal followed by in (the abbreviation for inches).	The left margin to use when creating the image.
rc:MarginRight	An integer or decimal followed by in (the abbreviation for inches)	The right margin to use when creating the image.
rc:MarginTop	An integer or decimal followed by in (the abbreviation for inches).	The top margin to use when creating the image.
rc:OutputFormat	BMP EMF GIF JPEG PNG TIFF	The graphics format to use.
rc:PageHeight	An integer or decimal followed by in (the abbreviation for inches).	The page height to use when creating the image.
rc:PageWidth	An integer or decimal followed by in (the abbreviation for inches).	The page width to use when creating the image.
rc:StartPage		The first page to render. A value of 0 causes all pages to be rendered. The default value is 1.

Table 18-6 *Image-Format Device Information (rc) URL Parameters and Their Possible Values*

Setting	Valid Values	Function
rc:JavaScript	True False	If true, JavaScript is supported in the rendered report.
rc:MHTMLFragment	True False	When this is set to true, the report is returned as a table, rather than a complete HTML page. This table can then be placed inside your own HTML page. The default value is false.

Table 18-7   *MHTML-Format Device Information (rc) URL Parameters and Their Possible Values*

The PDF-format device information parameters are shown in Table 18-8. Table 18-9 shows the device information parameters for the Word format. Table 18-10 shows the device information parameters for the XML format.

Setting	Valid Values	Function
rc:Columns		The number of columns to use when creating the PDF file.
rc:ColumnSpacing		The column spacing to use when creating the PDF file.
rc:DpiX		The number of dots per inch in the x-direction. The default is 300.
rc:DpiY		The number of dots per inch in the y-direction. The default is 300.
rc:EndPage		The last page to render. The default value is the value for the StartPage parameter.
rc:MarginBottom	An integer or decimal followed by in (the abbreviation for inches).	The bottom margin to use when creating the PDF file.
rc:MarginLeft	An integer or decimal followed by in (the abbreviation for inches).	The left margin to use when creating the PDF file.
rc:MarginRight	An integer or decimal followed by in (the abbreviation for inches).	The right margin to use when creating the PDF file.
rc:MarginTop	An integer or decimal followed by in (the abbreviation for inches).	The top margin to use when creating the PDF file.
rc:PageHeight	An integer or decimal followed by in (the abbreviation for inches).	The page height to use when creating the PDF file.
rc:PageWidth	An integer or decimal followed by in (the abbreviation for inches).	The page width to use when creating the PDF file.
rc:StartPage		The first page to render. A value of 0 causes all pages to be rendered. The default value is 1.

Table 18-8   *PDF-Format Device Information (rc) URL Parameters and Their Possible Values*

Setting	Valid Values	Function
rc:AutoFit	True False Never Default	If true, AutoFit is set to true on every Word table. If false, AutoFit is set to false on every Word table. If Never, AutoFit is not set on individual tables, so the behavior reverts to the Word default. If Default, AutoFit is set to true on all tables that are narrower than the physical drawing area.
rc:ExpandTools	True False	If true, all of the drilldown items are rendered in their expanded state. If false, all of the drilldown items are rendered in their collapsed state. The default is false.
rc:FixedPageWidth	True False	If true, the page width property in the resulting Word document is expanded to accomodate the width of the largest report page. If false, Word's default page width is used. The default is false.
rc:OmitHyperlinks	True False	If true, hyperlinks are not included in the resulting Word document. If false, hyperlinks are included. The default is false.
rc:OmitDrillThroughs	True False	If true, drill-through actions are not included in the resulting Word document. If true, drill-through actions are included. The default is false

Table 18-9 *Word Format Device Information (rc) URL Parameters and Their Possible Values*

Setting	Valid Values	Function
rc:Encoding	ASCII UTF-8 Unicode	The character-encoding scheme to use. The default is UTF-8.
rc:FileExtension		The file extension for the XML file. The default is .xml.
rc:Indented	True False	If true, the XML file is indented. The default is false.
rc:MIMEType		The MIME type of the XML file.
rc:OmitSchema	True False	If true, the schema name and XML Schema Definition (XSD) are not included in the XML file. The default is false.
rc:Schema	True False	If true, the XSD is rendered in the XML file. Otherwise, the report itself is rendered in the XML file. The default is false.
UseFormattedValues	True False	If true, the formatted value of each text box is included in the XML file. Otherwise, the unformatted value of each text box is included.
XSLT		The path in the Report Server namespace of an Extensible Stylesheet Language Transformation (XSLT) document to apply to the XML file. The XSLT must be a published resource on the Report Server and it must be accessed through the Report Server itself.

Table 18-10 *XML-Format Device Information (rc) URL Parameters and Their Possible Values*

Finally, you can specify the user name and password for data sources that prompt for credentials each time the report is run. This is done using the dsu and dsp prefixes. For example, to specify credentials for a data source called MaxMin, you would add the following to the end of the URL:

```
dsu:MaxMin=MyDBUser&dsp:MaxMin=DBPassword
```

where MyDBUser is a valid database logon and DBPassword is the password for that logon. This should only be done when using HTTPS:// to encrypt the URL information.

URL Access Using an HTTP Post

The previous examples demonstrate the use of URL access using the HTTP Get method. This method has several limitations. First, all parameter values are exposed in the URL itself. Second, the number of characters you can have in a URL is limited.

You can get around these limitations and still use URL access by employing the HTTP Post method. The HTTP Post method passes parameters as fields in an HTML form, so they are not exposed in the URL. Also, the HTTP Post is not subject to the same length restrictions as the HTTP Get.

The following HTML page uses the HTTP Post to request the Manufacturing By Machine Report for 2007 in the HTML 4.0, TIFF image, or Excel format:

```
<HTML>
<Head>
<title>
Reporting Services URL Post Demo
</title>
</Head>
<Body>
<FORM id= "frmRender"action="http://localhost/ReportServer?
           /MaxMinReports/BIStudioDeploy/Manufacturing
           By Machine Report"
           method="post" target="_self">
<H3>Manufacturing By Machine Report</H3><br>
<b>For 2007</b><br><br>
Render the Manufacturing By Machine Report
in the following format:<br>
<Select ID="rs:Format" NAME="rs:Format" size=1>
<Option Value="HTML4.0">HTML 4.0</Option>
<Option Value="IMAGE">TIFF Image</Option>
<Option Value="EXCEL">Excel File</Option>
```

```
</Select>
<Input type= "hidden" name="Year" value="2007">
<br><br>
<INPUT type= "submit" value="Render Report">
</FORM>
</Body>
</HTML>
```

The HTML form appears as shown in Figure 18-13.

Web Service Access

In addition to URL access, you can access reports using the web service interface. This is the same interface used by the Report Manager web-based application to interact with Reporting Services. This means anything you can do in Report Manager, you can also do through the web service interface.

The web service interface provides additional functionality unavailable through URL access. For example, the *web service interface* enables you to specify a set of credentials to use when executing a report. This allows your custom application to use a set of hardcoded credentials to access reports through the web service interface.

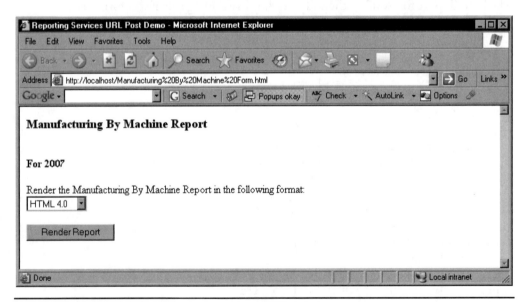

Figure 18-13 *The HTML form for requesting a report using an HTTP method*

This can be a big benefit in situations where you want Reporting Services reports to be exposed on an Internet or extranet site where each user does not have a domain account.

Using a Web Service Call to Execute a Report

This example takes you through the steps necessary to execute a report using the web service interface. In this example, you build a web application that acts as a front end for the Manufacturing By Machine Report.

Creating a Project and a Web Reference   First, you need to create an ASP.NET project with a reference to the Reporting Services web service.

1. Start Visual Studio 2008. (This example also works in earlier versions of Visual Studio.NET.)
2. Create a new project.
3. Select Visual Basic Projects in the Project Types area.
4. Select ASP.NET Web Application from the Templates area.
5. Enter an appropriate path for Location.
6. Click OK.
7. When the new project has been created, right-click the project folder for this new project in the Solution Explorer and select Add Web Reference from the Context menu. The Add Web Reference dialog box appears.
8. Enter the following address for the URL:

   ```
   http://localhost/ReportServer/ReportExecution2005.asmx
   ```

NOTE

Again, if Reporting Services is not on your computer, replace "localhost" with the name of the computer where Reporting Services is installed.

9. Click Go.
10. When the ReportExecution2005 description appears in the dialog box, enter an appropriate web reference name and click Add Reference. (The default web reference name is the name of the computer. The default name of "localhost" is used for this example.)

To use a web service, you need to create code that knows how to send data to and retrieve data from that web service. Fortunately, this code is generated for you by Visual

Studio through the process of creating a web reference. Once the web reference is in place, you can call the methods of the web service the same way you call the methods of a local .NET assembly.

A URL beginning with http://localhost was used to locate the web services on the local machine. Because of this, the Reporting Services web service uses localhost. ReportingService as its namespace.

Creating the Web Form   Now, we need to create the web form to serve as our user interface.

1. Change the name of Default.aspx to **ReportFrontEnd.aspx**.
2. Place two labels, one drop-down list, and a button on the web form, as shown in Figure 18-14.
3. Change the ID property of the drop-down list to **lstPicYear**.
4. Populate the Items collection of the list with 2006, 2007, and 2008.
5. Change the ID property of the button to **cmdExecute**.
6. Change the Text property of the button to Display Report.
7. Double-click the cmdExecute button to open the code window.

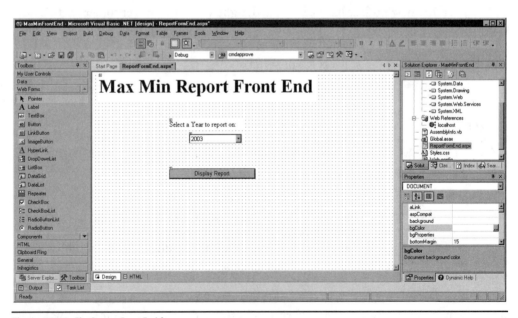

Figure 18-14 *The Report Front End form*

8. Enter the following code for cmdExecute_Click:

```
Private Sub cmdExecute_Click(ByVal sender As System.Object,-
                            ByVal e As System.EventArgs) _
                            Handles cmdExecute.Click
    Dim report As Byte () = Nothing

    ' Create an instance of the Reporting Services
    ' Web Reference.
    Dim rs As localhost.ReportExecutionService _
                        = New localhost.ReportExecutionService

    ' Create the credentials that will be used when accessing
    ' Reporting Services. This must be a logon that has rights
    ' to the Manufacturing By Machine report.
    ' *** Replace "LoginName", "Password", and "Domain" with
    ' the appropriate values. ***
    rs.Credentials = New _
            System.Net.NetworkCredential("LoginName", _
            "Password", "Domain")
    rs.PreAuthenticate = True

    ' The Reporting Services virtual path to the report.
    Dim reportPath As String = _
    "/MaxMinReports/BIStudioDeploy/Manufacturing By Machine Report"

    ' The rendering format for the report.
    Dim format As String = "HTML4.0"

    ' The devInfo string tells the report viewer
    ' how to display with the report.
    Dim devInfo As String = _
        "<DeviceInfo>" + _
    "<Toolbar>False</Toolbar>" + _
    "<Parameters>False</Parameters>" + _
    "<DocMap>True</DocMap>" + _
    "<Zoom>100</Zoom>" + _
    "</DeviceInfo>"

    ' Create an array of the values for the report parameters
    Dim parameters (0) As localhost.ParameterValue
    Dim paramValue As localhost.ParameterValue _
                            = New localhost.ParameterValue
    paramValue.Name = "Year"
    paramValue.Value = lstPicYear.SelectedValue
    parameters (0) = paramValue

    ' Create variables for the remainder of the parameters
    Dim historyID As String = Nothing
    Dim credentials () As _
                localhost.DataSourceCredentials = Nothing
```

```
      Dim showHideToggle As String = Nothing
      Dim encoding As String
      Dim mimeType As String
      Dim warnings () As localhost.Warning = Nothing
      Dim reportHistoryParameters () As _
                  localhost.ParameterValue = Nothing
      Dim streamIDs () As String = Nothing

      ' Prepare for report execution.
      Dim execInfo As New localhost.ExecutionInfo
      Dim execHeader As New localhost.ExecutionHeader
      rs.ExecutionHeaderValue = execHeader
      execInfo = rs.LoadReport(reportPath, historyID)
      rs.SetExecutionParameters(parameters, "en-us")

      Try
          ' Execute the report.
          report = rs.Render(format, devInfo, "", mimeType, _
                                  "", warnings,streamIDs)

          ' Flush any pending response.
          Response.Clear ()

          ' Set the HTTP headers for a PDF response.
          HttpContext.Current.Response.ClearHeaders ()
          HttpContext.Current.Response.ClearContent ()
          HttpContext.Current.Response.ContentType = "text/html"
          ' filename is the default filename displayed
          ' if the user does a save as.
          HttpContext.Current.Response.AppendHeader ( _
              "Content-Disposition", _
              "filename=""ManufacturingByMachineReport.HTM""")

          ' Send the byte array containing the report
          ' as a binary response.
          HttpContext.Current.Response.BinaryWrite(report)
          HttpContext.Current.Response.End ()
      Catch ex As Exception
          If ex.Message <> "Thread was being aborted." Then
              HttpContext.Current.Response.ClearHeaders ()
              HttpContext.Current.Response.ClearContent ()
              HttpContext.Current.Response.ContentType = _
                      "text/html"
              HttpContext.Current.Response.Write ( _
                  "<HTML><BODY><H1>Error</H1><br><br>" & _
                                  ex.Message & "</BODY></HTML>")
              HttpContext.Current.Response.End ()
          End If
      End Try
  End Sub
```

9. Click Save All on the toolbar.

10. Select Debug | Start from the Main menu. This executes your program.

11. When the browser window appears with the web application front-end page, click Display Report. The report appears using the dates selected on the front-end page.

12. Switch back to Visual Studio and select Debug | Stop Debugging from the Main menu.

You can refer to the comments in the code sample for information on the purpose of each section of code.

NOTE

The items in the DeviceInfo XML structure are the same rendering-specific, device information settings as those documented in the "URL Access" section of this chapter. Use the parameter name, minus the rc: prefix, as the element name.

Managing Reporting Services Through Web Services

In addition to executing reports through the web service interface, you can manage Reporting Services using the web services. If you choose, you can write an application that completely replaces the Report Manager web application for controlling Reporting Services.

The Report Viewer Control

The Report Server web service gives you a tremendous amount of control over report access. However, the web service simply provides our applications with a stream that contains the report. It is up to our applications to provide an appropriate method for viewing the content of that report stream.

The Report Viewer control in Visual Studio 2008 takes things one step further. Not only does it provide access to the reports, but it also provides a means to view them. In fact, the Report Viewer can even free you from the tether to the Report Server altogether. The Report Viewer control can be used in both Windows forms and web forms.

Displaying a Report from a Report Server

We first use the Report Viewer control to access a report on the Report Server. In this example, you build a Windows application that uses the Report Viewer to display the

Manufacturing By Machine Report. For this application to function properly, it must have access to the Report Server whenever a report is executed.

NOTE
_____
The web service example in the previous section works in any version of Visual Studio .NET. The Report Viewer examples in this section require Visual Studio 2005 or Visual Studio 2008.

Creating a Project and an Instance of the Report Viewer

First, you need to create a Windows application project in Visual Studio 2008.

1. Start up Visual Studio 2008.
2. Create a new project.
3. Select Visual Basic | Windows in the Project Types area.
4. Select Windows Forms Application from the Templates area.
5. Enter **MaxMinRVFrontEnd** for Name. Select an appropriate Location for this project.
6. Click OK. A Windows application project with a Windows form, called Form1, is created.
7. Expand Form1 so it adequately displays the report.
8. Select the Toolbox window.
9. Locate the Reporting section of the Toolbox and, if it is not already expanded, expand it.
10. Drag the Microsoft ReportViewer control from the Toolbox and drop it on Form1 (see Figure 18-15).
11. Click the Dock in Parent Container link in the ReportViewer Tasks dialog box.

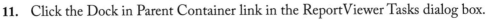

NOTE
_____
If you plan to put other controls on the same form with the Report Viewer, do not dock the viewer in the parent container.

Configuring the Report Viewer

Now we need to point the Report Viewer at a report. We need to make several selections from the ReportViewer Tasks dialog box. If this dialog box is invisible, click the small black triangle in the upper-right corner of the Report Viewer control, as shown in Figure 18-16.

1. In the ReportViewer Tasks dialog box, select <Server Report> from the Choose Report drop-down list.
2. Enter **http://ServerName/ReportServer** for Report Server URL, where *ServerName* is the name of the server hosting Reporting Services.

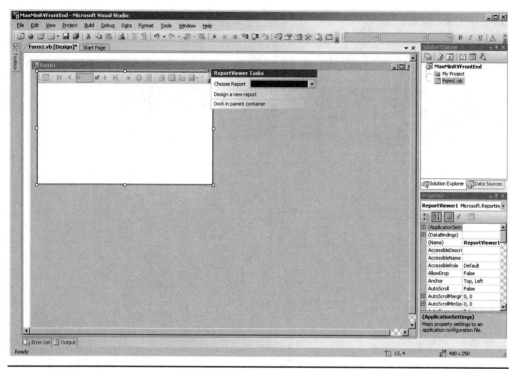

Figure 18-15 *Placing a Report Viewer control on a Windows form*

3. Enter **/MaxMinReports/BIStudioDeploy/Manufacturing By Machine Report** for Report Path.

4. Click Save All on the toolbar.

5. Select Debug | Start Debugging from the Main menu. Form1 executes and displays the Manufacturing By Machine Report from the Report Server.

6. Expand the Duramolder group. The interactive features, such as drilldown, work in the Report Viewer control, as shown in Figure 18-17.

Figure 18-16 *Opening the ReportViewer Tasks dialog box*

Machine Name	Product Name	Accepted Products	Rejected Product	Elapsed Time For Manufacture
⊞ BlandaCast 900		371,770	3,909	65,470
⊟ Duramolder		1,362,228	14,513	128,410
	Boston, MS Harbor Lighthouse	54,363	579	5,125
	Portland, ME Lighthouse	14,218	150	1,340
	Manitowoc, WI Lighthouse	4,932	53	465
	Marblehead, OH Lighthouse	6,634	70	625
	Chicago, IL Lighthouse	12,944	137	1,220
	Soaring Eagle	19,302	207	1,820
	Eagle Pair	75,057	797	7,075
	Nesting Eagle	17,240	183	1,625
	Eagle Paperweight	77,064	824	7,265
	Bear and Cub	94,079	1,002	8,870
	Eddistone Lighthouse	108,886	1,159	10,265
	Bear with Hive	5,572	60	525
	Howling Wolf	90,909	968	8,565
	Wolf Paperweight	17,605	189	1,660
	Moose with Calf	52,408	560	4,940

Figure 18-17 *The Report Viewer displaying a report with drilldown*

NOTE

You can use the ServerReport:ReportServerUrl and ServerReport:ReportPath properties of the Report Viewer control to programmatically change the report that the Report Viewer displays. In this way, a single Report Viewer control can display different reports, depending on user selection.

Displaying a Local Report in the Report Viewer

So far, all the methods of accessing reports we looked at in this chapter have required a Report Server. The Report Server provides a number of advantages for managing reports, including centralized control for updating report definitions and maintaining security. However, in some situations, it is impractical or undesirable for all installations of an application to pull reports from a Report Server.

The Report Viewer control provides an alternative. In addition to displaying reports rendered by a Report Server, the Report Viewer can render reports contained within the Visual Studio project. In this example, we create a simple report right in the Visual Studio project, and then display it with the Report Viewer.

Creating a Local Report   We begin by creating a report in the Visual Studio project.

1. Close Form1 and return to Visual Studio 2008, if you have not already done so.
2. Open the ReportViewer Tasks dialog box.
3. Click the Design a new report link. The Welcome page of the Report Wizard appears.
4. Click Next. The Choose a Data Source Type page of the Data Source Configuration Wizard appears.
5. Make sure Database is selected and click Next. The Choose Your Data Connection page of the Data Source Configuration Wizard appears.
6. Click New Connection. The Add Connection dialog box appears.
7. Create a connection to the MaxMinManufacturingDM database. Set the appropriate authentication. Test the connection to make sure you configured it correctly. When the connection passes the test, click OK to exit the Add Connection dialog box.
8. Click Next. The Save the Connection String to the Application Configuration File page of the wizard appears.
9. In most cases, it makes sense to store the connection information in the configuration file to make maintenance easier. Leave the default setting of Yes and click Next. The Choose Your Database Objects page appears.
10. Expand the tables node and place a checkmark next to DimProduct. Enter ProductList for the DataSet Name.
11. Click Finish. A typed dataset is created by the wizard for use with the report, and you are returned to the Select the Data Source page of the Report Wizard dialog box.
12. Select DimProduct and click Next. The Select the Report Type page of the Report Wizard appears.
13. Make sure Tabular is selected for the report type and click Next. The Design the Table page appears.
14. Click the Details button three times to place the ProductCode, ProductName, and ProductSubtypeCode fields in the Details area.
15. Click Finish. The Completing the Report Wizard page appears.
16. Enter **ProductList** for the name of the report. Click Finish again to exit the Report Wizard. The new report is opened in a Report Design tab.
17. Widen the middle column of the tablix. The report layout should appear similar to Figure 18-18.
18. Click Save All on the toolbar.

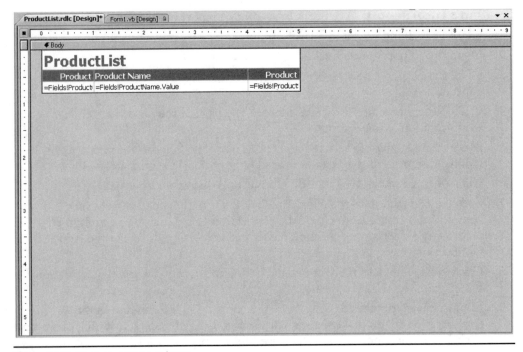

Figure 18-18 *The ProductList report layout*

Point the Report Viewer at the Local Report   Now, we point the Report Viewer at the new local report.

1. Click the Form1.vb [Design] tab in the layout area of Visual Studio 2008. Note that several items have been added to the area below the Form1 layout. These items will provide the data for the local ProductList report we just created.
2. Open the ReportViewer Tasks dialog box.
3. Select MaxMinRVFrontEnd.ProductList.rdlc from the Choose Report drop-down list.
4. Select Debug | Start Debugging from the Main menu. Form1 executes and displays the local report. The local report you just created displays a list of all Max Min products, as shown in Figure 18-19.
5. Close Form1 when you finish viewing this report.
6. Click Save All on the toolbar.

When you compile the MaxMinRVFrontEnd project, the Report1.rdlc report definition is compiled as an embedded resource in the executable. Therefore, nothing else except the data source is needed for the report to be rendered. The report always goes along with the application.

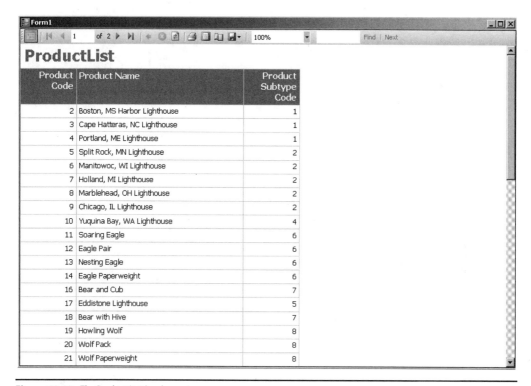

Figure 18-19 *The Product List local report*

Ready-Made Solution

In this chapter, we examined ways we can create our own custom interfaces to our business intelligence sources. In Chapter 19, we look at a familiar, decidedly noncustom environment that can be used for accessing OLAP data. This ready-made environment is none other than Microsoft Excel. Although the Excel environment may not have all the flash of a custom-made solution and all the enterprise-wide capabilities of Reporting Services, it still provides a capable environment for interactive and self-guided analysis of OLAP data.

Chapter 19

Another Point of View—Excel Pivot Tables and Pivot Charts

In This Chapter

- ► **Excel**
- ► **Great Capabilities, Great Opportunities**

If we spoke a different language, we would perceive a somewhat different world.
—Ludwig Wittgenstein

As we have stressed throughout this book, and especially in the past two chapters, business intelligence (BI) is not useful unless it can be delivered to decision makers at the most opportune moment. Perhaps we should add that the business intelligence must be delivered in a format and an environment that decision makers are comfortable with. Business intelligence must be timely and accessible.

In the previous two chapters, we examined tools that enable us to create our own business intelligence delivery methods. We saw how this can be done by building our own reports and by building our own custom applications. In this chapter, we explore a solution that, while not nearly as custom, may be able to fulfill some of our users' needs just as well as the custom solutions.

In many cases, the most comfortable format is the tried-and-true paper report. For this reason, Reporting Services is going to be a big part of our solution for delivering business intelligence. Perhaps Reporting Services can even serve as a comfortable mechanism for transitioning decision makers from hard copy to the more efficient and more capable interactive onscreen reports.

Using ADOMD.NET, we can integrate business intelligence information from Analysis Services with our line-of-business applications. Combining business intelligence and line-of-business information not only leads to efficiency, but it also makes the business intelligence information much more likely to be used. Having business intelligence information readily available as decision makers go about their daily tasks is an excellent approach.

Excel

In addition to hard copy reports and the daily line-of-business applications, most decision makers are comfortable with the applications that make up Microsoft Office. Spreadsheets were some of the first tools for doing what we now call ad hoc analysis and reporting. In almost every organization, decision makers depend heavily on spreadsheets as data repositories and tools for analysis. Wouldn't it make sense to allow our business intelligence information to be incorporated and manipulated in this comfortable and ubiquitous environment as well? Microsoft provides us the means to do this in Excel with the PivotTable and PivotChart Wizard.

Creating Pivot Tables and Pivot Charts

The PivotTable and PivotChart Wizard takes us step by step through the process of creating a pivot table and/or pivot chart. It first enables us to set the data source to be used for the pivot items. Fortunately, the data source can be an online analytical processing (OLAP) cube in an Analysis Services database. Once the data source is set, we can either lay out the report while we are still in the wizard or have the wizard create an empty pivot table, and then populate it after the wizard is complete.

Connecting to the Data

Pivot tables and pivot charts require a data source to work from. One option is to use data from cells right inside the spreadsheet. Pivot tables and pivot charts can also access data from external sources. This second option, of course, is the one we are most interested in. The wizard steps us through the process of setting up access to an external data source, which, in our case, is Analysis Services.

MDX Under the Hood

Like the MDX query screen on the Business Intelligence Development Studio Browser tab, the pivot table and pivot chart let us manipulate Analysis Services data. As you might guess, under the hood, the pivot table and pivot chart are sending MDX queries to Analysis Services. These tools provide an easy-to-use interface, so our decision makers do not need to know anything about the ins and outs of MDX. Behind the scenes, the SELECT ... ON COLUMNS, ... ON ROWS syntax is still being generated and utilized.

Layout

The pivot table layout is done in a manner similar to the drag-and-drop approach we saw on the MDX query screen on the Business Intelligence Development Studio Browser tab. One advantage of the Excel pivot table is that it not only includes row and column dimensions, but it can also include data in the pages dimension. We can, therefore, use these tools to look at three dimensions at a time.

As stated earlier, the pivot table layout can be created either as part of the PivotTable and PivotChart Wizard or after the wizard completes. In most cases, the layout is created after exiting the wizard. Waiting until after the wizard is complete provides a cleaner and more capable report creation environment. The one time we may want to create the layout in the wizard is in a situation where the underlying data has gotten large and unwieldy. By creating the layout in the wizard, we can specify a field to serve as the page grouping. Once this is done, data is retrieved one page at a time, eliminating the need to retrieve the entire data set before displaying results.

Pivot Table

The Excel pivot table is similar to the Browser tab in the Business Intelligence Management Studio in its implementation of drag-and-drop query creation. In format, the Excel pivot table is similar to the custom CellSet viewer we looked at in our

ADOMD.NET example in Chapter 18. After all, our CellSet viewer provided for a page dimension just like the pivot table. The difference is, our CellSet viewer supported only one hierarchy level on each dimension. The Excel pivot table allows for multiple hierarchy levels on each dimension. In addition, our CellSet viewer supported only one value in each cell. The Excel pivot table allows multiple values.

Learn By Doing—Creating an Excel Pivot Table

Feature Highlighted

▶ Creating a pivot table in Microsoft Excel

Business Need   The vice president (VP) of production for Maximum Miniatures, Incorporated would like to do some of his own analysis of the information in the MaxMinManufacturingDM cube. He is a big Excel user and is comfortable with this program. To fulfill the VP's needs, we show him how to create a pivot table in Excel, pulling data from the MaxMinManufacturingDM cube.

> **NOTE**
>
> Pivot tables can be created in either Excel 2003 or Excel 2007. Excel 2007 was used for the Learn By Doing exercises in this chapter.

Steps

1. Open Microsoft Excel.
2. Select the Insert ribbon and click the PivotTable icon, as shown in Figure 19-1. The Create PivotTable dialog box appears.

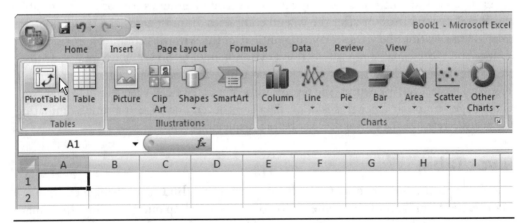

Figure 19-1 *Creating a pivot table in Excel*

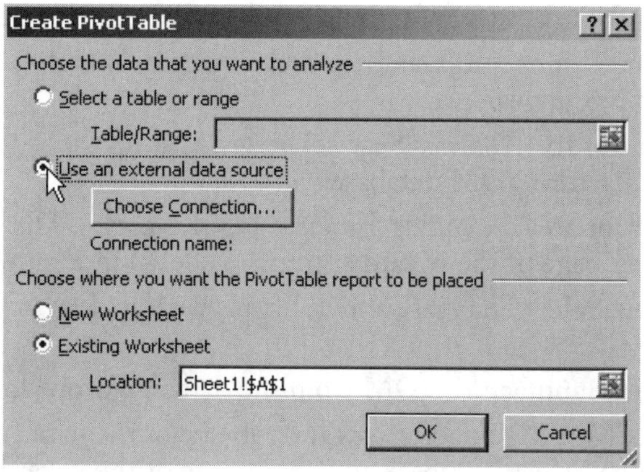

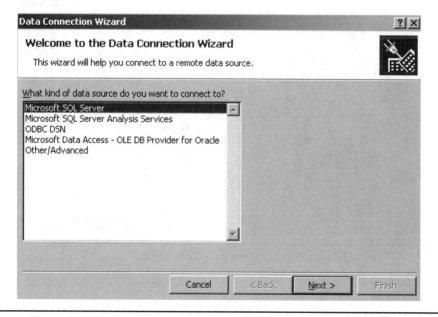

Figure 19-2   *The Create Pivot Table dialog box*

3. Select the Use external data source option to use data from outside the spreadsheet as shown in Figure 19-2.

4. Click the Choose Connection button. The Existing Connections dialog box appears.

5. Click the Browse for More button. The Select Data Source dialog box appears.

6. Click the New Source button. The Data Connection Wizard dialog box appears, as shown in Figure 19-3.

Figure 19-3   *The Data Connection Wizard dialog box*

7. Select Microsoft SQL Server Analysis Services from the list of data source types.

8. Click Next. The Connect to Database Server page of the Data Connection Wizard dialog box appears.

9. Enter the name of the Analysis Services server hosting the MaxMinManufacturingDM database.

10. Enter the appropriate credentials for accessing this server. The Connect to Database Server page of the wizard appears as shown in Figure 19-4.

11. Click Next. The Select Database and Table page of the Data Connection Wizard appears.

12. Select MaxMinManufacturingDM from the database drop-down list.

13. Select the Max Min Manufacturing DM cube from the list of cubes and perspectives. The Select Database and Table page of the wizard appears, as shown in Figure 19-5.

14. Click Next. The Save Data Connection File and Finish page of the Data Connection Wizard appears as shown in Figure 19-6.

15. Enter a description of the data source and click Finish. We return to the Create PivotTable dialog box.

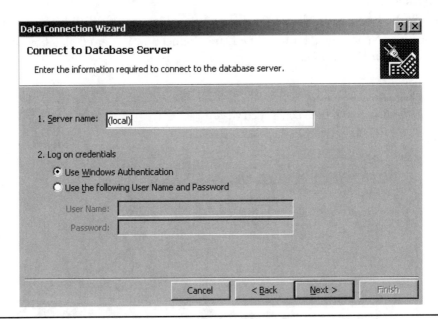

Figure 19-4   *The Connect to Database Server page of the Data Connection Wizard*

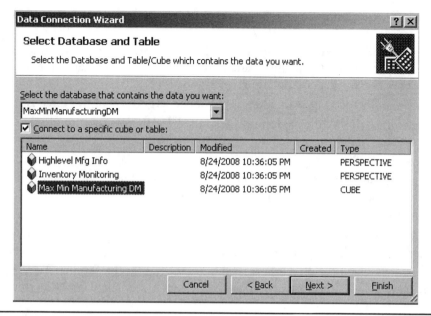

Figure 19-5   *The Select Database and Table page of the Data Connection Wizard*

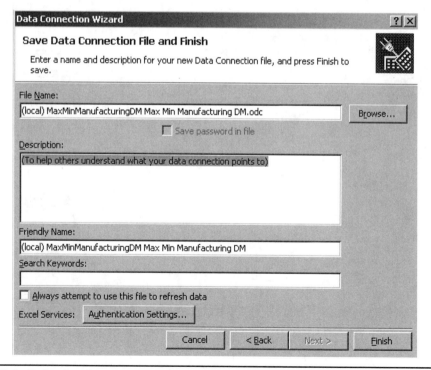

Figure 19-6   *The Save Data Connection File and Finish page of the Data Connection Wizard*

16. Click OK to exit the Create PivotTable dialog box. An empty pivot table is created, as shown in Figure 19-7.

17. In the PivotTable Field List, locate the Time Hierarchy. Drag the Time Hierarchy and drop it on the Report Filter area. This creates a report filter in the upper-left corner of the spreadsheet, as shown in Figure 19-8.

18. Click the filter icon next to 2008 in the upper-left corner of the spreadsheet.

19. Check the Select Multiple Items check box. We can now select multiple dimension members.

20. Expand the 2008 item in the list.

21. Uncheck the 2008Q3 and 2008Q4 items in the list. The Time Hierarchy drop-down window appears, as shown in Figure 19-9.

22. Click OK.

23. In the PivotTable Field List, locate the Product Hierarchy. Drag the Product Hierarchy and drop it on the Row Labels area.

24. Rows are created for the highest level in the hierarchy, the Product Type. Expand the Row Labels drop-down window.

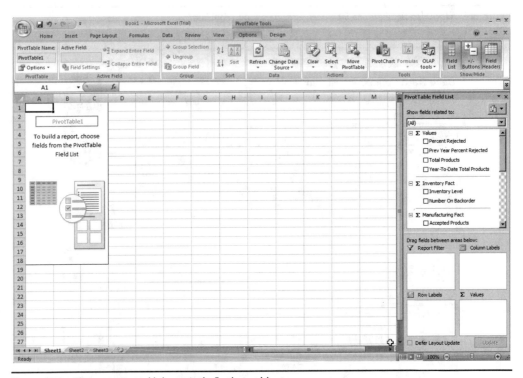

Figure 19-7 *The empty pivot table layout in the Excel spreadsheet*

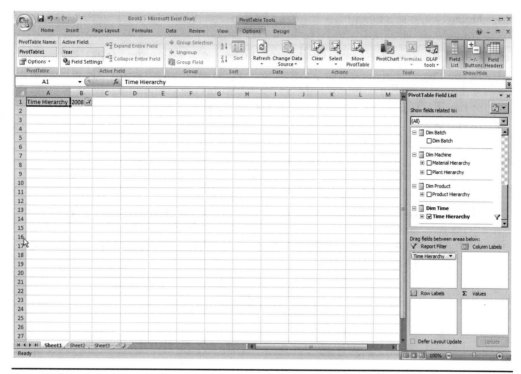

Figure 19-8   *A filter added to the pivot table layout*

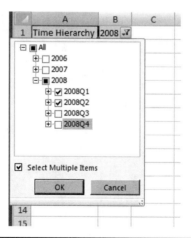

Figure 19-9   *The Time Hierarchy report filter*

25. Uncheck the Woodland Creatures and Warriors of Yore items. The Row Labels drop-down window is shown in Figure 19-10.

26. Click OK. Rows have been created for the two selected product types.

27. In the PivotTable Field List, locate the Plant Hierarchy. Drag the Plant Hierarchy and drop it on the Column Labels area. Columns are created for the highest level of the Plant Hierarchy, which is the country level.

28. In the PivotTable Field List, locate the Accepted Products measure. Drag the Accepted Products measure and drop it on the Values area. The Accepted Products measure is added to the pivot table, as shown in Figure 19-11. When a pivot table includes a single measure, the label for that measure appears in the upper-left corner of the pivot table.

29. Drag the Rejected Products measure and drop it in the area where you dropped the Accepted Products measure. Both measures are included in the layout. The labels for the measures are now at the top of each column, as shown in Figure 19-12.

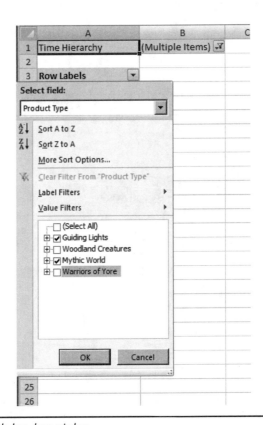

Figure 19-10 *The Row Labels drop-down window*

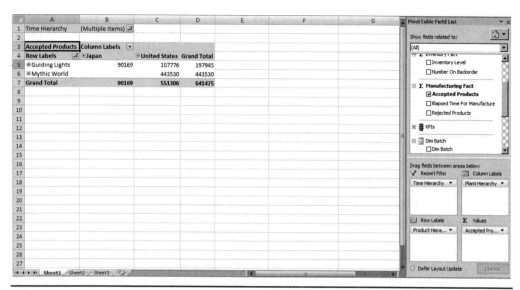

Figure 19-11 *A pivot table with a single measure*

30. Now that we are done placing items on the layout, we can close the PivotTable Field List window. We can close the window or click the Field List button in the Options ribbon, as shown in Figure 19-13. We can bring back the PivotTable Field List window by clicking this ribbon button a second time.

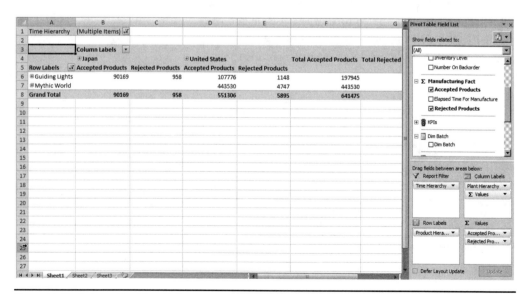

Figure 19-12 *A pivot table with multiple measures*

Figure 19-13 *The Field List button in the Options ribbon*

31. Select one of the cells containing the Accepted Products measure label. Change the text to **# Accepted**. When we exit the modified cell, all occurrences of the measure label are changed, as shown in Figure 19-14.

32. Change the Rejected Products measure label to **# Rejected**.

33. Let's format the text for the # Accepted cells. Select one of the cells containing a # Accepted amount.

34. Click the Field Settings button in the Options ribbon, as shown in Figure 19-15. The Value Field Settings dialog box appears.

35. Click the Number Format button. The Format Cells dialog box appears.

36. Select Number in the Category list. Set Decimal Places to 0. Check the Use 1000 Separator (,) check box.

37. Click OK to exit the Format Cells dialog box.

38. Click OK to exit the Value Field Settings dialog box.

39. Repeat Steps 33–38 to format the # Rejected cells. With some items expanded, the pivot table appears as shown in Figure 19-16.

40. Save the spreadsheet in an appropriate location.

	A	B	C	D	E	F	G
1	Time Hierarchy	(Multiple Items)					
2							
3		Column Labels					
4		⊞Japan		⊞United States		Total # Accepted	Total Rejected
5	Row Labels	# Accepted	Rejected Products	# Accepted	Rejected Products		
6	⊞Guiding Lights	90169	958	107776	1148	197945	
7	⊞Mythic World			443530	4747	443530	
8	Grand Total	90169	958	551306	5895	641475	
9							

Figure 19-14 *Changing a column label*

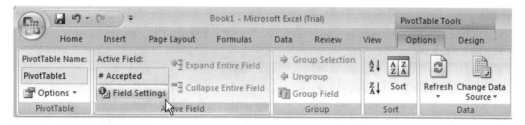

Figure 19-15 *The Field Settings button in the Options ribbon*

Pivot Chart

Learn By Doing—Creating a Pivot Chart

Feature Highlighted

▶   Creating a pivot chart in Microsoft Excel

Business Need   Our intrepid VP of production is extremely happy with the information he has been able to discover using the pivot table in Excel. Now, he would like to create a chart from this information to use at an upcoming presentation. We can show him how to create a pivot chart in Excel.

	A	B	C	D	E	F	G	H
1	Time Hierarchy	(Multiple Items)						
2								
3		Column Labels						
4		⊞ Japan		⊟ United States		United States # Accepted	United States # Rejected	Total # Acc
5				⊞ Maximum Miniatures - Fridley				
6	Row Labels	# Accepted	# Rejected	# Accepted	# Rejected			
7	⊟ Guiding Lights	90,169	958	107,776	1,148	107,776	1,148	1
8	⊞ Atlantic Coast Lighthouses	28,589	304	25,829	274	25,829	274	
9	⊟ Great Lakes Lighthouses	14,801	157	18,301	194	18,301	194	
10	Manitowoc, WI Lighthouse			4,932	53	4,932	53	
11	Marblehead, OH Lighthouse	637	6	637	6	637	6	
12	Chicago, IL Lighthouse	14,164	151	12,732	135	12,732	135	
13	⊞ World Lighthouses	46,779	497	63,646	680	63,646	680	1
14	⊞ Mythic World			443,530	4,747	443,530	4,747	4
15	Grand Total	90,169	958	551,306	5,895	551,306	5,895	6

Sheet1   Sheet2   Sheet3

Figure 19-16 *The completed pivot table*

Steps

1. Select the Sheet2 tab in the spreadsheet used in the first Learn By Doing exercise in this chapter.
2. Select the Insert ribbon.
3. Select PivotChart from the drop-down list below the PivotTable icon, as shown in Figure 19-17. The Create PivotTable with PivotChart dialog box appears.
4. Select the Use external data source option to use data from outside the spreadsheet and click Choose Connection. The Existing Connections dialog box appears.
5. Select the connection to the Analysis Services database you created in the previous Learn By Doing exercise.
6. Click Open to return to the Create PivotTable with PivotChart dialog box.
7. Click OK to exit the Create PivotTable with PivotChart dialog box. An empty pivot chart is created, as shown in Figure 19-18.
8. In the PivotTable Field List, locate the Plant Hierarchy. Drag the Plant Hierarchy and drop it on the Report Filter area.
9. Expand the Plant Hierarchy drop-down window in the upper-left corner of the spreadsheet.
10. Expand the All entry, and then expand the United States entry.
11. Select the Maximum Miniatures—Fridley entry.
12. Click OK.
13. In the PivotTable Field List, locate the Time Hierarchy. Drag the Time Hierarchy and drop it on the Row Labels area.

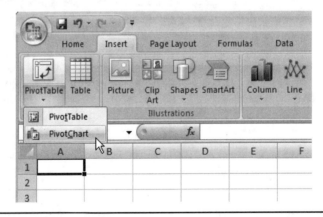

Figure 19-17 *Creating a pivot chart*

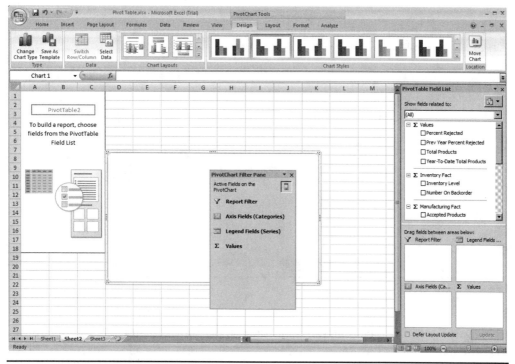

Figure 19-18 *An empty pivot chart*

14. In the PivotTable Field List, locate the Product Hierarchy. Drag the Product Hierarchy and drop it on the Column Labels area.

15. In the PivotTable Field List, locate the Total Products measure. Drag the Total Products measure and drop it on the Values area. The chart appears as shown in Figure 19-19.

16. Save the spreadsheet.

You can format the pivot chart in a similar manner to the method we used for formatting the Reporting Services chart item in Chapter 16. Select a section of the report you want to format: the axis labels, the legend, or a graph area itself. Right-click and use the context menu to carry out the desired formatting.

Additional Features

Microsoft Office 2007 and its Excel spreadsheet system allow for a workbook to be comprised of spreadsheets with Pivot Table and Chart pairs. So a workbook could be

Figure 19-19 *A pivot chart*

the viewer for several cube sources. Microsoft also has provided an Excel Accelerator for Reporting, which adds functionality to format Excel reports. This allows for locking down columns and rows in the spreadsheet and performing drilldown using the outline bar.

Another capability of Excel is to save the interactive spreadsheet using a pivot table or a pivot chart to a web page. This enables a user with a browser to perform interactive drilldown and drill across with integrated charts and other Office Web Component functions, such as top count, filters, sorting, and even creating new math formulas. Office Web Components (OWC) are growing in popularity as they are exposed through Microsoft's Portal product, Sharepoint Portal Services. A web part on a page in the portal is linked to an OLAP cube and uses Excel's charting, drilling, and filtering functions.

Great Capabilities, Great Opportunities

The business intelligence tools in SQL Server 2008 offer us tremendous capabilities. We can create powerful analysis tools to provide business intelligence to decision makers at every level of our organizations. We can define, construct, deploy, and analyze with greater speed and efficiency than ever before.

The complexity that made data warehousing, data mining, enterprise-wide reporting, and the integration of those items with line-of-business applications a lengthy, expensive, and risky venture has been reduced, if not eliminated.

The reputation of business intelligence projects as not worth the time, money, and headaches involved is widespread and deeply ingrained. Too many times, business intelligence projects delivered less than expected in a less effective manner than anticipated over a longer timeline than allowed for while requiring more money than budgeted. Most small and mid-size organizations would never dream of creating a data mart or using OLAP cubes or data mining. Yet, these are the same organizations that stand to benefit the most from what SQL Server 2008 has to offer. A number of large organizations have been down the business intelligence road with huge, all-encompassing projects that ended up failing miserably. With SQL Server 2008, these large organizations can implement business intelligence with an incremental approach that leads to a much higher success rate.

Those of us working with business intelligence in SQL Server 2008 have a job ahead of us. We need to let organizations of all sizes know that the tools, the architecture, and, indeed, the rules of business intelligence are changing. SQL Server 2008 allows for more of an iterative style and less of the all-or-nothing approach to business intelligence projects of the past. With SQL Server 2008, it is possible to get *more* than you expected in a *more* effective manner than anticipated with a *shorter* timeline than allowed requiring *less* money than budgeted.

Those organizations that hear this message can reap the rewards offered by the business intelligence tools in SQL Server 2008 and the strategic advantages that go along with them. They can efficiently create tools to achieve effective decision making!

Index

Note: Page numbers referencing figures are italicized and followed by an *"f"*. Page numbers referencing tables are italicized and followed by a *"t"*.

Symbols and numbers

- (except) operator, 461
- (negative) operator, 460
-- (single-line comment) operator, 459
- (subtraction) operator, 460
___$end_lsn column, 270
___$operation column, 270
___$seqval column, 270
___$start_lsn column, 270
___$update_mask column, 270
& (ampersand), 404
* (crossjoin) operator, 461
* (multiplication) operator, 460
/ (division) operator, 460
// (single-line comment) operator, 459
/*...*/ (multiline comment) operator, 459
: (range operator), 401–402
@Year query parameter, 577
@Year stored procedure parameter, 619
[ ] (square brackets), 392
{ } (curly brackets), 401, 438–439
+ (addition) operator, 460
+ (concatenation) operator, 460
+ (positive) operator, 460
+ (union) operator, 461
< (less than) operator, 460

<= (less than or equal to) operator, 460
<> (not equal to) operator, 460
= (equal) operator, 460
> (greater than) operator, 460
>= (greater than or equal to) operator, 460
' ' (single quotes), 448
3D Options page, *630f*

A

ABS function, *247t*
accounting system, 23
Action expression property, 364
Action page, 616
Action type action, 362
ActionAtEvent property, 173
ActionAtTimeout property, 173
Actions
    client software and, 365
    creating, 363–364
    Drillthrough, 364
    overview, 362–365
    Report, 364–365
    types of, 362–363
Actions tab, *363f*
activation function, 494
ActiveX objects, 654
ActiveX Script task, 155–156